CRITICAL ISSUES
IN POLICING

Seventh Edition

CRITICAL ISSUES IN POLICING

Contemporary Readings

Seventh Edition

Roger G. Dunham
University of Miami

Geoffrey P. Alpert
University of South Carolina

WAVELAND

PRESS, INC.

Long Grove, Illinois

For information about this book, contact:
Waveland Press, Inc.
4180 IL Route 83, Suite 101
Long Grove, IL 60047-9580
(847) 634-0081
info@waveland.com
www.waveland.com

Contents

Preface   ix

Section I
Introduction and Historical Overview   1
---

1   The Foundation of the Police Role in Society   3
    Roger G. Dunham & Geoffrey P. Alpert

2   The Development of the American Police: 11
    An Historical Overview
    Craig D. Uchida

3   Requests for Police Assistance, 2011   31
    Matthew Durose & Lynn Langton

4   You Can Observe a Lot by Watching: 46
    Contributions of Systematic Social Observation
    to Our Understanding of the Police
    Robert E. Worden, Sarah J. McLean, & Heidi S. Bonner

Section II
Police Socialization and the Police Subculture 75
---

5   Breeding Deviant Conformity: 79
    The Ideology and Culture of Police
    Victor E. Kappeler, Richard D. Sluder, & Geoffrey P. Alpert

6   Solidarity and the Code of Silence   106
    Geoffrey P. Alpert, Jeffrey J. Noble, & Jeff Rojek

7   Police Discretionary Behavior: A Study of Style   122
    Laure Weber Brooks

v

8   The Asshole   143
     John Van Maanen

9   Addressing Police Misconduct: 162
     The Role of Citizen Complaints
     Jeff Rojek, Scott H. Decker, & Allen E. Wagner

10   Ethics and Law Enforcement   183
     Joycelyn M. Pollock & Paul D. Reynolds

Section III
Management and Organization 217

11   How Police Supervisory Styles Influence   219
     Patrol Officer Behavior
     Robin Shepard Engel

12   Technological Innovations in Policing   229
     Meghan S. Stroshine

13   Introduction to Early Intervention Systems   244
     Samuel Walker

14   Evidence-Based Policing   260
     Cynthia Lum & Christopher S. Koper

15   Predictive Policing   275
     Justin Nix

16   Geographic Information Systems: Applications for Police   289
     William V. Pelfrey Jr.

17   The Practice of Crime Analysis   302
     Allison Rojek

Section IV
Issues in Policing 327

18   An Afrocentric Perspective on Policing   331
     Christopher Cooper

19   Women in Law Enforcement, 1987–2008   355
     Lynn Langton

20 Gender and Police Stress: The Convergent and   362
    Divergent Impact of Work Environment,
    Work-Family Conflict, and Stress Coping Mechanisms
    of Female and Male Police Officers
    Ni He, Jihong Zhao, & Carol A. Archbold

21 Toward an Understanding of the   385
    Physical Hazards of Police Work
    Steven G. Brandl & Meghan S. Stroshine

22 Beyond Boston: Applying Theory to   401
    Understand and Address Sustainability Issues
    in Focused Deterrence Initiatives for Violence Reduction
    Marie Skubak Tillyer, Robin S. Engel, & Brian Lovins

23 Campus Policing   421
    Andrea Allen

24 Police Response to Persons with Mental Illness   435
    Wesley G. Jennings & Edward J. Hudak

Section V
Community-Based Policing 453

25 Broken Windows   455
    James Q. Wilson & George L. Kelling

26 "Broken Windows" and Fractured History: 468
    The Use and Misuse of History
    in Recent Police Patrol Analysis
    Samuel Walker

27 Community Policing: Elements and Effects   481
    Gary W. Cordner

28 Problem-Oriented Policing   499
    John D. Reitzel, Nicole Leeper Piquero, & Alex R. Piquero

Section VI
Use of Force 513

29 The Split-Second Syndrome and   517
    Other Determinants of Police Violence
    James J. Fyfe

30   What We Know about Police Use of Force   532
      Kenneth Adams

31   Use-of-Force Policy, Policy Enforcement, and Training   548
      Lorie A. Fridell

32   State-Created Danger: Should Police Officers Be   567
      Accountable for Reckless Tactical Decision Making?
      Jeffrey J. Noble & Geoffrey P. Alpert

Section VII
The Future of Policing 583

33   What a Good Police Department Looks Like: 585
      Professional, Accountable, Transparent, Self-Monitoring
      Samuel Walker

34   The Challenge of Policing in a Democratic Society: 596
      A Personal Journey toward Understanding
      Charles H. Ramsey

      Index   611

Preface

The seventh edition of *Critical Issues* includes many updated and new articles reflecting changes in policing during the past several years. We are pleased that the authors we asked to update their material were willing to do so with dedicated attention, and we are proud to include the new articles that introduce fresh ideas on current topics.

It is instructive to view policing as an elastic profession. It changes shape, often appears different than it has in the past, may have a shift in focus but returns to an original function. The selected articles reflect that elasticity. Police work must be in concert with the community if it is to be successful. The agents of formal social control must rely on citizens—agents of informal social control—for effective performance of their duties, gaining respect, and earning a sense of satisfaction.

In choosing topics for *Critical Issues*, we selected those that have the broadest application. Rather than limiting the scope of our material to large, urban, suburban, rural, or small departments, we have selected issues that are applicable to all. As in *Policing: Continuity and Change*, a text designed to accompany *Critical Issues*, we are emphasizing the importance of involving community members in decisions concerning law enforcement—including tasks, objectives, and goals.

One of the major roles played by citizens is to help identify what is a proper measure of performance in law enforcement. In the past, the ultimate measure of police success was an evaluation of the crime rates. The comments from Durkheim through researchers today that crime rates are influenced by factors beyond the control of police, have fallen on deaf ears. Politicians and police officials still take credit when the reported crime rate decreases and are blamed when the reported rate of crime increases. The use of reported crimes as a measure of success for police demonstrates an unsophisticated understanding of the role and scope of police services. Different styles of policing can affect many performance measures including response time and the nature and extent of community contacts. However, understanding changes in the rates of crime requires a far more sophisticated analysis.

We have revised *Critical Issues* to include information on the tasks and objectives of law enforcement. We encourage readers to change from holding the police responsible for crime rates to holding them accountable for specific tasks and objectives and the goal of promoting secure communities.

Acknowledgments

We are indebted to many people for their contributions to this collection. The collaboration and friendship of our colleagues who wrote the excellent articles in this book are sincerely appreciated. Our collective ten children provided both incentive and distraction. Thanks to the many colleagues who used the sixth edition in the classroom and offered suggestions for the revision. This work was a cooperative effort, and we thank everyone who generously shared their time, knowledge, and expertise.

SECTION I

Introduction and Historical Overview

Like other social institutions, policing has evolved over time. There has been tremendous change in both the number of law enforcement agencies and their functions. There are nearly 18,000 state and local law enforcement agencies, with more than one million full-time employees (Bureau of Justice Statistics, 2011). These statistics touch on the enormity and complexity of modern policing in the United States. Changes will continue as policing is influenced by the social environment—forces that constantly reshape policing from its bureaucratic organization to specific policing strategies.

For example, research has found that, in many cases, crime is not evenly distributed geographically but is clustered in specific locales, or "hot spots," that generate half of all criminal events. A policing strategy responding to this information focuses policing efforts on those places and tries to identify and resolve the underlying problems that create the clustering of crime. Anthony Braga, Andrew Papachristos, and David Hureau (2012) conducted a systematic review and meta-analysis of 19 studies evaluating hot spot policing strategies. They concluded that hot spot policing yields noteworthy crime reductions, and the benefits diffuse into areas surrounding the hot spots. Further, they found that community members have positive evaluations of these focused policing strategies.

Our objective in this section is to provide some social context and historical perspective to our study of the police in the United States. "Standing back" to obtain a broader view of the role of the police in society and the storied history of policing provides a solid foundation for understanding policing today.

The first selection, "The Foundation of the Police Role in Society," sets the social context of policing by discussing how the institution of policing fits into a very complex U.S. society. Ideas concerning the social role of the police are introduced and analyzed, as are the foundations of police authority and power in a democratic society. Important issues are discussed including who has control over the police and what degree and types of control are feasible and necessary.

1

Craig Uchida's article, "The Development of the American Police: An Historic Overview," takes us from the colonial period of law enforcement to the present. Dr. Uchida provides us with an in-depth analysis of the changes in emphasis and form that have occurred in policing over this period of time. His article is divided into the various reform movements that have molded and changed police into our modern day departments. It is important to consider that many aspects of what we are now call community-oriented policing (COP) began in the early years of policing. It is interesting that Sir Robert Peele may be responsible for many aspects of modern law enforcement.

The third selection, "Requests for Police Assistance, 2011" by Matthew Durose and Lynn Langton is a special report from the Bureau of Justice Statistics that summarizes findings from the Police-Public Contact Survey. This survey collects information about experiences resulting from police-citizen contacts in a nationally representative sample of persons in U.S. households. It is noteworthy that very high percentages of people who have requested police assistance are very positive about the police response. Eighty-six percent of these people thought the police were helpful, 93% thought the police acted properly, and 85% were satisfied with the police response. Most importantly, there were no significant differences between the percentages of Hispanics (86%), Blacks (85%), and whites (83%) who reported a crime and felt the police were helpful.

Robert E. Worden, Sarah J. McLean, and Heidi S. Bonner review studies that have used systematic social observation of the police. In "You Can Observe a Lot by Watching," they discuss the benefits and limitations of this methodology for studying police practices. Further, they summarize and critique the principal contributions of these studies to our knowledge of policing. For example, these types of studies have shed light on a number of factors that shape police behavior, such as situational factors, officer characteristics and outlooks, and organizational structures.

REFERENCES

Braga, A. A., Papachristos, A. V., & Hureau, D. M. (2012). The effects of hot spots policing on crime: An updated systematic review and meta-analysis. *Justice Quarterly.* Retrieved from http://dx.doi.org/10.1080/07418825.2012.673632

Bureau of Justice Statistics. (2011). *Census of State and Local Law Enforcement Agencies, 2008* (NCJ 233982). Washington, DC: U.S. Department of Justice.

1

The Foundation of the Police Role in Society

Roger G. Dunham & Geoffrey P. Alpert

What is the basic role of the police in our society? What do we expect them to do—and *not* to do? And how do these expectations correspond to the actual day-to-day behavior of the police? If the police get out of line or begin using their authority in ways deemed inappropriate by a majority of citizens, does society have the right or even the ability to control their behavior? In order to answer these questions we must recognize that the police are an integral part of government. In fact, they are located at the interface between government and the private lives of individual citizens (Pollock, 1994). The police represent and implement the government's right to use coercion and force to guarantee certain behaviors from its citizens.

Carl Klockars (1984) has described police control as having four major elements: authority, power, persuasion, and force. Authority is the incontestable entitlement to be obeyed; citizens do not question the right to issue commands. Power is similar to authority but includes the possibility of meeting resistance, which will be defeated without compunction. Persuasion involves the use of symbols, words, and arguments to convince an individual that he or she ought to comply with the rules. Force involves something very different from the other elements of control: the element of physical control. Although the other three elements rely mostly on mental or psychological control, they function partially because of the underlying threat of force. All of these elements of control are used by the police, but the ultimate right to use force is what makes police unique and what allows the police to function successfully.

Prepared especially for *Critical Issues in Policing* by Roger G. Dunham and Geoffrey P. Alpert.

3

The Police Right to Use Force

Where do the police get the right to use force to control citizens? In a democracy, citizens grant the government (federal, state, and local) the authority to use force to uphold the law. The extent of this power sometimes leads us to question whether the tremendous power vested in government authorities is prudent. However, most of us realize that governments are a necessary feature of modern societies.

In fact, Mancur Olsen (1965) made the argument that governments are unavoidable features of human societies. He argued that we need public goods (e.g., public safety) and that public goods can only be created by coercion. It is through the formation of a state or government that force is legitimized to coerce citizens into contributing to the public good. Fortunately, it is not necessary to apply force most of the time; generally, a credible threat of force is sufficient to keep society functioning.

Richard Quinney (1970:9–10) said that "a society is held together by force and constraint . . . [that] values are ruling rather than common, enforced rather than accepted, at any given point in time." Although other institutional means exist to officially establish sets of values and rules (e.g., laws and fines), they mean little without some method of enforcement. To enforce the rules, we have created the social institution of police and authorized it to use physical force. In fact, the police are the only ones in our society who have the legitimate right to use force against citizens. In a sense, the government must use organized coercion to prevent private coercion (Quinney, 1970).

In sum, we need the police in order to have a civilized society, to ensure safety from being harmed by insiders, and to make sure we contribute to other needed public goods. In his *Leviathan*, Thomas Hobbes (1651) tried to describe what life would be like in a condition of anarchy.

> Hereby it is manifest, that during the time men live without a common power to keep them all in awe, they are in that condition which is called war . . . where every man is enemy to every man. . . . In such condition, there is no place for industry: because the fruit thereof is uncertain: and consequently no agriculture . . . no society; and which is worst of all, continual fear, and danger of violent death; and the life of man, solitary, poor, nasty, brutish, and short.

Historically, the state has often been an institution of repression. It seems to be in the disposition of most individuals that, when they are put in positions of authority and given the right to use force to maintain society, they succumb to the temptation to use that power and authority to exploit others. Most citizens will give in to the lure of power and force to benefit themselves individually. This has been called the great dilemma of the state: how to have the state and keep it benign, to avoid the exploitation of its citizens (Stark, 2000). Given that the police are at the interface of citizens and government, this also becomes the central dilemma of policing. How can we authorize the police to use force to maintain our safety, ensure that our laws are obeyed, and at the same time keep officers from using that force illegitimately? Most of the important issues concerning the police emanate from this basic problem. The greatest issues surrounding the police are misuse of force, police corruption, and methods employed to control these problems. Taming the police is a major aspect of the distinction between a police state and a democratic state. In a police state, the citizens do not have adequate control over the police. The police are therefore able to use their monopoly on physical force to exploit citizens. In a democratic state, the people maintain more control over the police; exploitation is accomplished less easily.

The Social Contract

Jeffrey Reiman (1985) explains that democracy does not guarantee that the judgments of public officials, such as the police, will uniformly replicate those of the public. The power is delegated and must be exercised according to the judgment of the individuals to whom it is delegated. However, Reiman makes clear that "the public has a right to spell out the criteria by which the judgments should be made, and to insist on both competence and good faith in the application of those criteria" (1985:237). He defines the social contract as "embodying a general test of the legitimacy of the acts and rules of public agencies of law enforcement, namely, that such acts or rules must be such that the limits on citizens' freedom that they bring must result in a net increase of that freedom all told" (p. 246). His test gives us a way to exercise public control over the police's right to use force. To refuse to give the police the right to use force to enforce the law would undermine our laws and freedom and compel us to devote much of our time and effort to self-protection. Thus, according to Reiman, the public surrenders its right to use force and loans that right to the police to use it in the name of the group and to protect each member of the group against the use of force by other members. The sacrifice of this individual right results in a net gain in real and secure freedom to live with minimal fear of victimization by others.

The important issue for citizens to consider is whether they really decrease their overall likelihood of harm when they delegate the right to the police to use force, compared to the potential of being harmed by the police misusing that force. In a video series on the U.S. Constitution entitled *Law and Order* (1987), a victim of police misuse of authority, who later was able to obtain justice in the courts, said that he would still vote to give the police greater authority and risk the potential for misuse, rather than to have to fend off violent offenders in his community. He felt that with the police he at least had a chance for justice in the courts.

An argument against the social contract theory is that the police have always been instruments of the dominant class and seldom look out for the interests of all citizens equally. In fact, historically, the police have been extremely partisan toward those in power by looking out for their interests and by enforcing laws against opposing classes and groups. However, the idea of citizens actually delegating power and authority to the police has some historical support. Samuel Walker (1992), a police scholar, attributes the rapid social change in the early to mid-1800s to the breakdown of the old system of law enforcement and the need to establish modern police forces. When many people thought the best solution to contemporary social disorder was to create modern police departments, modeled after the newly formed London police, Americans showed great uncertainty and hesitated to create them.

Walker noted that despite the breakdown in law and order, Americans moved very slowly in creating new police forces. New York City did not create a new police force until 1845, eleven years after the first outbreak of riots. Philadelphia followed a more erratic course. Between 1833 and 1854, in the face of recurring riots, the city wrestled with the problem of police reform before finally creating a consolidated, citywide police force based on the London model. Walker argues that these delays reflected deep public uncertainty about modern police methods. For many Americans, police officers dispersed throughout the community brought to mind the hated British colonial army. Others were afraid that rival politicians would fight for control of the police department to their own partisan advantage—a fear that proved to be correct (Walker, 1992:7–8).

The dilemma created by the desire for police protection and the fear of losing control of the police was a factor in deciding whether or not to establish modern police forces in American cities. The notion that the police received their authority and right to use force from the citizens of the young democracy was as much a part of policing in the United States as was the subsequent partisan policing and corruption.

This democratic model of police in society therefore retains a certain historical validity and also provides a valuable standard or ideal for modern policing. In the same way that much of our Constitution remains an unfulfilled ideal, so does our means of societal control: it seems evident that a democratic model of policing could provide a framework for improving the police and therefore society. It is encouraging to note that the history of the police, especially since the 1960s, supports the idea that policing is progressively moving closer to this democratic ideal.

Following this model, Reiman (1985) outlines the implications of the social contract perspective for modern policing. He argues that "any coercive practice by legal agents that constricts and endangers the freedom of the citizenry, rather than expanding and securing it, reproduces the very condition of the state of nature that coercive legal agencies are meant to remedy" (p. 240). In other words, if the police use their authority and force in an exploitative fashion, it would literally undermine their own justification, because it would subject citizens to precisely the sort of risks they were given special powers to prevent. With regard to this tension, Reiman continues, "if law enforcement threatens rather than enhances our freedom, the distinction between crime and criminal justice is obliterated" (p. 241).

This view of the police is consistent with the idea of legitimate public power in which the power flows from the citizens to the police. To make this a reality, Reiman argues that the police must be accountable for their use of publicly assigned power—and be accountable to the wider public, not just to other law enforcement agents. For the use of force to be legitimate, he maintains, it must be viewed as owned by the public and loaned to police officers for specific reasons; further, it must be exercised under specific conditions (Reiman, 1985). In fact, under the democratic model of policing, one major function of the police is to guarantee citizens their rights.

Throughout this book, many of the issues examined (especially the hotly debated ones) will tie into the dilemma of policing described above. We hope this general analysis provides a foundation for thinking about the many topics covered in the book.

The Citizens' Role in Assisting the Police

The social contract perspective discussed above demonstrates the important tie between the police and the public based on a moral or philosophical argument. Beyond this basis for authority, the police have learned that they need a cooperative public to be effective in controlling crime and maintaining order. This has been termed the "co-production of police services" (Reiss, 1971). Findings indicate that between 75 and 85 percent of police-citizen encounters are generated by citizens calling for police services. This reflects the recent trends in policing strategy, which focus more and more on citizen involvement and cooperation with the police (e.g., community-based policing and problem-oriented policing). The police are sensitized to the importance of citizens' attitudes toward the police and how the police go about doing their job. Favorable attitudes toward the police and a willingness to cooperate with them are crucial to the success of many important police initiatives.

Many police administrators have found that positive contacts between the police and citizens and good policing can overcome negative attitudes held by citizens. As a result, they are making strong efforts to foster a conciliatory atmosphere and to develop programs and strategies, such as community-based policing, to cultivate positive police-citizen encounters. Weitzer and Tuch (2006) found that "the existence of community policing in one's neighborhood increases satisfaction with the police . . . for whites and blacks." While there is still much room for improvement, all of these measures lead to more police accountability to citizens. It is noteworthy, in spite of the fact that the role of the police officer has become increasingly complex and that citizens' expectations of the police continue to broaden, that the attitudes citizens hold toward the police and toward how well they do their job are generally positive. Matthew Durose and Lynn Langton for the Bureau of Justice Statistics, summarized nationwide data collected in 2011 on requests for police assistance (Durose and Langton, 2012). Their analysis provides important information on who calls the police and their evaluation of the police response. Consistent with other evaluations of the police, the vast majority of callers were satisfied with the police response. Ninety-three percent of the persons requesting police assistance thought the officers acted properly, and 86% evaluated the officers as helpful. Also, 85% of the callers were satisfied with the police response. It was noteworthy that no statistical differences were found between the percentage of Latinos', Blacks', and Whites' evaluation of the helpfulness of the police officers on the scene.

The Increasing Complexity of the Police Role

August Vollmer, police chief of Berkeley, California, from 1905–1932, and one of the first great reformers, once observed:

> The citizen expects police officers to have the wisdom of Solomon, the courage of David, the strength of Samson, the patience of Job, the leadership of Moses, the kindness of the Good Samaritan, the strategic training of Alexander, the faith of Daniel, the diplomacy of Lincoln, the tolerance of the Carpenter of Nazareth, and finally, an intimate knowledge of every branch of the natural, biological, and social sciences. If he had all these, he might be a good policeman! (cited in Bain, 1939)

As problems of social control have grown and become more complex, so have the actions and reactions required of the police. Unfortunately, the tendency has been to proliferate new agencies to meet specific needs, rather than to consolidate or to improve the effectiveness of existing law enforcement organizations. The result has been an increasingly complex and uncoordinated development of law enforcement, mired in the multiplicity of agencies and overlapping jurisdictions and responsibilities. Simultaneous with these developments has been the growing complexity of police functions and the growing public expectation of a more professional and competent police force. All of this has made the study of modern policing an exciting yet complex topic.

There is a great deal of confusion over the terms "policing" and "law enforcement." These terms are often seen as interchangeable. In common usage, a police officer is a law enforcement officer, but a law enforcement officer is not always a police officer. Another important distinction is that many law enforcement officers are not involved in traditional police work such as patrolling, traffic enforcement, service calls, and so on. For example, a private security guard or store detective may spend considerable time trying to detect crimes, but he or she is not a police officer. In the same light, a detective for a police department, or an agent of one of many state or federal law enforcement agencies, may have police power and authority but does not participate in traditional police work.

Law enforcement, whether practiced by a specialist sitting in front of a computer terminal or investigating a crime scene, or by the general practitioner cruising in his or her car or walking the beat, has an important role to play in U.S. society. It is onerous to have to separate police work from that of law enforcement, as they overlap in many situations. However, it is the work of the local, uniformed officer that represents the major portion of police work and, consequently, is the major focus of this book.

Police agencies and departments come in all sizes and many shapes. The federal government supports more than fifty law enforcement agencies, including the Federal Bureau of Investigation (FBI), the Drug Enforcement Agency (DEA), the United States Marshals Service, the United States Secret Service, the Bureau of Alcohol, Tobacco, Firearms and Explosives (ATF), and the United States Customs and Border Protection, among others. There are close to 60,000 federal law enforcement personnel who work for these agencies. While it may be necessary to refer to the work of these and other agencies, we will focus our attention on the local police in urban areas of the United States.

According to the most recent Bureau of Justice Statistics (2011) report that summarizes the findings of the 2008 census of state and local law enforcement agencies, there are more than one million full-time employees, including 765,246 sworn police officers, in state and local police forces in America. The numbers range from approximately 36,023 sworn officers and a budget well over one billion dollars in New York to numerous rural areas that employ only one part-time officer. It is interesting to note that more than 70,781 sworn full-time officers work in the five largest departments, but there are more than 10,000 police departments with ten or fewer employees. Police officers work for a large number of departments, but these are mostly small departments with approximately five sworn officers. The focus of this book is on the larger urban departments and their problems (for information on crime and policing in rural and small-town America, see Weisheit, Falcone, and Wells, 2006).

The articles that follow provide an exciting selection of readings that offer valuable insights into many of the important issues concerning the police role and police work. We will begin with a historical overview of policing.

REFERENCES

Bain, Read. 1939. "The Policeman on the Beat," *Science Monthly* 48:5.

Bureau of Justice Statistics. 2011. *Census of State and Local Law Enforcement Agencies, 2008.* Washington, DC: U.S. Department of Justice, NCJ 233982 [www.bjs.gov/index.cfm?ty=pbdetail&iid=2216].

Durose, Matthew and Lynn Langton. 2012. *Requests for Police Assistance, 2011.* Washington D.C.: Bureau of Justice Statistics, Department of Justice, NCI 242938.

Hobbes, Thomas. 1651. *Leviathan.* Reprint 1956. Chicago: Henry Regnery.

Klockars, Carl. 1984. "Blue Lies and Police Placebos," *American Behavioral Scientist* 4(27):529–44.

Law and Order. 1987. Princeton, NJ: Films for the Humanities.

Olsen, Mancur. 1965. *The Logic of Collective Action.* Cambridge: Harvard University Press.

Pollock, Joycelyn. 1994. *Ethics in Crime and Justice: Dilemmas and Decisions,* 2d ed. Belmont, CA: Wadsworth.

Quinney, Richard. 1970. *The Social Reality of Crime*. Boston: Little, Brown, and Company.

Reiman, Jeffrey. 1985. "The Social Contract and the Police Use of Deadly Force." In *Moral Issues in Police Work*, edited by Frederick A. Ellison and Michael Feldberg. Savage, MD: Rowman & Littlefield Publishers.

Reiss, A. J. 1971. *The Police and the Public*. New Haven: Yale University Press.

Stark, Rodney. 2000. *Sociology*, 8th ed. New York: Wadsworth Publishing Company.

Walker, Samuel. 1992. *The Police in America*, 2d ed. New York: McGraw-Hill.

Weisheit, Ralph A., David N. Falcone, and L. Edward Wells. 2006. *Crime and Policing in Rural and Small-Town America*, 3rd ed. Long Grove, IL: Waveland Press.

Weitzer, Ronald and Steven A. Tuch. 2006. *Race and Policing in America: Conflict and Reform*. New York: Cambridge University Press.

2

The Development of the American Police
An Historical Overview

Craig D. Uchida

Introduction

During the past 30 years, scholars have become fascinated with the history of police. A plethora of studies have emerged as a result. Early writings were concerned primarily with descriptions of particular police agencies. Roger Lane (1967) and James F. Richardson (1970) broke new ground in describing the origins of policing in Boston and New York, respectively. Since that time, others have followed suit with narratives of police organizations in St. Louis (Maniha, 1970; Reichard, 1975), Denver (Rider, 1971), Washington D.C. (Alfers, 1975), Richmond (Cei, 1975), and Detroit (Schneider, 1980).

Other authors have focused on issues in policing. Wilbur R. Miller (1977) examined the legitimation of the police in London and New York. Samuel Walker (1977) and Robert Fogelson (1977) concentrated on professionalism and reform of errant police in the nineteenth and twentieth centuries. Eric Monkkonen (1981) took an entirely different approach by using quantitative methods to explain the development of policing in 23 cities from 1860 to 1920.[1]

Overall these histories illustrate the way in which police have developed over time. They point out the origins of concepts like crime prevention, authority, professionalism, and discretion. In addition, these historical analyses show the roots of problems in policing, such as corruption, brutality, and inefficiency.

The major emphasis of this article is to examine the development of the police since A.D. 900 and more specifically, to determine whether the role of the police has changed in American society over a period of about 300 years.

Prepared especially for *Critical Issues in Policing* by Craig D. Uchida.

This is not an easy task. The debate over the "true" or "proper" police function is an ongoing one and cannot itself be resolved in an article such as this.[2] However, by describing the various roles, activities, and functions of law enforcement over time, we can at least acquire a glimpse of what the police do and how their activities have varied over time. To do so, we rely on a number of important contributions to the study of the history of police.

The article is divided into eight parts and basically covers the history of law enforcement and its effect on colonial America to the present. Part I examines the English heritage of law enforcement and its effect on colonial America. The colonists relied heavily on the mother country for their ideas regarding community involvement in law enforcement.

Part II examines the problems of urban centers in the eighteenth and nineteenth centuries and turns to the development of the full-time uniformed police in England and America. The preventive approach to law enforcement became central to the police role in both London and American cities. Part III is concerned with police activity in nineteenth-century American cities. Patrol work and officer involvement in corruption are discussed.

In Part IV the reform movement of the Progressive Era is examined. From 1890 to 1920 reformers attempted to implement social, economic, and political change in the cities. As part of city government, police departments were targets of change as well.

In Part V we study a second reform era. From 1910 to 1960 chiefs became involved in a movement to professionalize the police. Part VI covers the riots and disorders of the 1960s and their immediate effect on policing across the country. Part VII discusses the long-term legacy of the 1960s. That is, we examine the developments of the police since 1969 in terms of research and public policy. Lastly, in Part VIII we describe a third reform movement in policing—the development of community oriented policing of the 1980s and 1990s.

I. Communities, Constables, and Colonists

Like much of America's common-law tradition, the origins of modern policing can be linked directly to its English heritage. Ideas concerning community policing, crime prevention, the posse, constables, and sheriffs developed from English law enforcement. Beginning at about A.D. 900, the role of law enforcement was placed in the hands of the common, everyday citizens. Each citizen was held responsible for aiding neighbors who might be victims of outlaws and thieves. Because no police officers existed, individuals used state-sanctioned force to maintain social control. Charles Reith, a noted English historian, refers to this model of law enforcement as "kin police" (Reith, 1956). Individuals were considered responsible for their "kin" (relatives) and followed the adage, "I am my brother's keeper." Slowly this model developed into a more formalized "communitarian," or community-based police system.

After the Norman Conquest of 1066, a community model was established, which was called frankpledge. The frankpledge police system required that every male above the age of twelve form a group with nine of his neighbors called a tything. Each tything was sworn to apprehend and deliver to court any of its members who committed a crime. Each person was pledged to help protect fellow citizens and, in turn, would be protected. This system was "obligatory" in nature, in that tythingmen were not paid salaries for their work, but were required by law to carry out certain duties (Klockars, 1985:21). Tythingmen were required to hold suspects in custody while they were awaiting trial and to make regular appearances in court to present information on wrong-doing by members of their own or other tythings. If any member of the tything failed to perform his required duties, all members of the group would be levied severe fines.

Ten tythings were grouped into a hundred, directed by a constable (appointed by the local nobleman) who, in effect, became the first policeman. That is, the constable was the first official with law enforcement responsibility greater than simply helping one's neighbor. Just as the tythings were grouped into hundreds, the hundreds were grouped into shires, which are similar to counties today. The supervisor of each shire was the shire reeve (or sheriff), who was appointed by the king.

Frankpledge began to disintegrate by the thirteenth century. Inadequate supervision by the king and his appointees led to its downfall. As frankpledge slowly declined, the parish constable system emerged to take its place. The Statute of Winchester of 1285 placed more authority in the hands of the constable for law enforcement. One man from each parish served a one-year term as constable on a rotating basis. Though not paid for his work, the constable was responsible for organizing a group of watchmen who would guard the gates of the town at night. These watchmen were also unpaid and selected from the parish population. If a serious disturbance took place, the parish constable had the authority to raise the "hue and cry." This call to arms meant that all males in the parish were to drop what they were doing and come to the aid of the constable.

In the mid-1300s the office of justice of the peace was created to assist the shire reeve in controlling his territory. The local constable and the shire reeve became assistants to the justice of the peace and supervised the night watchmen, served warrants, and took prisoners into custody for appearance before justice of the peace courts.

The English system continued with relative success well into the 1700s. By the end of the eighteenth century, however, the growth of large cities, civil disorders, and increased criminal activity led to changes in the system.

Law Enforcement in Colonial America

In Colonial America (seventeenth and eighteenth centuries), policing followed the English systems. The sheriff, constable, and watch were easily adapted to the colonies. The county sheriff, appointed by the governor, became the most important law enforcement agent particularly when the colonies remained small and primarily rural. The sheriff's duties included apprehending criminals, serving subpoenae, appearing in court, and collecting taxes. The sheriff was paid a fixed amount for each task he performed. Since sheriffs received higher fees based on the taxes they collected, apprehending criminals was not a primary concern. In fact, law enforcement was a low priority.

In the larger cities and towns, such as New York, Boston, and Philadelphia, constables and the night watch conducted a wide variety of tasks. The night watch reported fires, raised the hue and cry, maintained street lamps, arrested or detained suspicious persons, and walked the rounds. Constables engaged in similarly broad tasks—taking suspects to court, eliminating health hazards, bringing witnesses to court, and so on.

For the most part, the activities of the constables and the night watch were "reactive" in nature. That is, these men responded to criminal behavior only when requested by victims or witnesses (Monkkonen, 1981). Rather than preventing crime, discovering criminal behavior, or acting in a "proactive" fashion, these individuals relied on others to define their work. Public health violations were the only types of activity that required the officers to exercise initiative.

II. Preventive Police: Cops and Bobbies

The development of a "new" police system has been carefully documented by a number of American and English historians. Sir Leon Radzinowicz (1948–1968), Charles Reith (1956), and T. A. Critchley (1967) are among the more notable English writers. Roger Lane (1967), James F. Richardson (1970), Wilbur R. Miller (1977), Samuel Walker (1977), and Eric Monkkonen (1981) represent a rather diverse group of American historians who describe and analyze a number of early police departments. Taken together these works present the key elements of the activities of the first English and American police systems that used the preventive model.

During the mid- to late 1700s the growth of industry in England and in Europe led to rapid development in the cities. London, in particular, expanded at an unprecedented rate. From 1750 to 1820 the population nearly doubled (Miller, 1977) and the urban economy became more complex and specialized. The Industrial Revolution led to an increase in the number of factories, tenements, vehicles, and marketplaces. With industrial growth came a breakdown in social control, as a crime, riots, disorder, and public health problems disrupted the city. Food riots, wage protests, poor sewage control, pickpockets, burglars, and vandals created difficulties for city dwellers. The upper and middle classes, concerned about these issues sought more protection and preventive measures. The constable-watch system of law enforcement could no longer deal successfully with the problems of the day, and alternative solutions were devised.

Some of the alternatives included using the militia; calling out the "yeomanry" or cavalry volunteers for assistance; swearing in more law-abiding citizens as constables; or employing the army to quell riot situations (Richardson, 1974:10). However, these were short-term solutions to a long-term problem.

Another proposal was to replace the constable-watch system with a stronger, more centralized police force. Henry and John Fielding (magistrates in the 1750s), Patrick Colquhoun (a magistrate from 1792 to 1818), and philosopher Jeremy Bentham and his followers advocated the creation of a police force whose principal object was the prevention of crime. A preventive police force would act as a deterrent to criminals and would be in the best interests of society. But the idea of a uniformed police officer was opposed by many citizens and politicians in England. An organized police force too closely resembled a standing army, which gave government potentially despotic control over citizens and subjects. The proponents of a police force eventually won out, based primarily on the disorder and fear of crime experienced by London residents. After much debate in the early 1800s, the London Metropolitan Police Act was finally approved by Parliament in 1829 (see Critchley, 1967 and Reith, 1956).

The London Metropolitan Police Act established a full-time, uniformed police force with the primary purpose of patrolling the city. Sir Robert Peel, Britain's Home Secretary, is credited with the formation of the police. Peel synthesized the ideas of the Fieldings, Colquhoun, and Bentham into law; convinced Parliament of the need for police; and guided the early development of the force.

Through Peel and his two police commissioners, Charles Rowan and Richard Mayne, the role of the London Police was formulated. Crime prevention was the primary function, but to enforce the laws and to exert its authority, the police had to first gain legitimacy in the eyes of the public. According to Wilbur R. Miller (1977) the legitimation of the London police was carefully orchestrated by Peel and his associates. These men recognized that in order to gain authority police officers had to act in a certain manner or the public would reject them. To gain acceptance in the eyes of the citizen, Peel and his associates selected men who were even-tempered and reserved; chose a uniform that was unassuming (navy blue rather than military red); insisted that officers be restrained and polite; meted out appropriate discipline; and did not allow officers to carry guns. Overall, the London police emphasized their legitimacy as based on *institutional* authority—that their power was grounded in the English Constitution and that their behavior was determined by rules of law. In essence, this meant that the power of the London "bobby" or "Peeler" was based on the institution of the government.

American cities and towns encountered problems similar to those in England. Cities grew at phenomenal rates; civil disorders swept the nation and crime was perceived to be increasing. New York, for example, sprouted from a population of 33,000 in 1790 to 150,000 in 1830. Foreign immigrants, particularly Irish and Germans, accounted for a large portion of the increase. Traveling to America in search of employment and better lifestyles, the immigrants competed with native-born Americans for skilled and unskilled positions. As a result, the American worker saw Irishmen and Germans as social and economic threats.

Other tensions existed in the city as well. The race question was an important one in the northern cities as well as in the southern plantation. In fact, historians have shown that hostility to blacks was just as high in the North as in the South (Litwack, 1961). Those opposed to slavery (the abolitionists) were often met by violence when they attempted to speak out against it.

Between the 1830s and 1870s, numerous conflicts occurred because of ethnic and racial differences, economic failures, moral questions, and during elections of public officials. In New York, 1834 was designated the "Year of the Riots" because so many took place (Miller, 1977). The mayoral election and anti-abolitionist sentiment were the two main reasons for the disorders. Other cities faced similar problems. In Philadelphia, the Broad Street Riot of 1837 involved almost 15,000 residents. The incident occurred because native-born volunteer firemen returning from a fire could not get by an Irish funeral procession. In St. Louis, in 1850 a mob destroyed the brothels in the city in attempt to enforce standards of public decency. To quell most of these disturbances, the local militia was called in to suppress the violence, as the constables and the night watch were ineffectual.

At the same time that the riots occurred, citizens perceived that crime was increasing. Homicides, robberies, and thefts were though to be on the rise. In addition, vagrancy, prostitution, gambling, and other vices were more observable on the streets. These types of criminal activities and the general deterioration of the city led to a sense of a loss of social control. But in spite of the apparent immediacy of these problems, replacements for the constable-watch police system did not appear over night.

The political forces in the large industrial cities like New York, Philadelphia, Boston, and others precluded the immediate acceptance of a London-style police department. City councils, mayors, state legislatures, and governors debated and wrangled over a number of questions and could not come to an immediate agreement over the type of police they wanted. In New York City, for example, while problems emerged in 1834, the movement to form a preventive police department began in 1841, was officially created in 1845, but officers did not begin wearing uniforms until 1853.

While the first American police departments modeled themselves after the London Metropolitan Police, they borrowed selectively rather than exactly. The most notable carryover was the adoption of the preventive patrol idea. A police presence would alter the behavior of individuals and would be available to maintain order in an efficient manner. Differences, however, between the London and American police abounded. Miller (1977), in his comparative study of New York and London police, shows the drastic differences between the two agencies.

The London Metropolitan Police was a highly centralized agency. An extension of the national government, the police department was purposely removed from the direct political influence of the people. Furthermore, as noted above, Sir Robert Peel recruited individuals who fit a certain mold. Peel insisted that a polite, aloof officer who was trained and disciplined according to strict guidelines would be best suited for the function of crime prevention. In addition, the bobbies were encouraged to look upon police work as a career in professional civil service.

Unlike the London police, American police systems followed the style of local and municipal governments. City governments, created in the era of the "common man" and democratic participation, were highly decentralized. Mayors were largely figureheads; real power lay in the wards and neighborhoods. City councilmen or aldermen ran the government and used political patronage freely. The police departments shared this style of participation and decentralization. The police were an extension of different political factions, rather than an extension of city government. Police officers were recruited and selected by political leaders in a particular ward or precinct.

As a result of the democratic nature of government, legal intervention by the police was limited. Unlike the London police, which relied on formal institutional power, the American police relied on informal control or individual authority. That is, instead of drawing on institutional legitimacy (i.e., parliamentary laws), each police officer had to establish his own authority among the citizens he patrolled. The personal, informal police officer could win the respect of the citizenry by knowing local standards and expectations. This meant that different police behavior would occur in different neighborhoods. In New York, for example, the cop was free to act as he chose within the context of broad public expectations. He was less limited by institutional and legal restraints than was his London counterpart, entrusted with less formal power, but given broader personal discretion.

III. Police Activity in the Nineteenth Century

American police systems began to appear almost overnight from 1860 to 1890 (Monkkonen, 1981). Once large cities like New York, Philadelphia, Boston, and Cincinnati had adopted the English model, the new version of policing spread from larger to smaller cities rather quickly. Where New York had debated for almost ten years before formally adopting the London style of policing, Cleveland, Buffalo, Detroit, and other cities readily accepted the innovation. Monkkonen explains that the police were a part of a growing range of services provided by urban administrations. Sanitation, fire, and health services were also adopted during this period and the police were simply a part of their natural growth.

Across these departments, however, differences flourished. Police activity varied depending upon the local government and political factions in power. Standards for officer selection (if any), training procedures, rules and regulations, levels of enforcement of laws, and police-citizen relationships differed across the United States. At the same time, however, there were some striking similarities.

Patrol Officers

The nineteenth century patrolman was basically a political operative rather than a London-style professional committed to public service (Walker, 1977). Primarily selected for his political service, the police officer owed his allegiance to the ward boss and police captain who chose him.

Police officers were paid well but had poor job security. Police salaries compared favorably with other occupations. On average in 1880, most major cities paid policemen in the neighborhood of $900 a year. Walker (1977) reports that a skilled tradesman in the building industry earned about $770 a year, while those in manufacturing could expect about $450 a year. A major drawback, however, was that job security was poor, as their employment relied on election day events. In Cincinnati, for example, in 1880, 219 of the 295 members of the force were dismissed, while another 20 resigned because of political change in the municipal government. Other departments had similar turnover rates.

New officers were sent out on patrol with no training and few instructions beyond their rulebooks. Proper arrest procedures, rules of law, and so on were unknown to the officers. Left to themselves, they developed their own strategies for coping with life in the streets.

Police Work

Police officers walked a beat in all types of weather for two to six hours of a 12-hour day. The remaining time was spent at the station house on reserve. During actual patrol duty, police officers were required to maintain order and make arrests, but they often circumvented their responsibilities. Supervision was extremely limited once an officer was beyond the station house. Sergeants and captains had no way of contacting their men while they were on the beat, as communications technology was limited. Telegraph lines linked district stations to headquarters in the 1850s, but call boxes on the beat were not introduced until late in the nineteenth century, and the radio and motorized communications did not appear until the 1900s (Lane, 1980). Police officers, then, acted alone and used their own initiative.

Unfortunately, little is known about ordinary patrol work or routine interactions with the public. However, historians have pieced together trends in police work based on arrest statistics. While these data have their limitations, they nonetheless provide a view of police activity.

Monkkonen's work (1981) found that from 1860 to 1920 arrests declined in 23 of the largest cities in the United States. In particular, crimes without victims (vice, disturbances, drunkenness, other public order offenses) fell dramatically. Overall, Monkkonen estimated that arrests declined by more than 33 percent during the 60-year period. This trend runs contrary to "common-sense notions about the crime and growth of industrial cities, immigration and social conflict" (p. 75). Further analysis showed that the decline occurred because the police role shifted from one of controlling the "dangerous class" to one of controlling criminal behavior only. From 1860 to 1890, Monkkonen argues, the police were involved in assisting the poor, in taking in overnight lodgers, and in returning lost children to their parents or örphanages. In the period of 1890 to 1920, however, the police changed their role, structure, and behavior because of external demands upon them. As a result, victimless arrests declined, while assaults, thefts, and homicide arrests increased slightly. Overall, however, the crime trend showed a decrease.

Police Corruption and Lawlessness

One of the major themes in the study of nineteenth-century policing is the large-scale corruption that occurred in numerous departments across the country. The lawlessness of the police—their systematic corruption and nonenforcement of the laws—was one of the paramount issues in municipal politics during the late 1800s.

Police corruption was a part of a broader social and political problem. During this period, political machines ran municipal governments. That is, political parties (Democrats and Republicans) controlled the mayor's office, the city councils and local wards. Municipal agencies (fire departments, sanitation services, school districts, the courts, etc.) were also under the aegis of political parties. As part of this system, political patronage was rampant. Employment in exchange for votes or money was a common procedure. Police departments in New York, Chicago, Philadelphia, Kansas City, San Francisco, and Los Angles were filled with political appointees as police officers. To insure their employment, officers followed the norms of the political party, often protecting illicit activities conducted by party favorites.

Corrupt practices extended from the chief's office down to the patrol officer. In New York City, for example, Chief William Devery (1898–1901) protected gambling dens and illegal prize fighting because his friend, Tim Sullivan (a major political figure on the Lower East Side) had interests in those areas. Police captains like Alexander "Clubber" Williams and Timothy Creeden acquired extensive wealth from protecting prostitutes, saloonkeepers, and gamblers. Williams, a brutal officer (hence, the nickname Clubber), was said to have a 53-foot yacht and residences in New York and the Connecticut suburbs. Since a captain's salary was about $3,000 a year in the 1890s, Williams had to collect from illegal enterprises in order to maintain his investments.

Because police officers worked alone or in small groups, there were ample opportunities to shake down peddlers and small businesses. Detectives allowed con men, pickpockets, and thieves to go about their business in return for a share of the proceeds. Captains often established regular payment schedules for houses of prostitution depending upon the number of girls in the house and the rates charged by them. The monthly total for police protection ranged between $25 and $75 per house plus $500 to open or reopen after being raided (Richardson, 1970).

Officers who did not go along with the nonenforcement of laws or did not approve of the graft and corruption of others found themselves transferred to less-than desirable areas. Promotions were also denied; they were reserved for the politically astute and wealthy officer (promotions could cost $10,000 to $15,000).

These types of problems were endemic to most urban police agencies throughout the country. They led to inefficiency and inequality of police services.

IV. Reform, Rejection, and Revision

A broad reform effort began to emerge toward the end of the nineteenth century. Stimulated mainly by a group known as the Progressives, attempts were made to create a truly professional police force. The Progressives were upper-middle-class, educated Protestants who opposed the political machines, sought improvements in government, and desired a change in American morality. By eliminating machine politics from government, all facets of social services, including the police, would improve.

These reformers found that the police were without discipline, strong leadership, and qualified personnel. To improve conditions, the Progressives recommended three changes: (1) the departments should be centralized; (2) personnel should be upgraded; and (3) the police function should be narrowed (Fogelson, 1977). Centralization of the police meant that more power and authority should be placed in the hands of the chief. Autonomy from politicians was crucial to centralization. Upgrading the rank-and-file meant better training, discipline, and selection. Finally, the reformers urged that police give up all activities unrelated to crime. Police had run the ambulances, handled licensing of businesses, and sheltered the poor. By concentrating on fighting crime, the police would be removed from their service orientation and their ties to political parties would be severed.

From 1890 to 1920 the Progressive reformers struggled to implement their reform ideology in cities across the country. Some inroads were made during this period, including the establishment of police commissions, the use of civil service exams, and legislative reforms.

The immediate response to charges of corruption were to create police administrative boards. The reformers attempted to take law enforcement appointments out of the hands of mayors and city councilmen and place control in the hands of oversight committees. The Progressives believed that politics would be eliminated from policing by using this maneuver. In New York, for example, the Lexow Committee, which investigated the corrupt practices of the department, recommended the formation of a bipartisan Board of Police Commissioners in 1895. Theodore Roosevelt became a member of this board, but to his dismay found that the commissioners were powerless to improve the state of policing. The bipartisan nature of the board (two Democrats and two Republicans) meant that consensus could not be reached on important issues. As a result, by 1900 the New York City police were again under the influence of party politics. In the following year the Board of Commissioners was abolished and the department was placed under the responsibility of a single commissioner (Walker, 1977). Other cities had similar experiences with the police commission approach. Cincinnati, Kansas City, St. Louis, and Baltimore were among those that adopted the commission, but found it to be short-lived. The major problem was still political—the police were viewed as an instrument of the political machine at the neighborhood level, and reformers could not counter the effects of the Democratic or Republican parties.

Civil service was one answer to upgrading personnel. Officers would be selected and promoted based on merit, as measured by a competitive exam. Moreover, the officer would be subject to review by his supervisors and removal from the force could take place if there was sufficient cause. Civil service met with some resistance by officers and reformers alike. The problem was that in guarding against the effects of patronage and favoritism, civil service became a rigid, almost inflexible procedure. The civil service exam measured abstract knowledge rather than the qualities required for day-to-day work, and civil service procedures were viewed as problematic. Eventually, the program did help to eliminate the more blatant forms of political patronage in almost all of the large police departments (Walker, 1977).

During this 30-year period, the efforts of the Progressive reformers did not change urban departments drastically. The reform movement resulted, in part, in the elimination of the widespread graft and corruption of the 1890s, but substantive changes in policing did not take place. Chiefs continued to lack power and authority, many officers had little or no education, training was limited, and the police role continued to include a wide variety of tasks.

Robert Fogelson (1977) suggests several reasons for the failure of reform. First, political machines were too difficult to break. Despite the efforts by the Progressives, politicians could still count on individual supporters to undermine the reforms. Second, police officers themselves resented the Progressives' interventions. Reformers were viewed by the police as individuals who knew little about police work and officers saw their proposals for change as ill-conceived. Finally, the reforms failed because the idea of policing could not be divorced from politics. That is, the character of the big-city police was interconnected with policy-making agencies that helped to decide which laws were enforced, which public was served, and whose peace was kept (Fogelson, 1977). Separating the police completely from politics could not take place.

V. The Emergence of Police Professionalism

A second reform effort emerged in the wake of the failure of the Progressives. Within police circles, a small cadre of chiefs sought and implemented a variety of innovations that would improve policing generally. From about 1910 to 1960 police chiefs carried on another reform movement, advocating that police adopt the professional model.

The professional department embodied a number of characteristics. First, the officers were experts; they applied knowledge to their tasks and were the only ones qualified to do the job. Second, the department was autonomous from external influences, such as political parties. This also meant that the department made its own rules and regulated its personnel. Finally, the department was administratively efficient, in that it carried out its mandate to enforce the law through modern technology and businesslike practices. These reforms were similar to those of the Progressives, but because they came from within the police organizations themselves, they met with more success.

Leadership and technology assisted the movement to professionalize the police. Chiefs like Richard Sylvester, August Vollmer, and O. W. Wilson emphasized the use of innovative methods in police work. Samuel Walker (1977) notes that Sylvester, the chief of the Washington, D.C. police, helped to establish the idea of professionalism among police chiefs. As president of the International Association of Chiefs of Police (IACP), Sylvester inculcated the spirit of reform into the organization. He stressed acceptance of technological innovations, raised the level of discussion among chiefs to include crime control ideas, and promoted professionalism generally.

The major innovator among the chiefs was August Vollmer, chief of the Berkeley, California, police. Vollmer was known for his promising work in developing college-level police education programs, bicycle and automobile patrol, and scientific crime detection aids. His department was the first to use forensic science in solving crimes.

Vollmer's emphasis on the quality of police personnel was tied closely to the idea of the professional officer. Becoming an expert in policing meant having the requisite credentials. Vollmer initiated intelligence, psychiatric, and neurological tests by which to select applicants. He was the first police chief to actively recruit college students. In addition, he was instrumental in linking the police department with the University of California at Berkeley. Another concern of Vollmer dealt with the efficient delivery of police services. His department became the first in the nation to use automobiles and the first to hire a full-time forensic scientist to help solve crimes (Douthit, 1975).

O. W. Wilson, Vollmer's student, followed in his mentor's footsteps by advocating efficiency within the police bureaucracy through scientific techniques. As chief in Wichita, Kansas, Wilson conducted the first systematic study of one-officer squad cars. He argued that one-officer cars were efficient, effective, and economical. Despite arguments from patrol officers that their safety was at risk, Wilson claimed that the public received better service with single-officer cars.

Wilson's other contributions include his classic textbook, *Police Administration*, which lays out specific ideas regarding the use of one-man patrol cars, deployment of personnel on the streets, disciplinary measures, and organizational structure. Later in his career, Wilson accepted a professorship at U. C. Berkeley where he taught and trained law enforcement officers. In 1947 he founded the first professional School of Criminology.

Other chiefs contributed to the professional movement as well. William Parker changed the Los Angeles Police Department (LAPD) from a corrupt, traditional agency to an innovative, professional organization. From 1950 to his death in 1966, Parker served as chief. He was known for his careful planning, emphasis on efficiency, and his rigorous personnel selection and training procedures. His public relations campaigns and adept political maneuvers enabled him to gain the respect of the media and the community. As a result, the LAPD became a model for reform across the country.

Technological changes also enabled the police to move toward professionalism. The patrol car, two-way radio, and telephone altered the way in which the police operated and the manner in which citizens made use of the police. Motorized patrol meant more efficient coverage of the city and quicker response to calls for service. The two-way radio dramatically increased the supervisory capacity of the police. Continuous contact between sergeant and police officer could be maintained. Finally, the telephone provided the link between the public and the police. Though not a new invention, its use in conjunction with the car and two-way radio meant that the efficient response to calls for service would be realized.

Overall, the second reform movement met with more success than the Progressive attempt, though it did not achieve its goal of professionalization. Walker (1977) and Fogelson (1977) agree that the quality of police officers greatly improved during this period. Police departments turned away the ill-educated individual, but at the same time failed to draw college graduates to their ranks. In terms of autonomy, police reformers and others were able to reduce the influence of political parties in departmental affairs. Chiefs obtained more power and authority in their management abilities, but continued to receive input from political leaders. In fact, most chiefs remained political appointees. In terms of efficiency, the police moved forward in serving the public more quickly and competently. Technological innovations clearly assisted the police in this area, as did streamlining the organizations themselves. However, the innovations also created problems. Citizens came to expect more from the police—faster response times, more arrests, and less overall crime. These expectations, as well as other difficulties, led to trying times for the police in the 1960s.

VI. Riots and Renewal

Policing in America encountered its most serious crisis in the 1960s. The rise in crime, the civil rights movement, anti-war sentiment, and riots in the cities brought the police into the center of a maelstrom.

During the decade of the 1960s crime increased at a phenomenal rate. Between 1960 and 1970 the crime rate per 100,000 persons doubled. Most troubling was the increase in violent crime—the robbery rate almost tripled during these ten years. As crime increased, so too did the demands for its reduction. The police, in emphasizing its crime fighting ability, had given the public a false expectation they had created. As a result, the public image of the police was tarnished.

The civil rights movement created additional demands for the police. The movement, begun in the 1950s, sought equality for black Americans in all facets of life. Sit-ins at segregated lunch counters, boycotts of bus services, attempts at integrating schools, and demonstrations in the streets led to direct confrontations with law enforcement officers. The police became the symbol of a society that denied blacks equal justice under the law.

Eventually, the frustrations of black Americans erupted into violence in northern and southern cities. Riots engulfed almost every major city between 1964 and 1968. Most of the disorders were initiated by a routine incident involving the police. The spark that initiated the riots occurred on July 16, 1964, when a white New York City police officer shot and killed a black teenager. Black leaders in the Harlem ghetto organized protests demanding disciplinary action against the officer. Two days later, the demonstrators marched on precinct headquarters, where rock throwing began. Eventually, looting and burning erupted during the night and lasted two full days. When the riot was brought under control one person was dead, more than 100 injured, almost 500 arrested, and millions of dollars worth of property destroyed. In the following year, the Watts riot in Los Angeles led to more devastation. Thirty-four persons died, a thousand were injured, and 4,000 arrested. By 1966, 43 more riots broke out across the country, and in 1967 violence in Newark and Detroit exceeded the 1965 Watts riot. Disorders engulfed Newark for five days, leaving 23 dead, while the Detroit riot a week later lasted nearly seven days and resulted in 43 deaths with $40 million in property damages.

On the final day of the Detroit riot, President Lyndon Johnson appointed a special commission to investigate the problem of civil disorder. The National Advisory Commission on Civil Disorders (The Kerner Commission) identified institutional racism as the underlying cause of the rioting. Unemployment, discrimination in jobs and housing, inadequate social services, and unequal justice at the hands of the law were among the problems cited by the commission.

Police actions were also cited as contributing to the disorders. Direct police intervention had sparked the riots in Harlem, Watts, Newark, and Detroit. In Watts and Newark the riots were set off by routine traffic stops. In Detroit a police raid on an after-hours bar in the ghetto touched off the disorders there. The police thus became the focus of the national attention.

The Kerner Commission and other investigations found several problems in police departments. First, police conduct included brutality, harassment, and abuse of power. Second, training and supervision was inadequate. Third, police-community relations were poor. Fourth, the employment of the black officers lagged far behind the growth of the black population.

As a means of coping with these problems in policing (and other agencies of the criminal justice system) President Johnson created a crime commission and Congress authorized federal assistance to criminal justice. The president's crime commission produced a final report that emphasized the need for more research, higher qualifications of criminal justice personnel, and greater coordination of the national crime-control effort. The federal aid program to justice agencies resulted in the Office of Law Enforcement Assistance, a forerunner of the Law Enforcement Assistance Administration (LEAA).

VII. The Legacy of the 60s

The events of the 1960s forced the police, politicians, and policy makers to reassess the state of law enforcement in the United States. For the first time, academics rushed to study the police in an effort to explain their problems and crises. With federal funding from LEAA and private organizations researchers began to study the police from a number of perspectives. Sociologists, political scientists, psychologists, and historians began to scrutinize different aspects of policing. Traditional methods of patrol development, officer selection, and training were questioned. Racial discrimination in employment practices, in arrests, and in the use of deadly force were among the issues closely examined.

In addition, the professional movement itself came into question. As Walker notes, the legacy of professionalization was "ambiguous" (Walker, 1977:167). On one hand, the police made improvements in their level of service, training, recruitment, and efficiency. On the other hand, a number of problems remained and a number of new ones emerged. Corruption scandals continued to present problems. In New York, Chicago, and Denver systematic corruption was discovered. Political parties persisted in their links to policing.

The professional movement had two unintended consequences. The first involved the development of a police subculture. The second was the problem of the police-community relations. In terms of the subculture, police officers began to feel alienated from administrators, the media, and the public and turned inward as a result. Patrol officers began to resent the police hierarchy because of the emphasis on following orders and regulations. While this established uniformity in performance and eliminated some abuses of power, it also stifled creativity and the talents of many officers. Rather than thinking for themselves (as professionals would) patrol officers followed orders given by sergeants, lieutenants, or other ranking officers. This led to morale problems and criticism of police administration by the rank and file.

Patrol officers saw the media and the public as foes because of the criticism and disrespect cast their way. As the crime rate increased, newspaper accounts criticized the police for their inability to curtail it. As the riots persisted, some citizens cried for more order, while others demanded less oppression by the police on the streets. The conflicting message given to the patrol officers by these groups led to distrust, alienation, and frustration. Only by standing together did officers feel comfortable in their working environment.

The second unintended consequence of professionalism was the problems it generated for police-community relations. Modern technology, like the patrol car, removed the officer from the street and eliminated routine contact with citizens. The impersonal style of professionalism often exacerbated police-community problems. Tactics such as aggressive patrol in black neighborhoods, designed to suppress crime efficiently, created more racial tensions.

The problems called into question the need for and effectiveness of professionalism. Some police administrators suggested abandoning the movement. Others sought to continue the effort while adjusting for and solving the difficulties. For the most part, the goal of professionalization remains operative. In the 1970s and 1980s, progressive police chiefs and organizations pressed for innovations in policing. As a result, social science research became an important part of policy-making decisions. By linking research to issues like domestic violence, repeat offenders, use of deadly force, training techniques, and selection procedures, police executives increased their ability to make effective decisions.

VIII. From Reactive to Proactive: Community Policing Strategies

As a result of the problems of the 1960s and 1970s, a third wave of reform of police operations and strategies began to emerge—community-oriented policing.

Community policing came to light as an idea and philosophy in response to the communication gap between police and community and because of research studies that questioned police tactics and strategies. A new paradigm, which incorporated the "broken windows" theory, proactive policing, and problem-oriented policing shaped the community policing reform era.

Researchers began to question some of the basic premises of law enforcement. They found that randomly patrolling an area of a city does not deter crime (Kelling, et al., 1974). Other researchers found that detectives could not solve crime by simply gathering evidence from crime scenes—they needed witnesses and other information to assist them (Greenwood, Chaiken and Petersilia, 1977). Researchers also found that rapid response to calls for service does not always result in the apprehension of offenders (Spelman and Brown, 1984).

Police strategists recognized that simply reacting to calls for service limits the ability of law enforcement to control crime and maintain order. Police on patrol cannot see enough to control crime effectively—they do not know how to intervene to improve the quality of life in the community. The reactive strategy used during the professional era no longer was effective in dealing with complex problems in the 1980s and 1990s. Instead, Herman Goldstein (1979) and James Q. Wilson and George Kelling (1982) called for police to engage in proactive work and problem-oriented policing. A whole body of work from police researchers, strategists, and reformers laid the groundwork for the community policing movement.

Defining Community Policing

Community policing has a number of different definitions (Maguire, et al., 1997). For some, community policing means instituting foot patrols and bicycle patrols, getting out of patrol cars, and a host of other activities that are designed to bring police officers closer to the communities they serve. For others, it means order maintenance, cleaning up tattered neighborhoods, and fixing "broken windows" (Wilson and Kelling, 1982). For many agencies, community policing is simply implementing a series of community-relations programs, including Drug Abuse Resistance Education (DARE), Neighborhood Watch, and a variety of others.

Most supporters of community policing view it as a new philosophy of policing. In its ideal sense, it means changing the traditional definition of policing from one of crime control to one of community problem-solving and empowerment (Goldstein, 1990; Wilson and Kelling, 1982). In addition to redefining the police mission, a practical shift to a community policing strategy means changing the "principal operating methods, and the key administrative arrangements of police departments" (Moore, 1992:103). Three integral dimensions are consistently highlighted:

1. engaging and interacting with the community;
2. solving community problems; and
3. adapting internal elements of the organization to support these new strategies (Bayley, 1994).

In its ideal sense, community policing promises to fundamentally transform the way police do business. Reformers argue that police should not be so obsessed with routine "people-processing" activities (e.g., making arrests or filling out reports) but should focus instead on "people-changing" activities (Mastrofski and Ritti, 2000). These include building up neighborhoods, designing custom solutions to local problems, forging partnerships with other community agencies, and a variety of other non-routine police activities.

The Effects of Federal Funding

The Violent Crime Control and Law Enforcement Act of 1994 (Crime Act) gave a tremendous financial boost to the community policing movement. Under Title I, known as the "Public Safety Partnership and Community Policing Act of 1994," Congress and the Clinton Administration determined that 100,000 additional officers, new technology, and innovative programs should be provided to law enforcement agencies throughout the nation, with a particular emphasis on the implementation of community policing. Title I authorized the expenditure of $8.8 billion over six years for use in three primary approaches—hiring new officers for community policing, acquiring technology and hiring civilians to free up time for officers to engage in community policing, and implementing new programs. A new agency, called the Office of Community Oriented Policing Services (COPS Office) was formed within the Department of Justice specifically to distribute grants and carry out the statutory mandates of Title I (see Roth et al., 2000; Gest, 2001).

From 1995 to 2003, the COPS Office provided more than $6.9 billion to nearly 13,000 state and local law enforcement agencies to hire over 118,000 officers, deputies, and troopers. The COPS Office provided law enforcement agencies with an array of community policing training and technical assistance resources. In addition, new programs were developed and funded, including the use of problem-solving partnerships in schools, community-based efforts to combat domestic violence, and advancing community policing through demonstration centers.

As a result of these funds, by 1999 over 60 percent of municipal police agencies had developed a strategic plan that incorporated community policing principles (Hickman and Reaves, 2001). Almost all of the largest police agencies in the country had full-time community policing officers working the streets. In 1997 about 4 percent of all local police officers served as community policing officers. By 1999, the percentage had increased to 21 percent. In jurisdictions with 500,000 or more people, the percentage of full-time sworn personnel increased from 1.4 percent in 1997 to 24.1 percent in 1999.

In addition to the changes in strategic plans and the increase in officers on the street, independent evaluators found that the COPS Office programs accelerated the transition of community policing in three important ways. First, they stimulated a "national conversation about community policing and provided training and technical assistance to agencies." Second, hiring monies and innovative policing grants allowed chief executives to add community policing programs without cutting back other programs. Third, the funds created an incentive for agency executives to adopt community policing (Roth et al., 2000:23).

Concluding Remarks

With the onset of a new millennium, American police agencies face new challenges. The terrorist attacks on the World Trade Center and the Pentagon changed the way in which law enforcement collectively thinks about public safety and security. Priorities for training, equipment, strategies, and funding have transformed policing once again—this time focusing on homeland security. Time will tell us about the hows and whys of this transformation.

This article has examined the history of American police systems from the English heritage through the last years of the twentieth century. Major emphasis has been placed on the police role, though important events that shaped the development of the police have also been discussed. As can be seen through this review, a number of present-day issues have their roots in different epochs of American history. For example, the idea of community policing can be traced to the colonial period and to medieval England. Preventive patrol, legitimacy, authority, and professionalism are eighteenth and nineteenth century concepts. Riots, disorders, and corruption are not new to American policing, similar events occurred in the nineteenth century. Thus, by virtue of studying history, we can give contextual meaning to current police problems, ideas, and situations. By looking at the past, present-day events can be better understood.

NOTES

[1] This list of police histories is by no means a comprehensive one. A vast number of journal articles, books, and dissertations have been written since those cited.

[2] A number of scholars have examined the "police function." Among the most well-known are Wilson (1968), Skolnick (1966), Bittner (1971), and Goldstein (1977). Each of these authors prescribes to a different view of what the police should and should not do.

REFERENCES

Alfers, Kenneth G. 1975. "The Washington Police: A History, 1800–1866," Ph.D. dissertation, George Washington University.

Bayley, D. 1994. *Police for the Future.* New York: Oxford University Press.

Bittner, Egon. 1970. *The Functions of the Police in Modern Society.* Chevy Chase, MD: National Institute of Mental Health.

Cei, Louis B. 1975. "Law Enforcement in Richmond: A History of Police Community Relations, 1737–1974," Ph.D. dissertation, Florida State University.

Critchley, T. A. 1967. *A History of Police in England and Wales.* Montclair, NJ: Patterson Smith.

Douthit, Nathan. 1975. "August Vollmer: Berkeley's First Chief of Police and the Emergence of Police Professionalism," *California Historical Quarterly* 54 Spring: 101–124.

Fogelson, Robert. 1977. *Big-City Police.* Cambridge, MA: Harvard University Press.

Gest, Ted. 2001. *Crime and Politics: Big Government's Erratic Campaign for Law and Order.* New York: Oxford University Press.

Goldstein, Herman. 1977. *Policing a Free Society.* Cambridge, MA: Ballinger Press.

———. 1979. "Improving Policing: A Problem-Oriented Approach." *Crime and Delinquency* 25: 236–58.

———. 1990. *Problem-Oriented Policing.* New York: McGraw-Hill.

Greenwood, P. W., J. M. Chaiken, and J. Petersilia. 1977. *The Criminal Investigation Process.* Lexington, MA: D.C. Heath.

Hickman, Matthew J. and Brian A. Reaves. 2001. *Community Policing in Local Police Departments, 1997 and 1999.* Washington, DC: Bureau of Justice Statistics, U.S. Dept. of Justice, NCJ 184794.

Kelling, George T., T. Pate, D. Dieckman, and C. Brown. 1974. *The Kansas City Preventive Patrol Experiment: Final Report.* Washington, DC: Police Foundation.

Klockars, Carl. 1985. *The Idea of Police.* Beverly Hills, CA: Sage Publications.

Lane, Roger. 1967. *Policing the City: Boston, 1822–1285.* Cambridge, MA: Harvard University Press.

———. 1980. "Urban Police and Crime in the Nineteenth-Century America," in Michael Tonry and Norval Morris, eds., *Crime and Justice: An Annual Review of Research, Volume 2.* Chicago: University of Chicago Press.

Litwack, Leon. 1961. *North of Slavery.* Chicago: University of Chicago Press.

Maguire, Edward R., Joseph B. Kuhns, Craig D. Uchida, and Stephen M. Cox. 1997. "Patterns of Community Policing in Nonurban America," *Journal of Research in Crime and Delinquency,* Vol. 34 No. 3, August: 368–394.

Maniha, John K. 1970. "The Mobility of Elites in a Bureaucratizing Organization: The St. Louis Police Department, 1861–1961," Ph.D. dissertation, University of Michigan.

Mastrofski, S. and R. Ritti. 2000. "Making Sense of Community Policing: A Theoretical Perspective." *Police Practice and Research Journal* 1(2): 183–210.

Miller, Wilbur R. 1977. *Cops and Bobbies: Police Authority in New York and London, 1830–1870.* Chicago: University of Chicago Press.

Monkkonen, Eric H. 1981. *Police in Urban America, 1860–1920.* Cambridge: Cambridge University Press.

Moore, M. H. 1992. "Problem-solving and Community Policing," in Michael Tonry and Norval Morris, eds., *Modern Policing: Crime and Justice, an Annual Review of Research.* Chicago: University of Chicago Press.

Radzinowicz, Leon. 1948–1968. *History of the English Criminal Law, Volume 1–4.* New York: MacMillan.

Reichard, Maximillian I. 1975. "The Origins of Urban Police: Freedom and Order in Antebellum St. Louis," Ph.D. dissertation, Washington University.

Reith, Charles. 1956. *A New Study of Police History.* Edinburgh.

Richardson, James F. 1970. *The New York Police: Colonial Times to 1901.* New York: Oxford University Press.

———. 1974. *Urban Police in the United States.* Port Washington, NY: Kennikat Press.

Rider, Eugene F. 1971. "The Denver Police Department: An Administrative, Organizational, and Operational History, 1858–1905," Ph.D. dissertation. University of Denver.

Roth, Jeffrey, A., Joseph F. Ryan, Stephen J. Gaffigan, Christopher S. Koper, Mark H. Moore, Janice A. Roehl, Calvin C. Johnson, Gretchen E. Moore, Ruth M. White, Michael E. Buerger, Elizabeth A. Langston, and David Thacher. 2000. *National Evaluation of the COPS Program—Title I of the 1994 Crime Act.* Washington, DC: National Institute of Justice.

Schneider, John C. 1980. *Detroit and the Problems of Order, 1830–1880.* Lincoln: University of Nebraska Press.

Skolnick, Jerome. 1966. *Justice Without Trial: Law Enforcement in Democratic Society.* New York: John Wiley and Sons.

Spelman, William and Dale Brown. 1984. *Calling the Police: Citizen Reporting of Serious Crime.* Washington, DC: U.S. Government Printing Office.

Walker, Samuel. 1977. *A Critical History of Police Reform: The Emergence of Professionalism.* Lexington, MA: D.C. Heath and Company.

Wilson, James Q. 1968. *Varieties of Police Behavior: The Management of Law and Order in Eight Communities.* Cambridge, MA: Harvard University Press.

Wilson, James Q. and George Kelling. 1982. "Broken Windows: The Police and Neighborhood Safety." *Atlantic Monthly* 249: 29–38.

3

Requests for
Police Assistance, 2011

Matthew Durose & Lynn Langton

In 2011, an estimated 31.4 million U.S. residents age 16 or older, or 13% of the population, requested assistance from the police at least once. About 93% of persons who requested police assistance thought the officers acted properly, 86% felt the police were helpful, and 85% were satisfied with the police response (figure 1). About 93% of persons who requested police assistance reported that they were just as likely or more likely to contact the police again for a similar problem.

The findings in this report are based on the Bureau of Justice Statistics' (BJS) 2011 Police-Public Contact Survey (PPCS), a supplement to the National Crime Victimization Survey (NCVS), which collects information from a nationally representative sample of persons in U.S. households. The PPCS collects information on contact with police during a 12-month period. This report presents the characteristics and experiences of persons who contacted law enforcement for assistance in 2011, examining perceptions of officer behavior and response during these encounters. It details requests for police assistance to (1) report a crime, suspicious activity, or neighborhood disturbance; (2) report a noncrime emergency; and (3) seek help for a nonemergency or other reason.

An Estimated 1 in 8 Persons
Requested Police Assistance in 2011

During 2011, an estimated 26% of the 241.4 million U.S. residents age 16 or older had one or more contacts with police, such as calling to report a

Bureau of Justice Statistics. Special Report, September 2013, NCJ 242938, http://www.bjs.gov/content/pub/pdf/rpa11.pdf

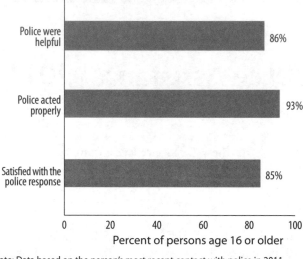

Police behavior and response

Percent of persons age 16 or older

Note: Data based on the person's most recent contact with police in 2011. Percentages exclude 1.7% of respondents who did not know or report whether the police were helpful, 2.9% who did not know or report whether the police acted properly, and 0.8% who did not know or report whether they were satisfied with the police response.

Source: Bureau of Justice Statistics, National Crime Victimization Survey, Police-Public Contact Survey, 2011.

Figure 1   Perceptions of police behavior and response following requests for assistance, 2011

crime, being stopped in a moving vehicle, or being approached by an officer in a public place (table 1). About 13% of the population requested assistance from the police at least once in 2011. For information on involuntary contacts with police that occurred during a traffic or street stop, see *Police Behavior during Traffic and Street Stops, 2011,* NCJ 242937, BJS web, September 2013.

The most common reason persons sought assistance from the police in 2011 was to report a crime, suspicious activity, or neighborhood disturbance (about 19.7 million persons or 8% of the population), followed by reporting a noncrime emergency (12.6 million or 5%), such as a medical issue or traffic accident. About 3.9 million persons, or 2%, sought help from the police for other reasons, such as having a problem with an animal, returning a lost item, or nonemergency matters (e.g., asking for directions).

In 2011, a similar percentage of females (13%) and males (13%) requested some type of assistance from the police (table 2 on p. 34). A greater percentage of non-Hispanic white persons (14%) than Hispanic persons (10%) contacted the police for assistance. A slightly larger percentage of

Table 1   U.S. residents age 16 or older who had contact with police, by reason for contact, 2011

Reason for contact with police	Number	Percent
Total	62,937,000	26.1%
Requested assistance	31,405,000	13.0%
Reported crime/disturbance/suspicious activity	19,737,000	8.2
Reported noncrime emergency	12,566,000	5.2
Other reason[a]	3,900,000	1.6
Stopped/approached by police[b]	35,425,000	14.7%
Involved in a traffic accident reported to police	7,434,000	3.1%
Participated in an anti-crime program with police	3,490,000	1.4%

Note: Data based on the 241,404,000 U.S. residents age 16 or older in 2011. Numbers and percentages include persons who experienced contact with police anytime during 2011. Detail sums to more than total because some persons had more than one type of contact with police in 2011. Number of persons who requested police assistance rounded to nearest thousand.

[a] Includes other reasons for approaching or seeking help from police, such as asking for directions, having a problem with an animal, or returning a lost item.
[b] Includes persons who had involuntary contact that was initiated by the police such as being pulled over in a moving vehicle, being arrested for a crime, or being approached for some other reason (e.g., police were providing a service or conducting a criminal investigation).

Source: Bureau of Justice Statistics, National Crime Victimization Survey, Police-Public Contact Survey, 2011.

white persons (14%) than black persons (12%) requested police assistance. In 2011, persons ages 25 to 44 contacted the police to request assistance at higher rates than younger persons (ages 16 to 24) and older persons (age 65 or older). The rates among persons ages 25 to 44 and 45 to 64 were not statistically different.

A similar percentage of males (8%) and females (9%) contacted the police to report a crime or neighborhood disturbance in 2011. Across all races and Hispanic origin, American Indians and Alaska Natives (15%) and persons of two or more races (15%) had the highest rates of reporting crime or neighborhood disturbances to the police. No statistical difference was observed between the percentage of white (9%) and black (7%) persons reporting a crime or neighborhood disturbance to police in 2011.

About 6 in 10 Requests for Police Assistance Involved Face-to-Face Contact with an Officer

In 2011, persons who requested assistance from law enforcement were asked about the methods used to contact the police and whether the contact was face-to-face. Persons who reported more than one contact with police in 2011 were asked to describe the most recent contact. About 24.2 million per-

Table 2 U.S. residents age 16 or older who requested assistance from police, by reason for contact and demographic characteristics, 2011

Demographic characteristic	Total	Reason for police contact		
		Reported crime/ disturbance/ suspicious activity	Reported noncrime emergency	Other reason[a]
Total	13.0%	8.2%	5.2%	1.6%
Sex				
Male	12.5%	7.8%	5.0%	1.5%
Female	13.5	8.5	5.4	1.7
Race/Hispanic origin				
White[b]	13.9%	8.6%	5.7%	1.8%
Black/African American[b]	12.0	7.5	4.5	1.4
Hispanic/Latino	10.1	7.0	3.6	0.9
American Indian/ Alaska Native[b]	17.0	15.2	4.8 !	3.1!
Asian/Native Hawaiian/other Pacific Islander[b]	8.5	5.2	3.1	1.3
Two or more races[b]	22.2	15.1	8.2	2.9
Age				
16–17	5.5%	2.3%	2.8%	0.6% !
18–24	12.7	7.5	5.2	1.5
25–34	15.0	10.1	5.8	1.4
35–44	15.1	9.7	6.0	1.7
45–54	14.1	8.8	6.0	2.1
55–64	13.3	8.3	5.1	2.0
65 or older	9.1	5.5	3.4	1.2
Number requesting assistance	31,405,000	19,737,000	12,566,000	3,900,000

Note: Data based on the 241,404,000 U.S. residents age 16 or older in 2011. Numbers and percentages include persons who requested assistance from police anytime during 2011. Number of persons who requested assistance from police rounded to nearest thousand.

! Interpret with caution. Estimate based on 10 or fewer sample cases, or coefficient of variation is greater than 50%.

[a]Includes other reasons for approaching or seeking help from police, such as asking for directions, having a problem with an animal, or returning a lost item.

[b]Excludes persons of Hispanic or Latino origin.

Source: Bureau of Justice Statistics, National Crime Victimization Survey, Police-Public Contact Survey, 2011.

sons reported that their most recent or only contact in 2011 was to request assistance from the police (table 3).

About 6 in 10 (62%) persons who requested police assistance in 2011 had face-to-face interaction with an officer during their most recent contact. Among persons who requested police assistance and had face-to-face contact with an officer, about 3 in 4 persons (75%) initiated the contact by telephone (not in table). The other 25% of contacts were initiated by the person approaching the police in public (e.g., the police station or on the street), the police coming to the person's house, a third party (e.g., a company or another person contacting the police), or another method.

Table 3   Persons who requested police assistance who had face-to-face contact with an officer, by reason for most recent contact, 2011

Reason for most recent contact	Number requesting assistance	Percent who had face-to-face with police after requesting assistance		
		Total	Yes	No
Total	24,227,000	100%	62.1	37.9
Reported crime/disturbance/ suspicious activity	14,523,000	100%	67.0	33.0
Reported noncrime emergency	6,477,000	100%	46.2	53.8
Other reason*	3,228,000	100%	72.1	27.9

Note: Percentages based on the 24.2 million persons who reported that their most recent contact in 2011 was to request assistance from the police. Percentages exclude less than 0.1% of respondents who did not report whether the contact was face-to-face. Number of persons who requested assistance from police rounded to nearest thousand.

*Includes other reasons for approaching or seeking help from police, such as asking for directions, having a problem with an animal, or returning a lost item.

Source: Bureau of Justice Statistics, National Crime Victimization Survey, Police-Public Contact Survey, 2011.

The Majority (93%) of Persons Who Requested Police Assistance Felt the Officers Acted Properly

Persons who requested assistance from the police (either in-person or not in-person) for any reason were asked if they felt police acted properly during the contact, were helpful, spent an appropriate amount of time with them, and improved the situation. In addition, persons were asked if they were satisfied with the police response and if they were likely to contact the police again for a similar problem.

During 2011, the majority of persons who requested assistance from the police for any reason felt the responding officers acted properly (93%) and were helpful (86%) (table 4). About 85% of persons who had contact with police to request assistance were satisfied with how the police handled the situation. The percentage of persons who were satisfied with the police response was not statistically different among requests for assistance that involved face-to-face contact with an officer (85%) and contacts that were not in-person (84%) (not in table).

Table 4   Perceptions of police behavior and response during contacts to request assistance, by reason for most recent contact and race/Hispanic origin of persons, 2011

Reason for most recent contact	All[a]	White[b]	Black/African American[b]	Hispanic/ Latino
Police were helpful				
Total	86.4%	86.7%	83.2%	87.9%
Reported crime/disturbance/ suspicious activity	84.0	83.5	85.0	86.0
Reported noncrime emergency	93.2	93.9	82.6	95.6
Other reason[c]	83.9	85.5	75.1	81.5
Police acted properly				
Total	93.1%	93.5%	90.4%	92.8%
Reported crime/disturbance/ suspicious activity	92.4	92.3	92.6	92.5
Reported noncrime emergency	95.6	96.3	88.1	96.0
Other reason[c]	90.9	92.5	83.5	86.9
Satisfied with police response				
Total	84.7%	85.8%	80.1%	81.4%
Reported crime/disturbance/ suspicious activity	82.0	82.7	80.5	79.0
Reported noncrime emergency	91.4	92.5	79.2	90.9
Other reason[c]	83.6	85.4	80.0	73.9

Note: Data based on the person's most recent contact with police in 2011. Percentages exclude 1.7% of respondents who did not know or report whether the police were helpful, 2.9% who did not know or report whether the police acted properly, and 0.8% who did not know or report whether they were satisfied with the police response.

[a]Includes estimates for persons identifying as white, black, Hispanic, American Indian, Alaska Native, Asian, Native Hawaiian, or other Pacific Islander, and persons of two or more races. Separate statistics on American Indians, Alaska Natives, Asians, Native Hawaiians, or other Pacific Islanders, and persons of two or more races are not shown due to too few sample cases to obtain reliable estimates.
[b]Excludes persons of Hispanic or Latino origin.
[c]Includes other reasons for approaching or seeking help from police, such as asking for directions, having a problem with an animal, or returning a lost item.

Source: Bureau of Justice Statistics, National Crime Victimization Survey, Police-Public Contact Survey, 2011.

While most people who requested police assistance believed the officers were helpful, a larger percentage of persons reporting noncrime emergencies (93%) than persons reporting crimes or neighborhood disturbances (84%) thought the police were helpful. Similarly, a larger percentage of persons reporting noncrime emergencies (91%) than persons reporting crimes or neighborhood disturbances (82%) were satisfied with the police response.

Among persons reporting noncrime emergencies, Hispanics (96%) and whites (94%) were more likely than blacks (83%) to feel the police were helpful. Among persons reporting a crime or neighborhood disturbance in 2011, no statistical differences were found between the percentage of Hispanics (86%), blacks (85%), and whites (83%) who felt the police were helpful.

While the large majority of white, black, and Hispanic persons who reported noncrime emergencies to law enforcement felt the officers provided a satisfactory response, blacks (79%) were less likely than whites (93%) and somewhat less likely than Hispanics (91%) to feel satisfied with the response. Among persons reporting a crime or neighborhood problem, a similar percentage of whites (83%), blacks (80%), and Hispanics (79%) were satisfied with the police response.

A similar percentage of males (86%) and females (86%) who requested assistance from the police felt the officers were helpful (table 5). No statistical differences were observed across age groups of persons who believed the police were helpful during requests for assistance.

Table 5 Perceptions of police behavior and response during contacts to request assistance, by sex and age of person, 2011

Demographic characteristic	Police were helpful	Police acted properly	Satisfied with police response
Total	86.4%	93.1%	84.7%
Sex			
Male	86.5%	93.4%	84.8%
Female	86.4	92.8	84.6
Age			
16–17	89.9%	94.7%	88.4%
18–24	87.1	94.3	81.5
25–34	85.0	91.0	82.9
35–44	87.4	93.6	85.2
45–54	85.4	92.9	84.4
55–64	86.4	93.4	84.8
65 or older	88.2	94.7	89.1

Note: Data based on the person's most recent contact with police in 2011. Percentages exclude 1.7% of respondents who did not know or report whether the police were helpful, 2.9% who did not know or report whether the police acted properly, and 0.8% who did not know or report whether they were satisfied with the police response.

Source: Bureau of Justice Statistics, National Crime Victimization Survey, Police-Public Contact Survey, 2011.

Among persons who requested assistance from the police in 2011, about 61% felt the police improved the situation, 21% felt the police did not improve the situation, and 18% were unable to say whether the situation did or did not improve (table 6). A larger percentage of persons reporting noncrime emergencies (70%) than persons reporting crimes or neighborhood disturbances (58%) felt the police improved the situation.

Table 6   Persons who felt police improved the situation during contacts to request assistance, by reason for most recent contact, 2011

Reason for most recent contact	Percent who felt the police improved the situation			
	Total	Yes	No	Don't know
Total	100%	61.3	20.9	17.8
Reported crime/disturbance/ suspicious activity	100%	57.7	25.6	16.7
Reported noncrime emergency	100%	69.9	8.4	21.7
Other reason*	100%	60.3	25.3	14.4

Note: Data based on the person's most recent contact with police in 2011. Percentages exclude 0.1% of respondents who did not report whether the police improved the situation.

*Includes other reasons for approaching or seeking help from police, such as asking for directions, having a problem with an animal, or returning a lost item.

Source: Bureau of Justice Statistics, National Crime Victimization Survey, Police-Public Contact Survey, 2011.

About 9 in 10 Persons Who Requested Police Assistance Felt the Police Spent an Appropriate Amount of Time with Them during the Contact

Overall, most (93%) persons who requested police assistance in 2011 felt the officers spent an appropriate amount of time with them during the contact (table 7). An estimated 2% of persons felt the police spent too much time with them, and 6% felt the police spent too little time with them.

Perceptions about whether police spent an appropriate amount of time responding to requests for assistance were related to views about the behavior and response of police during the contact. Among persons who believed the police had not behaved properly, about 37% thought the police spent an appropriate amount of time with them. In comparison, among persons who felt the police acted properly, 97% felt the police spent an appropriate amount of time with them. Among persons who felt the police did not provide a satisfactory response during a request for assistance, about 59% believed the offi-

Table 7   Persons who felt police spent an appropriate amount of time with them after requesting assistance, by perceptions of police behavior and response, 2011

Police behavior and response	Total	Percent who felt police spent an appropriate amount of time with them		
		Yes	No, too much	No, too little
Total	100%	92.9	1.5	5.6
Police were helpful				
Yes	100%	97.6	0.6	1.8
No	100%	60.0	8.1	31.8
Police acted properly				
Yes	100%	97.4	0.8	1.8
No	100%	36.7	11.7	51.5
Satisfied with police response				
Yes	100%	98.5	0.6	0.9
No	100%	59.3	7.0	33.8

Note: Data based on the person's most recent contact with police in 2011. Percentages exclude 3.5% of respondents who did not know or report whether the police spent an appropriate amount of time with them.

Source: Bureau of Justice Statistics, National Crime Victimization Survey, Police-Public Contact Survey, 2011.

cers spent an appropriate amount of time with them, compared to about 98% of persons who were satisfied with the police response.

About 9 in 10 Persons Who Requested Police Assistance in 2011 Stated They Were Just as Likely or More Likely to Contact Police Again for a Similar Problem

The large majority of persons who requested police assistance to report a crime or neighborhood disturbance (93%) or a noncrime emergency (96%) stated they were just as likely or more likely to contact the police again for a similar problem (table 8). In addition, the majority of persons reported being just as likely or more likely to contact the police again for a similar problem, even when the police were not helpful (65%), did not behave properly (53%), or did not provide a satisfactory response (66%). However, negative perceptions of police behavior were related to a lower likelihood of persons contacting the police in the future. For example, among persons requesting police assistance in 2011, about 47% of those who believed the police had not acted

Table 8   Persons who requested police assistance who reported how likely they were to contact police again for a similar problem, by reason for most recent contact, 2011

Reason for most recent contact	How likely to contact police again for a similar problem		
	More likely to call	Just as likely to call	Less likely to call
Total	33.9	59.2	6.9
Reported crime/ disturbance/suspicious activity	34.1	58.4	7.5
Reported noncrime emergency	34.0	61.7	4.2
Other reason*	33.0	57.5	9.5

Note: Data based on the person's most recent contact with police in 2011. Percentages exclude 1.8% of respondents who did not know or report how likely they were to contact the police again for a similar problem.

*Includes other reasons for approaching or seeking help from police, such as asking for directions, having a problem with an animal, or returning a lost item. Source: Bureau of Justice Statistics, National Crime Victimization Survey, Police-Public Contact Survey, 2011.

properly reported that they were less likely to contact the police again for a similar problem, compared to 4% of persons who felt the police behaved properly (table 9).

Methodology

Data collection

The Police-Public Contact Survey (PPCS) is a supplement to the National Crime Victimization Survey (NCVS). The NCVS annually collects data on crimes reported and not reported to the police against persons age 12 or older from a nationally representative sample of U.S. households. The sample includes persons living in group quarters (such as dormitories, rooming houses, and religious group dwellings) and excludes persons living in military barracks and institutional settings (such as correctional or hospital facilities) and the homeless. (For more information, see the *Survey Methodology* in *Criminal Victimization in the United States, 2008,* NCJ 231173, BJS web, May 2011.)

Since 1999, the PPCS has been administered every 3 years at the end of the NCVS interview to persons age 16 or older within households sampled for the NCVS. Proxy responders and those who complete the NCVS interview in a language other than English were not eligible to receive the PPCS.

Table 9   Persons who requested police assistance who reported how likely they were to contact police again for a similar problem, by perceptions of police behavior and response, 2011

Police behavior and response	How likely to contact police again for a similar problem		
	More likely to call	**Just as likely to call**	**Less likely to call**
Total	33.9	59.2	6.9
Police were helpful			
Yes	36.8	60.6	2.7
No	16.3	48.8	34.9
Police acted properly			
Yes	36.0	60.4	3.6
No	9.1	43.8	47.1
Satisfied with police response			
Yes	37.2	60.6	2.2
No	16.2	50.1	33.7

Note: Data based on the person's most recent contact with police in 2011. Percentages exclude 1.7% of respondents who did not know or report whether the police were helpful, 2.9% who did not know or report whether the police acted properly, 0.8% who did not know or report whether they were satisfied with the police response, and 1.8% of respondents who did not know or report how likely they were to contact the police again for a similar problem.

Source: Bureau of Justice Statistics, National Crime Victimization Survey, Police-Public Contact Survey, 2011.

The U.S. Census Bureau administered the 2011 PPCS questionnaire between July 1, 2011, and December 31, 2011, and processed the survey data. Respondents were provided a list of specific reasons for having contact with police and were asked if they had experienced any of those types of contacts during the prior 12 months. For example, persons interviewed in July 2011 were asked about contacts that occurred between August 2010 and July 2011. Persons who said they had a contact during 2011 were asked to describe the nature of the contact, and those who had more than one contact were asked about only their most recent contact during the period. To simplify the discussion of the findings, this report describes all contacts reported during the 12 months prior to the interviews as 2011 contacts.

PPCS nonrespondents consisted of persons whose household did not respond to the NCVS (NCVS household nonresponse), persons within an interviewed NCVS household who did not respond to the NCVS (NCVS person nonresponse), and persons who responded to the NCVS but did not complete the PPCS (PPCS person nonresponse). The NCVS household response rate was 89% and the person response rate was 88%. In 2011, PPCS interviews were obtained from 49,246 of the 62,280 individuals age 16 or older in the NCVS sample (79%). A total of 13,034 nonrespondents were excluded from the 2011 PPCS as noninterviews or as proxy interviews. Noninterviews (10,907) included respondents who were not available for the interview, those who refused to participate, and non-English-speaking respondents. (Unlike the NCVS interviews, PPCS interviews were conducted only in English.) The remaining 2,127 were proxy interviews representing household members who were unable to participate for physical, mental, or other reasons.

To produce national estimates on police-public contacts, sample weights were applied to the survey data so that the respondents represented the entire population, including the nonrespondents. After adjustment for nonresponse, the sample cases in 2011 were weighted to produce a national population estimate of 241,404,142 persons age 16 or older.

Despite the nonresponse adjustments, low overall response rates and response rates to particular survey items can still increase variance in these estimates and produce bias when the nonrespondents have characteristics that differ from the respondents. The Office of Management and Budget guidelines require a nonresponse bias study when the overall response rate is below 80%. The Bureau of Justice Statistics (BJS) and the Census Bureau compared the distributions of respondents as well as nonrespondents and nonresponse estimates for various household and demographic characteristics, and examined their impact on the national estimates produced for the 2011 PPCS. The study looked at household-level and person-level response rates and found some evidence of bias in the rates among blacks and persons of Hispanic origin. Blacks accounted for 12% of the U.S. population in 2011 but about 11% of PPCS respondents after weighting adjustments. Hispanics accounted for 14% of the U.S. population but about 12% of the PPCS respondents after weighting adjustments. Because the largest bias in person nonresponse was observed in the Hispanic origin characteristics, future iterations of the PPCS will address this issue by administering the survey in languages other than English and including Hispanic origin as a factor in the noninterview adjustment. Item nonresponse statistics were also computed for key survey questions from the PPCS, and no evidence of bias was found during the analysis.

Changes to the 2011 PPCS

Since its inception in 1999, the PPCS has captured information about in-person (i.e., face-to-face) contacts between police and the public. Telephone contacts were previously not included. The survey has also excluded face-to-face interactions in which persons approached an officer or an officer initiated contact with them in a social setting or because their work brought them into regular contact. In March of 2010, BJS hosted a series of meetings with subject-matter experts in the area of policing and police legitimacy to initiate discussion and work on substantive changes to the PPCS questionnaire. In 2011, based in part on these meetings, the PPCS was revised to expand the scope of the survey and to better capture contacts with police.

First, to determine if contact occurred and to enhance individuals' recollections about their interactions with police over a 12-month period, BJS implemented new screening procedures in the 2011 PPCS that describe a broad range of situations known to bring people in contact with police. Second, the scope of the PPCS was expanded to collect information about interactions that people had with the police that did not result in a face-to-face contact (e.g., reporting a crime to the police by phone or e-mail). Additionally, a new set of questions was added to the instrument to collect detailed information about requests for police assistance (e.g., reporting a crime or noncrime emergency) and contacts in which the police stopped someone in a public place or on the street but not in a motor vehicle (street stops).

The effects of these revisions, which included adding new questions and reordering existing questions, were significant when compared to the 2008 version of the questionnaire. To assess the impact of the survey redesign on trends in rates and types of contact, BJS administered a split-sample design in which a subset of the sample was interviewed using the 2008 version of the questionnaire, and the remaining sample was interviewed using the 2011 version. Based on the evaluation, it was determined that a 15/85 split would provide sufficient power to measure a 15% change in contact rate. In other words, about 85% of the 2011 sample was randomly assigned the revised questionnaire and the other 15% received the questionnaire designed for the 2008 survey. The Census Bureau completed interviews for 41,408 (79%) of the 52,529 persons who received the revised questionnaire.

The findings in this report are based on data collected from the revised questionnaire. An evaluation of the impact of the changes to the 2011 PPCS instrument on trends in contacts between the police and the public is underway, and the results of that assessment will be made available through the BJS website.

Police–Public Contact Survey questions pertaining to perceptions of police behavior and response following requests for assistance

Police behavior
Q. Looking back on this contact, do you feel the police behaved properly?

Q. Were the police helpful?

Police response
Q. Were you satisfied with the police response during your most recent contact?

Q. Did the situation improve after you contacted the police?

Amount of time police spent with the person during contact
Q. Do you believe the police spent an appropriate amount of time with you?

Likelihood of contacting the police again for a similar problem
Q. Would you be more likely, less likely, or just as likely to contact the police in the future for a similar problem?

Standard Error Computations

When national estimates are derived from a sample, as is the case with the PPCS, caution must be taken when comparing one estimate to another estimate. Although one estimate may be larger than another, estimates based on a sample have some degree of sampling error. The sampling error of an estimate depends on several factors, including the amount of variation in the responses, the size of the sample, and the size of the subgroup for which the estimate is computed. When the sampling error around the estimates is taken into consideration, the estimates that appear different may, in fact, not be statistically different.

One measure of the sampling error associated with an estimate is the standard error. The standard error can vary from one estimate to the next. In general, for a given metric, an estimate with a smaller standard error provides a more reliable approximation of the true value than an estimate with a larger standard error. Estimates with relatively large standard errors are associated with less precision and reliability and should be interpreted with caution.

In order to generate standard errors around estimates from the PPCS, the Census Bureau produces generalized variance function (GVF) parameters for BJS. The GVFs take into account aspects of the NCVS complex sample design and represent the curve fitted to a selection of individual standard errors based on the Jackknife Repeated Replication technique. The GVF parameters were used to generate standard errors for each point estimate (i.e., numbers or percentages) in the report.

In this report, BJS conducted tests to determine whether differences in estimated numbers and percentages were statistically significant once sampling error was taken into account. Using statistical programs developed specifically for the NCVS, all comparisons in the text were tested for significance. The primary test procedure used was Student's t-statistic, which tests the difference between two sample estimates. To ensure that the observed differences between estimates were larger than might be expected due to sampling variation, the significance level was set at the 95% confidence level.

Data users can use the estimates and the standard errors of the estimates provided in this report to generate a confidence interval around the estimate as a measure of the margin of error. The following example illustrates how standard errors can be used to generate confidence intervals:

> According to the PPCS, an estimated 13% of persons age 16 or older requested assistance from the police in 2011 (see table 1). Using the GVFs, BJS determined that the estimate has a standard error of 0.5. . . . A confidence interval around the estimate was generated by multiplying the standard error by ±1.96 (the t-score of a normal, two-tailed distribution that excludes 2.5% at either end of the distribution). Thus, the confidence interval around the estimate is 13% ± (0.5 × 1.96). In other words, if different samples using the same procedures were taken from the U.S. population in 2011, 95% of the time the percentage of persons age 16 or older who requested police assistance would be between 12% and 14%.

In this report, BJS also calculated a coefficient of variation (CV) for all estimates, representing the ratio of the standard error to the estimate. CVs provide a measure of reliability and a means to compare the precision of estimates across measures with differing levels or metrics. In cases where the CV was greater than 50%, or the unweighted sample had 10 or fewer cases, the estimate was noted with a "!" symbol (interpret data with caution; estimate is based on 10 or fewer sample cases, or the coefficient of variation exceeds 50%).

Many of the variables examined in this report may be related to one another and to other variables not included in the analyses. Complex relationships among variables were not fully explored in this report and warrant more extensive analysis. Readers are cautioned not to draw causal inferences based on the results presented.

See original publication for appendix tables 1–9 (standard errors).

4

You Can Observe a Lot by Watching
Contributions of Systematic Social Observation to Our Understanding of the Police

Robert E. Worden, Sarah J. McLean, & Heidi S. Bonner

Introduction

Yogi Berra, the Hall of Fame catcher for the New York Yankees in the 1950s, is reported to have said that "you can observe a lot by watching." Many such "Yogi-isms" are either tautological or internally contradictory: "it ain't over till it's over"; "baseball is ninety percent mental, the other half is physical"; and "nobody goes there anymore because it's too crowded." So we might be understandably skeptical about Yogi's insights into the benefits of watching. But the fact is that social scientists have learned quite a lot about the police by watching them do their jobs—that is, through observation.

The first observational studies of police (Westley, 1953, 1970) were anthropological or ethnographic, and such ethnographic research has been invaluable in understanding policing (Bittner, 1967; Manning, 1977; Moskos, 2008; Muir, 1977; Rubinstein, 1973; Skolnick, 1975; Van Maanen 1974). In this article, we focus on *systematic social observation* (SSO) of the police, introduced to criminology by Albert Reiss, Jr., in the 1960s (Mastrofski, Parks, and McCluskey, 2010). Reiss emphasized the value of precision in recognizing and recording observations, which he believed were an integral part of any science (Mastrofski et al., 1998). SSO has made very substantial contributions to our understanding of what the police do, the discretionary choices that they make, and the forces that influence those choices.

Like other forms of observation, SSO has provided for in-person observation of patrol officers during their regular tours of duty as they perform their work in natural settings. Unlike other forms of observation, SSO is sys-

Prepared especially for *Critical Issues in Policing* by Robert E. Worden, Sarah J. McLean, and Heidi S. Bonner.

tematic in two respects. First, the selection of officers to be observed is subject to probability sampling, so that inferences from analytic results can be drawn with the benefit of known statistical properties. Second, all observers are guided by the same structured coding protocol that is formulated prior to the field research, which directs observers' attention to specified features of police work. Researchers follow very specific procedures that can be duplicated; they are trained in what to look for and how to record/code it for data analysis. The observations are recorded in standardized measurement categories, which are quantifiable and replicable. SSO is, then, analogous to the structured interview common in survey research, in that both forms of data collection prescribe what to record and how to record it.

In this article we describe the more notable projects that have used SSO to study the police, including their designs and theoretical foundations, and we assess the benefits and limitations of the SSO methodology. We then summarize and critique the principal contributions of SSO-based research to our knowledge about police work. We conclude with a consideration of the future of SSO as a means to study police behavior.

Previous SSO Studies of the Police

Five Major Studies

As the research director for President Johnson's Commission on Law Enforcement and the Administration of Justice, Albert Reiss's 1966 study produced one of five large-scale sets of observational data that have together formed the basis for a large body of empirical evidence on the police. The other large-scale SSO projects are the "Midwest City" Study (1969–1971); the 1977 Police Services Study; the Project on Policing Neighborhoods conducted in 1996–1997; and the Policing in Cincinnati Project (1997–1998). The data generated by each of these five studies have formed the basis for numerous analyses. The range of research questions addressed in these analyses is testimony to the breadth and richness of the data sets. Some analyses have examined the functions that police perform and the time and effort that those functions demand. Many studies have examined the exercise of police authority: arrest, the use of force, stops, and searches. Some analyses have focused on police interactions with particular subsets of citizens, such as suspects, complainants, and juveniles. Others have focused on police responses to particular kinds of incidents, such as interpersonal disputes, domestic conflicts, drunk-driving, and traffic violations generally. All of these studies focus on police patrol, although the method could be adapted to the study of other police functions or units.

Theoretical Underpinnings.   The major SSO projects share some common elements of design and execution, with some common strengths and weaknesses, even though they have not shared common theoretical underpinnings. Reiss was a sociologist, and his project was guided by a theory that holds that the police–citizen encounter is a *social* transaction. The premise was that police action is affected by the citizen's social status (sex, age, race, class) and situational status (as complainant, suspect, witness, etc.) in the encounter, and by the citizen's "capability to undermine the means the police use to attain their goals" (Black and Reiss, 1967: 8–9). Thus, for each of up to five citizens in an encounter, observers coded the citizen's sex, age, race, and social class; the citizen's role in the encounter; the citizen's demeanor (civil, antagonistic, very deferential), emotional state (agitated, calm, detached) and sobriety; and the requests that the citizen made of police. Observers also coded police "manner" (e.g., "nasty," "bossy," or "business-like") and specific actions toward each citizen, including formal actions such as arrests or tickets, and informal actions such as threats and admonishments.

Richard Sykes and John Clark were also sociologists, but their perspective was a social behaviorist one, which emphasizes police–citizen interaction through verbal communication—"symbolic interaction." Officers handle or "regulate" situations mainly by talking: asking questions, making suggestions, making accusations, and issuing commands. They solicit information and establish identities. Citizens answer, evade, or decline to respond to questions, accept or deny accusations, follow or disobey commands (Sykes and Brent 1980, 1983). For their Midwest City study, the "utterance" was the fundamental unit of analysis. Observers captured data on utterances in real time in the field with a portable device that was developed for the project and called MIDCARS (Minnesota Interaction Data Coding and Reduction System).

Political scientists Elinor Ostrom, Roger Parks, and Gordon Whitaker approached the police as a municipal service, the delivery of which is fragmented across the thousands of local police agencies that comprise the police "industry" in the U.S. Many of these agencies are quite small, with a median size of 10 sworn officers (Reaves, 2010: 9). The Police Services Study (PSS) was designed to illuminate how these fragmented institutional arrangements affect the effectiveness, efficiency, equity, and responsiveness of police service delivery (Ostrom, Parks, and Whitaker, 2001) using SSO (and other methods) to examine policing in 60 neighborhoods spread across 24 jurisdictions in three metropolitan areas: Rochester, NY; St. Louis, MO; and Tampa-St. Petersburg, FL. Among the 24 agencies were the four major city departments and also county sheriff's departments and a number of small and medium-sized municipal agencies, including the "Lilliputs" of municipal policing (Ostrom and Smith, 1976)—agencies with as few as 10 to 25 sworn officers. Neighborhoods served by different agencies were matched in strata defined by median household income and racial composition. The researchers had previously found through surveys that the residents of neighborhoods served by small to medium-sized agencies rated their police services more favorably than their counterparts served by big-city departments (Ostrom, Parks, and Whitaker, 1973; Ostrom and Whitaker, 1973). The PSS included observation instruments that bore a strong resemblance to those fashioned by Reiss.

By the 1980s, policing had (arguably) entered the "community era" (Kelling and Moore 1988), and the Project on Policing Neighborhoods (POPN) was designed to describe community policing at the street level. POPN examined policing in two cities, Indianapolis and St. Petersburg, selected because these departments had made substantial progress in implementing community policing, albeit with different variants. Indianapolis practiced a "broken-windows" style of policing, while St. Petersburg emphasized problem-solving. But POPN was also intended to serve as the foundation for numerous replications, so that data collected according to the same protocol across many sites could support cross-jurisdictional analysis. Given this far-reaching, transdisciplinary purpose, the four POPN principal investigators sought to establish the broadest feasible base of SSO data. The investigators included Reiss and three political scientists: Stephen Mastrofski, Roger Parks (also an investigator for the PSS), and Robert Worden. The instruments provided for much of the same kind of data captured by Reiss in 1966 and the PSS in 1977 but with additional information on police and citizen requests, demands and responses to one another, and also the addition of items designed to tap behaviors that may be a part of community policing. Moreover, POPN added two forms of qualitative data to the coded observational data: *detailed* narrative accounts of encounters and "debriefings" of officers. Observers were instructed to describe every encounter they observed in details sufficient to stage a reenactment of the event. PSS had written narratives of some but not all events, and they tended to be fairly brief, so they were seldom used as a source of systematic information.[1] The POPN narratives, as we discuss below, have enabled researchers to supplement the coded data in key respects. The "debriefings" were added in an effort to gain insight into how officers make discretionary choices. Immediately (or as soon as possible) after an encounter, the observer invited the officer to share what s/he was thinking as s/he handled the situation. Data of this kind have been used in other contexts to learn more about how decision makers attend to and process information and make choices.

While POPN was still in the field, the Policing in Cincinnati Project (PCP) got underway using POPN's observation instruments (without debriefings), adapted as needed to the Cincinnati context. Directed by James Frank, the PCP's goal, like that of POPN, was to describe the contours of community policing. In a companion project, observations were also conducted in 21 small agencies, ranging in size from 9 to 56 sworn officers, serving suburban jurisdictions and small towns in the Cincinnati area (see Liederbach 2002).

Methods.   In general, the large-scale observational projects have sampled spatially and temporally, assigning observers to patrol units on selected shifts in selected beats/neighborhoods with oversampling on busier beats and shifts. A single observer accompanies the officer(s) assigned to a sampled beat on a sampled police work shift from start to finish. Data collection has been organized mainly around police–citizen encounters, providing for the coding of the characteristics and actions of citizens, the actions of the police (including the officer to whom the observer is assigned and any others who may be at or come to the scene), and other features of the interaction, such as the nature of its location. Observers record information at each of several levels, including: (1) the shift or "ride," such as the beat to which the observed officer was assigned, the time of day, and the officer's assignment (district/ beat officer or community policing specialist); (2) the encounter, such as how the encounter was initiated (e.g., a dispatched call, or officer-initiated), the type of location in which the encounter transpired (such as a private residence, a commercial business, or a parking lot), and actions taken by police that were not directed at individual citizens (such as searching the premises); and (3) the citizen, such as race, sex, and age; demeanor; requested actions by police; and actions taken by police toward the citizen. POPN also provided for another level, the "activity," which was anything that the observed officer did outside of the context of a police–citizen encounter, such as motor patrol. The PSS also captured these kinds of phenomena, albeit in less detail, as a part of the shift-level information (e.g., minutes spent on mobile patrol).

The notable exception to these more general rules of research design was the Midwest City study, with its in-field coding of "utterances." Capturing data at that level of detail leads to some burdensome data collection in the field, and utterances as units of analysis lead to some very complicated analysis, such as Markov chain models (see Sykes and Brent, 1983). POPN investigators contemplated the addition of a "transaction" level of data collection below that of citizen. Although they decided against it, transaction-like data have been distilled from POPN narratives.

Observers were graduate students and undergraduates trained in the observation instruments and procedures. Observers were supervised on a day-to-day basis, with quality-control checks of the data that they collected (for the mechanics of administering an SSO study, see Mastrofski et al., 1998; Mastrofski et al., 2010). PSS and POPN did not recruit observers who were local to the observation sites; instead, observers (and other field research staff) were recruited and trained at the home universities of the principal investigators and then housed at the research sites for the duration of a summer of field work. PCP, by contrast, recruited students from the University of Cincinnati (the investigator's home institution) to conduct observations locally, and hence conducted observations throughout the calendar year.

Observational data were in many instances supplemented with other forms of data. Four of the five large-scale studies provided for surveys of officers, which could be linked by an identifying number to rides on which officers had been observed and thus to the events associated with those shifts. Four of the studies also provided for surveys of the residents of the beats or neighborhoods in which observations were conducted, such that the character of the neighborhoods could be described and analyzed in conjunction with the description and analysis of beat or neighborhood patterns of police behavior. The President's Commission study and the PSS also provided for follow-up surveys of citizens who had been involved in observed encounters.

POPN observed not only patrol officers but also field supervisors, which researchers were subsequently able to link to the rides on which their respective subordinates were observed.

Other SSO Studies

In addition to these five large-scale projects, several smaller-scale and/or more focused SSO studies have also formed the basis for a number of analyses (Bayley, 1986; Bayley and Garofalo, 1987, 1989; Fyfe, 1988; Mastrofski and Snipes, 2002; Alpert et al., 2004; Schulenberg, 2014; Jonathan-Zamir et al., 2013; Worden and McLean, 2014b). Most of these studies did not provide for the same breadth of coding as those described above, and some of them were confined to particular kinds of encounters that suited their more focused purposes. Some of them also provided for sampling based not on shift or beat but on individual officer. For the Metro-Dade Violence Reduction Project, for example, James Fyfe conducted systematic observations of officers before and after the delivery of violence reduction training, in order to assess the effects of the training. Sample numbers of officers who received the training and of those who had not were observed, with observations focused on potentially violent situations: "incidents in which officers become aware that they are likely to confront citizens in adversarial contexts" (Fyfe, 1988: 1). David Bayley and James Garafolo's study in New York City similarly sampled among subsets of officers: 20 who had been nominated by peers as being skilled at handling potentially violent situations (1989: 2) and a comparison group of 26 officers who had not been nominated. Their objective was to ascertain the tactics used by skilled officers. Geoffrey Alpert and Roger Dunham fielded an SSO study in Savannah to examine how officers form suspicion and decide to stop motorists or pedestrians, observing and debriefing officers, and also querying officers when "they seemed to take notice of something but not act on it" (Alpert et al., 2004: 2–8).

Methodological Strengths and Weaknesses

Observational data have distinct and important advantages over many other forms of data on what officers do and the circumstances under which they do it (for a more extensive discussion of methodological issues, see Mastrofski et al., 2010; Worden and McLean, 2014a). Police dispatch records tend to omit or underrepresent proactive work, and officer activity logs are susceptible to reporting biases born of the organizational uses for which their completion is mandated (Whitaker, 1982). The use-of-force reports that many agencies require can be usefully analyzed, but we can have more confidence in the results when the findings are corroborated by analyses based on observations. The force reported by officers, and their reports of the situational conditions under which they used force, are subject to the same reporting biases that afflict activity logs. Even self-reports for only research purposes (Garner et al. 2002) are subject to misreporting that stems from officers' perceptual biases. The same concerns apply to police records of stops (the underreporting of which requires administrative auditing) and searches. Furthermore, some elements of the situations, such as citizens' demeanor toward the police, either do not appear (at all or systematically) in self-reports, or they are subject to concerns about the content and consistency of the definitions that officers apply. The seriousness of the offense (if any) and the strength of evidence are legal factors that have a significant bearing on police officers' choices. Sound measures of these factors are important in holding legal factors constant so that inferences can be drawn about the impacts of extralegal factors. Independent coding of both of these factors by observers obviates questions about what officers record and why; indeed, for the least serious offenses, no documentary record might exist.[2]

One of the most important potential drawbacks of SSO is the threat of reactivity, i.e., in the presence of observers, officers may behave differently than they normally do, engaging in some behaviors more frequently and refraining from other behaviors. For example, officers might be more proactive when an observer is present in an effort to demonstrate police work as well as their skills and work ethic. They might be more civil in their interactions with citizens than they would be without an observer. They might run fewer personal errands, and "loaf" less often or not at all. They might be more restrained in their use of physical force. Insofar as any of these reactions to observation contaminate observational data, the data will yield misestimates of the prevalence or frequency of certain behaviors. Several efforts to assess the bias introduced by reactivity suggest that the validity of observational data, in general, is quite high (Mastrofski and Parks, 1990), and some evidence has shown that the relationships between police behavior and other variables (such as characteristics of the situation) are unaffected by reactivity (Worden, 1989, fn 8). The most extensive catalog of forms of reactivity (Spano, 2003, 2005, 2006, 2007) indicates that officers are more proactive when with observers than they might normally be and that this is particularly pronounced when the observer is female; the arrest decision is similarly influenced by observer gender. But these effects diminish over the course of field work, and reactivity as a behavioral change is not universal. In general, as Reiss (1971b: 24) observed, "It is sociologically naive to assume that for many events the presence or participation of the observer is more controlling than other factors in the situation." In evaluating findings based on observational data, one should not assume that biases produced by reactivity are pervasive any more than one should assume that they are absent. It is, we believe, much more reasonable to begin with the premise that some forms of behavior are more susceptible to reactivity than others are, and also with the premise that steps can be taken to minimize reactivity during the field phase of research and to test the sensitivity of results to reactivity during the analysis phase.

A second concern is the reliability of observers' coded judgments. Reliability is maximized, we believe, through extensive training in the observation instrument and through quality-control checks that compare coded data to narrative data to test for logical patterns (e.g., the role of a citizen who is interrogated should be coded as that of a suspected offender). Nevertheless, the logistics and expense of in-person observation dictate the assignment of one observer to a sampled officer. Estimates of inter-rater reliability have been formed only by having groups of observers watch recorded police–citizen interactions and then code a set of items (see Mastrofski et al., 1998). Reliability appears to be fairly high, especially for items that require a minimum of judgment on observers' parts—e.g., whether the citizen was handcuffed by the officer. Reliability declines as the complexity and ambiguity of the phenomenon in question increases. For example, observers might reasonably interpret what they see and hear differently when deciding whether a citizen was disrespectful to an officer. Overall, however, the reliability of observational data is unknown.

What We Have Learned from SSO of Police

Police Role & Functions

Analyses of observational data have contributed to our understanding of the role of police in society: the nature of the incidents that officers handle, how those incidents come to police attention, and how police handle those incidents. Reiss (1971a: 70) showed that, in the 1960s, much of police work was reactive—87 percent of police mobilizations were initiated by citizens. Consequently, police tended to deal with problems that were defined as police business by citizens rather than by the police themselves. Observational (and other) studies challenged the popular characterization of police work as predominantly law enforcement and crime-fighting. Research showed that criminal matters comprised a minority of the encounters police had with citizens (Whitaker, 1982); disorders and service requests together were equally frequent. Moreover, officers were infrequently observed to make arrests, relying far more routinely on their interpersonal skills to maintain order and provide services than on their formal authority to take wrongdoers into custody.

Observations in the 1990s—during the community era—revealed somewhat different patterns. In Indianapolis and St. Petersburg, patrol generalists were far more proactive than the officers observed in the 1960s and 1970s, initiating about one-third of their encounters on their own authority, and community policing specialists were proportionally still more proactive (see Parks et al., 1999: 507; Frank et al., 2001: 51–52). The adoption of community policing presumably expanded the police role to better accommodate order maintenance, and this was confirmed in some but not all observations (see Worden and McLean, 2014a).

Use and Abuse of Police Authority

In general, police authority is invoked infrequently as a proportion of all police–citizen contacts. Many years ago, James Q. Wilson (1968) observed that the tendency of the police is to *underenforce* the law, declining to take legal action even when the circumstances authorize them to take legal action. Thus, it was not uncommon for police in the field to release offenders even when there was sufficient evidence to warrant an arrest. Wilson pointed out that police see their authority as a resource in accomplishing their objectives, such that the application of their authority is not an end but a means. In many instances, their objective is merely to "handle the situation"—that is, to restore order and to prevent immediate violence. When an arrest is made, the "formal charge justifies the arrest but is not the reason for it" (Bittner, 1974: 27). The reason for such an arrest is that the situation could not be handled in some other, informal fashion. Similarly, studies of the use of force have found that police seldom use physical force, and some research has found that police frequently refrain from using physical force when they could legally do so, or they use less physical force than the citizen's resistance would justify (Terrill, 2005).

In what is arguably the most fine-grained analysis of the use of force to date, Terrill (2005) distilled coded sequences of citizen resistance and police coercion (verbal and physical force) from the POPN narratives to describe officers' conformity with a use-of-force continuum. The narrative data enabled him to account for the temporal order of citizen and officer behavior and to determine when officers "jumped" the continuum (that is, used more force than warranted by the suspects' behavior), as well as when officers could have used more force than they did given the resistance they confronted. Terrill "provides the foundation for beginning to assess force appropriateness" (2005: 135), and it is thus one of only a few studies (Reiss, 1968; Friedrich, 1980; Worden, 1995) to examine the improper use of force. Many other studies—using observational or other kinds of data—have focused only on the use of force, whether it was proper or not. We would hope that more research of this kind will be done, because accounting for the improper use of force is a research task of overriding importance.

As police became more proactive, concerns arose about the disparate impact of their decisions to stop and detain people, especially racial and ethnic minorities. In the face of allegations of racial profiling, police departments across the country chose or were compelled to have their officers complete reports on stops. In the absence of a valid "benchmark"—the racial and ethnic composition of the population that would be properly stopped by police—the stop data were largely uninterpretable and the analyses inconclusive. Dunham and colleagues (2005) used debriefings of Savannah police to uncover the process by which officers form suspicion, as well as how they decide to stop a citizen based on that suspicion. They found that the process of forming suspicion is based largely on suspects' behavior, contrary to the hypothesis of racial profiling, and less frequently on offender appearance or presence in a given location at a particular time and place.

Officers' authority to conduct searches is also subject to abuse; even if it is not abused, its exercise can create the appearance of abuse. Gould and Mastrofski (2004) employed SSO data to investigate the frequency with which officers conduct searches (beyond "plain view") and how often the searches are unconstitutional (based on a matrix of Fourth Amendment court rulings). Legal experts evaluated encounter narratives to form judgments about the propriety of observed searches (rather than asking observers to make such judgments themselves). Gould and Mastrofski found that while searches were fairly infrequent, close to one-third of the searches conducted were unconstitutional. Further, unconstitutional searches were more common among suspects who were ultimately released as opposed to those who were arrested, which means that most unconstitutional searches would not be subjected to the scrutiny of the courts.

Scales of Police Authority. Much of what the police do is imbued with authority, so even when they resolve a situation without invoking the law, their actions are authoritative, and it is important to analyze what police do when they do not make arrests. It would be desirable to form a single measure of the authority that police apply, rather than analyze only the application of individual forms of authority—arrest, force, stop, search—one by one. But forming such a measure or scale of authority is complicated. Police intervene in widely diverse situations. Their latitude regarding how they will handle those situations is limited mainly by their ingenuity, and their approaches may shift over the course of a single encounter as they adapt to unfolding events. Consequently, it is difficult to construct a parsimonious set of categories for classifying police actions. Furthermore, one can make different assumptions about the relationships of behavioral categories to one another. Do they all lie on the same behavioral dimensions? What is the most appropriate level of measurement—nominal, ordinal, interval? What are the implications for analysis and interpretation? These complications make it difficult to develop measures of police behavior that have a high degree of verisimilitude and that can be subjected to analysis.

One of the first efforts to develop a framework in terms of which nonarrest behaviors might be distinguished from one another was that of Donald Black (1976, 1980), who suggested that analyses of legal action should distinguish among four "styles of social control": penal, conciliatory, compensatory, and therapeutic. In applying these concepts to police intervention into interpersonal disputes, Black (1980: ch. 5) indicated that each style of social control might take the form of one or more of a number of different actions, and that the acts of any one style can be distinguished in terms of the quantity of law they represent. For example, "in the penal style of social control, the deviant is defined as a violator of a prohibition, an offender deserving of condemnation and punishment" (Black, 1980: 131). Police officers adopt the penal style, according to Black, when they arrest one or both parties, compel the separation of the parties, threaten to arrest one of the parties, or merely scold or admonish. But not all of these actions represent equivalent amounts of law; an arrest is more law, according to Black, than separating the disputants, which in turn is more law than admonishing. For analysis, then, Black offered a nominal variable with four categories, each corresponding to a style of law, and four ordinal scales representing the quantity of each style of law.

Black's analysis of data on dispute resolution by the police revealed that police behavior is still more complex, inasmuch as officers' behavior could not always be classified in terms of the four styles. Moreover, the styles, particularly the penal and conciliatory styles, frequently occurred in combinations. Of the encounters that "police agreed to handle," 45 percent involved the combination of penal and conciliatory styles, and an additional 4 percent involved other combinations. Almost one fourth of the cases were handled in a purely conciliatory style, and more than one fifth in a purely penal style. While the compensatory and therapeutic styles were seldom adopted in disputes (less than 3 percent of the cases were handled in either fashion), they might occur with greater frequency in other types of police–citizen encounters. It is also possible, of course, that in other types of encounters, officers' behavior would more frequently defy classification in these terms.

Other analyses also reflect the complexity of police behavior, even when analysis focuses on a particular type of situation. Bayley's (1986) analysis of officers' "tactical choices" in disputes and in traffic stops breaks these police–citizen encounters into three stages—contact, exit, and a residual category of processing—and provides for a range of behavioral categories at each stage. In order to exhaustively account for officers' actions, Bayley specifies a rather large number of categories at each stage: thirteen contact actions, seventeen processing actions, and seventeen exit actions in disputes; ten contact actions, nine processing actions, and twelve exit actions in traffic stops. Moreover, these categories were not mutually exclusive, as officers might take multiple actions even at any one stage.

Likewise, Worden's (1989) analysis of police dispositions in disputes constructs a measure with fourteen categories of behavior. This measure captures the various combinations of four types of actions—coercion, separation, mediation, and counseling—that officers might take in an encounter and, in addition, arrest and inaction. Even with categories so numerous, however, this construction rests on a simplifying assumption: that different actions of the same type—e.g., coercive actions such as threatening and lecturing—are sufficiently similar for analytical purposes that they can be subsumed under a single analytic category.

Even these rather cumbersome measures arguably fail to capture all of the theoretically significant variation in police behavior. Klinger (1996a) argues that previous research has erred by not distinguishing solutions that are *imposed* by the police—albeit without arrest—from solutions that are *proposed* by the police. He explains, for example, that an officer might separate the parties to a dispute either by commanding one party to leave the scene or by suggesting or negotiating one party's departure. The difference is an important one in the amount of authority invoked by the police.

Klinger (1996a) proposed a "formal authority scale" (FAS) that encompasses many actions that police might take in their encounters with citizens.

Previous studies opted for nominal or ordinal measures. Klinger sought to form an interval scale, and so he grappled with the problem of developing commensurate metrics for different increments of police authority; as a result, the FAS is based on a series of arguable assumptions. The payoff is also questionable. Klinger's application using Metro-Dade data showed that the FAS is very similar to the arrest/no arrest dummy variable (the two measures were correlated at .85). The similarity stemmed largely from the fact that 85 percent of the encounters analyzed fell into the no-arrest category; of those, 71 percent fell into a single category of the FAS.

Procedural Justice. In the last ten years or so, research has reflected a better appreciation for how the quality of police performance might have as much (or more) to do with *how* authority is exercised as it does with what form of authority is exercised. A large body of social psychological research has shown that when people have contacts with the police, the procedural justice that they subjectively experience affects their trust and confidence in the police, their identification with the police, and their sense that the police deserve to be obeyed—that is, how officers are perceived to act affects the legitimacy of the police. Procedural justice, this research tells us, is a matter of treating people with dignity and respect, giving them an opportunity to explain their situations and listening to what they have to say, and explaining what police have done and/or will do so that it is clear that they are taking account of people's needs and concerns and basing their decisions on facts. This research further tells us that legitimacy is important not only for its own sake but also because it has consequences. People who believe that police are legitimate are more likely to accept police decisions and comply with police requests and directives, more likely to cooperate with the police, and more likely to abide by the law.

Observational research did not anticipate these developments, however, and extant data afforded only a limited opportunity to examine these features of police–citizen interactions. Mastrofski et al. (2002) operationalized one important aspect of the procedural injustice with which officers may act— disrespect—and found that police are typically civil toward citizens. When they are not, the disrespect that they display is most often an in-kind response to disrespect by the citizen; "unprovoked" disrespect was very uncommon. Analyzing citizen compliance with police requests, McCluskey (2003) distilled measures of procedural justice, as well as the temporal sequences of police action and citizen response, from POPN narratives. More recently, Jonathan-Zamir, Mastrofski, and Moyal (2013) conducted a small-scale observational study that pointedly captured elements of the procedural justice with which police act, finding fairly high levels of procedural justice in some respects (asking for and listening to citizens' viewpoints), moderate levels in some respects (treating citizens with respect), and low levels in other respects (showing care and concern for citizens' needs). Worden and McLean (2014b) distinguished procedurally just actions from procedurally unjust actions in observations of Schenectady (NY) police; they found moderate levels of procedural justice and low levels of procedural injustice.

"Good" Policing. Most police research describes and analyzes what officers do—arrest or not, use or refrain from using force—but it has tended *not* to address the normative dimensions of police authority—whether what individual officers do represents *good* police work. Others have lamented this shortcoming in police scholarship (see Bittner, 1983; Bayley, 1986; Fyfe, 1997). It is a deeply challenging gap to fill. The goals of policing are vague, ambiguous, and to some degree contradictory. The situations that police handle are complex, and so a normative judgment about the use of police authority is contingent on many factors. Moreover, the criteria against which such a judgment should be made are not at all clear. Officers' choices could be judged in terms of immediate outcomes, such as whether agitated citizens are calmed (McIver and Parks, 1983), or in terms of longer-term outcomes, such as whether a domestic assailant recidivates. Another potential criterion is a professional one of "workmanship," which as Bittner (1983) explains, concerns officers' "ability to call upon the resources of knowledge, skill, and judgment to meet and master the unexpected within one's sphere of competence." Similarly, Klockars (1996) proposed a "craft standard" against which the use of force could be compared, i.e., what a skilled police officer would have done under the circumstances.

As a general proposition, scholars agree that police should use their authority sparingly. Muir (1977) describes a "good" officer as one who can reconcile her personal moral code with the use of coercive power, but who uses it *only* as needed. Moore (2002) contends that police are more efficient when they use a minimum of authority. The use of police authority, he points out, depletes the "stock of private liberty" that the public enjoys, and the "net value" of policing must take account of the costs of policing, one of which is the use of authority (2002: 26). A somewhat broader view, about which there is also some agreement, is that "good" policing is at least as much a matter of process as outcome (Mastrofski, 1999; Reiner, 1998).

One approach to this problem is to identify officers with a reputation for effective performance and observe them in situations in which their skill is likely to manifest itself. Bayley and Garofalo (1987; 1989) did precisely that. They asked officers to identify peers whom they considered to be especially skilled in handling conflict. In the three NYPD precincts they studied, Bayley and Garofalo thereby identified a set of exceptionally skilled officers on whom they conducted systematic observations. They found that these officers exhibited somewhat distinctive patterns of interaction with citizens, particularly in situations that had the potential for conflict. Skilled officers "tended to be more concerned to get the fullest possible picture [of the incident] and to find a long-run solution, especially one that satisfied the complainant, while [comparison officers] showed less sympathy for complainants' problems, and were quicker to say that the police couldn't do anything" (1987: 13). They added that the more skilled officers "offered more information about ways to resolve problems, while [comparison officers] lectured citizens about how to act in the future and threatened a stern response if they were called back" (ibid.). But the detected differences were not large.

Factors that Shape Police Behavior

The discretionary use of police authority is a decision-making task. Officers make numerous choices in their encounters with citizens: to stop and question; to frisk or search; to arrest; to cite; to use any of a variety of forms of physical or verbal force. As an encounter with a citizen unfolds over time, the choices may recur. In general, behavioral choices can be predicted or explained when the premises for decision are known (Simon, 1976). Some of the premises are factual: the consequences of alternative police actions and the nature of the situation from which the consequences can be projected (see Worden and Brandl, 1990: 302–303). Other premises are matters of value: the goals of police intervention and the desirability of alternative sets of consequences. Most research on police behavior has treated the characteristics of police–citizen encounters—such as the nature of the offense, the demeanor of suspects, and the preferences of complainants for a disposition—as hypothesized decision premises. Some research has, in effect, allowed for variation in decision making among classes of decision makers, e.g., male and female officers, novice and experienced officers, college-educated and less-educated officers. Several studies have treated organizational policies, procedures, and informal norms as decision premises.

Explaining police decision making is complicated by the ambiguity and uncertainty of police officers' task environments. Situational cues are ambiguous in that the meaning or significance of any cue is subject to different interpretations. The credibility of citizens' testimony (which often is contradicted by the testimony of other citizens), the severity of injuries, the degree of citizens' sobriety, and many other features of police–citizen encounters are all matters of judgment, and these judgments can vary from situation to situation and from officer to officer. The same cue can be interpreted differently across multiple events, or even ignored as irrelevant in some instances. Similarly, organizational policies and group norms are ambiguous, requiring that officers interpret them as they are applied in individual cases.

Explanation is further complicated by uncertainty about cause-and-effect relationships. The choice of a course of action is based partly on the projected consequences of alternatives, but no body of scientific or other technical knowledge guides officers in making such projections (which would be probabilistic in any case). Officers may be socialized into some common working rules, but they also learn through their own idiosyncratic experiences, drawing from them some equally idiosyncratic lessons for practice. Thus, we can posit that the meaning and also the implications of situational and organizational cues are heterogeneous across officers, attenuating the explanatory power of situational and organizational variables.

Prior research on police decision making, for the most part, takes one of two approaches: ethnographic inquiry, and quantitative analyses of decision outcomes (e.g., police decisions to arrest or to use force) in terms of situational factors that are the hypothesized stimuli to which decision makers respond. The former has been very illuminating, although it is limited in its generalizability. The latter are scientifically rigorous, exploiting numerical data on the characteristics of the immediate decision task to estimate independent effects on decision outcomes. Researchers draw inferences about the forces that shape decision making from the regression coefficients, treating the process by which informational inputs are interpreted and judgments are made to reach decisions as a "black box." But these analyses are limited in their explanatory scope to factors that are of a priori significance, and we know that these factors fall far short of explaining police decisions.

Situational Factors. SSO is particularly well-suited to the examination of the socio-legal influences on police behavior, and much of the SSO-based research has focused on the effects of situational factors on police behavior. Some of this research is based on the theory that guided Reiss in his research, or on a variant thereof (e.g., Black, 1976), although any analysis that allows for variation in decision making across decision makers might begin with the analysis of situational factors (see, e.g., Worden and Pollitz, 1984; Smith, 1984b). Officers' choices take place in the context of particular situations and will inevitably be constrained by the varying encounter circumstances and citizen characteristics. Most studies have examined situational influences on relatively infrequent outcomes such as arrest and use of force because these actions represent the most consequential forms of authority police can invoke. They are, therefore, the areas of the greatest concern should police abuse that authority. Moreover, much of the research has been oriented not to explaining discretionary decision making but rather to determining whether and to what extent the application of police authority is influenced by extralegal factors, such as race, sex, and age. Thus, the analyses seek to control for the legal factors that legitimately shape police behavior, whereupon a determination can be made about whether residual variation is related to extralegal factors.

Research consistently finds that legal factors have significant effects on police decision making. Officers are more likely to invoke their authority for offenses that are serious and for those in which there is ample evidence. The strength of the evidence of wrongdoing also matters, although research reveals that police invoke their authority far less frequently than they have evidentiary cause to do so. Measures of the strength of evidence have improved over time, as instruments expanded to capture discrete forms of evidence (e.g., officer observed offense, suspect gave a confession, etc.) that could be combined to form a scale (Mastrofski, Worden, and Snipes, 1995).

One situational factor that attenuates the effects of offense seriousness and evidence is complainant preference. Research has consistently shown that officers tend to follow the preferences of complainants, particularly (but not only) if the offense is not serious or if the preference is for leniency. Thus, officers may consider complainant preference as a proxy for their likely cooperation with prosecution: when complainants prefer that police not take formal action, officers may treat that as an "instrumental" legal consideration (Mastrofski et al., 1995). This is particularly true when the relational distance between offender and victim is not that great (as discussed further below); requests for leniency often occur in domestic disputes.

The demeanor of a suspect has been a consistent predictor of police action—officers respond punitively to those who show a disregard for their authority. This has remained true despite a debate amongst researchers regarding the appropriate definition and operationalization of "demeanor." Klinger (1994) first questioned the measurement of demeanor in previous research, arguing that prior studies had failed to adequately isolate and control for crime committed by suspects during their encounter with police (in particular, crime *against* the police). Although subsequent research found that the original findings regarding the influence of demeanor were valid (e.g., Lundman, 1994, 1996; Worden and Shepard, 1996; Klinger, 1995a, 1996b; Worden et al., 1996), Klinger's critique pushed research to exercise greater care in the conceptualization and measurement of demeanor (and its separation from suspect resistance). However, despite all of the research conducted to date, the demeanor/resistance question has still not been conclusively answered. That officers react to negative behavior on the behalf of a citizen is not in dispute. The forms that such behavior takes, however, and the ways in which officers interpret representations of "attitude," remain open questions if we approach police behavior as the outcome of a decision-making process. Although some forms of resistance (e.g., passive) are legal, officers may not make such a distinction in the field. It may be that officers view both a disrespectful demeanor and forms of resistance as equal affronts to their authority. If that is the case, then additional work is needed to develop these constructs so that tests of their impact are accurate. Observational research is uniquely well suited to allowing researchers to examine these possibilities, and protocol analysis of debriefings (such as those collected during POPN) could help elucidate our understanding of officer interpretation of various forms of offender behavior.

Properly conceptualizing and measuring citizens' demeanor and resistance is important because it has been shown to affect our estimates of other predictors as well. In particular, early research on police indicated that minority status was a predictor of more punitive action. Later research, however, attributed these disparities to other factors including the more frequently disrespectful demeanor of black suspects (Black, 1971) as well as the greater likelihood of black complainants to request arrest (Black and Reiss, 1970). Other researchers have found that police were more likely to arrest in encounters without complainants when the poverty level of the neighborhood increased (Smith et al., 1984). Thus, differential treatment of minorities may be due to class differences as opposed to racial difference. In general, police are more likely to invoke their authority against citizens of lower social class (Lundman, 1994, 1996, 1998; Reiss, 1968; Worden, 1995; Terrill, 2001). Conclusions about the influence of social class (and its relationship with citizen race) based on observational study, however, may be problematic because observers must make inferences about social class, and there is no guarantee that observers' impressions match those of the officers they are observing (Mastrofski et al., 1995).

The sex of the suspect appears to influence both arrest and use of force decisions. Officers are more likely to use force against males (Worden, 1995; Terrill, 2001) and also use less force relative to resistance with female suspects than they do with males (Alpert and Dunham, 2004; Terrill, 2005). It might be that officers are being chivalrous to female offenders (Mastrofski et al., 1995; Worden, 1995; Terrill and Mastrofski, 2002), or it might be that female suspects simply require less force to control. In terms of the arrest decisions, most research has considered the influence of the gender makeup of the parties involved in terms of domestic incidents. Officers appear less likely to arrest when disputants are married (Fyfe et al., 1997; Worden and Pollitz, 1984; Black, 1971; cf. Klinger, 1995b), but it is not clear whether leniency in such cases is due to the marital relationship or because police tend to be more lenient in general as relational distance decreases (Fyfe et al., 1997).

As noted above, complainant requests for leniency are more likely in domestic incidents, as victims of domestic violence often indicate a reluctance to cooperate. Some research has also indicated that officers may discount evidentiary factors when deciding on a course of action in domestic encounters and, in terms of arrest decisions, some researchers have found that married disputants are less likely to be arrested than unmarried disputants (Worden and Pollitz, 1984; Black, 1971). Such considerations have prompted legislative and policy changes that are intended to attenuate the effect of complainant preference.

In general, research has not found that juvenile status affects the imposition of police authority (Worden and Myers, 2000; cf. Brown, Novak, and Frank, 2009). In concert with demeanor, however, there is some evidence that police might be giving breaks to youth who are deferential. As previously noted, police in general tend to invoke the law far less frequently than they have the authority to do so, but respectful youth (just like respectful adults) are more likely to benefit from an officer's lenience (Worden and Myers, 1999; Myers, 2002).

A few studies have utilized observational data to examine the process of decision making by police. Stroshine et al. (2008) enumerate informal "working rules" that serve to guide officers in performing their jobs, and they observe that "different officers look for different things and respond to suspects and situations differently" (2008: 335). They describe the cues to which officers attend in forming suspicion (e.g., time and place, and citizens' appearance and behaviors), the rules of thumb that they apply (e.g., with respect to the seriousness of violations, or the citizen's demeanor), and more general approaches that they take to their work (seeking out or avoiding opportunities for traffic enforcement). Schafer and Mastrofski (2005) utilized observation, debriefings, and structured interviews to analyze stop and sanction behavior in traffic enforcement. They found that each stage of an encounter was influenced by the context in which the encounter occurred—citizen demeanor and the officer's mood strongly influenced the ultimate sanction. Finally, Bonner (2012) utilized the POPN data to examine the process of decision making in dispute resolution encounters. She found that officers, on average, utilize less than half of the information available to them before rendering a decision, and further, officers are largely heterogeneous when it comes to what information is considered in an encounter and the relative importance it assumes in their individual decision-making process. Ultimately, a process model built around information from the narratives performed better in predicting an arrest outcome than the more conventional structural (regression-based) model. Although it has not been adopted frequently, a process approach provides an additional avenue to investigate the complexity of officer decision making.

Officer Characteristics and Outlooks.   Social scientists and police professionals often assume that the performance of individual police officers is shaped in important ways by their backgrounds and occupational attitudes. Given the breadth of discretion that officers exercise in handling the situations that routinely arise in their work, and in initiating contacts with the public, the proposition that their discretionary choices are influenced by their attitudes is intuitively plausible. Several studies have described marked differences in the ways that officers apply (or withhold) their authority and provide services; they have attributed those differences to corresponding variations in officers' outlooks. Such relationships are of more than theoretical significance, inasmuch as they underlie many initiatives to change the composition of—and thereby "upgrade"—police personnel. For example, administrators may believe that minority officers, female officers, or college-educated officers have different outlooks and therefore perform the police role differently. Efforts to inculcate different outlooks through training are also based on the belief that attitudes affect performance.

But the evidence that race, sex, and educational background affect how officers do their jobs is mixed and inconclusive (National Research Council, 2004), and systematic research has often failed to confirm that officers' attitudes and values bear a detectable relationship to their patterns of performance. One of the earliest and most striking findings from observational research on police was that, while many officers professed to be prejudiced against African Americans, officers did not act on that prejudice in their encounters with citizens (Reiss, 1968, 1971a). Another examination of these propositions (Worden, 1989) found only weak relationships between officers' occupational attitudes (e.g., their conceptions of the police role, attitudes toward citizens, attitudes toward legal restrictions) and their behaviors (e.g., proactivity in field interrogation, dispute resolution). Such results should not be surprising, in view of the ambiguity and uncertainty of police work. Officers with the same occupational outlooks might read the informational cues in a situation differently to reach a different conclusion, or they could perceive different ways of reaching the same objectives. Thus, officers' choices among alternative courses of action may be only loosely structured by their attitudes and values.

More recent findings, however, have provided more support for the hypothesized effects of officers' outlooks. This research analyzed attitudes as bundles (differentiating various subsets of attitudinally homogeneous officers), rather than estimating the additive effects of attitudes one by one. Terrill et al. (2003) reported that officers whose occupational attitudes conform more closely to the tenets of the traditional police culture are more prone to use coercive authority. That is, these officers emphasize law enforcement as their occupational role and espouse an aggressive approach that allows for occasional violations of civil liberties; they also hold negative attitudes toward the citizenry as well as toward police supervisors. Similarly, Paoline and Terrill (2005) found that such officers are more likely to conduct searches during traffic stops.

Organizational Structure.   Several efforts have been made to define and measure police performance in terms of citizens' evaluations of and satisfaction with their local police (Ostrom, 1975; cf. Sharp, 1981). Performance measures of this kind are based on a consumer model of the delivery of police services, questionnaires are administered to a sample of the residents of a municipality or other geographic unit. Respondents are asked to rate their local police, both in global terms and on more specific dimensions of service (e.g., courtesy, honesty, speed of response). Often they are also asked about their experiences with crime and with the police. Comparisons of departments using this type of measurement have revealed that small and medium-sized departments perform equally well or better than do large departments. Many of these studies use a "most similar systems" design, whereby neighborhoods that are served by different police departments—but which are alike in terms of selected demographic attributes—are compared directly, without statistical controls (see Ostrom and Whitaker, 1973: 56). These "matched neighborhood" studies have consistently shown that levels of citizen satisfaction with police are lower in those neighborhoods that are served by large departments. They have also indicated that in neighborhoods served by large departments, citizens are more likely to be victimized, less likely to report victimizations to police, and less satisfied with what the police do when they have direct contact with the police. Moreover, these results hold whether the neighborhoods are poor, black neighborhoods or middle-income, white neighborhoods.[3]

Although the results of previous empirical research are consistent, with only unimportant exceptions, the theoretical and practical implications of these results are not clear: many different hypotheses could account for the relationship between size and performance. One set of hypotheses concerns administrative features of police organizations. One of these hypotheses focuses on the "production strategies" adopted by police departments. It appears that smaller departments place a larger proportion of their personnel on patrol, which might enable them not only to be more visible but also to respond more quickly to citizens' calls for service (Ostrom, Parks, and Whitaker, 1978a; Parks, 1981). Insofar as citizens' perceptions of police response time influence their evaluations of police (Percy, 1980), these administrative decisions may account for all or part of the relationship between department size and performance.

Other hypotheses concern the development and supervision of police personnel (see Whitaker, 1983). Studies of supervision in larger departments found variation in supervisory "styles" that was for the most part unrelated to the behavior of subordinates (Engel, 2000; 2001), even finding that subordinates misperceived their supervisors' priorities (Engel and Worden, 2003). One might expect that smaller agencies are able to maintain closer supervision by using both formal and informal channels of communication; administrators in smaller departments can thereby better monitor patrol officers' behavior. One can find some empirical support for this proposition (Brown, 1981). Closer supervision might also enable and encourage supervisors to provide counsel and guidance, especially to inexperienced officers (see Muir, 1977). Furthermore, because task differentiation is lower and workgroup stability is higher in smaller departments, one might expect to find that the officers in smaller departments have higher morale, greater group esprit, and deeper loyalty to supervisors than do the officers in large departments.

If the administrative features of small police departments promote street-level behaviors that better satisfy the citizen-consumers of police services, then one would expect that these influences will be reflected in the experiences of citizens, *and* one would expect that the differences in citizen evaluations across departments would diminish when the effects of citizens' experiences are controlled. Previous research indicates that citizens' evaluations of the police are indeed influenced by their experiences with the police (Brandl et al., 1994; Reisig and Parks, 2000; Skogan, 2005; Rosenbaum et al., 2005), but it remains to be determined whether those experiences represent the causal linchpin between department size and citizen satisfaction.

Some research based on observational data has examined the formal structures of police organizations, including the degree of bureaucratization and the nature of administrative expectations, as a potential influence on officers' discretionary choices. Much of this research is based on James Q. Wilson's (1968) seminal study, which posited that in "professional," bureaucratic departments one tends to find "legalistic" patterns of policing (meaning that officers tend to be more proactive and to rely more on their legal authority), while in "fraternal," nonbureaucratic departments one tends to find "watchman" patterns of policing (meaning that officers tend to be reactive and to infrequently invoke the law). This research has been limited, however, by the very small number of police agencies (twenty-four for the PSS but only three in the Black-Reiss data and only one or two in all of the other projects) and the rather crude indicators of organizational structure that could be devised. Perhaps as a result, the research reports either null or countertheoretical findings (Friedrich, 1980; Smith, 1984b; Worden, 1989; 1995).

The Future of SSO

As it has been executed in the past, SSO is labor-intensive and hence expensive. By way of illustration: the two phases of the PSS cost $2,239,225 in 1974, or the equivalent of $10,663,843 in 2014 dollars; POPN cost $1,969,701 in 1995, or $3,034,438 in 2014 dollars. However, SSO can be done more economically: without the expense of instrumentation, the Policing in Cincinnati Project cost $234,908 in 1996, or $351,510 in 2014 dollars, and the further use of the POPN instruments in other sites would better enable researchers to conduct analysis whose findings cumulate.

With the increasing proliferation of technology (in-car cameras and especially body-worn cameras), SSO need not rely only on in-person observation. SSO can be done after-the-fact at a desktop computer using the video and audio recordings. Riley et al. (2005) analyzed Cincinnati traffic stops using video and audio recordings from CPD police units. Worden and McLean (2014b) used similar recordings in Schenectady (NY) to examine the procedural justice of police action in sampled encounters; they also collected data on citizens' subjective experience in the same encounters through a survey, which allowed them to compare citizens' judgments about how police acted against independent measures of police behavior.

This armchair observation can be done much more economically, and it enjoys other advantages over in-person observation. Reactivity, in the context of a police department whose officers are routinely subject to video and audio recording, may be eliminated. One recent study, in the Rialto (CA) Police Department, found that when officers were randomly assigned to wear audiovisual recording apparatus, they were less likely to use physical force (Farrar, 2014).

Arm-chair observation provides opportunities to reflect and to "revisit" an encounter by playing back audio and video, which is likely to enhance the validity and reliability of the coded observations. While observers in the field can refer back to their notes, these notes are gathered while an observer's brain is processing multiple sensory inputs. Observers are not exposed to risk. Furthermore, the observation is much less disruptive for the agency host, which might open doors that would otherwise be closed to observational study. Coding can be done at the encounter, citizen, and even transaction levels. Multiple observers can code the same encounters, providing for estimates of inter-coder reliability. Even debriefing could capitalize on the recordings, by asking officers to recount their thinking as the recording is played back (albeit in separate sessions and not as they go about their regular tours of duty).

Coding police–citizen interactions from video and audio recordings suffers some drawbacks compared with in-person observation, however. Even with body-worn video, the range of an observer's vision is limited, and nonverbal communication by the officer may not be observable. What officers do outside the context of police–citizen encounters may not be captured. Audio quality can be compromised by a host of factors, including: citizen and officer voice volume and speech clarity; noise inside the vehicle, such as a scanner or the radio; and noise outside the vehicle such as passing traffic or wind.

SSO as a method could be better adapted to empirical investigations grounded in perspectives other than the socio-legal perspective—i.e., psychological and organizational perspectives. Early police researchers (e.g., Muir, 1977; Brown, 1981) found evidence that officers exhibit "styles" of policing; these "typologies" of policing could be operationalized if SSO generated enough observations of individual officers. Similarly, data from SSO could provide additional insights (beyond the limited inquiry conducted thus far) on the effect of the formal structure of the police organization on officer behavior. The potential of SSO, however, turns on further development of the analytic constructs and their operationalization. Measures of occupational outlooks leave room for improvement, and other individual characteristics and traits surely have explanatory value. Concepts and measures of administrative priorities and expectations, and officers' perceptions of administrative priorities and expectations, are also in need of much greater elaboration.

We would be remiss if we failed to mention the contribution of SSO projects not only to substantive knowledge but also to the development of scholars. Many of these studies, and particularly the large-scale projects, have helped to launch the careers of a number of scholars. As graduate students, they worked on SSO projects as observers, supervisors, or site directors. Seven students worked on the PSS and based their dissertation research on PSS data; (at least) two additional dissertations have been based on PSS data. POPN yielded twelve doctoral dissertations, most of them authored by people who worked as POPN research assistants and/or field research staff. PCP also yielded a number of doctoral dissertations (at least six). Many of these students remain actively involved in police research today, as the citations in this essay (partially) document. We should count this as a prospective benefit of future SSO studies.

ENDNOTES

[1] Narratives were to be completed for selected types of encounters, e.g., domestic disturbances and juvenile problems, encounters with violence between officer and citizen, encounters in which officers from other police agencies participate, and encounters that the observer believed were too complex to adequately portray in coded data. Observers were advised to "[t]hink of the narrative as telling another observer what happened in a particular encounter. Write it similarly to the way you would tell someone about it verbally."

[2] Observation-based measures of these constructs have arguably left room for improvement. Offense seriousness has often been framed simply as a dichotomy: more serious and less seri-

ous (e.g., felony/misdemeanor). Klinger (1994) found fault with such measures as failing to capture much of the variation in seriousness. The addition of other binary variables for weapons and injuries, in his estimation, did not adequately complement the more/less serious dichotomy. Klinger suggested instead a 5-point, ordinal scale of offense seriousness: no crime; minor property crime; minor violent or major property crime; moderate violent crime; major violent crime. His advice has not been consistently heeded, and at this time, it is not clear how much difference it makes; some previous research has found that a binary measure captures much of the variation in the 5-point scale (Worden and Shepard, 1996).

[3] See Whitaker (1983) for a review. For the original findings, see Ostrom and Parks (1973); Ostrom, Parks, and Whitaker, (1973); Ostrom and Whitaker (1973). Pachon and Lovrich (1977) report contrary findings; but see Whitaker (1983) for a critique.

REFERENCES

Alpert, Geoffrey, and Roger G. Dunham, 2004. *Understanding Police Use of Force: Officers, Suspects, and Reciprocity.* Cambridge: Cambridge University Press.

Alpert, Geoffrey P., Roger G. Dunham, Meghan Stroshine, Katherine Bennett, and John MacDonald, 2004. *Police Officers' Decision Making and Discretion: Forming Suspicion and Making a Stop,* Report to the National Institute of Justice. Columbia: University of South Carolina.

Bayley, David H., 1986. "The Tactical Choices of Police Patrol Officers," *Journal of Criminal Justice* 14: 329–348.

Bayley, David H., and James Garofalo, 1987. *Patrol Officer Effectiveness in Managing Conflict During Police-Citizen Encounters.* Albany, NY: Hindelang Criminal Justice Research Center.

Bayley, David H., and James Garofalo, 1989. "The Management of Violence by Police Patrol Officers," *Criminology* 27: 1–25.

Bittner, Egon, 1967. "The Police on Skid-Row: A Study of Peace-Keeping," *American Sociological Review* 32: 699–715.

Bittner, Egon, 1974. "Florence Nightingale in Pursuit of Willie Sutton: A Theory of the Police," in Herbert Jacob, ed., *The Potential for Reform of Criminal Justice.* Beverly Hills: Sage.

Bittner, Egon, 1983. "Legality and Workmanship: Introduction to Control in the Police Organization," in Maurice Punch, ed., *Control in the Police Organization.* Cambridge, MA: MIT Press.

Black, Donald, 1971. "The Social Organization of Arrest," *Stanford Law Review* 23: 1087–1111.

Black, Donald, 1976. *The Behavior of Law.* New York: Academic Press.

Black, Donald, 1980. *The Manners and Customs of the Police.* New York: Academic Press.

Black, Donald, and Albert J. Reiss, Jr., 1967. "Patterns of Behavior in Police and Citizen Transactions," *Studies of Crime and Law Enforcement in Major Metropolitan Areas,* Volume II, Section I. Washington: U.S. Government Printing Office.

Black, Donald, and Albert J. Reiss, Jr., 1970. "Police Control of Juveniles," *American Sociological Review* 35: 63–77.

Bonner, Heidi S., 2012. *How Patrol Officers Make Decisions: Comparing a Structural Model to a Process Model.* Unpublished Ph.D. dissertation, University at Albany, SUNY.

Brandl, Steven G., James Frank, Robert E. Worden, and Timothy S. Bynum, 1994. "Global and Specific Attitudes Toward the Police: Disentangling the Relationship," *Justice Quarterly* 11:119–134.

Brown, Michael K., 1981. *Working the Street: Police Discretion and the Dilemmas of Reform.* New York: Russell Sage.

Brown, Robert, Kenneth Novak and James Frank, 2009. "Identifying Variation in Police Officer Behavior Between Juveniles and Adults," *Journal of Criminal Justice* 37: 200–208.

Dunham, Roger G., Geoffrey P. Alpert, Meghan S. Stroshine, and Katherine Bennett, 2005. "Transforming Citizens into Suspects: Factors that Influence the Formation of Police Suspicion," *Police Quarterly* 8:366–393.

Engel, Robin Shepard, 2000. "The Effects of Supervisory Styles on Patrol Officer Behavior," *Police Quarterly* 3: 262–293.

Engel, Robin S., 2001. "Supervisory Styles of Patrol Sergeants and Lieutenants," *Journal of Criminal Justice* 29: 341–355.

Engel, Robin Shepard, and Robert E. Worden, 2003. "Police Officers' Attitudes, Behavior, and Supervisory Influences: An Analysis of Problem-solving," *Criminology* 41: 131–166.

Farrar, William, 2014. "Operation Candid Camera: Rialto Police Department's Body-Worn Camera Experiment," *Police Chief* (January).

Frank, James, Kenneth Novak, and Brad W. Smith, 2001. *Street-level Policing in Cincinnati: The Content of Community and Traditional Policing and the Perceptions of Policing Audiences,* Final Report to the National Institute of Justice. Cincinnati: University of Cincinnati.

Friedrich, Robert J., 1980. "Police Use of Force: Individuals, Situations, and Organizations," *Annals of the American Academy of Political and Social Science* 452: 82–97.

Fyfe, James J., 1988. *The Metro-Dade Police/Citizen Violence Reduction Project: Final Report.* Washington: Police Foundation.

Fyfe, James J., 1997. "Good Policing," in Roger G. Dunham and Geoffrey P. Alpert, eds., *Critical Issues in Policing: Contemporary Readings,* 3rd ed. Long Grove, IL: Waveland.

Fyfe, James J., David A. Klinger, and Jeanne Flavin, 1997. "Differential Police Treatment of Male-on-Female Spousal Violence," *Criminology* 35: 455–473.

Garner, Joel H., Christopher D. Maxwell, and Cedrick Heraux, 2002. "Characteristics Associated with the Prevalence and Severity of Force Used by the Police," *Justice Quarterly* 19: 705–746.

Gould, Jon B., and Stephen Mastrofski, 2004. "Suspect Searches: Assessing Police Behavior under the Constitution," *Criminology and Public Policy* 3: 316–362.

Jonathan-Zamir, Tal, Stephen D. Mastrofski, and Shomron Moyal, 2013. "Measuring Procedural Justice in Police-Citizen Encounters," *Justice Quarterly* (on-line).

Kelling, George L., and Mark H. Moore, 1988. "From Political to Reform to Community: The Evolving Strategy of Police," in Jack R. Greene and Stephen D. Mastrofski, eds., *Community Policing: Rhetoric or Reality.* New York: Praeger.

Klinger, David A., 1994. "Demeanor or Crime? Why 'Hostile' Citizens are More Likely to be Arrested," *Criminology* 32: 475–493.

Klinger, David A., 1995a. "The Micro-Structure of Nonlethal Force: Baseline Data from an Observational Study," *Criminal Justice Review* 20: 169–186.

Klinger, David A., 1995b. "Policing Spousal Assault," *Journal of Research in Crime and Delinquency* 32: 308–324.

Klinger, David A., 1996a. "Quantifying Law in Police-Citizen Encounters," *Journal of Quantitative Criminology* 12: 391–415.

Klinger, David A., 1996b. "More on Demeanor and Arrest in Dade County," *Criminology* 34: 61–82.

Klockars, Carl B., 1996. "A Theory of Excessive Force and Its Control," in William A. Geller and Hans Toch, eds., *Police Violence: Understanding and Controlling Police Abuse of Force.* New Haven, CT: Yale University Press.

Liederbach, John, 2002. *Policing Small Towns, Rural Places, and Suburban Jurisdictions: Officer Activities, Citizen Interactions, and Community Context.* Unpublished Ph.D. dissertation, University of Cincinnati.

Lundman, Richard J. 1994. "Demeanor or Crime? The Midwest City Police-citizen Encounters Study," *Criminology* 32: 631–656.

Lundman, Richard J. 1996. "Demeanor and Arrest: Additional Evidence from Unpublished Data," *Journal of Research in Crime and Delinquency* 33: 306–323.

Lundman, Richard J. 1998. "City Police and Drunk Driving: Baseline Data," *Justice Quarterly* 15: 527–546.

Manning, Peter K., 1977. *Police Work: The Social Organization of Policing.* Cambridge, MA: MIT Press.

Mastrofski, Stephen D., 1999. *Policing for People*, Ideas in American Policing. Washington: Police Foundation.

Mastrofski, Stephen, and Roger B. Parks, 1990. "Improving Observational Studies of Police," *Criminology* 28: 475–496.

Mastrofski, Stephen D., Roger B. Parks, and John D. McCluskey, 2010. "Systematic Social Observation in Criminology." In Alex Piquero and David Weisburd (eds.), *Handbook of Quantitative Criminology.* New York: Springer-Verlag.

Mastrofski, Stephen D., Roger B. Parks, Albert J. Reiss, Jr., Robert E. Worden, Christina DeJong, Jeffrey B. Snipes, and William C. Terrill, 1998. *Systematic Observation of Public Police: Applying Field Research Methods to Policy Issues.* Washington: National Institute of Justice.

Mastrofski, Stephen, Michael Reisig and John McCluskey, 2002. "Police Disrespect Toward the Public: An Encounter-Based Analysis," *Criminology* 40:519–552.

Mastrofski, Stephen D., and Jeffrey B. Snipes, 2002. Impact of Community Policing at the Street Level: An Observational Study in Richmond, Virginia, 1992 [Computer file]. ICPSR version. Lansing, MI: Michigan State University [producer], 1998. Ann Arbor, MI: Inter-university Consortium for Political and Social Research [distributor], 2002. doi:10.3886/ICPSR02612.v1.

Mastrofski, Stephen D., Robert E. Worden, and Jeffrey B. Snipes, 1995. "Law Enforcement in a Time of Community Policing," *Criminology* 33: 539–563.

McCluskey, John D., 2003. *Police Requests for Compliance: Coercive and Procedurally Just Tactics.* New York: LFB Scholarly Publishing.

McIver, John P., and Roger B. Parks, 1983. "Evaluating Police Performance: Identification of Effective and Ineffective Police Actions," in Richard R. Bennett, ed., *Police at Work: Policy Issues and Analysis.* Beverly Hills, CA: Sage.

Moore, Mark H., 2002. *Recognizing Value in Policing: The Challenge of Measuring Police Performance.* Washington: Police Executive Research Forum.

Moskos, Peter, 2008. *Cop in the Hood: My Year Policing Baltimore's Eastern District.* Princeton, NJ: Princeton University Press.

Muir, William Ker, Jr., 1977. *Police: Streetcorner Politicians.* Chicago: University of Chicago Press.

Myers, Stephanie M., 2002. *Police Encounters with Juvenile Suspects: Explaining the Use of Authority and Provision of Support.* Unpublished Ph.D. dissertation, University at Albany, SUNY.

National Research Council, 2004. *Fairness and Effectiveness in Policing: The Evidence.* Washington: The National Academies Press.

Ostrom, Elinor, 1975. "The Design of Institutional Arrangements and the Responsiveness of the Police," in Leroy N. Rieselbach, ed., *People vs. Government.* Bloomington: Indiana University Press.

Ostrom, Elinor, Roger B. Parks and Gordon P. Whitaker, 1973. "Do We Really Want to Consolidate Urban Police Forces? A Reappraisal of Some Old Assertions," *Public Administration Review* 33: 423–432.

Ostrom, Elinor, Roger B. Parks and Gordon P. Whitaker, 1978a. "Police Agency Size: Some Evidence on its Effects," *Police Studies* 1: 34–46.

Ostrom, Elinor, Roger B. Parks and Gordon P. Whitaker, 1978b. *Patterns of Metropolitan Policing.* Cambridge, MA: Ballinger.

Ostrom, Elinor, Roger B. Parks, and Gordon Whitaker, 2001. *Police Services Study, Phase II, 1977: Rochester, St. Louis, and St. Petersburg* [Computer file]. ICPSR08605-v3. Ann Arbor, MI: Inter-university Consortium for Political and Social Research [distributor], 2001. doi:10.3886/ICPSR08605.v3

Ostrom, Elinor, and Dennis C. Smith, 1976. "On the Fate of 'Lilliputs' in Metropolitan Policing," *Public Administration Review* 36: 192–200.

Ostrom, Elinor, and Gordon P. Whitaker, 1973. "Does Local Community Control of Police Make a Difference? Some Preliminary Findings," *American Journal of Political Science* 27: 48–76.

Pachon, Harry P., and Nicholas P. Lovrich, Jr., 1977. "The Consolidation of Urban Police Forces: A Focus on the Police," *Public Administration Review* 37: 38–47.

Paoline, Eugene A. III, and William Terrill, 2005. "The Impact of Police Culture on Traffic Stop Searches: An Analysis of Attitudes and Behavior," *Policing: An International Journal of Police Strategies and Management* 28: 455–472.

Parks, Roger B., 1981. *Surveying Citizens for Police Performance Assessments,* Technical Report number 93. Bloomington, Ind.: Workshop in Political Theory and Policy Analysis.

Parks, Roger B., Stephen D. Mastrofski, Christina DeJong, and M. Kevin Gray, 1999. "How Officers Spend Their Time with the Community," *Justice Quarterly* 16:483–518.

Percy, Stephen L., 1980. "Response Time and Citizen Evaluation of Police," *Journal of Police Science and Administration* 8: 75–86.

Reaves, Brian A., 2010. *Local Police Departments, 2007.* Washington: Bureau of Justice Statistics.

Reiner, Robert, 1998. "Process or Product? Problems of Assessing Individual Police Performance," in Jean-Paul Brodeur, ed., *How to Recognize Good Policing: Problems and Issues.* Thousand Oaks, CA: Sage.

Reisig, Michael D., and Roger B. Parks, 2000. "Experience, Quality of Life, and Neighborhood Context: A Hierarchical Analysis of Satisfaction with Police," *Justice Quarterly* 17: 607–630

Reiss, Albert J., Jr., 1968. "Police Brutality—Answers to Key Questions," *Trans-action* 5: 10–19.

Reiss, Albert J., Jr., 1971a. *The Police and the Public.* New Haven, CT: Yale University Press.

Reiss, Albert J., Jr., 1971b. "Systematic Observation of Natural Social Phenomena," in Herbert L. Costner, ed., *Sociological Methodology 1971.* San Francisco: Jossey-Bass.

72   Section I: Introduction and Historical Overview

Riley, K. Jack, Susan Turner, John MacDonald, Greg Ridgeway, Terry L. Schell, Jeremy M. Wilson, Travis L. Dixon, Terry Fain, Dionne Barnes-Proby, and Brent D. Fulton, 2005. *Police-Community Relations in Cincinnati*. Santa Monica: RAND.

Rosenbaum, Dennis P., Amie M. Schuck, Sandra K. Costello, Darnell F. Hawkins, and Marianne K. Ring, 2005. "Attitudes Toward the Police: The Effects of Direct and Vicarious Experience," *Police Quarterly* 8: 343–365.

Rubinstein, Jonathan, 1973. *City Police*. New York: Ballantine.

Schafer, Joseph. and Stephen Mastrofski, 2005. "Police Leniency in Traffic Enforcement Encounters: Exploratory Findings from Observations and Interviews," *Journal of Criminal Justice* 33: 225–238.

Schulenberg, Jennifer L., 2014. "Systematic Social Observation of Police Decision-Making: The Process, Logistics, and Challenges in a Canadian Context," *Quality and Quantity* 48: 297–315.

Sharp, Elaine B., 1981. "Responsiveness in Urban Service Delivery: The Case of Policing," *Administration and Society* 13: 33–58.

Simon, Herbert A., 1976. *Administrative Behavior.* 3rd ed.; New York: Free Press.

Skogan, Wesley G., 2005. "Citizen Satisfaction With Police Encounters," *Police Quarterly* 8: 298–321.

Skolnick, Jerome, 1975. *Justice Without Trial: Law Enforcement in Democratic Society.* 2nd ed.; New York: John Wiley.

Smith, Douglas A., 1984a. "Police Control of Interpersonal Disputes," *Social Problems* 31: 468–481.

Smith, Douglas A., 1984b. "The Organizational Context of Legal Control." *Criminology* 22: 19–38.

Smith, Douglas A., Christy A. Visher, and Laura A. Davidson, 1984. "Equity and Discretionary Justice: The Influence of Race on Police Arrest Decisions," *Journal of Criminal Law and Criminology* 75: 234–249.

Spano, Richard, 2003. "Concerns about Safety, Observer Sex, and the Decision to Arrest: Reactivity in a Large-Scale Observational Study of Police," *Criminology* 41: 909–32.

Spano, Richard, 2005. "Potential Sources of Observer Bias in Police Observational Data," *Social Science Research* 34: 591–617.

Spano, Richard, 2006. "Observer Behavior as a Potential Source of Reactivity: Describing and Quantifying Observer Effects in a Large-Scale Observational Study of Police," *Sociological Methods & Research* 34: 521–553.

Spano, Richard, 2007. "How Does Reactivity Affect Police Behavior? Describing and Quantifying the Impact of Reactivity as Behavioral Change in a Large Scale Observational Study of Police," *Journal of Criminal Justice* 35: 453–465.

Stroshine, Meghan, Geoffrey Alpert, and Roger Dunham, 2008. "The Influence of 'Working Rules' on Police Suspicion and Discretionary Decision Making," *Police Quarterly* 11: 315–337.

Sykes, Richard E., and Edward E. Brent, 1980. "The Regulation of Interaction by Police: A Systems View of Taking Charge," *Criminology* 18: 182–197.

Sykes, Richard E., and Edward E. Brent, 1983. *Policing: A Social Behaviorist Perspective.* New Brunswick, NJ: Rutgers University Press.

Terrill, William, 2001. *Police Coercion: Application of the Force Continuum.* New York: LFB Scholarly Publishing.

Terrill, William, 2005. "Police Use of Force: A Transactional Approach," *Justice Quarterly* 22: 107–138.

Terrill, William, and Stephen D. Mastrofski, 2002. "Situational and Officer-Based Determinants of Police Coercion," *Justice Quarterly* 19: 215–248.

Terrill, William, Eugene A. Paoline III, and Peter K. Manning, 2003. "Police Culture and Coercion," *Criminology* 41: 1003–1034.

Van Maanen, John, 1974. "Working the Street: A Developmental View of Police Behavior," in Herbert Jacob, ed., *The Potential for Reform of Criminal Justice*. Beverly Hills: Sage.

Westley, William A., 1953. "Violence and the Police," *American Journal of Sociology* 59: 34–41.

Westley, William A., 1970. *Violence and the Police: A Sociological Study of Law, Custom, and Morality*. Cambridge, MA: MIT Press.

Whitaker, Gordon P., 1982. "What Is Patrol Work?" *Police Studies* 4 (1982): 13–22.

Whitaker, Gordon P., 1983. "Police Department Size and the Quality and Cost of Police Services," in Stuart Nagel, Erika Fairchild, and Anthony Champagne, eds., *The Political Science of Criminal Justice*. Springfield, IL: Charles C. Thomas.

Wilson, James Q., 1968. *Varieties of Police Behavior: The Management of Law and Order in Eight Communities*. Cambridge, MA: Harvard University Press.

Worden, Robert E., 1989. "Situational and Attitudinal Explanations of Police Behavior: A Theoretical Reappraisal and Empirical Assessment," *Law & Society Review* 23: 667–711.

Worden, Robert E. 1995. "The 'Causes' of Police Brutality: Theory and Evidence on Police Use of Force," in William A. Geller and Hans Toch (eds.), *And Justice for All: Understanding and Controlling Police Abuse of Force*. Washington: Police Executive Research Forum.

Worden, Robert E., and Steven G. Brandl, 1990. "Protocol Analysis of Police Decision Making: Toward a Theory of Police Behavior," *American Journal of Criminal Justice* 14: 297–318.

Worden, Robert E., and Sarah J. McLean, 2014a. "Systematic Social Observation of the Police," in Michael Reisig and Robert Kane, eds., *Oxford Handbook on Police and Policing*. New York: Oxford University Press.

Worden, Robert E., and Sarah J. McLean, 2014b. *Assessing Police Performance in Citizen Encounters*, Report to the National Institute of Justice (Albany, NY: John F. Finn Institute for Public Safety, Inc.).

Worden, Robert E., and Stephanie M. Myers, 1999. "Police Interactions with Juvenile Suspects," paper prepared for the National Research Council, Commission on Behavioral and Social Sciences and Education, Panel on Juvenile Crime.

Worden, Robert E., and Alissa A. Pollitz, 1984. "Police Arrests in Domestic Disturbances: A Further Look," *Law & Society Review* 18: 105–119.

Worden, Robert E., and Robin L. Shepard, 1996. "Demeanor, Crime, and Police Behavior: A Reexamination of Police Services Study Data," *Criminology* 34: 83–105.

Worden, Robert E., Robin L. Shepard, and Stephen D. Mastrofski, 1996. "On the Meaning and Measurement of Suspects' Demeanor toward the Police," *Journal of Research in Crime and Delinquency* 33: 324–332.

SECTION II

Police Socialization and the Police Subculture

Police administrators recognize that their department is only as good as the quality of its officers. As in many other organizations, police agencies are confronting a changing environment that is creating the need for adaptive changes in its workforce. Anthony Batts, Sean Smoot, and Ellen Scrivner (2012) discuss how changing environmental factors (such as the availability of new technologies, the changing nature of crime, and heightened budget concerns) have created opportunities for a new generation of police officers to meet the new challenges. They argue that the reliance on a paramilitary model, which does not adapt well to outside demands for accountability or change, constrains the police response. They conclude that many police leaders have recognized the need to alter some traditional structures to allow more flexibility for adaptation to changing circumstances and the characteristics of the new workforce.

The readings in this section provide students with a working knowledge of issues involving police personnel and of the images the police project as a result of their socialization into the world of policing. Where power exists, there also exists the potential to abuse that power. Two elements figure prominently in police corruption: opportunity and greed. In addition, there is always the possibility that bias and prejudice can creep into an officer's decision making concerning citizens, resulting in discriminatory treatment for some groups. For example, Lorie Fridell and Michael Scott (2010) reviewed the literature on racial profiling. They argue that this complex and challenging problem is not new, but law enforcement has never been better situated to address how law enforcement agencies perceive and respond to the problem of racially biased policing. Progressive chiefs and sheriffs across the nation are acknowledging the problem and implementing initiatives to create critically needed change.

In the first selection, "Breeding Deviant Conformity," Victor Kappeler, Richard Sluder, and Geoffrey Alpert describe how the real and exaggerated sense of the danger inherent in police work affects how the police picture the world. The worldview nurtures a police subculture that influences the behaviors of police officers that are deemed acceptable and effective in the world

75

they perceive. While these subcultural values often function to prepare the police to be more effective in fulfilling their difficult responsibilities, some extreme versions of the values can lead to police misconduct or corruption.

"Solidarity and the Code of Silence" by Jeffrey Noble, Geoffrey Alpert, and Jeff Rojek is a discussion of how the occupational subcultures existing in many police departments often create a sense of solidarity among police officers expressed as an "us against them" mentality that leads to a strongly enforced "code of silence" in the subculture. This situation often works against following many policies of the department and can lead to violations of departmental policies—and in extreme cases, serious corruption. The authors discuss ways to address the problem of extreme solidarity and the code of silence.

Next, Laure Weber Brooks presents an up-to-date review of the current research on police discretionary behavior, emphasizing the factors that affect police officers' behavioral choices. She notes that it is a collection of "rules of thumb" learned on the job through a combination of formal and informal socialization and training that best accounts for the officers' behavioral choices. She reviews the findings of research indicating the influence of a number of factors—including the gender of the officer, educational level, ethnicity, and job experience—on police behavior toward citizens.

The fourth article in this section, "The Asshole," by John Van Maanen, explores the negative labeling of certain citizens by police officers and how this stigmatizing label sets the stage for the ways the police approach situations, their attitudes toward citizens, and the actions officers deem appropriate for this type of citizen. This stereotyping creates expectations, thoughts, and feelings that result in officers behaving harshly. While this article was published many years ago (1978), the concept is timeless and still applies today.

Jeff Rojek, Scott Decker, and Allen Wagner examine the process that is initiated when a civilian files a complaint against a police officer. They suggest that the police have failed to effectively meet the challenges presented by citizen complaints. Perhaps the process of citizen complaints and police administrators' responses is akin to shutting the barn door after the horse escapes. One way to discover police behaviors that require more administrative oversight is to examine the information included in complaints made about the police by citizens.

In the final article in this section, "Ethics and Law Enforcement," Joycelyn Pollock and Paul Reynolds discuss the many ethical dilemmas that police officers frequently face. They also discuss various ways the police can resolve these ethical dilemmas, such as utilizing IACP's Code of Ethics for Law Enforcement, traditional ethical rationales, or some other ethical guidelines. They conclude that it is possible for officers to be "good" people and "good" police officers if they are aware of and use ethical decision making.

REFERENCES

Batts, A., Smoot, S., & Scrivner, E. (2012). Police leadership challenges in a changing world. *New Perspectives in Policing Bulletin.* Washington, DC: U.S. Department of Justice, National Institute of Justice. NCJ 238338.

Fridell, L., & Scott, M. (2010). Law enforcement agency responses to racially biased policing and the perceptions of its practice. In R. Dunham & G. Alpert (Eds.), *Critical issues in policing: Contemporary readings* (6th ed., pp. 343–360). Long Grove, IL: Waveland Press.

5

Breeding Deviant Conformity
The Ideology and Culture of Police

Victor E. Kappeler, Richard D. Sluder, & Geoffrey P. Alpert

Man is not just an individual, he belongs to the whole; we must always take heed of the whole, for we are completely dependent on it.
—Theodor Fontane (1819–1898)

Police learn a distinct orientation to their occupational role through formal and informal learning exchanges. This article examines police ideology by focusing on the processes that shape the cultural and cognitive properties of police officers.

Perspectives on the Development of Police Character

Before exploring the ideological and cultural attributes of the police, it is instructive to examine some of the different perspectives theorists and researchers have used to gain a better understanding of the character and behavior of the police as an occupational group. At the risk of oversimplification, one of three general perspectives or paradigms is commonly selected: psychological, sociological, or anthropological. In the sections that follow, the psychological and sociological perspectives of police character are discussed first to demonstrate the difference between researchers' perspectives on the police and to show the complexity of understanding police character. The anthropological perspective of police character is then given extensive treatment because it allows for the integration of research findings from the other areas and provides a broad framework for understanding both police character and behavior.

Adapted from *Forces of Deviance: The Dark Side of Policing*, 2/E. Long Grove, IL: Waveland Press (1998), pp. 83–108.

The Psychological Paradigm of Police Character

Many researchers adopt a psychological orientation to the study of police character. At one extreme, theorists taking this perspective limit their examination of the police to individual officers and attempt to understand how individual personality shapes behavior. According to this view, each person has a core personality that remains static throughout life (Adlam, 1982). Although events, experiences, and social situations change, an individual's basic personality is thought to stay the same. Behavior is structured by preexisting personality traits that are fixed early in life and remain intact.

When this fixed perspective of personality is applied to the police, researchers tend to focus on the personality characteristics exhibited by people who are attracted to the police occupation. Persons with certain personalities enter law enforcement and behave in distinct ways (Rokeach, Miller, & Snyder, 1971). Often this approach is limited to an examination of the personality structures of police recruits (see Burbeck & Furnham, 1985; Hannewicz, 1978). Theorists adopting this perspective think that people with certain personality characteristics are attracted to careers in law enforcement; those with other personality characteristics choose alternative career paths. From this perspective, researchers are inclined to examine the theorized "police personality." This perspective and research orientation has been referred to as a *predispositional model* of police behavior (Alpert, Dunham & Stroshine, 2015).

The predispositional model has led some to conclude that police recruits are more authoritarian than people who enter other professions. The *authoritarian personality* is characterized by conservative, aggressive, cynical, and rigid behaviors. People with this personality have a limited view of the world and see issues in terms of black and white. For the authoritarian personality, there is little room for the shades of gray that exist in most aspects of social life. People are either good or bad, likable or unlikable, friends or enemies. The authoritarian personality is characterized by a rigid view of the world that is not easily changed; they are, in essence, defenders of the *status quo* (Gaines & Kappeler, 2015). People with authoritarian personalities generally submit to superiors and are intolerant toward those who do not submit to them when they exert their own authority (Adorno, 1950). John J. Broderick (1987) has done an excellent job of capturing how the term authoritarian is used in discussions of the police.

> Those who . . . use it are usually referring to a person who has great respect for power and authority and strongly adheres to the demands of his or her own group. This person is also submissive to higher authority and hostile toward outsiders who do not conform to conventional standards of behavior. The characteristics of willingness to follow orders and respect for authority might seem to be virtues when possessed by police officers, but in the sense used here, the term authoritarian means an extreme, unquestioning willingness to do what one is told and an extremely hostile attitude toward people who are different than oneself. (p. 31)

While Broderick rejected the notion that police are more authoritarian than people who go into other occupations, some research supports the authoritarian police character. Research from this perspective focused on positive personality characteristics of the police. It identified police officers as conformists with personalities that more closely resemble the characteristics of military personnel than the attributes of people in other occupations. Carpenter and Raza (1987) found that police applicants differ from other occupational groups in several significant ways. First, police applicants, as a group, are psychologically healthy, "less depressed and anxious, and more assertive in making and maintaining social contacts" (p. 16). Second, police are a more homogeneous group of people and that this "greater homogeneity is probably due to the sharing of personality characteristics which lead one to desire becoming a police officer" (p. 16). Finally, they found that police were more like military personnel in their conformance to authority.

The psychological perspective on police and its premise that people attracted to law enforcement are more authoritarian than people in other occupations have been called into question by researchers who adopt a different perspective of police behavior. Researchers who take a more social psychological perspective see personality as developmental and, therefore, subject to change given differential socialization and experience (Adlam, 1982). Instead of assuming that personality is fixed, these researchers see personality as dynamic and changing with an individual's life experience. Essentially, researchers adopting this alternative orientation feel that personality cannot be divorced from the experience that shapes it. Other researchers focus on the role police perform in society and how training influences personality (Bahn, 1984; Putti, Aryee & Kang, 1988). From this perspective, researchers study the effects of police training, peer group support, and the unique working environment—all of which are thought to influence and shape police character and behavior. Many of these researchers, however, still view behavior from an individualistic level focusing on a single officer's unique experiences and the development of individual personalities. This limited view of the police character has been questioned by researchers adopting a sociological perspective.

The Sociological Paradigm of Police Character

Several studies elaborated a group socialization model of police culture (Stoddard, 2006). Arthur Niederhoffer (1967), David Bayley and Harold Mendelsohn (1969), as well as other social scientists, have rejected the notion that police have certain personality characteristics that might predetermine their behavioral patterns. Instead, they and others adopt the perspective that behavior is based on group socialization and professionalization. *Professionalization* is the process by which norms and values are internalized as workers learn their occupation (Alpert et al., 2015; Gaines & Kappeler, 2015). It is maintained that just as lawyers and physicians learn their ethics and values through training and by practicing their craft, so do the police. Exposure to a police training academy, regular in-service training, and field experience all shape occupational character. Police learn how to behave and what to think from their shared experiences with other police officers.

From this perspective, many researchers find that rookie police officers just beginning their careers are no more authoritarian than members of other professions who come from similar backgrounds (Broderick, 1987). This perspective on police behavior assumes police learn their occupational personality from training and through exposure to the unique demands of police work (Skolnick, 1994). If officers become authoritarian, cynical, hard, and conservative, it is not necessarily because of their existing personalities or because of their pre-occupational experiences. Rather, the demands of the occupation and shared experiences as law enforcement officers shape their development.

Research findings support the position that recruit and probationary officers are profoundly affected by their training and socialization. The socialization process experienced by the police affects their attitudes and values. Richard Bennett (1984) studied police officers from several departments and found that while recruit and probationary officers' values are affected by the training process, there was little support for the idea that police personalities were shaped by their peers in the department. This however, may be explained by the fact that new officers often do not become true members of the department until they are accepted by their peers and granted membership and acceptance into the police occupational culture. Others maintain that the full effect of the police socialization process is not felt during this initial "setting in" phase and may not develop until later in a police career (Bahn, 1984). Similarly, Joseph Putti and his colleagues (1988) stated their findings on police values "could be interpreted to mean that complete socialization into an occupational subculture is a function of time" (p. 253). While it is not known to what extent other reference groups shape personality in older officers, it seems that—at least initially—new police officers' values are shaped as they are trained for the demands of law enforcement and as they become accepted into the occupation.

The Anthropological Paradigm

The most dramatic change in the police social character occurs when officers become part of the occupational culture. The term *culture* is often used to describe differences among large social groups. Social groups differ in many aspects, and people from different cultures have unique beliefs, laws, morals, customs, and other characteristics that set them apart from other groups. These attitudes, values, and beliefs are transmitted from one generation to the next in a learning process known as socialization. Cultural distinctions are easy to see when one compares, for example, cultures of Japan and the United States. Both of these countries have laws, language, customs, religions, and art forms that differ significantly from each other. These differences provide each group with unique cultural identities.

There can also be cultural differences among people who form a single culture or social group. People who form a unique group within a given culture are called members of a *subculture*. The difference between a culture and a subculture is that members of a subculture, while sharing many values and beliefs of the larger culture, also have a separate and distinct set of values that set them apart. Clearly, police share cultural heritage with others in the United States—they speak the same language, operate under the same laws, and share many of the same values. There are, however, certain aspects of the police occupational subculture that distinguish the police from other members of society. The police are set apart from other occupational groups and members of society by their unique role and social status. Therefore, some scholars have adopted a *culturalization* perspective on the police as a unique occupational subculture.

The Police Worldview

The concept of *worldview* refers to the manner in which a culture sees the world and its own role and relationship to the world (Benedict, 1934; Redfield, 1952, 1953). This means that various social groups, including the police, perceive situations differently from other social or occupational groups. For example, lawyers may view the world and its events as a source of conflict and potential litigation. Physicians may view the world as a place of disease and illness. For the physician, people may become defined by their illness rather than their social character. Experiences, skills, and functions frame situations differently depending on one's occupational groups. Similarly, the police develop a framework for viewing interactions. The police worldview has been described as a working personality. According to Jerome Skolnick (1994), the police develop cognitive lenses through which to see situations and events—distinctive ways to view the world.

The way the police view the world can be described as a "we/they" or "us/them" orientation. The world is seen as composed of insiders and outsiders—police and citizens. Persons who are not police officers are considered outsiders and are viewed with suspicion. This "we/they" police worldview is created for a variety of reasons: the techniques used to select citizens for police service; the normative orientation police bring to the profession; an exaggeration of occupational danger; the special legal position police hold in society; and the occupational self-perception that is internalized by people who become police officers.

Before citizens can become police officers they must pass through an elaborate employment selection process—physical agility tests, background investigations, polygraph examinations, psychological tests, and oral interviews. These tools are used to screen out applicants who do not conform to a select set of norms and values. Many of the selection techniques that are used to determine the "adequacy" of police applicants have little to do with their ability to perform the real duties associated with police work (Cox, Crabtree, Joslin, & Millet, 1987; Gaines & Kappeler, 2015; Holden, 1984; Maher, 1988; Paynes & Bernardin, 1992). Often, these tests are designed merely to determine applicants' physical prowess, sexual orientation, gender identification, financial stability, employment history, and abstinence from drug and alcohol abuse.

If police applicants demonstrate conformity to a middle-class life style, they are more likely to be considered adequate for police service. The uniform interpretation of psychological tests, based on middle-class bias, tends to produce a homogeneous cohort. As one researcher has noted "the usefulness of psychological testing for police officer selection is, at best, questionable . . . no test has been found that discriminates consistently and clearly between individuals who will and who will not make good police officers" (Alpert, 1993, p. 100).

In part due to the traditional police selection process, the vast majority of people in policing have been (Kuykendall & Burns, 1980) and are today (Reaves, 2010), middle-class white males. Few municipal police departments employ personnel representative of the communities they serve in terms of race or gender. Every ten years, the Bureau of the Census collects information on the number and demographics of police officers. In 2010, more than 75% of cities had a police presence that was disproportionately white relative to the local population. In Niagara Falls, New York, for example, the population is 20% black, but the entire police force (250 officers) is white; in Florissant, Missouri, 25% of the population is black, but none of the 25 police officers are. The Census found that blacks were underrepresented on the police forces in more than 40% of cities. Black police officers are underrepresented in 72% of the communities where Blacks comprise at least 5% of the population. Hispanics are underrepresented in 66% of the cities where they make up at least 5% of the population (Keating, & Elliott, 2014).

A consequence of the police personnel system is that it selects officers who are unable to identify with groups on the margins of traditional society. The police process people and events in the world through cognitive filters that overly value conformity in ideology, appearance, and conduct. This conformist view of the world, derived from a shared background, provides police a measuring rod by which to make judgments concerning who is deviant and in need of state control (Matza, 1969) and what is "suspicious" (Skolnick, 1994) and in need of police attention.

This homogeneous group of police recruits experiences formal socialization when it enters the police academy. The police academy refines the cohort again by weeding out those recruits who do not conform to the demands of training. Police recruits soon learn

> that the way to "survive" in the academy . . . is to maintain a "low profile," by being one of the group, acting like the others. Group cohesiveness and mutuality is encouraged by the instructors as well. The early roots of a separation between "the police" and "the public" is evident in many lectures and classroom discussions. In "war stories" and corridor anecdotes, it emerges as a full blown "us-them" mentality. (Bahn, 1984, p. 392)

Some have argued that the paramilitary model of police training with a hierarchical organizational structure and those at the top determining the agenda is inconsistent with humanistic democratic values. It demands and supports "employees who demonstrate immature personality traits" (Angell, 1977, p. 105) and creates dysfunctional organizations (Argyris, 1957). The encouraged traits closely resemble attributes of the authoritarian personality. Traditional training teaches attitudes that suggest only skilled professionals can handle crime—differentiating the police from the public (Kappeler & Gaines, 2011). The emphasis on professional crime fighting can make recruits indifferent to the concerns of average people. Petty crimes affect far more people than, say, an armed bank robbery.

Skolnick (1994) noted that danger is one of the most important facets in the development of a police working personality. The relationship between the dangers associated with police work and the police perception of the job as hazardous is complex. Police officers uniformly perceive their work as dangerous, yet there is less agreement on the probabilities that they will be hurt on the job (Paoline & Terrill, 2014). Francis Cullen, Bruce Link, Lawrence Travis, and Terrence Lemming (1983) have referred to this situation as a paradox in policing. Their research in five police departments found that

> even though the officers surveyed did not perceive physical injury as an everyday happening, this does not mean that they were fully insulated against feelings of danger. Hence . . . it can be seen that nearly four-fifths of the sample believed that they worked at a dangerous job, and that two-thirds thought that policing was more dangerous than other kinds of employment. (p. 460)

David Bayley (1976) cogently explained the disjuncture between the potential for injury and the exaggerated sense of danger found among police officers.

> The possibility of armed confrontation shapes training, patrol preoccupations, and operating procedures. It also shapes the relationship between citizen and policeman by generating mutual apprehension. The policeman can never forget that the individual he contacts may be armed and dangerous; the citizen can never forget that the policeman is armed and may consider the citizen dangerous. (p. 171)

Police instructors are generally former street enforcement officers; their occupational experiences and worldview have been filtered through the cognitive framework described earlier. Thus, much of the material presented to new police officers serves to reinforce the existing police view of the world rather than to educate police recruits or to provide appropriate attitudes, values, and beliefs (Cohen & Feldberg, 1991; Delattre, 1989). Even though well intended, police instructors' ability to educate is restricted because most police training curricula overemphasize the potential for death and injury and further reinforce the danger notion by spending an inordinate amount of time on firearms skills, dangerous calls, and "officer survival." The training orientation often resembles preparation for being dropped behind enemy lines on a combat mission.

In 2013, 27 police officers were feloniously killed—the lowest number in more than 50 years. The average number of officers feloniously killed each year over the last decade was 51. The number of officers killed on duty has been falling since the mid-1990s. Assaults against police officers have also declined (Balko, 2014). This is not to dismiss the possibility of danger in police work. Certainly, police are killed and injured in the line of duty, but these figures remain relatively small in comparison to the time spent indoctrinating recruits with the notion that the world is a dangerous place for a police officer Kappeler & Potter, 2005).

As Table 1 shows, police training is dominated by an attempt to develop the practical rather than the intellectual skills of recruits. In addition to the substantial amount of time spent on the skills associated with officer safety, a large block of time is spent indoctrinating police on the basic elements of criminal law and the techniques to be used to detect criminal behavior. Little time is spent on developing an understanding of constitutional law, civil rights, or ethical considerations in the enforcement of the law. As the table indicates, police instructors evaluate student performance by weighting certain areas more heavily than others. Differential importance is given to the use of firearms, patrol procedures, and how to use force in arresting and restraining citizens. These three areas are seen as the most critical functions by instructors and are given greater emphasis in scoring the performance of recruits in the police academy.

Table 1   Typical Law Enforcement Basic Training Program

Topic	Hours Spent	Percent of Time	Weight
Administration	24.5	6.13	(—)
Introduction to Law Enforcement	20.5	5.00	1.00
Firearms (skills development)	56.5	14.10	2.00
Vehicle Operation (pursuit driving)	25.5	6.40	1.00
First Aid/CPR	16.0	4.00	.50
Accident Investigation	15.0	3.80	.50
Criminal Law (statutes)	55.5	13.80	1.00
Patrol Procedures (crime detection)	50.0	12.50	2.00
Criminal Investigation	19.0	4.80	.50
Specific Investigations (street crime)	31.0	7.80	1.00
Arrest and Restraint/Physical Fitness	67.5	16.90	2.00
Practical Performance Exercises	19.0	4.75	1.00

The real and exaggerated sense of danger inherent in police work contributes greatly to the police picture of the world (Gaines & Kappeler, 2015). As a result, the police may see citizens as potential sources of violence or as enemies. Citizens become "symbolic assailants" to the police officer on the street (Skolnick, 1994). The symbolic assailant is further refined in appearance by taking on the characteristics of marginal segments of society (Harris, 1973; Piliavin & Briar, 1964) and the characteristics of the populations police are directed to control (Sparger & Giacopassi, 1992). To the officer in southern Texas, the young Hispanic man becomes the potential assailant; in Atlanta, the poor inner-city black man becomes a source of possible injury; and in Chinatown, the Asian becomes the criminal who may resort to violence against the police.

Symbolic assailants, however, are not limited to those persons who pose a threat to the officer's physical safety, nor are they identified solely in terms of race or ethnicity. Jennifer Hunt's field study of police practice in one large urban police department found that officers also perceive certain types of citizens' actions as symbolic threats.

> Few officers will hesitate to assault a suspect who physically threatens or attacks them. . . . Violations of an officer's property such as his car or hat might signify a more symbolic assault on the officer's authority and self, justifying a forceful response to maintain control. (Hunt, 2006, p. 347)

She also found that some of the female officers she observed resorted to the use of force when their authority was explicitly denied by insults or highly sexualized encounters.

Emphasizing danger fosters the "we/they" worldview and focuses police attention on selective behaviors of certain segments of society. Research into the police culture over the course of thirty years has documented the changing nature yet sustained presence of danger and symbolic assailants as central themes in police culture. Perhaps the greatest change in this aspect of police culture is the growing abstraction of who and what constitutes symbolic danger.

The role and function of the police differ from the role and function of the military, but certain situations and events have increased the intersection. In the 1990s, the "War on Drugs" was in full force. Congress enacted the National Defense Authorization Act in response to the perceived drug crisis. Section 1208 allowed the transfer of surplus military equipment to law enforcement agencies for counter-drug activities. In 1997, Congress replaced Section 1208 with Section 1033, which extended the transfer of military property for use in law enforcement. The program has transferred more than $5.1 billion worth of property to more than 8,000 law enforcement agencies (Feldman, 2014). The proliferation of military weapons to police departments has been accompanied by the use of military tactics (Wofford, 2014).

The metaphor of war changes how people think about the police, priming the public to expect military tactics and weapons (Alpert et al, 2015). Police paramilitary units (PPUs) were originally established in large urban police departments for situations involving armed and dangerous individuals. The war on drugs greatly increased the number of activities in which they were involved. Joint task forces combined the efforts of local police departments, the National Guard, the Drug Enforcement Agency, and other federal agencies.

Many PPUs are used precisely for their symbolic or shock value. In urban areas, officers conduct "jump outs"—numerous officers exiting vehicles simultaneously and creating an enormous display of fire power.

> The military weapons, tactics, training, and drug-raids generate an intense feeling of "danger" among the officers. There exists of course a universal fear of being a victim of violence among regular police officers. . . . However, the preoccupation with danger in this special operations team, and the fear of being a victim of violence, is heightened. All the PPU officers expressed an extreme fear of the worst happening to them, emphasizing the "real possibility" that every call-out could end in tragedy. . . . The perception of danger and death serves to create a military-like camaraderie among PPU officers. Just as the fear of danger involved in the PPU is more intense than in normal policing, the camaraderie formed is also more intense. Officers emphasize that they must rely on fellow officers more, and their close bonding functions to protect each other's "backsides." (Kraska & Paulsen, 1997, p. 263)

In some situations, such as riot control, PPUs might limit the risk to the public. However, the use of PPUs has escalated. They have been used to raid medical marijuana shops, illegal poker games, businesses employing illegal immigrants, and to execute warrants (Balko, 2013). Officers may believe that military-style tactics provide more safety, but they can also contribute to making situations far more dangerous with disastrous consequences. The war on terror after the attacks of September 11, 2001, provided new reasons for militarizing the police. The Department of Homeland Security was created in 2002 and has distributed $35 billion in grants to departments, much of it to purchase military gear, including armored personnel carriers (Balko, 2013).

On August 9, 2014, in Ferguson, Missouri, a white police officer shot and killed Michael Brown, an unarmed 18-year old African American male. The community was outraged and took to the streets in protest. The protesters were black, and almost all of the officers were white. Ferguson's population (21,000) is 67% black, while the police force is almost entirely white (Jonsson, 2014). Ferguson officers responded militarily to the protesters. One magazine referred to the small town as looking like a "war zone." "Police— kitted out with Marine-issue camouflage and military-grade body armor, toting short-barreled assault rifles, and rolling around in armored vehicles—are indistinguishable from soldiers" (Wofford, 2014). Ferguson had acquired equipment from the 1033 program. The graphic images broadcast nationally of police officers deploying military-grade vehicles and weapons designed for foreign battlefields rather than city streets provoked widespread criticism.

> The needs of an occupying military force are—or at least should be—distinct from those of a local law enforcement agency. Effective policing requires much more than overwhelming firepower. It entails, among other things, working with the local community to gain its trust. But it's difficult to do that when you're staring community members down from atop the gun turret of an armored vehicle. (Ingraham, 2014)

When the police become more militaristic, the perceptions of danger may increase and officers may believe the only way to solve the problem is through military-style force—a mind-set more appropriate for the battlefield than for the community.

Skolnick (1994) has noted the importance of authority vested in the police as another important characteristic in the development of the police working personality. The law shapes and defines interactions between people and grants social status to members of society (Black, 1970, 1976). The police, by virtue of their social role, are granted a unique position in the law. Police have a legal monopoly on the sanctioned use of violence against other members of society (Bittner, 2006a; Bordua & Reiss, 1967; Reiss, 1971; Westley, 2006) and coercion (Bittner, 2006a; Westley, 2006). The legal sanctions that prevent citizens from resorting to violence are relaxed for police officers. Police often resort to coercion to accomplish their organizational goals of controlling crime and enforcing the existing social order. This legal distinction between citizens and police sets officers apart from the larger culture and other occupations.

Since the primary tools used by the police are violence and coercion, it was easy for the police to develop a paramilitary model of training and organization (Bittner, 2006b). In this model, likeness of dress, action and thought is promoted; homogeneity of appearance, ideology, and behavior is emphasized. The military model reinforces the "we/they" worldview of the police; it allows officers to see themselves as a close-knit, distinct group and promotes a view of citizens as "outsiders and enemies" (Westley, 1956). The strength of this conditioning is evident in the alienation felt by officers promoted to positions of management or by those who leave the profession. These individuals often feel isolated from their reference group when their organizational or occupational standing changes (Gaines & Kappeler, 2015).

Finally, the police worldview is intensified by the perception of policing as the most critical of social functions. As the process of socialization and culturalization continues, police begin to believe and project for the public the image that they are the "thin blue line" that stands between anarchy and order. "Brave police officers patrol mean streets" and are on the front lines of a war for social order and justice. The war for social order is seen by the police as so important that it requires sweeping authority and unlimited discretion to invoke the power of law—through the use of force if necessary.

The police believe in the goodness of maintaining order, the nobility of their occupation, and the fundamental fairness of the law and existing social order. Accordingly, the police are compelled to view disorder, lawbreaking, and lack of respect for police authority as enemies of a civilized society.

> They are thus committed ("because it is right") to maintain their collective face as protectorates of the right and respectable against the wrong and the not-so-respectable. . . . Thus, the moral mandate felt by the police to be their just right at the societal level is translated and transformed into occupational and personal terms and provides both the justification and legitimation for specific acts of street justice. (Van Maanen, 2006, pp. 310–311)

If law, authority, and order were seen as fostering inequity or injustice, the police self-perception would be tainted and the "goodness" of the profession would be questioned by the public. Police could no longer see themselves as partners in justice but rather partners in repression—a role most officers neither sought nor would be willing to recognize. Police who begin to question the goodness of the profession, the equity of law, or the criticality of maintaining the existing social order often quit or are forced out of the occupation for other careers, further solidifying the police social character of those who remain.

The Spirit of Police Subculture

The concept of *ethos* encompasses the distinguishing character, sentiments, and guiding beliefs of a person or institution. When this term is applied to the police subculture, three general ideas surface. First, the police value an *ethos of bravery*. Bravery is a central component of the social character of policing. As such, it is related to the perceived and actual dangers of law enforcement. The potential to become the victim of a violent encounter, the need for support by fellow officers during such encounters, and the legitimate use of violence to accomplish the police mandate all contribute to a subculture that stresses the virtue of bravery. The bravery ethos is so strong among police that

> merely talking about pain, guilt or fear has been considered taboo. If an officer has to talk about his/her personal feelings, that officer is seen as not really able to handle them . . . as not having what it takes to be a solid, dependable police officer. (Pogrebin & Poole, 1991, p. 398)

The military trappings of policing, organizational policies such as "never back down" in the face of danger, and informal peer pressure all contribute to fostering a sense of bravery. "Reprimand, gossip and avoidance constitute the primary means by which police try to change or control the behavior of co-workers perceived of as unreliable or cowardly" (Hunt, 2006, p. 344).

It is common for training officers to wait until a new recruit has faced a dangerous situation before recommending the recruit be given full status in the organization. Peer acceptance usually does not come until new officers have proven themselves in a dangerous situation. More than anything else, training officers and others in the police subculture want to know how probationary officers will react to danger—will they show bravery?

The importance of bravery in criminal justice occupational groups was highlighted in James Marquart's participant study of the prison guard subculture. Following a confrontation that required the use of force, Marquart (1986) found that:

> The fact that I had been assaulted and had defended myself in front of other officers and building tenders raised my esteem and established my reputation. The willingness to fight inmates was an important trait rewarded by ranking guards. Due to this "fortunate" event, I earned the

necessary credibility to establish rapport with the prison participants and allay their previous suspicions of me. I passed the ultimate test—fighting an inmate even though in self-defense—and was now a trustworthy member of the guard subculture. (p. 20)

An *ethos of autonomy* is also evident in the police subculture. As the first line of the criminal justice process, police officers make very authoritative decisions about whom to arrest, when to arrest, and when to use force. To this extent the police are the "gatekeepers" to the criminal justice system (Alpert et al., 2015). Police officers cling to their autonomy and the freedom to decide when to use force. The desire for autonomy often exists despite departmental, judicial, or community standards designed to limit the discretion of street enforcement officers. Personally defined justice, reinforced by subcultural membership, can lead to abuses of discretion. Any attempt to limit the autonomy of the police is viewed as an attempt to undermine the police authority to control "real" street crime and not as an attempt on the part of citizens to curb police abuses of authority.

A third ethos evident in police subcultures is the *ethos of secrecy.* William Westley, a leading scholar on policing, noted that the police "would apply no sanction against a colleague who took the more extreme view of the right to use violence and would openly support some milder form of illegal coercion" (Westley, 2006, p. 331). Similar conclusions were reached by William J. Chambliss and Robert B. Seidman (1971) in their consideration of police discretion. The police code of secrecy is often the result of a fear of loss of autonomy and authority as external groups try to limit police discretion and decision-making ability.

A second factor supporting the development of a code of secrecy is the fact that policing is fraught with the potential for mistakes. Police feel they are often called upon to make split-second decisions that can be reviewed by others not directly involved in policing. This "split-second syndrome" rationalization, however, has been used by the police "to provide after-the-fact justification for unnecessary police violence" (Fyfe, 2015, p. 526). The desire to protect one's coworkers from disciplinary actions and from being accused of making an improper decision can promote the development of a code of secrecy. John Crank (2004) observed that

the veil of secrecy emerges from the practice of police work from the way in which everyday events conspire against officers. . . . It is a cultural product, formed by an environmental context that holds in high regard issues of democratic process and police lawfulness, and that seeks to punish its cops for errors they make. (p. 278)

The police code of secrecy is also a product of the police perception of the media and their investigative function. The police perception of the media as hostile, biased, and unsupportive, contributes to friction in police-media relations and to increased police secrecy. However, it is sometimes mandatory for officers to refrain from making media releases, having public discussion, or commenting on current criminal investigations. Media Information Restrictions (Section 6.9) in Illinois prohibit a police department from releasing the name of an officer under investigation unless there has been a criminal conviction or a decision rendered by the Police Board. Police unions say these restrictions protect innocent officers from bogus claims, but they also provide police with protections not available to other citizens. In addition, they reinforce the wall of silence. By state law, police internal investigations are off-limits to the public and subject to only minimal review by a civilian oversight board. This is often interpreted by the media, citizens, and others as a self-imposed censorship of information. Perceptions of this nature can promote the separation of the public and the police and create the impression of a secret police society.

Cultural Themes in Policing

The concept of *themes* in a culture is related to the "dynamic affirmations" (Opler, 1945) maintained by its members. Themes help to shape the quality and structure of the group's social interactions. Themes are not always complementary to one another; however, they do occasionally balance or interact. This fact becomes readily apparent in studying the police subculture's dominant themes of social isolation and solidarity.

Isolation is an emotional and physical condition that makes it difficult for members of one social group to have relationships and interact with members of another group. This feeling of separateness from the surrounding society is a frequently noted attribute of the police subculture in the United States (Cain, 1973; Harris, 1973; Manning, 2006; Reiss & Bordua, 1967; Skolnick, 1994; Westley, 1956, 1970, 2006). Social isolation, as a theme of police subculture, is a logical result of the interaction of the police worldview and ethos of secrecy. Persons outside the police subculture are viewed somewhat warily as potential threats to the members' physical or emotional well-being, as well as to the officer's authority and autonomy. The emphasis on the dangers of the occupation prompts feelings of isolation (Kappeler & Gaines, 2011). If people outside the organization are viewed as potential threats, reliance on the police subculture is reinforced.

According to James Baldwin (1962) and Jerome H. Skolnick (1994), police impose social isolation upon themselves as a means of protection against real and perceived dangers, loss of personal and professional autonomy, and social rejection. Rejection by the community stems, in part, from the resentment which sometimes arises when laws are enforced (Clark, 1965). Since no one enjoys receiving a traffic ticket or being arrested and no one enjoys being disliked, the police tend to look inward to their own members for validity and support. Therefore, the police often self-impose restrictions on personal interactions with the community.

Bruce Swanton (1981) pointed out that two primary groups of determinants promote social isolation: those self-imposed by the police or those externally imposed on the police by the community. Self-imposed police determinants generally concerned work-related requirements of the police profession. These represent structurally induced determinants created by the organization and the police subculture. The most important of these include: administrative structures, work structures, and personality structures.

Swanton found that the traditional view of police work—enforcing the law, detecting, and apprehending criminals—created a sense of suspiciousness in police officers. This mistrust led to a false belief that positive community interactions or kindness from citizens were designed to compromise the officer's official position. A further deterrent to the maintenance of relationships with members of the general community was the police officer's on-duty and off-duty status. Swanton noted that the long and often irregular working hours—a result of shift schedules and possible cancellation of days off or vacations—contribute to the police officer's sense of isolation.

Swanton's (1981) externally imposed determinants of isolation included the public's suspicion that police officers' highest loyalty was to the department, thereby compromising outside friendships. Another external determinant was resentment over the police authority to issue tickets or other sanctions. The community sometimes views police work as socially unattractive.

Charles Bahn (1984) summarized the problem using a different perspective on the police.

> Social isolation becomes both a consequence and a stimulus. . . . Police officers find that constraints of schedule, of secrecy, of group mystique, and of growing adaptive suspiciousness and cynicism limit their friendships and relationships in the nonpolice world. (p. 392)

The second theme evident in the police subculture is *solidarity* (Banton, 1964; Harris, 1973; Skolnick, 1994; Stoddard, 2006; Westley, 1956, 1970, 2006). Traditionally, the theme of police solidarity and loyalty was seen as the result of a need for insulation from perceived dangers and rejection by the community. Michael Brown (1981) noted the importance of loyalty and solidarity among the police, citing one police officer's remarks.

> "I'm for the guys in blue! Anybody criticizes a fellow copper that's like criticizing someone in my family; we have to stick together." The police culture demands of a patrolman unstinting loyalty to his fellow officers, and he receives, in return, protection: a place to assuage real and imagined wrongs inflicted by a (presumably) hostile public; safety from aggressive administrators and supervisors; and the emotional support required to perform a difficult task. The most important question asked by a patrolman about a rookie is whether or not he displays the loyalty demanded by the police subculture. (p. 82)

Theodore N. Ferdinand (1980), however, has noted that solidarity and loyalty change in proportion to an officer's age and rank. He maintained that police cadets have the least amount of solidarity, and line officers have the greatest amount of solidarity. Ferdinand noted that until the age of forty, much of a police officer's social life is spent within the confines of the police subculture. However, solidarity declines as police move into higher ranks in the department. Indeed, members of the police administrative hierarchy are frequently categorized by line officers with nonpolice members of the community as threatening to the welfare of the subculture.

Police solidarity, therefore, may be said to be an effect of the socialization process inherent to the subculture and police work. New members are heavily socialized to increase their solidarity with the group, and those who move away from the subculture, either through age or promotion, are gradually denied the ties of solidarity. This cohesion is based in part on the "sameness" of roles, perceptions, and self-imagery of the members of the police subculture.

Postulates of Police Culture

Postulates are statements that reflect the basic orientations of a group (Opler, 1945). Postulates are the verbal links between a subculture's view of the world and the translation of that view into action. Because postulates and cultural themes may conflict, the degree to which they complement one another and are integrated is said to indicate the homogeneity and complexity of a culture. Postulates, then, are statements—expressions of general truth or principle that guide and direct the actions of subcultural members. These statements reveal the nuances of a subculture to a greater degree than do ethos or themes. Postulates act as oral vehicles for the transmission of culture from one generation to the next and reinforce the subcultural worldview.

Postulates basic to an understanding of the police subculture have been collected and arranged into an informal code of police conduct. Elizabeth Reuss-Ianni (1983), drawing from the research of many others (Manning, 1997; Rubinstein, 1973; Savitz, 1971; Skolnick, 1994; Stoddard, 2006; Westley, 1956, 2006), identified several of these postulates to demonstrate the conflict between administrators and line officers (see also Reuss-Ianni & Ianni, 1983). Reuss-Ianni's work is important because it illustrates the influence that line officers have on the total organization. Her work shows that despite administrative efforts to produce organizational change, substantive change is difficult to attain without the collective efforts of group members. In the case of the police, Reuss-Ianni recognized the importance of informal work groups and the influence those groups have on structuring social relationships both in and outside the police subculture. Hence, postulates are important in shaping not only the attitudes, values, and beliefs of police officers but also in shaping a shared understanding of unacceptable behaviors.

Postulates Shaping the Ethos of Secrecy and the Theme of Solidarity. The first group of postulates identified by Reuss-Ianni (1983, pp. 14–16) contribute to the ethos of secrecy that surrounds much of police work. This secrecy has many functions, three of which are especially important to the study of police deviance. First, the public is denied knowledge of many police activities because, in the eyes of the police, they have no "need to know." While it may be prudent to restrict access to certain types of sensitive information in law enforcement, the veil of secrecy that shields police from the public has the effect of minimizing public scrutiny of police activities and behaviors. Secondly, many of the postulates identified by Reuss-Ianni are guideposts which keep officers from relaying too much information to police supervisors. Line officers support these postulates as necessary protections to insulate themselves from punishment or challenges to their autonomy. Because police administrators are perceived as applying sanctions situationally and erratically, line officers develop postulates that bring predictability to their working world. Finally, perhaps the most important function is providing line officers with a sense of solidarity.

The Mollen Commission (1994) investigated the New York City Police Department and identified problems resulting from the police culture's emphasis on loyalty and secrecy.

> These aspects of police culture facilitate corruption primarily in two ways. First, they encourage corruption by setting a standard that nothing is more important than the unswerving loyalty of officers to one another—not even stopping the most serious forms of corruption. This emboldens corrupt cops and those susceptible to corruption. Second, these attitudes thwart efforts to control corruption. They lead officers to protect or cover up for others' crimes even crimes of which they heartily disapprove. (pp. 51–52)

A report in 2013 looked at five decades of misconduct in the Chicago police department (Hagedorn et al., 2013). Chicago police officers often resist reporting crimes and misconduct committed by fellow officers. "The 'blue code of silence,' while difficult to prove, is an integral part of the department's culture and it exacerbates the corruption problems" (p. 1). The report noted the finding of a federal jury in 2013 that found that the City of Chicago and its police culture were partially responsible for the brutal beating of a female bartender.

Off-duty Police Officer Anthony Abbate attacked and punched Karolina Obrycka in February 2007 when she refused to serve him more drinks. The bar's videotape system recorded Abbate going behind the bar and repeatedly punching and kicking Obrycka. He was convicted in 2009 in state court of aggravated battery and sentenced to community service, anger management counseling, and two years of probation. In a federal civil rights trial, the jury found that the police culture of impunity was a significant factor in the attack. Abbate believed that his status as a police officer would protect him from sanctions. Indeed, the officers who responded the night of the attack did not include Abbate's name in the report, did not identify him as a police officer, and did not mention existence of the video. Obrycka's lawyer argued that the "code of silence" for decades had protected police officers who committed crimes and that a history of ineffective disciplinary action against misconduct contributed to officers' beliefs that they were shielded from punishment. On November 14, 2012, the jury found both the City of Chicago and Abbate were responsible for the attack and awarded Obrycka $850,000 in damages (Hagedorn et al., 2013).

Some of the postulates reinforcing the ethos of secrecy and the theme of police solidarity include:

- *"Don't give up another cop."* As perhaps one of the most important factors contributing to secrecy and to a sense of solidarity, this postulate admonishes officers to never, regardless of the seriousness or nature of a case, provide information to either superiors or nonpolice that would cause harm to a fellow police officer. Reuss-Ianni notes that this postulate implicitly informs a police officer that abiding by this canon and never giving up another cop means others "won't give you up."

- *"Watch out for your partner first and then the rest of the guys working that tour."* This postulate tells police officers they have an obligation to their partners first, and then to other officers working the same shift. "Watching out," in this context, means that an officer has a duty not only to protect a fellow officer from physical harm, but also to watch out for their interests in other matters. If, for example, an officer learns that another member of his or her squad is under investigation by an internal affairs unit, the officer is obligated to inform the officer of this information. As with the postulate listed above, the implicit assumption here is that if you watch out for fellow police, they will also watch out for you.

- *"If you get caught off base, don't implicate anybody else."* Being caught off base can involve a number of activities, ranging from being out of one's assigned sector to engaging in prohibited activities. This postulate teaches officers that if they are discovered in proscribed activities, they should accept the punishment, not implicate others. This postulate insulates other police officers from punishment and reduces the possibility that organized deviance or corruption will be uncovered.

- *"Make sure the other guys know if another cop is dangerous or 'crazy.'"* Police are caught in a double-bind if they become aware that one of their fellow members is unstable or presents a safety hazard. The secrecy dictum prohibits a line officer from informing police supervisors of another officer's instability; at the same time, an officer has an obligation to watch out for his or her peers. In order to deal with such a contradiction, this rule of behavior tells an officer that there is an obligation to let other police know of potential safety risks but not to take formal action against another officer. This postulate allows "problem" officers to continue to operate within the profession and reduces the chances that they will be detected by the agency administration or the public. It does, however, allow informal sanctions of exclusion to be imposed.

- *"Don't get involved in anything in another cop's sector."* Reuss-Ianni notes that in older, corrupt departments, this dictum advised officers not to try to hedge in on another police officer's illegal activities. In essence, this rule informed police that officers "owned" certain forms of corruption in their sector. This rule of territoriality is believed necessary because officers are responsible for activities in their respective beats. This postulate serves to limit the spread of information making it easier for officers to deny knowledge of deviance, which in turn makes deviance appear to be a mere aberration.

- *"Hold up your end of the work; don't leave work for the next tour."* These postulates teach officers that if they neglect their work responsibilities, two results are likely to occur. First, other officers must cover for those who shirk their responsibilities. Second, malingerers call attention to everyone on a shift. Thus, there are pressures for all officers to carry their own weight to avoid being detected for deviance. If, however, an officer fails to follow this edict, other officers are expected to "cover" for the officer and to deflect attention away from the group.

- *"Don't look for favors just for yourself."* This dictum admonishes officers not to "suck up" to superiors. In essence, this rule tells officers that their primary responsibilities are to their peers and that attempts to curry favors with superiors will meet severe disapproval. This postulate prevents line officers from developing relationships with superiors that might threaten the safety of the work group.

Postulates Supporting Police Isolationism.   Reuss-Ianni (1983, pp. 14–16) identified several postulates that teach new officers that nonpolice simply do not understand the true nature of police work. These statements reinforce the notion that there are vast differences between police and citizens—who will never be able to understand the unique problems inherent in policing. In John Van Maanen's typology of how the police characterize outsider views of their occupation, these citizens are classified as "know nothings" (Van Maanen, 2006, p. 306). This we/they worldview increases police isolation from citizens.

- *"Protect your ass."* As perhaps one of the most important postulates leading to a sense of isolation, this rule teaches police to be wary of everyone including citizens and superiors. At the simplest level, the rule informs police that anyone who wants to cause trouble for an officer probably can; it teaches police that others cannot be trusted. Officers must be vigilant and take all steps necessary to protect themselves from any possible threat. While threats include the possibility of physical harm, they also include the possibility of disciplinary action by superiors and the potential for citizens to complicate the lives of police by filing complaints, making allegations, or uncovering deviance.

- *"Don't trust a new guy until you have him checked out."* Rookie police and officers who are new to a work group are not accorded status automatically. Instead, outsiders are treated cautiously until information about them can be obtained—until they have "proven" themselves. In some cases, rookie officers are "tested" to determine if they can be trusted—intentionally placed in situations to observe behavior and determine if they can be trusted.

- *"Don't talk too little or too much; don't tell anybody more than they have to know."* The themes of "don't talk too much," and "don't reveal more than necessary" inform new police officers that others including citizens and supervisors are not to be trusted. These dictates reinforce the notion that "loose lips sink ships" and that there is no need to provide others with information beyond the minimum required. Information can be distorted or used in other ways that are potentially harmful. At the same time, the dictate "don't talk too little" lets new police officers know that excessive silence or introversion will be seen as suspicious behavior by other officers. As Reuss-Ianni notes, the extremes of talking too much or too little are both viewed as suspicious behaviors by fellow officers. This postulate directs officers to maintain communications with the work group but to limit their exposure to administrators and citizens.

- *"Don't trust bosses to look out for your interests."* This maxim informs new police officers that when forced to make a choice, managers and administrators will look out for their own best interests rather than those of the officer. Whether true or not, this idea has the effect of further distancing officers from their superiors. Since line officers are taught that they cannot depend on either citizens or superiors, they are forced to align themselves with the only group left for protection—fellow police.

Postulates Indicative of the Ethos of Bravery. David H. Bayley and Egon Bittner (2001) have noted that a crucial part of a police officer's job is to take charge of situations and people. Taking charge, in this sense, involves developing a "presence" to handle incidents. In essence, this means that officers must be poised to take control regardless of the situation. Yet, it is crucial not to appear too ready, since overeagerness can escalate situations. In one officer's words, "Always act . . . as if you were on vacation." At the same time, however, "One must be keyed up but not 'choke'" (p. 28). Reuss-Ianni (1983, p. 16) identified two postulates that strongly suggest new officers must always, above all else, show bravery in the performance of police work.

- *"Show balls."* The police characterize their work as dangerous and fraught with hazards. This postulate counsels police that they are never to back down from a situation; backing down signals weakness. All police are harmed by the cowardice of an individual officer. Officers must have fortitude to control situations. When the authority of a single officer is challenged, the authority of the entire police group is challenged and must be addressed. While this is especially true for incidents that occur in view of the public, it is also important for an officer never to back down from a situation where other officers are present.

- *"Be aggressive when you have to, but don't be too eager."* This postulate reflects the idea that while officers should always be alert, they should not go out of their way to seek trouble. This is partly because overeagerness, or having a "chip" on one's shoulder, will only bring unneeded complications. In a sense, the maxim, "If you look for trouble, it will find you," applies here. Therefore, challenges to authority must be met and dealt with, but they should not be sought out. Police are to avoid acting in ways that cause the group to undergo unnecessary scrutiny. However, this postulate also reminds an officer to meet a challenge or confrontation as aggressively as necessary to handle it effectively.

Through exposure to these and other postulates, new generations of police officers learn to view the world from a particular perspective. These "truths," shape the officers' belief system, which dictates acceptable and unacceptable behavior. The postulates are part of the socialization process for members of the police occupation and reinforce the police worldview. Officers are taught the necessity for secrecy and solidarity among the ranks, and the belief that police are different and isolated from larger society. Violations of these canons may lead to immediate sanctions from fellow subculture members, frequently resulting in expulsion from the security of the group. It is ironic that police who violate the precepts of the subculture are doubly isolated—first from the community by nature of the occupation and later by the police subculture for violation of its informal norms of conduct. Police officers who do not conform to the postulates of the work group become outcasts who have been stripped of the benefits of group membership.

Earlier we mentioned protests in Ferguson, Missouri, over the death of Michael Brown. Other deaths of citizens during encounters with police in 2014 fueled public outcry over police deadly force and subsequent investigations into whether the actions were justified. A white rookie officer in Cleveland shot and killed a black 12-year-old who was waving a pellet gun. A white officer in Phoenix shot and killed an unarmed black man who the officer believed was reaching for a gun—it turned out to be a bottle of pills (Editorial, 2014). A rookie Asian officer participating in a violence-reduction detail at a public housing unit in Brooklyn where serious crimes had been reported shot and killed an unarmed African American resident, Akai Gurley, in a darkened stairwell (Clifford, 2014). Local business owners complained to the police that Eric Garner was selling "loosies" (single cigarettes) near the Staten Island Ferry Terminal on July 17, 2014. The police approached Garner, who accused the officers of hassling him and refused to cooperate. Bystanders recorded the encounter on their cell phones, including an officer wrapping his arm around Garner's throat and pulling him to the ground. Other officers participated in holding him down. The videos recording Garner saying "I can't breathe" were posted to the Internet and viewed millions of times. The medical examiner said Garner died from chest compression and from a choke hold applied by Officer Daniel Pantaleo. Nine days after the grand jury in

Ferguson did not charge Officer Darren Wilson with a crime, the grand jury in New York did not bring criminal charges against Pantaleo.

Protests against police brutality after the incidents listed above had fueled a countermovement from officers and their supporters. Officers saw the criticism as hostile and "anti-police" and were particularly critical of officials perceived as sympathizing with protesters. Resentment from officers in New York boiled over after the mayor, William de Blasio whose son is African American, remarked "Is my child safe, and not just from some of the painful realities of crime and violence in some of our neighborhoods but safe from the very people they want to have faith in as their protectors?" (Bouie, 2014).

On December 20, 2014, Ismaaiyl Brinsley shot his former girlfriend in Baltimore. Hours later, he ambushed and killed two police officers in their car in Brooklyn, New York, and then killed himself. He had posted anti-police messages on Instagram the day of the shooting. At the funeral for one of the officers, Mayor de Blasio called the killings a despicable act and an attack on everyone that "tears at the very foundation of our society" (Bouie, 2014). Some of the officers at the funeral turned their backs when the mayor was speaking. Reuss-Ianni identified hostilities that exist between street officers and management. The solidarity of members of the police subculture is acted out in the powerful traditions of police funerals (Crank, 2004). The tragedy of losing a colleague has far-reaching effects on the tightly knit culture, expressed in the collective grieving ritual that embodies powerful symbols of the image of the police, their occupation, and their role in society. The funeral projects the strength of the police in their role as social control agents—a "sea of blue" symbolizing the solidarity of members united in their battle against those who break the law.

Summary

Many approaches have been used to explain the unique character of the police. Scholars who endorse the psychological paradigm suggest that police character may be explained by one of two approaches. Personality theorists suggest that people with certain personality types—such as those who are authoritarian—are attracted to police work. Seen in this light, police character is a reflection of the unique personality characteristics of those who enter and remain in police work. An alternative social-psychological explanation for police character posits that the police working environment shapes the personality, character, and behavior of individual officers. Those who adopt this perspective believe that experiences such as recruit training and relationships with coworkers shape personality and, therefore, the behavior of individual officers.

The sociological paradigm rejects the idea that personality characteristics alone predetermine police character. Instead, this paradigm suggests that police character is molded and shaped by occupational experiences; police character is determined by the police working environment. Socialization experiences—including academy and on-the-job training—are responsible for the development of police values and ethics.

The anthropological paradigm offers perhaps the most complete explanation for the development of police character. The occupational culture provides police with a unique working personality. This working personality includes the development of a worldview that teaches police to distinguish between insiders and outsiders (i.e., police/nonpolice)—those who are okay versus those who must be watched.

The we/they perspective instills in officers a perpetual concern for the element of danger in their work. The police working personality reinforces the notion of "differentness" in three ways. First, police are taught that they are vested with the unique power to use force and violence in carrying out legal mandates. Second, the paramilitary nature of police work isolates police from others in society. Finally, police are indoctrinated with the idea that they are the "thin blue line" between anarchy and order.

Three guiding beliefs define the police ethos. The social character of policing is shaped by a reverence for bravery, autonomy, and secrecy. The police subculture stresses these sentiments and teaches new officers the value of adopting these attitudes—and the consequences of not conforming.

Cultural themes are also a part of the police culturalization process. Cultural themes are fairly specific rules of behavior that shape police interactions. A dominant cultural theme in policing is the idea that police are socially isolated from the rest of society. A second important cultural theme extols the need for police solidarity. Postulates are specific statements that guide and direct the actions of subcultural members. Postulates that reinforce the need for police secrecy and solidarity include instructions never to "give up" another cop and to watch out for other police, especially one's partner. Postulates that support police isolationism instruct police to "protect your ass" by being wary of everyone; not to trust new officers until they have proven themselves; and not to trust supervisors to look out for an officer's best interests. Postulates also instruct officers on the ethos of bravery: never back down and be aggressive but not overeager in handling situations.

REFERENCES

Adlam, K. R. (1982). The police personality: Psychological consequences of becoming a police officer. *The Journal of Police Science and Administration, 10*(3), 347–348.

Adorno, T. W. (1950). *The authoritarian personality.* New York: Harper.

Alpert, G. P. (1993). The role of psychological testing in law enforcement. In R. G. Dunham & G. P. Alpert (Eds.), *Critical issues in policing: Contemporary readings* (2nd ed., pp. 96–105). Long Grove, IL: Waveland Press.

Alpert, G. P., Dunham, R. G., & Stroshine, M. S. (2015). *Policing: Continuity and change* (2nd ed.). Long Grove, IL: Waveland Press.

Angell, J. E. (1977). Toward an alternative to the classical police organizational arrangements: A democratic model. In L. K. Gaines & T. A. Ricks (Eds.), *Managing the police organization.* St. Paul, MN: West.

Argyris, C. (1957, June). The individual and organization: Some problems of mutual adjustment. *Administrative Science Quarterly*, 1–24.

Badger, E., Keating, D., & Elliott, K. (2014, August 14). "Where minority communities still have overwhelmingly white police." *Washington Post*. Retrieved from http://www.washingtonpost.com/blogs/wonkblog/wp/2014/08/14/where-minority-communities-still-have-overwhelmingly-white-police/

Bahn, C. (1984). Police socialization in the eighties: Strains in the forging of an occupational identity. *Journal of Police Science and Administration, 12*(4), 390–394.

Baldwin, J. (1962). *Nobody knows my name*. New York: Dell.

Balko, R. "Five myths about policing" *Chicago Tribune*, December 9, 2014, p. 21.

Balko, R. *Rise of the warrior cop: The militarization of America's police forces*. New York: Perseus Book Group, 2013.

Banton, M. (1964). *The policeman in the community*. New York: Basic Books.

Bayley, D. H. (1976). *Forces of order: Police behavior in Japan and the United States*. Berkeley: University of California Press.

Bayley, D. H., & Bittner, E. (2001). Learning the skills of policing. In R. G. Dunham & G. P. Alpert (Eds.), *Critical issues in policing: Contemporary readings* (4th ed., pp. 114–138). Long Grove, IL: Waveland Press.

Bayley, D. H., & Mendelsohn, G, (1969). *Minorities and the police: Confrontation in America*. New York: The Free Press.

Benedict, R. (1934). *Patterns of culture*. Boston: Houghton Mifflin.

Bennett, R. R. (1984). Becoming blue: A longitudinal study of police recruit occupational socialization. *Journal of Police Science and Administration, 12*(1), 47–57.

Bittner, E. (2006a) The capacity to use force as the core of the police role. In V. E. Kappeler (Ed.), *The police & society: Touchstone readings* (3rd ed., pp. 123–133). Long Grove, IL: Waveland Press.

Bittner, E. (2006b). The quasi-military organization of the police. In V. E. Kappeler (Ed.), *The police & society: Touchstone readings* (3rd ed., pp. 190–200). Long Grove, IL: Waveland Press.

Black, D. (1970). Production of crime rates. *American Sociological Review, 35*, 733–748.

Black, D. (1976). *The behavior of law*. New York: Academic Press.

Bouie, J. (2014, December 23). "No, There Isn't a Broad Campaign against Police." *Chicago Tribune*, p. 15.

Bordua, D. J. & Reiss, A. J., Jr. (1967). Law enforcement. In P. Lazarsfeld, W. Sewell, & H. Wilensky (Eds.), *The uses of sociology*. New York: Basic Books.

Broderick, J. J. (1987). *Police in a time of change* (2nd ed.). Long Grove, IL: Waveland Press.

Brown, M. K. (1981). *Working the street: Police discretion and the dilemmas of reform*. New York: Russell Sage.

Burbeck, E., & Furnham, A. (1985). Police officer selection: A critical review of the literature. *Journal of Police Science and Administration, 13*(1), 58–69.

Cain, M. E. (1973). *Society and the policeman's role*. London, England: Routledge and Kegan Paul.

Carpenter, B. N., & Raza, S. M. (1987). Personality characteristics of police applicants: Comparisons across subgroups and with other populations. *Journal of Police Science and Administration 15*(1), 10–17.

Chambliss, W. J., & Seidman, R. B. (1971). *Law, order and power*. Reading, MA: Addison-Wesley.

Clark, J. P. (1965). Isolation of the police: A comparison of the British and American situations. *Journal of Criminal Law, Criminology and Police Science, 56*, 307–319.

Clifford, S. (2014, December 5). Brooklyn grand jury to examine Akai Gurley shooting death. *New York Times.*

Cohen, H. S., & Feldberg, M. (1991). *Power and restraint: The moral dimension of police work.* New York: Praeger.

Cox, T. C., Crabtree, A., Joslin, D., & Millet, A. (1987). A theoretical examination of police entry-level uncorrected visual standards. *American Journal of Criminal Justice, 11*(2), 199–208.

Crank, J. P. (2004). *Understanding police culture.* New York: Routledge.

Cullen, F. T., Link, B. G., Travis, L. F., & Lemming, T. (1983). Paradox in policing: A note on perceptions of danger. *Journal of Police Science and Administration, 11*(4), 457 462.

Delattre, E. J. (1989). *Character and cops: Ethics in policing.* Washington, DC: American Enterprise Institute for Public Policy Research.

Editorial (2014, December 5). "Black and Blue." *Chicago Tribune,* p. 22.

Feldman, L. (2014, August 16). "Ferguson: How Pentagon's 1033 program helped militarize small-town police." *Christian Science Monitor.*

Ferdinand, T. H. (1980). Police attitudes and police organization: Some interdepartmental and cross-cultural comparisons. *Police Studies, 3,* 46–60.

Fyfe, J. J. (2015). The split-second syndrome and other determinates of police violence. In R. G. Dunham & G. P. Alpert (Eds.), *Critical issues in policing: Contemporary readings* (7th ed., pp. 517–531). Long Grove, IL: Waveland Press.

Gaines, L. K., & Kappeler, V. E. (2015). *Policing in America* (8th ed.). Waltham, MA: Elsevier.

Hagedorn, J., Kmiecik, B., Simpson, D., Gradel, T. J., Mouritsen Zmuda, M., & Sterrett, D. (2013, January 17). Crime, corruption and cover-ups in the Chicago Police Department: Anti-corruption report #7. Retrieved from http://www.uic.edu/depts/pols/ChicagoPolitics/policecorruption.pdf

Hannewicz, W. B. (1978). Police personality: A Jungian perspective. *Crime and Delinquency, 24*(2), 152–172.

Harris, R. (1973). *The police academy: An insider's view.* New York: John Wiley.

Holden, R. (1984). Vision standards for law enforcement: A descriptive study. *Journal of Police Science and Administration, 12*(2), 125–129.

Hunt, J. (2006). Police accounts of normal force. In V. E. Kappeler (Ed.), *The police & society: Touchstone readings* (3rd ed., pp. 339–357). Long Grove, IL: Waveland Press.

Ingraham, C. (2014, August 14). "The Pentagon gave nearly half a billion dollars of military gear to local law enforcement last year." *Washington Post.* Retrieved from http://www.washingtonpost.com/blogs/wonkblog/wp/2014/08/14/the-pentagon-gave-nearly-half-a-billion-dollars-of-military-gear-to-local-law-enforcement-last-year/

Jonsson, P. (2014, August 12). "Mike Brown death, Ferguson riots raise questions about police immunity." *Christian Science Monitor.*

Kappeler, V. E. & Gaines, L. K. (2011). *Community policing: A contemporary perspective* (6th ed.). New York: Routledge.

Kappeler, V. E., & Potter, G. W. (2005). *The mythology of crime and criminal justice* (4th ed.). Long Grove, IL: Waveland Press.

Kraska, P. B. & Paulsen, D. J. (1997). Grounded research into U.S. paramilitary policing: Forging the iron fist inside the velvet glove. *Police and Society, 7,* 253–270.

Kuykendall, J., & Burns, D. (1980). The black police officer: An historical perspective. *Journal of Contemporary Criminal Justice, 1*(4), 103–113.

Maher, P. T. (1988). Police physical agility tests: Can they ever be valid? *Public Personnel Management Journal, 17*, 173–183.

Manning, P. K. (2006). The police: Mandate, strategies and appearances. In V. E. Kappeler (Ed.), *The police & society: Touchstone readings* (3rd ed., pp. 94–122). Long Grove, IL: Waveland Press.

Manning, P. K. (1997). *Police work: The social organization of policing* (2nd ed.). Long Grove, IL: Waveland Press.

Marquart, J. (1986). Doing research in prison: The strengths and weaknesses of full participation as a guard. *Justice Quarterly, 3*(1), 20–32.

Matza, D. (1969). *Becoming deviant.* Englewood Cliffs, NJ: Prentice-Hall.

Mollen Commission. 1994. *The City of New York Commission to Investigate Allegations of Police Corruption and the Anti-Corruption Procedures of the Police Department: Commission Report.* New York: City of New York.

Niederhoffer, A. (1967). *Behind the shield: The police in urban society.* Garden City, NY: Anchor Books.

Opler, M. E. (1945). Themes as dynamic forces in culture. *The American Journal of Sociology, 51,* 198–206.

Paoline, E. A. & Terrill, W. (2014). *Police culture: Adapting to the strains of the job.* Durham, NC: Carolina Academic Press.

Paynes, J., & Bernardin, H. J. (1992). Entry-level police selection: The assessment center is an alternative. *Journal of Criminal Justice, 20*, 41–52.

Piliavin, I., & Briar, S. (1964). Police encounters with juveniles. *American Journal of Sociology, 70*, 206–214.

Pogrebin, M. R., & Poole, E. D. (1991). Police and tragic events: The management of emotions. *Journal of Criminal Justice, 19*, 395–403.

Putti, J., Aryee, S., & Kang, T. S. (1988). Personal values of recruits and officers in a law enforcement agency: An exploratory study. *Journal of Police Science and Administration, 16*(4), 249–265.

Reaves, B. A. (2010). Local police departments, 2007. Washington, DC: Bureau of Justice Statistics, NCJ 231174.

Redfield, R. (1952). *The primitive worldview.* Proceedings of the American Philosophical Society, *96*, 30–36.

Redfield, R. (1953). *The primitive world and its transformations.* Ithaca, NY: Cornell University Press.

Reiss, A. J. (1971). *The police and the public.* New Haven: Yale University Press.

Reiss, A. J., & Bordua, D. J. (1967). Environment and organization: A perspective on the police. In D. J. Bordua (Ed.), *The police: Six sociological essays.* New York: John Wiley.

Reuss-Ianni, E. (1983). *Two cultures of policing.* New Brunswick, NJ: Transaction Books.

Reuss-Ianni, E., & Ianni, F. A. J. (1983). Street cops and management cops: The two cultures of policing. In M. Punch (Ed.), *Control in the police organization.* Cambridge: MIT Press.

Rokeach, M., Miller, M. G., & Snyder, J. S. (1971). The value gap between the police and the policed. *Journal of Social Issues, 27*(2), 155–177.

Rubinstein, J. (1973). *City police.* New York: Farrar, Straus and Giroux.

Savitz, L. (1971). The dimensions of police loyalty. In H. Hahn (Ed.), *Police in urban society.* Beverly Hills: Sage.

Skolnick, J. H. (1994). *Justice without trial: Law enforcement in a democratic society* (3rd ed.). New York: Macmillan.

Sparger, J. R., & Giacopassi, D. J. (1992). Memphis revisited: A reexamination of police shootings after the Garner decision. *Justice Quarterly, 9,* 211–225.

Stoddard, E. R. (2006). The informal code of police deviancy: A group approach to blue-collar crime. In V. E. Kappeler (Ed.), *The police & society: Touchstone readings* (3rd ed., pp. 201–222). Long Grove, IL: Waveland Press.

Swanton, B. (1981). Social isolation of police: Structural determinants and remedies. *Police Studies, 3,* 14–21.

Van Maanen, J. (2006). The asshole. In V. E. Kappeler (Ed.), *The police & society: Touchstone readings* (3rd ed., pp. 304–325). Long Grove, IL: Waveland Press.

Westley, W. A. (1956). Secrecy and the police. *Social Forces, 34*(3), 254–257.

Westley, W. A. (1970). *Violence and the police: A Sociological study of law, custom and morality.* Cambridge: MIT Press.

Westley, W. A. (2006). *Violence and the police.* In V. E. Kappeler (Ed.), *The police & society: Touchstone readings* (3rd ed., pp. 326–338). Long Grove, IL: Waveland Press.

Wofford, T. (2014, August 13). "How America's police became an army: The 1033 program. *Newsweek.* Retrieved from http://www.newsweek.com/how-americas-police-became-army-1033-program-264537

6

Solidarity and the Code of Silence

Geoffrey P. Alpert, Jeffrey J. Noble, & Jeff Rojek

David Émile Durkheim (1933) introduced social solidarity and collective conscience as related phenomena critical to understanding relationships among workers in like situations. Social solidarity refers to the set of shared beliefs, emotional links, work-related values, or bonds that are formed among members of a small group, organization, or a society. He emphasized the influence of the workplace and how it can produce or create a set of values shared by the employees. In fact, it is membership in an occupational or professional group that can provide a level of integration that creates a "collective conscience," the glue for social solidarity. Durkheim argued that these principles are necessary to understand rules of social conduct and explained that members protect their interests in a group because they identify with it and its values. They will also band together against a common enemy or threat. These broad sociological traditions can explain a wide range of behavior within a variety of complex social systems. The concept of unity and solidarity clearly varies among professions with different levels of responsibilities and consequences. Generally, they can explain the relationships within and among businesses, occupations or professions, and specifically they can explain the "code of silence" among the police.

The working environment of the police is characterized by a set of elements including danger, hostility, suspiciousness, unsympathetic media coverage, and relentless public scrutiny. These conditions have been used to explain why police officers tend to form a fiercely loyal and protective solidarity system that results in a code of silence (Chin & Wells, 1998; Crank, 2004; Dworkin & Baucus, 1998; Heck, 1992). Reciprocal silence is valued because police work can easily result in mistakes or regrettable behavior. Secrecy among officers can avoid consequences of oversight and managerial hindsight. Whistle-blowing by complaining about the actions of another offi-

Prepared especially for *Critical Issues in Policing* by Geoffrey P. Alpert, Jeffrey J. Noble, and Jeff Rojek.

cer or filing an internal complaint or grievance can threaten the solidarity that runs through the police organization.

The code of silence in any organization has multiple layers. First, there is a code not to "give up" fellow workers; second, there is a code not to give up management or the organization. Indeed, there are concerns that an agency that allows this silence is fostering or creating a custom, practice, and policy that encourages or allows silence. There are different reasons for each type of silence. Employees are concerned that speaking out about the failures or evils of fellow workers has a different meaning compared to complaining about the actions or inactions of management (Skolnick, 2002). While employees have a great deal at stake concerning internal complaints, an outsider who is injured by an employee may be more concerned about the policy and "deep pockets" of a city or municipality than the behavior or assets of an individual officer. The purpose of this article, therefore, is to explain that solidarity or the code of silence known to exist within policing is not unique—it is recognized in most if not all organizations. The "code" receives more attention in policing than in other professions not because the actors are more cynical, closed minded, or untrusting but because mistakes can result in serious injuries and fiscal damages, which are consequential and newsworthy. The media and the public have developed a great interest in police misbehavior, real or reported.

Social Unity or a Closed Shop?

The principles of solidarity suggest that many professionals band together and create a sense of unity by keeping like members secure and outsiders vulnerable and uninformed. Many professions have varying degrees of this organizational safeguard—a continuum of solidarity related to the degree of serious consequences for mistakes. For example, if a college professor errs, it is unlikely that someone will be injured or even harmed. At the other end of the continuum, mistakes made by engineers, builders, and architects can have serious consequences. (The work in these professions is subject to inspection and approval before being allowed to continue. While the peer-review process for professors serves as a type of "inspection" process, it is limited to documents and not other types of communication or products.)

Honest and dishonest citizens and criminal offenders often refuse to talk to others or the police about criminal conduct, for a variety of reasons and consequences (see Asbury, 2010–2011). Police officers, firefighters, emergency room physicians and other professionals who must make split-second decisions rely heavily on the likelihood that their fellow workers will not question their decisions or report them to management for decisions with which they disagree. While it is human nature to protect friendly and relied-upon fellow workers, there are actions or behavioral thresholds that when crossed will encourage fellow employees to report injurious behavior and turn to management for leadership and support.

Perhaps the most interesting code of silence exists in the medical profession—the most closed of any occupation. The 1982 movie, *The Verdict* provides a snapshot into the closed nature of this profession. One of the movie's important messages is the difficulty an injured patient has recovering monetarily from the actions of a negligent doctor. Specifically, it details the incredible problems involved with hiring a medical expert to testify against well-known and well-respected doctors. The takeaway message is that doctors weave a curtain of silence around their profession and protect—if not conceal—their mistakes. Kelner (1970–1971) provides a succinct description of the problem.

> Silence is golden—for the doctor not the patient. The sick, sore, lame or disabled patient wants to know his medical care is careful care, but his right to know conflicts with an unwritten code of the medical brotherhood—to see, hear and speak no evil against each other, whether they know each other or not.
>
> This is a mass "cop-out" of doctors in medical malpractice litigation—the silent treatment, even in the clearest cases of carelessness. Patients injured by negligent doctors must crack this "conspiracy of silence" before they can win malpractice damages. . . .
>
> Thus, to prove a doctor's careless departure from prevailing standards of care usually requires that another doctor testify against the defending doctor. It takes one to know one. But recruiting a doctor ready, able and willing to testify against the negligent doctor is like looking for the proverbial needle in the haystack. The doctor willing to testify is inviting social and professional ostracism in his county medical society—and worse.
>
> The curtain of silence is parted here and there by a few "renegade" doctors with enough courage to brave the taunts and penalties. (119, 122–123)

Similar to the medical profession, policing has historically been a closed shop, with a strong reluctance on the part of officers to criticize the decisions and actions of other officers and the organization. Our look into the policing profession will focus on understanding the code of silence and what to do about it. A good springboard is the information published from the Police Foundation survey on attitudes of police toward abuse of authority in the age of community policing (Weisburd et al., 2001). The study relied on an extensive and thorough questionnaire that asked officers to report their views on authority, use of force, and the code of silence. The authors concluded: "The responses suggest the possibility of a large gap between attitudes and behavior. That is, officers do not believe in protecting wrongdoers; nevertheless, they often do not turn them in" (p. 25). It may be that officers responded to the questions in ways they thought were socially acceptable, but even with that caveat, findings from the study point to potential concerns. First, it is not uncommon for officers to turn a blind eye to improper conduct by fellow officers (53%). Second, more than half of the officers (61%) do not think that police will always report serious criminal violations involving abuse of authority by fellow officers. Third, approximately one-fourth (25%) of the officers agreed that whistle-blowing is not worth it. Fifth, more than two-thirds (67%) reported that police officers who report incidents of misconduct are likely to be given a "cold shoulder" by fellow officers. Finally, more than 80 percent of police surveyed report that they do not accept the "code of silence" as an essential part of good policing. During the focus group discussions conducted for this study, the issue of the "code of silence" or "blue wall of silence" produced more controversy than any other topic. The discussion began with an officer making a harsh denial: "I've got to tell you: there is no code of silence." However, later in the discussion he admitted that a code of silence existed, but he called it "police subculture" (Greenspan et al., 2001: 25).

A major conclusion reported by Weisburd et al. (2001) is that officers may answer survey and focus group questions in the appropriate way but act differently. This distinction is a symptom of how little we know about the code of silence and whistle-blowing among the police or other professions. The research on this topic is difficult to conduct and does not provide us with answers to important questions about the nature, extent, or reality of the code of silence. The vast majority of the information known about the code of silence comes from survey research, which is frequently limited to time and place. A common finding that has been echoed by Wolfe and Piquero (2011) is that officers (in Philadelphia) are less likely to follow the code of silence when they perceive their agency's managerial practices as reasonable. Ivkovich and Sauerman (2013) report a different result from their sample of South African police. Perhaps the most consistent general result of the research on the code is the clear and convincing evidence that it exists within a variety of professions and specifically within the police. However, there is no evidence that it affects all officers in the same way or under all conditions. It is more likely that the impact of the code of silence on police officers waxes and wanes just as people drift in and out of other types of improper and criminal behavior depending on the severity, consequences, or circumstances of the behavior. In addition to external influences, internal controls and bonds clearly have an influence on the behavior of the police—and the willingness of officers not to hear things, not to report them, or to turn a blind eye. The frequent and increasing use of video recordings may also have a strong influence on how an officer responds and what she reports. The challenge is to determine in what agencies the code is influential, when it surfaces, and under what situations. A common response to this type of question, as seen above, is that the "culture" of an agency influences the behavior of officers. While this type of answer makes intuitive sense, there is no quality research that confirms the hypothesis or explains what it is about the police culture that impacts officers' silence (see Cockcroft, 2013 and Alpert et al., 2012).

While social science research lacks a strong foundation for the existence or impact of the code of silence, there is an interesting trend developing in the courts from plaintiffs suing officers and agencies for covering up abuses in a variety of ways. In *Nick Lynch v. Adam Barrett, et al.,* (2013) Nick Lynch claims officers Adam Barrett, Stephen Kenfield, and Michael Morelock all violated his constitutional right to access to the courts by refusing to disclose who used excessive force against him during an arrest. Lynch also claims the city of Denver violated his right to court access by adopting a custom, policy, and practice that precipitated the "conspiracy of silence" waged against him. While many of these factual issues will likely be resolved by a jury, other cases have been heard and resolved, including one involving the City of Chicago.

Karolina Obrycka v. City of Chicago

Karolina Obrycka was a bartender at Jesse's Shortstop Inn, a neighborhood bar in Chicago. Anthony Abbate was an off-duty Chicago police officer who was drinking at the bar. At about 3:00 P.M. on February 19, 2007, Abbate got into a fight at the bar and was told by the bartender at that time that she wouldn't serve him any more alcohol; he left. Around 8:00 P.M. that night, he returned to the bar and was served alcohol by Obrycka. As the night progressed, Abbate became more verbally and physically abusive and went behind the bar; Obrycka told him to get away and not come behind the bar. He replied no one tells him what to do, shouted "Chicago Police Department," flexed his biceps, and began kicking and punching Obrycka. After he left Jesse's, Obrycka called 911 and informed the operator that a person at the bar told her that her assailant was a Chicago Police Officer. Chicago police officers Peter Masheimer and Jerry Knickrehm responded to the call and spoke to Obrycka, who said she told them her assailant was a Chicago police officer named Tony and that the whole incident was caught on the bar's video cameras. Officers Masheimer and Knickrehm did not report that the perpetrator was a Chicago police officer and that the incident was taped by the bar's security cameras. In fact, they denied being provided any information that the assailant was a Chicago police officer.

Abbate had called other Chicago police officers, including his partner who, in-turn, called more officers and detectives. One of Abbate's friends (who worked for the city) approached Obrycka and said that Abbate would pay for her medical bills and time off if she did not file a complaint or sue Abbate, which constituted an attempted bribe. There was evidence that Abbate threatened Obrycka and stated that there would be problems for the bar and its employees if he were not provided the videotape. After a review of the tape, OPS officers contacted the Cook County's State's Attorney's Office for review. Having been told that an off-duty officer was involved in a bar fight and took several swings at an employee, the State's Attorney representative suggested a misdemeanor battery charge be filed against Abbate. Based on the minimal actions (and inactions) she perceived, Obrycka released the videotape to the media. It made its way to YouTube and went "viral." After the video was released, the State's Attorney filed felony charges for aggravated battery. After a bench trial, Abbate was found guilty of aggravated battery and was sentenced to two years of probation. Obrycka filed a civil suit and claimed that the "code of silence" that exists within the Chicago Police Department results in officers failing to report or investigate thoroughly each other's misconduct.

On November 13, 2012, a federal jury found the city liable, but the verdict was ambiguous in relation to the code of silence. However, many media reports included such a finding. For example, the day after the verdict, the *Los Angeles Times* reported: "In the end, federal jurors agreed with Obrycka's claims that the Chicago Police Department was operating under a code of silence, and decided that both the attack and the department's culture 'constituted an exercise of power without reasonable justification in a manner that shocks the conscience'" (Pearce, 2012). To complicate matters further, the city reversed its stated intention to appeal the verdict and award of $850,000. On December 3, 2012, it agreed to pay Obrycka the $850,000. The media reported that the reason for the change of strategy was based on an agreement that Obrycka request the court to erase the jury's finding that the police department had a code of silence and that the City of Chicago had a widespread practice of failing to investigate and discipline its officers adequately. The *Chicago Tribune* reported: "A federal jury's judgment that a 'code of silence' in the Chicago Police Department protects rogue officers will stand, the trial judge ruled Thursday, rejecting the Emanuel administration's attempt to erase the verdict from one of the department's most notorious scandals" (Heinzmann, 2012).

Whether there was such an agreement or not and whether the jurors believed the claims of a code of silence made by Obrycka (and supported by her expert witness) is not as important as the attention this case brought to the existence and practice of the code. The opinion in this case suggests that courts will be looking closely at how officers act when behavior of their fellow officers is questioned and sends a strong message to police administrators mandating action to understand, prevent, root out, and address the code of silence whether it exists among a few officers (bad apples) or is pervasive within the organization (rotten barrel).

State Trooper Donna Watts

The *Obrycka* case brought attention to the code of silence involving a few officers in a single department, but a case involving a Florida Highway Patrol officer suggests the code of silence is pervasive. In October 2011, Trooper Donna Watts saw a marked police vehicle that was being driven at 120 mph. Concerned that the cruiser was stolen, Watts turned on her siren and followed the vehicle. After seven minutes the driver, an off-duty City of Miami police officer in full uniform, finally stopped. Watts approached the vehicle with her gun drawn, only to be told by the officer that he was late for an off-duty job. The Miami officer asked for professional courtesy in an attempt to avoid arrest, but Watts arrested the off-duty officer for reckless driving. As a consequence of her professional actions, she was targeted by other officers who made her life miserable.

She filed lawsuits claiming that she was the victim of retaliation by other police officers throughout the state. She reported receiving prank phone calls, having pizzas delivered that she did not order, and seeing strange vehicles parked outside her home. Message boards and other social media that cater to police officers contained threats and lengthy tirades against Watts. Even other Florida Highway Patrol officers were the victims of retaliation. One trooper had his car covered in human excrement (DeFede, 2013). Another trooper was stopped by a Miami officer who asked, "How does it feel to be pulled over?" When the Miami officer discovered that the trooper's brother was an Internal Affairs sergeant with the Miami Police Department, he offered to buy the trooper dinner to avoid being reported. The trooper did not accept the offer, and the Miami officer was disciplined (Munzenrieder, 2011).

Watts alleged that officers were accessing her personal information through DMV records. The result of an investigation showed that at least 88 officers from 25 different agencies accessed her driver's license information more than 200 times. Many of those officers received some discipline after their misconduct was discovered, but it was usually in the form of a verbal warning or a written reprimand. One officer claimed he accessed the information as a matter of public safety because he was concerned for Watts' welfare (Anderson, 2014). It appears that none of the officers was terminated from their employment or criminally charged for violating the public trust of their position and unlawfully accessing a confidential database without just cause.

As part of her damage claims, Watts states that her career has essentially been taken from her and she is concerned for her safety. Even Watts' own supervisors believe that Watts will never be allowed to return to field duties because other officers would not respond if she were in a situation that required backup (Munzenrieder, 2012). Watts' lawsuit includes over 100 named police officers as well as more than two dozen police and sheriff's departments across the state. Eight of those agencies have already settled for over $66,000.

This case is perhaps the most egregious example of a code of silence that implicates the policing profession and culture as a whole, rather than incidents that are contained within a single agency. Not only were the actions of the involved officers unconscionable, but the failure of the agencies to affirmatively address the seriousness of the misconduct is indefensible.

The Blue Wall of Silence

While the behavior of officers in these cases is extremely disturbing, the lack of effort of the organizations to prevent and address the code of silence before it becomes systemic within the organization is an even greater concern. The *Obrycka* and *Watts* cases do, however, present the complicated struggle between officer and organizational interests. First, officers are concerned with their individual welfare, while organizations represented by management have broader, more political concerns. Officers must rely on their fellow officers for safety and social support while organizational managers shift the course and direction of the department based on their reading of the social, political, and economic climates (see Koepke, 2000). These competing and often conflicting goals present a challenge for the police chief, his or her command staff, and frontline officers. The demands on the officers and organizations also have an impact on the willingness of employees to respond formally to the mistakes and misdeeds of their peers. What we know about the police blue wall of silence comes from a limited literature comprised of scholarly contributions and commission reports as well as anecdotal and journalistic information. As noted above, the code of silence is not limited to the police, but it permeates high-risk professions and occupations where mistakes and abuses have the most serious consequences. Unfortunately, the academic and professional literature does not provide great insight into the nature and extent of mutual silence among workers. The literature on whistle-blowing is instructive and helps direct us to questions to ask about policing and its closed environment (Miceli & Near, 1992). What we know about the police code is quite limited and mostly based on self-reporting and anecdotes.

Jerome Skolnick (2002) provides an excellent review of the code of silence and the literature that convinces him that it is alive and thriving in police agencies throughout the world. He points to "loyalty," a form of solidarity among officers, as a key feature of police culture and the formation of the code of silence. He notes that this loyalty is not unique to the police but that the threat of danger and public scrutiny help form a mutually dependent working environment. The Christopher Commission (1991) identified the extreme power of the code, which "influences the behavior of many officers in a variety of ways, but it consists of one simple rule: an officer does not provide adverse information against a fellow officer" (p. 168). An example from Queensland, Australia, clarifies:

> The unwritten police code is an integral element of police culture and has been a critical factor in the deterioration of the police force. It has allowed two main types of misconduct to flourish. A practical effect of the code is to reduce, if not eliminate, concern at possible apprehension and punishment as a deterrent to police misconduct. (Fitzgerald, 1989: 202)

While loyalty is a positive reason for the existence of the code, the fear of retaliation is a negative reason. In any case, officers need to understand their responsibilities and the consequences of their silence.

> It should be clearly established that once misconduct is detected, those who ought to have known about it because of the nature of their work and their responsibilities will be dealt with for incompetence if involvement cannot not be proved. . . . There would have been much less likelihood of corruption in the Queensland Police Licensing Branch if those who were not involved had known that they faced dismissal and loss of benefits if they failed to take action against their corrupt colleagues. Similarly, it is likely that there would be a sharp reduction in police fabrication of evidence and other illegal practices if it were known that those involved would be prosecuted and their supervisors severely penalized. The efforts of those not involved in misconduct must be directed against those who engage in it. Police officers must not be permitted to sympathetically condone misconduct or even be neutral. (Fitzgerald, 1989: 180)

Bringing Down the Wall

The atmosphere and organization of work encourages solidarity among workers and a resultant code of silence. While codes range from weak to strong, it is impossible to eliminate totally the likelihood that officers will never be part of a code of silence. Fortunately, there are mechanisms that can be designed and enforced to educate, discourage, prevent, and send a clear message to officers that a code of silence will not be tolerated. Most importantly, while individual officers may engage in improper behavior, including the code of silence, organizations should not become a breeding ground for this behavior or allow misconduct of any type to fester. Organizational rules, mandatory reporting, ethics training, required acceptance of all complaints, proactive and reactive investigations, effective supervision, and the implementation of clear consequences are all tools to address the code of silence. Additionally, these procedures show that an agency does not have a custom, policy, or practice of allowing officers to protect others by failing to report misconduct.

Rules and Regulations

Organizational rules and regulations are the cornerstones for the prevention of misconduct and corruption. They define codes of conduct for an officer's behavior, separating the acceptable from the unacceptable. Policies are the foundational building blocks for the organization—statements of guiding principles that must be followed to achieve a specific organization objective or the overall organizational mission (Kappeler, Sluder, & Alpert 1998). Police departments develop policies, rules, and procedures to guide their employees' actions and to prevent employee misconduct by articulating the types of behaviors that are objectionable and to communicate that there are consequences for employees who fail to conform their behavior to departmental standards. All modern police organizations have policies, rules, and procedures that prohibit misconduct. Indeed, a lack of conduct policies is sufficient to signal inept leadership and a dysfunctional organization. But beyond the rules and regulations that all reasonable police agencies develop are specific policies that serve to address the code of silence. These policies include truthfulness, mandatory reporting, and retaliation.

Truthfulness. Police officers often tell lies in the performance of their duties (Noble & Alpert, 2008). Officers lie to suspects about witnesses and evidence; they engage in undercover activities; they even work to create a perception of community safety when they know that dangerous crime exists. Most of these deceitful actions by police officers are sanctioned, legal, and encouraged. Although police officers are allowed to be deceitful in certain circumstances, they are also required to be trustworthy and honest and to maintain the highest level of integrity. Police deception exists on a continuum, from deceitful conduct that is excusable (lies made in jest or socially acceptable lies) and justifiable (lies that may be defended based on the circumstances), to intentional, malicious, deceitful conduct that will take one of three forms:

- Deceptive action in a formal setting, such as testifying in court or during an investigation;
- Failure to bring forward information involving criminal action of other officers—the code of silence; and
- Creation of false evidence that tends to implicate another in a crime.

Intentional, malicious, deceptive misconduct in any of these three areas will permanently destroy an officer's credibility, and there is no alternative in the employment context other than termination or permanent removal from any possible activities that require a reliable, truthful officer. Any discoverable behavior involving intentional, malicious, and deceitful misconduct becomes evidence if an officer is called as a witness, effectively preventing the officer from performing a core job function of testifying in court.

Organizations that fail to take appropriate action by using euphemisms or mischaracterizations to minimize or shield an officer's untruthful conduct send a message to all of their employees that there are few, if any, meaningful consequences if an employee is untruthful. This allows employees to believe that the decision scales weigh in favor of being untruthful to protect another officer.

Mandatory Reporting. While mandatory reporting has been recommended for many years, the International Association of Chiefs' of Police issued a model policy in 2012 that requires all employees to report serious acts of misconduct. The failure to report will result in corrective or disciplinary action (IACP 2012). The IACP's model policy provides protection for the reporting officer from retaliation. The goal of mandatory reporting is to remove any level of discretion from the officers by creating an affirmative duty to report serious misconduct. Officers who fail to report will be disciplined, thus removing the stigma that was attached to voluntary reporting. Recognizing that the majority of officers are honest and creating disincentives for honest officers to remain quiet disrupts an environment where speaking out may have been implicitly or explicitly discouraged.

Retaliation. The fear of individuals that they may be ostracized from the group, treated differently, bullied, harassed, threatened, or that others may take actions that would impact the officer's safety forms the root of a code of silence. A mandatory reporting policy, combined with a retaliation policy that directly addresses any retaliation toward officers who report serious misconduct, is an effective tool to decrease the negative impacts of the code of silence. Retaliation policies not only protect individual officers who report misconduct of others but also create a disincentive for other officers who may be concerned about avoiding the social stigma of associating with those who report misconduct.

Ethics Training

Policies are the building blocks to prevent and address police solidarity, and training translates the department's written rules and regulations into practices that help officers apply the rules to real-world situations. Consistent, frequent, and ongoing ethics training is necessary to ensure that the organization's goal of ethical conduct is fulfilled. Comprehensive training on ethics and integrity involves critical-thinking, problem-solving, and decision-making strategies that should be fully integrated into both academy and post-academy instruction (Los Angeles Police Department, 2000). Simply stated, ethics training helps officers react and respond appropriately (Kappeler, Sluder & Alpert 1998).

Complaint Acceptance

There is wide agreement that all complaints of officer misconduct should be accepted, documented, and reviewed. Many agencies, however, still place impediments that discourage or prevent complaints of misconduct from being accepted or investigated. Requiring complainants to sign affidavits and to make complaints in person are barriers, as are refusing to accept complaints from juveniles, third persons, and attorneys or failing to address allegations made in lawsuits. In addition, supervisors frequently try to dissuade complainants from making a "formal complaint." They assure the complainant that a formal complaint is not necessary, saying they will address the concern directly with the officer. This behavior hides allegations of misconduct; the complaints are never documented, and they are seldom resolved appropriately.

Failure to accept complaints is a form of the code of silence—supervisors are preventing allegations of misconduct from being thoroughly investigated, reviewed, and tracked. Early warning signs that could suggest the need for intervention are missed, eliminating the opportunity to prevent more serious misconduct before it occurs.

Proactive and Reactive Investigations

The quality of administrative investigations should minimally be at a "reasonable" level, and organizations should strive to exceed basic standards. It is important to understand that no investigation is "perfect" and that there can always be "better" methods that may produce "better" results. To suggest a standard of "perfect" or even "best practices" for every investigation is unreasonable. Indeed, due process does not require that every conceivable step be taken, at whatever cost, to eliminate the possibility of an unjust result. To conclude otherwise would all but paralyze the organization tasked with completing an investigation. The only appropriate standard that may be applied is one of reasonableness based on the totality of the investigation while encouraging investigators and organizations to strive for continued improvement (Noble & Alpert, 2012).

The only method that may be used to determine the quality of an investigation is by reviewing each individual investigation. While it may be tempting to evaluate investigations through the use of statistics, the application of a sustained rate is not a valid indicator of overall integrity, efficiency, and quality of administrative investigations. There are no standards, protocols, or policies for complaint processes that are uniformly adhered to by police departments across the nation. The great disparity in the definition of terms, differences in investigative processes, variations in state and local laws, dissimilar collective bargaining agreements, and multiple organizational and political cultures makes achieving commonality unlikely. This lack of commonality of terms, processes, and reports makes it impossible to compare data from one agency to another without knowing the specifics of each individual agency. This lack of uniformity makes any estimate of a proper sustained rate for inter-department comparisons impossible.

Moreover, the meaning of a complaint rate is not entirely clear. A low force complaint rate could mean that police are performing well or that the complaint process is inaccessible; likewise, a high force complaint rate could mean that officers use force often or that the complaint process is more accessible (Hickman, 2006). Similarly, a low sustained rate may mean that the officers are performing their duties appropriately or that the investigative process is failing to identify misconduct.

Consequences

The Rampart Report found that a major cause in the lack of integrity in American police officers is mediocrity. Mediocrity stems from the failure to hold officers accountable and comes from a lack of commitment, laziness, excessive tolerance, and unduly inconsequential disciplinary actions (Los Angeles Police Department, 2000). Turning a blind eye to disciplining officers by failing to address observed misconduct, failing to accept complaints of misconduct, failing to reasonably investigate complaints, or failing to reasonably discipline officers for their misbehavior all send the message to officers that they may act with impunity as there are no penalties for their bad behavior—or if penalties are applied, they will be disproportionately slight compared to the officer's misconduct.

There must be clear, reasonable and meaningful consequences for those who breach the department's rules and community's expectations by engaging in a code of silence. Police officers who engage in misconduct must be held accountable for their actions (Kappeler, Sluder, & Alpert 1998). It is only through effective disciplinary actions that an employer sends an unequivocal message to the offending officer and others that serious misconduct will not be tolerated. Officers who protect other officers from allegations of criminal conduct or civil rights abuses by engaging in a code of silence should be separated from the organization; there is no other reasonable alternative. The separation of these employees sends a strong message to remaining employees of the consequences for shielding the misconduct of other officers.

While one avenue would be to seek evidence of significant disciplinary actions to support a conclusion that a department takes a firm stance on misconduct, minor disciplinary actions for administrative violations (e.g., tardiness, improper equipment, uniform appearance, etc.) are equally meaningful. One would expect that close relationships would exist between supervisors and the employees with whom they work daily. These types of relationships can tempt supervisors to turn a blind eye, especially to minor misconduct. Thus, a significant area of review would be to determine if supervisors and managers are able to overcome personal relationships with their subordinates and to take appropriate disciplinary measures for administrative rules violations. These types of disciplinary actions are the easiest for supervisors and managers to ignore if there were a pervasive code of silence because there is no public outcry and no formal complaint that can be tracked or questioned by other supervisors, managers, or outside assessors.

Supervision and Leadership

Strong supervision and leadership is critical to effective corruption controls. Supervisory failures are a major contributor to a climate of tolerance; they send a message that the department is not concerned about the integrity of their officers. The reasons for supervisors' blindness varies, but often supervisors find it difficult to transition from officer to supervisor, believe that management will not support them, and that their lives will be made miserable by both their subordinates and superiors alike. Ultimately, many supervisors find to "get along" they should "go along."

Organizational Intolerance

Law enforcement agencies are sometimes the subject of litigation where a code of silence is alleged to be the moving factor in a constitutional violation. For example, if an officer uses excessive force, the plaintiff may contend that the officer engaged in the constitutional violation based on a belief that there would be no negative consequences for his or her actions because the officer knew the bad acts would be concealed by the code of silence. These lawsuits are sometimes settled, and the settlement agreements almost always contain a confidentiality clause prohibiting the parties from engaging in future litigation or acknowledging liability. Lawsuits are settled for a wide variety of reasons that may, or may not, be evidence that the organization believed they were responsible for the plaintiff's damages. They may also be settled on a belief the plaintiff would prevail on a portion of his or her claim but not on claims that relate to the code of silence. The use of settlement agreements, and particularly confidentiality agreements, should not shield police administrators from their responsibility of addressing the code of silence when there is evidence that it may exist or from reassessing their systems to ensure that they have taken every reasonable measure to prevent, address, and resolve the code of silence within the organization. As with any litigation that requires the taxpayer to pay damages, elected officials approving the settlements should seek assurances that steps have been taken to prevent future similar actions and that the organization will not tolerate misconduct.

Conclusion

The phenomenon of social solidarity is not unique to policing; it exists in all organizations where relationships are formed and people interact to accomplish defined goals. However, the impact of social solidarity of the police is powerful because officer actions have dire consequences on the civil liberties and civil rights of individuals. There will always be unprincipled individuals or small social groups that may revert to silence to prevent the detection of their misconduct or the misconduct of a member of the group. While it is important to address these individuals and small groups, it is more important to ensure that such negative conduct does not become widespread or pervasive throughout the organization.

Entitlement and impunity are two overlapping characteristics that must be minimized or eliminated to thwart the code of silence. If officers develop a strong sense of entitlement, they are likely to view the code of silence as part of the job. For example, many officers habitually accept free or discounted meals and services; they believe that these "perks" are part of the job. If not offered or if taken away, officers can become frustrated or embittered (Ruiz & Bono, 2004; Coleman, 2004; Meyer, Steyn, & Gopal, 2013). This disappointment can impact officers' view of the job and can strengthen solidarity among officers while creating a division between the police and the public.

Once officers feel entitled, they can easily act with impunity. As an example, many officers do not expect to get a speeding ticket even if pulled over by officers from another agency. They expect the code of silence to protect them from their misconduct being identified (Kestin & Maines, 2012). Therefore, they drive with impunity believing there will be no consequences for their dangerous or illegal behavior. The belief that they will not be punished for indiscretions may affect other actions on and off the job.

All managers and administrators know that organizations best address employee concerns through well-developed and enforced systems. In policing, there are methods to address the code of silence and those systems are developed through policies and procedures; mandatory reporting policies; intolerance of untruthful employees and those who retaliated against truthful employees; ongoing effective ethics training; acceptance and documentation of all complaints of officer misconduct; proactive and reactive investigations; supervision and leadership; and perhaps most importantly consequences for those who fail to conform their behavior to organizational standards.

REFERENCES

Alpert, G., Rojek, J. & Porter, L. (2012). *Measuring the impact of organisational culture and climate on police officers' decisions and behaviour.* Centre of Excellence in Policing and Security: Brisbane, Australia.

Anderson, C. (2014, February). Florida trooper who stopped cop sues after harassment. Associated Press. Retrieved from http://bigstory.ap.org/article/fla-trooper-who-stopped-cop-sues-after-harassment.

Asbury, B. (2010–2011). Anti-snitching norms and community loyalty. *Oregon Law Review* 89: 1257–1500.

Chin, G. J., & Wells, S. C. (1998). The blue wall of silence and motive to lie: A new approach to police perjury. *University of Pittsburg Law Review* 59: 233–299.

Christopher, W. (1991). *Report of the independent commission of the Los Angeles Police Department*. Los Angeles: City of Los Angeles.

Cockcroft, T. 2013. *Police culture: Themes and concepts*. New York: Routledge.

Coleman, S. (2004). When police should say "no!" to gratuities. *Criminal Justice Ethics* 23: 33–44.

Crank, J. P. (2004). *Understanding police culture*. Cincinnati, OH: Anderson.

DeFede, J. (2013, November 26). FHP trooper Donna Watts' last stand. CBS Miami. Retrieved from http://miami.cbslocal.com/2013/11/26/fhp-trooper-donna-watts-last-stand/.

Durkheim, E. (1933) *The division of labor in society*. New York, The Free Press.

Dworkin, T. M., & Baucus, M. S. (1998). Internal vs. external whistleblowers: A comparison of whistle-blowing processes. *Journal of Business Ethics* 17: 1281–1298.

Fitzgerald, G. (1989). *Report of a commission of inquiry Pursuant to orders in council*. Government Printer: Queensland, Australia.

Greenspan, R., Weisburd, D., & Hamilton, E. E. (2001). Appendix C: Report on focus group of rank-and-file police officers October 20–21, 1997. In, David Weisburd, Rosann Greenspan, Edwin E. Hamilton, Kellie A. Bryant, and Hubert Williams (Eds.), *The abuse of police authority: A national study of police officers' attitudes*. Washington, DC: The Police Foundation.

Heck, W. P. (1992). Police who snitch: Deviant actors in a secret society. *Deviant Behavior: An Interdisciplinary Journal* 13: 253–270.

Heinzmann, D. (2012, December 21). "Code of silence" verdict stands in *Abbate* case: Judge denies city's request to erase jury's finding. *Chicago Tribune*. Retrieved from http://articles.chicagotribune.com/2012-12-21/news/ct-met-abbate-ruling-code-of-silence-20121221_1_code-of-silence-verdict-abbate-case-police-code.

Hickman, M. J. (2006, June). *Citizen complaints about police use of force*. Washington, DC: Bureau of Justice Statistics.

IACP. (2012) *Emerging use of force issues: Balancing public and officer safety*. Washington, DC: U.S. Department of Justice.

Ivkovich, S., & Sauerman, A. (2013). Curtailing the code of silence among the South African Police. *International Journal of Police Strategies and Management* 36: 175–198.

Kappeler, V. E., Sluder, D. & Alpert, G. E. (1998). *Forces of deviance: Understanding the dark side of policing*. Long Grove, IL: Waveland Press.

Kelner, J. (1970–1971). Silent doctors—The conspiracy of silence. *University of Richmond Law Review* 5: 119–127.

Kestin, S., & Maines, J. (2012, February 11). Cops among Florida's worst speeders, Sun Sentinel investigation finds. *Ft. Lauderdale Sun Sentinel*. Retrieved from http://www.sun-sentinel.com/news/local/speeding-cops/fl-speeding-cops-20120211,0,3706919.story.

Koepke, J. (2000). The failure to breach the blue wall of silence: The circling of the wagons to protect police perjury. *Washburn Law Journal* 39: 211–242.

Los Angeles Police Department. (2000). *The board of inquiry into the Rampart area corruption incident: Public report.* Los Angeles: Author.

Meyer, M., Steyn, J., & Gopal, N. (2013). Exploring the public parameter of police integrity. *Policing: An International Journal of Police Strategies & Management* 36: 140–156.

Miceli, M. P., & Near, J. P. (1992). *Blowing the whistle: The organizational and legal implications for companies and employees.* New York: Lexington Books.

Munzenrieder, K. (2011, November 18). FHP trooper pulled over by Miami cop in revenge is brother of MPD Internal Affairs officer. *Miami NewTimes.* Retrieved from http://blogs.miaminewtimes.com/riptide/2011/11/fhp_trooper_pulled_over_by_mia.php.

Munzenrieder, K. (2012, December 26). FHP trooper who pulled over Miami cop Fausto Lopez claims she was harassed and forced to live like a hermit. *Miami New Times.* Retrieved from http://blogs.miaminewtimes.com/riptide/2012/12/fhp_trooper_who_pulled_over_mi.php.

Nick Lynch, v Adam Barrett; Sgt. Stephen Kenfield; Michael Morelock; City and County of Denver, United States Court of Appeals Tenth Circuit. No. 12-1222. January 4, 2013.

Noble, J., & Alpert, G. (2012). Evaluating the quality of law enforcement investigations: Standards for differentiating the excellent, good and reasonable from the unacceptable. *Journal of California Law Enforcement, 46*: 18–25.

Obrycka v. City of Chicago, Case No. 07 C 2372. December 20, 2012.

Pearce, M. (2012, November 14). Jury rules Chicago police "code of silence" protected felon cop. *Los Angeles Times.* Retrieved from http://articles.latimes.com/2012/nov/14/nation/la-na-nn-chicago-police-code-silence-20121114.

Ruiz, J., & Bono, C. (2004). At what price a "freebie"? The real cost of police gratuities. *Criminal Justice Ethics* 23: 44–54.

Skolnick, J. (2002). Corruption and the blue code of silence. *Police Practice and Research* 3: 7–19.

Weisburd, D., Greenspan, R., Hamilton, E. D., Bryant, K. A., & Williams, H. (2001). *The abuse of police authority: A national study of police officers' attitudes.* Washington, DC: The Police Foundation.

Wolfe, S., & Piquero, A. (2011). Organizational justice and police misconduct. *Criminal Justice and Behavior* 38: 332–353.

7

Police Discretionary Behavior
A Study of Style

Laure Weber Brooks

Introduction

The exercise of discretion by police has been the focus of an enormous amount of research. The issues of how police spend uncommitted time, how quickly they respond to calls for assistance, and what police do when handling a call for service have all received attention. While all police officers exercise some discretion, not all exercise the same levels of discretion. There are many factors that affect the degree of leeway an officer has in determining outcomes. Officers may develop response styles, and these styles may affect not only police perceptions, but they may also predispose the officer to act in certain ways. Additionally, levels of discretion are contingent on the flexibility police departments allow their officers, by policy, in handling day-today calls for service. When organizational rules are strict, less discretion is afforded to police. Conversely, when rules are vague or lax, officers are allowed, or perhaps forced, to make their own decisions on how to conduct themselves.

Much research attention has been paid to the examination of what factors affect police discretionary behavior. To explain this behavior, research has focused primarily on the characteristics of the situation in which police act (Engel, Sobol, and Worden, 2000; Terrill and Mastrofski, 2002; Engel, 2003; Novak, Frank, Smith, and Engel, 2002; Brandl and Stroshine, 2012; Kochel, Wilson, and Mastrofski, 2011; Mastrofski, Reisig, and McCluskey, 2002; Mastrofski, Snipes, Parks, and Maxwell, 2000; Terrill and Reisig, 2003; Riksheim and Chermak, 1993; Klinger, 1994; Lundman, 1994; Klinger, 1996; Worden and Shepard, 1996; Worden, 1989; Friedrich, 1977; Smith and Visher, 1981; Ericson, 1982; Black, 1980; Sun, Payne, and Wu, 2008; Schafer, Carter, Katz-Bannister, and Wells, 2006; Sun and Payne, 2004; Alpert, Mac-

Prepared especially for *Critical Issues in Policing* by Laure Weber Brooks.

Donald, and Dunham, 2005; Dunham, Alpert, Stroshine, and Bennett, 2005; Terrill and Paoline, 2007; Schuck, Rosenbaum, and Hawkins, 2008; National Research Council, 2004). Other discretionary factors that have received scholarly attention include: characteristics of the police organization (Mastrofski, Ritti, and Hoffmaster, 1987; Crank, 1993; Riksheim and Chermak, 1993; Wilson, 1968; Smith, 1984; Brown, 1981; Mastrofski, 1981; Sherman, 1983), characteristics of the environment or neighborhood in which the police work (Crank, 1993; Terrill and Reisig, 2003; Klinger, 1997; Riksheim and Chermak, 1993; Rossi, Berk, and Eidson, 1974; Smith, 1986; Nardulli and Stonecash, 1981; Ostrom, Parks, and Whitaker, 1977; Brown, 1981; Mastrofski, 1981; Smith and Klein, 1983; Sun and Payne, 2004; National Research Council, 2004; Schuck, Rosenbaum, and Hawkins, 2008; Dunham, Alpert, Stroshine, and Bennett, 2005; Alpert, MacDonald, and Dunham, 2005; Terrill and Paoline, 2007; Sun, Payne, and Wu, 2007), and characteristics of the officer involved in the encounter (Crank, 1993; Brooks, Piquero, and Cronin, 1993; Dejong, 2003; Johnson, 2013; Paoline and Terrill, 2007; Terrill and Mastrofski, 2002; Riksheim and Chermak, 1993; Friedrich, 1977; Bloch and Anderson, 1974; Worden, 1989; Brown, 1981; Brooks, 1986; Mastrofski, 2004; Sun, Payne and Wu, 2007; Alpert, MacDonald, and Dunham, 2005; Dunham, Alpert, Stroshine, and Bennett, 2005; Sun and Payne, 2004; National Research Council, 2004; McCluskey and Terrill, 2005). Taken together, the research concerning these four dimensions (situational, organizational, environmental, and officer) provide us with information on the determinants of police behavior.

With the advent of community policing, which has as a basic tenet the recognition that law enforcement behavior is not always the best way to handle social problems, scholars have speculated about how police discretion may be influenced by this movement. Mastrofski, Worden, and Snipes (1995) studied the determinants of police discretion in a police department that had implemented community policing. They explored the possibility that, due to the focus on community preferences and less on legal requirements that community policing encourages, officers might tend to rely less on legal variables (strength of evidence, seriousness of offense, the preference of the victim, etc.) and more on extralegal variables (suspect and victim characteristics). They found, though, that legal variables actually showed a much stronger effect on the arrest decision than did the extralegal ones; however, this depended on the officer's attitude about community policing. Officers who were supportive of community policing were more selective in making arrests and tended to rely less on legal variables than were officers who were not supportive of community policing. Overall, the more positive the officers were toward community policing, the less likely they were to effect an arrest. These researchers concluded that pro-community policing officers arrest more selectively and rely less on legal variables but show no greater reliance on extralegal variables to guide their arrest decision than officers who are not pro-community policing.

Schuck and Rosenbaum (2006) argue there is evidence that community policing can have a positive impact on neighborhoods in that it appears to reduce fear of crime, as well as results in an increased positive attitude toward police and in better police–community relations; they contend, however, there is less evidence that community policing actually results in less crime or changes what police do. Novak, Frank, Smith, and Engel (2002), in comparing beat and community officers, found no significant direct influence of type of officer assignment on arrest decisions. Yet, in a study examining citizens' preference, Mastrofski, Snipes, Parks, and Maxwell (2000) found that officers with a strong proclivity for community policing were more responsive to requests by citizens. It has also been speculated that in the spirit of community policing, police administrators may demand that officers take a zero tolerance approach toward crime and thus increase police arrest behavior (Nowicki, 1998). Unfortunately, as Nowicki (1998) points out, a zero tolerance policy goes against community empowerment, problem solving, the exercise of discretion, and the involvement of the community, which are all basic tenets of community policing. Sun et al. (2008) found that assignment to a community policing unit was significantly related to the likelihood of engaging in a noncoercive action, with community-policing officers less likely to take such action.

This chapter first discusses the definition of police discretion to present a clear picture of the focus of this research, while revealing both the benefits and the problems associated with police discretion. Next, attention will turn to the role of police in society, followed by a discussion of police orientations or styles of policing. The chapter concludes with research findings concerning the determinants of police behavior.

Police Discretion

At least some discretion is exercised in every aspect of the police task. Some discretionary actions involve very subtle and perhaps minor decisions, while others involve blatant and important ones. Police discretion exists when officers have some leeway or choice in how to respond to a situation. The fewer the rules about handling incidents and situations, the more discretion officers have. Discretion involves both action and inaction (Davis, 1969; Ericson, 1982). Not doing something may be equally as important as doing something. Discretion involves having the power to decide which rules apply to a given situation and whether or not to apply these rules (Ericson, 1982). Both of these decisions have potentially significant implications for the community and for the police department.

Police discretion has been justified on many grounds including: the existence of vague laws, limited resources, community alienation, the need to individualize the law, and the fact that many violations are minor in nature. The exercise of police discretion poses some difficulties, such as: unequal treatment of citizens, interference with due process, a reduction in deterrent effects, and the hidden or unreviewable nature of many discretionary decisions. Police discretion exists at both the individual level (patrolling strategies, decisions to arrest, stop and frisk, write a report, etc.) and at the administrative or departmental level (manpower levels, allocation of personnel and resources, policies, training, etc.).

Police departments are encouraged and perhaps compelled to enact clear policies regulating officer actions. As Alpert and Fridell (1992) aptly point out, the purpose of departmental policy is to reduce officer or individual discretion, as well as to help officers prepare for situations they may confront. As Mastrofski (2004) points out, control over police discretion varies and covers an entire range of influence from very little to absolute. Clearly, some officer decisions, such as whether to arrest, how to patrol, and whether to stop and frisk, should be made with a considerable amount of individual discretion, while others, such as the use of deadly force and continuing a police pursuit, are clearly candidates for a reduced amount of discretion.

Mastrofski (2004) argues that while good studies have been conducted on police discretion, the generalizability of these studies is questionable. He contends that the small number of departments studied and the focus on large municipal departments, among other factors, make it difficult to generalize. Further, Mastrofski (2004) argues that this body of research often focuses on irrelevant measures of police practice and does not take into account the quality of the choices police make.

The Police Role

To understand the behavior of police, we need to first clarify the functions of police or the police role in society. The appropriate role of police is an area where there is some discord among scholars: Scholars generally agree that, in practice, police have multiple functions, many of which involve situations where no crime has occurred. While some scholars disagree that police response to such matters should be an appropriate police function, most would agree that they do represent a substantial portion of police activity (Goldstein, 1977; Nardulli and Stonecash, 1981; Scott, 1981; Reiss, 1971; Mastrofski, 1983). Thus, scholars recognize the existence of not only the *law enforcement* role of police but also the *order maintenance* component of policing. While this noncriminal component is referred to in different terms in the police literature, and not all scholars agree on the exact nature of the activities that comprise the noncriminal component, most recognize there is a distinction between traditional law enforcement response and this noncriminal dimension. Nevertheless, for certain situations (such as arrest for domestic violence), the distinction between law enforcement and order maintenance behavior is less clear. Of major importance is the recognition that the police role is one most accurately described as dealing with many different types of problems (Goldstein, 1979).

With the advent of community policing, the police role has changed somewhat. Community policing, which is generally expected to include creative problem solving, community partnership and empowerment, decentralization, flexible responses, supportive environments, and risk-taking behavior on the part of police (Greene, 2000; Skogan, 1998), requires more **effort** from our officers than ever before. It is clear then, that police in our society have multiple functions to perform. Additionally, the exercise of discretion depends on many factors. One important factor concerns the development of styles or orientations. This issue is discussed in the following section.

Orientations of Police or Styles of Policing

Given the wide discretion of police and their multiple functions, many of which are noncriminal, it is interesting to consider how these discretionary judgments are made. In view of suggestions made in previous research, we can no longer ignore the role that attitudes, orientations, or styles of policing play (Brown, 1981; Smith and Klein, 1984; Berk and Loseke, 1981; Brooks, 1986). Wilson (1968:38) contends that police make judgments about situations and individuals and practice distributive justice. They evaluate the moral character of victims and suspects, and these judgments determine action. Worden (1995:50) argues that a police officer's belief system is "comprised of beliefs, attitudes, values, and other 'subjective outlooks.'" Police develop indicators that are used to determine behavior. Past experience leads police to make conclusions concerning suspiciousness, crime proneness, and the moral character of certain types of individuals (Werthman and Piliavin, 1967). Police develop styles of policing that affect their discretionary behavior (Chatterton, 1983; Wilson, 1968; Brown, 1981). Some have argued that certain types of police departments encourage different styles of policing (Wilson, 1968).

Brown (1981), Muir (1977) and Ericson (1982) have been advocates of the need to consider police attitudes or orientations in our understanding of police discretionary behavior. Brown (1981) argues that to understand what determines the routine choices that patrol officers make, we need to examine the beliefs that officers hold toward their job, the law, and the events and people they confront in the daily course of their job. Police do not react to each incident as though it were unique; rather they generalize. They fashion a coherent set of beliefs or orientations that guide their behavior and develop an "operational style" (Brown, 1981:26). Ericson (1982:25) contends that officers develop a "recipe of rules" that guide their behavior. This recipe of rules is essentially a collection of rules-of-thumb learned on the job and mediate actual events, police departmental rules, and legal codes.

Stroshine, Alpert, and Dunham (2008:322–334), in their study of police officers in Florida and Georgia, argue that officers develop a set of "working rules" that influence their decisions to act. These "working rules" relate to such considerations as time and place, appearance, behavior, perceptions of fairness, safety, as well as other factors.

Predictors of Police Behavior

Much research has focused on determining what factors predict police behavior. While most of the attention has been paid to situational characteristics, however, research has also examined the police organization, the neighborhood, and the officer. Each level will be discussed in turn.

Organizational Variables

Organizational variables deal with characteristics of the police department in which the officer works and would include such factors as how bureaucratic and/or professional a police agency is, the size of the police department, whether the department rotates officers among different areas, and supervision levels. Research examining organizational variables and their effect on police behavior has been minimal in recent years. A review of the literature concludes that organizational variables: have largely been ignored in the study of police service behavior, appear to influence police use of force, and have not been clearly correlated to having an effect on police arrest behavior (Riksheim and Chermak, 1993).

The word "bureaucracy" has been used rather loosely in the police literature, but there does appear to be some consensus of the characteristics that bureaucratic police departments share. Bureaucratic police departments are thought to have a high degree of vertical differentiation (a tall rank structure), in which efficiency, discipline, and productivity are stressed (Bittner, 1970:52–62; Manning, 1977:193–197).

Skolnick (1966:11), in his case study of two police departments, contends that the degree to which a police department is organized around the military model, with its stress on regulations, hierarchy, and obedience, determines officers' "conception of order." He argues that in militaristic police departments, police members will have a rigid conception order and routinization. Officers from these departments will be so concerned with following the rules and regulations that they will feel compelled to follow them to the letter to avoid punishment; this rigid conception of order may result in an emphasis on crime control behavior (Skolnick, 1966:11).

Police departments may also be classified on the basis of professionalism. Professional police organizations have been characterized in many different ways but are thought to be agencies in which education, service, and citizen respect are central (Goldstein, 1977:2–3). Professional departments may have tall or shallow rank structure but generally have wide ranges of specialty units. These specialty units (various crime prevention, police–community relations, etc.) are thought to express the department's commitment to service and positive police–community relations. Professional police departments may be identified by factors such as college incentive pay, community relations training, and percent of officers who are college educated (Smith and Klein, 1984; Swanson, 1978).

Smith's (1984) research is one of the few attempts to clarify the issues of bureaucracy and professionalism in police departments. Smith (1984) found, when examining discretionary decisions by type of police organization, there were differences in factors that affect the decision to arrest. He found that increasing the degree of bureaucracy in professional departments resulted in a shift from conciliatory to punitive responses by police, at least in settling interpersonal disputes. Smith and Klein (1984) found that the probability of arrest increased as departments became more bureaucratic and more professional.

The size of a police department relates to how bureaucratic it is, and some research has examined the effect of an agency's size on police discretionary behavior. Mastrofski, Ritti, and Hoffmaster (1987) found that officers in larger, more bureaucratic police agencies were much less likely to arrest than were officers in smaller departments. Contrary to Brown's (1981) findings, Mastrofski, Ritti, and Hoffmaster (1987) found that as department size and level of bureaucracy increased, the willingness of officers to make DUI arrests decreased. They argued that this may be the result of the fact that small police departments may be easier to control by supervisors and that discretion in large police agencies is less accountable. It may be that large police departments are expected to have less effective controls on their members (due to the numerous members in the department), less group stability, and fewer and less effective links to the community—all of which detract from a service style of policing (Mastrofski, 1981).

How frequently police departments rotate their officers may also influence how officers behave. Departments that frequently rotate their personnel into different beats, shifts, or units inhibit close relations with community members (Brown, 1981:58, Murphy and Pate, 1977:39). Mastrofski (1981) argues that an officer's continued presence in a neighborhood increases the likelihood of repeated contact with citizens and helps officers develop empathy through an understanding of problems. He argues that this understanding will result in fewer instances of force and arrest. Murphy and Pate (1977:39, 225) use the phrase "stranger policing" to refer to jurisdictions that frequently rotate their officers. Davis (1978:135) discusses the "territorial imperative" that occurs when officers become protective of their area and their residents. This theme is central to the concept of community policing.

Neighborhood Variables

Prior research has identified several neighborhood or environmental variables that appear to be related to police discretionary behavior. They include: racial composition of a neighborhood, heterogeneity, socioeconomic status of an area, and the neighborhood crime rate. Some researchers have utilized a rate reflecting neighborhood "disadvantage," which includes variables relating to socioeconomic status, race, and the percentage of female-headed households (Terrill and Reisig, 2003; Novak et al., 2002; Sun and Payne, 2004; Mastrofski, 2004; Mastrofski, Reisig, and McCluskey, 2002).

Research has found that in poor neighborhoods and neighborhoods where the proportion of black residents was high, there was more of a demand for police intervention (Walker, 1991; Nardulli and Stonecash,

1981). This was due to the increased number of "happenings" in these areas, as well as a belief in the appropriateness of calling the police in these areas (Nardulli and Stonecash, 1981:86–88). Similar results were found with respect to low socioeconomic status neighborhoods. Research examining the relationship between neighborhood socioeconomic status and arrest found that these variables were significant predictors of this discretionary decision (Riksheim and Chermak, 1993; Smith, 1984; Smith and Klein, 1984; Smith, 1986) with the general finding being that higher arrest rates occur in poorer areas. It has also been argued that police are more likely to listen to a preference for arrest in a high socioeconomic status neighborhood than in a poorer one (Smith and Klein, 1984). Additionally, police respond differently to the settlement of disputes depending on the socioeconomic status of a neighborhood. Regardless of whether or not a preference for arrest was expressed, as the percentage of households below the poverty level increased, so did the probability of arrest (Smith and Klein, 1984).

Sun and Payne (2004) found that police are more likely to behave in a supportive fashion to residents in low-disadvantaged neighborhoods as compared to high-disadvantaged ones but did not find a significant effect of neighborhood racial composition, heterogeneity, or disadvantage on police coercive behavior. They did find that officer race may interact with neighborhood racial composition in that black officers were significantly more likely to engage in supportive behavior in predominantly black neighborhoods (Sun and Payne, 2004). Sun, Payne, and Wu (2008) found that socially disadvantaged neighborhoods were more likely to receive coercive actions from police than were less disadvantaged neighborhoods. Dunham, Alpert, Stroshine, and Bennett (2005) found that while some characteristics of an area were related to the likelihood of an officer conducting a frisk, they did not find the racial makeup of an area to be significant.

Research examining how the crime rate of a neighborhood affects police discretionary behavior has resulted in mixed findings (Riksheim and Chermak, 1993). Schuck and Rosenbaum (2006) contend that those exposed to violence or crime in their neighborhood are more likely to have other negative experiences (come from low income families, substance abuse or mental health problems, lack of education /employment opportunities, etc.). These factors may in turn lead to negative behavior on the part of the citizen (i.e., deviance) (Schuck and Rosenbaum, 2006). Perceptions of crime risk and the potential for danger to police may affect how police behave and may justify a coercive or aggressive police response in the minds of police (Mastrofski, 1981; Bayley and Mendelsohn, 1969). Klinger (1997) suggests that as crime increases in a neighborhood, police resources become scarce, and officers must respond less vigorously (i.e., fewer arrests and reports, and less thorough investigations).

The National Research Council (2004:189), in its examination of predictors of police behavior, argue that the research demonstrates that "disadvantaged and higher crime neighborhoods are more likely to receive punitive or enforcement-oriented policing, other things being equal." They acknowledge that the strength of these effects is small as compared to those of situational predictors. They further contend that the research indicates that police are more coercive in areas with inequality and racial diversity (National Research Council, 2004). Some research has also indicated that the neighborhood crime rate may influence officer attitudes (Brooks, Piquero, and Cronin, 1993).

Schuck, Rosenbaum, and Hawkins (2008) argue that middle-class African Americans and Hispanics living in disadvantaged neighborhoods are more likely to hold negative views toward police. They contend this could be a result of residents in these neighborhoods viewing police as an extension of the government who they hold responsible for the neighborhood conditions.

Terrill and Reisig (2003) found that police officers were significantly more likely to use higher levels of force when they encountered suspects in disadvantaged neighborhoods, that is, those neighborhoods with higher percentages of homes below the poverty level, unemployment, female-headed households, and African Americans. They also found that higher levels of force are used in neighborhoods with higher homicide rates, independent of suspect characteristics (e.g., resistance) and several officer characteristics (e.g., age, education, and training). They found evidence to support the finding noted by Smith (1986) that police "do act differently in different neighborhood contexts." Mastrofski, Reisig, and McCluskey (2002) found that police were significantly more likely to behave disrespectfully in disadvantaged neighborhoods but argued that suspect behaviors are the most powerful predictors of police disrespect.

Situational Variables

Situational variables have received most of the research attention in terms of their effect on police discretionary behavior and involve characteristics of the encounter between citizen(s) and the police. They include such variables as the characteristics of both the suspect and the complainant, the characteristics of the call for service or crime involved, and the visibility of the encounter.

One of the most frequently examined situational variables has been the race of the suspect, and the results found in research are mixed. Research covering many years has found that nonwhite suspects are more likely to be arrested and/or to be treated more punitively by police (Kochel, Wilson, and Mastrofski, 2011; Brame, Bushway, Paternoster, and Turner, 2014; Powell, 1990; Terrill and Mastrofski, 2002; Smith and Visher, 1981; Smith and Davidson, 1984; Brooks, 1986; Sun, Payne, and Wu, 2008; Dunham, Alpert, Stroshine, and Bennett, 2005; Alpert, MacDonald, and Dunham, 2005; Schafer et al., 2006), but other studies report no effect (Klinger, 1996; Smith and Klein, 1983; Smith, 1984; Sun and Payne, 2004). The National Research Council (2004) concludes that the evidence on this issue is mixed and dependent on many methodological variables, making it difficult to determine if patterns are present, while Kochel, Wilson, and Mastrofski (2011) confidently assert that race does matter, with their finding that minority suspects are more likely to be arrested than white suspects.

A study by Mastrofski, Reisig, and McCluskey (2002) found that in one city, minority suspects experienced disrespect from police less often than white suspects. They do acknowledge that this may be a result of a clear policy of the police chief in that city to curtail police abuse in that department. Engel (2003) found that nonwhite suspects were more likely to be noncompliant and to show all types of resistance toward police, with the exception of physical aggression. Schuck, Rosenbaum, and Hawkins (2008), in their study on the influence of neighborhood context on citizen attitudes toward police, found that African Americans reported a more negative view of police than white citizens. They found that African Americans have more negative global views toward police, less positive perceptions of police service, and are more fearful of police (Schuck et al., 2008).

Sun, Payne, and Wu (2008) found that males, minorities, and poor citizens were more likely to be the recipient of coercive actions by police, but this finding did not hold true for noncoercive actions. Dunham, Alpert, Stroshine, and Bennett (2005) found that males and minorities were more likely to arouse suspicion in police; however, the main reason that officers formed suspicion was the citizen's behavior. Suspicious behavior included traffic violations, showing signs of trying to avoid the officer, or acting nervous. They further found that once an officer became suspicious, race, gender, socioeconomic status, or age had no effect (Dunham et al., 2005). In a related paper, Alpert, MacDonald, and Dunham (2005) found that minority status influences the decision to form nonbehavioral suspicion but not the actual decision to stop and question the citizen.

Smith and Alpert (2007:1262) propose "a theory of individual police behavior that is grounded in social–psychological research on stereotype formation and that assumes a nonmotivational but biased response to minority citizens." They argue that this response is largely unintentional and a result of unconscious racial profiling. Stereotypes are the result of social conditioning and the "illusory correlate phenomenon," which results in police overestimating negative behaviors of minorities (Smith and Alpert, 2007:1262).

Schafer et al. (2006), in a study of traffic stops by police, found that race was among a number of important predictors, including a suspect's gender, age, and other situational characteristics. They concluded that African-American males, controlling for age and gender, were the most likely group to be searched by police (Schafer et al., 2006). In terms of predicting consent searches during these traffic stops, they found that the race of the driver was a significant predictor for the stop. While they found race/ethnicity to be a significant predictor of traffic stops, they contend that age and gender are important predictors as well (Schafer et al., 2006). Conversely, Sun and Payne (2004) did not find a relationship between citizen race and the amount of coercion that is used by an officer.

Brame et al. (2014) in their study of demographic patterns of arrest prevalence, found that black males have a significantly higher arrest rate than white males but that these race differences do not apply to the arrest rates of females. Additionally, they found no differences in arrest rates of Hispanic males as compared to white or black males.

Some research on deadly force found that blacks are disproportionately shot more often than are whites, however this may be due to a an overrepresentation in serious crime (Geller and Karales, 1981; Fyfe, 1980), while other research reported no racial effect on deadly force decisions (Blumberg, 1981).

Early research found gender differences in police treatment of suspects and complainants, but recent research is somewhat mixed. Some research has found that either no gender differences occur or that they are less prominent than previously thought (Klinger, 1996; Smith and Visher, 1980; Smith and Visher, 1981; Krohn, Curry, and Nelson-Krueger, 1983; Visher, 1983; Smith and Davidson, 1984; Smith and Klein, 1983; Smith, 1984), but others suggest gender differences do occur, with females being more likely to be treated forcefully, to be coerced, or to be arrested (Terrill and Mastrofski, 2002; Sun, Payne, and Wu, 2008; Novak et al., 2002). Some research has found that female suspects act more disrespectfully toward officers than male suspects (Engel, 2003), and others found that females hold more negative attitudes toward police and police service, particularly in minority and poor neighborhoods (Schuck et al., 2008).

There have been several recent studies that show a gender effect in terms of police behavior. Schafer et al. (2006) find that being young or male significantly predicts the likelihood of a consent search but acknowledge that they did not explore whether the consents were sought and not obtained, so their conclusions must be viewed as tentative. A recent study of cumulative arrest patterns by Brame et al. (2014) found that males have higher arrest rates than females. Sun and Payne (2004) found that police are more likely to coerce male citizens and that police are more likely to show supportive behavior toward female citizens. Dunham, Alpert, Stroshine, and Bennett (2005) found that male drivers were more likely to arouse suspicion or to be stopped by police than females. However, once suspicion was aroused, the gender effect, as did other citizen characteristics, disappeared. Further, males were five times more likely to be frisked than females; yet, if a female was stopped, she was twice as likely as a male to receive a ticket (Dunham et al., 2005).

It is generally supported in the literature that individuals in the lower socioeconomic strata receive harsher treatment by police (Black 1971; Reiss, 1971; Black and Reiss, 1967; Friedrich, 1977; Lundman, 1994; Terrill and Mastrofski, 2002; Sun, Payne, and Wu, 2008; Black, 1980; Riksheim and Chermak, 1993). Sun and Payne (2004) found that police were more likely to be supportive of citizens who were not poor. It is important to note that these general findings may be related to the race and demeanor of the suspect and the complainant. There is evidence that residents who live in poorer areas may hold more negative views of the police (Schuck et al., 2008), and these attitudes could influence their behavior and thus the police response to it (Schafer et al., 2006).

Research is also somewhat mixed regarding the effect of a citizen's age on police discretionary behavior. Some research found that young suspects are more likely to be arrested, less likely to comply with police, and more likely to be the recipients of deadly force by police and that older complainants are more likely to be taken seriously (Sherman, 1980; Terrill and Mastrofski, 2002; Novak et al., 2002; McCluskey, Mastrofski, and Parks, 1999; Friedrich, 1977), while other research indicated that suspect age is not an important predictor of police behavior (Klinger, 1996; Sun, Payne, and Wu, 2008; Smith and Visher, 1981; Smith and Davidson, 1983; Smith, 1984; Visher, 1983).

The demeanor, or attitude, of the suspect and the complainant has received considerable attention in the research literature. The general finding has been that disrespectful or uncooperative citizens are more likely to be treated punitively (arrested, targets of force, less often accommodated as complainants) (Black and Reiss, 1970; Black, 1971; Brooks, 1986; Piliavin and Briar, 1964; Friedrich, 1977; Engel, Sobol, and Worden, 2000; Terrill and Paoline, 2007; Novak, Frank, Smith, and Engel, 2002; Smith and Visher, 1981; Ericson, 1982; Black, 1970; Sherman, 1980; Visher, 1983; Smith, 1986; Smith, 1987). A hostile attitude may signify a threat to an officer's control or a challenge to his or her authority. However, questions concerning the measurement of demeanor have been raised (Klinger, 1994). Klinger (1994) argues that previous studies examining the effect of suspect demeanor on police behavior have been flawed due to the failure to properly measure "demeanor." Sun, Payne, and Wu (2008) found that the effect of citizen demeanor on officer coercive behavior depends on the shift the officer worked (day vs. evening). In this research, police who worked the evening and night shifts were more coercive toward hostile citizens than were day-shift officers. Further, in general, officers were more coercive toward citizens if they showed disrespect (Sun et al., 2008). The National Research Council (2004) concludes that there is a conflicting body of evidence about the demeanor effect but there does seem to be a high degree of support that demeanor is a powerful predictor of police use of force.

Research has been fairly consistent in the finding that when a complainant expresses a preference for arrest, an arrest is more likely to occur (Black, 1971; Black, 1970; Friedrich, 1977; Smith and Visher, 1981; Visher, 1983; Novak, Frank, Smith, and Engel, 2002; Smith, 1987; Worden, 1989; Brooks, 1986). The degree of relational distance or the degree of intimacy between suspects and complainants seems to be related to police behavior, as well. Research indicates that as relational distance decreases or intimacy increases, police are less likely to take official action (Black, 1971, 1970; Friedrich, 1977; Smith and Visher, 1981). It may be that police believe taking official action against a suspect who is in a relationship with the complainant may cause future problems, or they may feel that it is not part of police responsibility.

Characteristics of police–citizen encounters have received attention in the study of police discretionary behavior. Mastrofski, Snipes, Parks, and Maxwell (2000) found in studying officer characteristics and responsiveness to citizen requests, less experienced male officers who had a proclivity toward community policing were significantly more likely to give citizens what they requested. The National Research Council (2004) found that police behavior is mostly influenced by legalistic factors (seriousness of offense, evidence, complainant preference, etc.). Sun, Payne, and Wu (2008) contend that the strength of the evidence affects positively the likelihood of a coercive action but has no significant effect on a noncoercive action. Terrill and Paoline (2007) found that the "presence" of evidence is what affects police behavior, but not the strength of the evidence. They contend that "officers treat cases with little probable cause the same as those with a great deal of probable cause" (Terrill and Paoline, 2007:319).

Generally, research indicates that the more serious the offense that police encounter, the more likely a harsher disposition will be the result (Wilson, 1968; Ericson, 1982; Black, 1971; Piliavin and Briar, 1964; Smith and Visher, 1981; Brooks, 1986; Visher, 1983; Sherman, 1980; Smith and Klein, 1983; Smith, 1984). Terrill and Paoline (2007) found that the strongest effect on nonarrest decisions was the type of problem—noncoercive problems were almost four times more likely to end up with no arrest.

Police, with the many demands on their time, may have to prioritize and choose to take action when dealing with serious crimes. However, most research has found the presence of injuries was not an important determinant of arrest (Smith and Klein, 1984; Worden and Pollitz, 1984). Some research has found when an encounter is visible (public) or when others were present (including supervisors), police would be more likely to either write a report, make an arrest, or use force (Friedrich, 1977; Brooks, 1986; Reiss, 1971; Brandl and Stroshine, 2012; Smith and Visher, 1981; Smith and Klein, 1983; Smith, 1984). Police may behave aggressively or officially when encounters are visible to others due to a belief they must appear in control.

Officer Characteristics

Researchers have examined characteristics of the police officer (i.e., experience, race, gender, etc.) to determine how they may influence what police do. Overall, these characteristics have not been found to exert strong influences on police discretionary behavior (Riksheim and Chermak, 1993); however some significant findings do emerge. Some argue that officer-level predictors explain better the coercive actions of police as compared to noncoercive ones (Sun, Payne, and Wu, 2008).

Some research has shown that less experienced officers perform more "work" (are more aggressive, stop and frisk more often, arrest more often), but more experienced officers engage in higher quality work and/or are less likely to engage in a legalistic manner (Friedrich, 1977; Sherman, 1980; Crank, 1993), while other research has found no relationship between individual officer experience and arrest and/or use of force behavior (Smith and

Klein, 1983; Worden, 1989; Brandl and Stroshine, 2012). Paoline and Terrill (2007) found that officers with high levels of police experience were less likely to use both verbal and physical force. Some research has suggested a connection between officer experience and certain officer attitudes (i.e., cynicism, role definition, perception of the public, perception of support by the criminal justice system), which may relate to discretionary behavior (Brooks, Piquero, and Cronin, 1993; Canter and Martensen, 1990; Hayeslip and Corder, 1987).

Dunham, Alpert, Stroshine, and Bennett (2005), in their study of the formation of police suspicion, found that the officer's length of police experience was related to the levels of resistance offered by suspects. Specifically, they found that officers with more police experience were more likely to encounter a resistant suspect. They speculate that perhaps more experienced officers are rougher or less patient with suspects (Dunham et al., 2005). Alpert, Mac-Donald, and Dunham (2005) also studied the formation of suspicion and found that the longer the officer had been on the police department, the more likely he or she was to form suspicion based on nonbehavioral cues. While this finding was not statistically significant, due perhaps to a small sample size, they felt it was noteworthy (Alpert et al., 2005).

It has been assumed that the level of education of an officer affects police behavior, and the advent of police professionalism has definitely incorporated this premise. It has been argued that college-educated officers learn things that are independent of what is taught in their curriculum (Goldstein, 1977). The research, however, has resulted in some findings that suggest individual education has no effect on police behavior (Worden, 1989, 1990; Smith and Klein, 1983; Crank, 1993), but there may be a negative effect on arrest if officer education is measured at the departmental level (Smith and Klein, 1983). Some research has also suggested a link between officer education and certain attitudes (attitudes toward legal restrictions, attitudes toward discretion, perceptions of ethical conduct, cynicism, attitudes toward the community, solidarity, use of force, role), which may in turn influence police behavior (Shernock, 1992; Worden, 1990; Canter and Martensen, 1990; Hayeslip and Cordner, 1987; Brooks, Piquero, and Cronin, 1993).

Sun and Payne (2004) found an officer's educational background significantly affects his or her likelihood of providing supportive actions to citizens. Officers with college educations were more likely to employ some type of supportive action (i.e., counsel citizen to sign a formal complaint or to use the legal system, to offer information, to comfort or reassure, etc.) than those who did not possess a college degree. Mastrofski (2004) argues that in studies that show positive effects of college education on police behavior, it is unclear whether the positive effects result from actual experience in college or from the process of getting into college and completing a degree. The National Research Council (2004), in their examination of the effects on police behavior, argue there isn't enough evidence to determine whether college education impacts police behavior, and they cite methodological limitations, weak effect size, and mixed results as reasons for this position.

Paoline and Terrill (2007) found that the education level of the police officer does affect the officer's use of coercion. Specifically, they assert that officers with at least some college use significantly less verbal force as compared to officers with just a high school education. However, in terms of the use of physical force, significant differences emerged only when an officer had a 4-year degree, with these officers using significantly less physical force.

The race of an officer has been examined in terms of its effect on police behavior. Early research reported a link between officer race and police behavior (Sherman, 1980); however, other research finds no such effect (Worden, 1989; Alpert, MacDonald, and Dunham, 2005; Brandl and Stroshine, 2012; Smith and Klein, 1983). The National Research Council (2004) concluded there is little support that officer race has a significant impact on police behavior and argues that there is not credible evidence that officers perform differently toward citizens as a result of their race or ethnicity.

Some more recent research concerning race and the use of force has reported racial differences. Sun and Payne (2004) found that black officers were more likely to use force in disputes than were white officers. They contend that officer race exerts a significant influence on the level of force an officer uses, even when controlling for other characteristics (officer, citizen, and neighborhood levels). They argue that black officers are more active in resolving conflict, more likely to act coercively, and are more likely to engage in supportive behavior when the neighborhood is predominantly black (Sun and Payne, 2004). Dunham et al. (2005) find that officer race affects the likelihood of a suspect receiving a traffic ticket and contend that white officers are more than two times as likely to issue tickets during traffic stops than are nonwhite officers.

In general, the deadly force literature concludes that black officers are overrepresented in police shootings of citizens, although most researchers note that this relationship is most likely due to differential deployment of black officers in high crime areas and to the higher rate of black officers residing in these areas (Geller and Karales, 1981; Fyfe, 1978). However, Alpert, MacDonald, and Dunham (2005) find no evidence that an officer's race affects the likelihood of forming a nonbehavioral suspicion. There is, however, some evidence that race may play a role in officer attitudes, which may influence their behavior (Brooks, Piquero, and Cronin, 1993).

Generally, recent research has indicated that the gender of an officer exerts no influence on police behavior (Worden, 1989; National Research Council, 2004), while some earlier research found that females were less likely to make arrests, use deadly force, and be involved in deadly force situations (Sherman, 1980; Horvath, 1987; Grennan, 1987). A recent study by Brandl and Stroshine (2012) found that male officers are more likely to be involved in a high rate of use of force incidents. The National Research Council (2004) argues that the body of research on officer gender is too small and the findings are too mixed to provide any definitive word on the possible effects of gender on police behavior.

A few officer-level predictors that received some recent attention are officer complaint rate and work shift. A study by McCluskey and Terrill (2005) found that an officer's complaint rate for force and verbal discourtesy is related to an increase in coercive suspect encounters. Additionally, while the verbal–discourtesy complaint rate of an officer is related to higher levels of coercion, this is not apparent for complaints involving physical force (McCluskey and Terrill, 2005). Sun, Payne and Wu (2008) found that young, male, and evening-shift officers were more likely to engage in coercive behaviors, but these predictors were insignificant in the examination of noncoercive behavior. Brandl and Stroshine (2012) found that officers who patrol high crime areas and/or who work certain shifts (3 P.M.–11 P.M., 7 P.M.–3 A.M.) were more likely to be involved in a high rate of use of force incidents.

Research has also suggested that officer attitudes may be related to gender (Dorsey and Giacopassi, 1986; Brooks, 1986; DeJong, 2003; Brooks, Piquero, and Cronin, 1993, Brooks, Piquero, and Cronin, 1994). Johnson (2013:1149) argues "displaced aggression theory" may explain punitive police behavior. He contends that officers may be negatively primed from a personal family conflict and that this may result in a less lenient response to a minor violation. Unfortunately, there has been little empirical work examining police attitudes and their influence on police discretionary behavior, and the research that has been done on this issue has yielded disappointing results.

Conclusions

Since police exercise so much discretion, it is important to understand the factors that affect their discretionary choices. It appears as though organizational, situational, neighborhood, and officer characteristics all may play some part in the decisions police make. While much research has focused on the determinants of police behavior and much has been learned in the process, there is still a great deal that is unexplained. As researchers use more sophisticated designs and methods, it becomes apparent that the study of police discretionary behavior is a complicated endeavor. Adopting a community policing philosophy in police departments would seem to influence the discretionary choices police officers make, and future research might do well to explore this issue. Additionally, while attitudes of police officers appear to contribute little to our understanding of police behavior, more attention should be paid to this area.

REFERENCES

Alpert, G., and L. Fridell. 1992. *Police Vehicle and Firearms: Instruments of Deadly Force.* Long Grove, IL: Waveland Press.

Alpert, G. P., J. M. MacDonald, and R. G. Dunham. 2005. "Police Suspicion and Discretionary Decision Making During Traffic Stops." *Criminology* 43 (2): 407–434.

Bayley, D. H. and H. Mendelsohn. 1969. *Minorities and the Police.* New York: Free Press.

Berk, S. F., and D. Loseke. 1981. "Handling Family Violence: Situational Determinants of Police Arrest in Domestic Disturbances." *Law and Society Review* 15 (2).

Bittner, E. 1970. *The Functions of Police in Modern Society.* Rockville: National Institute of Mental Health.

Black, D. 1971. "The Social organization of Arrest." *Stanford Law Review* 23: 1087–1111.

———. 1980. *The Manners and Customs of Police.* New York: Academic Press.

Black, D., and A. Reiss. 1967. "Section I: Patterns of Behavior in Police and Citizen Transactions." *Studies of Crime and Law Enforcement in Major Metropolitan Areas.* Vol. 2. (Field Surveys III). Washington, DC: Government Printing Office.

———. 1970. "Police Control of Juveniles." *American Sociological Review* 35: 63–77.

Bloch, P., and D. Anderson. 1974. *Policewomen on Patrol: Final Report.* Washington, DC: Police Foundation.

Blumberg, M. 1981. "Race and Police Shootings: An Analysis in Two Cities." In J. J. Fyfe (ed), *Contemporary Issues in Law Enforcement.* Beverly Hills: Sage.

Brame, R., S. Bushway, R. Paternoster, and M. Turner. 2014. "Demographic Patterns of Cumulative Arrest Prevalence by Ages 18 and 23." *Crime and Delinquency* 60: 471–486.

Brandl, S., and M. Stroshine. 2012. "The Role of Officer—Attributes, Job Characteristics, and Arrest Activity in Explaining Police Use of Force." *Criminal Justice Policy Review* 24: 551–572.

Brooks, L. W. 1986. "Determinants of Police Officer Orientations and Their Impact on Police Discretionary Behavior." Unpublished PhD Dissertation. Institute of Criminal Justice and Criminology, University of Maryland.

Brooks, L. W., A. Piquero, and J. Cronin. 1993. "Police Officer Attitudes Concerning Their Communities and Their Roles: A Comparison of Two Suburban Police Departments." *American Journal of Police* 12: 115–139.

———. 1994. "'Workload' Rates and Police Officer Attitudes: An Examination of 'Busy' and 'Slow' Precincts." *Journal of Criminal Justice* 22.

Brown, M. K. 1981. *Working the Street: Police Discretion and the Dilemmas of Reform.* New York: Russell Sage Foundation.

Canter, P., and K. Martensen. 1990. "Neiderhoffer Revisited—Comparison of Selected Police Cynicism Hypotheses." Paper Presented to the 1990 American Society of Criminology Annual Meetings in Baltimore, Maryland.

Chatterton, M. 1983. "Police Work and Assault Charges." In M. Punch (ed.), *The Police Organization*, pp. 194–221. Cambridge: The MIT Press.

Crank, J. P. 1993. "Legalistic and Order-Maintenance Behavior Among Police Patrol Officers: A Survey of Eight Municipal Police Agencies." *American Journal of Police* 12: 103–126.

Davis, E. M. 1978. *Staff One: A Perspective on Effective Police Management.* Englewood Cliffs, New Jersey: Prentice-Hall.

Davis, K. C. 1969. *Discretionary Justice.* Westport, CT: Greenwood Press.

DeJong, C. 2003. "Gender Differences in Officer Attitude and Behavior: Providing Comfort to Citizens." An Unpublished Paper. School of Criminal Justice: Michigan State University.

Dorsey, R., and D. Giacopassi. 1986. "Assessing Gender Differences in the Levels of Cynicism Among Police Officers." *American Journal of Police* 5: 91–112.

Dunham, R. G., G. P. Alpert, M. S. Stroshine, and K. Bennett. 2005. "Transforming Citizens into Suspects: Factors That Influence the Formation of Police Suspicion." *Police Quarterly* 8 (3): 366–393.

Engel, R. S. 2003. "Explaining Suspects' Resistance and Disrespect toward Police." *Journal of Criminal Justice* 31: 475–492.

Engel, R. S., J. J. Sobol, and R. E. Worden. 2000. "Further Exploration of the Demeanor Hypothesis: The Interaction Effects of Suspects' Characteristics and Demeanor on Police Behavior." *Justice Quarterly* 17: 235–258.

Ericson, R. 1982. *Reproducing Order: A Study of Police Patrol Work*. Toronto: University of Toronto Press.

Friedrich, R. J. 1977. "The Impact of Organizational, Individual, and Situational Factors on Police behavior." PhD Dissertation. Department of Political Science: University of Michigan.

Fyfe, J. J. 1978. "Shots Fired: An Examination of New York City Police Firearms Discharges." PhD Dissertation. School of Criminal Justice: State University of New York at Albany.

———. 1980. "Geographic Correlates of Police Shootings: A Microanalysis." *Crime and Delinquency* 17: 101–113.

Geller, R., and K. Karales. 1981. *Split Second Decisions: Shootings of and by the Chicago Police*. Chicago: Chicago Law Enforcement Study Group.

Goldstein, H. 1977. *Policing a Free Society*. Cambridge, MA: Harvard University Press.

———. 1979. "Improving Policing: A Problem Oriented Approach." *Crime and Delinquency* 25: 236–258.

Greene, J. 2000. "The Road to Community Policing in Los Angeles: A Case Study." In G. Alpert and A. Piquero (eds.), *Community Policing: Contemporary Readings*. Long Grove, IL: Waveland Press.

Grennan, S. 1987. "Findings on the Role of Officer Gender in Violent Encounters with Citizens." *Journal of Police Science and Administration* 15: 78–85.

Hayeslip, D., and G. Cordner. 1987. "The Effects of Community-Oriented Patrol on Officer Attitudes." *American Journal of Police* 6.

Horvath, F. 1987 "The Police Use of Deadly Force: A Description of Selected Characteristics of Intrastate Incidents." *Journal of Police Science and Administration* 15: 226–238.

Johnson, R. 2013. "Arrest as Displaced Aggression." *Criminal Justice and Behavior* 40: 1149–1162.

Klinger, D. A. 1994. "Demeanor or Crime? Why 'Hostile' Citizens Are More Likely To Be Arrested." *Criminology* 32: 475–493.

———. 1996. "More on Demeanor and Arrest in Dade County." *Criminology* 34: 61–82.

———. 1997. "Negotiating Order in Patrol Work: An Ecological Theory of Police Response to Deviance." *Criminology* 35 (2): 277–306.

Kochel, T., D. Wilson, and S. Mastrofski. 2011. "Effect of Race on Officers' Arrest Decisions." *Criminology* 49: 473–512.

Krohn, M., J. Curry, and S. Nelson-Krueger. 1983. "Is Chivalry Dead? An Analysis of Changes in Police Dispositions of Males and Females." *Criminology* 21: 395–416.

Lundman, R. J. 1994. "Demeanor or Crime? The Midwest City Police-Citizen Encounter." *Criminology* 32: 631–656.

Manning, P. 1977. Police Work: The Social Organization of Policing. Cambridge: The MIT Press.

Mastrofski, S. 1981. "Policing the Beat: The Impact of Organizational Scale on Patrol Officer Behavior in Urban residential Neighborhoods." *Journal of Criminal Justice* 9: 343–358.

———. 1983. "The Police and Noncrime Services." In G. Whitaker and C. D. Phillips (eds.), *Evaluating Performance of Criminal Justice Agencies*. Beverly Hills: Sage.

———. 2004. "Controlling Street-Level Police Discretion." *The Annals of the American Academy of Political and Social Science* 593: 100–118.

Mastrofski, S. D., M. D. Reisig, and J. D. McCluskey. 2002. "Police Disrespect Toward the Public: An Encounter-Based Analysis. *Criminology* 40: 519–552.

Mastrofski, S. D., R. Ritti, and D. Hoffmaster. 1987. "Organizational Determinants of Police Discretion: The Case of Drinking-Driving." *Journal of Criminal Justice* 15: 387–402.

Mastrofski, S. D., J. B. Snipes, R. B. Parks, and C. D. Maxwell. 2000. "The Helping hand of the Law: Police Control of Citizens on Request." *Criminology* 38: 307–342.

Mastrofski, S. D., R. E. Worden, and J. B. Snipes. 1995. "Law Enforcement in a Time of Community Policing." *Criminology* 33: 539–563.

McCluskey, J. D., S. D. Mastrofski, and R. B. Parks. 1999. "To Acquiesce or Rebel: Predicting Citizen Compliance with Police Requests." *Police Quarterly* 2: 389–416.

McCluskey, J. D., and W. Terrill. 2005. "Departmental and Citizen Complaints as Predictors of Police Coercion" *Policing* 28 (3): 513–529.

Muir, W. K. 1977. *Police: Streetcorner Politicians.* Chicago: University of Chicago Press.

Murphy, P. V., and T. Pate. 1977. *Commissioner.* New York: Simon and Shuster.

Nardulli, P. F., and J. M. Stonecash. 1981. *Politics, Professionalism, and Urban Services: The Police.* Cambridge, MA: Oelgeschlager, Gunn, and Hain.

National Research Council. 2004. *Fairness and Effectiveness in Policing: The Evidence.* Washington, DC: The National Academies Press.

Novak, K. J., J. Frank, B. W. Smith, and R. S. Engel. 2002. "Revisiting the Decision to Arrest: Comparing Beat and Community Officers." *Crime and Delinquency* 48: 70–98.

Nowicki, D. 1998. "Mixed Messages." In G. Alpert and A. Piquero (eds.), *Community Policing: Contemporary Readings.* Long Grove, IL: Waveland Press.

Ostrom, E., R. B. Parks, and G. Whitaker. 1977. *The Police Services Study.* Bloomington: Workshop in Political Theory and Policy Analysis, Indiana University.

Paoline, E., and W. Terrill. 2007. "Police Education, Experience, and the Use of Force." *Criminal Justice and Behavior* 34: 179–196.

Piliavin, J., and S. Briar. 1964. "Police Encounters with Juveniles." *American Journal of Sociology* 70: 206–214.

Powell, D. D. 1990. "A Study of Police Discretion in Six Southern Cities." *Journal of Police Science and Administration* 17: 1–7.

Reiss, A. 1971. *The Police and the Public.* New Haven, CT: Yale University Press.

Riksheim, E. C., and S. M. Chermak. 1993. "Causes of Police Behavior Revisited." *Journal of Criminal Justice* 21: 353–382.

Rossi, P., R. Berk, and B. Eidson. 1974. *The Roots of Urban Discontent: Public Policy, Municipal Institutions, and the Ghetto.* New York: John Wiley & Sons.

Schafer, J. A., D. L. Carter, A. J. Katz-Bannister, and W. M. Wells. 2006. "Decision Making in Traffic Stop Encounters: A Multivariate Analysis of Police Behavior." *Police Quarterly* 9: 184–209.

Schuck, A. M., and D. P. Rosenbaum. 2006. "Promoting Safe and Healthy Neighborhoods: What Research Tells Us about Intervention." In K. Fulbright-Anderson and P. Auspos (eds.), *Community Change: Theories, Practice, and Evidence.* Washington, DC: Aspen Institute.

Schuck, A. M., D. P. Rosenbaum, and D. F. Hawkins. 2008. "The Influence of Race/Ethnicity, Social Class, and Neighborhood Context on Residents' Attitudes toward the Police." *Police Quarterly* 11: 496–519.

Scott, E. J. 1981. *Calls for Service: Citizen Demand and Initial Police Response.* Washington, DC: National Institute of Justice.

Sherman, L. 1980. "Causes of Police Behavior: The Current State of Quantitative Research." *Journal of Research in Crime and Delinquency* 17: 69–100.

———. 1983. "Reducing Police Gun Use: Critical Events, Administrative Policy, and Organizational Change." In M. Punch (ed.), *Control in the Police Organization.* Cambridge: The MIT Press.

Shernock, S. 1992. "The Effects of College education on Professional Attitudes among Police." *Journal of Criminal Justice Education* 3: 71–92.

Skogan, W. 1998. "Community Policing in Chicago." In G. Alpert and A. Piquero (eds.), *Community Policing: Contemporary Readings.* Long Grove, IL: Waveland Press.

Skolnick, J. 1966. Justice without Trial: Law Enforcement in a Democratic Society. New York: John Wiley & Sons.

Smith, D.A. 1984. "The Organizational Aspects of Legal Control." *Criminology* 22: 19–38.

———. 1986. "The Neighborhood Context of Police Behavior." In A. J. Reiss and M. Tonry (eds.), *Crime and Justice: An Annual Review of Research.* Vol. 8. Chicago: University of Chicago Press.

———. 1987. "Police Response to Interpersonal Violence: Defining the Parameters of Legal Control." *Social Forces* 65: 767–782.

Smith, D. A., and L. A. Davidson. 1984. "Equity and Discretionary Justice: The Influence of Race on Police Arrest Decisions." *Journal of Criminal Law* 75: 234–249.

Smith, D. A., and J. R. Klein. 1983. "Police Agency Characteristics and Arrest Decisions." In G. D. Whitaker and C. D. Phillips (eds.), *Evaluating Performance of Criminal Justice Agencies.* Beverly Hills: Sage.

———. 1984. "Police Control of Interpersonal Disputes." *Social Problems* 31: 468–481.

Smith, D. A., and C. Visher. 1980. "Sex and Involvement in Deviance/Crime: A Quantitative Review of the Empirical Literature." *American Sociological Review* 45.

———. 1981. "Street Level Justice: Situational Determinants of Police Arrest Decisions." *Social Problems* 29: 167–178.

Smith, M., and G. Alpert. 2007. "Explaining Police Bias: A Theory of Social Conditioning and Illusory Correlation." *Criminal Justice and Behavior* 34: 1262–1283.

Stroshine, M., G. Alpert, and R. Dunham. 2008. "The Influence of 'Working Rules' on Police Suspicion and Discretionary Decision Making." *Police Quarterly* 11: 315–337.

Sun, I. Y., and B. K. Payne. 2004. "Racial Differences in Resolving Conflicts: A Comparison Between Black and White Police Officers." *Crime and Delinquency* 50 (4): 516–541.

Sun, I. Y., B. K. Payne, and Y. Wu. 2008. "The Impact of Situational Factors, Officer Characteristics, and Neighborhood Context on Police Behavior: A Multilevel Analysis." *Journal of Criminal Justice* 36: 22–32.

Swanson, C. 1978. "The Influence of Organization and Environment on Arrest Policies in Major U.S. Cities." *Policy Studies Journal* 7: 390–318.

Terrill, W., and S. D. Mastrofski. 2002. "Situational and Officer-Based Determinants of Police Coercion." *Justice Quarterly* 19: 215–248.

Terrill, W., and E. Paoline. 2007. "Nonarrest Decision Making in Police-Citizen Encounters." *Police Quarterly* 10 (3): 308–331.

Terrill, W., and M. D. Reisig. 2003. "Neighborhood Context and Police Use of Force." *Journal of Research in Crime and Delinquency* 40: 291–321.

Visher, C. A. 1983. "Gender, Police Arrest Decisions, and Notions of Chivalry." *Criminology* 21: 5–28.

Walker, S. 1991. *The Police in America*. Second Edition. New York: McGraw-Hill.

Werthman, C., and I. Piliavin. 1967. "Gang Members and the Police." In D. Bordua (ed), *The Police: Six Sociological Essays*. New York: John Wiley & Sons.

Wilson, J. Q. 1968. *Varieties of Police Behavior*. Cambridge, MA: Harvard University Press.

Worden, R. E. 1989. "Situational and Attitudinal Explanations of Police Behavior: A Theoretical Reappraisal and Empirical Assessment." *Law and Society Review* 23: 667–711.

———. 1990. "A Badge and a Baccalaureate: Policies, Hypotheses, and Further Evidence." *Justice Quarterly* 1990: 565–592.

———. 1995. "Police Officers' Belief Systems: A Framework for Analysis." *American Journal of Police* 14: 49–81.

Worden, R. E., and A. A. Pollitz. 1984. "Police Arrests in Domestic Disturbances: A Further Look." *Law and Society Review* 18: 105–119.

Worden, R. E., and R. L. Shepard. 1996. "Demeanor, Crime, and Police Behavior: A Reexamination of the Police Services Study Data." *Criminology* 34: 83–105.

8

The Asshole

John Van Maanen

> I guess what our job really boils down to is not letting the assholes take
> over the city. Now I'm not talking about your regular crooks . . . they're
> bound to wind up in the joint anyway. What I'm talking about are those
> shitheads out to prove they can push everybody around. Those are the
> assholes we gotta deal with and take care of on patrol. . . . They're the
> ones that make it tough on the decent people out there. You take the
> majority of what we do and it's nothing more than asshole control.
>
> A veteran patrolman[1]

Police Typifications

The asshole—creep, bigmouth, bastard, animal, mope, rough, jerkoff,
clown, scumbag, wiseguy, phony, idiot, shithead, bum, fool, or any of a number of anatomical, oral, or incestuous terms—is a part of every policeman's
world.[2] Yet the grounds upon which such a figure stands have never been
examined systematically. The purpose of this article is to display the interactional origins and consequences of the label asshole as it is used by policemen, in particular, patrolmen, going about their everyday tasks. I will argue
that assholes represent a distinct but familiar type of person to the police and
represent, therefore, a part of their commonsense wisdom as to the kinds of
people that populate their working environment. From this standpoint, assholes are analytic types with whom the police regularly deal. More importantly, however, I will also argue that the label arises from a set of situated
conditions largely unrelated to the institutional mandate of the police (i.e., to
protect life and property, arrest law violators, preserve the peace, etc.) but
arises in response to some occupational and personal concerns shared by virtually all policemen.

Peter K. Manning and John Van Maanen, (Eds.), *Policing: A View from the Street,* (1978) pp. 221–
38. Reprinted with permission. Notes renumbered.

According to most knowledgeable observers, nothing characterizes policing in America more than the widespread belief on the part of the police themselves that they are primarily law enforcers—perpetually engaged in a struggle with those who would disobey, disrupt, do harm, agitate, or otherwise upset the just order of the regime. And, that as policemen, they and they alone are the most capable of sensing right from wrong; determining who is and who is not respectable; and, most critically, deciding what is to be done about it (if anything). Such heroic self-perceptions reflecting moral superiority have been noted by numerous social scientists concerned with the study of the police. Indeed, several detailed, insightful, and thoroughly accurate mappings of the police perspective exist.[3] For instance, learned discussions denote the various "outgroups" perceived by the police (e.g., Harris, 1973; Bayley and Mendelsohn, 1969); or the "symbolic assailants" which threaten the personal security of the police (e.g., Skolnick, 1966; Niederhoffer, 1967; Rubenstein, 1973); or the "suspicious characters" recognized by the police via incongruous (nonordinary) appearances (e.g., Sacks, 1972; Black, 1968). These reports provide the background against which the pervasive police tropism to order the world into the "for us" and "against us" camps can most clearly be seen.

Yet these studies have glossed over certain unique but together commonsensical properties of the police situation with the attendant consequence of reifying the police position that the world is in fact divided into two camps. Other than noting the great disdain and disgust held by many police officers toward certain predefined segments of the population they presumably are to serve, these studies fail to fully describe and explain the range and meaning attached to the various labels used by the police themselves to affix individual responsibility for particular actions occurring within their normal workaday world. Furthermore, previous studies do not provide much analytic aid when determining how the various typifications carried by the police are recognized as relevant and hence utilized as guides for action by a police officer in a particular situation. In short, if police typifications are seen to have origins as well as consequences, the popular distinction between "suspicious" or "threatening" and the almost mythologized "normal" or "respectable" is much too simple. It ignores not only the immediate context in which street interactions take place, but it also disregards the critical signs read by the police within the interaction itself which signify to them both the moral integrity of the person with whom they are dealing and the appropriate recipe they should follow as the interaction proceeds.[4] Therefore, any distinction of the "types" of people with whom the police deal must include an explicit consideration of the ways in which the various "types" are both immediately and conditionally identified by the police. Only in this fashion is it possible to accurately depict the labels the police construct to define, explain, and take action when going about their routine and nonroutine tasks.

To begin this analysis, consider the following typology which suggests that the police tend to view their occupational world as comprised exhaustively of three types of citizens (Van Maanen, 1974). These ideal types are: (1) "suspicious persons"—those whom the police have reason to believe may have committed a serious offense; (2) "assholes"—those who do not accept the police definition of the situation; and (3) "know nothings"—those who are not either of the first two categories but are not police and therefore, according to the police, cannot know what the police are about.

This everyday typification scheme provides a clue to the expectations, thoughts, feelings, and behaviors of the police. For example, "suspicious persons" are recognized on the basis of their appearance in public surroundings. Such an appearance is seen as a furtive, nonroutine, *de trop,* or, to use Sacks's (1972) nicely turned phrase, "dramatically torturous." Crucially, such persons, when they provide the police reason to stop and interrogate them, are treated normally in a brisk, though thoroughly professional, manner. It is not their moral worth or identity which is at issue, but rather it is a possible illegal action in their immediate or not-so-immediate past which is in question. From the patrolman's point of view, he is most interested in insuring that formal procedural issues are observed. Hence the personal production of a professional police performance is called for and is presented—at least initially.[5] On the other end of the continuum reside the "know nothings," the "average" citizens, who most generally come under police scrutiny only via their request for service. The "know nothing" may be the injured or wronged party or the seeker of banal information and as such is treated with a certain amount of deference and due respect by the patrolman.

"Assholes," by way of contrast, are stigmatized by the police and treated harshly on the basis of their failure to meet police expectations arising from the *interaction situation itself.* Of course, street interaction may quickly transform suspicious persons into know nothings and know nothings into assholes, or any combination thereof. But it is the asshole category which is most imbued with moral meaning for the patrolman—establishing for him a stained or flawed identity to attribute to the citizen upon which he can justify his sometimes malevolent acts. Consequently, the asshole may well be the recipient of what the police call "street justice"—a physical attack designed to rectify what police take as personal insult. Assholes are most vulnerable to street justice, since they, as their title implies, are not granted status as worthy human beings. Their actions are viewed by the police as stupid or senseless and their feelings as incomprehensible (if they can even be said to have feelings). Indeed, as I will show, the police consistently deny an asshole a rationale or ideology to support their actions, insisting that the behavior of an asshole is understandable only as a sudden or lifelong character aberration. On the other hand, suspicious persons are less likely candidates for street justice because, in the majority of cases, their guilt may still be in question, or, if their guilt has been in fact established, their actions are likely to seem at least comprehensible and purposeful to the police (i.e., a man steals because he needs money; a man shoots his wife because she "two-timed" him; etc.). Also, there are incentives for the suspicious person to cooperate (at least nominally) when subject to police attention.

The suspicious person may well be the most cooperative of all the people with whom the police deal on a face-to-face basis. This is, in part, because he is most desirous of presenting a normal appearance (unafraid, unruffled, and with nothing to hide), and, in part, because if he is in fact caught he does not want to add further difficulty to his already difficult position. Finally, know nothings are the least likely candidates for street justice since they represent the so-called client system and are therefore those persons whom the police are most interested in impressing through a polished, efficient, and courteous performance.

At this point, I should note that the above ideal types are anything but precise and absolute. One purpose of this article is to make at least one of these categories more explicit. But since I am dealing primarily with interior, subjective meanings negotiated in public with those whom the police interact, such typifications will always be subject to severe situational, temporal, and individually idiosyncratic restriction. Hence, an asshole in one context may be a know nothing in another, and vice versa. In other words, I am not arguing in this article that a general moral order is shared by all policemen as their personalized but homomorphic view of the world. Indeed, the moral order subscribed to by police is complex, multiple, and continually shifts back and forth between that which is individual and that which is collective. What I will argue, however, is that particular situational conditions (i.e., provocations) predispose most policemen toward certain perceptions of people which lead to the application of what can be shown to be rule-governed police actions. My objective, then, is simply to begin teasing out the underlying structure of police thought and to denote the features of what might be called the secondary reality of police work.

The remainder of this article is divided into four sections. The next section, "Patrol Work," describes very briefly certain understandings shared by street-level patrolmen as to what is involved in their work. In a sense, these understandings are akin to behavioral rules that can be seen to mobilize police action; hence they represent the grounds upon which the figure of the asshole is recognized. The following section, "Street Justice," deals with the characteristic processes involved in discovering, distinguishing, and treating the asshole. Some conclusions revolving around the relationship between the police and the asshole are suggested in the next section. And, finally, a few of the broad implications that flow from this analysis are outlined in the last section.

Patrol Work

Policing city streets entails what Hughes (1958) refers to as a "bundle of tasks." Some of these tasks are mundane; many of them are routine; and a few of them are dangerous. Indeed, patrol work defies a general job description since it includes an almost infinite set of activities—dogcatching, first-aid, assisting elderly citizens, breaking up family fights, finding lost children, pursuing a fleeing felon, directing traffic, and so forth. Yet, as in other lines of endeavor, patrolmen develop certain insider notions about their work that may or may not reflect what outsiders believe their work to be. Such notions are of course attached firmly to the various experientially based meanings the police learn to regularly ascribe to persons, places, and things—the validity of which is established, sustained, and continually reaffirmed through everyday activity. Because these meanings are, to some degree, shared by patrolmen going about similar tasks, their collective representation can be detailed and linked to certain typical practices engaged in on the street by the police. Thus, to understand the police perspective on, and treatment of, the asshole, it is necessary also to understand the manner in which the policeman conceives of his work. Below is a very short summary of certain interrelated assumptions and beliefs that patrolmen tend to develop regarding the nature of their job.

Real Police Work

Many observers have noted the pervasive police tendency to narrowly constrict their perceived task to be primarily—and to the exclusion of other alternatives—law enforcement. As Skolnick and Woodworth (1967:129) suggest evocatively, "when a policeman can engage in real police work—act out the symbolic rites of search, chase and capture—his self-image is affirmed and morale enhanced." Yet, ironically, opportunities to enact this sequence are few and far between. In fact, estimates of the time police spend actually in real police work while on patrol vary from 0 percent (as in the case of the quiet country policeman for whom a street encounter with a bona fide "criminal" would be a spectacular exception to his daily tour of duty) to about 10 or 15 percent (as in the case of the busy urban patrolman who works a seamy cityside district in which the presence of pimps, dealers, cons, and burglars, among others, are the everyday rule). Nonetheless, most of the policeman's time is spent performing rather dry, monotonous, and relatively mundane activities of a service nature—the proverbial clerk in a patrol car routinely cruising his district and awaiting dispatched calls (see Cain, 1971; Reiss, 1971; Webster, 1970; and Cumming, Cumming, and Edell, 1965, for further discussion on how the police spend their time).

Within these boundaries, notions of real police work develop to provide at least a modicum of satisfaction to the police. To a patrolman, *real police work* involves the use of skills and special abilities he believes he possesses by virtue of his unique experience and training. Furthermore, such a perspective results in minimizing the importance of other activities he is often asked regularly to perform. In fact, an ethos of "stay-low-and-avoid-trouble-unless-real-police-work-is-called-for" permeates police organizations (Van Maanen, 1973, 1974, 1975). Only tasks involving criminal apprehension are attributed symbolic importance. For the most part, other tasks, if they cannot be avoided, are performed (barring interruption) with ceremonial dispatch and disinterest.

Territoriality

A central feature of policing at the street level is the striking autonomy maintained (and guarded jealously) by patrolmen working the beat. All patrol work is conducted by solo officers or partnerships (within a squad to whom they are linked) responsible for a given plot of territory. Over time, they come to know, in the most familiar and penetrating manner, virtually every passageway—whether alley, street, or seldom-used path—located in their sector. From such knowledge of this social stage comes the corresponding evaluations of what particular conditions are to be considered good or bad, safe or unsafe, troubled or calm, usual or unusual, and so on. Of course, these evaluations are also linked to temporal properties associated with the public use of a patrolman's area of responsibility. As Rubenstein (1973) suggests, the territorial perspective carried by patrolmen establishes the basic normative standard for the proper use of place. And those perceived by patrolmen to be beyond the pale regarding their activities in space and time are very likely to warrant police attention.

Maintaining the Edge

Charged with enforcing ambiguous generalized statutes and operating from an autonomous, largely isolated position within the city, it is not surprising that police have internalized a standard of conduct which dictates that they must control and regulate all situations in which they find themselves. At one level, police feel they have the right to initiate, terminate, or otherwise direct all encounters with members of the public. Yet such perceptions penetrate more broadly into the social scheme of things, for police feel furthermore that the public order is a product of their ability to exercise control. The absence of trouble on their beat becomes, therefore, a personalized objective providing intimate feedback as to one's worth as a patrolman. Activity which may threaten the perceived order becomes intolerable, for it signifies to the patrolman that his advantage over the conduct of others (his "edge") is in question. It is a source of embarrassment in front of a public audience, and sometimes it is considered a disgrace to the police uniform if it is viewed by one's peers or departmental superiors. Clearly, such activity cannot be allowed to persist, for it may indicate both to a patrolman's colleagues and to his superiors that the officer no longer cares for his job and has, consequently, lost the all-important respect of those he polices (endangering, it is thought, other policemen who might work the same district). Hence, to "maintain one's edge" is a key concept vis-à-vis the "how to" of police work. And, as all policemen know, to let down the facade (for they do recognize the contrived nature of the front) is to invite disrespect, chaos, and crime.

The Moral Mandate

In light of the above three features of the police frame, it should be clear that police are both representatives of the moral order and a part of it. They are thus committed ("because it is right") to maintain their collective face as protectorates of the right and respectable against the wrong and the not-so-respectable. Situations in which this face is challenged—regardless of origin—are likely to be responded to in unequivocal terms. For example, Cain

(1971) writes that when the authority of an officer is questioned by a member of the nonpolice public, the officer has three broad responses available to him. He may (1) physically attack the offender; (2) swallow his pride and ignore the offender; or (3) manufacture a false excuse for the arrest of the offender. What this suggests is a highly personalized view on the part of the police as to their moral position and responsibility, one in which an attempt on the part of the citizen to disregard the wishes of a policeman may be viewed by the police as a profaning of the social and legal system itself. Such an act can also be seen to provoke moral and private indignation on the part of the officer as an individual, thus providing him with another *de rigueur* excuse to locate an appropriate remedy. Since the police personally believe that they are capable of making correct decisions regarding the culpability of an involved party, justice is likely, in the case of an offense to the moral sensibilities of a police officer, to be enacted quickly, parsimoniously, and self-righteously—whether it be the relatively trivial swift kick in the pants or the penultimate tragedy involved in the taking of a life. Thus, the moral mandate felt by the police to be their just right at the societal level is translated and transformed into occupational and personal terms and provides both the justification and legitimation for specific acts of street justice.

This truncated picture of the occupational frame involved in the doing of police work provides the rubric upon which we now can examine the making of an asshole. As one would expect, assholes are not afforded the protection of the more structured relationships police maintain with others of their categories of persons—the suspicious and the know nothings. Rather, they fall outside this fragile shelter, for their actions are seen as "senseless," so "aimless" and "irrational" that recognizable and acceptable human motives are difficult for the police to discover (i.e., from the patrolmen's perspective, there are not legitimate reasons to distrust, disagree with, make trouble for, or certainly hate the police). In this sense, it is precisely the "pointlessness" of an individual's behavior that makes him an asshole and subjects him to the police version of street justice.

Street Justice

Policeman to motorist stopped for speeding:
 "May I see your driver's license, please?"

Motorist:
 "Why the hell are you picking on me and not somewhere else looking for some real criminals?"

Policeman:
 "Cause you're an asshole, that's why . . . but I didn't know that until you opened your mouth."

The above sea story represents the peculiar reality with which patrolmen believe they must contend. The world is in part (and, to policemen, a large part) populated by individuals to whom an explanation for police behavior cannot be made, for, as the police say, "assholes don't listen to reason." The purpose of this section is to explore the commonplace and commonsense manner in which the tag asshole arises, sticks, and guides police action during a street encounter. This stigmatization process is divided into three stages which, while analytically distinct, are highly interactive and apt to occur in the real world of policing almost simultaneously. For convenience only, then, these phases are labeled *affront, clarification,* and *remedy.*

Throughout this discussion it should be remembered that the asshole is not necessarily a suspected law violator—although the two often overlap, thus providing double trouble, so to speak, for the labeled. Importantly, the police view of the asshole as deviant is a product of the immediate transaction between the two and not a product of an act preceding the transaction. This is not to say, however, that certain classes in society—for example, the young, the black, the militant, the homosexual—are not "fixed" by the police as a sort of permanent asshole grouping. Indeed, they are. Yet such bounded *a priori* categories can do policemen little good—except perhaps when dealing with the racial or bohemian obvious—for such stereotypes are frequently misleading and dysfunctional (e.g., the "hippie" who is a detective's prized informant; the black dressed in a purple jumpsuit who happens to be a mayor's top aide; the sign-carrying protestor who is an undercover FBI agent). And, even in cases in which *a priori character* judgments are a part of the decision to stop an individual, the asshole label, if it is to play a determining role in the encounter, must arise anew. That is to say, if the asshole distinction is to have a *concrete* as opposed to *abstract* meaning, it must in some manner be tied fundamentally and irresolutely to observable social action occurring in the presence of the labeling officer.

Certainly, a policeman's past experience with an individual or with a recognizable group will influence his street behavior. For example, a rookie soon discovers (as a direct consequence of his initiation into a department) that blacks, students, Mexicans, reporters, lawyers, welfare workers, researchers, prostitutes, and gang members are not to be trusted, are unpredictable, and are usually "out-to-get-the-police." He may even sort these "outsiders" into various categories indicative of the risk he believes they present to him or the implied contrast they have with his own life-style and beliefs. Yet, without question, these categories will never be exhaustive—although the absolute size of what patrolmen call their "shit lists" may grow over the years. Consequently, to understand the police interpretation and meaning of the term "asshole" we must look directly into the field situations in which it originates.

Affront: Challenge

When a police officer approaches a civilian to issue a traffic citation or to inquire as to the whys and wherefores of one's presence or simply to pass the time of day, he directly brings the power of the state to bear on the situation and hence makes vulnerable to disgrace, embarrassment, and insult that power. Since the officer at the street level symbolizes the presence of the Levi-athan in the everyday lives of the citizenry, such interactions take on dramatic properties far different from ordinary citizen-to-citizen transactions (Man-ning, 1974a; Silver, 1967). In a very real sense, the patrolman-to-citizen exchanges are moral contests in which the authority of the state is either con-firmed, denied, or left in doubt. To the patrolman, such contests are not to be taken lightly, for the authority of the state is also his personal authority, and is, of necessity, a matter of some concern to him. To deny or raise doubt about his legitimacy is to shake the very ground upon which his self-image and corresponding views are built.

An affront, as it is used here, is a challenge to the policeman's authority, control, and definition of the immediate situation. As seen by the police, an affront is simply a response on the part of the other which indicates to them that their position and authority in the interaction are not being taken seri-ously. It may occur with or without intent. Whether it is the vocal student who claims to "know his rights," the stumbling drunk who says he has had "only two beers," or the lady of the evening who believes she is being ques-tioned only because she is wearing "sexy clothes," the police will respond in particular ways to those who challenge or question their motive or right to intervene in situations that they believe demand police intervention. Clearly, overt and covert challenges to police authority will not go unnoticed. In fact, they can be seen to push the encounter to a new level wherein any further slight to an officer, however subtle, provides sufficient evidence to a patrol-man that he may indeed be dealing with a certifiable asshole and that the sit-uation is in need of rapid clarification. From this standpoint, an affront can be seen, therefore, as disrupting the smooth flow of the police performance. The argumentative motorist, the pugnacious drunk, the sometimes ludicrous behavior of combatants in a "family beef" all interfere [with], and hence make more difficult, the police task. Of course, some officers relish such encounters. In this sense, ironically, the asshole gives status to the police rather than takes it away. However, since the label is itself a moral charge (and it need not be made salient or verbally expressed), it is open theoretically for rebuttal and evidence may or may not be forthcoming which will substantiate or contradict the charge. Such evidence is gathered in the next analytic stage.

Clarification: Confrontation

Based upon a perceived affront, the patrolman must then attempt to determine precisely the kind of person with whom he is engaged. It is no lon-ger an idle matter to him in which his private conceptions of people can be kept private as he goes about his business. But the patrolman is now in a posi-tion wherein he may discover that his taken-for-granted authority on the street is not exactly taken for granted by another. Two commonsensical issues are critical at this point in an encounter. *First,* the officer must determine whether or not the individual under question could have, under the present circum-stances, acted in an alternative fashion. To wit, did the perceived affront occur by coercion or accident through no fault of the person? Did the person even know he was dealing with a police officer? Was he acting with a gun at his head? And so on. *Second,* and equally important, given that the person could have acted differently, the officer must determine whether or not the individual was aware of the consequences that might follow his action. In other words, was the action frivolous, naive, unserious, and not meant to offend? Did the person know that his actions were likely to be interpreted offensively by the police? The answers to these two questions provide patrolmen with material (or lack of it) to construct and sustain an asshole definition. Let us examine in some depth these questions, for they raise the very issue of personal responsibility which is at the nexus of the asshole definition.[6]

McHugh (1969) argues persuasively that the social construction of deviant categories is a matter of elimination which proceeds logically through a series of negotiated offers and responses designed to fix responsibility for a perceived deviant act (i.e., a deviant act requires a charge before it can be said to have happened). Police follow a similar paradigm when filling, emptying, or otherwise attending to their person categories. Again, the first item to be determined in this process is the issue of whether or not the person had alternative means available to him of which he could reasonably be expected to be aware. For example, the speeding motorist who, when pulled to the side of the road, could be excused for his abusive language if it were discovered by the officer that the motorist's wife was at the same time in the back seat giving birth to a child. Similarly, juveniles "hanging out" on a public street corner at certain times of the day may be sometimes overlooked if the police feel that "those kids don't have anyplace to go." On the other hand, if it can be determined that there is no unavoidable reason behind the affronting action, the individual risks being labeled an asshole. The drunken and remorseless driver, the wife who harangues the police officer for mistreating her husband after she herself requested police service to break up a family fight, or the often-warned teenager who makes a nuisance of himself by flagrantly parading in public after curfew are all persons whom the police believe could have and should have acted differently. Their acts were not inevitable, and it could be expected that they had available to them conventional alternatives.

Given that there are no compelling deterministic accounts readily available to the patrolman to excuse a particular affront, the officer must still make a judgment about the offender's motive. In other words, as the second issue listed above suggests, the policeman must decide whether or not the person knows what he is doing. Could the person be expected to know of the consequences which follow an affront to an officer of the law? Indeed, does the person even realize that what he is doing is likely to provoke police action? Could this particular person be expected to know better? All are questions related to the establishment of a motive for action. For example, the stylized and ceremonial upright third finger when attached to the hand of a thirty-year-old man is taken by the police very differently from the same gesture attached to the hand of a four-year-old child. Loud and raucous behavior in some parts of a city may be ignored if the police feel "the people there don't know any better." Or the claim that one is Jesus Christ resurrected and is out to do battle with the wages of sin may indicate to the police that they are either in the presence of a "dope-crazed radical hippie freak" or a "soft-brained harmless mental case," depending, perhaps, on the offender's age. If the person is young, for instance, responsibility is likely to be individualized—"it is his fault"; however, if the person is old, responsibility is likely to be institutionalized—"he can't help it, he's a nut."

Summarily, the police have available to them two principles of clarification. One concerns the means available to a person guilty of an affront, and the other concerns the purposes behind the affront itself. If the affront is viewed as unavoidable or unintended, the person is unlikely to be subjected to shabby or harsh treatment at the hands of the police. The asshole, however, is one who is viewed as culpable and blameworthy for his affronting action, and, as the next section details, he will be dealt with by the police in ways they feel appropriate.

Remedy: Solution

The above portrait of the clarification principles utilized by police in labeling assholes suggests that certain typical police responses can be displayed by a simple fourfold typology. Figure 1 depicts the relationship between the police officer's assessment of responsibility for the affront and denotes, within each cell, the typical police response given the various possible assessments.

Cell A represents the subject case of this essay since it involves a flagrant (inexcusable) disregard for the sentiments of the police. To the police, those falling into this category are unmistakably assholes and are therefore prominent candidates to be the recipients of street justice—the aim of which is to punish or castigate the individual for a moral transgression. Persons placed in this category are also the most likely to be placed under questionable arrest. This is not so because of the original intent of the encounter (which often, by itself, is trivial) but rather because of the serious extralegal means utilized by the police to enforce their particular view of the situation upon the recalcitrant asshole—"hamming-up" or "thumping" (beating).[7] And, as Reiss (1971) suggests, the use of force is not a philosophical question to the police but rather one of who, where, when, and how much.

		Does the person know what he is doing?	
		Yes	No
Could the person act differently	Yes	A Castigate	B Teach
under the circumstances?	No	C Ignore	D Isolate

Figure 1

The use of such means requires of course that the officer manufacture post facto a legally defensible account of his action in order to, in the vernacular of the day, "cover his ass."[8] Such accounts in legalese most often take the form of "disorderly conduct," "assaulting a police officer," "the use of loud and abusive language in the presence of women and children," "disturbing the peace," or the almost legendary—due to its frequent use—"resisting arrest." The asshole from this position is subject to a police enactment of double jeopardy—justice without trial in the streets and justice, perhaps with trial, in the courts. And regardless of the outcome in the latter case, there is usually only one loser. I should emphasize, however, that I am not saying the behavior of the asshole may not be brutish, nasty, and itself thoroughly vicious. I am simply suggesting that behavior violating extralegal moral codes used by police to order their interactions—whether it be inconsiderate, barbarous, or otherwise—will be responded to in what police believe to be appropriate ways.

Cell B of Figure 1 also represents a serious affront to police integrity, and it too may be an affront which calls for an extra-legal response. An illustration provided by the remarks of a patrolman is useful in this context:

> Those goddamn kids got to learn sooner or later that we won't take a lot of shit around Cardoza (a local college campus). Next time I see one of those punks waving a Viet Cong flag I'm gonna negotiate the little bastard back into an alley and kick his rosy red ass so hard he ain't gonna carry nothing for awhile. Those kids gotta be made to see that they can't get away with this type of thing.

Whether or not such a prediction was actually carried out does not matter, for the quotation itself indicates that "teaching" occupies a particularly prominent position in the police repertoire of possible responses. Thus, the uncooperative and surly motorist finds his sobriety rudely questioned, or the smug and haughty college student discovers himself stretched over the hood of a patrol car and the target of a mortifying and brusque body search. The object of such degradation ceremonies is simply to reassert police control and demonstrate to the citizen that his behavior is considered inappropriate. Teaching techniques are numerous, with threat, ridicule, and harassment among the more widely practiced. Other examples are readily available, such as the morally toned lectures meted out to those who would attempt to bribe, lie, or otherwise worm their way out of what a policeman sees to be a legitimate traffic citation, the traditional—but vanishing—"kick in the ass" administered to a youngster caught stealing an apple or cutting school. The intent in all these cases is clear. The person must be taught a lesson. And whether the teaching occurs in public or in the back of an alley, the person must be shown the error of his ways. He has acted perhaps out of ignorance, but nevertheless the police feel they must demonstrate that they will not casually overlook the action. However, I should note that the person in this category will remain an asshole in the eyes of the police until he has apparently learned his lesson to the satisfaction of the officers on the scene. Here a display of remorse is no doubt crucial to the police.[9]

Cell C represents the case in which the police are likely to excuse the affront due to the extenuating circumstances surrounding the affront. When it is clear to the police that there are indeed mitigating conditions, their response is to ignore the error—pretend, as it were, that such an affront never happened. For example, it is understandable to the police that the victim of a mugging may be somewhat abusive toward them when they interrogate him just after the crime (although there is a fine line to be drawn here). Similarly, if a teenage male vigorously defends the chaste and virtuous intentions of he and his girlfriend while questioned by the police in a concealed and cozy corner of a public park, it is understood by the police that the boy has few other acceptable alternative lines available. The police response is typically to adopt a somewhat bemused tolerance policy toward actions which under different circumstances may have produced the orb and scepter.

Finally, cell D in figure 1 concerns the case of an affront which police take to lie beyond the responsibility of the actor. While such action cannot normally be allowed to continue, the moral indignation felt by police is tempered by the understanding that the person is not aware nor could be easily made aware of the rule-breaking nature of his actions. The police response is to isolate the offender, not to punish him. Thus, the "mental case" is shipped to the county hospital for observation and treatment; the "foul-mouthed child" is returned to those responsible for his behavior; the out-of-state tourist prowling an area close to his hotel but frequented by prostitutes is informed of his "oversight" and told in unmistakable terms to vacate the territory. It is important to note that police feel justified in using only enough force or coercive power to seal off the offender from public (and, by implication, their own) view. To use more force would be considered unreasonable.

It has been my purpose here to suggest that much of what the general public might see as capricious, random, or unnecessary behavior on the part of the police is, in fact, governed by certain rather pervasive interpretive rules which lie close enough to the surface such that they can be made visible. Certain police actions, following the model presented above, can be seen, then, to be at least logical if not legal. Furthermore, much of the power of these rules stems from their tacit or taken-for-granted basis. Indeed, were the rules to be questioned, the game could not continue. However, while these rules are applied in a like fashion by all police in a given interactional episode, the specific situated behavior of a citizen that is taken as a sign which leads to isolating, ignoring, teaching, or castigating a given individual is no doubt quite different across patrolmen. Here, the police game continues as it does because, in part, the asshole label swallows up and hides whatever individual differences exist across patrolmen. Thus, language neatly solves the problem of misunderstanding that would arise among the police were the rules to be articulated and standards sought as to how they should be applied.

Some Conclusions

It is possible, of course, to see the preceding ritualized sequence as an isolated and rarely indulged propensity of the police. However, in this section, I will argue that indeed such a sequence and the corresponding identification and treatment of the asshole is intimately related to the police production and represents an aspect of policing that is near the core of the patrolman's definition of his task. In essence, the existence of an asshole demonstrates and confirms the police view of the importance and worth of themselves both as individuals and as members of a necessary occupation. However, several other, somewhat more practical and everyday features of police work insure the ominous presence of the asshole in the police world.

First, the labeling of individuals as assholes can be seen as a technique (although invisible to most) useful to patrolmen in providing distance between themselves and their segmented audiences—to be liked by the people in the street is, in the defensive rhetoric of patrolmen, a sign of a bad cop. By profaning and degrading the actions of another, social distance can be established and maintained—a guarantee, so to speak, that the other will not come uncomfortably close. Thus, the asshole simplifies and orders the policeman's world and continually verifies his classification scheme regarding those who are "like him" and those who are "unlike him." Relatedly the labeling serves also as an immediate call to action, denoting a consensually approved (by the police culture) means for remedying "out-of-kilter" situations.

Second, the label not only describes and prescribes but it also explains and makes meaningful the statements and actions of others. In fact, an entire set of action expectations (i.e., "they are out to make the police look bad") can be ascribed as motives to the asshole. In this sense, the police function in street interaction is not unlike that of a psychiatrist diagnosing a patient. Both explain perceived deviancy in terms of a characterological genesis. Hence, the label implies that a different, inappropriate, and strange motivational scheme is used by the "type of person" known as an asshole. In this manner, an act is made understandable by stripping away whatever meaning might be attributed to it by the actor. Thus, to make sense of the act is to assume that it does not make sense—that it is stupid, irrational, wrong, deranged, or dangerous. Any other assumption would be too threatening.

Third, the labeling process must be viewed as serving an occupational purpose. I suggested previously that the urban policeman is primarily a keeper of the peace yet he defines his job in terms of law enforcement. Furthermore, as others have noted, many patrolmen try to convert peacekeeping situations to those of law enforcement (e.g., Bittner, 1967, 1970; Wilson, 1967; Piliavin and Briar, 1964). Since real police work is seldom available, marginally legitimate arrests of assholes provide a patrolman excitement and the opportunity to engage one's valued skills. Perhaps the police cliché, "a good beat is full of deadbeats," reflects structural support for the asshole-labeling phenomena.

Fourth, the discovery and subsequent action taken when the police encounter the asshole provides an expressive outlet—almost ceremonial in its predictability—for much of the frustration policing engenders. To the patrolman, one particular asshole symbolizes all those that remain "out there" untouched, untaught, and unpunished. Such emotional outbursts provide, therefore, a reaffirmation of the moral repugnance of the asshole. Whether the officer responds by placing the handcuffs on the person's wrists such that they cut off circulation (and not incidentally cause intense, almost excruciating pain) or pushes a destitute soul through a shop window, these actions release some of the pent-up energies stored up over a period in which small but cumulative indignities are suffered by the police at the hands of the community elites, the courts, the politicians, the uncaught crooks, the press, and numerous others. The asshole stands, then, as a ready ersatz for those whom the police will never—short of a miracle—be in a position to directly encounter and confront.

Finally, the asshole can be seen as a sort of reified other, representing all those persons who would question, limit, or otherwise attempt to control the police. From this standpoint, knowing that there are assholes at large serves perhaps to rally and solidify police organizations around at least one common function. Thus, the police are, to a limited degree, unified by their disdain of those who would question their activities. Perhaps one could say that the police represent what Simmel (1950) referred to as an "invisible church" in which the faithful are fused together through their common relation to an outside phenomenon.

Consequently, assholes are not simply obscure and fanciful figments of the bedeviled imagination of the police. On the contrary, they define to a surprising degree what the police are about. And while the internal satisfactions and rewards involved in "slamming around" an asshole may seem esoteric if not loathsome to the outsider, to the patrolman who makes his living on the city streets it is not.

Postscript

The foregoing description and explanation of an overlooked aspect of urban policing highlights the fact that the police officer is anything but a Weberian bureaucrat whose discretion and authority are checked rigidly. The collective myth surrounding the rulebound "policeman-as-public-servant" has no doubt never been very accurate. By virtue of their independence from superiors, their carefully guarded autonomy in the field, their deeply felt notions about real police work and those who would interfere with it, and their increasing isolation from the public they serve (as a result of mobile patrol, rotating shifts, greater specialization of the police, and the growing segmentation of the society at large with its own specialized and emerging subcultures), police-community "problems" will not disappear. And, since the police view their critics as threatening and as persons who generally should be taught or castigated, one could argue that the explosive potential of citizen-police encounters will grow.

Additionally, if the police become more sensitive to public chastisement, it could be expected that something of a self-fulfilling prophecy may well become a more important factor in the street than it is presently. That is to say, if the police increasingly view their public audience as foes—whose views are incomprehensible if not degenerate or subversive—it is likely that they will also magnify clues which will sustain the stereotype of citizen-as-enemy escalating therefore the percentage of street interactions which result in improper arrest and verbal or physical attack. Thus, the fantasy may well become the reality as stereotypes are transformed into actualities. In fact, the future may make prophetic Brendan Behan's half-jesting remark that he had never seen a situation so bad that a policeman couldn't make it worse.

To conclude, this article has implied that there is a virtual—if unintended—license in this society granted to police. In particular, when it comes to the asshole, police actions are not governed at all, given the present policies of allowing the watchers to watch themselves. It would seem that something is amiss, and, if the practical morality in urban areas is not exactly inverted, it is at least tilted. If the asshole is indeed a critical aspect of policing, then there is serious risk involved in the movement to "professionalize" the police. As other observers have remarked, successful occupational professionalization inevitably leads to increased autonomy and ultimately increased power for members of the occupation (Becker, 1962; Hughes, 1965). Professionalism may well widen the police mandate in society and therefore amplify the potential of the police to act as moral entrepreneurs. From this perspective, what is required at present is not professional police but accountable police.

NOTES

[1] All police quotes are taken from field notes I compiled of conversations and observations taking place during a year of participant observation in what I have referred to anonymously in my writings as the Union City Police Department (a large, metropolitan force employing over 1,500 uniformed officers). The quotes are as accurate as my ear, memory, and notes allow. . . . I should note, also, that in this essay I use the terms "police," "police officer," "patrolman," and "policemen" somewhat interchangeably. However, unless I indicate otherwise, my comments are directed solely toward the street-level officer—the cop on the beat—and not toward his superiors, administrators, or colleagues in the more prestigeful detective bureaus.

[2] I chose the term "asshole" for the title of this essay simply because it is a favorite of working policemen (at least in Union City). The interested reader might check my assumption by a casual glance at what several others have to say about this linguistic matter. Most useful in this regard are the firsthand accounts police have themselves provided and can be found, for example, in Terkel (1968, 1974); Drodge (1973); Maas (1973); Olsen (1974); Whittemore (1973); Walker (1969). I should note as well that such labeling proceeds not only because of its functional use to the police but also because it helps officers to capture perceptual distinctions (i.e., labels are "good to think"). Thus assholes are conceptually part of the ordered world of police—the statuses, the rules, the norms, and the contrasts that constitute their social system.

[3] See, for example: Rubenstein's (1973) report on the Philadelphia police; Westley's (1970) study of a midwestern police department in the late 1940s; Wilson's (1968) global accounting of the police perspective; Reiss's (1971) research into police-community interactions; LaFave's (1965) treatment of the police decision to arrest; Cain's (1973) and Banton's (1964) observations on the British police; and Berkeley's (1969) cross-cultural view of policing in democratic societies. What comes out of these excellent works is tantamount to a reaffirmation of Trotsky's famous dictum, "There is but one international and that is the police."

[4] For example, Skolnick's (1966) idea that policemen are "afraid" of certain categories of persons distorts the nature of the occupational perspective. More to the point, policemen are disgusted by certain people, envious of others, and ambivalent toward most. At times they may even vaguely admire certain criminals—those that the British police call "good villains" (Cain, 1971). Fear must of course be given its due, but the occasion of fear hangs more upon unforeseen situational contingencies (the proverbial dark alley, desolate city park, or underlife tavern) than upon certain individuals.

[5] Certainly this may not always be the case. For example, some "suspected persons," due to the nature of their alleged crime (e.g., child molestation, drug dealing, indecent exposure, political sabotage, assault [or worse] upon a police officer, etc.) are likely to provide a strong sense of moral indignation on the part of the arresting (or stopping) officers. In such cases, once identity has been established to the satisfaction of the police (and it should be noted that errors are not unknown—particularly in these volatile cases), the person suspected is transformed immediately into an asshole and is subject to a predictably harsh treatment. Thus, in effect the label arises from an offense which occurred outside the immediate presence of the officers. However, since the spoiled identity must be reestablished anew in the immediate surroundings, the properties of the "affront" correspond analytically to the more familiar case outlines in the text. And while the distinction has theoretical value regarding the norms of the police culture (i.e., that it is not the denounced per se that is important, but rather it is the denouncer that matters—"says who?"), its practical implications are questionable because patrolmen rarely encounter such situations.

[6] In most regards, the asshole is a classic case of the deviant—although not transituationally so. See Matza (1969), Becker (1963), and Cohen (1965) for a systematic elaboration of the ideas which underpin this analysis.

[7] By the term "extralegal" I am merely implying that the formal police mandate excludes such moral considerations from actions inducing decisions made by officers on the street. The notion of professional policing makes this explicit when it is suggested that patrolmen must act impersonally without regard to individual prejudice.

[8] The "cover-your-ass" phenomena associated with urban policing is described in more depth in Van Maanen (1974). See also Manning (1974b) for a theoretical view of the more general construct, the police lie; and Chevigny (1968) for a presentation of numerous disturbing case studies.

[9] Arrests are, of course, sometimes used to teach someone a lesson. However, police believe that in many cases the asshole will arrange his release before the patrolman will have completed the paperwork necessitated by the arrest. And since the affront was moral, the legal justification to "make the case" in court may be lacking. Thus, the classroom more often than not is in the street. Given the opportunity to teach the asshole either by "turning him in" or "doing him in," most police would choose the latter.

REFERENCES

Banton, Michael (1964). *The Policeman in the Community*. New York: Basic Books.

Bayley, D. H., & Mendelsohn, H. (1969). *Minorities and the Police: Confrontation in America*. New York: Free Press.

Becker, Howard S. (1962). The nature of a profession. In *Education for the Professions*, 61st Yearbook of the Society for the Study of Education, Part 2. Chicago: University of Chicago Press.

——— (1963). *Outsiders.* New York: Free Press.

Berkeley, George E. (1969). *The Democratic Policeman.* Boston: Beacon Press.

Bittner, Egon (1970). *The Functions of the Police in Modern Society.* Washington, DC: United States Government Printing Office.

——— (1967). The police on skid row. *American Sociological Review,* 32:699–715.

Black, Donald (1968). Police Encounters and Social Organization: An Observational Study. Unpublished Ph.D. Dissertation, University of Michigan.

Cain, Maureen (1973). *Society and the Policeman's Role.* London: Kegan Paul.

——— (1971). On the beat: Interactions and relations in rural and urban police forces. In Cohen, S. (ed.). *Images of Deviance.* Middlesex, England: Penguin Books.

Chevigny, Paul (1968). *Police Power: Police Abuses in New York.* New York: Pantheon.

Cohen, Albert K. (1965). The sociology of the deviant act. *American Sociological Review,* 30:5–14.

Cumming, E., Cumming, I., & Edell, L. (1965). The policeman as philosopher, guide and friend. *Social Problems,* 12:276–286.

Drodge, Edward F. (1973). *The Patrolman: A Cop's Story.* New York: New American Library.

Harris, Richard N. (1973). *The Police Academy: An Inside View.* New York: John Wiley & Sons.

Hughes, Everett C. (1965). Professions. In Lynn, K. S. (ed.). *Professions in America.* Boston: Beacon Press.

——— (1958). *Men and Their Work.* Glencoe, IL: Free Press.

LaFave, W. R. (1965). *Arrest: The Decision to Take a Suspect into Custody.* Boston: Little, Brown and Company.

Maas, Peter (1973). *Serpico.* New York: The Viking Press.

Manning, Peter K. (1971). The police: Mandate, strategies and appearances. In Douglas, J. (ed.). *Crime and Justice in America.* Indianapolis: Bobbs-Merrill.

——— (1974a). Dramatic aspects of policing: Selected propositions. *Sociology and Social Research,* 59 (October).

——— (1974b). Police lying. *Urban Life,* 3 (October).

Matza, David (1969). *Becoming Deviant.* Englewood Cliffs, NJ: Prentice-Hall.

McHugh, Peter (1969). A common-sense perception of deviancy. In Douglas, J. (ed.). *Deviance and Respectability.* New York: Basic Books.

Niederhoffer, Arthur (1967). *Behind the Shield.* Garden City, NY: Doubleday.

Olsen, Jack (1974). *Sweet Street.* New York: Simon and Schuster.

Piliavin, I., & Briar, S. (1964). Police encounters with juveniles. *American Journal of Sociology,* 70:206–214.

Reiss, Albert J. (1971). *The Police and the Public.* New Haven: Yale University Press.

Rubenstein, Jonathan (1973). *City Police.* New York: Farrar, Straus and Giroux.

Sacks, Harvey (1972). Notes on police assessment of moral character. In Sudnow, D. (ed.). *Studies in Social Interaction.* New York: The Free Press.

Silver, Allen (1967). The demand for order in civil society. In Bordua, D. (ed.). *The Police: Six Sociological Essays.* New York: John Wiley & Sons.

Simmel, Georg (1950). *The Sociology of Georg Simmel.* Translated, edited, and with an introduction by Kurt H. Wolff. New York: The Free Press.

Skolnick, Jerome (1966). *Justice Without Trial.* New York: John Wiley & Sons.

Skolnick, Jerome, & Woodworth, J. R. (1967). Bureaucracy, information and social control. In Bordua, D. (ed.). *The Police: Six Sociological Essays.* New York: John Wiley & Sons.

Terkel, Studs (1968). *Division Street: America.* New York: Random House.
———— (1974). *Working.* New York: Pantheon.
Van Maanen, John (1972). Pledging the Police: A Study of Selected Aspects of Recruit Socialization in a Large Police Department. Unpublished Ph.D. Dissertation, University of California, Irvine.
———— (1973). Observations on the making of policemen. *Human Organizations,* 32:407–418.
———— (1974). Working the streets: A developmental view of police behavior. In Jacobs, H. (ed.). *Reality and Reform: The Criminal Justice System.* Beverly Hills: Sage Publications.
———— (1975). Police socialization. *Administrative Science Quarterly,* 20:207–228.
Walker, T. Mike (1969). *Voices from the Bottom of the World: A Policeman's Journal.* New York: Grove Press.
Webster, J. A. (1970). Police task and time study. *Journal of Criminal Law, Criminology and Police Science,* 61:94–100.
Westley, William (1970). *Violence and the Police.* Cambridge: MIT Press (originally a Ph.D. Dissertation, University of Chicago, 1951).
Whittemore, L. H. (1973). *The Super Cops.* New York: Stein and Day.
Wilson, James Q. (1967). Police morale, reform and citizen respect: The Chicago case. In Bordua, D. (ed.). *The Police: Six Sociological Essays.* New York: John Wiley & Sons.
———— (1968). *Varieties of Police Behavior.* Cambridge: Harvard University Press.

9

Addressing Police Misconduct
The Role of Citizen Complaints

Jeff Rojek, Scott H. Decker, & Allen E. Wagner

Introduction

The rule of law constrains the behavior of public agencies in American society. In no other case is this more apparent than for law enforcement agencies. The police are constrained by a variety of factors as they endeavor to go about their job. Perhaps it is the irony that the police sometimes act outside the law as they enforce the law, which makes police misconduct particularly troublesome in a democratic society. From a more pragmatic perspective, the police are dependent upon citizen cooperation to fulfill their crime control mandate. Absent such cooperation, the identification and apprehension of criminal suspects becomes a nearly impossible task, and misconduct undermines citizen cooperation.

One only need look at the national news media over the past couple of years to find cases of misconduct that question police legitimacy. In 1998, a New York City police officer was convicted of sexually assaulting a Haitian immigrant with an object. The Los Angeles Police Department experienced one of its worst cases of police misconduct stemming from officer corruption in a divisional gang unit (LAPD, 2000). Citizen complaints of officer misconduct, however, rarely rise to this level of seriousness or media coverage. The day-to-day cases of officer misconduct examined by police review systems range from complaints about an officer's attitude to complaints of excessive use of force. Nonetheless, the review of this wide range of complaints is an important function of a civilian law enforcement agency.

This article examines the process by which a civilian complaint against the police emerges and is resolved. The first half of this article gives discussion to the role of the police and how misconduct arises within this context.

Prepared especially for *Critical Issues in Policing* by Jeff Rojek, Scott H. Decker, and Allen E. Wagner.

Included in this discussion is an overview of the explanations for this misconduct. The latter half of the article is then directed at the citizen complaint process, acknowledging some of the pitfalls in this effort.

The Police Role and Complaints

Herman Goldstein cautions that "anyone attempting to construct a workable definition of the police role will typically come away with old images shattered and a new-found appreciation for the intricacies of police work" (1977:21). While definitions of the police role are divergent, the following list provided by former F.B.I. Director J. Edgar Hoover represents an often cited framework (Niederhoffer, 1969:7):

1. protection of life and property;

2. preservation of the peace;

3. prevention of crime;

4. detection and arrest of violators of the law;

5. enforcement of laws and ordinances; and

6. safeguarding the rights of individuals.

This list of police goals (or one similar) has been taught to recruit officers for at least a generation, and no one seriously doubts their foundation in the law. But the goals, laudable as they are, do not accurately reflect the vagaries of the police role.

What, then, is the role? Walker (1983:56–57) posits that, however one defines role, it is complex and ambiguous and leads to conflict within the individual officer and between the police and the public. Such conflicts often lead to the filing of a complaint against the police. Clearly, the diffuse and often contradictory roles of the police precipitate many police-citizen misunderstandings. Different expectations regarding the police role, differences that stem in part from the discretion exercised by officers, lead to citizen complaints.

The multifaceted nature of police discretion is best exemplified by Bittner's (1990) discussion of police working in skid row areas. The enforcement of minor offenses on skid row is often overridden by the desire to maintain the peace. In summation of skid row practices, Bittner states:

> The basic routine of keeping the peace on skid row involves a process of matching the resources of control with situational exigencies. The overall objective is to reduce the total amount of risk in the area. In this, practicality plays a considerably more important role than legal norms. Precisely because patrolmen see legal reasons for coercive action much more widely distributed on skid row than could ever be matched by interventions, they intervene not in the interest of law enforcement but in the interest of producing relative tranquility and order on the street. (1990:55)

Though the situational application of the law by police officers often has an internal logic, to the outsider it can often look arbitrary, and perhaps abusive.

This "discretionary" aspect of police work is sometimes at the cutting edge of dissonance between the police (indeed, individual police officers) and the public. Consider the citizen; the public has its own definition and expectations of the police role. Like police work, these expectations vary from community to community, individual to individual. Essentially, the general public believes that the police should enforce the law, prevent crime, and maintain order. But, as Ward points out, "a group of drug addicts might have different expectations than the local Chamber of Commerce with regard to the way policemen institute searches" (1975:215).

The officer, therefore, must learn to react to the situation and the individuals involved, keeping in mind the expected gains or losses. The officer must determine which of several options are open and then choose between one or more alternatives that may be at variance with the expectations of some of those concerned, including other police officers. Crank (1998:29) underscores this variation in expectations when he observes, "Line officers are not presented with a single monolithic environment in which they conduct their work, but instead confront a series of environments, each with its own particular expectations of the police." It can be easily observed that the ambiguous nature of the police role almost invites criticism. Perez (1994:36) notes, "police malpractice, in a real sense, is created by several dynamics that impact these average men and women who are trying to accomplish their multiple, 'impossible tasks.'"

Police Misconduct

In 1903, a New York City police commissioner turned judge noted that his court had seen numerous citizens with injuries received when the police effected their arrest. He felt that many of them had done nothing to deserve an arrest, but most of them had made no complaint. Said the judge, "If the victim complains, his charge is generally dismissed. The police are practically above the law" (Reiss, 1970:57). Almost seventy years later, Germann observes that "police attitudes for the most part, indicate no responsibility for unnecessary or illegal police violence, or abuses of police authority" (1971:418).

The key word is "authority." The laws of most states, coupled with department regulations, usually define the extent to which force may be used by a police officer in the performance of official duties. In addition to articulating the proper circumstances for police use of force, legal codes and department policies give vague boundaries to the authority of police to intervene in the lives of citizens. However, as noted above, police work unfolds in a dynamic environment that is often filled with ambiguity of the proper police role. The coexistence of formal regulations and the uncertainty of police work often results in a struggle between department accountability and officer autonomy, which Crank (1998:234–236) calls the "paradox of accountability." Police agencies, as well as legislative bodies, attempt to develop more accountability through elaborate rules that provide guidelines for police conduct. However, police officers will attempt to insulate themselves from a formal accountability system that cannot account for the dynamic and uncertain nature of their work. The result is Crank's paradox, where the department attempts to increase its control over police conduct, and officers further distance themselves from department accountability in an attempt to develop self-protection. This paradox provides difficult environment for a police department that seeks to provide accountability to its constituency.

Some Definitions of Police Misconduct

A variety of definitions of police misconduct have been developed. Field observers, working on a project for the Center of Research on Social Organization (CRSO) in the late 1960s, were given several guidelines to assist them in determining when police use of force was judged to be unnecessary or improper.

1. If a policeman physically assaulted a citizen and then failed to make an arrest; proper use involves an arrest.
2. If the citizen being arrested did not, by word or deed, resist the policeman; force should be used only if it is necessary to make an arrest.
3. If the policeman, even though there was resistance to the arrest, could easily have restrained the citizen in other ways.
4. If a larger number of policemen were present and could have assisted in subduing the citizen in the station, in lockup, and in the interrogation rooms.
5. If an offender was handcuffed and made no attempt to flee or offer violent resistance.
6. If the citizen resisted arrest, but the force continued even after the citizen was subdued (Reiss, 1970:64).

Stark notes that a set of guidelines was also prepared by the International Association of Chiefs of Police (IACP). While the IACP directions were longer and more legalistic in appearance than were those given the CRSO observers, they were similar in content (1972:57).

The unnecessary or excessive use of force by the police (both of which fit under the label of "physical abuse"), especially when a citizen is seriously injured, is often considered the most serious of these complaints. But, there are other abuses that, while they don't physically injure anyone, might be termed degrading, dehumanizing, or humiliating. Police departments around the country record these types of complaints under a variety of terms such as verbal abuse, discourtesy, harassment, improper attitude, and ethnic slur.

By the same token, Reiss (1970:59–62) discovered that citizens objected to, and complained about:

1. the way police use language (not necessarily the words they select);
2. the habit police officers have of "talking down" to them; and

3. the "harassing" tactics of the police—the indiscriminate stopping and searching of citizens on foot or in cars, commands to go home or to "move on."

In 1968, the National Advisory Commission on Civil Disorders (the Kerner Commission) reported the finding of similar abuses. While it noted that verbal abuse or discourtesy in urban areas was more likely to be directed at whites, such tactics were particularly distressing to blacks. Said the commission report, "In nearly every city surveyed, the Commission heard complaints of harassment of interracial couples, dispersal of social street gatherings, and the stopping of (blacks) on foot or in cars without obvious basis. These, together with contemptuous and degrading verbal abuse, have great impact in the ghetto . . ." (1968:299–322).

Reiss (1970:59) summarizes the ways in which police have traditionally dealt with certain citizens, particularly those in the lower class:

1. the use of profane and abusive language;

2. commands to move on or get home;

3. stopping and questioning people on the street or searching them and their cars;

4. threats to use force if not obeyed;

5. prodding with a nightstick or approaching with a pistol; and

6. the actual use of physical force or violence itself.

These acts articulated by Reiss are consistent with what Perez (1994:21) labels "police malpractice." Perez notes that these actions represent the common complaints received by police agencies, which he categorizes as use of excessive force and abuse of discretion. In fact, it is this second category, abuse of discretion, that represents the large portion of citizen complaints (Dugan and Breda, 1991:168). Perez (1994:25) notes that such acts as verbal abuse, harassment, discrimination, and failure to take action are representative of the abuse of discretion. This behavior on the part of police officers frequently results in citizen attempts at redress. Such redress often takes the form of a complaint.

Previous Studies in Police Misconduct

The President's Commission on Law Enforcement and Administration of Justice reported that earlier studies had shown that physical abuse was a significant problem. Said the commission:

> The National Commission on Law Observance and Enforcement (the Wickersham Commission), which reported to President Hoover in 1931, found considerable evidence of police brutality. The President's Commission on Civil Rights, appointed by President Truman, made a similar finding in 1947. And, in 1961, the U.S. Civil Rights Commission concluded that "police brutality is still a serious problem throughout the United States." (1967:193)

The commission stated that it did not feel that physical abuse was as serious a problem as in the past, saying "the few statistics . . . suggest small numbers of cases involving excessive use of force" (1967:193). Black and Reiss submitted a research study to the same commission. It was based upon seven weeks of observations of police-citizen interactions in Boston, Chicago, and the District of Columbia. The research was not particularly focused on physical abuse but on other forms of police abuse. The Black and Reiss (1967:35–107) study found that: (1) police tend to be hostile toward antagonistic citizens, offenders, and intoxicated persons (in some instances) during field interrogations; (2) permission of citizens was seldom requested before personal searches were made of subjects; searches were determined to be unnecessary as often as 86 percent of the time; and (3) black citizens objected the least to personal searches, were less apt to be taken to the station house and released without charge, and were less discriminated against, when antagonistic, than whites, at least in radio dispatch situations.

In 1971, Reiss addressed the subject of excessive force. This study determined that: (1) more than three-quarters of the cases involving excessive force took place in a patrol car, precinct station, or public place (primarily the streets); (2) almost all victims were offenders or suspects and were young, lower-class males from any racial group; and (3) persons regarded by the police as deviant offenders (drunks, homosexuals, drug addicts), or who were perceived (by the officer) to have defied the officer's authority, were the most likely victims of undue force (1971:1).

Reiss noted the disparity between his findings and popular opinion that black citizens are the primary victims of physical abuse. He suggested that, even though white officers might be prejudiced toward blacks, they did not discriminate in the use of excessive force. It was Reiss's contention that the police culture more readily explained the use of force than did prejudice (1971:76).

Studies conducted after Reiss, however, show that nonwhite citizens, especially blacks, *are* more often the victims of police misconduct. Hudson, in his study of complaints investigated by the Philadelphia Police Advisory Board, found that police encounters with nonwhite citizens more frequently led to altercations than did police encounters with white citizens. Nonwhite citizens also constituted 70 percent of the principal complainants in Hudson's study (1970:187). Wagner found that blacks constituted slightly more than two-thirds of those who filed complaints against the police (1980:249). Decker and Wagner determined that black complainants were more likely to have been injured in an incident that precipitated a complaint against the police and were also more likely to be arrested than their white counterparts (1982:116–117). Decker and Wagner also found that the incident which prompted the complaint was more likely to have occurred in police custody and out of public view, if the complainant was black (1985:111).

Studies by Lersch and Mieczkowski (1996:39) found that minority citizens are disproportionately represented among complainants. While minority citizens consisted of only 22.2 percent of the population studied by Lersch and Mieczkowski, they accounted for 50.5 percent of complaints. However, they found that minority officers disproportionately accounted for complaints by minority citizens. Minority officers represented 15 percent of the department's personnel, yet they accounted for 35 percent of complaints by minority citizens. Using the same data set, Lersch (1998:96) found that when controlling for complaint type, minority citizens had the same likelihood as whites of having their complaints sustained by police internal affairs divisions.

Causes of Police Misconduct

In addition to documenting its prevalence, research on police misconduct also attempted to explain the reason for its occurrence. Explanations of misconduct range from the individualistic "bad apples" approach to the institutional "police culture" perspective. Each of these frameworks has found support in the police literature.

Bad Apples. The bad apple analogy states that a few bad apples can ruin the entire barrel, suggesting that the rest of the apples in the barrel are otherwise good. In the case of police departments, the analogy suggests that the majority of police misconduct can be isolated to a small group of problem-prone officers. This approach has found some statistical support. For example, the Christopher Commission (1991) found that 183 of the department's more than 8,000 officers had four or more allegations of excessive use of force or improper tactics in a four-year period, and 44 officers had six or more allegations.

Consistent with the notion of concentrated misconduct, Lersch and Mieczkowski (1996:32) found that 35.5 percent of complaints about misconduct in a large southeastern police department was accounted for by 7.3 percent of the department's sworn personnel. These officers each had five or more complaints. Further, 46 percent of the officers did not receive a single complaint over the same three-year examination period. However, the bad apple theory cannot explain all misconduct, or even the modal category. Almost two-thirds of the complaints examined by Lersch and Mieczkowski were attached to officers not classified as problem prone.

Police Culture. Some researchers have suggested that misconduct can more readily be explained by the "police culture," which represents that various informal rules develop among officers. Chevigny observed that "police recruits are much like other young men of similar background; it is police mores and police role that make them adopt police attitudes" (1969:137), and "the challenge to police authority continues as a chief cause of force in all urban police departments" (1969:60). Similarly, Niederhoffer asserted, "At first impression it would appear that above all other groups the police ought to be tied to the law, but because they learn to manipulate it, the law can become nothing more than a means to an end" (1969:97). What each of these assertions allude to is that police culture supports the subversion of official rules and thus represents the cause of misconduct.

Recent literature on police culture has moved away from the deterministic approach of past scholars, however. Crank (1998:14) notes that police culture is a complex mixture of various themes, which unfold in the environmental context of police work. The culture develops out of the various exchanges and experiences that officers are exposed to in their day-to-day work environment. Police culture is a set of informal norms that develop in an occupation of uncertainty. As Crank (1998:94) observes, "What is often overlooked is the mediating influence of police culture on the relationship between unpredictable encounters and police administration. Officers deal with the unknown on a daily basis, and develop broad cultural adaptations to unknown situations." This perspective suggests that police culture is more than a basis for subverting formal regulations. It is not to say that such cultural themes as danger, morality, or solidarity cannot lead to misconduct. However, these themes of police culture are more commonly the basis for addressing the multiple and uncertain tasks of police work. As a result, these informal cultural adaptations will always exist to some extent as long as officers are asked to fulfill an undefined role. Thus, the informal norms that emerge among officers does not solely contribute to misconduct, and as a result it cannot be simply isolated and removed.

A review of police behavior and misconduct show that complaints are based on a variety of explanations. The actions that prompt citizen complaints can be a result of a mistake or the intended subversion of formal regulations. Nonetheless, in order for police agencies to provide accountability and an image of legitimacy, they must provide a process that allows citizens to file complaints about conduct they believe is improper or unjust. Such a process allows for the correction of behavior deemed undesirable or the dismissal of those who are unable to perform adequately the tasks required of police officers.

Filing a Complaint

When a breakdown in the management of a police-citizen encounter has occurred, the citizen may file a complaint. Russell, in his study in England and Wales, found that those citizens who did decide to file a complaint against the police did so only after giving consideration to one or more of the following:

1. the citizen was advised that he might well succeed in his complaint;
2. he was able and prepared to make the effort to complain in the belief that justice would be done;
3. he believed that by complaining a policeman might be deterred from misbehaving in the future and that the result could only be in the public interest; and
4. the complaining citizen does not believe that any effort will be made by the officer or his associates to seek revenge (1978:54).

Conversely, Russell found the following to be the reasons why citizens did not file a complaint:

1. the advice of significant others;
2. the apathy of the potential complainant;
3. the apprehensiveness of the citizen;
4. the fatalistic approach that no effective action will be taken by the police;
5. the belief that police work is sufficiently difficult and hazardous without making it more so; and
6. an unawareness of the complaint procedure (1978:52–53).

These reasons were used by Russell to form the following typology of individuals who fail to report misconduct.

The Advised

The advice not to complain against the police may be given by a professional (i.e., attorney, social worker) or another governmental agency based upon the facts given to the individual about the potential complaint. The advisor, perhaps more knowledgeable than the citizen, might "explain away" the basis for the citizen's feeling that the officer was not properly conducting himself or herself. Also a "significant other," such as a friend or relative, might advise that he or she had previously filed a complaint and received no satisfaction. The advice of this individual (not to bother to file a complaint) contributes to the fatalistic posture described below.

The Apathetic

Russell's survey of citizens disclosed that 14 percent were "apathetic potential complainants" who "could just not be bothered to become involved in the detailed procedures of making a complaint" (1978:52). The apathetic citizen has no other reason than a lack of desire to make a complaint.

Bayley and Mendelsohn found the same to be true in their study of complaints in Denver. They discovered that there was a minority of persons in Denver who just didn't want to take the time to complain. "People simply did not want to be bothered; the complaint was not as important as the time they would have to devote to it" (1969:132).

The Apprehensive

Apprehensive citizens indicated that they feared reprisals, whether by personal violence or extralegal means, which deterred them from filing a complaint. The 1967 President's Commission on Law Enforcement and Administration of Justice learned that such apprehensiveness was sometimes well founded. The commission noted that in one large eastern city "the police department used to charge many of those who filed complaints of police misconduct with filing false reports with the police" (1967:195). More recently, the police have begun filing civil suits for libel and/or slander against complainants whose complaints are not substantiated by the police department investigation or who have filed civil suits against the police and lost. While the police argue that they are within their rights in suing a complainant, others feel that they are simply nuisance suits to harass and intimidate not only the present complainant but potential complainants as well.

The National Advisory Commission on Criminal Justice Standards and Goals also expressed knowledge of the problem when it asserted that "personal fear of reprisal or harassment, complex and cumbersome filing procedures, and the highlighted possibility of criminal prosecution for making a false report are three conditions that can discourage the public from making even valid complaints" (1973:471). Reiss asserted that, "many citizens are reluctant to complain against agencies that hold power over them and could respond with punitive action" (1971:190).

The Fatalistic

Russell described the fatalistic person as "those citizens who do not utilize the complaint process because they believe that no effective action will be taken by the police" (1978:53). The potential complainant who believes that nothing will really be done by the police dominated the literature. Bayley and Mendelsohn, for example, stated:

> The evidence very clearly shows that people, regardless of ethnicity, do not complain against the police automatically when they feel aggrieved. People commonly accept what is done to them without trying to buck the system. . . . Willingness to complain seems to be a function of what happens to people and what they expect to be able to gain from it, and these factors are not class-specific. (1969:130)

The Public Spirited

Russell's survey located a group of citizens who believed that the police have a difficult and hazardous job and that they would only make it more difficult by filing a complaint. This notion is not indicated in other literature.

The Unaware

In contrast to the "Public Spirited," instances of potential complainants who either did not know how to initiate the complaint process or did not know that such a process existed are not unusual. The President's Commission commented that "the mechanics of receiving complaints often tends to discourage potential complainants from taking any action. Some procedures are so little known, so complex, or so hard to pursue that the ordinary citizen either gives up or never tries in the first place" (1967:196). Repeating a recommendation of the National Advisory Commission on Civil Disorders some three years earlier, the National Advisory Commission on Criminal Justice Standards and Goals warned that this might be the result of a misunderstanding by the public, and "if this is the case, it is incumbent on the police agency to educate the public in these areas" (1973:471).

172 Section II: Police Socialization and the Police Subculture

Police Accountability and the Citizen Complaint Process

The citizens of a democratic society should have the right to make complaints about the actions of public officials acting in their official capacity. Further, police officers should be no less accountable for their actions than the mayor or any other employee of a political subdivision. Establishing a process that provides such accountability can have both positive and negative aspects.

Positive Aspects of Citizen Complaints

Police administrators should look upon citizen complaints as a barometer of police performance. Police officers have little supervision as they go about their duties, and fellow police officers are not likely to report their colleagues' misconduct. Citizens can provide the police department with valuable information about how well the department is performing.

The United States Commission on Civil Rights believes that citizen complaints also provide another useful function, acting as "important indicators of public perception of the agency" (1981:50). Police departments, says the commission, can use information obtained through citizen complaints to improve the public image and community relations of the department as they strive to provide better service to the community.

The complaint system has also found a fiscal basis in recent years. The paying out of large sums of money in liability lawsuits stemming from police officer misconduct has become increasingly more common (del Carmen, 1993:87–90). Such court findings against the police not only damage department images of legitimacy but also affect the future funding of police departments and services provided by local government entities. The ability to identify problem officers via a complaint process, in order to provide them with additional training or to terminate those who are most problematic, can reduce future exposure to liability.

Negative Aspects of Citizen Complaints

Making a complaint often takes a great deal of time and effort. The citizen may not know where to go to make the complaint. Even if he or she *does* know where to make the complaint, several obstacles exist.

First, the complainant may discover that there are no complaint procedures established for that police department; the citizen may, at best, be introduced to a ranking officer who will listen to the complaint but will take no formal action. (One of the authors will long remember the comment made to him by a member of a rural police department that "we don't accept complaints.") Second, the complainant may be required to go to the police department, a seemingly simple requirement that may actually be a hardship or an impossibility for the poor, disabled, or busy. Third, the citizen who goes to the police department to make a complaint against an officer may be greeted with any number of reactions. The literature is rich with evidence of the close-knit police fraternity. Accordingly, the complainant may be treated with courtesy and respect or may meet with intimidation, threats, and hostility. Caiden and Hahn point out, for example, that some departments require that the citizen complete a complaint form that states that the complainant is subject to prosecution for making false statements if the information is not substantiated (1979:171). Finally, the complainant may discover that the police department has an arbitrarily assigned "statute of limitations" on citizen complaints; the complaint will not be accepted if it is made after a certain length of time following the precipitating incident.

The citizen who overcomes the obstacles to the process and files a formal complaint then learns, if it wasn't previously known, that the complaint will be investigated by officers of that police department. Whether the investigators will be one of the accused officer's supervisors or a member of an internal affairs unit, the complainant comes face-to-face with the reality that the police department is investigating itself, a fact that the complainant may find, at the least, disheartening. Whether the concern of the citizen that police investigating police will prove fruitless is justified or not, the police department must recognize that suspicion and take steps to avoid even the appearance that the investigation is anything but impartial.

All of these considerations, both positive and negative, are best addressed within the framework of a formal, written citizen complaint procedure.

Establishing a Proper Citizen Complaint Process

In its 1981 report to President Ronald Reagan, the United States Commission on Civil Rights (1981:v–vi) listed several reasons for "the continuous, thoughtful examination" of police conduct. "Police officers possess awesome powers . . . protection of civil rights demands close examination of the exercise of police authority . . . police officers exercise their powers with wide discretion and under minimal supervision . . . a single occurrence or a perceived pattern of discriminatory and unjustified use of force can have a powerful, deleterious effect on the life of the community." Finally, the commission noted:

> Thus, there is ample reason for studying police conduct even without further justification. However, the volume of complaints of police abuse received by the Commission has increased each year, and the nature of the alleged abuse has become more serious. *Patterns of complaints appear to indicate institutional rather than individual problems.* (1981:vi, italic added)

The International Association of Chiefs of Police (IACP) contributed its voice to a similar endeavor, publishing a detailed manual of rules and procedures for the management of effective police discipline. The lengthy IACP publication began with a sample policy statement that police departments might adopt. The model statement called for: "the establishment of a system of complaint and disciplinary procedures . . ." and "the prompt receipt, investigation and disposition of complaints regarding the conduct of members and employees of the Department . . ." (1976:40). The IACP policy statement also recognized the importance of citizen complaints in the management of a police department when it stated: "The Police Department welcomes from the people of the community constructive criticism of the Department and valid complaints against its members or procedures" (1976:40–41).

The Police Executive Research Forum (PERF) began its model police misconduct policy statement by asserting that "the purpose of this policy is to improve the quality of police services" (1981:1). PERF then listed three positive outcomes that could be accomplished:

1. through the provision of meaningful and effective complaint procedures, citizen confidence in the integrity of police increases and this engenders community support and confidence in the police department;

2. disciplinary procedures permit police officials to monitor officers' compliance with departmental procedures;

3. the third purpose is to clarify rights and ensure due process protection to citizens and officers alike (1981:1).

All three of the documents, those of the U.S. Civil Rights Commission, the International Association of Chiefs of Police, and the Police Executive Research Forum, are remarkably similar. These similarities include:

1. the publication and distribution by the police department of written rules and regulations guiding the conduct of officers as they perform the various duties required of them;

2. an emphasis on the importance of proper supervision as a means of reducing and controlling police misconduct;

3. the establishment of an internal affairs unit (or individuals in a small department) with written guidelines on conducting an internal investigation;

4. the creation of a citizen complaint system, one that: is not intimidating, is accessible, and accepts anonymous complaints;

5. the education of the public about the disciplinary process and how complaints against the police may be filed;

6. the use of complaint forms for recording citizen complaints and for forming the basis for an investigation (one copy would go to the accused officer); the Civil Rights Commission recommended, in addition, the use of bilingual forms;

7. a prompt investigation of the complaint; and

8. equally prompt notification of the complainant and the accused officer as to the results of the investigation and what channels of appeal are open.

The Structure of the Police Review Process

Much of the debate about citizen complaints against the police has focused on the structure of responses to such complaints. There is considerable evidence that police and citizens desire different structures to deal with such complaints. And there is also evidence to indicate that the structure, responsibility, jurisdiction, and staffing of such review boards have a significant impact on their decisions.

West (1988) noted that any determination about what form the complaint process should take must consider all actors. While the system must, he says, be thorough and impartial, it must also be equally acceptable "to the officers themselves, to members of the public, and to those elected political officials who are charged with the responsibility of ensuring that police agencies are effectively and efficiently managed" (101–102). Dugan and Breda (1991:171) asserted that the way that a police agency deals with criticism "will determine whether criticism is a positive management tool or a basis for low morale, cynicism, and nonprofessional behavior." We turn our attention now to the various structural aspects of the complaint process, and their impact on the process.

The review of police conduct is a complex process. There are both formal and informal controls on police behavior, subjecting it to review from a variety of different sources. Most important in the review process are the reviews that come from criminal justice institutions, including, most directly, courts, prosecutor's office, and police administration. It is obvious that each of these are entrusted with the formal responsibility of review of police procedures, policies, and actions, many on a daily basis. Even the potential for review by one or more of these agencies exerts a control on police behavior. In addition to these formal agencies entrusted with an oversight function, there are many groups and institutions, external to the justice system, that perform a similar function. Notable among these are the media. Newspapers, radio, and television are all actively engaged in reviewing police conduct through news reports and editorials. As such, their "reviews" of police behavior are likely to have a widespread impact, perhaps greater than those conducted within the criminal justice system.

The review of police conduct provided by these external groups is significant, but it tends to lack the focus of those formally entrusted with the direct responsibility of oversight of allegations of police misconduct. The central issue in the consideration of the formal structure of the process is the extent to which citizens are involved. The level of involvement by citizens in the formal police review process varies significantly. It is this level of involvement that distinguishes the several formal procedures now in use by police departments.

Traditionally, the police review process excluded citizens from the process altogether. In their review of the administrative structure of police complaint procedures in the 1960s, Beral and Sisk (1964) found that the model in which only police were involved predominated. This was true into the 1980s, as the research of Terrill (1982) and Kerstetter (1985) indicated; they estimated that perhaps as many as 80 percent of all administrative structures were composed of only police officers.

Walker and Bumphus (1991) have shown, however, that since 1986 there has been an increase in the number of cities involving citizens at some stage of the complaint review process. They found that investigations of police misconduct in 18 cities (36%) were solely internal, that is, had no citizen involvement. Another 6 cities (12%) had minimal civilian involvement; usually the complainant was given the opportunity to appeal the final disposition to a board that includes nonsworn personnel. The remaining 26 cities (52%) provided for greater involvement of citizen review.

Several arguments exist to support the police-only model. First is the expertise brought to a review process. Police officers are well versed in matters of law and police procedure and, it is argued, are thus in the best position to render informed and competent decisions regarding citizen complaints (Walker, 2000). Supporters of this model also argue that the process lacks credibility among police officers when it includes citizens. The effectiveness of the process is enhanced when police are the sole arbiters in the process, and thus outcomes are likely to have more significant consequences. Further arguments include the well-accepted notion that bureaucracies and public sector organizations are responsible for solving their own problems. Citizen involvement in the process is evidence of the inability of the police organization to deal effectively with the shortcomings or misbehavior of its members. While this list is not an exhaustive one,[1] it provides the major arguments presented in support of review structures that include only police personnel.

The other major structural alternative includes citizens in some part of the review process. It should be noted that the review process is a truncated one involving many different decision points. Prominent among those are the receipt of complaints, evaluation, investigation, adjudication, and disciplinary recommendations. There is considerable variation among those structures that allow citizen input as to what stages of the process that input is allowed. Kerstetter and Rasinski (1994) say, however, that their study of the Minneapolis Police Department underscores the value of even modest civilian participation in the process. We will examine each of the structures that allow citizen input, beginning with the least amount of involvement and stretching along a continuum to those that have full citizen involvement at each stage.

The structure allowing for the least amount of input by citizens is that which includes citizens who are employees of the police department in a nonsworn capacity. Typically, models that utilize this approach involve these "police-civilians" in the earlier stages of the complaint process (i.e., the receipt and/or investigation of complaints), reserving the latter stages (adjudication and assignment of penalties) to police personnel.

The remaining three models all involve citizens from outside the police department. They do, however, vary considerably as to the extent of that citizen involvement. Kerstetter (1985) has identified these models, which he refers to as the civilian monitor, civilian input, and civilian review complaint structures. Each progressively involves citizens to a greater extent.

The first of the models, the *monitor*, is the weakest of the three, allowing citizen input into the complaint review process only after the complaint has been reviewed and a punishment determined within the police structure.

Under this model, citizens provide a review of police decisions after the fact. The opportunity to have an impact on the process and outcome of any individual complaint is minimal. The next structure, *input*, allows citizen participation at the earliest stages of the complaint review process. In particular, citizen input is used at the stages of receipt and investigation of the complaint. However, the remaining stages (adjudication and punishment) are handed over to the police agency. The final model, *review*, is the strongest of the three in that citizens are involved in all of the meaningful stages of the complaint process, receipt, investigation, adjudication, and punishment.

In the first national survey of civilian review procedures in the United States, Walker and Bumphus (1991) found that 32 of the 50 largest cities had instituted civilian review procedures.[2] They observed that 17 of the 32, over half of the total, have been established only since 1986.

Walker and Bumphus found no two agencies whose civilian review procedures were identical. Thus, they divided the 32 systems along two general criteria:

1. who does the initial investigation of a citizen complaint; and

2. who reviews the investigative report and makes a recommendation for action (1991:1).

They call the models that emerged Classes I, II, and III.

Class I: (a) Initial investigation and fact-finding by nonsworn personnel; (b) Review of investigative report and recommendation for action by nonsworn person or board consisting of a majority of nonsworn persons.

Class II: (a) Initial investigation and fact-finding by sworn police officers; (b) Review of investigative report and recommendation for action by a nonsworn person or board that consists of a majority of nonsworn persons.

Class III: (a) Initial investigation and fact-finding by sworn officers; (b) Review of investigative report and recommendation for action by sworn officers; (c) Opportunity by the citizen who is dissatisfied with the final disposition of the complaint to appeal to a board that includes nonsworn persons (1991:1).

Walker and Bumphus (1991:3) note that the three classes are similar to Kerstetter's three models: Class III is "similar" to Kerstetter's "civilian monitor;" Class II is "similar" to "civilian input;" and Class I "is the same" as "civilian review."

As a result of their survey, Walker and Bumphus classified 12 (37.5%) of the 32 police agencies as Class I; 14 (43.7%) as Class II; and 6 (18.7%) as Class III. Thus, almost half of the 32 police departments with civilian review procedures have included some civilian input in the process.

While the Walker and Bumphus survey did not measure the effectiveness of civilian review procedures, the authors noted (1991:1) that, "the spread of civilian review represents a new national consensus on civilian review as an appropriate method of handling citizen complaints about police misconduct."

There are many dilemmas that emerge as a result of this consideration of the structure of the complaint review process. The clearest distinction between structures can be made between those that include meaningful citizen participation and those that do not. An issue of primary significance to the resolution of complaints—credibility—cuts both ways. West (1988:108) observes that those who favor external review argue that a closed system, where police investigate the police, is contrary to "the rules of natural justice." Those opposed to external review say that such review threatens police morale and professionalism. It seems imperative that citizen involvement be integrated into the police structure, but in such a way as to preserve the ability of the police to monitor themselves. Kerstetter (1985) has argued that the emphasis on the resolution of complaints should not be on punishment, but rather on conciliation, compensation, training, and assistance. Such a call is consistent with the emerging mediation models of citizen complaint resolution. Walker and Kreisel (1996) found that of 65 police departments they observed having some form of citizen review, 12 had some form of mediation available. Walker and Kreisel further state that at the present time there has been little evaluation of the effectiveness of the mediation approach.

The reintegrative or mediation approach, whatever merits its may have, ignores the obvious dilemma that in many departments a serious problem exists with many officers and indeed with the prevailing norms regarding citizen treatment. These problems may require solutions of a punitive nature, rather than the reintegrative ones recommended by Kerstetter.

A final reactive system must be included. A number of police departments have been the subject of external scrutiny, often in the form of commissions or investigations by the U.S. Justice Department. The Christopher Commission Report (1991) resulted from the beating of Rodney King and made several recommendations for changing police practice and culture. In Chicago, the Commission on Police Integrity (1997) examined police corruption following citizen complaints and formal investigations of misconduct. Such reports can be viewed as a form of reactive, external control of police departments, as they carry both the force of public opinion and political will. Another form of reactive, external institutional control of the police is the consent decree. A number of U.S. cities, notably, Cincinnati, Pittsburgh, and Los Angeles, have entered into such decrees with the U.S. Justice Department. These decrees represent an extreme form of the role that police complaints about police misconduct can play, as they invoke federal investigations and ultimately agreements about specific aspects of police behavior that must be implemented by the agency and then monitored by the Justice Department.

Proactive Efforts in Managing Misconduct

Our discussion of the response to police misconduct to this point has focused on reactive efforts, where agencies do not take corrective action until they receive a citizen complaint regarding an officer's behavior. Given the recognition in the policing literature that often a small number of officers account for a disproportionate number of complaints (e.g., Christopher Commission, 1991; Lersch and Mieczkowski, 1996), it stands to reason that a more proactive approach could pay dividends in reducing the total number of future complaints. Such an approach represents a risk management orientation that seeks to address hazards that increase an organization's exposure to loss or otherwise negative events (Head and Horn, 1991). In the context of officer misconduct, the hazards are officers who have routinely displayed problematic behavior (i.e., frequent improper use-of-force incidents, harassing citizens, etc.). Just such a proactive approach, referred to as "early warning systems," has slowly emerged within police departments over the past twenty-five years.

The typical early warning system is composed of a three-step process (Walker, Alpert, and Kenney, 2001). First, potentially problematic officers are identified through monitoring of a number of conduct indicators (e.g., citizen complaints, firearms-discharge reports, use-of-force reports, civil litigation, resisting arrest incidents, and pursuits and vehicular accidents). Second, officers who have a number of these indicators within a given period of time are diverted for intervention. The intention of the intervention process is to provide an informal corrective action to improve the officer's performance rather than applying the punitive responses found in the more reactive complaint process discussed above. Thus, the common intervention techniques include counseling from a supervisor or training in a related area where the officer is deficient (e.g., communication or decision-making skills). Third, once the intervention is applied the officer continues to be monitored. The monitoring provides feedback on the effectiveness of the intervention efforts and identifies the possible need to take stronger corrective action for those officers who are not responsive. (See Walker, Alpert, and Kenney in this volume for a more extensive discussion of early warning systems.)

A recent survey of law enforcement agencies has found that early warning systems are becoming more common, with 27 percent of the agencies that serve populations of 50,000 or more having such a process (Walker, Alpert, and Kenney, 2001). Further, a case study conducted in three of these agencies found that officer complaints were dramatically reduced for individuals who had received some form of intervention. For example, in the Minneapolis and New Orleans police departments the average number of citizen complaints for officers who went through the process dropped more than 60 percent in the year that followed the intervention. Although these findings are based on a limited number of agencies, they suggest that comprehensive efforts to address officer misconduct should include this proactive process.

Conclusion

This article has examined police misconduct and its review through the citizen complaint process. The nature of police work, particularly the enforcement aspect of the role, is adversarial by nature. Such interactions are likely to generate disagreement and hostility. That complaints eventuate from such interactions is not surprising. Campaigns to recruit more sensitive or less aggressive police officers would appear to have little if any effect in reducing citizen complaints. The evidence presented in this article suggests that the informal culture that develops among police officers has a contributing role in misconduct. Most commentators have pointed to the role of the police culture in shaping the actions that are most likely to result in citizen complaints. However, this article acknowledges that police culture often represents legitimate norms that allow officers to conduct their day-to-day activities in an uncertain environment. This creates a difficult situation in which a police department must find a way to curb norms that foster misconduct yet allow officers the flexibility to address the variety of situations they confront. The failure to do so may result in the greater application of formal controls on officers, which will in turn influence officers to become more evasive to accountability procedures.

Traditionally, police departments addressed citizen complaints through some form of internal review system. Claims that the internal review process was too lenient on officers prompted the creation of various levels of civilian input in the complaint resolution process. The assumption was that civilian input would create a process of greater officer and agency accountability. However, some observers have suggested that a civilian process tends to be more lenient on officers than the internal review system. There has been no empirical evaluation to support or deny this claim. Nonetheless, this position questions whether the goal of the complaint process is to project an image of legitimacy to the citizenry or to provide greater accountability to formal regulations. It is reasonable to assert that both of these are desirable goals (see Walker, 2000 for both perspectives on citizens review).

This article has presented various models of complaint response, and none of these have proven to be the perfect answer. Whatever the model chosen by a police agency, it is important that a citizen complaint process must address allegations of misconduct in a way that guarantees both due process for officers and accountability to the public. The process also has to be viewed as legitimate in order to instill confidence on the part of the citizenry. A society that places a high value on democracy and the preservation of civil rights requires some level of civilian participation in the control of law enforcement agencies. An adequate citizen complaint process plays an integral role in fostering citizen support for the institution of policing. Such support is necessary to the overall function of police agencies.

NOTES

[1] For a more exhaustive list, see Terrill (1982), and International Association of Civilian Oversight of Law Enforcement (IACOLE) (1989).

[2] The number of cities with civilian review procedures was listed as thirty in the original report. It was updated to thirty-two cities in a February 1992 addendum.

REFERENCES

Bayley, David H. and Harold Mendelsohn (1969), *Minorities and the Police,* New York: The Free Press.

Beral, Harold and Marcus Sisk (1964), "The Administration of Complaints by Civilians Against the Police," *Harvard Law Review,* Vol. 77.

Bittner, Egon (1990), *Aspects of Police Work,* Boston, MA: Northeastern University Press.

Black, Donald J. and Albert J. Reiss, Jr. (1967), "Patterns of Behavior in Police and Citizen Transactions," *Field Surveys III, Studies in Crime and Law Enforcement in Major Metropolitan Areas,* Vol. 2, Washington, DC: U.S. Government Printing Office.

Caiden, Gerald and Harlan Hahn (1979), "Public Complaints Against the Police," in Ralph Baker and Fred A. Meyer, Jr. (eds.), *Evaluating Alternative Law-Enforcement Policies,* Lexington, ME: Lexington Books.

Chevigny, Paul (1969), *Police Power,* New York: Vintage Books.

Christopher Commission (1991), Report of the Independent Commission on the Los Angeles Police Department, Los Angeles, California.

Commission on Police Integrity (1997), Report of the Commission on Police Integrity, Presented to the City of Chicago, Chicago, IL.

Crank, John (1998), *Understanding Police Culture,* Cincinnati, OH: Anderson.

Decker, Scott H. and Allen E. Wagner (1982), "Race and Citizen Complaints Against the Police: An Analysis of Their Interaction," in Jack R. Green (ed.), *The Police and the Public,* Beverly Hills, CA: Sage Publications.

——— (1985), "Black and White Complainants and the Police," *American Journal of Criminal Justice,* Vol. 10, No. 1.

del Carmen, Rolando V. (1993), "Civil Liberties in Law Enforcement: Where Are We and Where Should We Go From Here?" *American Journal of Police,* Vol. 12, No. 4.

Dugan, John R. and Daniel R. Breda (1991), "Complaints About Police Officers: A Comparison Among Types and Agencies," *Journal of Criminal Justice,* Vol. 19, No. 2.

Germann, A. C. (1971), "Changing the Police—The Impossible Dream?," *The Journal of Criminal Law, Criminology and Police Science,* Vol. LXII (September).

Goldstein, Herman (1977), *Policing a Free Society,* Cambridge, MA: Bailinger Publishing Company.

Head, G. and S. Horn (1991), *Essentials of Risk Management: Volume 1,* Malvern, PA: Insurance Institute of America.

Hudson, James R. (1970), "Police-Citizen Encounters That Lead to Citizen Complaints," *Social Problems,* Vol. 18, No. 2, 179–193.

International Association of Chiefs of Police (1976), *Managing for Effective Police Discipline,* Gaithersburg, MD: International Association of Chiefs of Police, Inc.

International Association of Civilian Oversight of Law Enforcement (IACOLE) (1989), *Compendium of International Civilian Oversight Agencies,* Evanston, IL: IACOLE.

Kerstetter, Wayne A. (1985), "Who Disciplines the Police? Who Should?" in William A. Geller (ed.), *Police Leadership in America: Crisis and Opportunity,* Chicago: American Bar Foundation.

Kerstetter, Wayne A. and Kenneth A. Rasinski (1994), "Opening a Window into Police Internal Affairs: Impact of Procedural Justice Reform on Third-Party Attitudes," *Social Justice Research,* Vol. 7, No. 2 (March).

Lersch, Kim M. (1998), "Predicting Citizen Race in Allegations of Misconduct Against the Police," *Journal of Criminal Justice,* Vol. 26, No. 2.

Lersch, Kim M. and Tom Mieczkowski (1996), "Who are the Problem-Prone Officers? An Analysis if Citizen Complaints," *American Journal of Police*, Vol. 15, No. 3.

Los Angeles Police Department (2000), Board of Inquiry Report into the Rampart Area Corruption Incident, *LAPD Online*, http://www.lapdonline.org/whats_new/boi/boi_report.htm.

National Advisory Commission on Civil Disorders (1968), *Report of the National Commission on Civil Disorders*, New York, NY: Bantam Books.

National Advisory Commission on Criminal Justice Standards and Goals (1973), *Police*, Washington, DC: U.S. Government Printing Office.

Niederhoffer, Arthur (1969), *Behind the Shield: The Police in Urban Society*, Garden City, NY: Anchor Books.

Perez, Douglas W. (1994), *Common Sense about Police Review*, Philadelphia, PA: Temple University Press.

Police Executive Research Forum (1981), *Police Agency Handling of Officer Misconduct: A Model Policy Statement*, Washington, DC: Police Executive Research Forum.

President's Commission on Law Enforcement and Administration of Justice (1967), *Task Force Report: The Police*, Washington, DC: U.S. Government Printing Office.

Reiss Jr., Albert J. (1970), "Police Brutality-Answers to Key Questions," in Michael Lipsky (ed.), *Law and Order Police Encounters*, New Brunswick, NJ: Aldine Publishing Co.

——— (1971), *The Police and the Public*, New Haven, CT: Yale University Press.

Russell, Ken (1978), *Complaints Against the Police: A Sociological View*, Glenfield, Leicester, England: Milltak Limited.

Stark, Rodney (1972), *Police Riots*, Belmont, CA: Wordsworth Publishing Company, Inc.

Terrill, Richard J. (1982), "Civilian Review Boards," *Journal of Police Science and Administration*, Vol. 10, No. 4.

U. S. Commission on Civil Rights (1981), *Who is Guarding the Guardians? A Report on Police Practices*, Washington, DC: U.S. Government Printing Office.

Wagner, Allen E. (1980), "Citizen Complaints Against the Police: The Complainant," *Journal of Police Science and Administration*, Vol. 8, No. 3.

Walker, Samuel (1983), *The Police in America*, New York: McGraw-Hill Book Company.

Walker, Samuel and Vic W. Bumphus (1991), *Civilian Review of the Police: A National Survey of the 50 Largest Cities*, Omaha, NE: Center for Public Affairs Research.

Walker, Samuel and Betsy W. Kreisel (1996), "Varieties of Citizen Review: The Implications of Organizational Features of Complaint Review Procedures for Accountability of the Police," *American Journal of Police*, Vol. 15, No. 3.

Walker, Samuel (2001), *Police Accountability: The Role of Citizen Oversight*, Belmont, CA: Wadsworth.

Walker, Samuel, Geoffrey P. Alpert, & Dennis J. Kenney (2001), *Early Warning Systems: Responding to the Problem Police Officer*. Research in Brief. Washington, DC: National Institute of Justice.

Ward, Richard H. (1975), "The Police Role: A Case of Diversity," in George G. Killinger and Paul F. Cromwell Jr. (eds.), *Issues in Law Enforcement*, Boston, MA: Holbrook Press.

West, Paul (1988), "Investigation of Complaints Against the Police: Summary Report of a National Survey," *American Journal of Police*, Vol. 7, No. 2.

10

Ethics and Law Enforcement

Joycelyn M. Pollock & Paul D. Reynolds

- Denver, Colorado: A former sheriff's deputy was sentenced to six years in prison for helping an inmate escape from the jail.
- East Haven, Connecticut: A former police officer was sentenced to five years in prison for violating the civil rights of Latinos. The case involved false arrest and excessive use of force.
- Normangee, Texas: A former police chief has pleaded guilty to abusing access to a crime database for a drug trafficking suspect.
- Mobile, Alabama: A police officer was fired for exchanging "sexual favors in return for not turning in citations" at adult entertainment establishments.
- Pomona, California: A jury has awarded a Los Angeles police officer $260,000 after finding that Pomona police unlawfully arrested and used excessive force on the police officer.

These entries were those cited in one week on the Cato Institute's website (http://www.policemisconduct.net/) "National Police Misconduct Reporting Project." Misconduct scandals capture the public's attention because of their notoriety and egregiousness. However, as serious as these events are, there are very few "criminal cops," and ethical dilemmas in law enforcement are more often a choice between two perfectly legal actions. In this chapter, we will explore the concept of a dilemma and describe some of the types of dilemmas that exist in law enforcement. Dilemmas may occur in two major areas of ethical decision making, which will be called "day-to-day ethics" and "noble cause ethics." Next, we will discuss police corruption and examine some of the explanations that have been proposed to explain police deviance and corruption. We will then describe some suggestions to improve ethical decision making in law enforcement.

Prepared especially for *Critical Issues in Policing* by Joycelyn M. Pollock and Paul D. Reynolds.

Ethical Dilemmas

Police officers are not the only professionals who face difficult decisions. Individuals in every profession encounter their own particular types of ethical dilemmas. Doctors are tempted to prescribe unneeded drugs because of huge incentives offered by pharmaceutical companies; lawyers face ethical dilemmas when their clients want them to pursue cases with no legal merit or suborn perjury; and business leaders are often tempted to engage in unethical or even illegal practices to improve the profitability of their company. However, the ethical dilemmas faced by law enforcement officers are different from those of other professionals because officers are public servants. Public servants typically have authority over others and/or make decisions that should contribute to the "public good." They have a great deal of power, and we expect them to wield this power fairly and without favor or prejudice (Delattre, 2011).

One aspect of being a public servant is that one's private life is judged by others. We are not particularly interested in the sexual peccadilloes of our plumber, nor do we care about his gambling or drinking habits outside of the job. Public servants, however, are subjected to a high degree of scrutiny even in their private lives. The private behavior of politicians, judges, and other public servants concerns us because we suspect that the decisions made regarding private behavior also affects, in some way, their role as a public servant. Police officers fall into this group of people who are held to a higher standard of behavior. Public service is, after all, a choice the individual makes, and the power we entrust to public servants is quite awesome.

Part of the reason that public servants are held to a higher standard is that they make decisions for and about the rest of us. The concept of the social contract, as derived from the writings of Thomas Hobbes (1588–1679), John Locke (1632–1704), and Jean-Jacques Rousseau (1712–1778), is that we give up certain rights in return for protection. We don't take the law into our own hands because we give our government the power to use force. In return for this power, we expect agents of the government to live up to a higher standard of behavior that includes objectivity, fairness, and lawfulness (Alderson, 1998; Pollock, 2014).

Law enforcement historians note that part of the trend of "professionalism" starting in the 1920s was spurred by several factors, one of which was to improve the image of police as objective enforcers of the law rather than enforcers for whomever happened to be in power. Part of this transformation involved the idea that police were like professional soldiers in the war on crime, a concept that implies objectivity, professional expertise, and specialized training (Kappeler, Sluder, and Alpert, 1998; Fogelson, 1977; Payne, 2002; Caldero and Crank, 2010). Part of the professionalization of law enforcement involved creating and promulgating a Code of Ethics. The Code of Ethics for Law Enforcement was written by the International Association of Chiefs of Police in 1956 and updated in 1991. It is an "aspirational" code, meaning that it promotes the model of a perfect police officer, one that mere mortals can only aspire to. It is interesting that the code has made few changes over the last decades, but one change that has been made has been to add the phrase, "I will cooperate with all legally authorized agencies and their representatives in the pursuit of justice." This phrase brings into bold relief the dilemma of the officer who must choose between loyalty to colleagues and loyalty to the organization and the community. There may be no issue more problematic in the application of the code to day-to-day decision making by individual officers. In law enforcement codes and most oaths of office, one can identify at least four major themes:

1. The principle of justice or *fairness* is the single most dominant theme in the law enforcement code. Police officers must uphold the law regardless of the offender's identity. They must not single out special groups or individuals for different treatment.

2. A second theme is that of *service*. Police officers exist to serve the community, and their role appropriately and essentially concerns this idea.

3. Still another theme is the *importance of the law*. Police are protectors of the Constitution and must not go beyond it or substitute rules of their own.

4. The final theme is one of *personal conduct*. Police must uphold a standard of behavior consistent with their public position. This involves a higher standard of behavior in their professional and personal lives than that expected from the general public (Bossard, 1981; Pollock, 2014).

Day-to-Day Ethics

Discretion can be defined as the power and authority to make a decision, and police officers have a great deal of discretion when performing their job. For instance, police have the authority to make an arrest or not in a wide array of circumstances. They don't ticket all motorists who break traffic laws and they don't arrest all barroom brawlers. What guides their discretion? Obviously police officers are trained to abide by the law and departmental policy, but individual ethics also guides officers' decision making.

In some instances there is a clearly "right" course of action, either because of law, policy, or consequence. In other instances, however, there is no decision that is clearly right. This may be because law or policy does not cover such a circumstance or because law or policy results in an effect that doesn't seem just or fair. In some situations, police officers temper the law with "street justice." In the situations below, many officers ignore the formal law to arrive at a result that they feel is more just. Other officers, however, would enforce the law "by the book" as they were trained to do.

- An officer responds to a shoplifting call and finds a 70-year-old lady being held for stealing batteries for her hearing aid. She is on a fixed income and can't afford them.

- A very poor woman is stopped for not having child seats for her two children. Since she can't afford the child seats to begin with, she certainly can't afford the ticket for not having them, yet she broke the law and endangered her children.

• An officer responds to a residence where a nine-year-old boy had grabbed a knife and threatened his mother, because she turned off his video game. However, the child has documented emotional-psychological issues and just recently changed to new medication.

In some situations, there is no clear legal response called for. In these circumstances, officers could rightfully argue that they have no role since there is no illegality involved, or they could perceive their role more broadly and help to solve problems. What is their ethical duty?

• An officer responds to a disturbance call and finds that a drunken father is trying to remove his son and daughter-in-law and their kids from his home. They refuse to leave and argue that he is drunk and will change his mind tomorrow.

• An officer responds to a call in a housing project to discover a distraught mother who has just chased a rat away from her newborn baby. The manager of the project is clearly unsympathetic and unwilling to do anything about the problem.

• An elderly woman constantly calls the station reporting burglaries or noises on her porch. The facts are that she is lonely and scared since the neighborhood has changed around her and she has no close friends or neighbors to check in on her.

The scope of a law enforcement officer's duty is a complicated issue and one we keep redefining. Community policing efforts dramatically enlarged the officer's role to include social service issues such as helping citizens clean up abandoned lots and fix broken streetlights. It should also be noted, however, that community policing seems to have faded as a favored model of policing, and it is unclear whether police departments continue to embrace the enlarged scope of duty consistent with the community policing philosophy (Chappell and Gibson, 2009; Oliver, 2006; Ortiz, Hendricks, and Sugie, 2007). The war on terror has created new roles for local law enforcement agencies such as investigating immigration violations and taking responsibility for guarding target sites such as power plants and airports. Duty may be defined by the organization, but each individual officer also shapes and personalizes his or her own parameters of duty. To not do what one is paid to do is an obvious ethical transgression, but beyond that, there are nuanced answers for how much an officer is or should be expected to do considering the complicated and difficult situations they encounter.

We expect police to utilize their discretion in an ethical manner, but what does that mean? The law gives police officers the power to ticket anyone they observe violating traffic laws, but officers also are legally allowed to give a warning rather than a citation. The only illegal use of his or her discretion is if the decision to ticket or not is based on a bribe or the driver's race (or membership in any other protected class). Formal policy may leave the decision to the officer's discretion; however, informal policy may impose quotas or other parameters for the decision. Absent legal or policy elements, officers rely on their personal ethics to decide when to ticket and when to issue only a warning. What are ethical versus unethical criteria for this decision? Ethical criteria may include the seriousness of the driving violation, whether the driver had prior tickets, and whether there was a reason for the violation (speeding to a hospital for instance). Unethical criteria may include the attractiveness of the driver or who the driver was (e.g. "professional courtesy" is often extended to other law enforcement officers and sometimes family members). Some criteria are less clear as ethical or unethical. Is the driver's bad attitude an ethical or unethical criterion to give a citation rather than a warning?

Gratuities

One instance where police officers receive (and, in some instances, expect) special treatment is the practice of gratuities. Gratuities can be defined as something given because of one's role or position as a matter of policy. Gratuities are distinct from gifts, but most departments prohibit both.

- An officer, new to his beat, stops at a convenience store. The clerk refuses to accept payment for his cold drink, even though the officer argues that he would prefer to pay. The clerk, now upset, accuses the officer of trying to be "better than the others" and says he will tell the officer's supervisor.

- An officer stops to help a motorist on the side of the freeway. The officer drives the individual to his home, which is only a short distance away, and, in appreciation, the man offers the officer $10 for breakfast.

In the first situation, the clerk was offering something simply because of the officer's uniform—this is the classic example of a gratuity. In the second situation, the person helped was offering a gift to a particular officer because of a kind act over and above the officer's duty. Neither gifts nor gratuities are usually acceptable under departmental policy; however, the rule against them is probably one of the least enforced of any department's rulebook.

Arguments for gratuities include the idea that such social interchanges cement public relationships and help officers with their networking. Another argument supporting the taking of gratuities is that some citizens are more frequent "consumers" of police services and so should expect to "pay more." Kania (1988, 2004) argues that one should look at the motivation and intent on the part of the officer and the giver. Arguments to support gratuities include:

1. Gratuities cement social relationships between officers and citizens, especially between those who require disproportional police service.

2. Gratuities should be accepted when there are good intentions on the part of both parties (no special service asked for or offered).

3. Other professionals accept gratuities.

4. There is nothing wrong with more frequent users of police services "paying" extra.

5. "No gratuity" rules are tools of playing "gotcha" since in some locales the practice is so common that most officers find it impossible to follow the rules strictly. In these departments, the rules are then something that can be enforced arbitrarily against some officers and not others. This erodes morale and reduces the legitimacy of administrative discipline procedures.

6. Educators and academics tend to distort the seriousness of gratuities (Kania, 1998, 2004).

Arguments against gratuities depend on the notion that police are public servants, and we do not expect to have to pay extra for public service, especially for those public servants who have discretionary power over us. Litigants do not give a judge a gratuity for a good decision, and residents do not give city council members gifts for a vote to pave their street or tip the zoning commissioner for pushing through an exemption application. We want these decision makers to be completely free of bias and they should not be influenced by anything other than the law and the public good.

The reason why many gifts, and even some gratuities, do not seem wrong for police officers is that they sometimes perform purely service functions without using their discretionary authority. In the situation above where the officer drove the motorist home, the officer is not using her discretionary power over the individual and that is why many people see nothing wrong with the person offering or the officer accepting the offer of $10 for breakfast. It is quite a different situation if an officer decided not to ticket a car that was double-parked and the car owner gives the officer $10 for not ticketing him. It should also be noted, however, that some ethicists would argue that allowing officers to receive gifts creates a slippery slope where officers might come to expect remuneration in more situations when interacting with the public.

Arguments against gratuities include the idea that there is an expectation of different or special service when gratuities are a store/restaurant policy. Officers may patrol differently or make decisions because of them, and this is unfair. Other arguments against gratuities include:

1. Police are professionals, and professionals don't take gratuities.

2. Gratuities are incipient corruptors because people expect different treatment.

3. Gratuities are an abuse of authority and create a sense of entitlement.

4. Gratuities add up to substantial amounts of money and can constitute as high as 30 percent of an officer's income.

5. Gratuities can be the beginning of more serious forms of corruption.

6. It is contrary to democratic ideals because it is a type of fee-for-service of public functions.

7. It creates a public perception that police are corrupt (Ruiz and Bono, 2004; Coleman, 2004a, 2004b; Prenzler, Beckley and Bronitt, 2013).

Drug and Alcohol Use

Recall that part of being a public servant means that private behavior is more scrutinized. We are concerned, for instance, when police officers engage in drug use or excessive alcohol use. Obviously drug use is a crime, and officers who use illegal substances in their private life and then arrest others for the same behavior are the worst type of hypocrites. We don't have good recent data on how many officers use drugs, although Carter (1999) reported findings that up to 20 percent of officers in one city used marijuana and other drugs while on duty. In Fyfe and Kane's (2006) study of police officers terminated for cause in New York City, the most common reason for termination was a failed drug test. Gorta (2007), studying drug use by police officers in New South Wales, did not report prevalence figures but did find that there was no typical age or rank for those officers who admitted drug use; older supervisor-level officers also reported illegal drug use despite the widespread belief that it is a problem only among younger officers.

Alcohol use is more socially acceptable than drug use, but excessive use can impair one's judgment, which is part of the reason why drinking is a concern. In one older survey it was found that about 8 percent of those in protective services occupations (which would include police officers) reported heavy alcohol use, compared to 12 percent of construction workers and 4 percent of sales workers (Mieczkowski, 2002: 179). If an officer carries his or her drinking over into the working shift, it is an even more serious concern. In one study, Barker and Carter (1994) reported that 8 percent of officers reported drinking alcohol on duty. A more recent study on police and problematic alcohol consumption by Swatt, Gibson, and Piquero (2007) reported that 68 percent of officers sampled reported drinking, but only 6 percent showed all three signs of problematic drinking behaviors. A recent study found probable signs of lifetime alcohol abuse among 7.8 percent of officers surveyed in the study (Ballenger et al., 2011: 25). More concerning in this report was 11 percent of male officers and 15.9 percent of female officers were classified in the "at risk" category, with an average number of 35 drinks in the prior week reported by survey respondents. One explanation of higher drinking percentages of female officers is the desire to gain acceptance in a predominately male profession. Also concerning was that over one-third of both male and female officers reported binge drinking (five or more drinks on a single occasion in the past 30 days). While drinking alcohol is not unethical in and of itself, drinking on duty, or drinking to the point where it impairs one's ability to perform one's duties adequately, is an ethical issue.

In another study, 10 percent of officers reported drinking four or more times a week, 10 percent reported drinking five or six drinks at a time, and 9.5 percent reported they drank six or more drinks in one occasion at least weekly (Chopko, Palmieri, and Adams, 2013). This study also reported a correlation between the level of alcohol use and the amount of stress experienced by the officer. Although these recent studies did not ask specifically about drinking on duty, the drinking patterns indicate that alcohol use may be impairing the officer's performance, and the decision to drink may be influenced by perceived stress.

Discrimination

Clearly, when officers discriminate on the basis of race, sex, or any other unfair categorization, they are using their discretionary power in an unethical way (Cohen, 1986, 1987). Many argue that police officers treat minority citizens differently. This is certainly the perception in the minority community (Cole, 1999; Walker, Spohn, and DeLone, 2000). African Americans have significantly more negative interactions with police, and many report disrespectful language or swearing by police officers (Weitzer, 1999; Weitzer and Tuch, 2000, 2002). Some research disputes this general view, finding that age, sex, and wealth were better predictors of whether police officers were disrespectful in citizen encounters. The researchers did point out, however, that blacks appeared in the pool of encounters at roughly 1.5 times their percentage in the general population. In other words, blacks were no more likely than whites to receive disrespect, but they were stopped 1.5 times as often as their population percentage would predict. Thus, the rate of all black citizens receiving disrespect was higher than that of white citizens (Mastrofski, Reisig, and McCluskey, 2002: 543). Race does seem to be a predictor in the use of verbal and physical coercion by officers observed in the encounters (Mastrofski et al., 2002; Terrill, 2001, 2005; Terrill, Paoline, and Manning, 2003). More recent research indicates that in one sample blacks and Hispanics were more likely than whites to perceive unfair treatment by police in *citizen*-initiated contacts while there were no statistically significant race or ethnic group perceptual differences in *police*-initiated contacts (Schuck and Martin, 2013).

Racial profiling refers to the practice of police officers targeting black drivers driving expensive cars or driving in "white" areas of town. In fact, the so-called "crime" of DWB (driving while black) has been denounced as the effect of the discriminatory practice of racial profiling. When young, black men are stopped frequently for little or no reason, the perceived harassment inevitably poisons the relationship between the community and the police department. Many states have now passed legislation requiring police departments to collect demographic information on police stops to determine whether racial profiling is an issue.

Racial profiling has been in the news most recently due to the policies and practices of the New York City Police Department. In a lawsuit against the city alleging police illegally stopped minorities, an analysis by criminologist Jeffrey Fagan was used that indicated that 84 percent of 4 million stops recorded by officers were of black or minority citizens. In about half of the stops, the officer indicated the stop was for "furtive movements," which was simply a box they could check on the forms they filled out. The records also indicated that only 6 percent resulted in arrests (Toobin, 2013). The city argued that the stop and frisk practices, especially targeting housing projects with high crime, were responsible for a dramatic and historic drop in crime. Judge Shira Scheinlin of the Federal District Court in Manhattan ruled in favor of the plaintiffs, but the city appealed. Before an appellate court could consider the case, the newly elected mayor, Bill D'Blasio, in January 2014, instructed the city to drop its appeal and appointed a new police commissioner, William Bratton. Bratton is serving a second term as commissioner after having been commissioner of NYPD in the mid-1990s. He has pledged that the department will follow the plan mandated by the judge, including hiring a monitor to develop widespread reforms and revising training (Weiser and Goldstein, 2014).

A different kind of racial profiling occurs when individuals who appear to be Latino are asked their citizenship status when they interact with police as victims, witnesses, or criminals. Local law enforcement is increasingly being utilized to enforce immigration laws, and this has created serious controversy. In 2010 the Arizona legislature passed HB 2162, which, among other things, mandated that police officers ask for proof of citizenship or residency if there was reasonable suspicion that the person was an illegal immigrant. Upon appeal, the Supreme Court ruled in *Arizona v. United States* (2012) that, although other sections of the law were unconstitutional, the section mandating law enforcement to check legal status was acceptable as long as the stop was for any other legal reason. The Supreme Court did indicate that they would be willing to revisit the issue if evidence emerged that race or ethnicity was being used as a sole reason to stop people.

Officers seem to use force at higher rates toward racial minorities—particularly blacks; however, other situational factors besides race or ethnicity have a greater influence on the likelihood and extent of the force, such as the individual's behavior toward the officer during the encounter (Hickman, Piquero, and Garner, 2008; Lawton, 2007). Some research has found Hispanics are twice as likely to be the target of Taser use compared to whites. Interestingly, there was no difference between blacks and whites regarding Taser use (Gau, Mosher, and Pratt, 2010).

One explanation for the greater use of force against blacks is the racial threat theory. Research has shown that black males are perceived by officers as posing a greater threat to their safety. Due to this perceived threat, officers are more likely to use force and a greater degree of force. For example, a recent decision-to-shoot study comparing officers' responses to threats using a computer simulation showed that white participants were more likely to react with lethal force toward black males (Plant, Goplen, and Kunstman, 2011). What research shows is that racial bias may exist but stem from unconscious attitudes and beliefs. In other words, decisions may not be unethical uses of discretion so much as well-intentioned decisions based on unconscious biases.

There are many other ethical issues that arise during the course of day-to-day decision making. Ultimately, police officers on the street typically make these decisions to the best of their ability, in the heat of the moment, under the guidelines of law, policy, and ethics. Noble cause ethics is another type of law enforcement dilemma and decision making that merits a separate discussion.

Noble Cause Ethics

In an early discussion of police practices, Klockars (1983) asked whether it was ethically acceptable for a police officer to inflict pain on a suspect in order to acquire information that would save an innocent victim. He called this dilemma the "Dirty Harry" problem, which is derived from Clint Eastwood's *Dirty Harry* movies. This discussion has been elaborated on by others, most notably by Caldero and Crank (2010), who proposed that such practices as "testilying" (committing perjury to obtain a conviction) and coercion are not caused by selfishness but by "ends-oriented thinking." The "noble cause" of police officers is crime fighting and making the world a safer place (Caldero and Crank, 2010). The discussion of "noble cause corruption" draws heavily from Herbert Packer's (1968) two models of law enforcement—crime control and due process. The crime control model operated under certain principles, including repression of criminal conduct as the most important function of law enforcement, efficiency as a top priority, and an emphasis on speed and finality. Under this model a failure of law enforcement signals a breakdown of order. The due process model, on the other hand, operates under the principles that efficiency is less important than eliminating error and the protection of the process of law is more important than any end result of conviction. Under this model there is a recognition that the coercive power of the state is sometimes subject to abuse, and that must be guarded against by due process.

Noble cause corruption is a type of wrongdoing that stems from a crime control orientation. It is a type of "means-end" thinking where the results of crime control justify the means, even if the means are otherwise unethical or illegal. Therefore, police officers may feel compelled to lie either while testifying or to support a warrant request, use physical coercion during an interrogation, ignore exculpatory evidence if they feel they have the guilty party in custody, overlook the criminal acts of an informant, and/or plant or manufacture evidence in order to secure a conviction against someone they believe to be guilty. What sets apart these acts from other ethical issues is that they are done for arguably good motives. The trouble is that many activities that might be categorized under the label of noble cause corruption are neither ethical nor sometimes even effective in gaining convictions of guilty defendants.

Rossmo (2008) discusses investigative errors that occur when police officers focus too soon on one specific suspect and ignore protocols in investigation. This can take the form of ignoring witnesses or evidence or even manufacturing evidence to shore up a case against a suspect. Investigations fail because of the very human tendency to ignore evidence that does not fit preconceived notions. In the cases that Rossmo describes, the true criminal was not discovered and others were suspected, and sometimes charged and convicted, because police officers did not follow proper protocol in the collection and interpretation of evidence.

Undercover Investigations and Testilying

In undercover operations, lying is a necessity and is perfectly legal (Skolnick, 1982; Marx, 1985, 1991). Undercover officers lie about who they are; informants lie and are lied to; suspects are lied to on the street and in the interrogation room. In undercover investigations, there is a continuum of deception that starts with a simple buy-bust scenario where an officer lies about wanting to buy drugs. At the other end of the continuum are the most elaborate and profound deception scenarios where officers engage in fairly intimate relationships in order to gather information on suspects. These are the most problematic, and some ethicists have remarked that the end rarely justifies the means in these cases of trust violation (Schoeman, 1985, 1986; Sherman, 1985b; Pollock, 2014).

Undercover work carries risks to officers as well. Carter (1999: 316) discusses the phenomena of police officers who go undercover and become socialized to the drug culture. They may adapt norms conducive to drug taking. Elements of police work that lead to drug use include: the exposure to a criminal element, relative freedom from supervision, and the uncontrolled availability of contraband.

Another problem with lying at the investigative phase is that it sometimes leads to a temptation to lie at the trial stage. One of the most well-known cases of testilying occurred in Tulia, Texas. In this small town, 43 people were arrested after an undercover drug operation. The police officer who gathered evidence was hired from outside the town and targeted mostly African Americans. Convictions were obtained almost solely on his testimony with no corroborating evidence. After an investigation by the ACLU and NAACP, it was discovered that the officer had lied in his affidavits and on the witness stand and there was ample exculpatory evidence in many cases, which should have alerted the prosecutor and the officer's superiors to the problem. In their zeal to obtain convictions, however, this evidence was ignored. The scandal resulted in sanctions against the prosecutor, criminal charges against the narcotics officer, and a special gubernatorial pardon for all convicted, but not before many had served many months in jail and/or prison (Herbert, 2002).

While testilying and other forms of dishonesty on the part of police officers occur extremely infrequently, such incidents affect the entire force and make it more difficult for prosecutors to win convictions because jurors are less likely to believe police officer-witnesses who have been found to have lied in the past. The Cato Institute's National Police Reporting Web site lists incidents that have ruined officers' lives and tainted their department's reputations. In January 2014, the following incidents were reported:

- Windermere, Florida: A former police chief was found guilty of lying under oath during a friend's trial who was convicted of raping children and sentenced to life in prison.
- East Haven, Connecticut: A former officer received a 30 month prison sentence for civil rights charges, including writing a false arrest report.
- Los Angeles County, California: A former deputy pleaded guilty to one count of perjury in a probable cause declaration and one count of filing a false report.

Interrogation

The desire to gain a confession sometimes leads to unethical actions during the interrogation phase. The "third degree" (using the infliction of pain to obtain a confession) was eliminated in interrogations long ago. The use of physical coercion to obtain confessions is considered unethical, illegal, and ineffective in that victims might confess to stop their suffering. Many would argue that whatever information is gained from an individual who is physically coerced into confessing or giving information is not worth the sacrifice of moral standards even if the information is truthful, and human rights treaties signed by the majority of free countries condemn such practices.

Police, however, continue to use mental coercion and deception during interrogation. Skolnick and Leo (1992) present a typology of deceptive interrogation techniques. The following is a brief summary of their descriptions of these practices:

- calling the questioning an interview, questioning in a noncustodial setting, or telling the suspect that he or she is free to leave (thus eliminating the need for Miranda warnings)
- presenting Miranda warnings in a way designed to negate their effect (mumbling or by using a tone suggesting that they are unnecessary)
- misrepresenting the nature or seriousness of the offense
- using manipulative appeals to conscience through role playing or other means
- misrepresenting the moral seriousness of the offense
- making promises beyond the power of the police to offer
- misrepresenting identity by pretending to be lawyers or priests

The Supreme Court has basically approved of most types of deception during interrogation. Police are taught various tricks of interrogation, including pretending that a crime partner is "rolling over" on the defendant, pretending that they have found overwhelming physical evidence at the crime scene, and so on. Most people don't have a problem with these examples. However, police also threaten female defendants that they will lose their children if they don't cooperate, or promise to put the word out on the street that the defendant is a snitch. Are these as defensible? The question is whether the coercion used (whether physical or mental) would be enough to make an innocent person confess.

Can innocent people be coerced to confess to a crime they didn't commit? It happened in the Central Park jogging case where teenage boys confessed and spent years in prison before the true rapist was discovered through a spontaneous confession and confirmation by DNA (Getlin, 2002; Tanner, 2006). In fact, in many of the cases of exonerated individuals, freed by Innocence Commissions across the country with DNA evidence, their conviction was obtained partially through a false confession. A study of these cases indicates that many of the defendants were very young, mentally handicapped, or influenced by extreme stress and coercion on the part of police officers (Garrett, 2012).

Use of Force

Police officers have a legal right (and duty) to utilize necessary force to subdue a suspect, for self-defense or defense of others. Use of force, even lethal force, is not an ethical issue unless it is excessive, and excessive is defined as that over and above what is required to subdue the suspect or neutralize a threat (Alpert and Dunham, 2004). In a National Institute of Justice study, about a quarter of police respondents agreed or strongly agreed that sometimes *illegal* force is acceptable (Weisburd and Greenspan, 2000: 5). This acceptance of extra-legal or illegal force has long been described as an element of the police subculture and can be considered a type of noble-cause corruption since the officers involved often have a sense that they are inflicting a type of street justice by administering corporal punishment to those who deserve it.

It should be noted that *any* use of force by officers occurs in a very small percentage of all police–citizen encounters. The Bureau of Justice Statistics estimates there are over 40 million police–citizen contacts each year, yet less than 2 percent involved threats or use of force (IACP, 2012: 11). Terrill (2001, 2005), in a study based on participant observations of police–citizen encounters, reported that officers did not even use the level of force that they were legally and (by policy) entitled to use in the majority of encounters based on the resistance of the suspect. However, it appears that some departments have a culture that creates a greater potential for excessive force.

Any incident of excessive force galvanizes citizen distrust and has the potential to expose the city to large monetary judgments and even criminal charges against the officers involved. For instance, the Kelly Thomas case in Fullerton, California, involved a mentally ill homeless man who would not (some say could not) follow the instructions of the police officers to put his hands on his knees and sit on the curb. Before the altercation was over, Thomas suffered broken facial bones, a conducted energy device (CED) was used on him five times, and he suffered asphyxia from chest compression. He ended up in a coma and died five days later. The incident was recorded on a security camera and was widely distributed and is still accessible via the

Internet. Three officers were eventually charged with involuntary manslaughter, but when two were acquitted in January 2014, the district attorney dropped the charges against the third. Like the Rodney King case, the acquittal has sparked protests and widespread opposition against the police department. The legal definitions that are applied if an officer is charged with a crime are hard for people to understand and, even if an officer is not guilty of a crime, he or she may still face departmental sanctions because of not following policies. In these situations, even though the officer was within the law in his or her use of force during the incident, actions taken before the need for the use of force may have been contrary to policy and created the situation where force was ultimately necessary. In the Thomas case, investigators concluded that the officers did not take Thomas' mental illness into account and the violence could have been avoided. The city has paid the mother of Kelly Thomas $1 million, and another lawsuit brought by his father is still pending (Associated Press, 2014).

Again, the Cato Institute's web page provides some cases from the month of January 2014:

- Salem, New Hampshire: A police officer was fired in connection with excessive force allegations.
- New York, New York: Witnesses reported that police officers assaulted an 84-year-old man when he jaywalked and didn't follow their orders to stop. The man ended up in the hospital.
- West Valley City, Utah: Two drug defendants have had their criminal cases dismissed and have filed a lawsuit alleging that members of the police department's narcotics unit used excessive force when they slammed one of the defendant's heads into a wall, cutting it open.
- Painesville, Ohio: An excessive force lawsuit claims that a man suffered brain damage caused by police using a Taser on him at his home.
- Oklahoma City, Oklahoma: An attorney alleges his deaf client was the victim of excessive force during a traffic stop and at the hospital and jail because the man would not comply with the officer's orders to display his hands.
- Salem, New Hampshire: A police officer is on unpaid leave and charged with two counts of simple assault from an incident where he is alleged to have struck the victim on the head with a flashlight and stepped on his hand while the man was handcuffed and sitting on the ground.

While some argue that CEDs (often called Tasers because that is the name of one of the devices) are a welcome addition to police efforts to subdue or control suspects without resorting to lethal force; others have alleged that there is abuse and some police officers use the device in illegal and unethical ways. Amnesty International alleges that police use CEDs in hundreds of cases in which their use is unjustified and "routinely" inflict injury, pain, and death. Its investigation uncovered the fact that CEDs were used on unarmed suspects 80 percent of the time and for verbal noncompliance in 36 percent of the cases. They have allegedly been used on "unruly schoolchildren," the "mentally disturbed or intoxicated," and those who do not comply immediately with police commands (Dart, 2004).

One instance of the use of a CED in Austin, Texas, has been widely viewed on the Internet and illustrates different perceptions sometimes occur in whether or not its use is appropriate. From a dashboard camera, a police officer is seen stopping a vehicle for a traffic offense and asking for a license and registration. When the black driver argues with the officer, the officer uses his Taser against the man. The chief of police made an unprecedented decision to release the tape and use it for training purposes. The officer was suspended, and members of the police officer's union apologized to the public at large for the actions of this one officer (Plohetski, 2007). (You can view the tape at http://www.youtube.com/watch?v=8RGe8fJ597w.)

As previously stated, officers use force rarely and there are extremely few instances of excessive force. However, any single incident has widespread effects on the police department and reduces public confidence that police officers follow the law. Another way excessive force becomes an ethical issue is when police officers cover up incidents for the offending officer by falsifying police reports that the subject was resisting or testifying that they didn't see anything. The so-called Blue Curtain of Secrecy is an undeniable element of the police subculture.

The Blue Curtain of Secrecy and Whistle-Blowing

In situations where an officer knows of the wrongdoing of another officer, the conflict is between loyalty to one's friend/colleague and loyalty to the organization or to one's own integrity (Wren, 1985; Ewin, 1990). If one has no loyalty to friends, there would be no dilemma in exposing an offending officer; if one has no integrity or loyalty to the organization, there would be no inclination to do anything at all when a partner or friend commits a wrongful or illegal act. Officers experience conflict only when they are loyal and honest. These examples might be categorized as noble cause corruption because the officers involved believe that it is right to protect each other because they are the "thin blue line" that separates the citizenry from criminals. Officers who come forward against other officers are considered traitors.

One of the most extreme examples of a law enforcement cover-up was the Abner Louima case in New York where a Haitian man, arrested for a dispute at a bar, was anally assaulted by Officer Justin Volpe in the station house. The incident was witnessed by at least one other officer and others were implicated in the cover-up. It was only when officers were threatened with criminal action that they cooperated with prosecution efforts. Volpe received a 30-year prison sentence and another officer received a five-year sentence for perjury. The question remains, however, as to why some officers would conceal such a heinous act.

Although the "blue curtain" of secrecy (the practice of protecting fellow officers) is, perhaps, breaking down, it is still a strong element in most departments. In a survey sponsored by the National Institute of Justice, a large percentage of police officers (67 percent) agreed that someone who reported another officer's misconduct would be ostracized and 50 percent disagreed that police officers would always report serious criminal violations of other officers (Weisburd and Greenspan, 2000: 2). In a study by Klockars and colleagues (Klockars, Ivkovic, and Haberfield, 2000, 2004), officers were presented with a hypothetical involving excessive force and asked if they would report their fellow officers. Findings varied quite a bit between departments. In one department, less than 10 percent indicated that they would definitely *not* report it, whereas over 40 percent in another department indicated that they would definitely *not* report the incident. Similar differences were found in all hypotheticals between these two departments indicating substantial differences exist in what might be considered a police subculture.

Noble cause corruption has been a helpful concept to understand that some of the decisions of police officers are made not for self-gain, but rather to pursue their mission of crime control and protection. The discussion also illustrates, however, that such decisions can result in wrongful convictions. Some might argue that the consequences of ignoring the law to gain a conviction are always worse because the law and police credibility are always more important than single convictions. In one exploration of trying to measure noble cause values and their relationship to crime, researchers found that there were wide variations in support for noble cause statements and that adherence to noble cause did not seem to be related to a perception of level of crime (Crank, Flaherty, and Giacomazzi, 2007).

Police Deviance and Corruption

One way to identify and categorize unethical police behavior is offered by Barker and Carter (1994), who propose that police abuse of authority comes in three different areas: (1) physical abuse—excessive force, physical harassment; (2) psychological abuse—disrespect, harassment, ridicule, excessive stops, intimidation; and (3) legal abuse—unlawful searches or seizures, manufacturing evidence.

The following is an outline of the types of police misconduct (see Fyfe and Kane, 2006, for a detailed discussion):

- *Police crime* involves situations where police officers violate criminal statutes, either with crimes that have nothing to do with their position (e.g., burglaries or insurance fraud), or crimes that are related to their position (e.g., theft from an evidence locker or identity theft using information obtained by writing tickets).
- *Police corruption* refers to offenses where the officer uses his or her position, by act or omission, to obtain improper financial benefit (e.g. bribes, kickbacks, protection).

- *Abuses of power* can be physical, psychological or legal. Physical abuse can be divided into "brutality," which occurs when officers inflict physical abuse on persons to teach them a lesson, and unnecessary force, which occurs when police officers make mistakes that lead them to resort to force that would not have been necessary had he or she followed proper procedures. Psychological abuse ranges from deception during an interrogation to intimidation on the street. Legal abuse involves various forms of wrongdoing designed to convict wrongdoers, including perjury, planting evidence, and hiding exculpatory evidence. Another type of abuse of power involves off-duty misconduct (e.g., driving while intoxicated or physical assaults) with the expectation that the wrongdoing will be covered up by fellow officers.

Some police departments seem to have a consistent history of corruption. Wide-scale investigations and exposés regarding the New York Police Department occurred in 1894, 1913, 1932 (the Wickersham Commission), 1949 (the Kefauver Commission), 1972 (the Knapp Commission), and 1993 (the Mollen Commission). Los Angeles has also had its share of scandals (Rodney King, Ramparts Scandal). More recent scandals have taken place in Honolulu, Hawaii, Washington D.C., Minneapolis, Minnesota, and Seattle, Washington. It is also possible that big cities may receive the most coverage and are not necessarily more prone to corruption than smaller agencies.

Quite a bit of academic literature exists that discusses the prevalence, origin, and reasons for the existence of corruption (Murphy and Moran, 1981; Barker and Carter, 1991, 1994; Murphy and Caplan, 1989; Souryal, 2007). Klockars and colleagues (2000, 2004) investigated the concept of integrity in police departments by asking officers to rank the seriousness of a number of hypotheticals involving wrongdoing. They also asked if the officer would report the behavior and what level of discipline would probably result. Although the rank-order of the hypotheticals were the same across the many departments surveyed, there were differences in the level of seriousness ascribed, as well as willingness to report. Another finding was that the officers' perceptions of seriousness correlated with the level of discipline they expected would be the result for each incident (Klockars et al., 2004: 280).

It should be emphasized that although police scandals occur regularly, they involve an extremely small percentage of all officers and departments and the vast majority of police officers are honest, ethical, and do their job to the best of their ability. Interestingly, the public seems to understand this fact. In 1977, 37 percent of the public rated police integrity and ethics as high or very high and 12 percent rated it as low or very low. By 1997, the percentage of those who rated police high or very high went up to 49 percent and those who rated them low or very low was only 10 percent. By 2007, 53 percent of the public rated police integrity as high or very high and only 9 percent of the population rated them as low or very low (Pastore and Maguire, 2007). Over the last five years perceptions have remained relatively constant. Results from

2013 show 54 percent of citizens rate police officers with having high/very high honesty and ethical standards (Gallup, 2014).

Explanations for Police Deviance and Corruption

There are a variety of explanations for the presence of corruption in police organizations. Some point to weaknesses in the recruiting and training practices (Dorschner, 1993). Some point to the police subculture, and some to more systemic elements of policing that set the groundwork for a network of corruption to exist. We can group explanations into the categories of individual, organizational, and societal (Pollock, 2014).

Individual

The "rotten apple" explanation of police deviance and corruption is that individual officers are either already deviant when they enter policing or become so after they join. There is no fail-safe method to eliminate dishonest officers from an applicant pool, although psychological testing continues to improve the hiring process. Once hired, some officers may be tempted by the opportunities unique to policing. Officers are also exposed to a fairly steady diet of deviance. After years of policing, some officers may become convinced that everyone is dishonest and so they might as well profit from wrongdoing as well.

The slippery slope explanation is that some officers start down the path of deviance with relatively minor transgressions and then proceed to more serious misconduct in a slow but steady progression (Sherman, 1982, 1985a; Malloy, 1982). Because most officers engage in their share of minor transgressions they are unable to point fingers at those who commit serious violations.

Organizational

Organizational explanations of police deviance and corruption point to the police subculture, management and administration, or both. The parameters and elements of the police subculture have been described by many authors (Muir 1977; Reuss-Ianni, 1983; Sherman 1982; Scheingold, 1984; Crank, 1998; Ingram, Paoline & Terrill, 2013). Some elements of the subculture support unethical behavior on the part of officers. For instance, the premise that some people deserve extra-legal uses of force and that covering up the wrongdoing of other officers is the right thing to do (the blue curtain of secrecy) have been described as elements of a police subculture, and both would encourage unethical actions.

The subculture of policing obviously doesn't support the worst forms of deviance, such as drug dealing and theft, but what the culture does do is create an atmosphere where individuals come to feel that the law does not apply to them. Many citizens criticize officers who drive too fast, park in the road and block traffic, leave restaurants without paying, give "professional courtesy" to fellow officers who have broken traffic laws, and otherwise let it be known that even though they enforce the law against the rest of us, they don't have to follow it. The culture creates an "us-versus-them" attitude that fosters the blue curtain of secrecy, which protects even the more deviant members of the profession.

It should also be noted that the subculture may be breaking down. Barker (2002), for instance, reported on some research indicating that minorities and women have torn the solidarity that once existed, and this can be seen by the proliferation of complaints against fellow officers. For instance, he notes that there were more than 30 cases in Los Angeles where officers were the primary witnesses against other officers. Another survey study found that police respondents were more likely to report misdemeanors and felonies of their fellow officers than were civilian employee-respondents in other agencies. On the other hand, Weisburd and Greenspan (2000), in their large survey of police officers, discovered that although 80 percent of police officers did not feel that the "code of silence" was essential for police trust and good policing, fully two-thirds reported that a "whistle-blower" would encounter sanctions. Further, more than half agreed that it was not unusual for police to ignore improper conduct on the part of other officers, and 61 percent indicated that police officers do not always report even the most serious violations/crimes of other officers. Another study found that police officers were more likely to report the wrongdoing of other officers if it involved the acquisition of goods or money (except for gratuities) rather than if the wrongdoing was excessive force or "bending" rules. In this study, even though almost all respondents thought that stealing from a burglary scene was very serious, about a quarter thought that their colleagues would not report it (Westmarland, 2005).

Most agree that the strongest correlate to the level of dishonesty among employees is the level of dishonesty among administrators. If there is wide-scale corruption in a police department, inevitably that corruption has reached high levels of management that protected and even encouraged dishonesty on the part of the rank and file. Even honest administrators and managers can foster and encourage corruption when they do nothing about it. In most wide-scale corruption scandals there was an attempted cover-up from high in the management ranks. There is an aversion to "airing dirty laundry" in law enforcement that influences decisions to curtail investigations of dirty cops and keep evidence of corruption under wraps. Ironically, this often results in worse publicity in the long run.

Organizational justice research supports the premise that misconduct and corruption is at least partially influenced by organizational aspects. Organizational justice focuses on how employees define fair treatment within their organization and how their perceptions of how just their organizations are influence both positive and negative work-related outcomes (Colquitt, Greenberg, and Zapata-Phelan, 2005). The concept of organizational justice can be explained using three primary dimensions: distributive, procedural, and interactional justice (Cohen-Charash and Spector, 2001), although some researchers recommend a four-dimensional model, suggesting it would be more descriptive and explanatory to separate interactional justice into interpersonal justice and informational justice (Colquitt, Conlon, Wesson, Porter, and Ng, 2001). Distributive justice refers to the perceived fairness of an outcome or decision (e.g., rewards or disciplinary). Procedural justice refers to the processes used to determine the outcome (e.g., departmental policies). Interactional justice involves how information is communicated and the manner in which the employee is treated during the process. Interactional justice is sometimes viewed as two separate dimensions: interpersonal and informational. Interpersonal justice focuses on if supervisors treat employees with dignity and respect and refrain from demeaning or inappropriate comments. Informational justice is the perceived fairness in organizational explanations for the existence of certain procedures and distributions in the workplace (Cohen-Charash and Spector, 2001; Colquitt, et al., 2001; Colquitt, et al., 2005).

Research has found that perceptions of fairness are related to positive work outcomes; while perceptions of unfairness are related to negative performance. For instance, perceptions of interpersonal justice have been found to be negatively associated with retaliatory behaviors (behaviors used to punish or get even with the organization and its representatives, including decreased performance such as work slowdowns) (Cohen-Charash and Spector, 2001; Colquitt, et al., 2001). Conversely, employees' perceptions of fairness in the organization have been shown to foster employee cooperation. Cooperative behaviors include: rule compliance, voluntary deference, extra-role and in-role performance (Tyler, Callahan, and Frost, 2007; Tyler, 2011).

Research on organizational justice in law enforcement agencies sheds light on how perceptions of organizational justice can influence officers' behaviors (Tyler, Callahan, and Frost, 2007; Wolfe and Piquero, 2011). Organizational justice research in law enforcement agencies has reached similar conclusions as the research described above (Farmer, Beehr, and Love, 2003; Harris and Worden, 2014; Tyler, Callahan, and Frost, 2007; Wolfe and Piquero, 2011). For example, Farmer, Beehr, and Love (2003) examined the relationship between perceptions of distributive and procedural dimensions of organizational justice and job performance, satisfaction, and organizational commitment among police officers. A survey was administered to a sample of 271 police officer applicants to measure officers' reactions to the department's undercover officer selection system. The results showed that both distributive and procedural perceptions of justice were positively related to the undercover officers' job performance, job satisfaction, and organizational commitment. Wolfe and Piquero (2011) examined perceptions of organizational justice utilizing survey data from a random sample of police officers. Topics surveyed included: officer misconduct, adherence to the code of silence, and justifications for noble cause corruption. The findings indicated that officers who perceive that organizational procedures are fair are less likely to engage in police misconduct. In addition, favorable perceptions of organizational justice are related to lower likelihood of adhering to the code of silence or perceptions that corruption in pursuit of a noble cause is justified.

Societal

Police departments probably represent the communities they police. Cities torn by racial strife will probably have a police department that plays racial politics. Communities where corruption is endemic among local politicians rarely escape similar corruption in their police departments. Communities that turn a blind eye to police violence (as long as it is visited upon less desirable groups) will probably have a police department marked by brutality.

Much of what is defined as unethical on the part of officers is supported by the public itself. If the "end" of catching criminals is more important than the "duty" of protecting the sanctity of the law, then unethical actions are sure to follow because anything can be justified. If we accept unethical practices when they benefit us, then we can hardly cry out when unethical practices flourish and spread to other behavioral decisions. Historically some police have had some degree of community support for unethical practices, such as harassing and brutalizing labor union organizers in the early part of the twentieth century and civil rights demonstrators in the 1950s and 1960s (Fogelson, 1977; Crank, 1998; Skolnick and Fyfe, 1993; Nelson, 2000). Certainly the public does not seem to care if drug dealers' civil liberties are violated. The trouble is that once those protections are removed from one group, it becomes easier to ignore due process protections for everyone.

When police departments emphasize crime control over community relations, there are consequences. In New York City, the implementation of a zero tolerance mandate toward petty crime and street people supposedly contributed to the city's dramatic decline of crime. Others noted complaints against police increased 75 percent during the same time period (Greene, 1999: 176). In the following 15 years, the NYPD dramatically increased the number of stop-and-frisks, and there was a rising disagreement among civil libertarians and ordinary citizens as to the legitimacy of these stops. Recently, William Bratton indicated that the cost of the tremendous increase in stop-and-frisks, especially of minority boys and men, was a deterioration of rights enjoyed by the citizenry and a decrease in public trust toward police. He indicated changes will be made; thus, the community does have a voice in what happens within their police department (Weiser and Goldstein, 2014).

Improving Ethical Decision Making in Law Enforcement

Officers themselves typically identify several standard elements important to being a "good officer." These elements include: legality (enforcing and upholding the law), service (protecting and serving the public), honesty and integrity (telling the truth, being honest in action), loyalty (to other police officers), and the golden rule (treating people with respect or the way one would like to be treated) (Pollock and Becker, 1996). These elements seem to be universal with those officers who are committed to doing their best.

The question is how to create a situation wherein all officers in a division or department try to uphold these standards of behavior. Carter (1999) identified the following steps:

- leadership from the chief's office,
- management and supervision,
- supervisory training,
- organizational control and information management,
- internal auditing of the use of informants,
- internal affairs,
- drug enforcement units having audit controls and turnover of staff,
- better evidence handling,
- early warning systems, and
- training and discipline.

Hunter (1999) discussed the following approaches:

- decertifying officers who have committed serious misconduct,
- community policing,
- college education,
- enhanced discipline,
- civilian review boards, and
- training.

These answers fall into three general categories: better selection which is an individual deviance response, better training and management, which are organizational level responses, and the societal response of the public being involved in a shared vision of what law enforcement should be in that community.

Selection

The process of selecting the appropriate individuals for hire in law enforcement is one that continues to be improved. Psychological testing is now fairly standard and helps, to some extent, weed out those who are not qualified to take on the responsibilities of the role. The MMPI and similar tests do not adequately measure one's moral development, nor do they accurately predict how the individual will respond to ethical dilemmas; however, they do provide some information about a person's personality characteristics (Sanders, 2008).

Higher education continues to be debated as a requirement of hire. There are findings on both sides of the argument, but no one has definitively proven that education insulates someone from unethical decisions. Thus, those who examine the applicant pool continue to look at their past experience and use "gut instinct" to determine the best among those who pass the preliminary battery of tests. It is possible that better tests will be developed, but they do not exist today.

Training and Management

The informal police subculture and the Code of Ethics are sometimes in conflict. Academy and in-service training attempt to thwart some of the most negative aspects of the subculture, but often with limited success. Often, the field training officer (FTO) will start his or her training by first telling the rookie, "Forget everything you learned in the academy. . . ." Thus, in some departments, there is a disconnection between training and what happens on the street.

Many departments have instituted various models of ethical training as part of the academy training and/or as an in-service class (Pollock-Byrne, 1988; Pollock and Becker, 1996; Swift, Houston, and Anderson, 1993; Kleinig, 1990; Sherman, 1981; Martinelli, 2000). No doubt the effect of such training lies in the perception that the leaders of the organization take it seriously. New training components or entirely revised training employ elements of procedural justice. According to Jonathan-Zamir, Mastrofski, and Moyal (2013), previous research has identified four elements related to citizens' perceptions of fair treatment and decisions by police during police–citizen interactions. The first is participation in the process. For example, an officer listens to the citizen's concerns and views before deciding what to do. The second aspect is neutrality, which refers to the officer being impartial or unbiased. For instance, the officer should explain why the decision or outcome is being made. By doing so, the officer may reduce perceptions of preferential or disadvantageous treatment due to an individual's racial, ethnic, or socioeconomic class. The third is dignity and respect. Officers can show people respect and dignity by not violating an individual's rights and talking in a polite and courteous manner. The final element is trust. Officers can garner trust with individuals by performing their duties in manner that shows that they care for the individuals and the community they serve. As noted by Tyler and Hou (2002), a primary ingredient needed to build trust among individuals is to act in a manner that they will perceive as fair. Several academies across the country are employing these concepts in their training of recruits.

Probably the single most important element in minimizing corruption in police departments is how the organization is managed. Generally, police officials prefer to manage the investigation of and discipline for corruption internally; however, communities are increasingly demanding a role in the monitoring and enforcement of discipline. All departments have some version of internal affairs and an internal discipline process (Prenzler and Ransley, 2002). There is no research that evaluates the effectiveness of internal anticorruption units (Walker, 2007); however, they may be perceived by the public to be the least effective way to deal with misconduct. In one Toronto study, 70 percent of people who filed complaints were not confident with the process, and only 14 percent felt their complaint was handled fairly (Prenzler and Ronken, 2001b: 180). Some departments have "beefed up" their internal anticorruption units. These units, especially in other countries, now undertake a mission of not only investigation and punishment but also deterrence and prevention. Such units may undertake integrity testing, promote awareness, improve selection and screening procedures, develop performance standards, and, in other ways, "police" the police to minimize corruption (Moran, 2005). Integrity testing is widely condemned by officers, but it has been used by many departments to test officers' honesty. In one agency, almost 30 percent of officers failed to turn in "found" money (Prenzler and Ronken, 2001a: 322).

Another internal method is to employ an "early warning" system that alerts management to officers who have excessive citizen complaints or other specified indications that intervention is needed. Walker and Alpert (2002) noted that these programs have been endorsed by the National Institute of Justice and have been incorporated into several consent decrees between cities and federal courts to avert civil rights litigation. Walker (2007) reports that early warning systems are different in what elements they count and where they set the threshold of concern. They also have different objectives: while some departments use them to punish, others use them to provide assistance.

Civilian review boards or other citizen oversight mechanisms (such as independent monitors) have been created in several cities to monitor and review the investigation and discipline of officers who have complaints filed against them. There are many models that exist for the idea of civilian review, and no one model has been reported to be more effective or better than any other. Prenzler and Ronken (2001b) argue that it is difficult to analyze the success of such bodies because a high level of complaints may mean that there is greater trust in the process rather than a spike in misconduct. Recent descriptions of citizen overview mechanisms indicate that they are opposed by police unions in some cities, but other cities have had some type of system in place since the 1970s. Researchers note that, as of 2011, more than 120 citizen oversight agencies operate across the country (Ferdik, Rojek and Alpert, 2013). There are also additional models that provide overview, such as monitors in the executive branch (e.g. Austin, Texas).

Another intervention that is becoming more common is the use of "consent decrees" between the department and the Department of Justice. The Department of Justice (DOJ) has been given the legal authority to investigate allegations of constitutional violations. After an investigation, the DOJ may pursue a lawsuit against the police department, but, much more often, there is a written "consent decree" between the DOJ and the police department in lieu of a lawsuit. Consent decrees have been entered into by many police departments around the country including: Pittsburgh (1997), New Jersey State Police (1999), Los Angeles (2001), Detroit (2002), New Orleans (2012), and Seattle (2012). One of the elements of these decrees is that a police monitor is appointed to measure progress and report back to the court as to whether the decree should be extended or terminated. While there have been rancorous relationships between department officials and monitors in some cities, other city officials admit that the experience improved their department (Police Executive Research Forum, 2013).

Law enforcement administrators do not have to be corrupt to encourage corruption. Administration can encourage corruption through poor or ill-conceived management practices. Previously mentioned was the practice of covering up the wrongdoing of individual officers. While the intent may be to protect the department, the effect is to broadcast a message to the rank and file that wrongdoing will be ignored or protected. When the honest officer isn't supported, the dishonest officer wins. Management practices may encourage corruption by imposing pressures for arrest quotas or make it acceptable to cut corners to effect arrests. A recent controversy concerns the COMPSTAT program in New York City, widely hailed as William Bratton's greatest contribution to police management (in his first term as police commissioner of the NYPD). The practice of almost immediate crime statistics and comparison of districts in management meetings has been identified as one of the reasons New York City experienced a dramatic decline in crime because it showed management where crime was occurring and added a competitive edge to reducing numbers. Recently, Eterno and Silverman (2012) generated a firestorm of controversy when they published their research findings that COMPSTAT has led to widespread "fudging" of figures to make it appear as if crime has been reduced. They used a survey of retired NYPD field commanders, statements by union officials, internal NYPD reports, comparisons of trends in index versus nonindex crimes and of index crimes versus hospital records, and undercover recordings of supervisors' instructions to patrol officers to conclude that COMPSTAT encouraged a culture of downgrading crime reports and coercing officers to convince crime victims not to file reports of crime. Their research has been criticized, but it does bear noting that the situation is not too dissimilar to the test-score cheating scandals that occur in school districts, and for the same reason: when an agency is evaluated on numbers, there is an inevitable temptation to manipulate those numbers.

The research of Klockars et al. (2000, 2004) described earlier shows that the discipline practices of management has a direct bearing on how serious officers perceive various forms of wrongdoing. Other research indicates that close supervision, especially by mid-level managers such as sergeants, reduces the use of force and incidences of misconduct by officers (Walker, 2007). Research by Lee et al. (2013), also found that when supervisors discipline more severely for corrupt behavior, frontline officers perceive corruption as more serious.

In another study, it was found that role modeling was significant in limiting unethical conduct of an interpersonal nature (sexual harassment, discrimination, bullying), while strictness in supervision seemed to be more important in controlling the misuse of resources, fraud, and other forms of financial corruption. A third component of leadership was described as openness when leaders encouraged subordinates to talk to them about ethical dilemmas. This was associated with lower violations in a number of areas, especially in favoritism and discrimination. Interestingly, this study of over

6,000 police officers found that strictness had no effect on reducing the gratuitous use of violence but role modeling and openness did. This seems to support a police culture explanation of excessive force (Huberts, Kaptein, and Lasthuizen, 2007).

The concept of organizational justice can provide guidance to administrators on how to improve officer accountability by simply treating officers fairly. Perceived unfair or harsh treatment by police leaders, particularly concerning disciplinary or complaint processes, increases negative work-related behaviors. Harris and Worden (2014) examined the effect of the severity of police disciplinary sanctions on future incidents of police misconduct, measured by citizen complaints on officers with at least one previous sustained complaint during their career at a large northeastern police department. The findings from this longitudinal cohort study show that officers who received more severe punishments were more likely to receive a future complaint compared to officers who received lesser sanctions. However, the severity of the punishment may not be as important as the officers' perceptions of fairness during the disciplinary process. For instance, Shane (2012) found officers were more likely to perceive the disciplinary process as fair when supervisory discretion and the unpredictability of decisions were reduced by utilizing a disciplinary matrix for disciplinary outcomes. Research is beginning to accumulate that police officers engage in less negative behaviors when departments apply the elements of organizational justice by having fair outcomes (distributive justice), based on fair procedures (procedural justice); treat employees with dignity and respect; and provide information on how disciplinary decisions are made (interactional justice) (Cohen-Charash and Spector, 2001).

Societal Intervention

Societal interventions that might decrease police misconduct and encourage ethical performance of duty in police departments generally involve communication and participation. As mentioned above, citizen oversight review has been a method that, if both police departments and citizens are open-minded and committed to a process that is fair and just for complainants and officers alike, can improve community relations and lead to a better functioning police department. Citizen police academies are offered by some departments in an effort to engage citizens to show them the reality of policing instead of the steady diet of fiction that is portrayed on television. The community must make clear what it won't tolerate in the performance of public servants. Generally, if community expectations are clear and reasonable, public agencies respond.

Conclusion

The ability for legal authorities to be effective is dependent upon people to be willing to follow and obey the law, so legal authorities should act in a manner that promotes compliance (Tyler, 2006). Police legitimacy is important because officers need public support and cooperation to be successful in their order- maintenance role. This support derives from people's perception that the police are legitimate legal authorities and therefore should be obeyed (Tyler, 2006; Jonathan-Zamir, Mastrofski, and Moyal, 2013). Officers can maintain and protect their legitimacy by performing their duties in a manner that is reflective of both the law and their law enforcement code of ethics and oaths of office, as noted earlier in this chapter.

In general, when citizens perceive that they are being treated in a procedurally fair manner, they are more likely to view the police as legitimate (Mazerolle, Antrobus, and Bennett, 2013, Tyler, 2004), more likely to obey law (Tyler, 2006), comply with the demands and cooperate with police officers (Tyler, 2004; Tyler, 2006, Tyler and Huo, 2002), experience increased satisfaction with the experience (Jonathan-Zamir, Mastrofski, and Moyal, 2013), and have increased trust and confidence in the police (Murphy, Mazerolle, Bennett, 2013), regardless of the experience outcome (Tyler and Fagan, 2008). Furthermore, perceptions of legitimacy and citizen's reactions and behaviors toward authorities can be positively influenced by single incidents (Mazerolle et al., 2013; Murphy, et al., 2013), such as a traffic stop that is conducted using procedurally fair principles. It is important for police to understand not only how their actions and decisions impact the lives of the citizens they interact with but also how society ultimately will perceive police officers in general and the legitimacy of their role in society.

Individual officers will continue to wield their discretion in a multitude of situations. They must make those decisions using the law and policy as their guide, but oftentimes, their ethics also come into play to determine the right thing to do. There are day-to-day decisions and "noble cause" situations where they must make difficult choices. Ultimately, they must hold themselves accountable for their own individual behavior. It is possible to be a "good" person and a "good" police officer when one takes the time to define the terms, is aware of the ethical nature of decision making, and has the courage to live up to one's own principles.

The explanations of police misconduct (individual, organizational, and societal) can also form the basis for interventions and innovations to improve the ethical climate of law enforcement agencies. Better selection of officers is an individual response. Organizational responses include training that employs procedural justice concepts and management that is consistent with organizational justice principles. Another response that is both organizational and societal is the inclusion of citizens in the process of discipline and oversight. Citizens are the ones who suffer when police officers are not ethical; therefore, they have a right and a duty to participate in the process to ensure that law enforcement officers follow law, policy, and ethics in their decision making and, for those very few who do not, fair and just consequences ensue. In this way, the social contract is honored.

REFERENCES

Alderson, J. 1998. *Principled Policing: Protecting the Public with Integrity.* Winchester, MA: Waterside.

Alpert, G., and R. Dunham. 2004. *Understanding Police Use of Force.* New York: Cambridge University Press.

Arizona v. United States, 567 U.S. ____ (2012).

Associated Press. 2014. "Kelly Thomas Trial: Officers Acquitted in Homeless Man's Death." Foxnews.online, January 14. Retrieved from http://www.foxnews.com/us/2014/01/14/kelly-thomas-trial-officers-acquitted-in-homeless-man-death/.

Ballenger J., S. Best, T. Metzler, D. Wasserman, D. Mohr, A. Liberman, and C. Marmar. 2011. "Patterns and Predictors of Alcohol Use in Male and Female Urban Police Officers." *The American Journal on Addictions,* 20(1): 21–29.

Barker, T. 2002. "Ethical Police Behavior." In *Policing and Misconduct,* ed. K. Lersch, 1–25. Upper Saddle River, NJ: Prentice-Hall.

Barker, T., and D. Carter. 1991. "Police Lies and Perjury: A Motivation-Based Taxonomy." In *Police Deviance,* 2d ed., ed. T. Barker and D. Carter. Cincinnati: Anderson.

Barker, T., and D. Carter (Eds.). 1994. *Police Deviance,* 3rd ed. Cincinnati: Anderson.

Bossard, A. 1981. "Police Ethics and International Police Cooperation." In *The Social Basis of Criminal Justice: Ethical Issues for the 80's,* ed. F. Schmalleger and R. Gustafson, 23–38. Washington, DC: University Press of America.

Caldero, M., and J. Crank. 2010. *Police Ethics: The Corruption of Noble Cause,* 3d ed. Cincinnati: Anderson.

Carter, D. 1999. "Drug Use and Drug-Related Corruption of Police Officers." In *Policing Perspectives,* ed. L. Gaines and G. Cordner, 311–324. Los Angeles: Roxbury.

Chappell, A., and S. Gibson. 2009. "Community Policing and Homeland Security Policing: Friend or Foe?" *Criminal Justice Policy Review* 20(3):326–343.

Chopko, B., Palmieri, P. and Adams, R. 2013. "Association between Police Stress and Alcohol Use: Implications for Practice." *Journal of Loss and Trauma: International Perspectives on Stress and Coping* 18: 482–497.

Cohen, H. 1986. "Exploiting Police Authority." *Criminal Justice Ethics* 5(2): 23–31.

Cohen, H. 1987. "Overstepping Police Authority." *Criminal Justice Ethics* 6(2): 52–60.

Cohen-Charash, Y., and P. Spector. (2001). "The Role of Justice in Organizations: A Meta-analysis." *Organizational Behavior and Human Decision Processes* 86: 278–321.

Cole, D. 1999. *No Equal Justice.* New York: Free Press.

Coleman, S. 2004a. "Police, Gratuities, and Professionalism: A Response to Kania." *Criminal Justice Ethics* 23(1): 63–65.

Coleman, S. 2004b. "When Police Should Say 'No!' to Gratuities." *Criminal Justice Ethics* 23(1): 33–44.

Colquitt, J. A., D. Conlon, M. Wesson, C. Porter, and K. Ng. 2001. "Justice at the Millennium: A Meta-analytic Review of 25 Years of Organizational Justice Research." *Journal of Applied Psychology* 86(3): 425–445.

Colquitt, J., J. Greenberg, and C. Zapata-Phelan. 2005. "What is Organizational Justice? A Historical Overview." In *Handbook of Organizational Justice,* ed. J. Greenberg and J. Colquitt, 3–56. Mahwah, NJ: Lawrence Erlbaum.

Crank, J. 1998. *Understanding Police Culture.* Cincinnati: Anderson.

Crank, J., D. Flaherty, and A. Giacomazzi. 2007. "The Noble Cause: An Empirical Assessment." *Journal of Criminal Justice* 35(1): 103–116.

Dart, B. 2004. "Police Use Taser Guns 'Excessively,' Rights Group Asserts." *Austin American-Statesman*, November 30: A14.

Delattre, E. 2011. *Character and Cops: Ethics in Policing*. Washington, DC: American Enterprise Institute for Public Policy Research.

Dorschner, J. 1993. "The Dark Side of the Force." In *Critical Issues in Policing*, 2d ed., ed. R. Dunham and G. Alpert, 254–274. Long Grove, IL: Waveland Press.

Eterno, J. and E. Silverman. 2012. *The Crime Numbers Game: Management by Manipulation*. Boca Raton, FL: CRC Press.

Ewin, R. 1990. "Loyalty and the Police." *Criminal Justice Ethics* 9(2): 3–15.

Farmer, S. J., T. Beehr, and K. Love. 2003. "Becoming an Undercover Police Officer: A Note on Fairness Perceptions, Behavior, and Attitudes." *Journal of Organizational Behavior* 24: 373–387.

Ferdik, F., Rojek, J. and G. Alpert. 2013. "Citizen Oversight in the United States and Canada: An Overview." *Police Practice and Research: An International Journal* 14: 104–118.

Fogelson, R. 1977. *Big City Police*. Cambridge, MA: Harvard University Press.

Fyfe, J., and R. Kane. 2006. *Bad Cops: A Study of Career-ending Misconduct among New York City Police Officers* (Document #215795). Washington, DC: U.S. Department of Justice.

Gallup. 2014. "Honest/Ethics in Professions." Gallup. Retrieved from http://www.gallup.com/poll/1654/honesty-ethics-professions.aspx.

Garrett, B. 2012. *Convicting the Innocent: When Criminal Prosecutions Go Wrong*. Boston, MA: Harvard University Press.

Gau, J., C. Mosher, and T. Pratt. 2010. "An Inquiry into the Impact of Suspect Race on Police Use of Tasers." *Police Quarterly* 13(1): 27–48.

Getlin, J. 2002. "DA Suggests Overturning Convictions in Jogger Case." *Austin American-Statesman*, December 6: A16.

Gorta, A. 2007. "Illegal Drug use by Police Officers: Using Research and Investigation to Inform Prevention Strategies." *International Journal of Police Science and Management* 11: 85–96.

Greene, J. 1999. "Zero Tolerance: A Case Study of Police Policies and Practices in New York City." *Crime and Delinquency* 45(2): 171–187.

Harris, C., and R. Worden. 2014. "The Effect of Sanctions on Police Misconduct." *Crime & Delinquency* 60(8): 1258–1288.

Herbert, B. 2002. "In Tulia, Justice Has Gone into Hiding." *Austin American-Statesman*, August 13: A9.

Hickman, M., A. Piquero, and J. Garner. 2009. "Toward a National estimate of Police Use of Nonlethal Force." *Criminology and Public Policy* 7 (4): 563–604.

Huberts, L., M. Kaptein, and K. Lasthuizen. 2007. "A Study of the Impact of Three Leadership Styles on Integrity Violations Committed by Police Officers." *Policing: An International Journal of Police Strategies & Management* 30(4): 587–607.

Hunter, R. 1999. "Officer Opinions on Police Misconduct." *Journal of Contemporary Criminal Justice* 15(2): 155–170.

IACP. 2012. *Emerging Use of Force Issues: Balancing Public and Officer Safety*. Washington, DC: International Association of Chiefs of Police. Retrieved from: http://www.theiacp.org/portals/0/pdfs/EmergingUseofForceIssues041612.pdf/.

Ingram, J., E. Paoline III, and W. Terrill. 2013. "A Multilevel Framework for Understanding Police Culture: The Role of the Workgroup." *Criminology* 51(2): 365–397.

Jonathan-Zamir, T., S. Mastrofski, and S. Moyal. 2013. "Measuring Procedural Justice in Police-Citizen Encounters." *Justice Quarterly*. Forthcoming, DOI: 10.1080/07418825.2013.845677.

Kania, R. 1988. "Police Acceptance of Gratuities." *Criminal Justice Ethics* 7(2): 37–49.

Kania, R. 2004. "The Ethical Acceptability of Gratuities: Still Saying 'Yes' After All These Years." *Criminal Justice Ethics* 23(1): 54–63.

Kappeler, V., R. Sluder, and G. Alpert. 1998. *Forces of Deviance: Understanding the Dark Side of Policing*, 2d ed. Long Grove, IL: Waveland Press.

Kleinig, J. 1990. "Teaching and Learning Police Ethics: Competing and Complementary Approaches." *Journal of Criminal Justice* 18: 1–18.

Klockars, C. 1983. "The Dirty Harry Problem." In *Thinking About Police: Contemporary Readings*, ed. C. Klockars and S. Mastrofski, 428–438. New York: McGraw-Hill.

Klockars, C., S. Ivkovic, and M. Haberfeld. 2004. *The Contours of Police Integrity*. Thousand Oaks, CA: Sage.

Klockars, C., S. Ivkovic, W. Harver, and M. Haberfeld. 2000. *The Measurement of Police Integrity: NIJ Research in Brief*. Washington, DC: U.S. Department of Justice.

Lawton, B. 2007. "Levels of Non-Lethal Force: An Examination of Individual, Situational, and Contextual Factors." *Journal of Research in Crime and Delinquency* 44(2):163–184

Lee, H., L. Hyeyoung, D. Moore, and K. Jeonglim. 2013. "How Police Organizational Structure Correlates with Frontline Officers' Attitudes Toward Corruption: A Multilevel Model." *Police Practice and Research: An international Journal* 14(5): 386–401.

Malloy, E. 1982. *The Ethics of Law Enforcement and Criminal Punishment*. Lanham, NY: University Press.

Martinelli, T. 2000. "Combating the Charge of Deliberate Indifference through Police Ethics Training and a Comprehensive Risk Management Policy." Paper presented at the 2000 Annual Meeting of the Academy of Criminal Justice Sciences, New Orleans, LA.

Marx, G. 1985. "Police Undercover Work: Ethical Deception or Deceptive Ethics?" In *Police Ethics: Hard Choices in Law Enforcement*, ed. W. Heffernan and T. Stroup, 83–117. New York: John Jay Press.

Marx, G. 1991. "The New Police Undercover Work." In *Thinking About Police: Contemporary Readings*, ed. C. Klockars and S. Mastrofski, 240–258. New York: McGraw-Hill.

Mastrofski, S., M. Reisig, and J. McCluskey. 2002. "Police Disrespect Toward the Public: An Encounter-Based Analysis." *Criminology* 40(3): 519–551.

Mazerolle, L., E. Antrobus, and S. Bennett. 2013. "Shaping Citizen Perceptions of Police Legitimacy: A Randomized Field Trial of Procedural Justice." *Criminology* 51(1): 33–63.

Mieczkowski, T. 2002. "Drug Abuse, Corruption, and Officer Drug Testing." In *Policing and Misconduct*, ed. K. Lersch, 157–192. Upper Saddle River, NJ: Prentice-Hall.

Moran, J. 2005. "'Blue Walls,' 'Grey Areas' and 'Cleanups'": Issues in the Control of Police Corruption in England and Wales." *Crime, Law & Social Change* 43: 57–79.

Muir, W. 1977. Police: *Streetcorner Politicians*. Chicago: University of Chicago Press.

Murphy, K., Mazerolle, L. and S. Bennett. 2013 "Promoting Trust in Police: Findings from a Randomised Experimental Field Trial of Procedural Justice Policing." *Policing and Society* 24(4): 405–424.

Murphy, P., and D. Caplan. 1989. "Conditions That Breed Corruption." In *Critical Issues in Policing*, ed. R. Dunham and G. Alpert, 304–324. Long Grove, IL: Waveland Press.

Murphy, P., and K. Moran. 1981. "The Continuing Cycle of Systemic Police Corruption." In *The Social Basis of Criminal Justice: Ethical Issues for the 80's*, ed. F. Schmalleger and R. Gustafson, 87–101. Washington, DC: University Press of America.

Nelson, J. 2000. *Police Brutality*. New York: Norton.

Oliver, W. 2006. "The Fourth Era of Policing: Homeland Security." *International Review of Law, Computers, and Technology* 20: 49-62.

Ortiz, C., N. Hendricks, and N. Sugie. 2007. "Policing Terrorism: The Response of Local Police Agencies to Homeland Security Concerns." *Criminal Justice Studies* 20(2): 91-109.

Packer, H. 1968. *The Limits of the Criminal Sanction*. Stanford, CA: Stanford University Press.

Pastore, A. C., and K. Maguire (Eds.) 2007. "Respondents' Ratings of the Honesty and Ethical Standards of Police." Table 2.20.2007. *Sourcebook of Criminal Justice Statistics*. Retrieved from http://www.albany.edu/sourcebook/pdf/t2202007.pdf.

Payne, D. 2002. *Police Liability: Lawsuits against the Police*. Durham, NC: Carolina Academic Press.

Plant, A., J. Goplen, and J. Kuntsman. 2011. "Selective Response to Threat: The Role of Race and Gender in Decisions to Shoot." *Personality and Social Psychology Bulletin* 37(9): 1274-1281.

Plohetski, T. 2007. "From Officer's Order to Taser: 45 Seconds." *Austin American-Statesman*, Sunday, September 30: A1, A6.

Police Executive Research Forum. 2013. *Critical Issues in Police Series. Civil Rights Investigations of Local Police: Lessons Learned*. Washington, DC: Police Executive Research Forum.

Pollock, J. 2014. *Ethical Dilemmas and Decisions in Criminal Justice*, 8th ed. Boston: Wadsworth/Cengage.

Pollock, J., and R. Becker. 1996. "Ethical Dilemmas in Police Work." In *Justice, Crime and Ethics*, ed. M. Braswell, B. J. McCarthy, and B. R. McCarthy, 83–103. Cincinnati: Anderson.

Pollock-Byrne, J. 1988. "Teaching Criminal Justice Ethics." *The Justice Professional* 3(2): 283–297.

Prenzler, T., A. Beckley, and S. Bronitt. 2013. "Police Gifts and Benefits Scandals: Addressing Deficits in Policy, Leadership and Enforcement." *International Journal of Police Science and Management* 15(4): 294–304.

Prenzler, T., and J. Ransley. 2002. *Police Reform: Building Integrity*. Sydney, Australia: Hawkins.

Prenzler, T., and C. Ronken. 2001a. "Police Integrity Testing in Australia." *Criminal Justice* 1(2): 319–342.

Prenzler, T., and C. Ronken. 2001b. "Models of Police Oversight: A Critique." *Policing and Society* 11: 151–180.

Reuss-Ianni, E. 1983. *Two Cultures of Policing: Street Cops and Management Cops*. New Brunswick, NJ: Transaction.

Rossmo, D. K. 2008. *Criminal Investigative Failures*. Boca Raton, FL: Taylor & Francis.

Ruiz, J., and C. Bono. 2004. "At What Price a 'Freebie'? The Real Cost of Police Gratuities." *Criminal Justice Ethics* 23(1): 44–54.

Sanders, B. 2008. "Using Personality Traits to Predict Police Officer Performance." *Policing: An International Journal of Police Strategies and Management* 31(1): 129–147.

Scheingold, S. 1984. *The Politics of Law and Order.* New York: Longman.

Schoeman, F. 1985. "Privacy and Police Undercover Work." In *Police Ethics: Hard Choices in Law Enforcement*, ed. W. Heffernan and T. Stroup, 133–153. New York: John Jay Press.

Schoeman, F. 1986. "Undercover Operations: Some Moral Questions about S. 804." *Criminal Justice Ethics* 5(2): 16–22.

Shane, J. 2012. "Police Employee Disciplinary Matrix: An Emerging Concept." *Police Quarterly* 15(1): 62–91.

Sherman, L. 1981. *The Teaching of Ethics in Criminology and Criminal Justice.* Washington, DC: Joint Commission on Criminology and Criminal Justice Education and Standards, LEAA.

Sherman, L. 1982. "Learning Police Ethics." *Criminal Justice Ethics* 1(1): 10–19.

Sherman, L. 1985a. "Becoming Bent: Moral Careers of Corrupt Policemen." In *Moral Issues in Police Work*, ed. F. Elliston and M. Feldberg, 253–273. Totawa, NJ: Rowman and Allanheld.

Sherman, L. 1985b. "Equity against Truth: Value Choices in Deceptive Investigations." In *Police Ethics: Hard Choices in Law Enforcement*, ed. W. Heffernan and T. Stroup, 117–133. New York: John Jay Press.

Schuck, A. and C. Martin. 2013. "Residents' Perceptions of Procedural Injustice during Encounters with the Police." *Journal of Ethnicity in Criminal Justice* 11(4): 219–237.

Skolnick, J. 1982. "Deception by Police." *Criminal Justice Ethics* 1(2): 40–54.

Skolnick, J., and J. Fyfe. 1993. *Above the Law: Police and the Excessive Use of Force.* New York: Free Press.

Skolnick, J., and R. Leo. 1992. "Ideology and the Ethics of Crime Control." Criminal Justice Ethics 11(1): 3–13.

Souryal, S. 2007. *Ethics in Criminal Justice: In Search of the Truth*, 4th ed. Cincinnati: Anderson.

Swatt, M., C. Gibson, and N. Piquero. 2007. "Exploring the Utility of General Strain Theory in Explaining Problematic Alcohol Consumption by Police Officers." *Journal of Criminal Justice* 35: 596–611.

Swift, A., J. Houston, and R. Anderson. 1993. "Cops, Hacks and the Greater Good." Academy of Criminal Justice Sciences Conference, Kansas City, MO.

Tanner, R. 2006. "Bad Science May Taint Many Arson Convictions." *Austin American-Statesman*, Wednesday, May 3: A1, A5.

Terrill, W. 2001. *Police Coercion: Application of the Force Continuum.* New York: LFB Scholarly Publishing.

Terrill, W. 2005. "Police Use of Force: A Transactional Approach." *Justice Quarterly* 22(1): 107–139.

Terrill, W., E. Paoline, and P. Manning. 2003. "Police Culture and Coercion." *Criminology* 41(4): 1003–1034.

Toobin, J. 2013. "Rights and Wrongs." *The New Yorker*, 89(15): 36–43.

Tyler, T. 2004. "Enhancing Police Legitimacy." *The Annals of the American Academy of Political and Social Science* 593(1): 84–99.

Tyler, T. 2006. *Why People Obey the Law.* Princeton, NJ: Princeton University Press.

Tyler, T. 2011. *Why People Cooperate: The Role of Social Motivations.* Princeton, NJ: Princeton University Press.

Tyler, T., E., Callahan, and J. Frost. 2007. "Armed, and Dangerous (?): Motivating Rule Adherence among Agents of Social Control." *Law & Society* 41(2): 457–492.

Tyler, T., and J. Fagan. 2008. "Legitimacy and Cooperation: Why Do People Help the Police Fight Crime in Their Communities?" *Ohio State Journal of Criminal Law* 6:231–75.

Tyler, T., and Y. Huo. 2002. *Trust in the Law: Encouraging Public Cooperation with the Police and Courts.* Vol. 5. New York: Russell Sage Foundation.

Walker, S. 2007. "Police Accountability: Current Issues and Research Needs." Paper presented at the National Institute of Justice, Policing Research Workshop: Planning for the Future, Washington DC, November 28–29, 2006. Available through the National Institute of Justice, Washington DC.

Walker, S., and G. Alpert. 2002. "Early Warning Systems as Risk Management for Police." In *Policing and Misconduct*, ed. K. Lersch, 219–230. Upper Saddle River, NJ: Prentice-Hall.

Walker, S., C. Spohn, and M. DeLone. 2000. *The Color of Justice.* Belmont, CA: Wadsworth.

Weisburd, D., and R. Greenspan. 2000. *Police Attitudes toward Abuse of Authority: Findings from a National Study.* NIJ Research in Brief. Washington, DC: U.S. Department of Justice.

Weiser, B. 2014. "New York Reaches Agreement to End Battle over Stop-and-Frisk." *New York Times*, January 30.

Weitzer, R. 1999. "Citizens' Perceptions of Police Misconduct: Race and Neighborhood Context." *Justice Quarterly* 16(4): 819–846.

Weitzer, R., and S. Tuch. 2000. "Reforming the Police: Racial Differences in Public Support for Change." *Criminology* 38(2): 391–416.

Weitzer, R., and S. Tuch. 2002. "Perceptions of Racial Profiling: Race, Class, and Personal Experience." *Criminology* 40(2): 435–456.

Westmarland, L. 2005. "Police Ethics and Integrity: Breaking the Blue Code of Silence." *Policing and Society* 15(2): 145–165.

Wolfe, S., and A. Piquero. 2011. "Organizational Justice and Police Misconduct." *Criminal Justice and Behavior* 38(4): 332–353.

Wren, T. 1985. "Whistle-blowing and Loyalty to One's Friends." In *Police Ethics: Hard Choices in Law Enforcement*, ed. W. Heffernan and T. Stroup, 25–47. New York: John Jay Press.

SECTION III

Management and Organization

The purpose of policing, beyond protecting life, is to control crime and maintain order, which involves the unique right to use force to accomplish this responsibility. Administrators can use several methods to control officer discretion in using force. The articles chosen for this section describe potential conflicts that will test the ability of officers to act fairly and impartially. Unlike conflicts in other organizations, those faced by the police can result in violence, injury, or death.

In the first selection, "How Police Supervisory Styles Influence Patrol Officer Behavior," Robin Shepard Engel addresses the question of how much a field supervisor's style of supervision influences officers' performances. She uncovers four supervisory styles that have different impacts on officers' behaviors, such as use of force, problem solving, and proactivity.

Meghan Stroshine then discusses information technology innovations in policing. She describes the profound changes in computer-aided dispatch, record keeping, crime mapping and analysis, and operations. She also discusses how police administrators use information technology to enhance management, accountability, and personnel/resource allocations.

Samuel Walker explains how police agencies are using early intervention (EI) systems to improve accountability for officer behavior. These data-based programs identify officers with problems and provide the basis for intervention to correct those problems before they develop into serious incidents such as lawsuits, citizen complaints over excessive force, or another type of public crisis. EI systems are growing in popularity, but they are still in the early stages of development. Some difficult and important issues concerning the structure and use of EI systems will need to be addressed in evaluating the effectiveness of the programs.

The next selection, written by Cynthia Lum and Christopher Koper, presents evidence-based policing, an emerging law-enforcement perspective that argues that scientific research, evaluation, and analysis should inform police decision making. Scientific research can guide policing on a wide variety of subjects and issues—from evaluations of interventions and tactics to analysis of various police behaviors, activities, and issues of internal management. This perspective involves two important elements: (1) using the results of scientifically rigorous evaluations of law-enforcement tactics and strategies to

217

guide decisions, and (2) generating and applying analytic knowledge derived from the agency's analysis of its own internal issues and crime problems.

Justin Nix discusses and critiques the strategy of using advanced analytical techniques to identify times and places where crimes are most likely to occur and then deploying personnel accordingly to prevent the crimes. He argues that this is preferable to responding to crimes after they have occurred. The strategy refocuses policing from reactive to proactive. He concludes that while the analytical techniques are not perfect, they yield enough information to justify the reallocation of police resources.

Another innovation in policing is the use of geographic information systems (GIS). William Pelfrey explains GIS and the many ways it can assist in understanding crime patterns and planning police responses to them. GIS allows police agencies to compare layers of crime data with census information, identify vulnerable areas of a city, and develop geographic profiles of crime patterns and individual criminals.

The tragic terrorist attacks on the United States on September 11, 2001, have transformed law enforcement activities in important ways. One important change is the strategic integration of intelligence through the networking of large databases. In the final selection, "The Practice of Crime Analysis," Allison Rojek discusses the role that crime and intelligence analysis now play in criminal justice organizations. She outlines the specific tasks that analysts are expected to perform, as well as the tools and software they use to accomplish the tasks. In addition, she provides a penetrating review of the challenges faced by analysts and the organization in maximizing the usefulness of the crime analysis process.

11

How Police Supervisory Styles Influence Patrol Officer Behavior

Robin Shepard Engel

Does field supervision of patrol officers matter? Chances are that personal experience, common sense, and intuition would elicit a quick "yes" from most police administrators and managers. But does street-level evidence justify that viewpoint?

The answer is a qualified yes, according to recent field research. Research findings not only confirm that view but also shed light on how frontline supervisory styles can influence such patrol officer behavior as making arrests, issuing citations, using force, and engaging in community policing.

The study involved field observations of and interviews with sergeants and lieutenants who directly supervised patrol officers in the Indianapolis, Indiana, Police Department and the St. Petersburg, Florida, Police Department. The research is based on data from the Project on Policing Neighborhoods (POPN), a 2-year research project sponsored by the National Institute of Justice that broadly examined policing issues, especially the effects of community policing initiatives on police and the public (see "The Project on Policing Neighborhoods").

The most important finding was that style or quality of field supervision can significantly influence patrol officer behavior, quite apart from quantity of supervision.[1] Frontline supervision by sergeants and lieutenants can influence some patrol officer behavior, but the study found that this influence varies according to the style of supervision. An "active" supervisory style— involving leading by example—seems to be most influential despite potential drawbacks. Indeed, active supervisors appear to be crucial to the implementation of organizational goals.

NIJ Research for Practice, June 2003, NCJ 194078.

This report in NIJ's Research for Practice series addresses three principal questions:

- What are the four supervisory styles identified by the research?
- How do those styles influence patrol officer behavior?
- What are the implications for departmental policy and practice?

Frontline Supervisory Styles

The study's field observations and interviews identified four main supervisory styles: traditional, innovative, supportive, and active. Supervisor characteristics include personal features such as age as well as level of training and experience (see exhibit 1). Each of the four styles encompasses about 25 percent of the 81 field supervisors (see exhibit 2). In general, none of the four supervisory styles was found to be ideal. Each style has benefits and drawbacks. (See "Study Methodology.")

The active style of supervision emerged as having the most influence over patrol officers' behaviors. Officers with active supervisors were more likely than those with other types of supervisors to use force and spent more time on self-initiated activities, community policing activities, and problem solving.

Traditional Supervisors

Traditional supervisors expect aggressive enforcement from subordinates rather than engagement in community-oriented activities or policing of minor disorders. They are more likely than other types of supervisors to make

Exhibit 1   Characteristics of 81 Supervisors

Characteristics	Minimum	Maximum	Mean
Supervisor age (years)	31	70	44
Years of experience as a supervisor	1	33	10
Percentage of supervisors who were female			15
Percentage of supervisors who were nonwhite			15
Percentage of supervisors who held a 4-year college degree			51
Amount of training* in community policing	1	5	4
Amount of knowledge† about community policing	1	3	2
Amount of training in supervision, management, leadership	1	5	4
Amount of knowledge about supervision, management, leadership	1	3	1

Note: 17 lieutenants and 64 sergeants.

*Amount of training: 1 = none, 2 = less than 1 day, 3 = 1–2 days, 4 = 3–5 days, 5 = more than 5 days.
†Amount of knowledge: 1 = very knowledgeable, 2 = fairly knowledgeable, 3 = not very knowledgeable.

Exhibit 2   Distribution of Supervisory Styles, in Percent

	Traditional	Innovative	Supportive	Active
Gender				
Male ($n = 69$)	22	30	25	23
Female ($n = 12$)	50	8	17	25
Race				
White ($n = 69$)	26	26	25	23
Nonwhite ($n = 12$)	25	33	17	25
Location				
Indianapolis lieutenants ($n = 17$)	12	35	24	29
Indianapolis sergeants ($n = 39$)	18	28	26	28
St. Petersburg sergeants ($n = 25$)	48	20	20	12
Total ($N = 81$)	**26**	**27**	**23**	**23**

Note: Each percentage is the proportion of field supervisors associated with the style noted in the far left column. Thus, traditional supervisors constituted 26 percent of all 81 supervisors, 22 percent of 69 male supervisors, etc.

decisions because they tend to take over encounters with citizens or tell officers how to handle those incidents.

Traditional sergeants and lieutenants are highly task oriented and expect subordinates to produce measurable outcomes—particularly arrests and citations—along with paperwork and documentation.

Less inclined toward developing relationships, traditional supervisors give more instruction to subordinates and are less likely to reward and more likely to punish patrol officers. The traditional supervisor's ultimate concern is to control subordinate behavior.

Traditional supervisors are more likely to support new policing initiatives if they are consistent with aggressive law enforcement. More than 60 percent of these supervisors "agree strongly" that "enforcing the law is by far a patrol officer's most important responsibility," compared with 14 percent of innovative supervisors, 11 percent of supportive supervisors, and 11 percent of active supervisors. Along with their no-nonsense approach to policing, traditional supervisors strictly enforce rules and regulations and adhere to the chain of command.

Innovative Supervisors

Innovative supervisors are characterized by a tendency to form relationships (i.e., they consider more officers to be friends), a low level of task orientation, and more positive views of subordinates. These supervisors are considered innovative because they generally encourage their officers to embrace new philosophies and methods of policing. Innovative supervisors are defined by their expectations for community policing and problem-solving efforts by subordinates. For example, 96 percent of these supervisors reported that they "agree strongly" that "a good patrol officer will try to find out what residents think the neighborhood problems are," compared to 48 percent of traditional supervisors, 68 percent of supportive supervisors, and 68 percent of active supervisors.

One goal of innovative supervisors is to help subordinates implement community policing and problem-solving strategies by coaching, mentoring, and facilitating. They are less concerned with enforcing rules and regulations, report writing, or other task-oriented activities than traditional supervisors.

Unlike traditional supervisors, innovative supervisors generally do not tell subordinates how to handle situations and do not take over the situations themselves. They are more likely to delegate decision making. They spend significantly more time per shift dealing with the public or other officers than other supervisors do (15 percent compared with 9 percent).

Supportive Supervisors

These supervisors support subordinates by protecting them from discipline or punishment perceived as "unfair" and by providing inspirational motivation. They often serve as a buffer between officers and management to protect officers from criticism and discipline. They believe this gives their officers space to perform duties without constant worry of disciplinary action for honest mistakes.

In some cases, supportive supervisors do not have strong ties to or positive relations with management. They may attempt to shield patrol officers from the police administration. Thus, some supervisors classified as supportive may function more as "protectors" than "supporters."

Of supportive supervisors, 68 percent reported that "protecting their officers from unfair criticism and punishment" is one of their most important functions, compared with 10 percent of traditional supervisors, 5 percent of innovative supervisors, and no active supervisors.

The protective role adopted by some supportive supervisors can be a problem, however. Other research has found that shielding officers from accountability mechanisms within the department can lead to police misconduct.[2]

Supportive supervisors are less concerned with enforcing rules and regulations, dealing with paperwork, or ensuring that officers do their work. They may encourage officers through praise and recognition, act as counselors, or display concern for subordinates' personal and professional well-being. The study found that supportive supervisors praise or reward subordinate officers significantly more often during an average shift (3 times per shift) than do other supervisors (2 times per shift).

Active Supervisors

Active supervisors embrace a philosophy of leading by example. Their goal is to be heavily involved in the field alongside subordinates while controlling patrol officer behavior, thus performing the dual function of street officer and supervisor.

Almost all active supervisors (95 percent) report that they often go on their own initiative to incidents that their officers are handling, compared to 24 percent of traditional supervisors, 55 percent of innovative supervisors, and 68 percent of supportive supervisors.

Active supervisors also give importance to engaging in patrol work themselves. They spend significantly more time per shift than other supervisors on general motor patrol (33 percent compared with 26 percent) and traffic encounters (4 percent compared with 2 percent). These supervisors attempt to strike a balance between being active in the field and controlling subordinate behavior through constant, direct supervision. Supervisors with an active style are characterized by directive decision making, a strong sense of supervisory power, and a relatively positive view of subordinates.

Although active supervisors believe they have considerable influence over subordinates' decisions, they are less likely to encourage team building, coaching, or mentoring. One possible explanation for this is that they are reluctant to become so involved that they alienate subordinate officers. A fine line separates an active supervisor from being seen as overcontrolling or micromanaging.

Impact of Supervisory Style on Patrol Officers

What impact does supervisory style have on patrol officer activities? The study examined the influence of 64 sergeants' supervisory styles on the behavior of 239 patrol officers, having identified the sergeant-supervisor of each officer. The study's findings focus on how likely officers were to make arrests, issue citations, and use force as well as how much time per shift they allocated to community policing activities, administrative duties, and personal business.

Arrests and Citations

Supervisory style did not affect the likelihood that patrol officers would make arrests or issue citations in either traffic or nontraffic situations. In nontraffic encounters, however, the mere presence of a field supervisor, regardless of style, significantly influenced officer behavior; the longer a supervisor was present, the more likely patrol officers were to make an arrest.

Use of Force

Patrol officers with active supervisors were twice as likely to use force[3] against suspects as officers whose supervisors employ other styles. In addition, active supervisors themselves used force against suspects more often than other types of supervisors. The mere presence of a supervisor at the scene, however, did not have a significant influence on police use of force.

Self-Initiated Activities

Patrol officers with active supervisors spent more time per shift engaging in proactive (self-initiated) activities than officers with other supervisors. The former spent 15 percent of their time per shift being proactive, in contrast to 14 percent, 13 percent, and 11 percent for officers under supportive, traditional, and innovative supervisors, respectively. Proactivity excludes time spent on dispatched or supervisor-directed activities, general patrol, traveling to a location, personal business, and administrative activities.

Community Policing and Problem Solving

Officers with active supervisors spent more time per shift engaging in problem solving and other community-policing activities than officers with other types of supervisors. Officers under active supervision spent 11.3 percent of their time per shift on problem solving, compared with 10.7 percent for officers with supportive supervisors, 9.4 percent for those with traditional supervisors, and 8.0 percent for officers with innovative supervisors. Although differences between these percentages seem small, they can produce substantial differences in the amount of time spent on community policing by an entire patrol force over the course of a year.

At first glance it appears contradictory that officers with innovative supervisors spent the least amount of time on community policing and problem solving. This finding suggests that simply having an innovative supervisory style does not necessarily translate into more innovative activities from subordinates. Possibly, innovative supervisors may be more inclined to encourage community-building tactics, while active supervisors may encourage more aggressive enforcement, which may lead active supervisors and their subordinates to be more engaged with problem solving and other citizen interactions.

Administrative Activities

Patrol officers with active supervisors spend significantly less time per shift on administrative tasks. Officers under active supervision spent 13 percent of their time dealing with administrative matters, compared with 19 percent for patrol officers with traditional supervisors and 17 percent for those with innovative or supportive supervisors.

Community Policing in Field Training and Supervision

Although not part of POPN research, a study conducted by Robin N. Haarr Ph.D., under NIJ grant 96-IJ-CX-0060, also looked at influences on patrol officer behavior, particularly new recruits. This research also found that field supervisors have crucial influence, although in a different context.[a]

A separate study of how police recruits are taught community policing principles provides some guidance for police managers on how field training and actual policing experience may supersede academy training in influencing the attitudes and beliefs of new officers.

The 3-year study surveyed police recruits at four intervals[b] during their training and first year on the job. It focused on academy "reform training"[c] designed to change recruits' attitudes positively toward community-oriented policing and problem-solving policing.

The research found that academy reform training often proved ineffective because it was not followed up during field training, and factors contradicting academy training[d] dominated recruits' actual policing experiences.

The study also found that recruits' beliefs about the nature of policing were firmly established before training even begins:

> The best predictors of attitude change were by far the attitudes that recruits brought with them to the academy. In other words, police recruits are not empty vessels to be filled with new attitudes and values related to policing.[e]

Nonetheless, academy reform training did influence recruits' beliefs about police work before field training. But the study found "little evidence of a formal and/or systematic approach to incorporating community policing and/or problem-solving training into the field training process."[f] Thus, community policing principles—already on shaky ground because of recruits' previously held beliefs—often appeared to be academic:

> It seems unreasonable to expect police recruits to continue their commitment to community policing and problem-solving policing principles and practices if they leave the training academy and return to a police agency that does not require its officers to engage in community policing or problem-solving activities.[g]

It falls to police leadership, the study concluded, to set the tone for community policing. When supervisors and the organization practice community-oriented and problem-solving policing, recruits will too. The study recommends that academy-taught principles be' coupled more closely with field training and actual police practices.

Notes
[a] Haarr, R. N., *The Impact of Community Policing Training and Program Implementation on Police Personnel*, final report for the National Institute of Justice, grant number 96-IJ-CX-0060, Washington, DC; National Institute of Justice, 2000, NCJ 190680.
[b] Surveys were administered on the first day at the academy, near the last day at the academy, 12 weeks later (near the end of field training), and at the end of 1 year on the job.
[c] "Reform training" is defined as "training designed to alter an officer's perception of the world and/or police work. . . . In the case of community policing training, the goal is to replace outdated attitudes and beliefs about policing with new attitudes and beliefs that are consistent with community policing and problem-solving policing philosophies and strategies." (Haarr, *The Impact of Community Policing Training end Program Implementation on Police Personnel*, pp. 3–4.)
[d] Such as shift, coworkers' attitudes, and precinct location.
[e] Haarr, p. v.
[f] Ibid., p. 176.
[g] Ibid., p. 175.

Personal Business

Supervisory style has little effect on the time patrol officers spend conducting personal business (nonwork-related encounters and activities, including meal and restroom breaks). Overall, officers spent 16 percent of their time on personal business.

Implications for Policy and Practice

Collectively, the research findings indicate that supervisory styles affect some types of subordinate behavior. Police administrators are encouraged to consider supervisory style in setting department goals and training.

Compared with other styles, an active supervisory approach appears to wield the most influence over patrol officer actions. The findings suggest that to best influence their patrol officers' behavior, field supervisors must lead by example—the hallmark of an active style.

One clear implication of the research is that police administrators and managers would be well-advised to direct and train field supervisors to become more involved and set an example of the behavior they expect from subordinates. (For discussion of a different study that examined supervisory practices and officer training, see "Community Policing in Field Training and Supervision.")

An active supervisory style, however, has potential problems. Leading by example can be positive or negative, depending on the example set. As noted previously, for instance, active supervisors and their subordinates are more likely to use force against suspects.

One reason why active supervisors might promote greater use of force and proactivity (which could expose the officer to greater risk if things go wrong) is that by taking precisely the risks that he/she wants the officer to take, the active supervisor demonstrates that "if it's safe for Sarge, then it's safe for me, too."

Supervisory styles influenced only those officer behaviors that are hardest to monitor and measure, such as use of force, problem solving, and proactivity. Conversely, supervisory styles did not significantly affect officer behaviors that are relatively easy to monitor and measure, such as making arrests and issuing citations. One reason may be that supervisors have more influence in situations where patrol officers have the most discretion. Perhaps the less certain the task and the less visible its performance, the more opportunity a sergeant may have to define the duties of subordinates, who may appreciate such clarification of their roles.

Another possible explanation is that such easily measured officer activities as arrests and citations may be most influenced by policy guidelines from higher ranking officials. This effect is likely to be relatively uniform regardless of field supervisors' styles. Thus, the place to look for supervisory influence over these activities may be at the district or departmental level, not the field supervisory level.

Leading by example is an effective frontline supervisory tool only if the example supports departmental goals. For instance, many officers at both sites had received relatively little training in community policing and were skeptical about its worth. Sergeants who practiced an active supervisory style supplemented training deficiencies while building the self-confidence of subordinate officers.

These findings strongly suggest that police administrators are more likely to achieve departmental goals if they align them with supervisory practice and encourage field supervisors to "get in the game."

Study Methodology

This study used data collected for the POPN multimethod study of police patrol in the Indianapolis, Indiana, and St. Petersburg, Florida, police departments, which were implementing community policing at the time of the study.

The core methodology was systematic social observation of patrol officers in the field. Trained observers accompanied officers on their work shifts and took field notes. Officers assigned to each of the 24 study beats were observed for approximately 240 hours. Researchers observed more than 5,700 hours of patrol work during the summer of 1996 in Indianapolis and the summer of 1997 in St. Petersburg. From their field notes, observers prepared narratives and coded data items about officer activities.

Researchers also interviewed patrol officers and frontline supervisors about their personal characteristics, training and education, work experience, perceptions of their beats, attitudes toward the police role, and perceptions of their department's implementation of community policing and problem solving. Participation was voluntary and confidential. To encourage candid responses to potentially sensitive questions about the quality of supervision, officers were not asked for their supervisors' names. Officers were matched with sergeants through other information.

Review of prior research identified 10 attitudinal dimensions that potentially shape supervisors' styles:

• How they make decisions.

• How they distribute power.

• The extent to which they attempt or avoid exerting leadership.

• The priority they place on aggressive enforcement.

• The priority they attach to community policing and problem solving.

• How they view subordinates.

• Whether they engage in inspirational motivation.

• How task oriented they are.

• Whether they focus on building friendships and mutual trust with subordinates.

• Whether they focus on protecting subordinates from unfair criticism and punishment.

Factor analysis of these dimensions revealed the four individual supervisory styles: traditional, innovative, supportive, and active.

NOTES

[1] "Quantity" is used here in the sense of amount of supervision, i.e., the number of supervisors, the amount of interaction between supervisors and subordinates, and time spent on supervised encounters between patrol officers and citizens. This study is unique in its focus on the quality and style—as well as quantity—of patrol officer supervision.

[2] For example, see Christopher Commission, *Report of the Independent Commission on the Los Angeles Police Department*, Los Angeles Independent Commission on the Los Angeles Police Department, 1991; Mollen Commission to Investigate Allegations of Police Corruption, *Commission Report*, New York: The Mollen Commission, 1994; Skolnick, J.H., and J.J. Fyfe, *Above the Law: Police and the Excessive Use of Force*, New York: Free Press, 1993; and Kappeler, V.E., R.D. Sluder, and G.P. Alpert, *Forces of Deviance: Understanding the Dark Side of Policing*, 2d edition, Long Grove, IL: Waveland Press, 1998.

[3] Use of force includes firm grip or nonpain restraint, pain compliance (hammerlock, wristlock, finger grip, carotid control, bar arm lock), impact or incapacitation (striking with body or weapon, mace, taser), or drawing or discharging a firearm.

BIBLIOGRAPHY

Engel, R., "Patrol Officer Supervision in the Community Policing Era," *Journal of Criminal Justice* 30(1) (January/February 2002): 51–64.

Engel, R., "Supervisory Styles of Patrol Sergeants and Lieutenants," *Journal of Criminal Justice* 29(4) (July/August 2001): 341–355.

Engel, R., "The Effects of Supervisory Styles on Patrol Officer Behavior," *Police Quarterly* 3(3) (September 2000): 262–293.

Bergner, L., "Building Teamwork Among Officers," *Law Enforcement Trainer* 12(6) (November/ December 1997): 10–12.

Haarr, R., "Making of a Community Policing Officer: The Impact of Basic Training and Occupational Socialization on Police Recruits," *Police Quarterly* 4(4) (December 2001): 402–433.

Mastrofski, S., R. Parks, A. Reiss, Jr., and R. Worden, *Policing Neighborhoods: A Report from St. Petersburg*, Research Preview, Washington, DC: U.S. Department of Justice, National Institute of Justice, July 1999, NCJ 184370.

Mastrofski, S., R. Parks, A. Reiss, Jr., and R. Worden, *Policing Neighborhoods: A Report from Indianapolis*, Research Preview, Washington, DC: U.S. Department of Justice, National Institute of Justice, July 1998, NCJ 184207.

Mastrofski, S., R. Parks, and R. Worden, *Community Policing in Action: Lessons from an Observational Study*, Final Report to the National Institute of Justice, 1998.

Office of Community Oriented Policing Services Web site, www.usdoj.gov/cops/

Weisburd, D., and R. Greenspan, et al., *Police Attitudes Toward Abuse of Authority: Findings From a National Study*, Research in Brief, Washington, DC: U.S. Department of Justice, National Institute of Justice, May 2000, NCJ 181312.

12

Technological Innovations in Policing

Meghan S. Stroshine

Walking the beat is now a matter of "walking" through the reporting process with a keyboard rather than a nightstick in hand. (Ericson & Haggerty, 1997, p. 395)

As suggested by Ericson and Haggerty (1997) nearly 20 years ago, the means by which policing is being transformed by technological innovations is profound. The technological advances that arguably caused the most substantial changes in policing to date occurred in the early twentieth century. The inventions of the automobile, telephone, and two-way radio had dramatic effects on the way police performed their functions. Once relegated to walking a limited geographical beat with a nightstick in hand, automobiles allowed for greater geographical coverage, a rapid response to calls, and ultimately, less face-to-face contact with the citizenry. The telephone, in combination with the two-way radio, also had a significant impact on the police profession in America. Once restricted to seeking out police officers walking beats in their neighborhoods, citizens were able to mobilize the police simply by picking up the telephone. Moreover, the telephone served to make police accessible to the public at any time of the day or night, 365 days a year. The two-way radio not only allowed police departments to dispatch officers in response to calls for service, but it also revolutionized police supervision, allowing police supervisors to closely monitor the actions of their officers. These technologies were closely related to the crime fighting mission of the police and allowed police to be more effective at it (Wexler, 2012).

In the last 30 years, the mission of the police has changed. The police have adopted a much broader mission: working with citizens to solve and prevent crime, ultimately resulting a reduction in crime rates (Wexler, 2012).

Prepared especially for *Critical Issues in Policing* by Meghan S. Stroshine.

Once again, technology is playing a pivotal role in allowing police to achieve their mission. For instance, the dramatic reduction of violent crime in the 1990s was clearly related to technology: "Compstat would not have been possible without accurate, timely information about where and when crimes are being committed, and computers made it possible to gather crime data on a weekly or daily basis" (Wexler, 2012, p. iii). In fact, it can be argued that technology is more important today than ever before. The United States is currently experiencing some of the worst economic conditions in decades. The collapse of the country's financial system in 2008 had devastating effects on many American institutions, governmental agencies included. Police agencies have experienced budgetary cuts that have had dire consequences in the form of hiring freezes and large-scale layoffs. Many of the officers who remain employed are being forced to take mandatory furloughs (unpaid days off) (Office of Community Oriented Policing Services, 2011).

While budget cuts have threatened the jobs of many police officers, law enforcement agencies are facing pressure to maintain the same level of public safety as in years past (Office of Community Oriented Policing Services, 2011). As a result, many departments have turned to technology as a type of "force multiplier"—"using various technologies to mitigate the effects of a shrinking workforce" (Wexler, 2012, p. iii). Policing experts expect that the importance of technology will only increase in the years to come. According to Chuck Wexler, Executive Director of the Police Executive Research Forum (PERF): "We expect to see a new Age of Technology in policing over the next 10 to 20 years, as the technologies that we are currently testing really take hold, and new technologies that we aren't even aware of yet take hold" (2012, p. iii).

This chapter highlights recent technological advances in the areas of communications, record keeping, analysis of police data, operations, and administration that are significantly changing the nature of policing in the United States.

Communications

911/311

After the invention of the automobile, telephone, and two-way radio, the next major advance in policing occurred in 1968 when the President's Crime Commission argued that a national emergency number was necessary, which led to the adoption of 911 by the Federal Communications Commission (FCC) and AT&T (Abt Associates, 2000). In 2007, 91% of local police departments used a 911 or a similar emergency telephone system. Most (74%) 911 systems are "enhanced," meaning that the systems are capable of pinpointing the number, location, and any special needs of the caller (Reaves, 2010). As of 2005, the FCC required that wireless services have the technology in place to allow police to identify the location and number of incoming cell phone calls to 911 (McEwen et al., 2003). Eighty-four percent of the "enhanced" 911 systems in place in 2007 were capable of displaying the phone number of wireless callers, and 62% could display the general location of wireless callers (Reaves, 2010).

Since its introduction over 40 years ago, our emergency call system has been remarkably successful—perhaps too successful. While 911 was explicitly designed and marketed for use as an emergency call number, police dispatchers are regularly inundated with nonemergency calls for service, ranging from complaints about unkempt lawns to requests for driving directions. These nonemergency calls for service have created backlogs, inefficiency, and in some cases, death or other tragic consequences when citizens calling for assistance have received busy signals or a delayed response time due to an overload on the emergency call system (Harris, 2003).

In response to this burden on police agencies, several jurisdictions have implemented a three-digit alternative to 911 for nonemergency calls for service (e.g., 311). "The 311 technology allows police to focus their emergency and patrol response capacity on high-priority incidents while applying a more long-term, problem-solving approach to calls that citizens consider nonemergencies" (National Institute of Justice, 2005, p. 5). Baltimore was the first city in the United States to adopt a 311 alternative to 911 in 1996, and by 1997, the FCC had designated "3-1-1 as a national, voluntary, non-toll number for non-emergencies" (McEwen et al., 2003). Other departments that have adopted 311 as a number for nonemergencies include Dallas, Texas; Buffalo, New York; and Phoenix, Arizona (National Institute of Justice, 2005). Data from the pilot project in Baltimore demonstrate the effectiveness of 311 as an alternative to 911. During the study period, the volume of calls to 911 was reduced by 25% and there was widespread community acceptance of 311 as an alternative number (Mazerolle et al., 2001). Moreover, the average time taken to answer 911 calls was reduced by 50%, and the total number of calls dispatched to police units was reduced by 12% (Harris, 2003).

Another advance in communications technology is the auto-dialing system, also referred to as "reverse 911." This system allows law enforcement agencies to send prerecorded messages to every telephone in a predefined area (e.g., a neighborhood). These messages may contain information about crime trends, suspicious persons, and suggestions for reducing victimization. In addition, some auto-dialing software systems are capable of tracking outcomes after the system is activated, allowing police to gauge the effectiveness of these efforts.

Computer-Aided Dispatch (CAD)

Enhanced 911 systems have been augmented by computer-aided dispatch (CAD) systems. Traditionally, calls for service were handled by dispatching an officer to the scene as quickly as possible. This was not the most efficient use of police resources, however, since not all calls for service merited an emergency response. In fact, one study showed that 50–90% of calls to 911 were nonemergency in nature (Harris, 2003). Computer-aided dispatch (CAD) systems now allow for the prioritization of calls by providing an automated means of classifying and prioritizing calls for service. Urgent calls are handled by immediately dispatching an officer to the scene, while calls for which a delayed response will suffice are "stacked" until an officer becomes available.

CAD systems were first adopted by larger departments across the country (e.g., New York, Boston, Detroit) in the early 1970s with funds made available by the Law Enforcement Assistance Administration (LEAA). In 1990, 40% of police departments across the United States used CAD; by 1999 this figure had grown to 56% (Hickman & Reaves, 2001). By 2007, 86% of all local police officers worked for a department that used computers for dispatch purposes (Reaves, 2010).

Internet

By the beginning of the 2000s, the majority of all local police departments used computers for Internet access (Hickman & Reaves, 2006). Today, many local police departments operate an Internet home page (Hickman & Reaves, 2001). Police departments can facilitate communication with the public by using their home page in a variety of ways. First, departments can provide a directory of their personnel, including names, phone numbers, and/or e-mail addresses, thereby facilitating the ability of the public to make contact with members of the agency. The Web site can also serve as an important vehicle for the posting and distribution of a wide variety of information, such as crime prevention information, a "most wanted" page, crime maps, and the like. Finally, the Internet may also be used to obtain information from citizens. Some departments have features on their Web sites that allow citizens to submit complaints, commendations, crime reports, and even crime tips online (McEwen et al., 2003).

More recently, departments have been using social media platforms (e.g., Facebook, YouTube, Twitter) to both disseminate and receive information from the public. According to one nationwide survey of law enforcement agencies, 83% of police departments use social media to share information with the public; 70% use social media outlets to receive information from the public (Police Executive Research Forum, 2012). As an example, the Boca Raton Police Department has created VIPER (Visibility, Intelligence, Partnerships, Education, and Resources), a social media project designed to enhance police services to the public. VIPER provides residents "with a forum to share crime tips, view recent mug shots, receive information, or even request emergency services" (Madeiros, 2011; as cited in Office of Community Policing Services, 2011, p. 28).

Record Keeping

In the past, records collected by police departments (e.g., crime incident reports, arrest records, field interview cards) were manually recorded, first with pen and paper and then the typewriter. Technological advances, particularly the invention of the computer, have made possible the collection, collation, and sharing of this information. "One of the earliest uses of computers in law enforcement was records storage and retrieval" (Craig-Moreland, 2004, p. 300). Since the introduction of computers, data from handwritten or typewritten "hard copies" can be entered into computer databases, which allow for their storage and then retrieval at a later time. Since 1990, the use of computers by law enforcement agencies for maintaining various records has increased substantially (Hickman, 2001). In 2007, the majority (79%) of local police departments used computers for records management (Reaves, 2010).

As the number of local police departments maintaining computerized files has increased, so, too, has the use of computers to submit crime incident reports to the agency's central records system. In 2007, 60% of local departments used computers for this purpose. This figure represents a significant increase; between 1997 and 2007, the number of local police departments using computers to transmit crime incident reports increased more than sixfold, from 9% in 1997 (Hickman & Reaves, 2006) to 60% in 2007 (Reaves, 2010).

In order to allow for the efficient querying and analysis of data, however, databases must be linked. Nowadays, in addition to linking different databases within departments, there are a number of initiatives designed to help departments link databases across jurisdictions. One very successful example of using computers for linking disparate databases is CopLink. Work on CopLink began in 1996 at the Artificial Intelligence Laboratory at the University of Arizona (in conjunction with the Tucson, Arizona, Police Department) with the assistance of a National Institute of Justice grant (Falcon, 2005). It is now commercially available and used by over 100 jurisdictions nationwide (Falcon, 2005). CopLink is a software program that "enables vast quantities of seemingly unrelated data, currently housed and scattered among incompatible agency record management systems, to be organized within and accessed through a single, highly secure Intranet," earning it the nickname "Google™ for law enforcement" (Falcon, 2005, p. 24). The Intranet can be accessed by an individual police agency, agencies within a given region, and even agencies across state lines.

CopLink allows for the identification of criminal suspects, relationships, and patterns. The premise behind CopLink is that most crime is committed by persons who are already in police records. They may have arrest records, be found in mug shot archives, be registered sex offenders, or have motor vehicle violations. Before CopLink, police officers would have had to search multiple databases (e.g., records management systems, jail records, gang offender registries) in an arduous and time-consuming process of linking suspect and crime information. With CopLink, police can link disparate sources of data and match suspects to crimes in ways that would have been impossible before. "Partial names, monikers, physical descriptions, and vehicle descriptions are but some of the information that these systems pull out from other participating records systems to identify suspects" (Schultz, 2008). One study found that a police agency using CopLink was able to save 104 full-time equivalents, and then redeploy those forces to other tasks (Davis, 2007).

More recently, the FBI launched the National Data Exchange (N-DEx). This is a larger vehicle for information sharing among law enforcement agencies at every level of government in the United States (Mitchell, 2013). The purpose of N-DEx is to "establish a set of data sharing standards and a central hub, a giant data warehouse into which CJIS [the FBI's Criminal Justice Information Services division] could pull together law enforcement incident reports from thousands of disparate, proprietary and often incompatible federal, state, local and regional databases and data sharing networks" (Mitchell, 2013). N-DEx is essentially a repository for investigative data (e.g., incident and case reports, corrections data, arrest reports, warrants, missing person reports) collected from criminal justice agencies across the country. These data have allowed law enforcement personnel to identify patterns of criminal activity that span jurisdictions such as state borders (Mitchell, 2013). Like CopLink, N-DEx has been compared to a giant search engine for law enforcement (Mitchell, 2013). CopLink and N-DEx are not just similar by way of comparison; they share a business relationship as well. All of CopLink's users who have software maintenance contracts (approximately 4,000) can now access the N-DEx (Mitchell, 2013).

Analysis of Police Data

Crime Analysis

Melissa M. Reuland stated that there are three primary functions of crime analysis:

> (1) assess the nature, extent, and distribution of crime in order to efficiently and effectively allocate resources and personnel, (2) identify crime-suspect correlations to assist investigations, and (3) identify the conditions that facilitate crime and incivility so that policymakers may make informed decisions about prevention approaches. (as cited in O'Shea & Nicholls, 2003, p. 8)

The ability of law enforcement agencies to engage in crime analysis for these purposes has been greatly enhanced by technological innovations. CAD systems and the computer have had a tremendous impact on the ability of the police to analyze calls for service. CAD systems automatically collect certain information on every call—type of call, location, date, and time. Based on this information and other information routinely provided by officers to dispatchers (e.g., time of arrival, time back in service), officer response time and the time spent at each call can be easily calculated. When these data sources are linked with others, crime analysts are capable of identifying patterns, trends, the modus operandi of criminals, and other factors or conditions that may contribute to crime.

According to a 2007 survey of local police departments, over one-third (38%) of departments used computers for crime analysis. Larger departments are more likely than smaller departments to use computers for this purpose; all police departments serving populations of 250,000 or more use computers for crime analysis. Crime analysis is a critical component of what has now become known as "predictive policing," defined as "the advanced use of information/technology to predict and prevent crime" (Police Executive Research Forum, 2012, p. 1). A nationwide survey of law enforcement agencies on the current state of technology in policing found that 70% of agencies said they currently use a form of predictive policing. Ninety percent of responding agencies said they planned on increasing the use of predictive policing in the next 5 years (Police Executive Research Forum, 2012).

Crime Mapping

Crime mapping, at one time performed by placing "pushpins" in maps displayed on precinct station walls, is now significantly more sophisticated. Early manual maps using pushpins allowed for a simple visual representation of crime. Today, due to computer, hardware, and software advances, police are able to create maps that allow for the analysis of data. Crime mapping is based on geographic information systems (GIS) technology. As defined by Boba (2001):

> a geographic information system (GIS) is a set of computer-based tools that allow a person to modify, visualize, query and analyze geographic and tabular data. A GIS is a powerful software tool that allows the user to create anything from a simple point map to a three-dimensional visualization of spatial or temporal data. (p. 19)

Different types of data may be used with crime mapping, much of which is regularly collected by law enforcement agencies (e.g., calls for service, arrests). After beginning with a map, different databases serve as thematic layers. Maps can be designed to depict different information, utilizing different databases. For example, a map might be designed to depict only the location of burglaries in a city, thus drawing solely on the database that stores this information. This type of map is a "spot" map and might be used to assist police in identifying hot spots of crime. A more complex type of map, referred to as a "thematic map," allows police to access far more information. For example, using a thematic map, it would be possible for police to access several off-screen databases—in addition to the information depicted on a "spot map." These databases can contain information about victim, offender, and crime characteristics. With this type of map, analysts are able to manipulate and analyze the data behind the geographical representations on the map.

In 2007, 27% of local police departments, employing 75% of all officers, used computers for crime mapping purposes (Reaves, 2010). Many of the departments using crime mapping software and hardware have acquired their technology with the assistance of federal grants, particularly those funded through the Office of Community Oriented Policing Services (COPS) and the Making Officer Redeployment Effective (MORE) program (Boba, 2001). An example is CrimeStat III, "a stand-alone spatial statistics program for the analysis of crime incident locations," which is free and can be downloaded from the National Archive of Criminal Justice Data (Falcon, 2005, p. 25).

Operations

Computers in the Field

Police now have the capability to use computers in the field. These computers are often referred to as mobile data/digital terminals (MDTs) or computers (MDCs). The use of infield computers has increased dramatically since 1990. The percentage of local police departments using infield computers increased from 5% in 1990 (Hickman & Reaves, 2006) to 59% in 2007 (Reaves, 2010).

Computers in the field can serve a variety of functions. Approximately half of agencies with infield computers use them to prepare field reports (57%) or for communications (35%) (Reaves, 2010). Field reports prepared using infield computers may be saved to a thumb drive and submitted at a later point at the station house, or, depending on the software used by a particular jurisdiction, submitted online.

Used in conjunction with CAD systems, officers are able to obtain a variety of information about a call for service before ever arriving on the scene, such as the nature of the call, the location of the call, and the history of prior calls for service to the address. Police can also use infield computers to collect a variety of information about the persons and places with whom they come into contact. Figure 1 depicts the various types of information accessible to officers through their infield computers.

While the effectiveness of officers in the field has undoubtedly been improved due to the increased accessibility of various types of data, there has also been an effect on communications. The ability of officers to collect the types of information depicted in Figure 1 has had a significant impact on the demands placed on police dispatchers and the amount of time officers spend on the radio. While officers were once reliant upon dispatchers for information on suspects or driving records, it is now possible to obtain this information without using scarce airtime or bothering dispatchers.

Video Cameras

Video cameras are also becoming more commonplace in police work. In 2007, the majority of local police departments (66%) used video cameras in some capacity (Reaves, 2010). Most often, video cameras are installed in squad cars and are used to capture interactions with citizens. The resulting video recordings can be used refresh an officer's memory as to suspect statements and behaviors while report writing, or can be submitted at a later date as evidence in criminal proceedings. A 2011 survey of law enforcement agencies found that 71% of departments had in-car video recording capabilities,

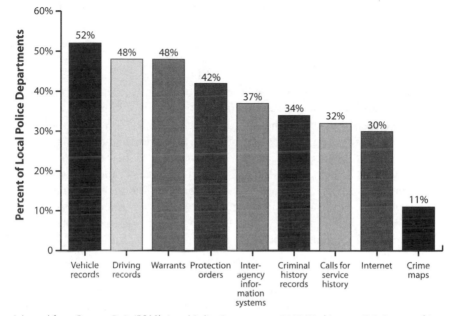

Adapted from Reaves, B. A. (2010). *Local Police Departments, 2007*. Washington, DC: Bureau of Justice Statistics, p. 23.

Figure 1   Computerized Information Available to Local Police Officers Using Infield Computers

with 25% of agencies reporting that they have video recorders in *all* squad cars (Police Executive Research Forum, 2012).

Video cameras in squad cars have many advantages, but one problem is that their range of vision may be limited. Improving upon this concept, most recently officers have begun wearing video cameras. Body-worn cameras are worn by officers (on their head, chest, etc.) and are thus more versatile than video cameras that are mounted in fixed locations in squad cars. In addition to improving the camera's range of vision, body-worn cameras have the added benefit of discouraging police misconduct, as they document police behavior in addition to the behavior of those with whom the police are interacting (Walker and Katz, 2013). For instance, a study by the Police Foundation found that officers who knew they were being watched (i.e., were wearing body cams) engaged in more pro-social behavior than the comparison group—in this case, 50% fewer incidents of excessive force (Police Foundation, 2013).

While not yet the norm, some larger and urban departments have begun using fixed-site surveillance cameras at intersections and in other places, giving police the ability to track individuals' movements (Reaves, 2010). These cameras have other abilities as well; the Camden (New Jersey) police, for instance, use CCTVs "to identify problem areas and dispatch officers to those places, which is more efficient than waiting for calls for service" (Office of Community Oriented Policing Services, 2011, p. 27).

Less-Lethal Weapons

Technological advances have also led to the improvement of less-than-lethal weapons, and they are now far more commonplace than in years past. In 2007, nearly all local police departments authorized officers to carry at least one type of less-than-lethal weapon (Reaves, 2010). While police were once relegated to using their batons, fists, or firearms in situations requiring physical force, officers today have far more options at their disposal: pepper spray, conducted energy devices (CEDs) such as Tasers ® and stun guns, and soft projectiles. These less-than-lethal weapons and others like them have significantly reduced the likelihood of injury to officers, innocent bystanders, and suspects (Terrill & Paoline, 2011; Kaminski et al., 2013; Paoline, Terrill, & Ingram, 2012; Kaminski, Edwards, & Johnson, 1999; Smith et al., 2007).

License Plate Readers

License plate readers (LPRs) are another emerging use of technology by law enforcement; over 70% of departments surveyed by PERF on the state of technology in policing reported using LPRs to at least some extent (Police Executive Research Forum, 2012). LPRs (also known as tag readers) are installed on police vehicles or in fixed locations such as traffic intersections. Most commonly, LPRs are used to detect stolen license plates and vehicles. LPRs scan the license plates of vehicles, which are then compared against a variety of different databases, and officers are immediately alerted if the plates or vehicle have been reported as stolen. LPRs have other uses. While less common, these uses can be far more sophisticated. For instance, as outlined by Walker and Katz (2013), LPRs may be used to track the movements of certain individuals (e.g., gang members, drug dealers, fugitives), to identify previously undetected crime, and for crime analysis.

Global Positioning Systems

Eighty-three percent of departments who participated in the PERF study mentioned above reported using Global Positioning System (GPS) technology to track criminals. For instance, GPS devices may be attached to a suspect's vehicle to monitor his or her whereabouts. While tracking criminals is the main use of GPS technology today, 69% of responding agencies in the PERF study also use them to track officers. Tracking officers can serve multiple purposes. For safety purposes, officers can be tracked so dispatchers know the officer's exact location if he or she becomes endangered or disabled in some way. The Camden (NJ) Police use GPS technology to assist in the patrolling of hot spots of crime. The GPS devices attached to officers' vehicles are linked with crime data, which can then trigger alerts that encourage officers to spend more time in their "hot spots" (Police Executive Research Forum, 2012).

Administrative

Technological innovations have had an impact on the ability of police to perform a variety of administrative functions. Technological innovations are making an impact particularly in two areas: (1) management and accountability and (2) personnel/resource allocation.

Management and Accountability

Technology has aided police managers and supervisors in tracking and monitoring the behavior of subordinate officers. In the past, and to a large extent today, subordinate officer behavior has been monitored by supervisors directly, either in person or over the radio, and by administrators or internal affairs (IA) personnel who might take the time to look at an officer's personnel file. Performance evaluations and interventions tended to be reactive and piecemeal. If an officer received a citizen complaint, the situation was largely evaluated as an isolated matter, and any disciplinary action taken was in response to that incident. Today, over half of all local police departments use computers to maintain personnel records (Reaves, 2010), and innovations in computing technology are allowing for the identification of problems in a much more holistic fashion (e.g., taking into account an officer's assignment, activity level, past complaints or commendations). In addition, the performance of an officer relative to other officers working the same area and shift may be compared, providing supervisors with a better distinction between "problem" behavior and incidents that might be considered reasonable based on an officer's working environment. Based on this information, management can take a variety of preventive and preemptory actions.

Early warning (EW) systems, also known as early intervention (EI) systems, are one such example. Data on officer performance (e.g., use-of-force reports, citizen complaints, pursuits, traffic accidents) are either entered into preexisting or new databases, which are then linked. Different software programs are then used in a systematic fashion to evaluate officer performance, and to identify any area(s) of performance in need of correction. According to Walker (2003):

> The major contribution of an EI system is its capacity to spot patterns of performance and to intervene before problems lead to a serious incident such as a lawsuit, a citizen complaint over excessive force, or some other public crisis involving the department. (p. 8)

Many departments, particularly larger departments, have EW/EI systems in place today. Three case studies were conducted in departments using an EI system (Miami-Dade, Minneapolis, and New Orleans), and results indicated that an EI system can have a substantial effect on officer behavior, with a significant decrease in problem behaviors after supervisory intervention (Walker et al., 2001).

Just as EW/EI systems might be conceived as data-driven systems of behavioral accountability and important management tools, so, too, might systems such as Compstat and its successors. Compstat is a management tool that was first adopted in 1994 by the New York City Police Department to hold officers and precinct commanders accountable for crime and the quality of life in the city. A critical piece of the Compstat system is the analysis and mapping of data. In fact, Compstat is an abbreviation for "computer comparison statistics" (Walsh, 2001). Each week, maps and statistics on crime in each of the department's 76 precincts are calculated. Compstat meetings, attended by precinct commanders and executive staff, are held as forums in which precinct commanders are held accountable for the crime figures in their precincts. Attendees also can discuss patterns of crime, high-profile incidents, and the effectiveness of various tactics and strategies being used to combat crime and disorder (Silverman, 1999; Walsh, 2001).

Exact numbers on the prevalence of departments using the Compstat model are unavailable, but estimates suggest that up to one-third of major cities across the country had adopted this or a similar model of accountability as of the early 2000s (McDonald, 2002; Weisburd et al., 2003); today that number is likely greater. The available research suggests a substantial effect on crime; in New York City, crime statistics for the seven major index crimes declined by more than 50% between 1993 and 1998 (Silverman, 1999). Other cities (e.g., New Orleans, Minneapolis, Los Angeles) have also reported double-digit decreases in reported crime after the implementation of a Compstat model (Walsh, 2001).

Personnel/Resource Allocation

In 2007, 27% of local police departments used computers for fleet management; 20% used computers for resource allocation (Reaves, 2010). Traditionally, law enforcement agencies have deployed officers on the basis of the personnel available and workload demands. The extent to which these deployment decisions were based on an in-depth analysis of data, however, varied considerably. The introduction of CAD systems into policing had a significant impact on the ability of administrators to make more informed decisions regarding the allocation of patrol resources. By analyzing CAD data, administrators were able to confirm that some areas, shifts, and days of the week were busier than others, and were able to make resource allocation decisions accordingly.

Today, personnel allocation decisions may also be the result of crime analysis or crime mapping. Some departments use Automated Emergency Dispatch systems (AEDs), which allow for the automated "locating and dispatching the nearest available patrols" (Cordero, 2011; as cited in Office of Community Oriented Policing Services, 2011, p. 27). As Schultz (2008) notes, "The days when officers patrolled random areas hoping to catch the bad guys are giving way to a new era in which agencies use crime maps of every patrol district to assign officers to patrols in a reasonable and logical manner" (p. 8). In departments practicing community- or problem-oriented policing, or using a management model similar to Compstat, personnel from multiple units and functions could be deployed in response to a specific problem. In this way, technological innovations are helping police managers be more flexible and effective in their allocation decisions, adapting to particular situations that may require more personnel.

Challenges Ahead

Technological advances have allowed police departments across the country to improve police services, increase consumer satisfaction, and become much more sophisticated in their ability to fight crime. In the current fiscal climate, technology has become a "force multiplier." Police chiefs across the country have set about "identifying the most cost conscious ways to deliver police services, and developing a new model of policing that will ensure that communities continue to receive the quality police protection they are entitled to" (Office of Community Oriented Policing Services, 2011, p. 3).

The technological advances outlined here are just a few of many that are revolutionizing police work. As technology continues to evolve and is adopted by law enforcement agencies, opportunities for improvement in policing will increase dramatically. That said, there are challenges. Perhaps the greatest dilemma for police administrators is that technology is increasing in importance at the same time their budgets are being slashed. "Never before has the law enforcement community experienced such significant cuts to operating budgets and available resources" (Office of Community Oriented Policing Services, 2011, p. 34). As a result, most law enforcement agencies are not well equipped technologically (Mitchell, 2013).

Politics—and egos—play a role in limiting the effectiveness of technology. Some law enforcement agencies have been reluctant to participate in the N-DEx (described earlier in this chapter), which is an FBI initiative. Departments at the state and local levels are weary of sharing too much information with the Feds. There is concern of sharing too much information with "Big Brother," a view that will have to be overcome if progress is to be made (Mitchell, 2013).

The ability of most officers to utilize the technology available is also in question. Although it is becoming more and more common that at least some college education is a necessary condition of employment, many forms of data analysis (e.g., crime mapping) require special expertise not readily found in most police applicants (or the population at large, for that matter).

Finally, as technology advances, questions arise as to the legality or constitutionality of various technologies. For instance, in 2012, the U.S. Supreme Court heard a case related to the use of GPS devices (*United States v. Jones* 132 U.S. 949 2012). In it, the Court was asked to decide whether GPS tracking of suspect vehicles violates the Fourth Amendment ban on unreasonable searches and seizures. The Court ruled that attaching a GPS device to a suspect's vehicle does amount to a search under the Fourth Amendment, which necessitates a warrant.

These challenges must be overcome, however, as the computer and Internet have become major breeding grounds for crime. Correia and Bowling (2004) cautioned that law enforcement, particularly agencies at the local level, are ill-prepared to deal with the burgeoning problem of cyber crime.

These scholars suggest that there is hope, however. As they stated, "just as law enforcement has adapted to the automobile, radio, and telephone, so too can they become a formidable foe of the cybercriminal" (p. 294).

REFERENCES

Abt Associates (2000). *Police Department Information Systems Technology Enhancement Project (ISTEP)*. Washington, DC: U.S. Department of Justice, Office of Community Oriented Policing Services.

Boba, R. (2001). *Introductory Guide to Crime Analysis and Mapping*. Washington, DC: U.S. Department of Justice, Office of Community Oriented Policing Services.

Correia, M. E., & Bowling, C. (2004). "Veering toward digital disorder," in *Contemporary Policing: Controversies, Challenges, and Solutions*, ed. Q. C. Thurman and J. Zhao, pp. 285–298. Los Angeles: Roxbury Press.

Craig-Moreland, D. E. (2004). "Technological challenges and innovation in police patrolling," in *Contemporary Policing: Controversies, Challenges, and Solutions*, ed. Q. C. Thurman and J. Zhao, pp. 299–303. Los Angeles: Roxbury Press.

Davis, P. (2007). "Technology serves as a force multiplier." *Law Enforcement Technology*, 34(6): 28–35.

Ericson, R. V., & Haggerty, K. D. (1997). *Policing the Risk Society*. Toronto: University of Toronto Press.

Falcon, W. (2005). "Special technologies for law enforcement and corrections." *National Institute of Justice Journal*, 252: 23–27. Washington, DC: U.S. Department of Justice, Office of Justice Programs.

Harris, E. (2003). *311 for Non-Emergencies: Helping Communities One Call at a Time*. Washington, DC: U.S. Department of Justice Office, Office of Community Oriented Policing Services.

Hickman, M. J., & Reaves, B. A. (2001). *Local Police Departments, 1999*. Washington, DC: U.S. Department of Justice, Office of Justice Programs, Bureau of Justice Statistics.

Hickman, M. J., & Reaves, B. A. (2006). *Local Police Departments, 2003*. Washington, DC: U.S. Department of Justice, Office of Justice Programs, Bureau of Justice Statistics.

Kaminski, R. J., Edwards, S. M., & Johnson, J. W. (1999). "Assessing the incapacitative effects of pepper spray during resistive encounters with the police." *Policing: An International Journal of Police Strategies and Management*, 22: 7–29.

Kaminski, R. J., Engle, R. S., Rojek, J., Smith, M. R. & Alpert, G. (2013). "A quantum of force: The consequences of counting routine conducted energy weapon punctures as injuries." *Justice Quarterly*. DOI: 10.1080/07418825.2013.788729.

Mazerolle, L., Rogan, D., Frank, J., Famega, C., & Eck, J. E. (2001). *Managing Citizen Calls to the Police: An Assessment of Non-Emergency Call Systems*, Final Report Submitted to the National Institute of Justice. Washington, DC: U.S. Department of Justice, Office of Community Oriented Policing Services.

McDonald, P. P. (2002). *Managing Police Operations: Implementing the New York Crime Control Model*. Belmont, CA: Wadsworth.

McEwen, T., Spence, D., Wolff, R., Wartell, J., & Webster, B. (2003). *Call Management and Community Policing: A Guidebook for Law Enforcement*. Washington, DC: U.S. Department of Justice, Office of Community Policing Services.

Mitchell, R. L. (2013, October 24). "It's criminal: Why data sharing lags among law enforcement agencies." *Computerworld*. Retrieved from http://www.computerworld.com/s/article/9243354/It_s_criminal_Why_data_sharing_lags_among_law_enforcement_agencies.

National Institute of Justice. (2005). *Managing Calls to the Police with 911/311 Systems.* Washington, DC: U.S. Department of Justice, Office of Justice Programs.

Office of Community Oriented Policing Services (2011). *Impact of the Economic Downturn on American Police Agencies.* Washington, DC: U.S. Department of Justice, Office of Community Policing Services.

O'Shea, T. C., & Nicholls, K. (2003). *Crime Analysis in America: Findings and Recommendations.* Washington, DC: U.S. Department of Justice, Office of Community Oriented Policing Services.

Paoline, E.A., Terrill, W., & Ingram, J. R. (2012). "Police use of force and officer injuries: Comparing conducted energy devices (CEDs) to hands- and weapon-based tactics." *Police Quarterly,* 15: 115–136.

Police Executive Research Forum (2012). *How Are Innovations in Technology Transforming Policing?* Washington, DC: Police Executive Research Forum.

Police Foundation. (2013). *Self Awareness to Being Watched and Socially Desirable Behavior: A Field Experiment on the Effect of Body-Worn Cameras on Police Use-of-Force.* Washington, DC: Police Foundation.

Reaves, B. A. (2010). *Local Police Departments, 2007.* Washington, DC: U.S. Department of Justice, Bureau of Justice Statistics.

Schultz, P. D. (2008). "The future is here: Technology in police departments." *Police Chief,* 75(8): 13–24.

Smith. M. R., Kaminski, R. J., Rojek, J. Alpert, G. P., & Mathis, J. (2007). "The impact of conducted energy devices and other types of force and resistance on officer and suspect injuries." *Policing: An International Journal of Police Strategies and Management,* 30: 423–446.

Silverman, E. (1999). *NYPD Battles Crime: Innovative Strategies in Policing.* Boston: Northeastern University Press.

Terrill, W. and Paoline, E. A. (2011). "Conducted energy devices (CEDs) and citizen injuries: The shocking empirical reality." *Justice Quarterly,* 29: 153–182.

United States v. Jones, 132 U.S. 949 (2012).

Walker, S. (2003). *Early Intervention Systems for Law Enforcement Agencies: A Planning and Management Guide.* Washington, DC: U.S. Department of Justice, Office of Community Oriented Policing Services.

Walker, S., Alpert, G. P., & Kenney, D. J. (2001). *Early Warning Systems: Responding to the Problem Police Officer* (Research in Brief). Washington, DC: U.S. Department of Justice, Office of Justice Programs.

Walker, S., & Katz, C. M. (2013). *The Police in America: An Introduction* (8th Ed.). New York: McGraw-Hill.

Walsh, W. F. (2001). "Compstat: An analysis of an emerging police managerial paradigm." *Policing: An International Journal of Police Strategies and Management,* 24(3): 347–362.

Weisburd, D., Mastrofski, S. D., McNally, A., Greenspan, R., & Willis, J. J. (2003). "Reforming to preserve: Compstat and strategic problem solving in American policing." *Criminology and Public Policy,* 2: 421–456.

Wexler, C. (2012). "How are innovations in technology transforming policing?" Washington, DC: Police Executive Research Forum.

13

Introduction to Early Intervention Systems

Samuel Walker

The Concept of Early Intervention

An Early Intervention (EI) system is a data-based management tool designed to identify officers whose performance exhibits problems, and then to provide interventions, usually counseling or training, to correct those performance problems. EI systems have emerged as an important mechanism for ensuring police accountability.[1]

EI systems do more than just focus on a few problem officers. As a 1989 report by the International Association of Chiefs of Police (IACP) explains, an EI system is "a proactive management tool useful for identifying a wide range of problems [and] *not just a system to focus on problem officers.*"[2]

In an EI system, performance data are entered into a computerized database. These data include departmental use-of-force reports, citizen complaints, officer involvement in civil litigation, resisting arrest charges, and other performance indicators. Some current EI systems use a dozen or more performance indicators while others use a smaller number.

An EI system is early in the sense that it helps to identify officer performance problems that do not warrant formal disciplinary action but suggest that an officer is having problems dealing with citizens. The major contribution of an EI system is its capacity to spot patterns of performance and to intervene before problems lead to a serious incident such as a lawsuit, a citizen complaint over excessive force, or some other public crisis involving the department. An EI system warns an officer to the extent that it sends an informal but nonetheless clear message that his or her performance needs improvement.

Early Intervention Systems for Law Enforcement Agencies: A Planning and Management Guide. Washington, DC: Office of Community Oriented Policing Services, 2003, ch. 1.

An EI system is officially separate from the formal disciplinary system. It is designed to help officers improve their performance through counseling, training, or coaching. No record of participation in an EI program is placed in an officer's personnel file, although a separate record of participation is usually maintained by the internal affairs or professional standards unit. One or more of the incidents identified by an EI system may warrant formal disciplinary action that is officially recorded, but identification by the EI system remains separate from the disciplinary process.

EI systems are data-driven mechanisms of accountability, providing systematic data as a basis for performance evaluations of officers. They differ from traditional performance review systems that rely heavily on subjective assessments such as "works well with people" or "demonstrates initiative."[3] The database can identify specific areas of performance that need correcting (e.g., a pattern of citizen complaints alleging rudeness).

Bob Stewart, former Executive Director of the National Organization of Black Law Enforcement Executives (NOBLE), says that "If I could choose only one accountability mechanism, it would be an early intervention system." Stewart has seen police performance problems from several perspectives: he was a police officer in Washington, DC, the chief of police in Ormond, Florida, and is now a consultant to communities and law enforcement agencies around the country. Based on this long experience, he now regards EI systems as the single most valuable tool for achieving accountability, primarily because of their capacity to monitor a wide range of officer activities and to spot performance problems at an early stage.[4]

EI systems are retrospective performance reviews. They do not attempt to predict officer performance based on background characteristics or other factors, rather they indicate that current performance levels, while not warranting disciplinary action, still warrant improvement. Past efforts to develop a methodology for predicting which applicants for police employment will perform well and which are not likely to perform well have not proven successful.[5] An EI system provides a basis for counseling or warning an officer that his or her performance needs to improve in the future, and in successful cases, for documenting that the improvement has occurred.

EI systems are designed to help officers improve their performance. The names of several EI systems reflect this orientation. The New Jersey State Police EI system is known as the Management Awareness Program (MAP), indicating its purpose of assisting management. In this respect, EI systems represent a significant departure from traditional police disciplinary practices. Law enforcement agencies have been punishment-oriented bureaucracies, with innumerable rules and regulations that can be used to punish an officer, but with few procedures for either rewarding good conduct[6] or helping officers with problems. Apart from employee assistance programs (EAP) designed to address substance abuse or family problems, police departments have done relatively little in a formal way to correct problem behavior.[7] An EI system helps to identify specific performance problems that need to be addressed (e.g., a tendency toward verbal abusiveness, frequent charges of resisting arrest, etc.).

EI systems represent a problem-solving approach to officer performance. The problem in this instance involves questionable officer performance. The problem-solving involves identifying officers in need of assistance and providing that assistance through counseling or training. (The EI problem-solving process is discussed in detail later in this article.) As one commander with EI system experience explained, his agency's EI system "provides a way for the department to provide non-disciplinary direction and training before the officer becomes a liability to citizens, the department, and him/herself" (*Early Intervention Systems for Law Enforcement Agencies*, p. 78).

EI systems are very similar to COMPSTAT programs. COMPSTAT is one of the most important innovations in police management. It is a data-based system designed to help law enforcement agencies respond effectively to crime and disorder and to hold their managers accountable for their performance.[8] Both EI systems and COMPSTAT programs rely on the analysis of systematic and timely data—in the case of COMPSTAT the data involve crime and disorder, with EI systems the data involve individual officer performance.

EI systems are consistent with the basic principles of personnel management and human resource development.[9] Employers recruit, select, and train employees to effectively serve the goals and objectives of their organizations. Effective personnel management assumes that employee performance is assessed and evaluated on a regular basis, and that the organization takes steps to correct unsatisfactory performance.

Contrary to the expectations of many people, EI systems have not encountered significant opposition from police unions representing rank and file officers.[10] To be sure, there has usually been grumbling and fear of the unknown, but in practice unions have not succeeded in blocking the operation of an EI system once it is in place. The police managers' survey found that only 16 percent of managers had encountered serious opposition from police unions (*Early Intervention Systems for Law Enforcement Agencies*, p. 79). Potential opposition from unions is best overcome by involving union representatives in the planning of an EI system.

EI systems are consistent with the goals of community oriented policing (COP). Community policing creates demands for responsiveness to community residents and in the process new measures of police performance. The traditional measures of the crime rate and the clearance rate are no longer adequate. EI systems have the capacity to quickly document the performance of officers who are not effectively serving the community and provide a basis for remedial action by the department.

The available evidence indicates that EI systems are successful in achieving their goals of reducing officer misconduct. An NIJ study of EI systems in three police departments found significant reductions in use-of-force and citizen complaints among officers following EI intervention.[11] Commanders with EI system experience, meanwhile, are able to report specific examples of individual officers whose performance improved as a result of intervention. One commander, for example, has described an officer who had on-the-street problems because of an excessive fear of being struck in the face. Intervention counseling identified the problem, and retraining in tactics helped the officer overcome the problem. Commanders report many other such success stories. In the survey of managers, about half (49 percent) reported that the system has had a positive impact on the on-the-street performance of their officers, while almost a third (28 percent) reported a mixed impact. No commanders reported a negative impact. Generally, managers have had very positive experiences with the impact of their systems of supervision and accountability (*Early Intervention Systems for Law Enforcement Agencies*, p. 76).

Box 1   EI Systems: An Overview

- Data-based management information system
- Capacity for identifying and correcting performance problems
- Recommended police accountability "best practice"
- Separate from the formal disciplinary system
- Consistent with the goals of community policing
- Consistent with the process of problem-oriented policing
- Rely on systematic and timely data
- Consistent with the process of COMPSTAT
- Careful planning is needed for development and implementation

---

A Word about Terminology

Early Intervention

This report uses the term *early intervention*. It does not use the more widely used term *early warning*. *Early warning* has a negative connotation, suggesting that the system is primarily oriented toward discipline. One department with a comprehensive EI system found through interviews with officers that they did not like the phrase *early warning* because of its "big brother" connotation. EI systems are evolving in the direction of more comprehensive personnel assessment systems, for the purpose of examining a broad range of performance issues. For this reason, the more positive *early intervention* term is used here. Other terms are also appropriate. These include *Personnel Performance Index*, as used by the Los Angeles County Sheriff's Department, or the *Personnel Assessment System* (PAS), as used by the Phoenix Police Department.

Officers with Performance Problems

This report uses the term *officers with performance problems* rather than the commonly used term *problem officers*. The latter terms unfairly labels officers and suggests that their performance cannot change. The term *officers with performance problems* focuses on behavior without labeling an officer and conveys the message that performance can improve.

A Recommended Best Practice in Police Accountability

EI systems have been recommended by a wide range of organizations as a best practice in police accountability.

- A January 2001 report by the U.S. Department of Justice, *Principles for Promoting Police Integrity*, includes EI systems among its recommended best practices.[12]

- The Commission on Accreditation for Law Enforcement Agencies (CALEA, 2001) has adopted Standard 35.1.15 mandating EI systems for large agencies. The CALEA Standard states that:

   A comprehensive Personnel Early Warning System is an essential component of good discipline in a well-managed law enforcement agency. The early identification of potential problem employees and a menu of remedial actions can increase agency accountability and offer employees a better opportunity to meet the agency's values and mission statement.[13]

The CALEA Standard warns that a department should not be faced with a situation where an officer is alleged to have committed a serious act of misconduct where "there was an escalating pattern of less serious misconduct, which could have been abated through intervention." The Standard suggests but does not require the use of such performance indicators as use-of-force incidents, citizen complaints, and disciplinary actions.

- A 1989 report by the International Association of Chiefs of Police (IACP) (1989:80) recommends EI systems as a means of controlling corruption and building integrity in police departments.[14]

- The U.S. Civil Rights Commission was the first agency to recommend EI systems, in its 1981 report, *Who is Guarding the Guardians?*[15]

- Since 1997, EI systems have been included in consent decrees and memoranda of understandings settling law suits brought by the Civil Rights Division of the U.S. Justice Department under the "pattern or practice" clause of the 1994 Violent Crime Control Act. EI systems are mandated in the agreements related to the Pittsburgh Police Bureau; the New Jersey State Police; the Metropolitan Police Department of Washington, D.C.; the Los Angeles Police Department; and the Cincinnati Police Department.[16]

The consent decree settling the Justice Department suit against the New Jersey State Police, for example, requires the development of a Management Awareness Program (MAP) for the purpose of "maintaining and retrieving information necessary for the supervision and management of the State Police to promote professionalism and civil rights integrity, to identify and modify potentially problematic behavior, and to promote best practices . . ."[17] The consent decree with the Los Angeles Police Department (LAPD) sets requirements for an EI system, known as TEAMS (Training Evaluation and Management System). The consent decree specifies seventeen categories of data to be collected and entered into the system.[18]

Box 2   EI Systems Recommended By:

• U.S. Department of Justice

• U. S. Civil Rights Commission

• Commission on Accreditation for Law Enforcement Agencies

• International Association of Chiefs of Police

EI Systems and Other Best Practices

EI Systems are the centerpiece of an emerging package of best practices designed to enhance police accountability. The other elements in the package of best practices, as recommended by the U.S. Department of Justice report *Principles for Promoting Police Accountability (2001)*, include a comprehensive use-of-force reporting system and an open and accessible citizen complaint system. Data on officer traffic enforcement can also be entered into an EI system and can be used to address the issue of potential racial bias in traffic stops.[19] The EI system is the central repository of data on use-of-force and citizen complaints (and other indicators). In this new paradigm of accountability, particular issues such as use-of-force performance are no longer treated as separate items but are linked to all areas of officer performance in a systematic fashion.

A Vera Institute evaluation of the implementation of a consent decree in Pittsburgh commented that "the early warning system is the centerpiece of the Police Bureau's reforms in response to the consent decree."[20] It is the mechanism by which these performance data become useful to managers committed to enhancing accountability and reducing officer misconduct.[21]

Goals and Impacts of EI Systems

The goals and potential impacts of EI systems are broader than generally understood. When the EI concept originally developed more than twenty years ago, EI systems had a narrow focus on "problem" police officers. The implicit idea was to "catch" the "bad" cops. As EI systems have developed over time, however, police managers increasingly understand that they have broader goals and potential impacts, including individual officers, supervisors, and the department as a whole.

Individual Officers

EI systems have a major focus on individual officers. The goal of the system is to correct the performance of officers who appear to be having performance problems. The NIJ study found that the EI systems investigated did succeed in reducing citizen complaints and officer use of force among officers subject to intervention. . . .

One important change that has occurred is that there is now a broader definition of a "problem" employee. Originally, problem officers were defined primarily as those who frequently used excessive force and received a large number of citizen complaints. Reflecting a broader approach, however, the commander responsible for the Pittsburgh Police Bureau's PARS reports that the system allows them to identify their "top performers" and their "under-performers" as well as their "problem officers." Another police department with a comprehensive system, for example, identified an officer who had made no arrests, no pedestrian stops, and no traffic stops in a given time period. The data also indicated that this officer was working the maximum number of permissible hours of off-duty employment. These indicators allowed the department to take the appropriate corrective action.

The capacity to identify top performers as well as officers with performance problems requires a comprehensive EI system such as the Pittsburgh PARS. Most of the early EI systems are not able to identify under-performers, however, because they do not collect the necessary performance data, such as arrest activity. . . .

Supervisors

An EI system also reorients the role of supervisors in a department. An EI database provides first-line supervisors with documentary evidence of officers' performance and permits both a detailed analysis of individual officers and comparisons among officers. In the survey of police managers . . . one manager reported that the EI system as "A useful tool to involve supervisors and lieutenants in non-traditional models of problem solving. It has served to enhance their management skills and help round out their people interaction skills" (*Early Intervention Systems for Law Enforcement Agencies*, p. 78).

At the same time, however, orienting supervisors to their new role is one of the major challenges facing EI systems. Engaging an officer with performance problems and helping that person to recognize his or her performance problems is a role that many supervisors are reluctant to undertake. Some prefer to define their role as friend and supporter of their officers. Some do not have the skills for the task. Most have not been properly trained for this new role. Supervisor training tends to emphasize the formal disciplinary aspects of the job. The intervention phase of an EI system requires supervisors to be a combination of coach and trainer, providing a delicate mix of support, criticism, and help.[23]

As already mentioned, the Pittsburgh PARS takes a special approach to reorienting the role of supervisors. Sergeants are required to access the system's database and review the performance of officers under their command. In addition, as mentioned earlier, the PARS requires sergeants to conduct "roll-bys" of officers who have been identified by the system. In this way, PARS creates a structured and systematic form of intensive supervision for officers who have been identified as having performance problems. (In this and other systems, a supervisor has a password granting access to all officers under his or her command but no other officers. A district commander at the rank of captain, for example, would have access to the records of all lieutenants, sergeants, and officers in that district.)

Some EI systems record each supervisor's access of the system. Thus, the performance review of a sergeant can include a review of the extent to which he or she accessed the system during the period under review.

An evaluation of the consent decree in Pittsburgh concluded that the department's PARS "marks a sweeping change in the duties of the lowest level supervisors." Supervisors log on to the PARS each day prior to roll call. The screen notifies each supervisor of any critical incident involving an officer under his or her command since the last time that supervisor logged on.[24]

The consent decree regarding the Los Angeles Police Department requires that "on a regular basis, supervisors review and analyze all relevant information in TEAMS II about officers under their supervision. . . ."[25] Additionally, the consent decree requires that "LAPD managers on a regular basis review and analyze relevant information in TEAMS II about subordinate managers and supervisors in their command . . . and that managers' and supervisors' performance in implementing the provisions of the TEAMS II protocol shall be taken into account in their annual personnel performance

---

Box 3   Goals and Impacts of EI Systems

The Individual Officer
• Improved Performance
• Higher Standards of Accountability

Supervisors
• Improved Supervisory Practices
• Higher Standards of Accountability as Supervisors

The Department
• Higher Standards of Accountability
• Reduction in Litigation
• Improved Community Relations

evaluations."[26] The consent decree involving the Cincinnati Police Department contains a similar requirement that supervisors be evaluated on the basis of "they're to use the risk management system to enhance department effectiveness and reduce risk."[27]

EI systems can also address the problem that, with regular shift changes, sergeants often find themselves responsible for officers who they do not know. As one commander reports, "There is a lot of movement of personnel, so supervisors often do not know the histories of their officers. The EWS report brings them up to speed in a much more timely fashion" (*Early Intervention Systems for Law Enforcement Agencies*, p. 78).

The San Jose Police Department has taken EI systems to a new level by developing a Supervisor's Intervention Program (SIP) that addresses the performance of supervisors as well as rank and file officers. Whenever the team of officers under a supervisor's command receives three or more citizen complaints within a six-month period, the supervisor is required to meet with his or her chain of command and the head of Internal Affairs. (The San Jose EI system relies only on citizen complaints.) In the first year of the SIP program, four supervisors met the thresholds and were counseled by the department.[28]

Some departments are exploring ways to use their EI system to hold sergeants accountable. The San Jose Police Department, for example, identifies sergeants when officers under their command receive a certain number of citizen complaints. This approach recognizes that many officer performance problems are the result of inadequate supervision.[29]

The Department

An EI system also has the potential for considerable impact on the department as a whole. The system defines standards of conduct and provides a database for measuring officer performance and identifying substandard performance. At the same time, a fully operational system redefines the role of supervisors, giving them specific duties related to supervision of officers with performance problems. And as mentioned in the previous section, the more sophisticated EI systems have the capacity to monitor supervisors' use of the system and to grade their performance accordingly.

Problems identified by the EI system can also lead to changes in departmental policy. The consent decree between the Justice Department and the New Jersey State Police, for example, requires that "Each supervisor shall, consistent with his or her authority, implement any appropriate changes or remedial measures regarding traffic enforcement criteria, training, and enforcement practices for particular units or subunits . . ."[30]

Over the long run, the cumulative effect of the changes in the role of supervisors and changes in departmental policy has the potential for changing the organizational culture of a police department and establishing new standards of accountability. In the police commander survey, one commander explained that over time rank and file officers came to accept the goals of the EI system: "Most no longer believe this system is out to 'get' them, but rather to assist them" (*Early Intervention Systems for Law Enforcement Agencies*, p. 81). A top commander in the Pittsburgh Police Bureau claims that PARS has begun to change the culture within the department. Two impacts are particularly notable. First, the system forces a more intensive form of supervision on the part of sergeants. Second, by identifying officers who are underperforming because they are devoting too much time to off-duty employment, and then correcting that problem, PARS helps to develop a greater commitment by officers to their primary employment.[31]

The positive impact on the organizational culture of a department is not guaranteed, however. If there is little effective use of the EI system—as in failure to conduct meaningful interventions with officers—the impact could easily be negative: reinforcing officer cynicism about the gap between stated ideals and actual practice.

Learning from the Corrections Profession

The corrections profession has already begun to incorporate the EI concept into its accreditation process. The American Correctional Association (ACA) is adopting a "performance-based" approach to accreditation. The indicators for agency performance are essentially the same as those used in law enforcement EI systems. The Performance-Based Standards for Adult Community Residential Services, for example, includes the following standard:[32]

> Number of offenders' grievances filed alleging inappropriate use of force in the past 12 months, divided by [the] Average daily offender population in the past 12 months.

The approach used by the ACA focuses on the agency, with organizational-level performance measures, while law enforcement EI systems focus on individual officers. There are good reasons for suggesting that the ACA approach is the better of the two. It properly focuses on organizational-level issues of management and supervision where corrective action can prevent future misconduct. The current law enforcement focus on individual officers tends to make scapegoats of a few officers, generate hostility from the rank and file, and ignore important issues of management and supervision.

Early Intervention and Community Policing

EI systems are fully compatible with the goals of community oriented policing (COP). In particular, the community policing movement has created demands for new measures of police performance.[33] Because COP reorients the goals of policing, new measures of are needed for both individual police officers and entire departments. The traditional measures of the crime rate and the clearance rate are no longer adequate.

Traditional police performance measures are inadequate in several regards. They emphasize crime, to the neglect of quality-of-life issues; they fail to take into account perceived community needs; and they fail to reward adequately good police performance.[34] By systematically identifying and attempting to control inappropriate behavior, an EI system can potentially reduce the number of incidents that alienate communities from the police.

One of the basic goals of COP is to establish closer ties to the communities receiving police services. COP places particular emphasis on being more responsive to community concerns about the quality of police services, particularly with respect to racial and ethnic minority communities' concern about excessive force or other forms of inappropriate behavior by officers.

In this regard, Alpert and Moore recommend "the development of statistical evidence on the use of force and the incidence of brutality, discourtesy, and corruption . . ." This is precisely what an EI system does. Indeed, Alpert and Moore's approach suggests that a law enforcement agency's personnel data system should transcend a narrow focus on suspected officers with performance problems and include all current sworn officers.[35]

Early Intervention and Problem-Oriented Policing

EI systems are also consistent with the principles of problem-oriented policing (POP). In this case, the problem is not graffiti or public drunkenness, but those officers with performance problems. As initially formulated by Herman Goldstein, POP holds that law enforcement agencies should desegregate the various aspects of their role and, instead of attempting to address "crime" and "disorder" as global categories, should identify particular problems within each category and develop narrowly tailored responses appropriate to each. In addition, they should develop the appropriate performance measures for each problem.[36]

The POP process of scanning, analysis, response, and assessment (SARA) is, for all practical purposes, the way an EI system operates:

- Scanning: review of data in the EI system database
- Analysis: identification and selection of potential officers with performance problems
- Response: intervention with selected officers
- Assessment: post-intervention review of officers' performance

Early Intervention and COMPSTAT

EI systems are very similar to COMPSTAT programs in terms of both purpose and process. Both rely on the analysis of systematic data for the purpose of addressing problems and holding police managers accountable for problems under their command. An evaluation of the Pittsburgh PARS (its EI system) described one key element as modeled after COMPSTAT. The Quarterly COMPSTAT meetings in Pittsburgh involve a review of officers who have been identified by PARS. Area commanders make presentations about any officers under their command who have been identified and conclude with a recommendation regarding formal intervention. After a discussion, the chief of police makes a final decision on what course of action to take.[37]

COMPSTAT is one of the most notable police innovations in recent years, and has been widely adopted across the country. A COMPSTAT program involves a computerized database of timely and systematic data on criminal activity. Analysis of the data provides a means of developing rapid and narrowly targeted responses designed to reduce crime. Regular COMPSTAT meetings are designed to hold police managers accountable by requiring them to describe crime trends in their areas of responsibility and to explain what responses they have developed.

Early Intervention and Risk Management

EI systems can be a key component in a risk management system (RMS).[38] Risk management is a process for reducing an organization's exposure to financial loss due to litigation. In law enforcement, the major civil litigation costs arise from fatal shootings, excessive physical force, and high-speed pursuit incidents. An EI system database can readily identify patterns of individual officers and situations that represent actual or potential risks. It also provides a structured process for correcting those problems and reducing the potential financial risk. In fact, the expanded EI system in the Cincinnati Police Department, as mandated by a memorandum of understanding with the Justice Department, is called the Risk Management System.

Early Intervention and Police-Community Relations

EI systems represent a potentially effective response to the historic problems of officer misconduct and tensions between law enforcement professionals and the communities they serve. For many decades, alleged police officer misconduct, including misuse of deadly force, use of excessive physical force, and discourtesy, has been a major cause of tensions between the police and racial and ethnic minority communities. Civil rights leaders have alleged that minority citizens are not only the targets of police misconduct at a rate disproportionate to their presence in the population, but that police departments have failed to investigate citizen complaints about misconduct and discipline guilty officers.[39]

To an unfortunate extent, police abuse of citizens has been explained in global terms, typically labeling all police officers with a broad brush. Abusive behavior for example, has been attributed to a general police subculture, with the implicit assumption that certain attitudes and behaviors are common to all officers in all police departments.[40] Other observers have attributed abusive behavior to race, arguing that abuse reflects racist attitudes and behavior on the part of white police officers toward citizens of color.[41] Some observers have attributed overly aggressive or abusive behavior to gender, holding that reflects male norms of behavior.[42] Still other observers have attributed police misconduct to organizational dysfunction, arguing that poor leadership and low standards of professionalism have tolerated many different forms of police officer misconduct.[43]

The great virtue of an EI system is that it can pinpoint specific actions that are creating conflict with the community and the particular officers responsible for them. For example, if there are complaints in one neighborhood about frequent use of force, an EI system can help to confirm or refute the allegations, and if confirmed, identify the officers involved. At the same time, it can help to identify those officers who are engaged in active police work (e.g., a high volume of arrests) without resorting to inappropriate behavior.

Early Intervention and Racial Profiling

A comprehensive EI system has the potential for addressing the issue of racial profiling. The Pittsburgh and Phoenix EI systems collect data on traffic stops, including data on the race and gender of drivers. These data make it possible to identify officers who are stopping a suspiciously high number of racial or ethnic minority drivers. As a discussion paper by Samuel Walker argues, an EI system solves many of the problems associated with interpreting traffic stop data. Rather than use resident population data, as many reports do, an EI system permits comparisons among officers working similar assignments.[44]

In a predominantly Latino neighborhood, for example, it is to be expected that a high percentage of all stops would involve Latino drivers. The EI system database can help identify officers who are stopping far more Latino drivers than their peers. The data alone would not prove that racial profiling exists. Rather, it would be the starting point for supervisory review that would determine whether or not an officer's activities involve racial or ethnic bias. The peer officer comparison approach . . . is the methodology currently used in the Pittsburgh PARS.[45]

In one department, the EI system identified an officer who had a practice of stopping female drivers for questionable purposes. The department received a formal citizen complaint from one female driver who alleged that the officer made improper sexual advances during a traffic stop. A review of the EI database revealed a very high rate of traffic stops of female drivers. Combined with the original complaint, these data were sufficient to cause a formal departmental intervention.

Using peer officers as the comparison group solves the most vexing problem with regard to the analysis of traffic stop data. Most current data collection efforts use the racial and ethnic composition of the resident population as the baseline or denominator.

One Size Does Not Fit All Departments

There is no single model for EI systems. The outline of the basic components of a system described above represents a single framework. Each department can develop an EI system appropriate to its needs. These needs will vary significantly according to the size of the department.[46]

Medium-sized and small agencies do not need as complex and sophisticated a system as do large departments. Most of the available information about EI systems at present, however, is derived from large law enforcement agencies. Consequently, at this time it is not possible to specify the exact needs of medium-sized and small departments. Developing those needs is on the list or priorities for future research and program development. . . .

A Work in Progress

Although EI systems are increasingly popular and have been recommended by a wide range of professional groups, they are far more complex than is generally realized. They require making a number of difficult choices regarding their design, and once operational require close, ongoing administrative attention.

EI systems are in a state of continuing development. There is no solid consensus regarding a single best way to operate a system. Local police departments have found that they need to continually revise and fine-tune their EI systems. As one police manager explains, "this is a new practice that may, and has, changed over time. It continues to evolve." Another explains that an EI system "needs to continuously evolve and expand" (*Early Intervention Systems for Law Enforcement Agencies*, p. 84).

Additionally, our understanding of EI systems is experiencing a paradigm shift. First, they are no longer seen only as a means of identifying officers with performance problems, but instead are recognized as an effective data-based tool for general personnel assessment. Second, instead of focusing exclusively on rank and file officers they are seen as a tool for promoting the accountability of supervisors.

Conclusion

Early Intervention systems are an important new tool for police accountability. They are data-based programs for identifying officers with performance problems and providing the basis for departmental intervention to correct those problems.

EI systems have emerged as a recommended best practice in police accountability. They have been recommended by a wide range of professional associations. In addition, EI systems are consistent with the goals of both community policing and problem-oriented policing.

Although they are growing in popularity, EI systems are still in the early stages of development. Departments are still wrestling with a number of difficult and important issues. These issues are addressed in the remaining chapters of this report.

NOTES

[1] Samuel Walker, Geoffrey P. Alpert, and Dennis Kenney. 2001. *Early Warning Systems: Responding to the Problem Police Officer*. Research in Brief. (Washington, DC: National Institute of Justice, 2001). Available on the Web at www.ncjrs.org. NCJ 188565.

[2] International Association of Chiefs of Police, *Building Integrity and Reducing Drug Corruption in Police Departments* (Washington, DC: Government Printing Office, 1989), p. 80.

[3] Frank Landy, *Performance Appraisal in Police Departments*. (Washington, DC: The Police Foundation, 1977).

[4] Bob Stewart, Comments, Focus Group Session, Nebraska State Patrol, June 9, 2003.

[5] Gary Stix, "Bad Apple Picker: Can A Neural Network Help Find Problem Cops?" *Scientific American* (December 1994): 44–45. Bernard Cohen and Jan M. Chaiken, *Police Background Characteristics and Performance* (Lexington, MA: Lexington Books, 1973).

[6] Herman Goldstein, *Police Corruption* (Washington, DC: The Police Foundation, 1975).

[7] It is significant, for example, that a recent National Institute of Justice (NIJ) publication on developing programs to deal with law enforcement officer stress includes a section on "Selecting Target Groups" but contains no reference to specific performance indicators such as are commonly used in EI systems. Peter Finn and Julie Esselman Tomz, *Developing a Law Enforcement Stress Program for Officers and Their Families* (Washington: Government Printing Office, 1997), pp. 23–26. Available on the Web at www.ncjrs.org. NCJ163175.

[8] David Weisburd, Stephen Mastrofski, Ann Marie McNally, and Rosann Greenspann, *Compstat and Organizational Change: Findings from a National Survey* (Washington, DC: The Police Foundation, 2001). Eli B. Silverman, *NYPD Battles Crime: Innovative Strategies in Policing* (Boston: Northeastern University Press, 1999).

[9] Robert L. Mathis and John H. Jackson, *Human Resource Management*. Michael Poole and Malcolm Warner, *The IEBM Handbook of Human Resource Management* (London: International Thomson Business Press, 1998).

[10] One large city on the West Coast the union demanded that the EI system be subject to collective bargaining or meet and confer. The issue remained unresolved at the time this report was written. Nonetheless, this remains the only known case of union opposition to date.

[11] Walker, Alpert, and Kenney, *Early Warning Systems: Responding to the Problem Police Officer*.

[12] U.S. Department of Justice, *Principles for Promoting Police Integrity* (Washington, DC: Department of Justice, 2001). Available on the Web at www.ncjrs.org, NCJ # 186189.

[13] Commission on Accreditation for Law Enforcement Agencies, Standard 35.1.15. "Personnel Early Warning System" (2001). Commission on Accreditation for Law Enforcement Agencies, *Standards for Law Enforcement Agencies*, 4th ed. (Fairfax, VA: CALEA, 1999). www.calea.org.

[14] International Association of Chiefs of Police, *Building Integrity and Reducing Drug Corruption in Police Departments*.

[15] U.S. Commission on Civil Rights, *Who is Guarding the Guardians?* (Washington DC: The United States Commission on Civil Rights, 1981).

[16] The various consent decrees and memoranda of understanding, along with other related documents, are available at www.usdoj.gov/crt/split.

[17] *United States v State of New Jersey*, Consent Decree (1999), Parag. 40. Available at www.usdoj.gov/crt/split.

[18] *United States v Los Angeles*, Consent Decree (2000), Section II. Available at www.usdoj.gov/crt/split.

[19] Department of Justice, *Principles for Promoting Police Integrity*.

[20] Robert C. Davis, Christopher Ortiz, Nicole J. Henderson, Joel Miller and Michelle K. Massie, *Turning Necessity into Virtue: Pittsburgh's Experience with a Federal Consent Decree* (New York: Vera Institute of Justice, 2002), p. 37. Available at www.vera.org.

[21] Samuel Walker, "The New Paradigm of Police Accountability: The U.S. Justice Department 'Pattern or Practice' Suits in Context," *St. Louis University Public Law Review*, XXII (No. 1, 2003): 3–52.

[22] Walker, Alpert, and Kenney, *Early Warning Systems: Responding to the Problem Police Officer*.

23 Early Intervention System State of the Art Conference, Report (Omaha, 2003). Available at www.policeaccountability.org.

24 Davis, et al., *Turning Necessity into Virtue*, pp. 44 (quote), 43.

25 *United States v City of Los Angeles*, Consent Decree, Sec. II, Para. 47.

26 The Los Angeles and other consent decrees are available on the U.S. Department of Justice Web site: www.usdoj.gov/crt/split.

27 *United States v Cincinnati*, 2002: Sec. VII. 62. i.

28 San Jose Independent Police Auditor, *2001 Year End Report* (San Jose: Independent Police Auditor, 2002), pp. 48–49.

29 This program is described in Special Counsel Merrick J. Bobb, *16th Semiannual Report* (Los Angeles: Special Counsel, 2003), pp. 79–80.

30 *United States v. State of New Jersey*.

31 Unpublished Remarks. Early Intervention State of the Art Conference (2003).

32 American Correctional Association, *Performance-Based Standards for Adult Community Residential Services*, 4th ed. (Lanham, MD: American Correctional Association, 2000), Appendix B, p. 82.

33 Timothy N. Oettmeier and Mary Ann Wycoff, *Personnel Performance Evaluations in the Community Policing Context* (Washington, DC: The Police Foundation, 1997).

34 Geoffrey Alpert and Mark H. Moore, "Measuring Police Performance in the New Paradigm of Policing," Bureau of Justice Statistics, *Performance Measures for the Criminal Justice System* (Washington, DC: Government Printing Office, 1993), pp. 109–140.

35 Ibid.

36 Herman Goldstein, "Improving Policing: A Problem-Oriented Approach," *Crime and Delinquency*, 25 (1979): 236–258. Tara O'Connor, Shelley and Anne C. Grant, eds., *Problem-Oriented Policing* (Washington: Police Executive Research Forum, 1998).

37 Davis, et al., *Turning Necessity into Virtue*, pp. 45–47.

38 Carol Archbold, "Innovations in Police Accountability: An Exploratory Study of Risk Management and Police Legal Advising." (March 2002). Available at www.policeaccountability.org.

39 National Advisory Commission on Civil Disorders, *Report* (New York: Bantam Books, 1968). NAACP, *Beyond the Rodney King Story* (Boston: Northeastern University Press, 1995). Human Rights Watch, *Shielded From Justice: Police Brutality and Accountability in the United States* (New York: Human Rights Watch, 1998).

40 William A. Westley, *Violence and the Police* (Cambridge: MIT Press, 1970).

41 The argument is implicit in the long-standing recommendations that police departments diversify their workforces and actively recruit more racial and ethnic minority officers. See, for example, National Advisory Commission on Civil Disorders, *Report*, 315.

42 Catherine H. Milton, *Women in Policing* (Washington: The Police Foundation, 1970).

43 This view is central to the movement for police professionalism and the reform proposals that dominated the professionalization from about 1900 to the present. Samuel Walker, *A Critical History of Police Reform* (Lexington, MA: Lexington Books, 1977).

44 On using peer officers to evaluate officers' performance, see Special Counsel, *16th Semiannual Report*, p. 74.

45 Samuel Walker, Internal Benchmarking for Traffic Stop Data: An Early Intervention Approach. Discussion Paper. Omaha, NE, 2003. Available at www.policeaccountability.org.

46 Early Intervention State of the Art Conference, *Report*.

14

Evidence-Based Policing

Cynthia Lum & Christopher S. Koper

What Is Evidence-Based Policing?

Evidence-based policing is a law-enforcement perspective and philosophy that implicates the use of research, evaluation, analysis, and scientific processes in law-enforcement decision making. This research could cover a wide array of subject matters, from evaluations on interventions and tactics to analysis of police behavior, activities, and internal management. In his 1998 "Ideas in American Policing" lecture for the Police Foundation, Lawrence Sherman gave one of the most well-known articulation of evidence-based policing. He posited that "police practices should be based on scientific evidence about what works best" (p. 2). In particular, Sherman focused on two dimensions of a research orientation in policing: (1) using the results of scientifically rigorous evaluations of law-enforcement tactics and strategies to guide decisions, and (2) generating and applying analytic knowledge derived from an agency's analysis of its own internal issues and crime problems. Although using research and analysis was not a new concept in governance and social interventions when Sherman gave this lecture, what was innovative was his assertion that police should use research and analysis more frequently, substantively, and directly, discontinuing the use of tactics that were shown not to be effective.

The idea of using objective scientific information and criteria to inform public policy and agency decision making reflects a common value in modern liberal democracies: there must be evaluative and objective accountability for governmental actions and spending (Chalmers 2003; National Research Council 2004; Sherman et al. 2002; Sherman 2003). Sherman has argued that

This chapter is reprinted and minimally modified, with kind permission from Springer Science+Business Media, from "Evidence-Based Policing" by Cynthia Lum and Christopher Koper, 2013. *The Encyclopedia of Criminology and Criminal Justice* (Gerben Bruinsma and David Weisburd, Editors), pp. 1426–1437. New York, NY: Springer-Verlag.

this is especially important in policing, given the important mandate the police have to ensure the rule of law. In a lecture at the Royal Society for the Encouragement of Arts, Manufactures, and Commerce (RSA) in November 2011, Sherman emphasized this point when he said (quoting the text of the speech):[1]

> The competence we achieve today stems largely from the eighteenth century Enlightenment, when the Royal Society of Arts was founded. The unifying theme of the extraordinary competence produced by that Enlightenment is *objective* knowledge about technically complex matters. The debt we owe to that era is the great transition in so many professions from customs to science, from opinions to proofs. As the late US Senator Patrick Moynihan observed, "Everyone is entitled to his own opinion, but not to his own facts."
>
> That Enlightenment idea of objective knowledge is also crucial to the success of our liberal democracy, in which the rule of the majority protects individual liberty under a rule of law. No institution is more important to that success than the police, whose competence at insuring the rule of law is constantly challenged by thousands of different opinions on how police should do their job. It is therefore essential that our society constantly improves the competence of its police not merely with our opinions, but primarily with facts derived from objective knowledge.

This notion that evidence-based approaches are implicated in the values and ethics of modern democratic governance—particularly of government accountability and reducing harm (Chalmers 2003)—is mirrored in many social arenas, but especially in public health and medical practices. There are many requirements (and laws) stipulating that medical treatments and remedies must be supported by believable and rigorous scientific testing and replication and that those treatments must provide the least amount of harm or negative side effects (or at least report those side effects). Our demand for evidence-based treatment is so strong that doctors spend a large proportion of their income insuring themselves against lawsuits if they commit malpractice. However, when the police carry out an intervention that does not work, or that increases crime or recidivism, or worsens police-community relations, it is much less likely that they will be held similarly responsible.

The ideology behind evidence-based policing, however, suggests nurturing similar expectations. Former National Institute of Justice Director Jeremy Travis went so far as to assert in his keynote address at the Sentencing Project's 25th anniversary celebration in 2011 that "[w]e need a professional ethic that views failure to adopt those proven policies and practices as a form of justice malpractice." While this type of legal accountability is not likely to be soon adopted in American criminal justice practice, the idea behind evidence-based policing emphasizes that law enforcement should at least be held accountable to the knowledge already known about policing interventions and also to crime analysis generated in their own jurisdictions. Police should be deploying patrol officers, specialized units, detectives, supervisors and commanders in ways that can be shown to achieve results, whatever results are sought (i.e., crime or fear reduction; legitimate, fair, and respectful treatment; or responsiveness).

Adopting an evidence-based approach to police decision making may bring numerous benefits to the police. Most obvious are the rewards reaped from employing strategies and tactics that have been shown to reduce crime, increase legitimacy, reduce internal problems, address community concerns, or reduce fear (Lum 2009; National Research Council 2004; Sherman and Eck 2002). Policies deemed harmful or ineffective could be discarded (or at least critically questioned), potentially saving law enforcement agencies time, money, frustration, and blame. Using more objective judgments regarding deploying tactics also seems more ethically justifiable than other nonscientific methods such as best guessing or strategies based on anecdotes or personal preferences. This approach to policing may lead to greater transparency, legitimacy, and accountability in practice, which could improve police-citizen relations and trust.

There may be additional benefits of such an approach. Evidence-based policing requires agencies to access their information and data capabilities regularly to carry out outcome evaluations or analysis. This may lead to improvements in managerial accountability and efficiency, better data recording, collection and analysis, and a push to improve information technology systems to accommodate these needs. Other decision-making perspectives in policing, including community-oriented policing, problem-oriented policing, and professionalism, could be strengthened through the inclusion and use of scientific information and analysis. Problem-oriented policing, for example (see Braga, 2013; Eck and Spelman 1987; Goldstein 1979, 1990), demands analyzing crime problems, using interventions that have been shown to be effective, evaluating interventions against sought outcomes, and potentially discarding interventions that are not shown to be effective through rigorous evaluation. Community policing might also be strengthened from an evidence-based approach, given that many different types of community-based strategies have been developed and also evaluated, some which have not been shown to either reduce crime or improve legitimacy (see Sherman and Eck 2002; Gill, forthcoming). Research has also played—and can continue to play—an important role in developing professional policing, especially for police concerns such as the use of force, racial profiling, or internal corruption.

An evidence-based approach may also increase satisfaction in police work by providing creative ways to carry out the profession and also challenge the status quo. Many strategies shown to be effective run counter to professional mainstays, such as rapidly responding to 911 calls, randomly patrolling one's beat, or making arrests. Weiss and Bucuvalas (1980) found that challenging the status quo is one reason bureaucrats may be receptive to research in the first place. Related to this, applying critical, analytic, and proactive thinking in police work is also more akin to transformational, as opposed to transactional, leadership and deployment styles. Transformational approaches implicate more satisfaction among both supervisors and subordinates because more creative and proactive thinking is involved (Bass 1985; Burns 1978; McCardle 2011). In this manner, evidence-based policing, as with problem-oriented policing, could influence organizational and cultural forces that can inhibit both growth and a dynamic learning environment in policing. If using certain strategies, tactics, and internal practices lead to more positive results, this may then lead to greater motivation and job satisfaction.

Yet, despite these potential benefits, laments continue about the proverbial "gap" between research and practice (Bayley 1998; Lum 2009; Lum et al. 2012; Mastrofski 1999; National Research Council 2004; Weisburd 2008; Weiss and Bucuvalas 1980). Even in the field of medicine, where we might expect that practices are guided by the best scientific research, these gaps persist (Chalmers 2003; Sherman 2003). In policing, Weisburd (2008) points out that the best example of the disconnect between the evidence and its use in practice is the general failure of police agencies to regularly adopt hot spots, or place-targeted patrol, despite the strong evidence of the efficacy of this approach for crime and disorder reduction (National Research Council 2004) and the clear criminological support for the spatial concentration of crime (Weisburd 2008). Further, Koper (2008) found that while many agencies claim to be doing hot spot policing, much of the strategies agencies discussed appear to be consistent with more traditional beat- and neighborhood-based strategies. Other examples are the continued use of the DARE program (Drug Abuse Resistance Education), reactive arrests, rapid response to 911 calls, and gun buybacks—all strategies that have evidence showing ineffectiveness.

Reasons for the lack of evidence-based approaches in policing are many. Transforming more abstract and general research findings and experiences into tangible and specific law-enforcement tactics, practices, and strategies is a difficult and hard-to-measure venture, just as is applying one's education or training to any workplace task. Research knowledge often is not written in ways that make it straightforward for officers to receive or use in practice. Police chiefs often cite the lack of resources, political will, and the potential for police unions to object as challenges to adopting an evidence-based approach. There are also false expectations and beliefs about the role of researchers and research in policing. Despite what some have argued (see Sparrow 2011), researchers have rarely claimed that research or scientific processes can run a police department's daily operations or resolve law-enforcement concerns, just as problem-oriented policing, community-oriented policing, or professionalism cannot. However, incorrect beliefs and prejudices about research and researchers may lead to a widening communication gap between researchers and practitioners.

Further, implementing evidence-based policing is a challenge because its principles of decision making compete with an organizational culture in which decisions are influenced by other philosophies and processes. These include hunches and best guesses; traditions and habits; anecdotes and stories; emotions, feelings, whims, and stereotypes; political pressures or moral panics; opinions about best practices; or just the fad of the day (Lum 2009).

Granted, sometimes these processes and best practices can be influenced by knowledge, information, and analyses. However, they are also highly vulnerable to personal opinions, ideology, and stereotypes.

Thus, the difficulty of evidence-based policing lies not only in the transformation of research into practice but also in adjusting the culture to be more receptive to research and scientific processes. Some have also argued that evidence-based policing needs to acknowledge that crime control research sometimes focuses on outcomes that are not as practical as initially believed. For example, Mastrofski and Willis (2010) suggest that police visibility and responsiveness are how the public judges effectiveness of policing, not necessarily some abstract notion of crime reduction. In turn, this may explain why police have not fully adopted an approach that targets crime concentrations. Citizens may want to see police patrolling their own neighborhoods, irrespective of where crime is most prevalent. And they may focus on other performance measures when judging the police, such as quick response and fairness.

Whether there are valid reasons why police have been reluctant to move from a reactive to a more proactive patrol strategy should itself be subjected to study. Nonetheless, these are important debates about the utility of evidence-based policing and its focus. As Professor Mastrofski emphasized in personal correspondence to the authors, "for evidence-based policing to be useful in a democratic setting, it needs to measure success with sufficient sensitivity to the diversity of values that come to play in making choices about policy and practice. An evidence-based policing strategy that focuses on only a narrow range of values is more appropriately termed 'blinder-based policing.'"

Thus, while the notion of evidence-based policing may in theory seem reasonable, rational, and even democratic, using research in police daily practice is much more complex and nuanced in reality. Building on Sherman's discussion, therefore, Lum et al. (2012) add three further distinctions into the definition of evidence-based policing, which in turn highlight the difficulty in the fulfillment of its own definition:

> Evidence-based policing is a decision-making perspective, not a panacea.
>
> It is grounded in the idea that policies and practices should be supported by research evidence and analytics, not blindly determined by them.
>
> It suggests that research is not ignored and that it at least becomes a part of the conversation on what to do about reducing crime, increasing legitimacy, or addressing internal problems.

The Research Supporting Evidence-Based Policing

Given that evidence-based policing requires the use of research in practice, what then is the research evidence that supports it? There have been decades of policing and criminal justice research that can benefit police decision making across multiple areas of police practices and activities, as most recently reviewed by a special committee of the National Research Council (National Research Council 2004). Below, we focus on the research evidence regarding crime control and prevention of police interventions as only one example. We italicize "one example" because some critics view evidence-based policing as a "what works" movement, focused only on experimental evaluations of crime prevention interventions. However, we remind and caution the reader that there is much evidence in policing that is not about tactical interventions, which is also part of the research base in evidence-based policing, as Moore (2006) and Willis (2012) point out. Evidence-based policing is a general reform concept about the use of research in policing, not about the specific areas of research or the type of researcher that should be its focus.

But even though research can span the gamut of areas and types, it should also be mentioned that no matter what area of research is used to underpin law-enforcement decisions, a fundamental tenet of an evidence-based approach is that not all research in that area should be used. Research in policing uses a wide gamut of methods, including experiments, quasi-experiments, before-and-after designs with (and without) control groups, correlational research, case studies, ethnographies, and other qualitative studies. An evidence-based approach posits that agencies should make use of what Sherman (1998) calls the "best available" evidence—research that is of high quality, scientifically sound, believable, and therefore of high internal and external validity (Boruch et al. 2000; Campbell and Boruch 1975; Farrington 2003; MacKenzie 2008; Weisburd 2000). However, like the "what works" critique mentioned above, what constitutes high-quality research is also debated (Moore 2006). For example, with crime-control evaluation research, not all research evidence is created equal (Sherman et al. 2002). What is the threshold of methodological rigor by which an evaluation study should matter? Further, there are ranges of quality and fidelity in the implementation of research designs. Various sampling and measurement issues may also influence the validity of findings.

At the same time, we know there are many examples of criminal justice interventions that were deemed effective using scientifically weak assessments (or no assessment at all) and that were later discovered to be ineffective or even harmful (DARE, boot camps, reactive arrests, some community policing strategies, intensive supervised probation). As Weisburd et al. (2001) discovered, evaluation studies of lower quality in criminal justice, which may be less valid and reliable, are also more likely to report positive findings. While there are specific debates regarding the utility and ability of experimentation to evaluate crime prevention interventions (see Berk 2005), there is general agreement that an evidence-based approach posits that the rigor of the science behind an evaluation is an important consideration in the believability (and utility) of any particular study.

Thus, many reviews of research attempting to synthesize crime prevention and control research for practical use have been sensitive to the methodological rigor of studies. One of the more influential and recent reviews was conducted by Sherman as part of the University of Maryland Report to Congress on "What Works, What Doesn't, and What's Promising" in crime prevention (Sherman 1997), later updated by Sherman and Eck (2002) in Sherman and colleagues' (2002) study. Each policing evaluation was scored with regard to rigor of method used for evaluation, and then, based on evidence and the methodological rigor underpinning that evidence, a judgment was made about the effectiveness of policing interventions. Relying on the studies exhibiting strong internal validity, Sherman and Eck (2002) concluded in their update that directed patrols to hot spots, proactive arrests of serious repeat offenders and drunk drivers, arrest for employed suspects for domestic violence, and problem-oriented policing seemed to be evidence-based policing approaches. On the other hand, minor juvenile arrests, arrest for unemployed suspects of domestic violence, drug market arrests, some community policing approaches, or increasing police numbers did not seem evidence based.

In addition to—and prompted by—the Maryland Report were a number of subsequent reviews of the evidence of policing interventions promoted by the Campbell Collaboration, specifically its Crime and Justice Coordinating Group (see Farrington and Petrosino 2001). Similar to the Maryland Report, Campbell reviews emphasize that more weight should be given to research evidence with high levels of internal validity. In many reviews, only experiments and multi-subject quasi-experiments are considered in making final determinations about interventions in which multiple studies have been undertaken. Unlike the Maryland Report, Campbell reviews hone in on specific areas of policing and law enforcement. In policing and security, the most highly cited is likely the systematic reviews of the research evidence on hot spot policing (Braga 2007), which have shown place-based targeted patrol to be effective in reducing crime at places. The problem-oriented policing review (see Weisburd et al. 2010) indicates that specific and tailored approaches, in particular focusing on small places, can be effective. Bennett et al.'s (2008) neighborhood watch review found positive effects of neighborhood watch, although studies with lower internal validity were included in this review, and the conclusions of which counter Sherman and colleagues' (2002) more pessimistic findings. In their review of gun-carrying suppression, Koper and Mayo-Wilson (2006) found that police crackdowns on gun carrying are effective in reducing gun crime in crime hot spots.

Further, contrary to the Braga hot spots review, Mazerolle et al.'s (2007) systematic review of evaluations regarding street-level drug enforcement interventions found that problem- and community-oriented approaches were more effective in reducing drug calls and incidents than only focusing law enforcement at drug hot spots using standard tactics. In a review of second-responder programs for family abuse, Davis et al. (2008) found that such programs do not reduce the likelihood of future violence. Upcoming reviews include studies on pulling levers (Braga and Weisburd 2012) and community policing (Weisburd et al. in progress). These systematic reviews examine multiple studies on the same subject to draw conclusions and generalizations about the evidence, so that law-enforcement entities can better digest large amounts of research in an organized way.

Recently, a committee of policing scholars conducted a broader review of law-enforcement research for the National Research Council. Writing about the Fairness and Effectiveness in Policing (National Research Council 2004), the committee found that with regard to research on the "effectiveness of police activities in reducing crime, disorder and fear," the committee noted four key propositions about the state of research evidence in policing (summarized from National Research Council 2004: pp. 246–247, with parenthetical references added):

1. The standard model of policing that emphasizes random patrol, rapid response to calls for service, follow-up investigations by detectives, and unfocused enforcement efforts has not been effective in reducing crime (see also Sherman 1997; Sherman and Eck 2002).

2. Some of the strategies falling under the umbrella of community policing have been effective in reducing crime, disorder, or fear of crime, while others have not (also see Bennett et al. 2008; Sherman 1997; Sherman and Eck 2002).

3. Police strategies that are more focused and tailored to specific types of crimes, criminals, and places are more effective (also see Braga 2007; Koper and Mayo-Wilson 2006; Mazerolle et al. 2007; Weisburd et al. 2010).

4. Problem-oriented policing—a strategy involving systematic analysis of crime and disorder problems and the development of tailored solutions (Goldstein 1979)—is effective (also see Weisburd et al. 2010).

Supporting many of the findings from the Campbell reviews and Sherman (1997) and Sherman colleagues' (2002) reviews, place-focused, hot spot policing strategies—that is, patrol, problem-solving, and/or other interventions focused on small areas or specific places of crime concentration—have proven particularly effective in several rigorous outcome interventions (Braga 2007). In the judgment of NRC, the research on hot spot policing constitutes the "strongest collective evidence of police effectiveness that is now available" (National Research Council 2004, p. 250).

Finally, and most recently, Lum (2009) and Lum et al. (2011) have developed the Evidence-Based Policing Matrix (http://cebcp.org/evidence-based-policing/the-matrix/) an interactive web-based tool which houses and updates yearly all police crime-control intervention research of moderate to high methodological quality. As with other reviews, the Matrix's intentions are to provide easy ways for the evidence base to be accessed and used by decision makers (i.e., practitioners, policy makers, and researchers). However, the goal of the Matrix is not just to show but also to refine knowledge and to facilitate its translation and implementation through the application of the online tool. The idea of evidence-based policing translation tools suggest that such tools can draw out generalizations of tactics that are effective by examining a range of studies and then transform and apply that knowledge to specific problems an agency faces.

The Matrix uses a classification system for police interventions based on three very common dimensions of crime prevention strategies: the nature and type of target, the degree to which the strategy is reactive or proactive, and the strategy's level of focus (the specificity of the prevention mechanism it used). Using this three-dimensional "matrix," Lum (2009) and Lum and colleagues (2011) map all moderately rigorous to highly rigorous research evidence on police crime-control interventions according to how they might be characterized on these three dimensions (see Fig. 1, from Lum et al. 2011, and at http://cebcp.org/evidence-based-policing/the-matrix/). By doing this, clusters of studies (and their findings) illustrate the distribution and concentration of evaluations and effective practices along intersections of dimensions. In other words, police might be able to better glean generalizations from a large body of research about what intersecting dimensions tend to characterize effective interventions.

In general, the Matrix indicates the following general principles of the evidence base of police crime-control interventions:

- A large majority (79% at the time of writing) of successful interventions studied occur at "micro-places" or "neighborhoods."

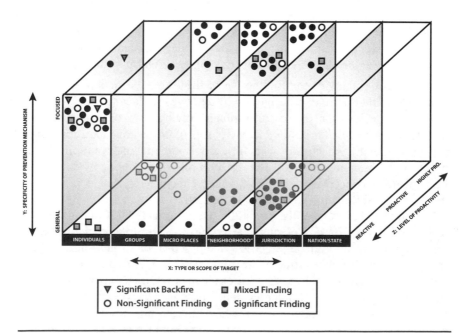

Figure 1   The Evidence-Based Policing Matrix

- 64% of successful interventions are "focused" or tailored strategies.
- 80% of successful interventions are either "proactive" or "highly proactive."
- 53% of interventions that show "no effect" or a "backfire effect" focus on targeting individual(s).

The evidence from the Matrix suggests that when police build strategies and tactics that are more proactive (or are based on using information-led and problem-solving approaches to reduce crime and related problems), when they target problems with greater specificity as to place and prevention mechanism, and when they shift from only a reactive/individual approach to incorporating more proactive place-based approaches, they will likely be more effective in reducing crime and disorder (see Lum et al. 2011). These findings are even more marked when only considering studies within the Matrix that are high-quality quasi-experimental and experimental research.

Although reviews of evaluation research by Campbell reviews, the Matrix, or the Maryland Report help to organize studies by rigor or type, there are other sources that could also be used to support an evidence-based approach in policing. For example, Crimesolutions.gov, an Office of Justice Programs web site, reviews a number of studies across multiple criminal justice arenas. The Center for Problem-Oriented Policing (http://www.popcenter.org/) houses a number of guides, which emphasize not only the application of research knowledge but also systematic problem-solving approaches using crime analysis. Numerous centers and universities also house information and research regarding faculty areas of expertise.

What Would an Evidence-Based Policing Agency "Look Like"?

Additional insights into defining "evidence-based policing" can be gleaned from a discussion of what an evidence-based law-enforcement agency might look like given this specific research base. Again, the examples used here focus on the crime-control research base reflected in the Matrix, but other research categories could also be similarly applied (e.g., research on what strengthens police legitimacy). Given the evidence, at the most basic level, an evidence-based policing agency requires an effort to at least balance traditional and reactive deployment approaches with other types of patrol and investigative techniques that are generally supported by research evidence. But what are these more evidence-based patrol and investigative techniques? From the knowledge gained from the last three decades of research, an agency would be more "evidence-based" if it shifted its deployment strategy from one primarily spent on rapid response and random patrol to more proactive, directed, and problem-oriented targeting of crime hot spots. The research also indicates in its totality that a shift from vague community-oriented approaches to more targeted, problem-solving approaches at specific places involving multiple agencies may be more effective (Weisburd and Eck 2004; Weisburd et al. 2010). If agencies want to focus on individuals, focusing on repeat violent offenders and strengthening post-arrest case enhancement and the use of DNA analysis may be important. Further, research on other values and priorities, such as due process, respectfulness, and fairness, would also have to be considered in developing these different patrol approaches.

Another basic requirement for an agency to be more research-oriented is that it has to have some way of assessing tactics and strategies and gathering knowledge about crime, the community, and internal issues. This involves having personnel assigned and committed to data collection, analysis, and evaluation, as well as having regular systems and procedures for using research and analytic evidence for various organizational functions (e.g., in managerial meetings, promotions, and assessments). This can include strengthening crime analysis and research and planning units, as wells as establishing standard operating procedures that ensure that units apply this information.

Finally, at the most basic level, knowledge from research, whether it comes from evaluations of policing interventions, research on racial profiling or traffic stops, or research regarding different ways to interact with the community, must be incorporated into academy and in-service training. This is a basic requirement that seems the easiest (and most obvious) to implement yet is likely furthest from reality. As indicated by Bureau of Justice Statistics data on academies (see Reeves 2009), it would not be surprising to find that many police academies and in-service systems do not seriously incorporate the latest information on what are the most effective ways police can use to reduce crime, increase legitimacy in the community, or reduce problem behaviors within the agency. Academies traditionally teach reactive skills such as applying police procedures and the law, writing reports and submitting evidence, or using firearms and motor vehicles. All of these focus on police reactive response to crime. Yet, a large portion of an officer's time is not committed to reactive procedural response but is uncommitted, leaving room for high levels of officer discretion (see Famega et al. 2005). Given this, the proactive skills and knowledge base that are needed to carry out effective and legitimate crime prevention during this discretionary time are often not taught. Yet a large portion of an officer's time is not committed to reactive procedural response but is open to use at the officer's discretion (see Famega et al. 2005). Further, knowledge disseminated about respectful and fair policing may build a more respective and legitimate police force.

Such efforts only reflect what an evidence-based approach would be at the minimum. Agencies that want to be more advanced in using analytic and research knowledge may pursue these with greater intensity and innovation. For example, mid-level achievement in evidence-based policing might be reflected in an agency having an active crime analysis culture (and specifically allocated resources) that constantly generates information for proactive enforcement and assessment of activities. In even more intense versions of evidence-based policing, these analysts become criminologists, seeking to find underlying reasons for crime problems and patterns and also assisting the agency in evaluating both its strategies and tactics to reduce crime and its approaches to addressing internal concerns.

More intensive evidence-based approaches might include not only incorporating research and analytic knowledge into academy and in-service training but also using it to rewrite standard operating procedures (SOPs) to conform more to research knowledge. An example might be the SOPs related to preventive patrol and noncommitted time. Currently, SOPs may not include guidance or directives on what officers should be doing when they are not answering calls or writing reports. By building research knowledge into SOPs, such knowledge also becomes part of the information base used for decisions about issues such as promotions and transfers. Further, when police receive research information through familiar agency sources, it increases their receptivity to the information—(Lum et al. 2012). In these agencies, commanders, first line supervisors, and officers ideally would develop a more sophisticated understanding of these issues which become part of their technical expertise (and a requirement for promotion).

Agencies well entrenched in an evidence-based approach work regularly with researchers inside and outside of their agencies and use that knowledge and those relationships to mold both officer and citizen expectations of the law-enforcement role and function in society. The sheriff or chief might even take an active role in reminding his or her political counterparts in the city council or state governments about outputs from research as justifications for activities and resource allocation. Agencies committed to evidence-based approaches would have a portion of their budget specifically devoted to research and analysis of the agency's activities and behaviors.

These are only just a few examples of how research might be incorporated into police practices. Institutionalizing the use of research in practice involves many adjustments to organizational, personnel, incentive, and policy structures in policing. (For more in-depth discussion and examples of these ideas, see the Matrix Demonstration Project (http://cebcp.org/evidence-based-policing/the-matrix/matrix-demonstration-project/) as well as Lum et al. 2012 and Weisburd and Neyroud 2011.) Further, achieving evidence-based policing cannot rely only on the will of police leaders or the merits and volume of the research base. Police must be receptive to such an approach; the research must be useful, and there needs to be a demand for such knowledge in policing. The logic and rationality of evidence-based policy more generally in medicine, governance, or social interventions can be overshadowed by stronger human tendencies of habit, tradition, and culture that can block receptivity toward research use in policing. The example of the continued use of DARE (Drug Awareness Resistance Education) comes to mind (Birkeland et al. 2005). Despite research evidence showing DARE's ineffectiveness, police, schools, and parents support the program for reasons other than meeting its intended outcome. Overcoming a culture of reactivity, low use of analysis, weak supervision and accountability, and a suspicion of researchers, research, and scientific processes will be keys to successfully implement such an approach. This not only requires a sea change in law enforcement culture but also real changes in organizational infrastructure that allows for research to be better received and digested by members of the agency.

ENDNOTE

[1] In this reprint, the text of this passage is presented, which is a slight modification from the oral speech given by Professor Sherman in accepting the Benjamin Franklin Award from the Royal Society of Arts. Both the text and video recording of this speech can be downloaded at http://www.thersa.org/events/audio-and-past-events/2011/professional-policing-and-liberal-democracy.

REFERENCES

Bass, B. (1985). *Leadership and performance beyond expectations.* New York: Free Press.

Bayley, D. (1998). *Policing in America: Assessments and prospects.* Ideas in American Policing Lecture Series. Washington, DC: Police Foundation.

Bennett, T., Holloway, K., and Farrington, D. (2008). The effectiveness of neighborhood watch. Retrieved January 10, 2012, from Campbell Collaboration Systematic Reviews: http://campbellcollaboration.org/lib/download/248/

Berk, R. (2005). Randomized experiments as the bronze standard. *Journal of Experimental Criminology,* 1(4), 417–433.

Birkeland, S., Murphy-Graham, E., and Weiss, C. (2005). Good reasons for ignoring good evaluation: The case of the Drug Abuse Resistance Education (D.A.R.E.) program. *Evaluation and Program Planning,* 28, 247–256.

Boruch, R., Snyder, B., and DeMoya, D. (2000). The importance of randomized field trials. *Crime and Delinquency,* 46, 156–180.

Braga, A. (2007). Effect of hot spots policing on crime. Retrieved January 10, 2012, from Campbell Collaboration Systematic Reviews: http://campbellcollaboration.org/lib/download/118/

Braga, A. (2013). Problem-oriented policing. In G. Bruinsma and D. Weisburd (Eds.), *Encyclopedia of criminology and criminal justice.* New York: Springer.

Braga, A. and Weisburd, D. (2012). The effects of focused deterrence strategies on crime: A systematic review and meta-analysis of the empirical evidence. *Journal of Research in Crime and Delinquency,* 49(3), 323–358.

Burns, J. (1978). *Leadership.* New York: Harper and Row.

Campbell, D. T. and Boruch, R. F. (1975). Making the case for randomized assignment to treatments by considering the alternatives: Six ways in which quasi-experimental evaluations tend to underestimate effects. In C. A Bennett and A. A. Lumsdaine (Eds.). *Evaluation and experience: Some critical issues in assessing social programs* (pp. 195–296). New York: Academic Press.

Chalmers, I. (2003). Trying to do more good than harm in policy and practice: the role of rigorous, transparent, and up-to-date evaluations. *Annals of the American Academy of Political and Social Science,* 589, 22–40.

Davis, R., Weisburd, D., and Taylor, B. (2008). Effects of second responder programs on repeat incidents of family abuse. The Campbell Collaboration library. http://campbellcollaboration.org/lib/download/233/

Eck, J. and Spelman, W. (1987). *Problem solving: Problem-oriented policing in Newport News.* Washington, DC: Police Executive Research Forum.

Famega, C., Frank, J., Mazerolle, L. (2005). Managing police patrol time: the role of supervisor directives. *Justice Quarterly,* 22, 540–559.

Farrington, D. (2003). Methodological quality standards for evaluation research. *Annals of the American Academy of Political and Social Science,* 587, 49–68.

Farrington, D. and Petrosino, A. (2001). The Campbell Collaboration crime and justice group. *Annals of the American Academy of Political and Social Science,* 587, 35–49.

Gill, C. (Forthcoming). What have we learned from systematic reviews of community interventions? In D. Farrington and D. Weisburd (Eds.), *Systematic reviews in criminology: What have we learned?* New York: Springer.

Goldstein, H. (1979). Improving policing: A problem-oriented approach. *Crime and Delinquency,* 25(2), 236–258.

Goldstein, H. (1990). *Problem-oriented policing.* New York, NY: McGraw Hill.

Koper, C. (2008). The varieties and effectiveness of hot spots policing: Results from a national survey of police agencies and a re-assessment of prior research. Paper presented November 14 at the American Society of Criminology meeting, St. Louis, MO.

Koper, C. and Mayo-Wilson, E. (2006). Police crackdowns on illegal gun carrying: A systematic review of their impact on gun crime. *Journal of Experimental Criminology,* 2, 227–261.

Lum, C. (2009). Translating police research into practice. Ideas in American Policing Lecture Series. Washington, DC: Police Foundation.

Lum, C., Koper, C., and Telep, C. (2011). The Evidence-Based Policing Matrix. *Journal of Experimental Criminology,* 7, 3-26.

Lum, C., Telep, C., Koper, C., and Grieco, J. (2012). Receptivity to research in policing. *Justice Research and Policy,* 14, 61–95.

MacKenzie, D. (2008). Reentry: examining what works in corrections. Keynote Address for the 16th Annual ICCA Research Conference, St. Louis, MO.

Mastrofski, S. (1999). Policing for people. Ideas in American Policing Lecture Series. Washington, DC: Police Foundation.

Mastrofski, S. and Willis, J. (2010). Police organization continuity and change: Into the twenty-first century. *Crime and Justice: A Review of Research,* 39, 55–144.

Mazerolle, L., Soole, D., and Rombouts, S. (2007). Street-level drug law enforcement: A meta-analytic review. Retrieved January 10, 2012, from Campbell Collaboration Systematic Reviews: http://campbellcollaboration.org/lib/download/123/

McCardle, B. (2011). Activating officers: the relationship between leadership styles and officer engagement. (Unpublished master's thesis). Cambridge, UK: Cambridge University.

Moore, M. H. (2006). Improving police through expertise, experience and experiments. In D. Weisburd and A. Braga (Eds.), *Police innovation: Contrasting perspectives* (pp. 322–338). New York, NY: Cambridge University Press.

National Research Council (NRC), Committee to Review Research on Police Policy and Practices. W. Skogan and K. Frydl (Eds.). (2004). *Fairness and effectiveness in policing: The evidence.* Washington, DC: The National Academies Press.

Reeves, B. (2009). *State and local law enforcement training academies, 2006.* Publication NCJ 222987. Washington, DC: Bureau of Justice Statistics, US Department of Justice.

Sherman, L. (1997). Policing for crime prevention. In L. Sherman, D. Gottfredson, D. MacKenzie, J. Eck, P. Reuter, and S. Bushway (Eds.), *Preventing crime: What works, what doesn't, what's promising.* Washington, DC: National Institute of Justice, U.S. Department of Justice.

Sherman, L. (1998). Evidence-based policing. Ideas in American Policing Lecture Series. Washington, DC: Police Foundation.

Sherman, L. (2003). Misleading evidence and evidence-led policy: Making social science more experimental. *Annals of the American Academy of Political and Social Science*, 589, 6–19.

Sherman, L. (November 1, 2011). Professional Policing and Liberal Democracy. The 2011 Benjamin Franklin Medal Lecture. Royal Society for the Encouragement of Arts, Manufactures and Commerce, London, UK.

Sherman, L. and Eck, J. (2002). Policing for crime prevention. In L. Sherman, D. Farrington, B. Welsh, and D. MacKenzie (Eds.), *Evidence-based crime prevention* (pp. 295–329). New York: Routledge.

Sherman, L., Farrington, D., Welsh, B., and MacKenzie, D. (Eds.). (2002). *Evidence-based crime prevention*. New York: Routledge.

Sherman, L., Gottfredson, D., MacKenzie, D., Eck, J., Reuter, P., and Bushway, S. (1997). *Preventing crime: What works, what doesn't, what's promising*. Washington, DC: National Institute of Justice.

Sparrow, M. (2011). Governing science: New perspectives in policing, Harvard Executive Session on Policing and Public Safety. Washington, DC: U.S. Department of Justice, National Institute of Justice.

Weisburd, D. (2000). Randomized experiments in criminal justice policy: Prospects and problems. *Crime and Delinquency*, 46, 181–193.

Weisburd, D. (2008). Place-based policing. Ideas in American Policing Lecture Series. Washington, DC: Police Foundation.

Weisburd, D. and Eck, J. (2004). What can the police do to reduce crime, disorder, and fear? *Annals of the American Academy of Political and Social Science*, 593, 42–65.

Weisburd, D. and Neyroud, P. (2011). Police science: Toward a new paradigm. New Perspectives in Policing. Washington, DC: National Institute of Justice.

Weisburd, D., Lum, C., and Petrosino, A. (2001). Does research design affect study outcomes? *Annals of the American Academy of Political and Social Science*, 578, 50–70.

Weisburd, D., Telep, C., Hinkle, J., and Eck, J. (2010). Is problem-oriented policing effective in reducing crime and disorder? Findings from a Campbell systematic review. *Criminology and Public Policy*, 9, 139–172.

Weiss, C. and Bucuvalas, M. (1980). *Social science research and decision-making*. New York: Columbia University Press.

Willis, J. (2012). The craft of policing. Ideas in American Policing Lecture Series. Washington, DC: The Police Foundation.

15

Predictive Policing

Justin Nix

Prediction is a part of our everyday lives. We often check the weather forecast before deciding whether to wear a jacket or grab an umbrella prior to stepping outside. When budgeting our money, we make predictions about how much money we should allot for various expenses such as bills, food, gas, and so on. And when hosting a cookout, we make predictions about how many guests will be attending so that we know how much food to prepare. Accurate or not, we are shaping our behavior based on what we believe the future holds.

Recently the police have begun to experiment with prediction in order to more effectively combat crime in their jurisdictions. Rather than responding to crimes after they have already occurred, *predictive policing* entails using advanced analytical techniques to identify times and locations where crimes are most likely to occur and deploying personnel accordingly to prevent them (Perry, McInnis, Price, Smith & Hollywood, 2013). Although it is a relatively new buzzword among the police, prediction is not new to the criminal justice system. Prison systems use classification instruments to estimate the security risk posed by incoming inmates (Bonta & Motiuk, 1992). Judges have been using recidivism prediction instruments since the 1920s to determine who should be released on parole and who should not (Hoffman, 1994). And while the term *predictive policing* itself may be relatively new, the police have long analyzed past crime patterns in the interest of anticipating where crimes are more or less likely to occur. The use of crime mapping and policing "hot spots" has been popular for over twenty years now (see, e.g., Sherman, Gartin & Buerger, 1989), but technically these are still reactive strategies as the police are shaping their behavior based on past trends.

One might naturally ponder: Is predictive policing a new concept—or is it merely a collection of old ideas with a catchy new title? Can the police actu-

Prepared especially for *Critical Issues in Policing* by Justin Nix.

ally predict when and where crime is going to occur? The current review will attempt to provide an answer to these questions. It is divided into three main sections. The first provides a brief overview of the different perspectives that paved the way for predictive policing. Then, predictive policing is defined and three particular approaches to prediction are presented along with empirical evidence where applicable. The final section contemplates the future of predictive policing, including its potential drawbacks.

From Reactive to Proactive Policing

Prior to the advent of community and problem-oriented policing in the 1990s, policing in the United States was anything but proactive. Rapid response to 911 calls and deterrence via randomized patrol were the primary goals of most agencies under what has been referred to as the "professional" or "standard" model of policing (Goldstein, 1990; Weisburd & Eck, 2004). Tilley (2003, p. 313) used the term "fire brigade policing" to characterize the standard model, whereby officers quickly respond to a crime, handle the case, then wait for the next incident to occur. When not responding to a call for service, officers randomly patrol their jurisdictions in their vehicles without much (if any) regard to crime patterns. Indeed, this style of policing is still favored by many agencies today despite empirical research as early as the 1970s indicating that randomized preventive patrol is not an effective deterrent (Kelling, Pate, Dieckman & Brown, 1974).

Rising crime rates, civil unrest, and growing concern about the legitimacy of police actions throughout the late 1960s and 1970s caused scholars to question the utility of the standard model. For example, Goldstein (1979) criticized the standard model for being overly concerned with randomized patrol and criminal investigations in light of evidence that these were ineffective procedures (Greenwood, Petersilia & Chaiken, 1977; Kelling et al., 1974). Then in 1982, *Atlantic Monthly* published an article by criminologists James Q. Wilson and George Kelling, in which they outlined their theory of "broken windows." The theory holds that the police can both reduce crime in the community and decrease fear among citizens by proactively policing disorder offenses such as panhandling or vandalism. Doing so should indirectly reduce crime by sending the message to offenders that the community does not tolerate criminal behavior of *any* kind (Wilson & Kelling, 1982). Wilson and Kelling's theory fueled the community policing movement, gaining widespread support from both the left and the right. It also represented a major step forward in terms of the police thinking more proactively about crime.

An equally important perspective that gained popularity around the same time as community policing was problem-oriented policing—an even more proactive approach to crime reduction. As the name suggests, it requires police officers to engage in problem solving, which entails more than simply responding to incidents (Goldstein, 1979, 1990). The SARA model outlined by Eck and Spelman (1987) has become practically synonymous with problem-oriented policing over the last twenty-five years. The acronym—which stands for *Scanning, Analysis, Response,* and *Assessment*—is an easy way for police to conceptualize the problem solving approach advocated by Goldstein (1979, 1990). More important, it reinforces the emphasis of proactivity in policing. The police *scan* their community for problems that need to be addressed and gather information (i.e., *analyze*) in order to garner a better understanding of the underlying causes of the identified problems. *Response* is the third phase of the SARA model, which serves to reiterate the importance of identifying and understanding the nature of a problem before attempting to address it. Finally, the police must conduct an *assessment* of their response, which "can be used to change the response, improve the analysis, or even redefine the nature of the problem" (Eck & Spelman, 1987, p. 50).

While forward thinking in the sense of proactivity, community- and prob-lem-oriented policing lacked the sophisticated analytical approach of today's predictive policing. This foundation would come from the Compstat model of policing.[1] Compstat gained popularity as a police managerial perspective throughout the United States after Commissioner William Bratton imple-mented the model in the NYPD the mid-1990s. The model consists of four basic principles: "gathering accurate and timely intelligence, designing effec-tive strategies and tactics, the rapid deployment of personnel and resources, and relentless follow-up and assessment" (Dabney, 2010, p. 28). District com-manders are given clearly defined objectives and weekly meetings are held during which they must demonstrate that they are on pace to meet said objec-tives. Crime mapping, the use of computerized data, and crime statistics are all vital components of the Compstat model. Like problem-oriented policing, Compstat moved the field another step closer to predicting crime. Still, strate-gies developed under the Compstat model are technically reactive strategies, as they are based entirely on past patterns of criminal activity. Furthermore, the model is vulnerable to human error and biases because it relies on human interpretation of simple patterns and basic statistics.

Intelligence-led policing (ILP) gained popularity in the United States after the World Trade Center was attacked on September 11, 2001. The Kent Police in the United Kingdom is recognized as being one of the first police agencies to practice ILP, originally using it as an operational tactic aimed at crime reduction through proactive policing (Ratcliffe, 2008). Over time, ILP has evolved into more of a management model than an operational tactic. According to Ratcliffe (2008):

> [I]ntelligence-led policing is a business model and managerial philosophy
> where data analysis and crime intelligence are pivotal to an objective,
> decision-making framework that facilitates crime and problem reduction,
> disruption and prevention through both strategic management and effec-
> tive enforcement strategies that target prolific and serious offenders. (p. 6)

Driven by the limitations of the professional model of policing, the increasing threat of organized and international crime, as well as rapid advances in technology, ILP is the epitome of proactive policing. It represents an organization-wide model of policing that emphasizes inter-agency sharing of information and places the intelligence unit at the center of the decision-making process. It encourages the police to collaborate and refer to evidence-based practices to come up with strategic crime solutions.

Each of the aforementioned policing models seeks to reduce crime using evidence-based, proactive tactics. That is, they draw upon well-established criminological theories and/or require the police to make tactical decisions based on patterns uncovered by various data. Community policing is grounded in broken windows (Wilson & Kelling, 1982) and social disorganization theory (Shaw & McKay, 1942), while problem-oriented policing draws on routine activity theory (Cohen & Felson, 1979) and the rational choice perspective (Clarke, 1992; Cornish & Clarke, 1986). Compstat and ILP rely on mapping hot spots of crime (Sherman et al., 1989) as well as identifying and dealing with chronic offenders in the community (Wolfgang, Figlio & Sellin, 1972). To be sure, these philosophies are not mutually exclusive—they overlap and in some ways complement each other. Collectively, they illustrate that scholars and police alike realize that crime is not random. Why then, should the police patrol their communities randomly and wait for crime to occur? Certain locations are more amenable to crime than others and a small percentage of offenders account for a disproportionate share of crime. Armed with this knowledge—and given recent advances in technology—predicting crime seems a natural "next step" for the police.

From Proactivity to Prediction

Predicting crime represents the ultimate form of proactive policing. In 2008, William Bratton (chief of the LAPD at the time) started a national discussion on predictive policing, which he claimed would be the next phase in the evolution of the field. He suggested that while it is not an entirely new concept (i.e., it builds upon the tenets of Compstat and intelligence-led policing), the fact that police can now gather and analyze information faster than ever provides them with the opportunity to predict and ultimately prevent crime. Since 2009, the National Institute of Justice (NIJ) and the Bureau of Justice Assistance (BJA) have held two symposia in Los Angeles and Providence during which practitioners and researchers discussed the potential of this "new" style of policing that has caught the attention of police around the world. In 2009 the NIJ awarded over $1 million in grant funding to RAND (Research and Development) Corporation to provide technical assistance for seven pilot projects being carried out by law enforcement agencies across the United States.[2] Two of the agencies—Chicago and Shreveport—received additional funding in 2011 to continue their work and evaluate the effectiveness of their programs. In 2013, NIJ awarded two grants totaling over $880,000 to the NYPD and Justice & Security Strategies, Inc., to test geospatial predictive policing strategies in New York City and Columbia, South

Carolina. Indeed, the possibility of preventing crimes before they transpire is especially appealing at a time when the police are being asked to do more with less.

With that in mind, it is important to be clear about what predictive policing is and is not. Media coverage from outlets such as the *New York Times* seem to imply that the police can use futuristic software to determine precisely when and where a crime is going to occur (Goode, 2011). Similarly, an article published in 2011 by *Popular Science* features an image of a town with a superimposed red circle that reads "Probability of crime tomorrow: 2.17%"—as though the police can forecast crime the same way meteorologists forecast the chances of precipitation (Thompson, 2011).[3] Yet, as Perry et al. (2013) point out, predictive policing is neither a "crystal ball" nor a real-life version of *The Minority Report* (a science-fiction film in which the police arrest citizens for crimes they have not yet committed). Rather, it is "the application of analytical techniques—particularly quantitative techniques—to identify likely targets for police intervention and prevent crime or solve past crimes by making statistical predictions" (pp. 1–2). A strict interpretation of this definition suggests that predictive policing is not an entirely new concept (nor is it one specific tactic). Indeed, at the first Predictive Policing Symposium in Los Angeles, speakers agreed that predictive policing borrows principles from many of the models outlined above (Pearsall, 2010). The police have been trying to predict crime for several decades now. However, with newer, more advanced technologies, innovative thinking, and help from university-based researchers, the police are equipped to take prediction to an entirely new level.

Can the Police Really Predict Crime?

George Mohler, a mathematician at Santa Clara University, and Jeff Brantingham, an anthropologist at UCLA, are listed as two of the co-creators of PredPol, predictive software being used by police in Los Angeles and elsewhere. The two researchers developed an algorithm—based on the same formulas used by seismologists to predict earthquake aftershocks—to predict when and where crime is likely to occur (Mohler, Short, Brantingham, Schoenberg & Tita, 2011). The software produces maps (updated daily) with 500- by 500-foot boxes that represent the areas that are most likely to experience crime on a given day. According to PredPol's website, predictive policing is suitable for jurisdictions of any size and can help "bring newer police officers up to speed more quickly" (PredPol: Predictive Policing in a Box, 2013). For example, the Santa Cruz Police Department identified fifteen hot spots using a predictive algorithm and then asked veteran and newer officers to point out hot spots on a map. Veteran officers were able to pinpoint just over half of the fifteen hot spots while newer officers were able to identify only one or two (Friend, 2013). This simple experiment illustrates that, as Predpol's website points out, predictive policing is not a replacement for officer intuition or experience. At the same time, the fact that veteran officers were only able to identify just over half of the fifteen hot spots suggests that predictive policing can supplement their existing knowledge. Moreover, it can standardize knowledge of hot spots across the entire department (i.e., shorten the "learning curve" for new officers).

Preliminary trials in Santa Cruz and Los Angeles suggest that predictive algorithms have enormous potential for crime reduction. Burglaries were down 19 percent in Santa Cruz after the first 6 months in 2012 (when the department began using a predictive algorithm) compared to the same period in 2011—despite no new officers being hired, shift lengths remaining the same, and no changes being made to patrol structure (Heaton, 2012). The LAPD conducted a controlled experiment to compare the utility of a predictive algorithm to their current practices. Officers were given maps at the beginning of each of their shifts. On some days, the maps were created using standard hot spot techniques (i.e., business as usual)—on other days, they were created using the algorithm. The officers had no knowledge of how the maps were created and they looked essentially the same. The program proved to be twice as accurate as LAPD's current practices, and property crime declined in their Foothill division by 12 percent (Friend, 2013).

It bears repeating that there is no single approach to predictive policing. Rather, as Perry and his coauthors (2013) have defined it, the term refers to analyzing data in order to anticipate and ultimately prevent crime. It is not as simple as purchasing and installing software like PredPol, Bair Analytics, or SPSS Modeler. Indeed, many agencies—especially smaller agencies with smaller budgets—may not be able to afford new software. That does not mean they cannot engage in some form of predictive policing. Using theory and research as a guide, the police can use existing data to anticipate when and where crime is most likely to occur in their community—as well as who may be the perpetrators or victims. The police have been collecting a wealth of data for decades now—they just have to exploit it in order to better understand crime in their communities. This will undoubtedly involve cleaning data, merging databases, and improving the way new data is collected and recorded. The phrase "garbage in, garbage out" should serve as a reminder that useful intelligence can only be extracted from data to the extent that useful data is recorded. A capable crime analyst (or intelligence unit) is almost a requisite to accomplish these tasks. Three promising concepts will be discussed below which can be valuable to any agency dedicated to predictive policing: the near repeat phenomenon, predictive crime mapping, and social network analysis.[4]

The Near Repeat Phenomenon. A growing body of literature indicates that crime is not only spatially concentrated but temporally clustered as well (Johnson, 2008; Johnson & Bowers, 2004a; Ratcliffe, 2004). Optimal foraging theory suggests that animals strategically forage in order to maximize reward while simultaneously minimizing both the amount of time they spend searching for food and the risk of being attacked by another predator (Kamil, Krebs

& Pulliam, 1987). It seems reasonable to assume that offenders have a similar mentality when selecting their targets. For example, Johnson and Bowers (2004b) have shown that repeat burglaries account for a disproportionate share of the total number of burglaries in an area over a given period of time. Furthermore, there is a contagion effect whereby residential burglaries tend to cluster for a period of 1 or 2 months and up to 400 meters around an initial burglary. In a similar vein, Haberman and Ratcliffe (2012) demonstrated that armed street robberies displayed a near repeat pattern in Philadelphia: a repeat armed street robbery was 80 percent more likely to occur within one block and 31 percent more likely to occur within two blocks following an initial robbery for a period of up to one week. Perhaps thieves like their chances of burglarizing the same residence again in hopes of stealing replaced items more than attempting to burglarize an unfamiliar residence that might present a greater risk of being caught. Similarly, offenders who seek to rob people likely stick to places they know. Whatever the offenders' rationale, police can use knowledge of this "near repeat phenomenon" to predict where burglaries or street robberies are most likely to occur in their communities at any given time.

Studies conducted in England and Australia suggest that simply reducing repeat crimes can have a meaningful impact on the overall crime rate in a community. In Huddersfield, police adopted a tiered response to residential burglaries as part of a larger initiative, the Police Operations against Crimes program. Victims received the bronze response after an initial burglary, the silver response after a second burglary, and the gold response after a third burglary. The idea was to prioritize burglaries according to need: rather than uniformly responding to all burglaries as though they were equal, repeat burglaries received extra attention from the police. The bronze tier involved mailing the victim a personalized letter with crime prevention tips and discount vouchers for security equipment, the silver tier included a visit from a Crime Prevention Officer, and the gold tier entailed loaning the victim temporary alarms and covert cameras (Anderson, Chenery & Pease, 1995). Upon completion of the project, Chenery, Holt, and Pease (1997) reported that there was a greater decline in repeat burglaries in Huddersfield relative to other areas. Furthermore, domestic burglaries and motor vehicle thefts declined 30 and 20 percent, respectively, relative to other areas. Police in Queensland carried out a similar initiative, which they dubbed "Lightning Strikes Twice." Budz, Pegnall, and Townsley (2001) found that repeat burglaries declined by 16 percent in the target area upon completion of the project and more than 80 percent of victims reported that the advice they received from police was helpful. These two cases illustrate the potential crime reduction benefits that can be achieved if the police focus on reducing repeat incidents.

Predictive Crime Mapping. Crime mapping has proliferated throughout the field of policing over the last forty years, but until recently it has been based exclusively on past data. Looking back at past crimes in order to detect patterns can certainly be informative, but it would be somewhat of a stretch to deem this a predictive technique. At most, it represents the most basic form of prediction (Chainey, Tompson & Uhlig, 2008). Predictive crime mapping represents a practical alternative to police agencies that would like to engage in predictive policing but cannot afford to purchase predictive software. It can be accomplished with programs such as ArcGIS that are already widely used and do not require the training that other software would likely necessitate. There are a variety of approaches that can be used to generate predictive crime maps (see, e.g., Groff & LaVigne, 2002).

Prospective hot-spotting is one form of predictive crime mapping that involves generating hot spot maps on a daily basis, which take into consideration past events in order to predict where crime is most likely to occur (Bowers, Johnson & Pease, 2004; Johnson & Bowers, 2004b). Hot spot maps are typically created using area-based crime rates, but Bowers et al. (2004) argue that the police should create their maps using individual events. The advantage of using individual events to create hot spot maps is that they can be summed and weighted according to their *current* predictive power, then used to detect patterns. That is, given what prior research has shown about the near-repeat phenomenon, the police could expect a burglary that occurred more than two months ago to have less "predictive power" than a burglary that occurred one week ago. In this case, prospective hot-spotting would take such information into consideration and assign the older burglary less weight than the more recent one. Moreover, as Johnson and Bowers (2004b) point out, hot spot maps generated using area crime rates may fail to reveal clusters of near repeat burglaries that could occur in areas that are not experiencing high volumes of crime. Prospective hot-spotting is straightforward, based on sound empirical research, and involves only a slight (but critical) modification to the way many agencies currently generate their crime maps. As a whole, predictive crime mapping exemplifies a data-driven approach to anticipating where crime is most likely to occur in the community.

Social Network Analysis.   The police regularly make contact with individuals in the community during calls for service, terry stops, traffic stops, and arrests. In many cases, these encounters involve multiple parties. Simply observing two or more people associating with one another can amount to valuable intelligence. To illustrate, suppose an officer pulls over a speeding vehicle containing a driver and three passengers. Suppose in addition the officer recognizes the driver because he is a known heroin user who has been arrested on numerous occasions. Even if the officer knows nothing else about the three passengers, he/she might suspect that they, too, are heroin users simply because they are associating with a heroin user. Likewise, if an officer observed a teenager hanging out with several verified gang members on more than one occasion, he/she might wonder if the teenager is a new member of the gang.

Social network analysis is widely used by researchers in a variety of fields including the social sciences, economics, and marketing. It refers to the study of relationship patterns among social entities rather than the entities themselves (Wasserman & Faust, 1994) and can be a great way for police to garner a better understanding of both offenders and victims in their community. Scholars have explored social networks among a variety of populations of interest to the police such as gangs (McGloin, 2004, 2005; Radil, Flint & Tita, 2010), deviant peer groups (Haynie, 2001), drug trafficking organizations (Natarajan, 2000), and residents of disadvantaged neighborhoods (Papachristos, Braga & Hureau, 2012; Schreck, McGloin & Kirk, 2009). For example, starting with 238 known gang members, Papachristos and his colleagues (2012) constructed a network of 763 individuals in Boston's Cape Verdean community and found that "the closer one [was] to a gunshot victim, the greater the probability of one's own victimization, net of individual and other network characteristics" (p. 999). Schreck et al. (2009) demonstrated that network ties in Chicago neighborhoods influenced the type of crime that occurred in those neighborhoods, and Haynie (2001) revealed that individuals who held more central positions in deviant peer networks were more likely to engage in delinquent acts than those who held peripheral positions. Radil et al. (2010) used social network analysis to better understand the spatial dynamics of gang violence in Los Angeles. These are just a few examples that illustrate the potential value of social network analysis as a predictive tool.

Research has shown that one of the most reliable predictors of criminal behavior is association with deviant peers (McGloin, 2009; Pratt et al., 2009). In a similar vein, individuals who have been previously victimized are at a higher risk of experiencing future victimization than individuals who have not been previously victimized (Farrell, Phillips & Pease, 1995; Hindelang, Gottfredson & Garofalo, 1978). Equipped with knowledge of these empirical findings, the police can use social network analysis to predict who in their community is (a) more likely to commit crime or (b) at a greater risk of being victimized. The police could even go a step further and use social network analysis to disrupt criminal organizations (e.g., gangs, drug cartels, prostitution rings, etc.), likely preventing future crimes in the process. In large networks, there are often a number of densely clustered subgroups connected to each other via *structural holes* (Burt, 1992). These structural holes are crucial to the overall network because they are the only avenue for communication to flow from cluster to cluster. If the police can successfully identify the individuals who represent the structural holes of a network, they could perhaps employ a "pulling levers" strategy (see Braga, Kennedy, Waring & Piehl, 2001) to remove them from said network. Whatever the strategy adopted, social network analysis can certainly help the police predict crime.

Concerns for the Future

In 2013, the Deputy Director of NIJ published an article entitled "The Pitfalls of Prediction" in which he outlined seven potential drawbacks of the use of prediction by the criminal justice system. These include trusting expert prediction too much, clinging to rudimentary statistical techniques, assuming one approach can be used for all problems, trying to interpret too much from the data, forsaking model simplicity for predictive strength (and vice versa), expecting perfect predictions, and failing to think about unintended consequences (Ridgeway, 2013). Perry et al. (2013, pp. 118–125) list five pitfalls that partially overlap with Ridgeway's concerns: focusing on predictive accuracy rather than tactical utility, basing predictions on poor-quality data, misunderstanding the factors behind the prediction, failing to conduct an assessment and evaluation, and overlooking civil and privacy rights. Both Ridgeway (2013) and Perry et al. (2013) warn about the danger of becoming overly concerned with predictive accuracy. Predictive algorithms can be of little use to the police if they are too complex to inform tactical operations. Data quality is something that the police must be ever-mindful of, as predictions based on inaccurate data can be misleading. With that said, police must be realistic about what can and what cannot be inferred from their data—whatever its quality. Ridgeway (2013) cautions against becoming too enamored or comfortable with any one predictive technique and thinking it can be used as a "one size fits all" approach. For example, the near repeat phenomenon seems to apply well to burglaries and perhaps even street robberies, but it would be a mistake to assume that it could be used to explain homicide patterns. And with regard to civil and privacy rights, Ferguson (2012) provides an in-depth discussion of how predictive policing could raise Fourth Amendment concerns. If a computer algorithm predicts a certain area to be at an increased risk of experiencing crime, does that constitute probable cause for an officer to stop and search an individual within that area? These are just some of the issues the police will have to wrestle with as they move forward with prediction.

Conclusion

Prediction has been a buzzword in the field of policing since 2008 when William Bratton started a national discussion on the idea of predictive policing. Since then, two national symposia have been convened by NIJ and BJA, during which practitioners and scholars debated and deliberated over the concept. The thought of police issuing a crime forecast much like meteorologists forecast the weather is indeed alluring. PredPol, for instance, has received considerable attention from the media over the last few years. There is no doubt that predictive policing is currently the leading perspective within the field.

Two questions were posed at the onset of this review. The first inquired whether predictive policing was a new concept or merely "old wine in a new bottle"; the second, whether or not the police can actually predict when and where crime is going to occur. The answer to the first question, it appears, is that predictive policing is not new. Since the community policing movement, police have sought to be more proactive about crime. Ultimately, the only difference is that technology has advanced to a point such that the police can engage in much more sophisticated predictive techniques. The answer to the second question—whether the police can *actually* predict crime—is "somewhat." As other writers have stated before, predictive policing is not a crystal ball. The police can never be certain about when or where a particular type of crime is going to occur. However, they are perhaps better equipped now than ever before to put themselves in the best position to prevent crime before it transpires.

Predictive software can potentially have a substantial impact on crime. Unfortunately, many agencies are faced with a conundrum: the appeal of predicting and preventing crime is that it would enable them to "do more with less," but what if an agency cannot afford to purchase (and train its officers to use) new software? Fortunately, predictions can be made using a variety of promising techniques. Three concepts were presented above—the near repeat phenomenon, predictive crime mapping, and social network analysis—that can be used as a means to engage in predictive policing. This is by no means an exhaustive list of options, but it illustrates the point that the police need not obtain expensive software to predict crime. Many agencies will find that what they already have is sufficient—access to an abundance of data which, if recorded and interpreted correctly, can be used to guide tactical decisions and ultimately stop crime before it occurs.

NOTES

[1] There does not appear to be a universally agreed upon meaning for the acronym "Compstat." Bratton (1998, p. 233) submits that Compstat is an acronym for "Computer-Statistics meetings." Elsewhere it has been referred to as an acronym for "Compare Stats" (Silverman, 1999, p. 98) or "Computerized Statistics" (Bratton & Malinowski, 2008, p. 261).

[2] These include the Maryland State, Boston, Chicago, Metropolitan (Washington, DC), New York, and Shreveport police departments, as well as the Los Angeles Police Foundation.

[3] Programs like PredPol do in fact forecast the likelihood of a crime being committed *in a hot spot* on a given day, making it easier for police to decide where to focus more of their attention. However, the articles referenced here could easily be misinterpreted as suggesting that predictive policing is an exact science.

[4] For a review of additional predictive techniques being used in Shreveport, Memphis, Nashville, Baltimore, Minneapolis, Charlotte-Mecklenburg, and Iraq, see Perry et al. (2013, pp. 64–76).

REFERENCES

Anderson, D., Chenery, S. & Pease, K. (1995). *Biting back: Tackling repeat burglary and car crime.* London: Home Office.

Bonta, J., & Motiuk, L. L. (1992). Inmate classification. *Journal of Criminal Justice,* 20(4), 343–353.

Bowers, K. J., Johnson, S. D., & Pease, K. (2004). Prospective hot-spotting: The future of crime mapping? *British Journal of Criminology,* 44, 641–658.

Braga, A. A., Kennedy, D. M., Waring, E. J., & Piehl, A. M. (2001). Problem-oriented policing, deterrence, and youth violence: An evaluation of Boston's Operation Ceasefire. *Journal of Research in Crime and Delinquency,* 38(3), 195–225.

Bratton, W. J. (1998). *Turnaround: How America's top cop reversed the crime epidemic.* New York: Random House.

Bratton, W. J. & Malinowski, S. W. (2008). Police performance management in practice: Taking COMPSTAT to the next level. *Policing, 2*(3), 259–265.

Budz, D., Pegnall, N., & Townsley, M. (2001). *Lightning strikes twice: Preventing repeat home burglary.* Queensland, Australia: Criminal Justice Commission.

Burt, R. S. (1992). *Structural holes: The social structure of competition.* Cambridge, MA: Harvard University Press.

Chainey, S., Tompson, L., & Uhlig, S. (2008). The utility of hotspot mapping for predicting spatial patterns of crime. *Security Journal, 21*, 4–28.

Chenery, S., Holt, J. & Pease, K. (1997). *Biting Back II: Reducing Repeat Victimisation in Huddersfield: Crime Detection and Prevention Series Paper 82.* London: Home Office, Police Research Group.

Clarke, R. V. (1992). *Situational crime prevention.* New York: Harrow and Heston.

Cohen, L. E., & Felson, M. (1979). Social change and crime rate trends: A routine activity approach. *American Sociological Review, 44*, 588–608.

Cornish, D. B. & Clarke, R. V. (1986). *The reasoning criminal.* New York: Springer-Verlag.

Dabney, D. (2010). Observations regarding key operational realities in a Compstat model of policing. *Justice Quarterly, 27*(1), 28–51.

Eck, J. E. & Spelman, W. (1987). *Problem solving: Problem-oriented policing in Newport News.* Washington, DC: Police Executive Research Forum.

Farrell, G., Phillips, C., & Pease, K. (1995). Like taking candy: Why does repeat victimization occur? *British Journal of Criminology, 35*, 384–399.

Ferguson, A. G. (2012). Predictive policing and reasonable suspicion. *Emory Law Journal, 62*(2), 259–325.

Friend, Z. (2013, April 9). Predictive policing: Using technology to reduce crime. *FBI Law Enforcement Bulletin.* Retrieved from http://www.fbi.gov/stats-services/publications/law-enforcement-bulletin/2013/April/predictive-policing-using-technology-to-reduce-crime.

Goldstein, H. (1979). Improving policing: A problem-oriented approach. *Crime and Delinquency, 25*, 236–258.

Goldstein, H. (1990). *Problem-oriented policing.* Philadelphia: Temple University Press.

Goode, E. (2011, August 15). Sending the police before there's a crime. *The New York Times.* Retrieved from http://www.nytimes.com/2011/08/16/us/16police.html?_r=0

Greenwood, P. W., Petersilia, J., & Chaiken, J. (1977). *The criminal investigation process.* Lexington: D. C. Health.

Groff, E. R. & LaVigne, N. G. (2002). Forecasting the future of predictive crime mapping. *Crime Prevention Studies, 13*, 29–57.

Haberman, C. P. & Ratcliffe, J. H. (2012). The predictive policing challenges of near repeat armed street robberies. *Policing, 6*(2), 151–166.

Haynie, D. L. (2001). Delinquent peers revisited: Does network structure matter? *American Journal of Sociology, 106*(4), 1013–1057.

Heaton, B. (2012, October). Predictive policing a success in Santa Cruz, Calif. *Government Technology.* Retrieved from http://www.govtech.com/Behavioral-Data-and-the-Future-of-Predictive-Policing.html.

Hindelang, M. J., Gottfredson, M. R., & Garofalo, J. (1978). *Victims of personal crime: An empirical foundation for a theory of personal victimization.* Cambridge, MA: Ballinger.

Hoffman, P. B. (1994). Twenty years of operational use of a risk prediction instrument: The United States Parole Commission's Salient Factor Score. *Journal of Criminal Justice*, 22(6), 477–494.

Johnson, S. D. (2008). Repeat burglary victimization: A tale of two theories. *Journal of Experimental Criminology*, 4, 215–240.

Johnson, S. D. & Bowers, K. J. (2004a). The stability of space-time clusters of burglary. *British Journal of Criminology*, 44, 55–65.

Johnson, S. D. & Bowers, K. J. (2004b). The burglary as cue to the future: The beginnings of prospective hot-spotting. *European Journal of Criminology*, 1(2), 237–255.

Kamil, A. C., Krebs, J. R., & Pulliam, H. R. (1987). *Foraging behavior*. New York: Plenum Press.

Kelling, G., Pate, A. M., Dieckman, D., & Brown, C. (1974). *The Kansas City preventive patrol experiment: Technical report*. Washington, DC: Police Foundation. Retrieved from https://www.ncjrs.gov/pdffiles1/Digitization/42537NCJRS.pdf

McGloin, J. M. (2004). Associations among criminal gang members as a defining factor of organization and as a predictor of criminal behavior: The gang landscape of Newark, New Jersey (Doctoral dissertation, Rutgers University).

McGloin, J. M. (2005). Policy and intervention considerations of a network analysis of street gangs. *Criminology & Public Policy*, 4(3), 607–635.

McGloin, J. M. (2009). Delinquency balance: revisiting peer influence. *Criminology*, 47(2), 439–477.

Mohler, G. O., Short, M. B., Brantingham, P. J., Schoenberg, F. P, & Tita, G. E. (2011). Self-exciting point process modeling of crime. *Journal of the American Statistical Association*, 106(493), 100–108.

Natarajan, M. (2000). Understanding the structure of a drug trafficking organization: A conversational analysis. *Crime Prevention Studies*, 11, 273–298.

Papachristos, A. V., Braga, A. A., & Hureau, D. M. (2012). Social networks and the risk of gunshot injury. *Journal of Urban Health: Bulletin of the New York Academy of Medicine*, 89(6), 992–1003.

Pearsall, B. (2010, May). Predictive policing: The future of law enforcement? *NIJ Journal*, 266, 16–19.

Perry, W. L., McInnis, B., Price, C. C., Smith, S. C. & Hollywood, J. S. (2013). *Predictive policing: The role of crime forecasting in law enforcement operations*. Rand Corporation.

Pratt, T. C., Cullen, F. T., Sellers, C. S., Winfree, L. T., Madensen, T., Daigle, L. E., Gau, J. M. (2009). The empirical status of social learning theory: A meta-analysis. *Justice Quarterly*, 27, 765–802.

PredPol: Predictive policing in a box. (2013). Retrieved from http://www.predpol.com.

Radil, S. M., Flint, C., & Tita, G. E. (2010). Spatializing social networks: Using social network analysis to investigate geographies of gang rivalry, territoriality, and violence in Los Angeles. *Annals of the Association of American Geographers*, 100(2), 307–326.

Ratcliffe, J. H. (2004). The hotspot matrix: A framework for the spatio-temporal targeting of crime reduction. *Police Practice and Research*, 5(1), 5–23.

Ratcliffe, J. H. (2008). *Intelligence-led policing*. Portland: Willan Publishing.

Ridgeway, G. (2013, February). The pitfalls of prediction. *NIJ Journal*, 271, 34–40.

Schreck, C., McGloin, J. M., & Kirk, D. (2009). A study of the contrast between violent and nonviolent neighborhood crime rates in Chicago: What factors make for a violent neighborhood? *Justice Quarterly*, 26, 771–794.

Shaw, C. R. & McKay, H. D. (1942). *Juvenile delinquency and urban areas.* Chicago: University of Chicago Press.

Sherman, L. W., Gartin, P., & Buerger, M. E. (1989). Hot spots of predatory crime: Routine activities and the criminology of place. *Criminology, 27,* 27–55.

Silverman, E. (1999). *NYPD battles crime: Innovative strategies in policing.* Boston: Northeastern University Press.

Thompson, K. (2011, November). The Santa Cruz experiment: Can a city's crime be predicted? *Popular Science.* Retrieved from http://www.popsci.com/science/article/2011–10/santa-cruz-experiment

Tilley, N. (2003). Community policing, problem-oriented policing and intelligence-led policing. In T. Newburn (Ed.), *Handbook of policing* (pp. 311–339). Cullompton, UK: Willan Publishing.

Wasserman, S. & Faust, K. (1994). *Social network analysis: Methods and applications.* Cambridge, UK: Cambridge University Press.

Weisburd, D. & Eck, J. E. (2004). What can police do to reduce crime, disorder, and fear? *The ANNALS of the American Academy of Political and Social Science, 593,* 42–65.

Wilson, J. Q. & Kelling, G. L. (1982). Broken windows: The police and neighborhood safety. *Atlantic Monthly,* 249(3), 29–38.

Wolfgang, M. E., Figlio, R. M., & Sellin, T. (1972). *Delinquency in a birth cohort.* Chicago: University of Chicago Press.

16

Geographic Information Systems
Applications for Police

William V. Pelfrey Jr.

Introduction

American law enforcement agencies are regularly asked to increase their efficiency and productivity despite limited resources. One of the tools that police can use to facilitate a more efficient and effective response is a geographic information system (GIS). A GIS is a software package that links datasets (such as arrest reports, gang intelligence, or census information) with computerized base maps to tell the police where crime occurs most frequently. Fifteen years ago, only 13% of all police departments regularly used geographic information systems (National Institute of Justice, 1999). Now, that number is much higher. A review of police websites found that 42 of the 50 largest law enforcement agencies in the United States use a crime-based mapping program (Leong and Chan, 2012). As the vast majority of patrol officers now have access to a mobile data terminal in their vehicle, software like a GIS is within reach of most police officers and agencies.

Using a GIS has two key benefits for police agencies. First, by deploying officers in a more intelligent fashion, police agencies will have officers available for proactive work (such as problem solving). Second, by identifying crime patterns and inferring where crime is likely to develop, police can engage in preventive work to reduce their future workload.

To take advantage of a geographic information system's capabilities, an agency must develop the appropriate layers of data, obtain base maps of the city or region, and make sure the personnel who will use them can understand and process the information. Next, maps can be developed to serve a variety of different purposes: describing crime patterns, linking crime to various factors or correlates, or using maps to predict future crime patterns and subsequent

Prepared especially for *Critical Issues in Policing* by William V. Pelfrey Jr.

resource allocation. This chapter will describe the process of developing maps, including data requirements, software options, and layer assembly, and will then consider some of the ways these programs can benefit police agencies.

Crime Mapping Process

Electronic maps are usually developed within one of several software frameworks. An individual obtains a data set (for example, all the arrests made by the Gotham Police Department in 2013) then imports those data into a mapping program. When the data are overlaid with streets, city boundaries, and landmark maps, the operator can produce any of a variety of map types. The process of obtaining the right data, cleaning the data, and mapping the results can be somewhat daunting the first time, but once the infrastructure for data handling is in place, it is easily updated from month to month or year to year with new data. Some agencies have officers who are trained to implement and use these systems while other agencies hire consultants and trainers to develop the basic system and train officers to use them. There are several important steps in the process of developing these electronic maps.

Data Collection

The first, and most important, piece of the mapping puzzle is the data. For law enforcement agencies, the most common data sets are *Arrests, Offenses, and Calls for Service*. Most large to medium-sized police departments have a computer system that works in conjunction with dispatchers to track calls for service, commonly called a CAD (Computer Aided Dispatch). Every time an individual calls for police assistance with a problem, a line of data gets created. These *Calls for Service* files can be complicated: Philadelphia, a city of approximately 1.5 million residents, annually generates 3.5 million or more calls for service. Many of these calls are redundant, which means several people call in the same event. For example, eight people may call in a gun shot at the corner of 1st and Main streets. A good dispatcher will code all these calls as a single event. Unfortunately, proper coding does not always occur. A single gunshot could be coded as an assault, attempted murder, discharging a firearm, possession of a firearm, or several other charges. At this point the *Offense* file becomes most useful.

The *Offense* files are based on police reports that are usually handwritten and then entered into a computer (although many police departments are now equipping officers with laptops and data are simply downloaded). When the officer arrives on the scene of the gunshot, he or she will create a report describing what happened, names of witnesses, details about the offender and the victim, and the resolution of the event.

The final, and smallest, data set is the *Arrest* file. This spreadsheet presents details of all individuals arrested for crimes within a given district, precinct, or city. A common line of data in an *Arrest* file would contain an event code number; date, time, location of the offense and of the arrest; arresting officer's badge number; name, address, age, sex, and race of the offender; the charges for which he or she is being arrested; and any extenuating circumstances of the arrest (possession of weapons or drugs). For a single event, the gun shot on 1st and Main, there may be seven or eight *Calls for Service*, at least one *Offense* report, and one or more *Arrest* reports. All of these are assembled into data sets that can be mapped for future use.

A number of other data sets are available to law enforcement agencies to provide depth and meaning to a simple map of crime. Census information presents much more than just the number of people in a city or county. The Census collects a host of information on income, education, employment, number of people in a dwelling, whether people rent or own (a good indicator of the stability of a neighborhood), race, sex, and age breakdown of a community, and even how far people travel to get to work. These data are broken down by census tract (which usually contain between 2,500 to 8,000 people) and can be specified down to the city block level, although with less information. A police analyst could add census information to crime information to determine what area characteristics are most related to crime and use that information to develop preventive programs or assign officers. More information on these topics can be found at the Census website: www.census.gov.

These data sets are all very interesting but are of limited use, from a GIS perspective, without a frame of reference. Maps of the county, the city, the streets, and the important geographic features (lakes, rivers, valleys, even street lights) are an absolute necessity to geographic information systems. Most maps of these types are available from geographic clearinghouses like universities, city planning groups, or even utility companies. For small or relatively new cities, maps of the city and all the streets may not yet exist and must be created. These files are not easy to generate but, once available, need only be updated occasionally. As cities change street names, build or close roads, and change geographic features (e.g., damming a stream into a lake), maps must be updated. A common way to develop or update maps relies on global positioning systems (GPS). A GPS links to satellites and uses a triangulation process to provide precise latitude and longitude coordinates. Another option for this process lies in Orthophotos. A plane with a photographic system can fly over a city and take detailed photos that are then scanned into a computer and converted to a database. These photos can aid in keeping data sets current or in enhancing the level of detail of existing map sets.

Data sets are limited only by the creativity of the analysts and available resources. Databases frequently used by police departments include: lists of all pawnshops, bars, liquor stores, hospitals, fire departments, subway entrances, churches, convenience stores, parking lots, and many others. Sitting down with a phone book and a spreadsheet program may be the only step required to develop these databases. In other cases, particularly for illicit venues (an illegal casino, crack house, prostitution den, etc.) data collectors may have to find these locations and note physical addresses. After these data sets are collected they can prove very valuable to law enforcement agencies.

Data Reduction

While collecting the data sets is the first step in developing a geographic information system, the geographic portion has not yet emerged. The second step in the process is Data Reduction. This means the datasets have to be reduced to a manageable, geographically useful data set. The key step in this stage is geocoding. Geocoding refers to assigning a geographic reference point to a bit of data. A person may be able to give directions using landmarks (go down past the Big Deal grocery store and turn left at the hot dog stand), but maps work best with latitude and longitude figures. To convert data points into information a mapping program can handle, each address has to be assigned a latitude and longitude code. This can be done by hand with a global positioning system if one only has a few addresses (i.e., all the movie theaters of a city), but for big groups of data, like all the houses in a city, driving to each address and recording the "lat" and "long" figures would take years. Instead, analysts acquire a list of all the addresses and run a geocoding program. The program "knows" where the street is and estimates where the address is on that block. For example, a geocoding program knows the latitude and longitude figures for Broad Street. The program knows odd number addresses are on the east side and even addresses are on the west side. The program knows the 1400 block is between 14th and 15th streets, which also have set latitude and longitude figures. The program would then take an address and estimate where it is on the street. The address 1450 Broad Street would be placed in the middle of the block on the west side and assigned a latitude and longitude code. Once the program repeats this process for every home, building, and business address a database is produced, which combines addresses with a geographic reference point. A mapping program can then tie these geographic reference points to known reference points (the streets, the borders of the city or county) and place the address on a computerized map. This base map of all the addresses can then be tied to a data set of crimes, perhaps homicides, and the location of all the homicides for a given year can be mapped.

While this process may sound simple, in practice it is much more complicated. The old adage of "Garbage in, garbage out" pervades the geocoding process. Addresses with a single typo are enough to throw a geocoding program into a tailspin. Coding a mugging as 131 Main Street is very different than the actual location of 1311 Main Street. Many cities have streets with similar, or sometimes identical, names. Atlanta, Georgia, has dozens of streets named Peachtree. King Street can be on the opposite side of town from King Avenue. Many of these quirks have to be corrected, or smoothed out, by hand to develop an accurate base map of the city with streets, landmarks, and addresses.

Once the base map is assembled, data sets can be compared to the base map. All the auto thefts for the month of August can be listed in a data set and then mapped onto the base map. Each auto theft may appear using a symbol of a little car sitting on top of an address. Address matching is the process of assigning an address to each event, or auto theft. Every little letter and number has to be just right or the map can misrepresent the event.

It is important to remember that every piece of information carries significant weight. An error entering a social security number can prevent authorities from identifying a repeat offender. A typo in the name column can do the same. My name could be entered as William Pelfrey, William V. Pelfrey, Jr., Will Pelfrey, W. Pelfrey, Bill Pelfrey, or the dreaded Willy Pelfrey. These are all reasonable permutations of my name and a computer might not tie any of them to my arrest record.

Layer Assembly

The first two steps of the crime mapping process have occurred: data sets have been collected and have been converted into geocoded spreadsheets. These data sets must now be matched to existing or newly created maps of the city, streets databases, and other templates. This is usually done within a mapping software package. These programs take spreadsheets of data and link them with maps to generate maps with data points of an event (e.g., a map of homicides) or some other descriptor of events (e.g., maps of hot spots of drug activity). Some of the most commonly used programs are: ArcGIS, CrimeStat, and MapInfo. Each is marketed on a detailed website demonstrating how the software functions.

It is best to think of these maps as layers. Imagine a series of clear plastic sheets with pieces of information on each one. These sheets can be layered on top of each other to produce different maps or coverages. The first transparency has an outline of the city. The second transparency might have an outline of all the major streets. The third transparency might have labels of these streets. A fourth transparency might describe the major geographic landmarks (rivers, forests, etc.). With these base maps, different data sets of information can be layered on top. A map of all the drunken driving accidents may be the next layer. Another map of all the bars may be interesting. A final layer of all the DUI checkpoints used by the police might also be linked. Clearly, these different layers can get complicated and cluttered. The mapping software allows the user to turn different layers on or off as they wish. If all the layers on the computer screen become too confusing, the analyst might turn off the street names layer, or use a less detailed layer of geographic features. A good mapping program, matched with a skilled user who has access to many data sets and coverages can produce brilliant maps and answer (or sometimes raise) hundreds of questions.

There are a variety of these maps available for public use and exploration. The National Institute of Justice assisted and funded online map development in several cities. An evaluation of this publicly available mapping program, called COMPASS, was conducted in East Valley, California (Boba, Weisburd, and Meeker, 2009). Researchers found that the data-sharing process between partners was very complicated, these data have important problem-solving implications.

An example of COMPASS in a major city, Milwaukee, Wisconsin, is easily accessible online. Simply search for "COMPASS Milwaukee," visit the website, select *Public Applications*, then select *Community Mapping*. An interactive map will pop up and you can add and subtract layers, zoom into different regions of the city, and observe where crime happens. One can turn on layers of crime (including homicide, robberies, aggravated assault, property crime, etc.) depending on your interests. Next, pair those with layers, such as community indicators like rental-occupied housing (an indicator of transience, as opposed to a neighborhood where most residents own their housing), foreclosed properties, and tax delinquent properties. This will provide a perspective of crime relative to socioeconomic conditions. The website also provides data for several years so you can investigate patterns. Many cities have these kinds of websites, and they can be tracked down with some investigation.

Map Production

The simplest map is much like the police pin maps of the old days. The mapping software places a colored dot or a symbol at a location. This point represents some offense, crime, or arrest. Most mapping programs come with their own set of predefined symbols (a skull equals a homicide, a syringe equals a drug offense, and so on). These symbols are usually tied back to the original data set so clicking on a skull will bring up a box that contains a snapshot of the event (indicating how the victim died, whether anyone has been arrested for the offense, and the age, race, or sex of the victim or offender).

However, an analyst has many other options that can provide significantly greater depth of information. Mapping all the incidences of an event, perhaps all the burglaries in a city, would produce a single giant blur of symbols. Aggregating information and mapping the concentrations, perhaps across census tracts or police districts, provides less detail but is much more intelligible. A color range (bright red to dark red) or different colors (red equals high, blue equals average, green equals low) can produce a thematic map of an area that is informative and easily understood. These chloropleth maps often resemble a weather map, which uses different colors to define the level of precipitation.

Another option is to use graduated circles to represent an event. A small circle may mean a small number of events (1 to 5 larcenies) and four progressively larger circles mean progressively higher rates of the event. Varying the colors of these graduated circles allows the analyst to plot different types of crimes. For example, one could plot three common crimes using three different colors, each of which has three different ranges. Green circles could equal burglary, red could equal larceny, and yellow could equal robbery, and each color could come in three size ranges (small, medium, or large) to represent the frequency of the event. Alternatively, the three different colors could represent years. Robberies from 1997 could be in green, robberies from 1998 in red, and robberies from 1999 could be blue. Yet another option uses contour maps, which look like topographic maps and trace different grades of crime throughout a city. Different software packages have their own set of maps and mapping tools that analysts can use to determine the most appropriate map style to convey their information.

Ethical Issues

There are important ethical issues in the mapping and geocoding process. The most important of these issues concerns the victim's right to privacy. As the level of specificity of crime and offense information increases, the possibility of embarrassment and secondary victimization by the media or general public likewise increases. If a map of all the rapes or sexual assaults in a city were released to the media, victims would be victimized a second time by the publication of such a list. Even diffusing the information by describing rapes at the block level instead of the address level could be problematic. On many blocks there are no more than a dozen residences. If a teenage female was sexually assaulted, it would be a simple matter for a reporter to determine which of these residences was home to a teenage female.

A second ethical issue concerns the problem of aggregating data. Crime reports may indicate the Riverfront District of Gotham City has a high rate of robberies. The robberies may in fact be isolated in a small portion of the Riverfront District, but such a report could scare tourists and consumers from the entire District. This error is known as the Geographic Fallacy—generalizing the problems within a region to all the locations or individuals within that region. The South Side may have a high number of drug arrests, but that does not mean everyone in the South Side is a drug dealer or user.

Reports of aggregated crime figures may hurt business or land values in an area; however, extremely specific reports of crime may compromise victims' privacy. While law enforcement has a responsibility to make the public aware of crime in their city and neighborhood, the police must tread a careful line to insure the privacy of victims is not violated.

Role of Hypotheses in Map Production

At this stage in the crime mapping process an analyst has collected and assembled data sets and is now prepared to generate some interesting and useful maps. Simply printing out all the possible combinations of maps is unrealistic. Intelligent questions have to be formulated, which link events or locations to each other. These hypotheses are based on one of several factors. *Experience* or *Common Sense* may suggest certain things tend to coexist—such as parking lots and thefts from autos. A *Theory* may indicate some relationship between factors is likely to exist. For example, routine activities theory suggests criminals will commit crimes near their travel patterns, so main roads and bus routes see high levels of victimization. Once the hypothesis is formed, data can be arranged into coverages or layers to answer the question. If an analyst hypothesized that there was a relationship between reports of mail theft and the location of check-cashing businesses, data could be assembled to answer that question empirically. While maps have tremendous descriptive uses, formulating intelligent hypotheses can significantly extend the capabilities of geographic information systems.

Uses of Crime Maps

The process of developing crime maps is sometimes tedious but, once created, these maps have any number of applications. Maps can describe events, help identify patterns, suggest a relationship between factors, and be used for projective analysis.

Descriptive Component

The most common use of crime maps is to describe crime for a given area. Using points, graduated circles, or chloropleth maps (which, as mentioned previously, assign different colors representing different intensity levels to areas of a region, such as counties in a state), analysts can arm officers and supervisors with detailed descriptions of the crime for their district or precinct. Buslik and Maltz suggest that officers who have spent a significant amount of time assigned to a single beat usually feel like they know their beats well: "who the bad actors are, what to watch out for, how and when things happen" (1997: 121). In Joseph Wambaugh's classic police tale, *The Blue Knight* (1973), Officer Bumper Morgan knows the bad guys so well he can complete the boxes in an arrest report from memory, having arrested the same people over and over. But police officers only work their beat during a given shift and during a set schedule of days. Thus, no one officer truly knows what happens on a beat all the time. A descriptive map can show the locations, times, and suspect description to an officer who might not have been on duty when the offense happened but may have knowledge about the offender or area.

Identification of Patterns

An observant officer or analyst who views a series of descriptive maps is likely to start looking for patterns. Crime maps are especially useful in this endeavor. By layering offenses from different periods of time, one can conduct trend analysis. Considering how offenses change during the seasons can provide important information regarding resource allocation and manpower distribution. If robberies in city parks significantly increase during the summer (as more pedestrians spend time outside) then assigning more officers to these regions during the summer and fewer in the winter should be the natural outcome. Police in Richmond, Virginia, have incorporated several important elements with their GIS to identify patterns of commercial robbery (Monroe, 2008). By linking their GIS with a statistics program and business intelligence databases, they can describe historical patterns of crime and then take action to prevent subsequent crime.

Identifying patterns of crime has important accountability implications. District and precinct commanders are, to some degree, held responsible for the crime in their district. As patterns of crime develop, police chiefs want to know what their district commanders are doing to resolve these problems. One of the best examples of this accountability process exists in New York City through the CompStat program. The Computerized Statistics program began in 1994 and has been replicated or adopted in many law enforcement departments (Harries, 1999). District commanders attend a weekly or biweekly meeting where crime maps of their district are projected on a screen. A police administrator then identifies the crime patterns that exist in that district and asks the district commander how they are handling that particular problem. Other district commanders can offer advice about programs that have succeeded or failed to address that particular problem. Thus, district commanders are held accountable for crime in their area and they are given a series of possible solutions to the problem so they do not have to "reinvent the wheel" in every police district. If a district commander fails to adequately address the problem, they may be replaced by someone who will try a different tact. CompStat and similar procedures force the police to make data-driven decisions and be more efficient with their resources.

The success of CompStat in New York inspired police agencies all over the United States to design their own versions. In Ft. Worth, Texas, regular meetings with police administrators, predicated on crime maps and analysis of crime data, were linked to specific crime prevention strategies. Through time-series analysis, Jang, Hoover, and Joo (2010) found reductions in violent and property crime, and total index crimes. Much like CompStat in New York, CompStat in Ft. Worth guided the police towards more effective efforts.

Another pattern identification approach is the mapping of *Hot Spots*. A *Hot Spot* is a small area, address, or region of a city or county that has an unusual concentration, or a clustering, of a particular crime. Crime maps often present hot spots as an ellipse around a region, a brightly colored street block, or a symbol over an address. These hot spots signal officers to focus their attention on that area or indicate a need for some program or initiative to resolve the problem. One of the tenets of problem-oriented policing (Goldstein, 1979, 1990) is that police agencies should leverage intelligence (such as tips from informants or business owners) with initiatives to combat crime. Ratcliffe (2004, 2008) describes a model linking crime analysts, intelligence officers, and GIS with decisions on allocation of resources. By identifying patterns of criminal behavior (via crime analysts and GIS) and linking police intelligence to decision makers, agencies can decide which problems have the greatest potential for resolution and the appropriate resources. This approach, known as *Intelligence Led Policing*, assesses crime risk, and location and guides police initiatives and action. Identification of hot spots or problem crime locations, followed by a well-conceived program or intervention, which is then evaluated empirically, is precisely what Goldstein envisioned.

In an exercise called "Operation Heat Wave" a contingent of Dallas Police Department officers focused on burglaries, particularly residential, commercial, and motor vehicle burglaries. They defined Targeted Area

Action Grids (TAAGs) that represented regions where conditions were favorable for burglaries, based on event- and place-based indicators. Detectives, while in uniform, interacted with community members, solicited information and intelligence on criminal activity, and operated as a deterrent element (Gassaway, Arnon, and Perez, 2011). This kind of initiative links GIS data, hot spot definitions, and police initiatives to a specific issue, maximizing resources and reducing crime.

It is important to note that there are limitations with the hot spot approach. Concentrations of people tend to be hot spots. Places where calls for service are clustered represent hot spots. These could include bars, bus stops, or apartment buildings (Sherman and Weisburd, 1995). The process of drawing hot spots is sometimes misleading and inaccurate—hot spots may not fit the descriptive method used to present them (i.e., shading of a single block or an ellipse). Despite these limitations the hot spot approach represents a valuable tool for law enforcement agencies in the identification of crime patterns.

The identification of patterns is not limited to the local level. Broader, macro-level research has been conducted, which specifies the relationship of various factors (such as socioeconomic status and racial diversity) to the occurrence of homicides across the entire United States. These analyses (Baller et al., 2001; Messner et al., 1999) use county-level homicide data and investigate regional patterns of violence. They noted, for example, that the South tends to have higher rates of homicide than most other parts of the country (Baller et al., 2001). They also suggest that a spillover effect may occur: that is, in urban areas with high violence rates, surrounding counties may experience higher rates of violence than one would otherwise expect (Messner et al., 1999). While these macro-level studies may not be particularly useful to local law enforcement, they are invaluable to researchers who are attempting to define the causes and correlates, and subsequently the *predictors* of crime.

Interaction of Factors

One of the most common uses of geographic information systems by law enforcement departments is to identify factors that are related to the production, or prevention, of crime. There are many obvious examples of correlated factors that most departments have already explored—the locations of bars and drunk driving accidents, thefts and the locations of pawn shops, abandoned houses and drug markets. There are other factors related to crime that agencies can identify and subsequently address.

Where and how people travel can influence crime rates. Studies addressing the routes students use when they walk to school indicated a need for "safe corridors" for children. Police can consider where assaults or drug sales occur within or around a school and then take specific steps to address these problems.

Defining important interactions of factors is not limited to crime issues. These analyses can be conducted to assist officers in the prevention of problems, especially traffic accidents. Reviewing data on drunk driving usually suggests problem locations within cities and can signal a need for DUI checkpoints or strict enforcement of drunk driving laws. In Houston, through a process called Crash Mapping, researchers and police identified DUI hot spots and establishments which produced high numbers of drunk drivers. They then worked with the City Council to deter drunk driving from these problem locations (Kaufman, 2008).

Police officers can also assist businesses in addressing or identifying security concerns and possible remedies for these problems. By first identifying high larceny and theft areas, then suggesting locations of lights, alarms, and secure access points, police can assist businesses in deterring criminals and cut down on crime rates.

Projective Analysis

The two primary uses of geographic information systems for law enforcement agencies have been in the areas of describing crime problems or patterns and considering factors that are highly correlated in the production of crime. The next step for law enforcement and researchers lies in the area of predicting crime. These projective, or inferential, analyses estimate where crime is likely to occur based on a series of factors. For example, if we know that drug sales are likely to increase as the number of rental properties increases in an area (as home owners move out and slumlords take over), once a certain threshold has been passed police can begin to pay special attention to an area to *prevent* the expected increases in drug sales. By identifying a series of factors related to the production of crime, analysts can help law enforcement deter the development of problem areas.

This type of work is exemplified by the research of George Rengert and his colleagues (2005). They suggested that analysts could predict where drug markets would develop based on the presence of a fence. Fences buy stolen property and are necessary for the drug users who steal property, sell it to the fence, and then use the cash to purchase drugs. If the locations of fences are known, one can predict where property crimes may occur and where drug sales are likely to happen. These pieces of information can help police maintain a watch over fences to deter the development of drug markets.

Geographic Profiling

A unique and progressive use of crime mapping has been defined by Kim Rossmo, a Canadian police detective and scholar (2000). He uses a technique called Criminal Geographic Targeting (CGT) based on theories from environmental criminology and routine activities theory. Rossmo suggests that a serial criminal is likely to commit his or her crimes in a specific pattern, which can then be analyzed to predict where the criminal lives. Based on a distance decay function simulating the journey to the crime, a probability is assigned to each point and the offender's residence is projected. There are four steps to the model:

- Map boundaries, which delineate the hunting area, are drawn.
- Distances along a grid from every point on the map are calculated.
- Distances are then used as independent variables in an equation.
- Figures are combined to generate a probability that a point represents the offender's residence.

This technique does not produce specific addresses of offenders. Instead, it identifies neighborhoods from which the offenders probably traveled to commit their crimes. Those areas, which are defined as high probability neighborhoods, are then exposed to increased patrol, surveillance, and investigation. Rossmo has found this technique to be effective in the apprehension of serial criminals and now teaches it to other law enforcement groups.

Conclusions

Geographic Information Systems have evolved since the police pin maps of earlier decades. Police agencies can now compare layers of crime data with census information, identify vulnerable areas of a city, and develop geographic profiles of criminals. Geographic Information Systems have many more uses than could be described in this chapter. Some agencies are using them to map the locations of paroled sex offenders to reduce the likelihood of offenders gaining access to a target population (e.g., a playground or nursery school). Some police agencies are mapping zoning restrictions and using these zoning laws as a way to close problematic bars and businesses. A GIS can be used to evaluate existing police programs and identify overlapping efforts (such as surveillance teams observing gang activity) or to reduce the chances of police teams running into each other while serving warrants or making arrests. As technology becomes more portable, officers can download crime maps to their mobile data terminals, cell phones, or personal digital assistants. These sources can inform responses to specific incidents or help identify patterns from previous events.

As the public demand for more efficient police services increases, police managers must become innovators. Police chiefs and sheriffs can no longer rely on a reactive style of policing—they must be proactive in identifying and preventing crime. A key tool in the drive for improved police services is the geographic information system. If agencies are willing to allocate funds and personnel to the development of GIS, they will see a significant return on their investment.

WORKS CITED

Baller, R. D., L. Anselin, S. F. Messner, G. Deane, & D. Hawkins. (2001). Structural covariates of U.S. County homicide rates: Incorporating spatial effects. *Criminology*, 39, 561–590.

Boba, R., D. Weisburd, & J. W. Meeker. (2009). The limits of regional data sharing and regional problem solving: Observations from the East Valley, CA COMPASS initiative. *Police Quarterly*, 12(1), 22–41.

Buslik, M. & M. D. Maltz. (1997). Power to the people: Mapping and information sharing in the Chicago Police Department. In D. Weisburd and T. McEwen (Eds.), *Crime Mapping and Crime Prevention*. Monsey, NY: Criminal Justice Press.

Gassaway, B., S. Armon, & D. Perez. (2011). Engaging the community: Operation Heat Wave. *Geography & Public Safety*, 3(1), 8–9.

Goldstein, H. (1979). Improving policing: A problem-oriented approach. *Crime and Delinquency*, 25, 236–258.

Goldstein, H. (1990). *Problem Oriented Policing, Second Edition*. New York: McGraw-Hill.

Harries, K. (1999). *Mapping Crime: Principle and Practice*. Washington D.C.: US Department of Justice.

Jang, H., L. T. Hoover, & H. Joo. (2010). An evaluation of Compstat's effect on crime: The Fort Worth Experience. *Police Quarterly*, 13(4), 387–412.

Kaufman, J. (2008). Creating a safer Houston through crash mapping. *Geography and Public Safety*, 1, 2, 2–5.

Leong, K. & Chan, S. (2012). A study of predictors and the extent of web-based crime mapping adoption by a police agency. *Security Journal*, 1–22.

Messner, S. F., L. Anselin, R. D. Baller, D. F. Hawkins, G. Deane, & S. E. Tolnay. (1999). The spatial patterning of county homicide rates: An application of exploratory spatial data analysis. *Journal of Quantitative Criminology*, 15, 423–450.

Monroe, R. (2008). High-tech crime fighting: Richmond, VA police gain valuable perspective with software. *American City and County*, January.

National Institute of Justice. (1999). *The Use of Computerized Crime Mapping by Law Enforcement: Survey Results*. Washington D.C.: US Department of Justice.

Ratcliffe, J. (2004). Crime mapping and the training needs of law enforcement. *European Journal on Criminal Policy and Research, 10*, 1, 65-83.

Ratcliffe, J. (2008). Intelligence-led policing. Cullompton, Devon: Willan Publishing.

Rengert, G. F., J. H. Ratcliffe, & S. Chakravorty. (2005). *Policing Illegal Drug Markets*. Monsey, NY: Criminal Justice Press.

Rossmo, D. K. (2000). *Geographic Profiling*. Boca Raton, FL: CRC Press.

Sherman, L. & D. Weisburd. (1995). General deterrent effects of police patrol in crime: A randomized, controlled trial. *Justice Quarterly*, 12, 4, 625–649.

Wambaugh, J. (1973). *The Blue Knight*. Boston: Little, Brown.

17

The Practice of Crime Analysis

Allison Rojek

Crime and intelligence analysis are relatively new in the history of law enforcement, but even in their brief history, they have already undergone significant changes that coincide with the larger shifts in policing. This purpose of this chapter is to capture the role that crime and intelligence analysis have come to play in criminal justice organizations. After providing a brief review of this role, attention is given to specific tasks analysts are expected to perform, as well as the tools and software they use to complete such tasks. This is followed by a review of the challenges faced by the analyst as well as the organization of finding ways to fully utilize the capacity of qualified analysts.

The Story of Crime Analysis

The history of modern policing in the United States is a story of evolution. Within that history, crime and intelligence analysis has undergone its own set of transformations. Police officers and investigators have been tracking crimes for the past 100 years, placing pins on paper maps on the wall to represent a criminal event (Ratcliffe, 2004); it just was not referred to as crime analysis. Departments also gathered basic statistics about where crime was occurring and the specific characteristics of these events, again without labeling it crime analysis. Police records and reports were manually recorded in the past, making it a cumbersome process to search through the records, so "analysis" was limited. However, the integration of computers in law enforcement for record storage and retrieval purposes (Craig-Moreland, 2004) opened a whole new world for people examining patterns and trends in crime.

The utilization of computers for maintaining records dramatically increased the amount of data being stored as well as the ability to access the data. This new access to data created opportunities to conduct more in-depth analysis on a larger set of records at one time than one can manually assess.

Prepared especially for *Critical Issues in Policing* by Allison Rojek.

In addition to the increases in database capacity and access to records, other technological changes had a significant impact on how police examined and responded to crime. The development and adoption of geographic information systems (GIS) technologies across law enforcement agencies increased the efficiency of plotting crimes for a visual assessment. GIS technology allowed for agencies to map a greater amount of information in a shorter period of time and created the ability to share this information between colleagues as well as other departments (Taylor et al., 2007). In addition, it increased their knowledge and ability to effectively respond to crime.

As the use of GIS technologies expanded across law enforcement, so did the use of analytical software to assess patterns in criminality. Software companies, realizing the essentially untapped market in law enforcement, began to create analytical packages specifically designed for use by police personnel. Some agencies also began to adopt software and statistical packages typically used in academia for analytical purposes. These changes in technology created opportunities for more sophisticated, efficient, and inventive crime and intelligence analysis, but this shift did not occur in a vacuum; a simultaneous shift occurred in the *style* of American policing, creating an environment ripe for analytical frameworks.

Prior to the shift in policing style, which occurred in the late 1970s and early 1980s, policing in America can be characterized as reactive; police waited for crimes to occur and then responded to them. Scholars in the 1970s and 1980s called for a shift in policing to a more proactive style; instead of responding to crimes after they occurred, try to prevent crime before it ever occurs. Weisburd and Lum (2005) argue this shift occurred after a "crisis confidence in standard American police practices" (420). Scholars and police administrators alike were looking toward a more analytical approach to solving crime problems, which is seen first in the problem-oriented policing style introduced by Goldstein (1979). Goldstein argued that officers need to identify the problems in their community, analyze them, and come up with unique strategies to address these problems, which sometimes means thinking outside the box. The technological advances discussed above fit perfectly into this framework and offered a tool for officers to use in gaining a better understanding of their communities. Goldstein's framework was further expanded by Eck and Spelman's (1987) SARA model—Scanning, Analysis, Response, and Assessment—to understand problems in a community. Crime analysis was a tool utilized to assist in the SARA model and the two evolved together to substantially impact policing across the US.

Policing in the 1980s focused on utilizing technology to help direct resources to crime-prone areas. For example, Sherman et al.'s (1989) examination of calls for service data in Minneapolis concluded that crime in fact is not randomly distributed across a geography, but rather concentrated in certain areas deemed "hot spots." They found that nearly 50% of the calls were generated from approximately 3% of all places. In order to effectively and efficiently solve crime problems then, resources must be directed at the problem places. These results have since been replicated in other jurisdictions across a variety of crime problems (Weisburd et al., 2004), and research has consistently shown that when agencies direct resources at hot spots, they are able to reduce levels of criminal activity (Uchida & Swatt, 2013; Ratcliffe et al., 2011; Braga & Bond, 2008; Sherman & Weisburd, 1995). Crime mapping was essential in identifying these hot spots and took the forefront in the larger crime analysis picture.

Generating hot spots maps on a routine basis and the reports based on these crimes was at the center of the next major paradigm in policing—Compstat. Compstat was more than just a style of policing—it represented a comprehensive police managerial system (Walsh, 2001). In Compstat (developed under Chief William Bratton of the NYPD in the early 1990s), police commanders were routinely brought together to discuss crime patterns in the area for which they were responsible. Crime maps provided a visual tool to display the patterns, while corresponding statistical reports showed the changes in crime numbers over time. Based on the information in the maps and reports, commanders were held accountable for crime trends in their area. They were put on the spot to discuss the problems, and if solutions were not effective in reducing the crime numbers, commanders were demoted or reassigned in the department. Compstat used computer statistics and technology to create substantial change within the department. Many agencies followed suit with the NYPD and developed similar programs across the country using a variety of acronyms (Weisburd et al., 2003).

While Compstat used technology and statistics to try and reduce crime, it was not without its faults. For some, Compstat simply became a numbers game and commanders just wanted to get their numbers down, regardless of how it would actually solve a crime problem. It also became a game of cops and dots—commanders would send their officers to the dots (hot spot locations), but the data were at least a week or a month old, thus they were going back to a reactive style of policing by responding to the problem after the fact instead of really trying to prevent it (Willis et al., 2007; 2004; Moore, 2003). Research has assessed the impact of Compstat on crime rates in New York City and the results are inconclusive (Rosenfeld et al., 2005; Berk, 2005). Nonetheless, it created a shift in the utilization of data and research to drive police decision making in operations.

Policing beyond Compstat has centered on the idea of intelligence-led policing (ILP), largely derived from the British National Intelligence Model (NCIS, 2000). The National Intelligence Model (NIM) came from a push to create a more effective and efficient style of policing without increasing resources or budgets, and the key to this efficiency and effectiveness was putting intelligence analysis at the forefront of police operations (Audit Commission, 1993; Her Majesty's Inspectorate of Constabulary, 1997; Ratcliffe, 2008). "This intelligence-led strategy called for the institutionalization of data collection and analysis into everyday policing practices in order to produce intelligence on criminal activity that aids agency leaders in strategic decision making and guides operational personnel on tactical actions" (Rojek et al., 2010, p. 4) and thus took crime analysis in a new direction to examine patterns not just in crime trends but also in offenders and groups to provide a more complete picture of the crime problem. Moreover, this strategy places the crime analyst as a central player in organizational decision making on how to address crime and disorder.

Since the events of 9/11, ILP has also gained increasing popularity among law enforcement agencies in the United States (Ratcliffe, 2008; Carter & Carter, 2009), to some degree replacing Compstat. More recently, however, ILP has evolved with the Smart policing framework. Smart policing, officially launched in 2009 by the Bureau of Justice Assistance (BJA), is a new police paradigm that emphasizes crime reduction through evidence-based policing. It is based on data and analysis, evaluation research, and innovation and includes a police practitioner-researcher partnership with scholars to create empirically based solutions to crime problems (Coldren et al., 2013). The role of analysts is again central to this new shift in policing, which also promotes the use of predictive analysis to identify where crimes may happen in the future.

This brief review does not do justice to the many nuances within these various changes in law enforcement. However, at a minimum, it highlights that as these shifts in American law enforcement have influenced the style of policing; they have also created the need for crime analysts in agencies and influenced the type and quality of analysts employed. Analysts have had to adapt and expand their knowledge base and skill sets with each of these shifts to provide their agencies with the most informed products on which to base operational decisions. The following discussion examines the various tasks and tools of an analyst to achieve this goal.

Tasks and Tools of an Analyst

The structure of crime analysis/intelligence analysis units in law enforcement organizations is as diverse as the agencies they serve. The presence of a crime or intelligence analyst is influenced by many factors such as agency size and budget (Rojek et al., 2010). The larger the agency, the more likely it is to employ full-time analysts. These larger agencies are also more likely to adopt advanced technologies at a more rapid pace (Weisburd & Lum, 2005). Agency type and budget also influence the number of analysts employed—larger agencies tend to employ more full-time analysts as they are more likely to have to resources to support the positions. Some agencies have distinct positions of crime analyst and intelligence analyst, whereas others may have only one of these types of analysts. Many agencies combine the positions into a crime/intelligence analyst, with the analyst conducting both types of analysis. Regardless of the structure of position or unit, analysts in law enforcement conduct multiple types of analysis and have a variety of tools at their disposal to conduct such tasks. The following description of the tasks and tools of an analyst is by no means an exhaustive list, but are those consistently conducted and used by the crime analysis community.[1]

Reports, Statistics, and Requests

According to Cope (2004), "crime analysis is the process of identifying patterns and relationships between crime data and other relevant data sources to prioritize and target police activity" (188). Analysts evaluate crime data to uncover patterns in location (Sherman 1990), time, and types of offenders to help police managers effectively allocate resources.[2] There are a variety of statistics and reports they generate to disseminate these patterns to command decision makers, which are produced with varying time intervals. One such report that typically generated by an analyst is a daily crime/intelligence report. This normally consists of a listing of all the crimes that happened the previous day, which is then distributed across the department. In addition to distributing this to the line officers as well as supervisors, the analyst also explores this report for any patterns in offending, time, place, etc. Crime-specific reports may also be generated on a weekly or monthly basis at different geographic levels for specific members of the department (e.g., a weekly burglary report generated for a burglary detective). Crime analysis also consists of monthly and annual reports to command-level staff to explore how crime is trending compared to last month or last year. These reports can be especially useful for administration when responding to requests from the press or political officials regarding the state of crime in the jurisdiction.

The above mentioned reports and statistics are routinely performed by an analyst at regular intervals and help evaluate overall crime trends in a jurisdiction or smaller unit of the department. In addition to these routinely generated statistics, analysts also conduct analyses upon request for individuals either internal or external to the department. Internal requests may come from patrol-level officers curious about a pattern in their patrol area, line-level supervisors looking for information to help with deployment of resources, task forces or special operations being conducted that need detailed intelligence before deploying, and investigative staff working a particular string of cases. These analyses and reports vary in depth of analysis and can consume a great deal of an analyst's day or sometimes weeks. Organizational members may request things such as lists of crimes in a given area, statistics comparing one time period to another, analysis on times of day/days of week crimes are occurring, patterns in modus operandi or theft of items, as well as many other things. The vast difference across requests requires an analyst to think and plan on the fly as most individuals requesting data or reports want them as quickly as possible.

Another source of requests of a crime/intelligence analyst is people external to the organization. This may include requests from the media on recent crimes that have occurred, statistics comparing one location to another, or a host of other requests. Media outlets can request a report through the Freedom of Information Act (US Department of Justice, n.d.) as much of the information in a crime or arrest report is public information. These requests sometimes take additional time to process as not all the information is meant to be publicly available and must be redacted for privacy purposes. Private citizens may also request reports on crime in a specific area, for example if they are considering relocating and want a list of crimes in the prospective area. Agencies have different policies in place regarding the level of detail to provide in such requests. Local politicians (mayor, city or county council, etc.) may also request crime analysis products from the organization in order to provide information to their constituents.

Data and Software

In order to generate the statistics and reports described, crime analysts can gather data from a number of sources and databases both internal and external to the organization. Two of the most widely used databases by analysts are computer-aided dispatch (CAD) and records management systems (RMS). A CAD system allows for prioritization of calls for service, the most prioritized calls getting immediate response while nonemergency calls get stacked for a response when an officer becomes available. CAD systems create a more efficient way to respond to calls, but also create a data system for analysts to mine. Each call generates a line of data, which can then be searched, filtered, and extracted for analysis. Essentially there is a record for each call made for police services. This can be a valuable database for analysts to access because not all calls for police service are going to generate a police report as a crime may not have actually been committed (Klinger, 1997), but the activity may still be of value to analyze to look for patterns and trends. CAD databases include each call for service, but they also include all actions of officers (traffic stops, suspicious persons, sign-on and sign-off), which can all be of utility to the organization.

A records management system (RMS) is a central database utilized by law enforcement agencies to house a variety of records. The information typically found in a RMS includes crime reports, arrest reports, and traffic citations. Some agencies also use their RMS to house/store investigative reports from the detective unit, field interviews generated by patrol officers, as well as a number of other records, depending on the capability of the RMS software. In the past, reports were handwritten in the field and subsequently entered into RMS by records personnel. Many police departments have now equipped officers with laptops or mobile data terminals in the field to electronically submit their reports (Pelfrey, 2015). This electronic submission allows for much more timely entry into the RMS, which translates into more timely analysis. Both the CAD and RMS can be queried by analysts and data extracted on which to perform the various analytical techniques.

While CAD and RMS are the most consistent data sources queried and analyzed to generate statistics and reports, there are additional external sources that can be very valuable to crime and intelligence analysts. Some analysts also have access to the following databases:

- jail inmates, probationers/parolees, corrections inmates
- department of motor vehicles
- Violent Criminal Apprehension Program (ViCAP)—the largest investigative depository for major violent crime cases in the US (FBI, n.d.a)
- National Crime Information Center (NCIC)—an "electronic clearinghouse of crime data" (FBI, n.d.b) including stolen articles, boats, guns, license plates, vehicles; sex offender registry; missing persons, unidentified persons, gang/terrorists, wanted persons; and criminal backgrounds to name a few
- court records

In order to access some of these databases, analysts have to undergo specific training, which provides the appropriate clearances as well as certification to enter and query the databases. For example, in order to access NCIC, an analyst must complete 16 hours of training on the system with recertification every two years. Such training helps ensure the security of the system as well as the accuracy and integrity of the data (FBI, n.d.b).

The various databases provide a plethora of information for analysts to extract and pour through, but simply collecting and extracting the data is not true analysis. In order to conduct the analytical component, analysts enter the extracted data into a software or statistical package to look for patterns and trends. Some of the software packages that are popular among analysts include Microsoft Office, BAIR Analytics, and a host of products from IBM (i2, modeler, SPSS, etc.). While it may seem simplistic for crime analysis purposes, Microsoft Office can be very useful for analysts with Excel and Access. Excel can perform a host of statistics while Access also has this ability with the benefit of query options. Microsoft also has the advantage in that most departments widely use the software, meaning there is not an additional cost for analysis software. BAIR Analytics provides multiple software packages, some for analysts and others for online data sharing with the public. Their analytical software, ATAC Workstation (Automated Tactical Analysis of Crime) provides crime pattern and predictive analysis, as well as crime mapping and reporting for investigation and intelligence analysis (BAIR Analytics, n.d.). Other aspects of BAIR will be discussed in more detail later with intelligence analysis and data sharing.

Crime Mapping and Analysis

Analysts spend a large portion of their time completing the above reports and requests using the data sources and analytical tools just described, but another significant portion of a crime analyst's time is spent mapping crimes and analyzing the spatial trends of crime. Crimes can be mapped to help explore the patterns identified in the reports and requests above, providing a visual representation of crime to commanders, investigators, and the public. The idea of providing a picture of crime is by no means a new idea, and police have been doing so for at least the past 100 years by sticking pins into paper maps on the wall (Ratcliffe, 2004). However, as technology has changed over time, the ability to map and the efficiency in doing so using computers has catapulted crime mapping into a whole new realm. The field of geographic information systems (GIS) is dominated by two main companies, MapInfo and ESRI (Ratcliffe, 2004), with the majority of law enforcement agencies using the ArcView and ArcGIS components of ESRI. Research on utilization of crime mapping in agencies suggests large agencies (typically defined as those with 100 or more sworn personnel) were the first to adopt crime mapping into their departments, but the trend has been increasing steadily over time (Weisburd & Lum, 2005). Of agencies surveyed by Weisburd and Lum, 62% responded they had adopted computerized crime mapping by 2001.

In the past, investigators would simply map the locations where crime occurs, and while this is still the most common piece of information mapped, analysts are now mapping anything and everything with location information. Some common locations mapped by law enforcement agencies include but are not limited to, calls for service, field interviews, known drug houses, traffic stops, car accidents, gang territories, and known offender addresses. Locations can be mapped using a street address, intersection, or latitude and longitude coordinates from GPS data. To map the geographic location of events, people, or places, analysts extract data from the above mentioned sources and input that data into a mapping software. The software then geocodes (provides the geographic coordinates) the location and marks it on the map. Doing this task by hand is undoubtedly time-consuming, but computerized crime mapping can plot thousands of addresses in mere minutes. The maps of known locations are typically overlaid onto police beats/districts, census boundaries, or other spatial boundaries to conduct analysis at different spatial levels. This allows for crime comparisons across different regions, districts, beats, and census geographies like tracts and blockgroups.[3]

Early forms of crime mapping produced maps to help in investigation and identify where crime is concentrated, but as crime analysis has advanced, so have the techniques to analyze spatial data. Crime mapping is typically utilized for three different functions across law enforcement agencies: hot spot mapping, Compstat, and geographic profiling (Ratcliffe, 2004).

Crime is not randomly distributed across communities but rather are concentrated in certain areas—hotspots—areas of high crime intensity (Sherman et al., 1989). These hot spots are of interest to academics and practitioners alike. Academic interest lies in the theoretical explanations for such hot spots, while practitioner interest lies in identifying the hot spots and their characteristics to engineer effective methods of crime control and prevention at such high crime areas. Much of the law enforcement focus on hot spots comes from the shift towards problem-oriented policing (Goldstein, 1990) and SARA models (Eck & Spelman, 1987), and intelligence-led policing (Ratcliffe, 2008). Police practitioners operate in a world of limited financial resources, and they need to maximize their results while being fiscally responsible, thus focusing on the hot spots in their jurisdiction. A key job of an analyst is identification of these hot spots.

The concentration of crime and hot spots on a map can be depicted in multiple ways. Most simply, a pin map can be used where a pin or dot is placed in each location where a crime occurred. This presents a very straight-forward picture of crime dispersion; the area with the most pins has the most crime. However, it can also be somewhat misleading. If there are five crimes at one address, the pins are placed directly on top one another and it appears only one crime occurred at that location. To rectify this, analysts can produce a graduated symbols map. This map varies the size of the symbol or pin to reflect the amount of crime occurring at a specific address. The bigger the pin, the more crime there is. This works well for smaller geographic locations but can be overwhelming when looking at, for example, an entire jurisdiction's crime for a year. In cases with larger areas or longer time frames, kernel density maps can be a better way to depict hot spots. These are similar to weather maps depicting rainfall or accumulation, different colors or grada-tions represent the varying levels of crime. Kernel density maps also have the added benefit of not specifically identifying any one address, which can be advantageous when releasing maps to the public.[4]

Crime mapping also plays a key role in police strategies such as Comp-stat in the NYPD and various cities that followed this practice. One of the tools police administrators used to hold commanders accountable for crime in their districts was maps depicting the patterns and trends in crime. The maps provided a quick, easy way to show the crime problem so commanders could explain the nature of the problem and, more specifically, what they were doing to fix it. While many agencies have evolved beyond Compstat-type approaches and responding to dots on a map, maps still provide a visual representation of crime that can be used to show problems in an area and help strategies for crime reduction.

The more recent and progressive utilization of maps and spatial analysis in law enforcement has been in the practices of geographic profiling and predic-tive analysis, more intelligence-led approaches to crime prevention and reduc-tion. Geographic profiling is defined as "an information management strategy for . . . crime investigations that analyzes crime site information to determine the most probable area of offender residence" (Rossmo, 2000, p. 259). Instead of trying to come up with a psychological profile of an offender, geographic profiling tries to determine a spatial profile of a serial offender. Based on the distance-decay principle from the journey to crime research (Koppen & Kei-jser, 1997; Rengert et al., 1999), geographic profiling suggests offenders com-mit their crimes in a specific pattern, which can be analyzed to identify an area where the offender likely lives (Pelfrey, 2015). Offenders typically won't go far-ther than needed to commit their crime, and they target locations that follow the nodes and paths of their routine activities, making rational choices along the way (Cohen & Felson 1979; Cornish & Clarke, 1986).

By mapping the locations of committed crimes, analysts can run spatial analysis on the locations to calculate the likelihood of an offender's residence in a particular area. Such analyses can be performed when there are as few as six data points (Rossmo, 1995) and on a number of different crime types such as homicide, arson, burglary, or theoretically any crime with an outdoor opportunity element (Ratcliffe, 2004). While this tool can be beneficial to law enforcement to narrow down suspect pools or areas for patrol saturation, research suggests geographic profiling software is not particularly accurate and works better for some crimes than others (Paulsen, 2006). Also, when law enforcement officers are armed with a little bit of knowledge on heuristics and journey to crime research, they more accurately predict the home area of the offender than the computer models (Bennell et al., 2007).

Intelligence Analysis

Another component of a crime or intelligence analyst's role in a law enforcement agency is conducting intelligence analysis. Agencies have moved beyond tracking dots on a map and focused on more intelligence-led policing styles largely derived from the British Intelligence Model of policing. Intelligence-led policing moves beyond the reactive form of policing following crime and offenders from one place to another, to integrating multiple data and information sources to provide a better picture of the criminal element (Ratcliffe, 2008). Intelligence-led policing focuses on a more holistic approach to crime control; gathering raw data from multiple sources, scrutinizing and processing it into something more accurate, valuable, and usable than just the raw data itself (Taylor and Davis, 2010). The goal is to create an intelligence product that can inform police decision-makers on the best approaches at crime prevention and reduction (Peterson, 2005). There are a variety of data and information sources an analyst can draw from to create multiple types of intelligence products.

According to the National Intelligence Model, there are four key intelligence products to help in decision making and guiding investigations and deployment of law enforcement efforts (NCIS, 2000):

- Strategic assessments
- Tactical assessments
- Target profiles
- Problem profiles

Strategic assessments aim to identify longer-term issues in an areas looking at current and future trends in criminality. They help establish law enforcement priorities, inform senior administration, as well as determine resource allocation. Tactical assessments aim to identify short-term issues in an area, which require immediate attention from the law enforcement community and can be based on crime series, hot spots, as well as preventive measures for these problems (NCIS, 2000).

Target profiles, instead of focusing on a crime problem, focus on a criminal target(s) or group. These profiles seek to gather as much information about a specific person or group to initiate an operation or support a current operation against the target or group. Examples of things that may be found in a target profile include habits, lifestyle, addresses, places frequently visited, family members and associates, risk posed to self and others, firearms possession, criminal history, all contact information available, and any other details that may be gathered about a suspect. This information is gathered by analysts from a number of sources, including many of those described under crime analysis. In order to establish a target's family, associates, and personal networks, analysts can use a form of analysis known as "link analysis." Link analysis is a data-analysis technique used to evaluate relationships between people, locations, events, and items. Arrest data, field interviews, gang databases (in-house, state, or regional), informant information, and investigative notes are common data that form the basis of link analysis between people, places, and things.

A more analytical approach to link analysis involves social network analysis (SNA). SNA is commonly used in other disciplines to identify the formal and informal structures of organizations and other groups. Within the law enforcement context, it is commonly used to examine gangs, organized crime, drug networks, and other criminal networks. The same data as described above can be utilized for SNA to identify the number of connections (ties) between people (nodes) along with identifying individuals who are central to a grouping such as those who have the most ties or connect two groups within the organization (McGloin, 2005; Sparrow, 1991; Van der Hulst, 2009; Coles, 2001). This information can be used to gain a better understanding of these criminal networks and to establish law enforcement investigative efforts. For example, identifying a key figure within a drug network to be targeted can help shape law enforcement efforts to more effectively disrupt the network as well as identify individuals who were previously unknown to be involved.

In addition to the traditional data sources mined for crime and intelligence analysis described above, analysts are also looking to new web-based sources of data to define target profiles. One of the most recent trends in data mining has been exploring social media accounts such as Facebook, Twitter, Instagram, among others. Some people post an extraordinary amount of personal information on these sites (see Moule et al., 2013; Pyrooz et al., 2014), much of it publicly available, which means law enforcement has access as well. The relationships and who people are connected to via social media provide yet another tool for law enforcement in building their target profiles. In addition, much of the information added to social networking sites has a geographic location attached, allowing law enforcement to track the whereabouts and comings and goings of offenders and criminal groups.

LexisNexis Accurint for Law Enforcement is another tool utilized in building target profiles. "Accurint for Law Enforcement is an investigative technology that can expedite the identification of people and their assets, addresses, relatives, and business associates by providing instant access to a comprehensive database of public records" (LexisNexis, n.d.). Typically, searching all these databases would take days, assuming one could even gain access. The system also helps identify evidence of financial distress and prior criminal activity, can set up alerts on specific people when information changes, as well as put investigators and analysts in contact with other federal, state, and local agencies using Accurint to share information. All of the above data sources can be used in combination to enter into link analysis software to generate intelligence products.

The most common software utilized to conduct link analysis are i2 and UCINET. i2 is a product of IBM and has multiple components available, with Analyst's Notebook and COPLINK being the most utilized. IBM i2 Analyst's Notebook is a visual analysis environment that helps discover networks, patterns, and trends inside volumes of data (IBM, n.d.). These analyses can produce complex data, and Analyst's Notebook can help simplify the communication of that data to decision makers in a timely and accurate manner (IBM, n.d.). It provides a valuable visual representation of the links across people, places, and things and also allows for documents, photos, video, and other forms of media to be embedded into the link charts. In practical terms, i2 Analyst Notebook is useful for maintaining a visual display of intelligence efforts where the analyst can maintain and build on a file of a criminal network. This creates the opportunity to organize an immense amount of information on the links between people, places, and things, as well as discover previously unknown links. One of the limitations to i2 Analyst Notebook is that much of the information used to form the link charts has to be manually entered by the analyst. However, this limitation can be partially solved through the use of COPLINK.

COPLINK can consolidate data from multiple source and helps generate tactical leads. The benefit of COPLINK is that it automatically produces link charts of people, places, and things by data mining agency (and possibly external) databases. The downside of COPLINK is that the link charts are not as easily manipulated to incorporate various forms of information (such as pictures, reports, and notes) for display as in i2. However, the combination of i2 and COPLINK, both from IBM, provide a useful tool set for the analyst. Alternatively, UCINET is a more analytically based software for examining links. UCINET was created in the early 1980s for social network analysis (UCINET, n.d.), which links to a much broader body of theory and research on social relationships. For the crime analyst, UCINET provides an analysis software for such factors as strength of ties and central figures.

The final type of intelligence product identified by the National Intelligence Model is problem profiles. A problem profile identifies established and emerging crime trends and crime hot spots (NCIS, 2000). In the past this has typically involved deploying resources across areas, managing hot spots, and crime reduction initiatives. While these tasks are still vital today, a new form of problem profile has recently emerged—predictive analysis or crime forecasting. Instead of responding to crime problems, agencies are attempting to predict where crimes are most likely to occur next and create tailored crime-prevention measures to reduce the likelihood of them actually occurring. PredPol and IBM SPSS Modeler are two predictive software products that law enforcement agencies use to try and achieve this goal. PredPol seeks to place officers in the right place at the right time to give them the best chance to prevent crime (PredPol, n.d.). PredPol processes crime data and assigns probabilities of future crime events to regions of space and time, presents an estimated crime risk to law enforcement decision makers, and can lead to the more efficient and accurate resource deployment by agencies (PredPol, n.d.). IBM SPSS Modeler uses a wide variety of algorithms and techniques to bring predictive intelligence to decision makers in agencies (IBM, n.d.). While predictive analysis or crime forecasting is an emerging trend in law enforcement, it is not without its critics.[5]

As crime and intelligence analysis continue to proliferate in law enforcement and more agencies shift toward a smart policing or intelligence-led framework, the work of analysts becomes increasingly important. They will continue to develop new techniques and types of analysis, as well as be armed with additional tools to do so. New software is constantly being developed, promising bigger and better things for law enforcement, especially in the realm of predicting or forecasting crime.

Issues for Analysts

Even as crime and intelligence analysis have grown over time and become a larger part of the law enforcement community, and the tasks and tools described above have advanced, the job of an analyst does not come without its challenges. The inclusion of an analyst in an agency is not a guarantee the efficiency and effectiveness of the agency will improve. Analysts face challenges, both analytical and organizational, which impede their ability to maximize their impact on crime reduction and efficiency.

Analytical Issues

The analysis an analyst can provide an agency is only as good as the data that are collected, and therein lies one of the greatest problems analysts face—quality of data (Cope, 2004). Several factors influence the quality of data available to analysts. Data issues can stem from the very beginning of the intake process—the officer who responds to the call and writes the initial report. In these reports, officers can fail to include details that would be important to establish patterns and trends, can commit errors when entering the data into the report (especially on mobile data terminals where they perhaps check the wrong box or click on a wrong field in a drop-down menu), as well as can hold up the data by failing to submit in a timely manner.

In an ideal setting, supervisors would review all submitted reports with a high level of scrutiny and bounce back problem reports to be fixed immediately, but this is not always the norm in agencies. When officers leave their shift without submitting their reports, it may be days before the data is actually entered into the system and is in the hands of the crime analyst, thus creating missing pieces when looking for patterns and trends. In addition, when new information about a crime is gathered, reports should be updated and supplemented to reflect such changes. Unfortunately such changes, typically done by investigators, are often not filtered back to the analyst. Crime data are not stagnant, but rather fluid and ever changing, and in order to produce accurate information, analysts must have the most up-to-date information on cases. The next stage at which error can occur in crime reporting is the data entry process into the RMS. Many agencies have electronic submissions via the mobile data terminals in patrol cars, but records personnel must still validate these reports to ensure accuracy, especially in submission to state or national crime statistics such as the FBI's Uniform Crime Reports. Human error in entering codes for variables such as weapon, type of injury, race, gender, age, among many others, can dramatically distort a crime report, thus introducing error into it as well as any analysis derived from it.

In addition to problems with poor and missing data, analysts also face challenges with the databases and software they use. In some cases, the databases housing the different data collected in an agency may be outdated or antiquated, or in a worst case scenario, may not be electronic. If reports are not in an electronic format, an analyst has to manually enter the reports into his or her own database for analysis, a time-consuming and cumbersome process. Databases in the agency may be electronic but outdated, or very cumbersome to query, making it hard to extract data. In addition, some agencies store their data in multiple databases, and those databases are not integrated and are unable to speak with one another, meaning the data must be extracted and then merged into some other system for analysis. All of these things take time, thus making the information outdated and of less value for creating immediate responses to current problems.

Software can pose another set of problems for an analyst when it is old or dated. It cannot perform the functions an analyst needs to conduct current or new types of analysis that could be beneficial to the organization. Perhaps an even greater problem with software is when purchases are made without consulting the analyst who will actually be using the software. Many companies now market crime or intelligence analysis software and pitch their products to those in a position to authorize purchases. In some cases, the software (when presented by the seller) seems as though it would be an asset to the organization and is purchased without the analyst vetting the software and evaluating whether or not it will be useful given the databases and software already being utilized in the department. Software may look great in a demonstration but may not function how an analyst needs it to when he or she imports the agency's own data. Resources are limited and analysts should be directly involved in vetting and recommending all software and databases the department decides to purchase.

Organizational Issues

The quality of data, databases, and software all pose challenges to a crime or intelligence analyst, but typically they can find solutions to address or work around these problems. The greatest issues that impede the ability of an analyst to function successfully and assist the department are organizational and structural. How the analyst is valued (or devalued) and placed in the organization, the culture of the department, as well as how the analyst is tasked all influence an analyst's function and contribution in effectively and efficiently preventing, reducing, and solving crime problems.

As discussed above, research suggests larger agencies are more likely to hire analysts than smaller ones, and larger agencies were also the first to employ crime and intelligence analysts. Much of this has to do with the resources available to larger agencies. Simply put, they operate with larger budgets and have more room to hire personnel other than sworn officers. They are also more likely to have the resources to purchase the software (database management and analytic) needed to conduct analysis. Agencies without such budgets are left to make a difficult decision—use the limited resources to hire additional sworn officers for patrol or hire a crime analyst to help maximize the efficiency of the officers the agency already has. This question is brought to light in the National Institute of Justice's *New Perspectives in Policing* Series, "One Week in Heron City" (Sparrow, 2009). This is a fictional case study of a new police chief who has to address several crime concerns in her agency, including considering if the department is using its resources most efficiently and effectively. The case study includes multiple scenarios where the chief speaks with analysts and realizes the value they offer to the agency, adding details the detectives and officers could not. The value of an analyst is directly tied to the culture of the department and how open the officers, investigators, and administration are to trying new crime reduction approaches. This case study highlights that a well-trained and well-utilized civilian analyst can increase the capacity and effectiveness of an agency without adding sworn personnel.

When analysts are initially hired in an agency, there will always be people who support bringing in new ideas and tactics, but there will also be a portion of the department that is skeptical and believes hiring more officers would have been a better use of resources—they fail to see the value an analyst can bring. Over time, some of these skeptics will switch over and become full supporters of their new asset. This typically happens when the analyst provides information that helps solve a problem. To provide an example, as an analyst, I had several investigators who consistently came to me when they had a trend they were examining, requesting additional information. When the information the investigators already had, along with the information I provided, helped solve cases, the skeptics quickly realized I could be of value to them and they routinely stopped by my office seeking advice. This involves changing the mind-set of the people in the department. The intelligence provided can be used not only to help work cases but also to help the people in the department to be open to sharing the knowledge they have, which benefits other cases. An open exchange of intelligence is key to becoming a more effective department.

Department culture and buying into the value of an analyst are also seen in situations where the analyst is placed in an organization. According to Ratcliffe's model of intelligence-led crime reduction (2003), analysts interpret the criminal element and use their intelligence products to influence decision makers, who subsequently make command decisions to impact the criminal environment. In order for this process to be effective, the analyst must be in a position to be able to first identify decision makers, and second, have a relationship with them (Ratcliffe, 2004) where the decision makers rely on this knowledge to take informed action. Analysts can produce intelligence products all day long, but if they do not have a direct line of communication to the key decision makers, what purpose does it serve?

The role an analyst has in a department can also be impacted by the chain of command and who oversees the analyst or unit. If the agency places a strong value on analysis, the analyst or unit is likely placed close to the agency leadership in the organizational structure, again allowing for direct communication with key decision makers. When an analyst has a direct connection to the top and is seen to be of value, it helps the analyst understand his or her role as well as the role of intelligence and empirical analysis in the organization. The discussion thus far has focused on the philosophical location of the analyst in an agency, but the physical location in the building is also important. When analysts are seen as key players in crime reduction, they typically have offices or cubicles within proximity of the decision makers. They are placed in a centralized location where everyone has access to them and where they have direct access to those in command.

Just as there are varying degrees of support for an analyst across an agency, there are also varying assumptions of what an analyst can and should do. Some personnel assume analysts can do everything they see on television and are disappointed when their requests are denied or an analyst says something cannot be done. Others, as previously discussed, assume analysts can offer little assistance or think the information they can produce is of little value (Ratcliffe, 2005) and are resistant to elicit their help. The primary duties of crime and intelligence analysis involve studying the criminal environment, but analysts are often tasked with administrative-based orders as well. The administration may use the analyst to conduct performance measures such as response times, analysis of calls for service, officer productivity, etc., to assist in the efficiency of the agency and reducing costs. While these are important measures to monitor in an agency and analysts are tasked to do them because of their unique analytical skill set, an analyst that spends his or her time primarily conducting these statistics does not have time to focus on the crime reduction aspect of the job.

Trusting an analyst is also key to maximizing the potential benefit of the position. While the tasks and intelligence products generated at the request of department personnel are critical to a crime reduction strategy, they must also be free to conduct analyses on their own. If they spend all day completing requests from others, they may not have time to explore the data to uncover their own patterns and trends, ones that others may not even be aware of yet. Their freedom to explore with no boundaries is essential, as is trusting the crime analysis and intelligence products they generate, even if it goes against the preconceived notions of the "right" way to do things. There can be a great deal of resistance to change in law enforcement, and analysts sometimes upset the status quo with their recommendations.

As an analyst, I was approached by a specialized unit commander during the late fall to conduct an analysis on armed robberies during the holiday season. The commander wanted the analysis to show there was an increase in armed robberies during this season so she could justify overtime for an armed robbery suppression team. I conducted the analysis as requested and found there was no increase in armed robberies during the holiday season. I ran the same analysis for a series of years in the past and found there had never been an increase in armed robberies. The commander, who was not pleased with the analysis, was convinced I was incorrect because that is what they had always done and needed to do it again. I did uncover a pattern that larcenies from autos went up during the holiday season, and we then set up an operation to address that crime-specific problem. Had I not challenged the status quo with this analysis, the department would have continued to waste officer overtime fighting a crime problem that did not even exist. In this case, the commander came to the analyst to learn about the nature of the crime problem, but often analysts are left completely out of the loop when their insight and knowledge could make for a far more efficient operation.

Who Is the Analyst?

The tasks and tools of an analyst vary across agencies, as do some of the issues described above, depending on how intelligence and analysis are viewed by a department. Other changing factors among analysts are their backgrounds, training, and official position in a department. Typically analysts have an educational background that has generated the specialized skill set they use to perform their jobs. Most analysts have at least an undergraduate degree in a field related to criminal justice, criminology, or perhaps statistics, and many also hold masters degrees as well. While the education is fairly consistent among analysts, this is not at all the case with their training. There is no academy to send analysts to like there is for officers to teach them the skills they need to do the job. Much of an analyst's training comes from his or her experience in college, and most analysts are self-taught. Very few have received formal training, so there is a wide range of abilities across analysts (Ratcliffe, 2005). Even when analysts do receive some formal training, data systems can sometimes be so unique to individual agencies that generic training is of little value. When analysts have different backgrounds and analytical capabilities, it creates problems with continuity and efficiency in the analysis unit. If a new analyst is hired, it may take weeks or sometimes months to get that person up to speed, all the while taking the current analyst away from his or her tasks to assist the department. The greatest reason for lack of formal training for analysts is lack of resources. Agencies face tight budgets, and if the decision is between sending an officer for training or sending an analyst, the officer almost always wins out.

Many of the training opportunities available are hosted by software companies (teaching analysts how to use their specific software) or crime/intelligence analyst associations. There are state, national, and international associations of crime analysts, which offer training on specialized issues to their members. For example, the International Association of Law Enforcement Intelligence Analysts (IALEIA) provides training, holds conferences, and provides various publications and related resources. The IALEIA has also put considerable effort into establishing basic and intermediate standards for analysts and guidelines for analysis as model policy.[6] They are offered at various locations covering a variety of topics which can be very useful to analysts. The downside to the training is that there are usually very limited spots, and even if the training is free, the department still has to pay an analyst's travel expenses to attend. The Florida Department of Law Enforcement (FDLE) has a unique program to specifically address training of analysts. In 2003, FDLE developed the first analyst academy where analysts are taught the specific skills they need to prevent crime, conduct complex investigations, and other analytical skills. The program has subsequently been divided into a number of different courses and certifications for analysts of varying abilities—a basic 40-hour course for new analysts as well as more advanced courses covering topics such as intelligence-led policing, geographic profiling, social networking, and advanced computer skills (FDLE, n.d.). These FDLE programs were federally funded and with government cuts, no classes are currently being offered and it is unclear if they will be in the future (FDLE, n.d.).

In addition to possessing the necessary analytical skill set, the personality and communication style of an analyst are essential. Analysts who thrive and who are sought out by agency personnel are those that are professional, confident, and stand firm behind their work. As previously discussed, some people in an agency will not be supportive of the analytical work and will question, critique, and attempt to refute the knowledge products. A confident analyst will stand behind his or her intelligence products and not back down just because a commander argues "Well, that's how we've always done it." Analysts can be put in precarious positions where they have to deliver news people do not want to hear, and it takes a strong personality to sometimes stand up to a commander or chief and offer contradictory evidence.

The ability to communicate well with both commanders and patrol officers is a key requirement of an analyst. An analyst who is central to the agency is going to interact with people of all ranks and be confident and collected without being condescending to those who may not understand the science used to generate empirical evidence. Analysts rely on the officers to input knowledge into the system for them to analyze, so they must be able to effectively communicate with the patrol officers. However, this should not be a one-way knowledge transfer. Analysts must make sure the intelligence produced from frontline officers' information is returned back to them as well, not just to the decision makers. Frontline officers in Sheptycki and Ratcliffe's (2004) study equated the intelligence unit to a "black hole"—they send information in but nothing ever comes out.

The ability of the analyst to communicate with all ranks in the agency is important in establishing rapport with colleagues. Frontline officers who trust the analyst will generate knowledge and send it to the analysis unit, and decision makers will use the intelligence products to inform their assessments on the best ways to prevent, reduce, and respond to crime. The trust an analyst builds in a department cannot be overstated, but trust is something in law enforcement that can be very difficult for an analyst to build for a number of reasons. First, many crime/intelligence analysts are not sworn but rather civilian employees. Sworn personnel are sometimes distrustful of civilian employees and their recommendations on a crime problem because they are not cops. They are not out there on the streets but rather sit in an office all day, so cannot possibly understand the crime problem since they have not seen it firsthand. Some analysts argue their work is sometimes overlooked by the sworn officers simply because they are civilian employees (Cope, 2004). The civilian job position adds a unique challenge as well because civilians are not in the same chain of command necessarily as sworn personnel, sometimes confusing their role. From my personal experience, as a civilian analyst I had a captain as a direct supervisor, but I would often take my results directly to the head of the agency instead of going through the chain of command. Sworn personnel could not imagine doing so and often questioned me about my ability to go directly to the top. They were also sometimes resentful of my direct access and ability to supersede the chain of command, in spite of the agency head requesting I do so.

Second, trust can also be difficult to earn because analysts tend to have higher levels of education than most officers which can also create animosity. Again, frontline officers are sometimes skeptical of the analysis produced and believe it lacks credibility because it was generated from a computer (Cope, 2004), not generated from being out on the street seeing the events as they unfold. Some officers (and commanders) will also be distrustful simply because an analyst has not been a cop, so he or she can never really understand. Third, although not experienced by everyone, the demographics of the analyst may inhibit the formation of trust. As a young, female analyst in a male-dominated department, some officers were skeptical simply because of my age and gender. While this was rare, if a key decision maker feels this way, an analyst will likely never be utilized to full potential in an agency.

Looking Forward

In the history of law enforcement, crime and intelligence analysis are fairly new on the scene. As more software companies become involved in analysis and personnel continue to learn new skills, the knowledge to be produced is virtually limitless. However, as the field moves forward, there are several issues agencies and analysts still face. Regarding data and software, analysis is only as good as the data that comes in from the street—garbage in equals garbage out. In order for analysts to create informed, accurate intelligence products, the quality of the data coming in needs to improve. The best way to do this is to train officers from the beginning when they first come into the organization. It is always easier to train someone to do it the right way the first time than retrain them after they have been doing it one way for years. However, retraining is also necessary for current officers. As was the case with multiple retraining sessions I conducted with officers during my time as an analyst, once the officers saw what we were trying to produce and how important their role was, they were fairly quick to convert over to the new method or approach, thus improving the quality of the data coming in. In addition to improving quality of data, training and retraining all officers creates consistency across the agency, something analysts often argue is lacking in report writing (Innes et al., 2005).

In addition to training officers, law enforcement agencies must provide additional training for their analysts. Some analysts have software on their computers they do not know how to use because they were not involved in the procurement process. Providing training on the software will be a short-term loss in training costs but a long-term gain in terms of increasing the analysts' capabilities. Programs like the FDLE's analyst academy and advanced analytical courses offer an innovate way for a state to consistently train analysts and seem to be a promising approach. With additional funding either at the state or federal level, creating more programs like FDLE's seems to be a promising direction for the future, especially in establishing consistency in analysis across a state, which would allow for easier sharing of data and products across agencies.

From the position of the organization, resources are always limited and law enforcement administrative staff must use them in the most efficient and effective manner. This involves having to make difficult decisions about where to allocate resources, and unfortunately supporting crime or intelligence analysis may not win out over providing more resources to deploy and equip officers. Supporting analysis may seem frivolous to some, but it is truly an investment in the agency that, with the right analyst and skills, can produce a long-term gain and will likely pay for itself times over by increasing the efficiency and effectiveness of the agency both in where and how to deploy officers. They can also perform analysis on administrative issues like productivity, response time, etc.

For agencies that have analysts and value their contribution to the department, the next problem is retention. Due to their specialized skill sets, analysts could likely make far more in the private sector than they do working for government organizations. When faced with limited opportunity for advancement in a law enforcement agency, analysts are sometimes forced to leave to increase their income opportunities. Most crime and intelligence analysts like the work they do, but economic constraints in the job sometimes make it difficult to stay. Providing opportunities for advancement and training to learn new skills to be applied on the job, as well as other perks such as take-home vehicles, good benefits, and having freedom and flexibility in the job may increase the likelihood of retaining analysts.

All the above mentioned challenges can only be remedied if there are innovative law enforcement executives that see the value crime and intelligence analysts can offer their departments. Analysts must be placed in a position in the organization where they have direct access to the decision makers, they have rapport and trust with the decision makers, and their work is directly utilized in deciding how to effectively and efficiently manage crime problems in a jurisdiction. Without crime and intelligence analysts being placed in centralized roles in a department, the true extent of their contribution to the agency will never be fully realized.

NOTES

[1] Ratcliffe (2007) notes that over time the distinction between crime analyst and intelligence analyst has blurred, where the roles are highly interrelated and often carried out by the same personnel. As such, I will use the terms interchangeably throughout the chapter.

[2] See Clarke and Eck (2005) for a more in-depth discussion of crime analysis.

[3] See Harries (1999) for a more detailed discussion on crime mapping.

[4] See Eck et al. (2005) for a more extensive discussion of hot spots and mapping techniques.

[5] For additional discussion of predictive analysis, see the chapter by Nix in this book, Ridgeway (2013), and Perry (2013).

[6] See http://ialeia.org/

REFERENCES

Audit Commission. (1993). Helping with enquiries: Tackling crime effectively. London: HMSO.

BAIR Analytics. (n.d.). ATAC Workstation. Retrieved from http://www.bairanalytics.com/software/atac/.

Bennell, C., Snook, B., Taylor, J. P., Corey, S., & Keyton, J. (2007). It's no riddle, choose the middle: The effect of number of crimes and topographical detail on police officer predictions of serial burglars' home locations. *Criminal Justice and Behavior*, 34(1), 119–132.

Berk, R. (2005). Knowing when to fold 'em: An essay on evaluating the impact of Ceasefire, Comstat, and Exile. *Criminology and Public Policy*, 4(3), 451–466.

Braga, A. A., & Bond, B. J. (2008). Policing crime and disorder hot spots: A randomized controlled trial. *Criminology*, 46(3), 577–607.

Carter, D. L. & Carter, J. G. (2009). Intelligence-led policing: Conceptual and functional considerations to public policy. *Criminal Justice Policy Review*, 20, 310–325.

Clarke, R. V., & Eck, J. E. (2005). *Crime Analysis for Problem Solvers*. Washington, DC: Center for Problem Oriented Policing.

Cohen, L. E. & Felson, M. (1979). Social change and crime rate trends: A routine activity approach. *American Sociological Review*, 44, 588–605.

Coldren, J. R., Huntoon, A., & Medaris, M. (2013). Introducing Smart Policing: Foundations, principles, and practice. *Police Quarterly*, 16(3), 275–286.

Coles, N. (2001). It's not what you know—It's who you know that counts. Analysing serious crime groups as social networks. *British Journal of Criminology*, 41(4), 580–594.

Cope, N. (2004). "Intelligence led policing or policing led intelligence?": Integrating volume crime analysis into policing. *British Journal of Criminology*, 44(2), 188–203.

Cornish, D. & Clarke, R. (1986). *The Reasoning Criminal: Rational Choice Perspectives on Offending*. New York: Springer.

Craig-Moreland, D. E. (2004). Technological challenges and innovation in police patrolling. In Q. C. Thurman & J. Zhao (Eds.), *Contemporary policing: Controversies, challenges, and solutions* (pp. 299–303). Los Angeles: Roxbury Press.

Eck, J., Chainey, S., Cameron, J., & Wilson, R. (2005). Mapping crime: Understanding hotspots. United States Department of Justice, Office of Justice Programs: Washington, DC.

Eck, J. E. & Spelman, W. (1987). *Problem Solving: Problem-oriented Policing in Newport News*. Washington, DC: Police Executive Research Forum.

FBI. (n.d.a). Wanted by the FBI. Retrieved 12 February 2014 from http://www.fbi.gov/wanted/vicap.

FBI. (n.d.b). National Crime Information Center. Retrieved 12 February 2014 from http://www.fbi.gov/about-us/cjiis/ncic.

Florida Department of Law Enforcement. (n.d.). Florida Law Enforcement Analyst Program. Retrieved 20 February 2014 from http://www.fdle.state.fl.us/content/getdoc/586c5070-fac8-44a2-8e53-661bef41b425/Analyst-Home.aspx.

Goldstein, H. (1990). *Problem-oriented Policing*. Philadelphia: Temple University Press.

Goldstein, H. (1979). Improving policing: A problem-oriented approach. *Crime and Delinquency*, 25, 236–258.

Harries, K. (1999). *Mapping crime: Principle and practice*. Washington, DC: United States Department of Justice, Office of Justice Programs.

Her Majesty's Inspectorate Constabulary. 1997. Policing with intelligence. London: Her Majesty's Inspectorate Constabulary.

IBM. (n.d.). SPSS Software: Predictive analytics software and solutions. Retrieved 4 March 2014 from http://www-01.ibm.com/software/analytics/spss/.

Innes, M., Fielding, N., & Cope, N. (2005). The application of science? The theory and practice of crime intelligence analysis. *British Journal of Criminology*, 45(1), 39–57.

Klinger, D. (1997). Measurement error in calls-for-service as an indicator of crime. *Criminology*, 35(4), 705–276.

Koppen, P. J., & Keijser, J. W. (1997). Desisting distance decay: On the aggregation of individual crime trips. *Criminology*, 35(3), 505–515.

LexisNexis. (n.d.). Accurint for law enforcement. Retrieved from 4 March 2014 http://www.lexisnexis.com/government/solutions/investigative/accurint-le.aspx.

McGloin, J. M. (2005). *Street gangs and interventions: Innovative problem solving with network analysis*. Washington, DC: US Department of Justice, Office of Community Oriented Policing Services.

Moore, M. H. (2003). Sizing up Compstat: An important administrative innovation in policing. *Criminology & Public Policy*, 2(3), 469–494.

Moule Jr., R. K., Pyrooz, D. C., & Decker, S. H. (2013). From "What the f#@% is a Facebook?" to "Who doesn't use Facebook?": The role of criminal lifestyles in the adoption and use of the Internet. *Social Science Research,* 42(6), 1411–1421.

NCIS (2000). The National Intelligence Model. London: National Criminal Intelligence Service.

Paulsen, D. J. (2006). Connecting the dots: Assessing the accuracy of geographic profiling software. *Policing: An International Journal of Police Strategies and Management,* 29(2), 306–334.

Pelfrey, Jr., W. V. (2015). Geographic information systems: Applications for police. In R. G. Dunham & G. P. Alpert (Eds.), *Critical Issues in Policing: Contemporary Issues* (7th ed., pp. 289–301). Long Grove: Waveland Press.

Perry, W. L. (2013). *Predictive Policing: The Role of Crime Forecasting in Law Enforcement Operations.* Santa Monica, CA: RAND Corporation.

Peterson, M. B. (2005). Intelligence-led policing: The new intelligence architecture. Washington, DC: US Department of Justice. Retrieved 20 March 2014 from https://www.ncjrs.gov/pdffiles1/bja/210681.pdf.

PredPol. (n.d.). PredPol: Predict crime in real time. Retrieved 4 March 2014 from http://www.predpol.com/.

Pyrooz, D. C., Decker, S. H., & Moule, R. K. (2014). Criminal and routine activities in online settings: Gangs, offenders, and the internet. *Justice Quarterly.* Online http://www.tandfonline.com/action/showCitFormats?doi=10.1080/07418825.2013.778326

Ratcliffe, J. H. (2008). *Intelligence-led Policing.* Portland: Willan Publishing.

Ratcliffe, J. H. (2007). Integrated intelligence and crime analysis: Enhanced information management for law enforcement leaders. Washington, DC: Police Foundation.

Ratcliffe, J. H. (2005). The effectiveness of police intelligence management: A New Zealand case study. *Police Practice and Research,* 6(5), 435–451.

Ratcliffe, J. H. (2004). Crime mapping and the training needs of law enforcement. *European Journal on Criminal Policy and Research,* 10(1), 65–83.

Ratcliffe, J. H. (2003). *Intelligence-led policing: Trends and issues in crime and justice,* 248, Griffith, ACT: Australian Institute of Criminology.

Ratcliffe, J. H., Taniguchi, T., Groff, E. R., & Wood, J. D. (2011). The Philadelphia foot patrol experiment: a randomized controlled trial of police patrol effectiveness in violent crime hotspots. *Criminology,* 49(3), 795–831.

Rengert, G. F., Piquero, A. R., & Jones, P. R. (1999). Distance decay reexamined. *Criminology,* 37(2), 427–446.

Ridgeway, G. (2013). The pitfalls of prediction. *NIJ Journal,* 271, 34–40.

Rojek, J., Kaminski, R., Smith, H., & Cooney, M. (2010). 2010 South Carolina Law Enforcement Census: Local Law Enforcement Use and Evaluation of the South Carolina Intelligence and Information Center. Columbia, SC: University of South Carolina Department of Criminology and Criminal Justice.

Rosenfeld, R., Fornango, R. & Baumer, E. (2005). Did Ceasefire, Compstat, and Exile reduce homicide? *Criminology and Public Policy,* 4(3), 451–466.

Rossmo, D. K. (2000). *Geographic Profiling.* Boca Raton: CRC Press.

Rossmo, D. K. (1995). Overview: Multivariate special profiles as a tool in crime investigation. In C. Block, M. Daboub, & S. Fregly (Eds.) *Crime analysis through Computer Mapping* (pp. 65–97). Chicago: Police Executive Research Forum.

Sheptycki, J., & Ratcliffe, J. H. (2004). Setting the strategic agenda. In J. H. Ratcliffe (Ed.), *Strategic Thinking in Criminal Intelligence* (pp. 194–216). Sydney: Federation Press.

Sherman, L. W., & Weisburd, D. (1995). General deterrent effects of police patrol in crime "hot spots": A randomized, controlled trial. *Justice Quarterly*, 12(4), 625–648.

Sherman, L. W. (1990). Police crackdowns: Initial and residual deterrence. In M. Tonry & N. Morris (Eds.), *Crime and Justice: An Annual Review of Research* (pp. 1–48). Chicago: University of Chicago Press.

Sherman, L. W., Gartin, P. R., & Buerger, M. E. (1989). Hot spots of predatory crime: Routine activities and the criminology of place. *Criminology*, 27(1), 27–54.

Sparrow, M. K. (2009). One week in Heron City (Case A): A case study. *New Perspectives in Policing*. Harvard Kennedy School. Retrieved 15 February 2014 from https://www.ncjrs.gov/pdffiles1/nij/227664.pdf.

Sparrow, M. K. (1991). The application of network analysis to criminal intelligence: An assessment of the prospects. *Social Networks*, 13(3), 251–274.

Taylor, R. W. & Davis, J. E. (2010). Intelligence-led policing and fusion centers. In R. G. Dunham & G. P. Alpert (Eds.), *Critical Issues in Policing: Contemporary Issues* (6th ed., pp. 224–244). Long Grove: Waveland Press.

Taylor, B., Kowalyk, A., & Boba, R. (2007). The integration of crime analysis into law enforcement agencies: An exploratory study in the perceptions of crime analysts. *Police Quarterly*, 10(2), 154–169.

Uchida, C. D., & Swatt, M. L. (2013). Operation LASER and the Effectiveness of Hotspot Patrol: A Panel Analysis. *Police Quarterly*, 16(3), 287–304.

UCINET. (n.d.). UCINET Software. Retrieved 4 March 2014 from https://sites.google.com/site/ucinetsoftware/home.

US Department of Justice. (n.d.) What is FOIA? Retrieved 15 February 2014 from www.foia.gov.

Van der Hulst, R. C. (2009). Introduction to Social Network Analysis (SNA) as an investigative tool. *Trends in Organized Crime*, 12(2), 101–121.

Walsh, W. F. (2001). Compstat: An analysis of an emerging police managerial paradigm. *Policing: An International Journal of Police Strategies and Management*, 24(3), 347–362.

Weisburd, D., Bushway, S., Lum, C., & Yang, S. M. (2004). Trajectories of crime at places: a longitudinal study of street segments in the city of Seattle. *Criminology*, 42(2), 283–322.

Weisburd, D. & Lum, C. (2005). The diffusion of computerized crime mapping in policing: Linking research with practice. *Police Practice and Research*, 6(5), 419–434.

Weisburd, D., Mastrofski, S. D., McNally, A., Greenspan, R., & Willis, J. J. (2003). Reforming to preserve: Compstat and strategic problem solving in American policing. *Criminology & Public Policy*, 2(3), 421–456.

Willis, J. J., Mastrofski, S. D., & Weisburd, D. (2007). Making sense of COMPSTAT: A theory–based analysis of organizational change in three police departments. *Law & Society Review*, 41(1), 147–188.

Willis, J. J., Mastrofski, S. D., & Weisburd, D. (2004). COMPSTAT and bureaucracy: A case study of challenges and opportunities for change. *Justice Quarterly*, 21(3), 463–496.

SECTION IV

Issues in Policing

Police departments confront a number of important issues, from hiring officers representative of the community served to handling stress and physical hazards to deterring violence to policing populations with specific characteristics or special needs.

Historically the majority of police officers have been white males. Although the proportion of officers who are members of minority groups has been increasing, it is still quite low in some departments and is a cause of concern to many, including community members who see the need for the police to be more representative of the populations they serve. One approach to resolving this problem is to recruit more African Americans and women (as well as members of other minority groups) into police work. Unfortunately, there has not been a great deal of research or literature directed toward the problems faced by minority officers or toward the impact of hiring those officers. Yet, the calls for community-based policing strategies, which emphasize the integration of the formal control system of the police with the informal control system of the community, require minority participation in policing. Further, the values of affirmative action, equal opportunity, and involvement of minorities encourage the hiring and advancement of minorities in law enforcement.

One problem that hasn't been resolved is the small number of women being promoted into the higher ranks of police organizations. For example, Chief Karin Montejo, from the Miami-Dade Police Department, argues that in spite of increasing numbers of women in entry-level and mid-manager positions in policing, female officers are still underrepresented and face discriminatory treatment that limits their career mobility and options for advancement. She discusses specific obstacles that make it very difficult for women to achieve command-level positions. Further, she discusses the results from her study of success factors of women who have overcome these obstacles and have achieved positions of command in law enforcement. Further, Chief Montejo suggests specific changes in police departments that will remove some of the obstacles to the advancement of women to command positions (Montejo, 2010). This section includes two articles that address the issues of how blacks and women interact within the institution of policing.

Police work incorporates a number of situations that present police officers with an unusual and unique set of personal hazards. Although rare, the possibility of being killed or assaulted while carrying out one's duties as an officer does exist. In addition, there is an unusual degree of stress involved in police work linked to the possibility of danger to oneself or to others, particularly in situations involving the potential or actual use of (deadly) force. Stress has been identified as a factor in divorce, alcoholism, suicide, and physical illnesses. Over the past decade, law enforcement administrators have increasingly become concerned about the personal hazards of police work and have focused on the identification and prevention or treatment of these problems.

Professor Chris Cooper presents some important suggestions for the study of police. His ideas focus on the Afrocentric perspectives on the history of policing in the United States and how the current customs and practices are interpreted by African Americans. His article presents a view of policing that is not readily available but deserves critical attention. He argues that the personal and collective experiences of black people with police officers gives African Americans a reality different from that of white Americans.

In "Women in Law Enforcement," Lynn Langton discusses the trends of hiring women law enforcement officers from 1987 to 2008. During this time period, the proportion of women in law enforcement positions increased only slightly and differed depending on the type and size of the law enforcement agency. For example, women comprise about 25% of the officers in the Offices of Inspectors General but less than 10% of the officers in small and medium sized police departments. About 20% of the officers in police departments with 500 or more officers are women. Even though law enforcement agencies are opening up to women, it appears that we have reached a threshold for the number of women who desire to become police officers.

"Gender and Police Stress: The Convergent and Divergent Impact of Work Environment, Work-Family Conflict, and Stress Coping Mechanisms of Female and Male Police Officers" by Ni He, Jihong Zhao, and Carol Archbold, explores the impact of work environments on the physical and psychological stresses of police officers. The authors find that work-family conflict and destructive coping mechanisms are the main factors leading to physical and psychological problems. They also found that the problems differ for male and female officers. Their research emphasizes that police administrators should devise management programs to minimize stress as much as possible and to train officers in effective coping strategies for the stressors inherent in police work.

Steven Brandl and Meghan Stroshine examine the hazards of policing by distinguishing between injuries that occur as a result of accidents and injuries that result from felonious acts. In "Toward an Understanding of the Physical Hazards of Police Work," the authors note that assaults on officers are relatively rare events, as are serious injuries and death; most of the incidents resulting in injury are the result of accidents. The authors conclude that policies must deal with both accidental and felonious hazards to be effective in creating a safer work environment for officers.

Next, Marie Tillyer, Robin Engel, and Brian Lovins address sustainability issues of deterrence initiatives to reduce violence. Previous assessments of deterrence initiatives, such as Operation Ceasefire in Boston, have found that the initial positive effects are not sustained in the long-term. Drawing on the success of the Cincinnati Initiative to Reduce Violence, the authors use criminological theory to explain why focused deterrence works and how the model can be improved to leverage long-term benefits.

The sixth article by Andrea Allen includes a discussion and analysis of campus police agencies. The author provides a brief history, beginning in 1894 when Yale University hired the first campus police officers. She outlines the characteristics of current campus police agencies and highlights their unique role among law enforcement agencies. Because campus police agencies are relatively new to law enforcement, they are understudied. The author offers a number of fruitful issues for future research on campus policing.

In the final article in this section, Wesley Jennings and Edward Hudak discuss law enforcement's role in applying power and authority to protect the safety and welfare of the community, while balancing their *parens patriae* obligations to protect offenders with mental disabilities. They stress the importance of officer training in reducing the risks of mishandling encounters with this special population and in decreasing the risk of injury to themselves, the public, and especially to the mentally ill citizens they confront.

REFERENCE

Montejo, K. (2010). Women in police command positions: How their investment in human capital influences career success. In R. Dunham & G. Alpert (Eds.), *Critical issues in policing: Contemporary readings* (6th ed., pp. 387–404). Long Grove, IL: Waveland Press.

18

An Afrocentric Perspective on Policing

Christopher Cooper

As a U.S. Marine, I was told that I was green, hence to discard my blackness. As a black policeman in America, there were many times when it was suggested that I disregard recognizing that I didn't look like most other officers—we were all supposed to be blue. As a scholar, there are just as many, if not more, times that I am reminded by my colleagues that to champion causes of people of color is to jeopardize tenure and publication possibilities. I choose to notice my societal position as a black man in America. To discard it is to avoid realizing and challenging the injustices that come with my societal position. The same people who tell you to forget who you are, are the same people who will not let you forget who you are.

—The author

The Afrocentric perspectives on the history of policing in the United States, the policing institution, and its day-to-day practices differ from the perspectives held by many people not of African descent. This article presents the "other side," the way that people of color see policing in the United States. It bolsters its points by reliance on empirical data and attention to factual information and events.

In the twenty-first century, black people are unavoidably intertwined with the institution of U.S. policing. The reasons lie with crime problems in some black communities that prompt police–black citizen interaction, with racism in the form of police officers who choose not to have a good relationship with people of color, and with officers singling out people because of their skin color (racially discriminatory policing). These phenomena have meant that scholarly discourse on policing, police programs, initiatives, and strategy are often about or directed at black people and often imposed on black people

Prepared especially for *Critical Issues in Policing* by Christopher Cooper.

(i.e., community policing in many jurisdictions). No other racial group in U.S. society is as much the focus, and at the nucleus, of policing policy. Under these conditions, an open-minded person would think that black people would be invited to proffer their perspectives on policing their communities; that black scholars (Ph.D.s) with sociological and criminological expertise would be included by their white colleagues in research efforts to identify causes and solutions and ultimately to make recommendations to policy makers.

The situation is quite to the contrary. Black people are often objects of policing, and the experts in the black community are treated by many of their white colleagues with disdain. It is white police scholars who assert that they know what is best for policing black communities. Case in point, an entire industry, criminal justice, has been built around analyzing the social interactions (e.g., police–black citizen) and day-to-day lives of black and brown people. Whether it is classroom instruction concerning policing black communities or a panel established to make recommendations regarding police–black citizen relations, the players are seldom if ever black. Black social scientists are available, and the black community is available—available to function as integral parts of society in discussions on policing and policy making around policing.

The black social scientists are prepared to present their perspective on U.S. policing. What they have to say about policing has merit, but seldom are there mainstream outlets welcoming the Afrocentric perspective on policing. Scholarly work concerning policing written by African Americans having an Afrocentric perspective, if published at all, is most often found in the black press or in black scholarly journals. This article's presence in a mainstream publication is unusual. Hopefully, its appearance indicates that some positive changes are coming from the scholarly policing field.

This article presents the Afrocentric perspective on three policing phenomena that adversely impact black communities. The first is an Afrocentric perspective on status-quo police scholars: how they perpetuate racism and exacerbate poor police–minority relations. Most importantly, the status-quo police scholars deny the existence of racism and have misquoted policing history (by presenting a Eurocentric perspective). The second perspective is the use of race by some police officers as a factor in deciding whether or not to use deadly force. In instances of interactions with persons of color, such decisions can lead to dispensing with protocol, as in "shooting first and asking questions later." The third and final perspective calls attention to how black people are often excluded, by the media, police administrations, and government from discourse and decision-making processes regarding policing of their communities. These three perspectives combine to present the reader with the other side of the story.

The Perspective of the Police Scholars

Police scholars are usually social scientists with doctorate degrees. Many are academicians, while others are a combination of practitioner and academician. Most of those who study and write about U.S. policing are white males. There are legitimate concerns by people of color that this is a scholarship lacking racial and ethnic diversity.

The words conservative, status quo, mainstream, and traditional best describe the majority of police scholars. Sadly, the status-quo mainstream scholars have the podium. What they have to say about policing in the United States is taken seriously and given great weight by policy researchers and much of the lay populace. In this way, these scholars influence and shape the perception of policing in the United States for many Americans. For example, they influence judges, prosecutors, and the public about what constitutes the crime of police brutality versus a mere mistake.

Often, scholars convey information about the police in the form of scientific research. The social scientists who analyze phenomena do so with an objective of ameliorating conditions and alleviating problems. In the end, they give their findings to policy makers in the form of recommendations. The public receives the findings in lay terms (e.g., via the newspaper or a television news program) and is supposed to add the new information to what it believes it already knows about policing.

The problem lies with the fact that from an Afrocentric perspective, the status-quo police scholars (especially those who undertake historical analyses) are not truthful concerning policing in the United States. Much like the history lessons of the past, which did not divulge that Native Americans occupied North America when Christopher Columbus arrived, the police scholars present a Eurocentric perspective of policing in the United States. It excludes mention of people of color, the events, epidemics, tragedies, and triumphs to which black people were and are connected.

The Hidden History

With few exceptions, the status-quo police scholars do not address the fact that early policing was for the purpose of maintaining slavery—black people were policed by organized police long before these scholars say formal policing was established (Dulaney, 1996). The brutality of the police during the slavery era is sometimes denied or mitigated by the status-quo scholars. As an example, Monkkonen (1981) asserts that reports of Southern police in the 1860s being repressive and brutal are the result of sentiments that reflect an anti-Southern bias (p. 198, n96). He likened the observers of police brutality to people who would have said that they had witnessed brutality even if they had not.

With the abolition of slavery, the police establishment embarked on a new style of class control. This included enforcing segregation and championing white supremacy,[1] but a reader would not learn this from twenty-first century, status-quo policing textbooks and lecture instruction. Rather, the status-quo or Eurocentric version (e.g., Carte and Carte, 1975) reveals a period of varying police functions, such as giving shelter to the homeless and garbage collection, and the resultant identity crisis of the vocation. Not far behind is discourse on the realization that policemen needed uniforms and that corrupt behavior by many of them spawned major "clean house" initiatives in 1884, 1890, and 1894, to name just a few (Fogelson, 1977). What the reader is not told by most Eurocentric writers, for example, is how blacks were often excluded from becoming police officers and that in many communities the Ku Klux Klan and police were either complicit or one and the same.

The policing literature places emphasis and significance on the police reform movement—the period in U.S. history in which, according to the Eurocentric perspective, the policing establishment is said to have gotten a moral and professional conscience. The corrupt establishment was called to task by innovators from within the ranks as well by a concerned external populace. Much of the Eurocentric police literature describes the reform era as an epiphany. We are to believe that the people rose up, realized the pathetic character of the policing establishment, then called for law and order to be taken seriously and administered equally. No doubt the reform movement was a pivotal moment in removing politics from policing and upgrading the establishment's status. However, its inattention to racial injustice makes the reform movement also a pivotal point of increased intolerance. Why the recent policing literature (post–civil rights era of the twentieth century, and the twenty-first century) conveniently leaves out the racial issues that were intertwined with the police reform movement is baffling. The policing establishment was concerned with defining its mandate and with maintaining segregation laws.

To this day, in classroom instruction, the Eurocentric heroes of policing are individuals who made their mark in the reform movement era: August Vollmer, Bruce Smith, Herbert Jenkins, and William Parker, to name a few. The movement's leaders are portrayed as benevolent and having had few faults. Their motives are said to have been for the good of all people. In reality, they were often upper-class men attempting to protect upper-class interests (Fogelson, 1981). The Afrocentric perspective is that the reformers had a primary, glaring fault—not paying attention to social justice as it applied to all people. The criminal justice student wouldn't learn this fact from the typical police history textbook published by Eurocentric police scholars.

Sparrow, Moore, and Kennedy (1990) are among the many policing scholars who have written and published about the history of policing in the United States. From their work, the reader would know how political patronage could land an individual a police position but would find no mention of how the reformers shirked their responsibility to society by not addressing racially discriminatory policing. It is not sufficient to argue that blacks did not meet the higher educational standards put in place by the reform movement. Many blacks who satisfied the educational criteria applied to police agencies but were not hired because they were black (Dulaney, 1996, p. 65).

The reform era of policing, in particular, provided the stage for race-based, violent, and brutal behavior by police officers, including lynch mobs comprised of police officers and officers who hunted and shot black people like animals. Violence by police officers would in large part give way to some of the most serious race riots that the United States has ever experienced (e.g., Watts and Newark). Yet, the mainstream literature scarcely mentions that police provoked the rioting.[2] The race riots that rocked the nation were spawned by one standard of policing for whites and another for blacks. They were propelled by horrific police brutality from dogs set on people because they were black to jail-house beatings of people of color because they were black. It only makes sense that there would be poor police–community relations following the civil rights era riots. Moreover, the provocation by police that led to most of the race riots is referenced by police scholars of color (e.g., Alex, 1976; Cooper, 1980; Dulaney, 1996) and a few white scholars (e.g., Fogelson, 1977).

The late Arthur Niederhoffer (1969), police sociologist, included issues of race in his brief discussion of the history of U.S. policing in his work, *Behind the Shield*. He called attention to occupational issues of black police officers and how officers abridged the civil rights of black and Puerto Rican people. Niederhoffer was an anomaly in the police scholarly field in 1969 and would be in the early twenty-first century because he revealed a connection to policing and the John Birch Society (among other things). He referenced a November 8, 1965, *New York Times* article announcing that the former chief of the Salt Lake City police department (a reform and professionalization era chief) was scheduled to be a keynote speaker at a John Birch Society function (in spite of the society's white supremacist views and support of racial segregation).[3]

In a 1982 issue of *Atlantic Monthly*, police scholars Wilson and Kelling published "Broken Windows."[4] The article is held in the highest esteem by conservative police academia. For good reason, many students of color find the article racially offensive. From an Afrocentric perspective, the article is condescending and reflects narrow-mindedness. Recall that the article is largely based on Kelling and Wilson's (two white men) observations and study of how black people felt about, and interacted with, police officers assigned to foot patrol in Newark housing projects in the 1970s. For example, the authors assert that although "the neighborhoods were predominantly black and the foot patrolmen were mostly white, this 'order maintenance' function of the police was performed to the general satisfaction of both parties" (p. 30). This statement is problematic for obvious reasons. In the twenty-first century, black citizen–white police relations are incredibly strained. At the time of Kelling and Wilson's observations, relations were worse or equal to the current climate. They chose to imply that black people were not astute enough to be suspicious of racial hostility from the police or that the police–citizen relationship was tense. This same argument was posited in the slavery era by proslavery observers. They described slave masters and slaves in close physical proximity as having a peaceful coexistence.

Most patronizing and racially insensitive is that "Broken Windows" (and a subsequent article by Mark Moore and George Kelling, entitled, "To Serve and Protect: Learning from Police History" [1983]) suggests that the policing of yesteryear was so wonderful and beneficial that the United States should restore the "good ol' days," or the reform model. From an Afrocentric perspective, police scholar Samuel Walker (1984) is correct when he calls attention to how the authors not only misinterpreted police history but also were not truthful in describing the past. Walker adds, "the tradition of policing cited by Wilson, Kelling, and Moore never existed."[5] McNamara (1982), in an article with a fitting title, "Dangerous Nostalgia for the Cop on the Beat," bolsters Walker's position in pointing out that the good old days were not all that good.

A more recent reminder of the status-quo position and its insensitivity are the remarks from a professor of criminal justice about a conservative Web site for police officers operated by a Chicago police officer. Although the Web site included racial slurs and sexual innuendoes, the professor said he found the site "more positive than negative" because it allows police to vent.[6]

On Contributions by Black Police

There were black police officers prior to the Civil War (Dulaney 1996), but that is a fact not easily found in the status-quo literature or passed on to college students studying criminal justice. In most publications, the tremendous contributions of black people to policing are not mentioned at all or are mentioned in passing. Instead, people like Darryl Gates, the former Los Angeles police chief, are often praised. To people of color, Gates was known for the terror that he imposed on communities of color; his name conjures memories of random sweeps of black and Mexican people and the most cruel and sadistic police brutality.[7] Yet this man was described (shortly before the Rodney King incident) by Harvard University professors (police scholars) Sparrow, Moore, and Kennedy "as a pioneering police chief" who had "pointed the way forward" (1990, p. ix). In complimenting "progressive" police departments, the authors described Gates as handsome, honest, and professional. They described him as "the epitome of the reform police chief and his department a shining example of the best in reform policing" (p. 60).

The Eurocentric perspective on Gates's tenure is completely distinguishable from the Afrocentric perspective. King's beating was not an aberration of Gates's reign. Atypical was that the beating was videotaped. It is likely that Gates's tyranny would have continued had the country not seen the brutality. The infamous Mark Fuhrman served under Gates's watch. In 1994, by his own admission, Fuhrman told how he and other members of the police department beat people mercilessly because they were black, planted evidence on people because they were black, and routinely referred to black people as "niggers."[8] Presently, the Los Angeles Police Department is in the midst of what could turn out to be the largest police scandal in U.S. history. Dubbed the "Rampart scandal," it includes admissions by police officers that they sought Latino victims because they were people of color, planted evidence on them, and filed countless false police reports about them, some of which were to cover for police officers who had committed murder (Cohen,

2000). Not surprisingly, the LAPD faces a federal civil rights suit alleging a "pattern and practice" of abuse and racial discrimination and the possibility of federal oversight for the department. By June 2000, eighty-one criminal cases brought by officers of the Rampart Division had been overturned (Murr, 2000). The truth of how the Los Angeles Police Department operates (and has always operated) is finally subject to unfiltered public view. In fact, the multiple lawsuits against the LAPD may result in the agency being considered an ongoing criminal enterprise subject to RICO statues for the recovery of damages.

In contrast to the publicity given to flawed reform initiatives and out-of-control police departments like the LAPD, contributions to policing by black people have been underreported. Accomplishments of black police executives include team policing established in Newark by Hubert Williams. Lee Brown was instrumental in bringing community policing to New York City. Sadly, he never received the support from his middle managers that was needed to make it a success (Dulaney, 1996). To Brown's credit, his community-policing model has been replicated by other jurisdictions.

The fact that the accomplishments of black police executives are reported primarily in Afrocentric publications calls attention to denial and bigotry within policing academia. It is status-quo work that is accepted for publication, even though it presents an inaccurate portrayal of the history of policing in the United States. Many phenomena (e.g., how black officers are often physically harmed by white officers in the twenty-first century) worthy of presentation, and of social utility to black people, are censored or simply not published. Equally guilty are the journal editors and reviewers who allow writing that contains falsehoods to be published or who oppose publication of Afrocentric manuscripts, alleging that the writing is scientifically invalid (something that black authors often hear concerning their research from close-minded peer reviewers; commonly, it is an accusation that the black author has misinterpreted policing history).

On Police Brutality

The mainstream, status-quo, twenty-first-century police scholar bristles at notions that police brutality could be a widespread problem. He/she sees policing as having followed a steady progression of improvement over time. For example, review of the policing literature shows that the Knapp Commission (1973) investigation into police corruption in New York City reduced corruption there and had reverberations nationwide. There is a false sense of confidence that contributes in some part to the Eurocentric position that police brutality could not in fact be widespread in the twenty-first century following a "clean house" investigation of such magnitude. While financial crimes (e.g., shakedowns) by police have declined, the same cannot be said for police brutality.

When research on police brutality has been conducted, status-quo (Eurocentric) methods are suspect. An example of one such method is the use of police reports without other corroboration. Police scholars know that police reports alone yield invalid information; therefore, one can assume that researchers who use reports do so knowing that the documents produce scientifically invalid research.[9] For other researchers, it is their naiveté (sometimes from not having had police experience before becoming academicians) that causes them to fail to realize that an officer can write a police report in any way that he or she chooses. The authoritative version is often shaped so that illegal use of force is masked. Reports are written to mitigate the use of force and/or to deny its very occurrence.[10] In spite of these obvious shortcomings, many of those charged with informing the public (e.g., academicians) concerning the extent of such a serious social concern continue to champion this methodological method. As a result, many acts of police brutality are not recorded in status-quo police scholarly research.[11]

Status-quo police scholarship discourages attention, especially from policy makers, on police brutality. These academicians assert that incidents of police brutality are mere aberrations—the "rotten apple theory"[12] (notwithstanding all of the evidence and common sense that shows the theory to be a falsehood). As an example, Kelling (1997/1999) commented about the Abner Louima[13] case: "The assault and torture of Abner Louima by New York City police officers . . . was an appallingly deviant act, not representative of the New York City Police Department, of policing generally, or of good order-maintenance tactics," (p. 48).

To prove their position that brutality is rare, the scholars raise an argument that arouses suspicions that they are contradicting themselves. They point to the difficulty in collecting data about the extent of police brutality. Essentially, the scholars take a position that if you "can't quantify it, it doesn't exist." This is absolute ignorance of the fact that a great deal of physical police brutality is never reported. Furthermore, they are seldom willing to give credence to self-reports from victims and other nonpolice sources. These are sources that from an Afrocentric perspective are very reliable—and indicative of an epidemic of police brutality. For example, data derived via content analysis (e.g., analyzing periodicals), when coupled with other empirical data, are extremely helpful. Content analyses findings present a strong case for a scientifically generalizable pattern and conclusions about police practices. Other examples include reliance on existing data. These secondary analyses include figures kept by the Department of Justice (Civil Rights Division) based on the number of complaints received by it. Additional sources of information for gauging the extent of police brutality are the many civil lawsuits alleging police brutality. Most significant are those for which a jurisdiction settles out of court.[14]

In an effort to deny the existence of the systemic problem of police brutality in the United States, status-quo scholars write off a large chunk of police brutality as good faith—not criminal—mistakes. For example, Fyfe (1995) argues that many instances are examples of excessive or unnecessary force, not police brutality. He claims the harm and excessive physical punishment are the result of "ineptitude or carelessness and occurs when well meaning officers prove incapable of dealing with situations they encounter" (p. 163). Said another way, Eurocentric scholars attribute the harm to the victim as the result of well meaning officers incapable of dealing with situations they encounter.

Because of the influence of mainstream policing literature on policy making and the criminal justice system, it is not uncommon that defense attorneys representing police officers charged with police brutality call upon scholars championing the good-faith-mistake position as expert witnesses. Court characterizations of police brutality as noncriminal and mere mistakes perpetuate an unwillingness of fact finders to find officers guilty of police brutality. The acquittal of the officers who killed Amadou Diallo (discussed later in this article) is an example of this phenomenon. The state of affairs (as well as race relations in the United States) will not change anytime soon as long as the powerful mainstream police academic lobby is able to persuade fact finders (judge or jury) to choose mistake over crime.

Even worse, a number of scholars (e.g., Stoddard, 1968; Fyfe, 1982, 1995) place blame for the behavior on macrophenomena. Officers are said to have guns that fire too quickly, supervisors who don't supervise, and a police subculture, or an administration, that is so powerful that it takes away an individual officer's ability to function on his/her own volition. A notion that more training is the solution rather than better pre-employment screening further insults the reality that human beings participating in police work possess free agency. From an Afrocentric perspective, it is racially offensive to hear from police administrators and scholars that horrific acts (e.g., sodomization of Abner Louima) are indicative of a need for more training. It seems more prudent to realize that many individuals hired as police officers should not have been hired because of their racial bias or lack of respect for human life. To suggest that training is to blame or that it is the panacea for police brutality is to disavow the seriousness of "individualistic" racial intolerance and its ingrained mind-set character.

The problem with placing blame on macrophenomena is that it prompts people (prosecutors and jurors for example) to allow individual officers to escape responsibility for their actions. Research by Brown (1981) among others, as well as common sense, show that U.S. police officers are not robots but possess extensive autonomy, notwithstanding the influences of their subculture.

Race and Use of Deadly Force

When making a decision to use deadly force, the problem is that for many police officers the race of the "other" is an impacting factor. Race prompts an officer's fears, or race prompts his/her aversions, or race prompts him/her to marginalize another's self-worth. An officer's fear can cause indifference, reckless acts, or irrational interactions with a member of a racial group. This is one possible explanation of why police officers killed Amadou

Diallo. Aversion can be another impetus for an officer's behavior. The officer manifests his or her racial hatred, very often with physical violence. Marginalization (treating a person's self-worth as insignificant) explains a police officer knowingly using unnecessary violence on a person: the officer has marginalized the person because of that person's race. These race-based impetuses (except fear in some cases, although still acting with depraved indifference to human life) increase the likelihood of shooting when you know that you don't have to shoot, but shooting anyway because you know that your actions will be justified.

Many police–black citizen interactions have a connection to racial profiling, since it is the race of the citizen that prompts the officer to confront the citizen in the first place. All of the aforementioned impetuses for deadly force are equally impetuses for why an officer engages in racial profiling.

Whether race was the factor that motivated the officer to behave the way that he/she did is the million-dollar question. As fast as some will argue that race was not a factor, they should, as quickly, consider the possibility that race was involved. Problematic for people of color is the Eurocentric presumption that race could *never* have been the reason why an officer used deadly force. Such denial happens within hours (or a short time thereafter) of the use of deadly force by a white police officer against a person of color. The denial is always based on automatic, unquestionable deference for the authoritative (police) version of what happened—and preconceived notions held about a particular racial group. Additionally, it is "white privilege" that stands in the way of many white people realizing the Afrocentric version of what happened on the "scene." Moreover, where blacks are unwilling to pay automatic deference to an authoritative version, many whites, on the other hand, have no such problem.[15]

Again and again, lay people of color—supported by their own personal experiences, research findings of scholars of color, and expertise in the minority community—show how a police officer's actions were motivated by race. This conclusion is an understanding that all human beings carry sociological baggage. Within that baggage may be stereotypical or adverse perceptions about particular racial groups, for example. The Afrocentric perspective is that many individuals who have in their baggage race-based fear and animus are hired as police officers (to the detriment of visible minorities). This is a deserving indictment, indicative of inadequate recruitment and screening processes of many police departments. These departments have shirked their responsibility to use methods (and there are many) to determine the applicant's mind-set—essentially, to probe what he or she has in his or her sociological baggage concerning race. So, people of color have a right to be offended by a white professor's assertion about the shooting death of a black policeman by his white colleagues: "Even if these officers were both awful racists, it wouldn't matter. [What matters is] whether their conduct was objectively reasonable based on the totality of circumstance" (Breton, 2000, p. 8A).

This typical Eurocentric conclusion influences prosecutorial decisions about police brutality and the likelihood of criminal convictions when cases are prosecuted. It fails to take into account race-based fear and aversion manifested by the officer via recklessness and depraved indifference to human life (both of which are elements of crimes such as second-degree murder). Both the fear and aversion are unreasonable, but the aversion is especially a catalyst for the actions of the officer. The legal test is not whether a reasonable white police officer who has issues about black people would have shot. The test is whether a reasonable police officer in similar circumstances would have shot. But this is the Afrocentric perspective,[16] not the way that the status-quo scholars see things. This is why a white law professor says it should not matter if the officers were awful racists when it should. Although *Scott v. U.S.* (1978) is not a criminal case, the Court's holding gives direction to the thinking needed in assessing race-based police brutality: "Of course, in assessing the credibility of an officer's account of the circumstances that prompted the use of force, a fact finder may consider, along with other factors, evidence that the officer may have harbored ill will toward the citizen" (139, n. 13).

All human beings carry stereotypical notions. In determining an individual's fitness to be a police officer, the following measurements are important: the degree from the norm that his/her stereotypical perceptions extend and or deviate; the manner (reasonable versus unreasonable) in which he/she reacts to his/her sociological baggage; the ability to remain objective in the face of stereotypical perceptions; and the degree of ease with which he or she can dispel stereotypical notions. For critics to say, for example, that both black and white police officers are equally likely to mistake an undercover black officer for a suspect is, unfortunately, true. However, the critics fail miserably when they do not recognize the high likelihood that black officers would not shoot the suspect. The data show that black officers are *not* responsible for friendly fire that has wounded or killed black police officers. Even if it should happen one day, the sheer number of friendly-fire incidents involving white against black is overwhelming. These criteria should call attention to the dynamics of the social interaction between black plain-clothes cops and black uniformed cops as opposed to white–black cop interaction.

Shootings and Lowered Threshold

Is there a "shoot first, ask questions later" policy (a police subcultural norm) that applies when the citizen is black? The evidence certainly supports such a conclusion. One example taken from the vast evidence available is the recorded radio transmissions received by the Christopher Commission (1992) investigating police brutality by the Los Angeles Police Department following the Rodney King riots. One officer says to another: "If you encounter these Negroes shoot first and ask questions later." The commission goes on to say that "officers also used the communications system to express eagerness to be involved in a shooting incident" (pp. 4–5).

Said another way, the issue is whether some police officers dispense with protocol when interacting with people of color. From an Afrocentric perspective, many do. In other words, a white police officer sees a lone black man holding a gun. The man does not know of the officer's presence, hence the man is not threatening the officer. Instead of shouting to the man "police, drop the weapon" (or something to that effect) as protocol would require, the officer commences gunfire. If this sounds unbelievable in the post–*Tennessee v. Garner* (1985) era, there are countless such cases in communities of color. Of course, there is almost always a dispute between police and black citizens and blacks and whites as to whether protocol was ignored.

One such case is the death of Cornel Young, Jr. at the hands of his fellow police officers. It was a cold January night in 2000 when an off-duty Young (required by law to act when he observed a crime) attempted to apprehend a gun-toting suspect outside of a diner in Providence, Rhode Island. As Young was closing in on the suspect, he was shot to death by two white Providence police officers, who said they mistook their colleague for a suspect. Soon after, the two officers would tell a wild story of having instructed their fellow officer to drop his weapon six to seven times, but that he refused.[17]

In controversy are several things, one of which is whether the officers dispensed with protocol. Many black police officers, based on having been the victims of friendly fire (or "friendly" beatings) at the hands of fellow officers, coupled with their knowledge of police subcultural norms that encourage shooting blacks first and then asking questions, believe that the facts of the Young case do not give rise to a dispute.[18] For them, the officers dispensed with protocol. A grand jury in declining to indict the Providence officers held that the officers did not violate protocol. Notwithstanding acknowledgment that the grand jury proceedings were secret, the grand jurors obviously believed the officers when they said that they repeatedly ordered Young to drop his weapon and that Young refused.[19] Further, they accepted an authoritative (police) version that Young placed the officers in a position in which they feared for their lives. The Afrocentric perception is that Young's life was marginalized by the officers. After all, the officer who fired rounds at Young from within approximately fifteen feet had been Young's classmate in the academy. Additionally, the two men had worked together in a unit car for two weeks.[20]

Consider the statements of a white law school professor[21] who was asked about the actions of the two white police officers several days after the shooting. "They were doing their job. If they felt this guy was threatening the other people with a gun, their job is to protect people from the threat of harm" (Mingis, 2000, p. 1A). Unless new evidence emerges, she said, "there's no question in my mind that these officers would not be held liable for anything here" (Breton, 2000, p. 8A). On February 12, 2000, approximately 14 days following Young's death, a Providence Police Department official, Lieutenant Timothy M. Lee, said in a television interview that he believed the two white officers who shot Officer Young would be exonerated. The black community responded, appropriately, with anger. Finally realizing that the statement was presumptuous and racially offensive, the Providence Police Department issued a statement regarding Lee's statement: "The Providence Police Department regrets and specifically disavows any and all statements tending to express an opinion regarding the outcome of this case and is committed to a fair and impartial investigation" (Sabar, 2000, 1A).

People of color find the authoritative (police) version of the Young case suspicious because of many prior similar cases in which the police versions are almost identical. The officers who killed Young asserted the same thing that other white police officers who have killed black police officers (and people in general) have asserted: "I told him to drop the gun and he disobeyed my command." All of the authoritative reports regardless of the venue (from New York City to Los Angeles to Washington, D.C.) read almost identically (Duggan, 1995).

The Afrocentric perspective is that some police officers dispense with use of deadly force protocol via not shouting a command(s) or shouting a command(s) contemporaneously with firing their weapons. The latter is the likely explanation of how a Providence police officer died in a pool of his own blood one cold January night. Why Young died had everything to do with how his colleagues perceived black men (as dangerous) and the amount of policy they felt should be afforded to black men confronted by the police.

Police officers are in numerous situations in which they do not shoot, although the rules of deadly force allow them to shoot. There is evidence that many officers don't use the discretion that is expected of a police officer. Instead, they shoot according to the minimum criteria allowed for use of deadly force, knowing that the shooting will probably be ruled justified. Consider domestic calls-for-service (and the author can speak from considerable experience with such calls when he was a police officer). A cop with more than a month on the street knows that a woman who is abused by her boyfriend, husband, or another male may grab a knife to defend herself from her attacker. Seven out of ten times, she will drop the knife if the officers give her a chance—they don't need to shoot her! But many officers do. Decisions to punish or prosecute police officers usually don't consider that the officer did not have to shoot (McGriff, 1999).

Officers learn very early on in their police tenure that they will be exonerated when they state that their subjective state of mind was that they feared for their lives (or something to that effect). Officers are just as aware (as are civilians) that police officers are seldom if ever prosecuted for police brutality; if they are prosecuted, they are seldom convicted. Officers know that the prosecutor's investigations into use of deadly force rarely second guess what the officer says was his/her state of mind at the time. Even more problematic, officers know that the norms of the police subculture mean that fellow police officers are not supposed to "sell them out" (Reuss-Ianni, 1982). So, some officers, when dealing with people of color, shoot at the mere flicker of a green light from the deadly force policy. In many cases, this is abuse of the furtive gesture rule—a slight harmless movement by a citizen is known to be harmless by the officer, but the officer shoots since he/she knows that he/she can describe the movement as threatening.

This raises the issue of police shootings of black people who were not involved in criminal activity and did not initiate contact with the police. Two recent cases illustrate the concerns of people of color. First, Amadou Diallo was shot and killed February 4, 1999; the police say he refused their commands and then reached for what they say they believed was a gun. From an Afrocentric perspective, it is questionable whether he reached for anything. If he did reach for something, it was his wallet. Of particular importance is the fact that Diallo was approached by the police although he had not committed a crime. The police say that they wanted to ask him questions. A criminologist testified at the trial of the police officers who shot Amadou Diallo that the officers simply made a mistake. Following the trial, several jurors said that they were persuaded by the testimony (see Barry, 2000 and Barry and Waldman, 2000).

Another example was Patrick Dorismond, shot and killed March 16, 2000. He was hailing a taxi on a New York City street when he was approached by an undercover police officer posing as a drug user. The officer asked Dorismond where he could buy marijuana. Dorismond told the officer he could not assist him and continued to look for a taxi. A scuffle ensued when the officer became offended by Dorismond's rebuffing him. The officer's partner, standing nearby, shot Dorismond in the chest at point blank range (Alpert, 2000).

While black people know that many black victims of police gunfire were not criminals or committing a felony, the Eurocentric perspective believes otherwise. As an example, Fyfe (1982) states "there is little to support the contention that Blacks are shot disproportionately in relatively trivial and nonthreatening situations" (p. 190). This denial is contradicted by case after case.

There seems to be an unwritten criminal justice system rule that black victims of police brutality should know the protocol for interacting with the police (e.g., hands placed on the steering wheel; do not reach for anything unless instructed; etc.) This is an offensive and constitutionally invalid requirement. The Afrocentric perspective is that a person of color who does not know the protocol can expect that he or she may be harmed or even killed. Case in point, Latanya Haggerty, killed June 4, 1999, by a Chicago police officer. She was described by the Chicago Office of Corporation Council as causing her own death, because she did not behave as a suspect.[22] Had the unarmed, terrified Haggerty followed the expected protocol of exiting the vehicle when told to do so, she would be alive today.[23]

In an episode of the popular sitcom, *Fresh Prince of Bel-Air*, savvy, street-conscious, African-American Will Smith was visiting his cousin in a posh California community far away from urban Philadelphia. Smith was a passenger in a vehicle pulled over by the police. Without direction from the officer, Smith stepped outside of the automobile and assumed a spread-legged position at the rear of the vehicle. Smith's elitist cousin, Carlton, is baffled and unaware of the motivation for Smith's behavior. Carlton's not recognizing the unwritten rule is similar to Latanya Haggerty's tragic unawareness of the consequences of not responding in the "expected" manner or to Amadou Diallo, if the position is taken that Diallo wanted to show the officers his identification as is customarily done in the country in which he was raised.

There are many situations in which black people follow the unwritten rule and are shot and killed anyway. On Christmas Day 1997 NYPD Officer Michael Davitt, who in fourteen years as a police officer had been involved in approximately eight shootings, shot and killed Michael Whitfield, an unarmed black man. Whitfield ran and hid in a grocery store when he saw police because he was afraid there was a warrant out for his arrest for not having paid child support. He was following police instructions coming out from behind a set of boxes with his arms outstretched when Davitt shot and killed him. Davitt was not terminated by the police department or charged criminally (McFadden, 1997).

In citizen–police interaction, body movements that are accepted from whites are not allowed for blacks. An otherwise harmless body movement by a person of color is suspicious, described as a furtive gesture. Furtive gestures by people of color are what many white officers say caused them to respond with gunfire. In response to learning of a death of a black person over a harm-less gesture, the Eurocentric scholars and many prosecutors shirk their duty by classifying the use of force as a mistake. So, it is a gesture by a black person that warrants suspicion and use of deadly force, but that same movement by a white person invites no similar reaction. Something to consider: the Bronx district attorney who prosecuted the officers who killed Amadou Diallo, Robert Johnson, was black. How likely is it that a white district attorney would have brought charges against the officers?

For those cases of police brutality against black victims that make it to trial, stereotypical perceptions of minorities lead fact finders to blame the police brutality on the victim. Both Rodney King and Amadou Diallo, for example, were misrepresented as superhuman. King was said to have resisted with unbelievable strength; therefore, it was argued, the force was commensurate. Diallo was said to have contributed to his death by his body movements. Further, the defense characterized Diallo as remaining standing after a volley of bullets, so forty-one bullets were said to have been needed to "bring him down" and to protect the police and the "public." These xenophobic characterizations are often followed by problematic instructions to juries by the judge—problematic since they are riddled with victim-blaming suppositions. What should be judged a crime is reduced to a mistake or "terrible" happening. Avoidable, says the judicial system, had the victim not contorted his body, had not been recalcitrant, and had submitted to the police inquiry without questioning authority.

Investigations of Police

In the twenty-first century, police officers who patrol in a racially discriminatory manner have learned to conceal racial epithets. Police officers are cognizant of their speech because of the consequences of revealing racist attitudes; they know that epithets satisfy the elements of a hate crime. It is therefore difficult (but not impossible) for investigators and prosecutors to show that the officer engaged in behavior because of a racial aversion, for example.

Problematic is that even if the officers' actions were prompted by the race of the citizens, investigations into use of deadly force seldom if ever explore for race-based phenomena. Typically, investigations into use of deadly force by police involve a forensics analysis (e.g., ballistics) and eliciting the subjective state of mind of the officer at the time of the situation, according to the officer him/herself. What the officer declares was his or her subjective state of mind is almost always accepted without further inquiry. This is the principal problem. In every case, the officer will state, "I feared for my life" or something to that effect. Sadly, it is the script learned in the police academy (the author also learned it when he began police work but, like some other officers, rejected it as a universal). In some cases, the officer is being truthful, but in others the officer is to be doubted. But we won't find out if we don't fully investigate the officer's sociological baggage.

From an Afrocentric perspective, consideration must be given to the role that the norms of the police subculture play in a use of deadly force situation. A firm, conceptual understanding of the police literature and police subculture can offer a great deal of insight as to what happened on a scene. Both enable an investigator to ask the right questions and to know when to be suspicious of the answers.

Although the policing literature has its biases and problems as noted throughout this article, the policing literature has documented a great deal about the way that day-to-day police duties are performed and why particular actions occur (e.g., see Reuss-Ianni, 1982). Specifically, the literature has documented the inner workings of the police subculture. Take, for instance, the subcultural norm that "if you run from the poe-lice you get fucked-up."[24] (The videotaped beating of Thomas Jones by Philadelphia police in July 2000 is a vivid example of this phenomenon.[25]) When an investigator and/or prosecutor is faced with a case in which the victim/defendant says that a police officer kicked him in the face as he lay prone on the ground or that he ran out of fear after he saw a police car, the investigator or prosecutor should possess a willingness to investigate further. Police officers learn early in their career that people who run from the police are to be abused. To accept at face value the officer's account that the victim is lying, in the face of overwhelming documentation that there is a subcultural norm that calls for "street justice" when you run from the police, is to commit a more serious injustice and to demonstrate utter indifference coupled with ignorance of pragmatic reality. Even United States Supreme Court justices, in *Illinois v. Wardlow*,[26] acknowledge that minorities often run from the police—not because they committed a crime but because they have credible reasons to fear an encounter with police.

Cops talk with each other about how they take the legal use of force right to the edge. As a cop you learn how to create situations that are legally indecipherable (see Crank, 1998, p. 65), such as intentionally placing yourself in front of an automobile so a fear of loss-of-life claim can be made. For investigators and prosecutors to get a clear sense of what happened at scenes where an officer said that the victim tried to run him or her over, they need to consider this phenomenon.[27] It is a pattern that an investigator will recognize if he/she looks at similar cases and examines police subcultural norms. Having discovered the pattern, he/she can see if the code dictated when and in what manner force was likely employed in the situation under investigation. No doubt, no two scenes are alike; however, pattern and practice (based on past scenes) suggest what questions to ask and what suspicions to maintain.

Other subcultural norms include "dead men tell no tales." Once you have shot and wounded a man, you are supposed "to put a cap in him"—otherwise he will sue you or file a complaint against you (the officer) littered with falsities. This norm is relevant to an investigator's toolbox, since a common problem with prosecuting police officers for "bad shootings" is that of being able to rebut effectively the officer's explanation as to why he or she shot a person. In this regard, the police subculture has a script already prepared to handle bad shootings. It includes, first and foremost, asserting that you feared for your life or something to that effect. It is followed by one of these primary assertions: (1) he tried to run me over with his car; (2) he pointed a gun at me; (3) he lunged at me with a knife. There is a cartoon that is passed out in police locker rooms that is referred to as the "Police Shooting Report Checklist," which includes the aforementioned choices.

Consider perhaps the most popular script and falsity: "he tried to run me over." In December 1998, a Pittsburgh police officer was arrested and charged with the murder of Deon Grimmitt, an unarmed black male. The officer, who was alleged to belong to a white supremacist group, became upset when Mr. Grimmitt slowed down his vehicle to observe the police making an arrest. The officer asserted that he wanted to question Grimmitt about his interest and that when he approached the automobile, Grimmitt tried to run him over. The autopsy revealed that Grimmitt had been shot in the head through a side window. Even with this information, the officer was acquitted at trial. In 1999 Louisville police shot Rudolph Desmond, an African American, as he sat inside an incapacitated automobile. Yet, the officers, who were white, said Desmond attempted to run them over. In Saint Louis in June 2000, two white police officers approached two black men in a vehicle. The officers shot and killed both men and claimed that the victims tried to run them over. In July 2000, a white Omaha police officer shot and killed George Bibbins, an unarmed black man who took police on an eight-minute car chase. Bibbins was shot as he sat inside the vehicle after it crashed into a telephone pole.

These cases are just the tip of the iceberg of an epidemic of officers shooting—not because they are justified, but because they know they can most likely get away with it. In the Louisville case, some law enforcement personnel publicly expressed doubt about the officers' claims.[28] In the Omaha case, the police chief, who is white, stated publicly that he couldn't pinpoint a reason why the officer shot George Bibbins. The chief stated, "As we indicated, there are concerns about what happened. We can't put our finger on the justification."

The fact that "he tried to run me over" claims sometimes make it to a grand jury is not much solace to communities of color. Many prosecutors act as gatekeepers to protect officers from prosecution for police brutality. They intentionally present facts to grand juries in such a way that the grand jurors will find that the officers acted properly. In other words, the rash of grand jury declinations to indict in police brutality cases in the United States where the officers are white and the victims are black or Latino is indicative of many prosecutors who "throw the fight."

It is not by accident or simply the result of rehearsal that the testimony of the officers indicted for killing Amadou Diallo was virtually identical (whether you believe that the officers acted properly or improperly in the shooting). *New York Times* reporters Dan Barry and Amy Waldman (2000) wrote "prosecutors have . . . encountered a blue wall . . . [in] which officers used almost identical language to defend their actions" (p. B1). Familiarity with the subculture socialization process should alert the investigator not just to what the defendant officer will say at trial but also to what really happened at the scene. The Code provides trial preparation long before any action takes place. Because many prosecutors know little to nothing about the premeditation for police brutality that the police subculture provides, they are not aware of the need to be suspicious. There are prosecutors who do know about and accept the premeditation perversion, yet do nothing, while others refuse to believe that it exists. The result is unchecked, egregious human rights violations.

Stakeholders Excluded

There is no other racial group in the United States that has been policed as long as and as much as people of African descent (cf., Dulaney 1996). Initially, it was the phenomenon of organized policing to maintain slavery. Over time, it became policing of black people and those classes considered unpopular for the benefit of the upper-middle, wealthy, and elite classes (Niederhoffer, 1969; Fogelson, 1981). It has always been the contention of the wealthy that the police may use whatever means necessary to keep the unpopular classes from interrupting the "flow" of their quality of life. This explains how a bombing of a church by the Ku Klux Klan in 1968 in which four children were killed ("Six Dead . . . ," 1963) did not shock many Americans who were not of color. Or that a California sheriff's deputy, Jeffrey Coates, in 1999 candidly told a journalist that he has one traffic-stop protocol for whites and another for black and Latino males. He says that he orders black or Latino males out of their automobiles and has them place their hands on the roof of the police cruiser; however, whites receive the mainstream treatment, no need to exit the automobile or stand hunched over. Even worse, the deputy killed a black man in 1998, admits to racial profiling, and like other officers in his unit, wears a "Grim Reaper" tattoo on his ankle—this is the insignia worn by white police officers signifying membership in a white supremacist gang (Goldberg, 1999). The fact that Coates is still employed by the Los Angeles Sheriff's Department is appalling to black and Latino people, but apparently to few white people.

The lack of concern expressed by whites about illegal and brutal policing practices in black communities has meant that the burden of raising awareness and pushing for change (justice) has been undertaken almost entirely by black police organizations, black elected officials, and scholars who are people of color.[29] Racial profiling, for example, now has a national forum not because of efforts by white policy researchers or police department self-analysis, but because of efforts by people of color themselves. This fact contributes to why black people are unavoidably connected to just about every facet of U.S. policing, both internal and external. One would think and expect that black people would have a role in the creation and implementation of police policy. Yet, black people are routinely excluded from discussion about these matters by: (1) white scholars, (2) media outlets, and (3) government.

The status-quo scholars hold themselves out to the media and policy makers as authorities on what is best for policing black communities. It is not uncommon to see a talk-show panel of all white people talking about police–black community relations on the heels of a violent encounter between a white police officer and a black citizen. In some cases, under pressure, the media will concede and invite a black panelist. Unfortunately, they often invite a black panelist who is an authority on certain subject matter but not necessarily on that which is the focus of the news television program. This discredits Afrocentric concerns and positions. For example, black clergy are experts who rightfully and often spearhead battles for social justice. However, it is disingenuous to include them with a white police scholar (Ph.D.) on a program about policing phenomena from a scientific or research perspective. By all appearances, it is media that are either indifferent (because of "racial privilege") or maliciously trying to portray an image of black "position/perspective" ineptness. If a person were to step off of a spaceship, never having been to earth, on the heels of a violent encounter between a white police officer and a black person, that alien would never know that there is one black Ph.D. or expert in this country, since typically the guests (experts) selected by the media are almost always white.[30]

Scholars of color are often excluded by their status-quo colleagues in discourse (e.g., debates, studies, dialogue) concerning police tragedies involving black victims. Consider that status-quo scholars are often given the authority and responsibility to form the commissions, and other investigatory or oversight bodies, that are concerned with policing phenomena. They decide who is appointed and who is not appointed or who will be appointed as a consultant and who will not. In some cases, commission appointments are not the responsibility of the status-quo scholars, but their influence is felt. Not surprisingly then, commissions and committees established to investigate poor community relations between black residents and the police (e.g., the Christopher Commission) are almost always headed by whites and comprised of whites. The Select Commission on Race and Police-Community Relations in Providence, established in 2000 on the heels of Cornel Young's death, is among the few commissions truly representative of all the people affected by an issue.[31]

Many white scholars deserve criticism because they do not take responsibility for calling media attention to the lack of racial diversity on a panel, for example. Status-quo reluctance to advocate for inclusion is most evident in the refusal to acknowledge how privilege[32] has enabled status-quo scholars to be the focus of the media or government in the establishment of a commission. They refuse to alert the media and policy makers to the need for black voices in talking about policing phenomena affecting black people.

Publishing also deserves criticism. This is evident by a vast amount of published work on policing black communities, little of which is written by black people. Publishing companies appear to be indifferent to the need for publications written by blacks on the subject of policing.

Conclusion

When talking about policing in the United States, there are two very different audiences. What white citizens find implausible or hard to believe is everyday experience for black people. Hence, it was no surprise to black people to learn in 1992 that a New Orleans Police officer had a mother of two murdered because she filed a complaint against him for police brutality. Fortunately, the officer's telephone call to the "hit man" was tape-recorded by federal law enforcement officers who were investigating the officer pursuant to another matter (Nossiter, 1994). Without incontrovertible evidence (the tape recording), the tendency to believe officer denials might well have allowed him to escape punishment. The officer is presently awaiting execution for the murder.

It is the personal and collective experiences of black people with police officers and other people of color that enables these minorities to understand without the aid of videotaped footage, or knowledge of a victim's feces on a broken broomstick (the Louima case), or hearing a tape-recorded call to a hit man that a law enforcement officer committed an inhumane act of brutality. Few visible minorities in the United States can speak of not having experienced nor having been an eyewitness to a police action that many white people would claim the police would never do.

Consider the outlandishness of blanket statements by some police administrators that their officers don't engage in racial profiling or that their officers would never behave in a racially discriminatory manner. These statements are made by people who do not spend eight hours a day riding around with their police officers, yet they make assertions that suggest that they know their officers' every move. It was refreshing to people of color when two New Jersey state troopers explained how they regularly engaged in racial profiling. Governor Christine Todd Whitman was left with no choice but to acknowledge the Afrocentric perspective. She retracted her statements that racial profiling didn't happen in New Jersey.[33]

The reality is that policing is just one microcosm in the scheme of life. In life there is racism. Some of those who choose to manifest their biases are police officers. It is not so far-fetched that a police officer would shoot and kill a man simply because the man is a person of color. From an Afrocentric perspective, there is more than enough reason in twenty-first-century United States for status-quo scholars to refrain from giving automatic deference to authoritative versions of encounters between black people and the police. For the Eurocentric/status-quo scholar not to consider seriously that the system may have erred greatly in hiring an officer who acted out of racial animus is to display the highest level of "white privilege" and ignorance.

NOTES

[1] cf. Dulaney, 1996.

[2] Fogelson, a historian rather than a police sociologist, presents an Afrocentric perspective. He says of race riots that gripped the nation in the 1960s, ". . . some of the blue-ribbon commissions appointed to look into the disorders issued reports that placed much of the blame on the local police" (Fogelson, 1977, p. 240).

[3] While Niederhoffer can be categorized as friendly to people of color by his exposition of police work phenomena, there are times when his opinions show otherwise.

[4] The article is reprinted in this volume, article 20.

[5] Article 21 in this collection.

[6] Van Slyke and Gordo. 1999. The Web site is www.PONetwork.com.

[7] Serrano, 1991; Tobar and Connell, 1991.

[8] See Marriott, 1995. Marriott writes, "Mark Fuhrman has expressed his racial hatred so bluntly that he may become a foil for the racism of others."

[9] Reasons include that policy makers who commissioned the research do not want to know the extent of police brutality.

[10] cf. Troutt, 1999; Prial, 1987.

[11] Chevigny's 1969 findings that many officers will legitimatize their actions in police reports via reporting falsely are still timely. He called attention to the practice of catchall offenses (e.g., resisting arrest and disorderly conduct) for which citizens are charged following having been brutalized. This author (Cooper) learned early on in his police tenure that officers who brutalized people were supposed to find something to charge them with in order to justify the beating. Often that charge was disorderly conduct.

[12] Defined as only a few aberrant police officers who engage in police brutality.

[13] See Kappeler, et al., 1998, pp. 272–275 for a discussion of this case.

[14] cf. Sontag and Barry, 1997.

[15] See June 17, 1999, Quinnipiac College Polling Institute Poll, which found that whites and minorities are sharply divided in their views of police brutality.

[16] and, the perspective of other people of color.

[17] See Marion Davis, 2000; Rockoff, 2000, "Officer."

[18] See Rockoff, 2000, "Grand jury."

[19] Since normally a prosecutor can get a grand jury to do whatever he or she wants it to do, one can safely assume that the prosecutor(s) in the Young case did not desire that the officers be indicted.

[20] See Rockoff, 2000, "How it all happened."

[21] Why Karen Blum was interviewed is puzzling, since she has never been a police officer and she is not a police scholar.

[22] See Lithty and Wilson, 1999; Lithty, 1999.

[23] The shooter of Haggerty was a black female officer. This tragedy has no indications that it was connected to race-based fear, animus, or marginalization, rather, the perception by the officer that Haggerty should have known "how the game is played," because she was black.

[24] As a rookie, the author remembers having to witness these violent attacks. These were vicious attacks that were almost always followed by a false arrest for disorderly conduct. It wasn't long before I started pulling officers off of people.

[25] See Cooper, 2000. Recall that the police said that Jones fled from officers and shot an officer. It turned out that Jones fled, but he did not shoot an officer, rather an officer shot another officer in the hand.

[26] *Illinois v. Wardlow*: No. 98–1036 (full opinion not yet in print); see dissent opinion by Justice Breyer.

[27] See McGriff (1999) for a report on the *Hood* case in which the Philadelphia P.D. said that its officer had lied.

[28] See Zambroski, et al., 2000. In this case, the nine-page police investigation noted numerous instances in which the officers who killed Rudolph committed tactical errors. When asked if the shooting could have been avoided, the lead investigator said, "One could come to that conclusion." A grand jury was convened and voted along racial lines. Since there were fewer blacks than whites, the grand jury voted not to indict. Even with the incriminating report, the officers were given medals of valor for shooting Rudolph.

[29] E.g., The National Black Police Association (NBPA) advocates for black police officers and represents the interests of the black community with regard to policing issues.

[30] The media must take some blame, for it is not uncommon for them to seek out white expertise when they know of qualified black people. The author is reminded of hearing so many times from the media that they didn't know where to find an African American to participate in the panel discussion.

[31] See Karen Davis, 2000, p. A1.

[32] That of being Caucasian or Caucasian in appearance for others.

[33] See Peterson, 1999; Peterson writes: "Gov. Christine Todd Whitman and her Attorney General conceded today for the first time that some state troopers singled out black and Hispanic drivers on the highway" (p. 1A).

REFERENCES

Alex, N. (1976). *New York cops talk back: A study of a beleaguered minority.* New York: John Wiley & Sons.

Alpert, L. I. (2000, March 25). Funeral of Patrick Dorismond ends in violence. *Associated Press.*

Barry, D. (2000, February 27). Diallo Legacy: Myriad Questions About Tactics for Policing Streets. *New York Times*, p. A1.

Barry, D., & Waldman, A. (2000, February 22). Erecting a blue wall of silence. *New York Times*, p. B1.

Breton, T. (2000, February 8). Experts: Criminal charges against officers unlikely. *Providence Journal*, p. 8A.

Brown, M. (1981). Working the street: Police discretion and the dilemmas of reform. New York: Russell Sage Foundation.

Carte, G. E., & Carte, E. H. (1975). *Police reform in the United States: The era of August Vollmer, 1905–1932.* Berkeley: University of California Press.

Chandler, G. F. (1974). *The policeman's art as taught in the New York State School for Police.* New York: AMS Press.

Chevigny, P. (1969). *Police power: Police abuses in New York City.* New York: Vintage.

Cohen, A. (2000, March 6). Gangsta cops: As the LAPD scandal keeps growing, a city asks itself, how could the police have gone so bad? *Time Magazine*, pp. 30–34.

Cooper, C. (2000, July 21). Entrenched subculture is at root of police brutality and bias cases. *Philadelphia Inquirer*, p. A27.

Cooper, C. (1995, October 6). The O. J. Simpson trial and rotten apples: Academics are to blame for the neglect of police racism unmasked by the O. J. Simpson trial. *Times Higher Education Supplement* (London), p. 12.

Cooper, J. L. (1980). *The police and the ghetto.* Port Washington, NY: Kennikat Press.

Crank, J. P. (1998). *Understanding police culture.* Cincinnati: Anderson Publishing.

Christopher Commission. (1992, July). *Report of the Independent Commission on the Los Angeles Police Department.* City of Los Angeles.

Davis, K. A. (2000, May 4). Board chosen to explore police-minority relations: Almond picks URI scholar to lead panel. *Providence Journal,* p. A1.

Davis, M. (2000, January 30). Friendly fire victims haunt fellow police. *Providence Journal,* p. A1.

Duggan, P. (1995, February 14). Praise and tears for officer slain in the line of duty: DC leaders laud dedication of policeman shot by colleague. *Washington Post,* p. E1.

Dulaney, M. (1996). *Black police in America.* Bloomington: Indiana University Press.

Fogelson, R. M. (1977). *Big-city police.* Cambridge, MA and London, England: Harvard University Press.

Fyfe, J. J., ed. (1982). *Readings on police use of deadly force.* Washington, DC: Police Foundation.

Fyfe, J. J. (1995). "Training to Reduce Police-Civilian Violence." In *And justice for all: Understanding and controlling police abuse of force.* William Geller and Hans Toch, (Eds.), Washington, DC: Police Executive Research Forum.

Goldberg, J. (1999, June 20). The color of suspicion. *New York Times Magazine,* 51–57, 64–65, 85–86.

Kappeler, V. E., Slader, R. D., & Alpert, Geoffrey P. (1998). *Forces of deviance,* 2d ed. Long Grove, IL: Waveland Press.

Kelling, G. L. (1997/1999). Efforts to reduce police brutality should not interfere with effective crime control. In T. L. Roleff (Ed.), *Police brutality* (pp. 48–51). San Diego: Greenhaven Press.

The Knapp Commission report on police corruption. (1973). New York: George Braziller.

Lane, R. (1967). *Policing the city: Boston 1822–1905.* Cambridge: Harvard University Press.

Lithty, T. (1999, September 2). City plays both sides in killing by officer. *Chicago Tribune,* p. 1.

Lithty, T., & Wilson, T. (1999, July 13). Cop chief moves to fire 4. *Chicago Tribune,* p. 1.

Marriott, M. (1995, September 3). Race lies & audiotape. *New York Times,* p. D4.

McFadden, R. (1997, December 27). After man is slain by officer, anger and calls for patience. *New York Times,* p. B1.

McGriff, M. (1999, May 28). Officer on patrol awaiting disciplinary hearing. *Philadelphia Tribune,* p. 3A.

McNamara, J.D. (1982, May 2). Dangerous nostalgia for the cop on the beat. *San Jose Mercury News.*

Mingis, K. (2000, January 28). Off-duty Providence police officer shot, killed by 2 other officers. *Providence Journal,* p. 1A.

Monkkonen, E. H. (1981). *Police in urban America 1860–1920.* Cambridge: Cambridge University Press.

Moore, M. H., & Kelling, G. L. (1983). To serve and protect: Learning from police history: *The public interest,* 70, 49–65.

Murr, A., (2000, June 12). "A murder in the family," *Newsweek,* p. 64.

Niederhoffer, A. (1969). *Behind the shield: The police in urban society.* Garden City, NY: Doubleday.

Nyden, P., Figert, A., Shibley, M., and Burrows, D. (1997). *Building community: Social science in action.* Thousand Oaks, CA: Pine Forge.

Nossiter, A. (1994, December 19). Officer linked to killing shocking a jaded city. *New York Times,* p. A14.

Olmsted, F. L. (1860). *A journey in the back country.* New York: Mason Brothers.

Peterson, I. (1999, April 21). Whitman says troopers used racial profiling. *New York Times*, p. 1A.

Prial, F. (1987, February 27). Judge acquits Sullivan in shotgun slaying of Bumpurs. *New York Times*, p. B1.

Quinnipiac College Polling Institute Poll. (1999, June). Hampden, CT: Quinnipiac College.

Reuss-Ianni, E. (1982). *Two cultures of policing*. Englewood Cliffs, NJ: Transaction.

Rockoff, J. (2000, April 19). Grand jury clears officers in Young's shooting death. *Providence Journal*, p. 1A.

Rockoff, J. (2000, February 3). How it all happened: A diner fight escalates, an officer is killed. *Providence Journal*, p. 1A.

Rockoff, J. (2000, January 29). Officer involved in peer's death had shot and wounded before. *Providence Journal*, p. 1A.

Sabar, A. (2000, February 12) The death of Sergeant Cornel Young, Jr.; The protest continues: Young's father joins call for outside probe. *Providence Journal*, p. 1A.

Serrano, R. A. (1991, July 10). Chief refuses to step down, defends police. *Los Angeles Times*, p. A1.

Sontag, D., & Barry, D. (1997, September 17). Using settlements to gauge police abuse: The price of brutality. *New York Times*, p. A1.

Sparrow, M., Moore, M. H., & Kennedy, D. M. (1990). *Beyond 911: A new era for policing*. New York: Basic Books.

Stoddard, E. R. (1968). The informal "code" of police deviancy: A group approach to "blue-coat crime." *The Journal of Criminal Law, Criminology and Police Science, 59*(2), 201–213.

Tobar, H., & Connell, R. (1991, July 10). Gates defends police at fiery council meeting; Violence: Commission gets briefing on charter provisions that could be used to discipline the chief. *Los Angeles Times*, p. A1.

Troutt, D. D. (1999). Screws, koon, and routine aberrations: The use of fictional narratives in federal police brutality prosecutions. *New York University Law Review, 74*, 18–122.

Six dead after church bombing: Blast kills four children; riots follow; two youths slain; state reinforces Birmingham police. (1963, September 16). *United Press International*.

Van Slyke, T., & Gordo, D. (1999, September). Controversial Web site vents Cops' fears, anger. *Chicago Reporter*, pp. 3,4.

Wade, R. (1964). *Slavery in the cities: The south, 1820–1860*. New York: Oxford University Press.

Walker, S. (1984). "Broken windows" and fractured history: The use and misuse of history in recent patrol analysis. *Justice Quarterly, 1*, 57–90.

Wilson, J. Q., & Kelling, G. L. (1982, March). The police and neighborhood safety: Broken windows. *Atlantic Monthly, 249*(3), 29–38.

Zambroski, J., Shafer, S. S., & Tangonan, S. (2000, March 3). Louisville police chief fired. *The Courier Journal*, p. 1.

Cases

Scott v. U.S. 436 U.S. 128 (1978)
Tennessee v. Garner 471 U.S. 1 (1985)
Illinois v. Wardlow 528 U.S. 119 (2000)

19

Women in Law Enforcement, 1987–2008

Lynn Langton

During the 1990s and 2000s, the percent of sworn law enforcement officers who were women increased only slightly in federal, state, and local agencies.

By 2007 nearly 4,000 state police, 19,400 sheriffs', and 55,300 local police officers were women.[1] In 2008, across 62 reporting federal law enforcement agencies there were about 90,000 sworn officers, of whom approximately 18,200 (20%) were women.[2] These 2007 and 2008 numbers suggest a combined total of almost 100,000 female sworn officers nationwide in federal, state, and local law enforcement agencies.

Using data primarily from the Bureau of Justice Statistics' Census of Federal Law Enforcement Officers (FLEO) and the Law Enforcement Management and Administrative Statistics (LEMAS) series, this report examines the current state of and trends in the employment of female sworn officers in federal, state, and local law enforcement agencies.

Of all the federal law enforcement agencies with sworn officers, the Offices of Inspectors General had the largest percent of female officers (25%) (figure 1). Among other agencies, those with more than 500 sworn officers employed more than double the percent of officers who were women (21%), compared to both medium-sized (9%) and small (10%) agencies. The Federal Bureau of Investigation (19% women), Federal Bureau of Prisons (14% women), and the Administrative Office of the U.S. Courts (46% women) (not shown) were the largest employers of female officers. These three agencies each employed more than 2,000 female officers.

Due to the reorganization of several large federal law enforcement agencies after the September 11, 2001 terrorist attacks and inconsistencies among some agencies in the reporting of data on the sex of officers, the trend analy-

Bureau of Justice Statistics. Crime Data Brief, June 2010, NCJ 230521. http://www.bjs.gov/index.cfm?ty=pbdetail&iid=2274

Percent of officers who are women

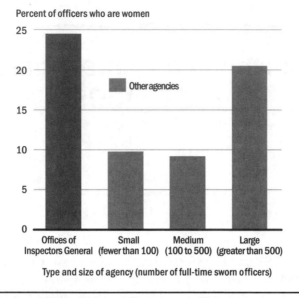

Figure 1   Percent of federal law enforcement officers who are women, by type and size of agency, 2008

sis was limited to 53 agencies that were consistently organized and had data available on the sex of officers from 1998 to 2008. Among these common reporting agencies, there was relative stability in the percent of female sworn officers. Over the 10-year period, the percent of officers who were women increased slightly from 14.0% in 1998 to 15.2% in 2008 (figure 2).

Among federal law enforcement agencies employing more than 500 full-time sworn officers and reporting data on the sex of officers in both 1998 and 2008, women accounted for approximately 16% of the total sworn force (not shown). From 1998 to 2008, the U.S. Postal Inspection Service (USPIS) and the Internal Revenue Service (IRS) had the greatest increase in the percent of law enforcement officers who were women (7%) (table 1). In 2008 the USPIS employed just over 500 (22%) women out of about 2,300 total officers. The agency employed nearly the same number of female officers in 2008 as in 1998, but employed about 1,200 fewer law enforcement officers overall in 2008.

The U.S. Forest Service, U.S. Fish and Wildlife Service, and the Veterans Health Administration (VHA) each experienced slight declines in the percent of women in law enforcement positions. The percent of female officers among Forest Service law enforcement officers decreased marginally from 16.1% in 1998 to 15.9% in 2008. The total number of Forest Service officers who were women increased slightly, from 97 to 103. Both the overall size of and the number of female law enforcement officers employed by the Fish and Wildlife Service decreased during the 10-year period, from 84 female officers out of 836 officers total in 1998 to 50 female officers out of 565 total in 2008.

Percent of officers who are women*

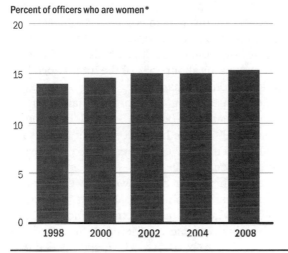

Note: Data obtained from the BJS Census of Federal Law Enforcement Officers.

*Includes the 53 federal agencies that were consistently organized and consistently reported data on the sex of officers from 1998 to 2008.

Figure 2   Percent of federal law enforcement officers who are women, 1998–2008

Table 1   Percent and number of full-time sworn officers who are women, by federal law enforcement agencies employing 500 or more full-time officers, 1998 and 2008

	Percent		Number	
Agency	1998	2008	1998	2008
Internal Revenue Service, Criminal Investigation	25%	32%	848	835
U.S. Postal Inspection Service	15	22	513	516
Federal Bureau of Investigation	16	19	1,816	2,428
National Park Service - Ranger Division	15	19	230	263
U.S. Capitol Police	18	19	189	303
U.S. Forest Service	16	16	97	103
Federal Bureau of Prisons	12	14	1,545	2,304
National Park Service - U.S. Park Police	9	13	62	72
Bureau of Alcohol, Tobacco, Firearms & Explosives	12	13	211	333
Bureau of Diplomatic Security	8	11	33	113
Drug Enforcement Administration	8	10	261	421
U.S. Fish and Wildlife Service	10	9	84	50
Veterans Health Administration	9	8	24	248

Note: Does not include U.S. Customs and Border Protection and U.S. Immigration and Customs Enforcement because these did not exist in 1998. U.S. Marshals Service and U.S. Secret Service did not provide 2008 data on the sex of officers, and the Administrative Office of the U.S. Courts and Pentagon Force Protection Agency did not provide 1998 data on the sex of officers; these four agencies are also excluded from the table.

From 1998 to 2008, the VHA police force grew substantially, from 262 to 3,175 sworn officers. Although the percent of female officers in the VHA declined from 9% to 8% over the 10-year period, the number of sworn officers who were women increased by more than 200, from 24 to 248 female officers.

In 2007 women accounted for about 15% of the total sworn law enforcement officers in large local police departments (figure 3). In large sheriffs' offices, female officers comprised about 13% of the total sworn officers. In contrast, local police departments with between 1 and 10 full-time sworn officers employed fewer than 2,000 female law enforcement officers nationwide (6%). Small sheriffs' offices across the county employed just over 200 total sworn officers who were women (4%) in 2007.

From 1987 to 2007 trends in the percent of sworn law enforcement officers who were women varied among state police departments, local police departments, and sheriffs' offices. The percent of female officers in local police departments increased steadily over the two decades, from 7.6% in 1987 to nearly 12% in 2007 (figure 4). From 1987 to 2007, state police departments also increased the percent of sworn officers who were women, but at a slower rate than the local police departments. In 2007, 6.5% of state police officers were women, compared to 3.8% in 1987. While the percent of female officers was higher in 2007 than in 1987, state police departments did experience a slight decline in the percent of female officers from 2003 (6.7%) to 2007 (6.5%).

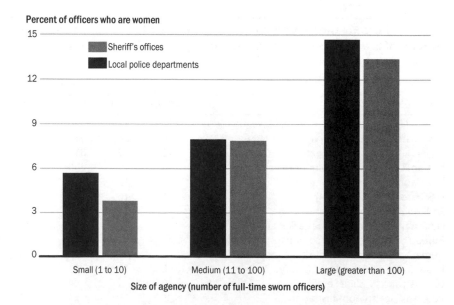

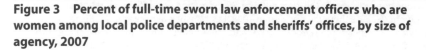

Figure 3   Percent of full-time sworn law enforcement officers who are women among local police departments and sheriffs' offices, by size of agency, 2007

Percent of officers who are women

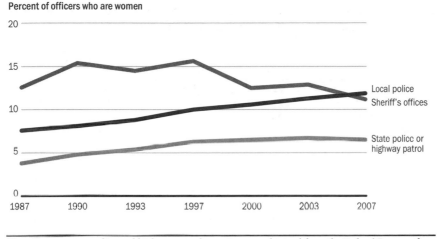

Note: Data on state police and highway patrol agencies were obtained from the Federal Bureau of Investigation's Uniform Crime Reports. Data on local police departments and sheriffs' offices were obtained from the BJS Law Enforcement Management and Administrative Statistics (LEMAS) series.

Figure 4   Percent of full-time sworn law enforcement officers who are women among state and local law enforcement agencies, 1987–2007

After reaching a high of 15.6% female officers in 1997, the percent of sheriffs' officers who were women declined to 11.2% in 2007. The 2007 survey excluded sheriffs' offices that did not perform law enforcement functions. The decline in female officers may be due in part to this exclusion.

In 2007, women accounted for an average of 18% of the officers among local police departments with 2,000 or more sworn personnel. The Detroit Police Department had the highest percent of female officers (27%) among the largest police departments (table 2).

From 1997 to 2007, 12 of the 13 largest police departments that reported data on the sex of officers had increases in the percent of sworn officers who were women. The Detroit Police Department had the largest increase in the percent of female officers, from 22% in 1997 to 27% in 2007. Because the Detroit Police Department decreased in size by over 1,000 sworn officers overall from 1997 to 2007, the number of female officers actually declined by approximately 50 officers.

The District of Columbia Metropolitan Police Department had a 2% decline in the percent of officers who were women, though the number of female officers in the department increased by 12 officers from 1997 to 2007.

Methodology

Data on local police departments and sheriffs' offices were compiled from the BJS Law Enforcement Management and Administrative Statistics

Table 2   Percent and number of full-time sworn officers who are women among the largest police departments, 1997 and 2007

Agency	Percent		Number	
	1997	2007	1997	2007
Detroit	22%	27%	880	829
Philadelphia	22	25	1,461	1,666
District of Columbia	25	23	904	916
Chicago	19	23	2,549	3,097
Memphis	17	19	250	386
New York City	15	17	5,743	6,151
Dallas	16	17	444	527
San Francisco	15	16	303	378
Baltimore	14	16	432	485
Boston	13	14	275	293
Houston	12	13	637	656
Las Vegas Metro*	8	9	113	219

Note: Data obtained from the BJS 1997 and 2007 Law Enforcement Management and Administrative Statistics (LEMAS) surveys. Includes police departments with 2,000 or more sworn officers in 2007. Phoenix police department did not provide a distribution of officers by sex and was excluded.

*Las Vegas Metro numbers do not include correctional officers.

(LEMAS) survey. LEMAS collects data from all state and local agencies with 100 or more sworn officers and a nationally representative sample of smaller agencies. Agencies that did not primarily perform law enforcement functions were excluded in 2007. For local police in 2007, the 95% confidence interval around the number of officers was between 51,600 and 59,000 and around the percent of female officers was between 11.1% and 12.7%. Among the agencies that responded to LEMAS in 2007, over 99% of local police and 98% of sheriffs' offices provided data on the sex of officers. See Local Police Departments, 2003 (http//bjs.ojp.usdoj.gov/content/pub/ pdf/lpd03.pdf) and Sheriffs' Offices, 2003 (http://bjs.ojp.usdoj.gov/content/pub/pdf/so03.pdf) for more information on the LEMAS survey. Data on state police agencies were compiled from the Federal Bureau of Investigation's Crime in the United States series (http://www.fbi.gov/ucr/ucr.htm).

Data on federal agencies with full-time sworn law enforcement officers were compiled from the BJS Census of Federal Law Enforcement Officers (FLEO). In 2008, FLEO data were collected from 62 of 67 federal agencies. The U.S. Supreme Court, Environmental Protection Agency, Agency for International Development, Bureau of Industry and Security, and U.S. Immigration and Customs Enforcement did not provide 2008 data on the number and sex of law enforcement officers. The sex of officers in the U.S. Secret Service and U.S. Marshals Service was estimated using the ratio of male to female officers from 2004, applied to the total number of officers in 2008. See http//www.ojp.usdoj.gov/bjs/pubalp2.htm#fleo for more information on the FLEO survey methodology.

ENDNOTES

[1] Data for sheriffs' offices and local police departments are estimated from a nationally representative sample.

[2] Data available for 62 of 67 federal law enforcement agencies. In 2004, four of the five missing agencies reported an estimated 11,000 sworn officers of whom approximately 1,500 were women.

20

Gender and Police Stress
The Convergent and Divergent Impact of Work Environment, Work-Family Conflict, and Stress Coping Mechanisms of Female and Male Police Officers

Ni He, Jihong Zhao, & Carol A. Archbold

Introduction

Police work is often considered to be a highly stressful occupation. Not only are police officers frequently exposed to the most violent, antisocial, and mistrustful elements of society, they are also expected to exercise discretion under critical circumstances (Crank and Caldero, 1991; Violanti and Aron, 1994). Researchers have long argued that police officers' job performance can be affected deleteriously, when officers experience chronic stress (McGreedy, 1974; Goodman, 1990). However, most of the early research fails to examine the differences of the impact of stress among both male and female police officers. Early police stress studies focus primarily on male police officers.

Observations and subsequent policy implications derived from police stress research based solely on male police officers may not be applicable to female police officers. Research on stress and gender in occupations outside of the scope of policing indicates that there are significant differences in the perceptions and coping skills of male and female workers (Barnett et al., 1987). Though limited, there is also research that suggests that female police officers experience stress derived from sources that are different from male police officers, and that female officers cope with stress differently than male officers (Pendergrass and Ostrove, 1984; Brown and Campbell, 1990). There

Reprinted with permission of Emerald Journals, from *Policing: An International Journal of Police Strategies & Management*, 25(4) (2002): 687–708.

have been few studies that examine stress coping mechanisms of both male and female officers through direct comparison.

The concern of the impact of stress and female police officers should be given more attention now that female police officers have become a steadily growing demographic in many police agencies. The representation of female police officers in U.S. police agencies grew from 4.6 percent in 1980 to 14.3 percent in 1999 (National Center for Women and Policing, 2000; Martin, 1993). The increase in the presence of female police officers, coupled with research findings that suggest that stress can have a negative impact on job performance, provides justification for additional research on gender and police stress.

In spite of the plethora of literature on the general relationship between police work and job-related stress, there is a paucity of empirical evidence pertaining to the study of gender differences in coping with police stress. Most of the earlier studies on police stress did not have sample sizes large enough to allow for meaningful comparisons between male and female police officers (Burke, 1993). The current study uses survey data from a large metropolitan police department located in the New England area to explore the impact of work environment, work-family conflict, and coping mechanisms on physical and psychological stresses of both male and female police officers. Among those who responded to the survey, there were 943 male officers and 157 female officers. This relatively large sample size allows us to perform an in-depth analysis of gender-specific police stress using clinical measurements.

The purpose of the current study is to investigate whether levels of clinically developed measures of psychological and physical stress are similar between male and female police officers, and the impact of work environment, work-family conflict, and stress coping mechanisms on the stress of both male and female police officers. In our analysis, we use three indexes to measure the levels of physical and psychological stress in the workplace considering both male and female officers. Four categories of explanatory variables including work environment, work-family conflict, coping mechanisms, and demographic variables are also employed to predict levels of stress among male and female police officers.

Literature Review

Researchers who study stress across a wide variety of professions often utilize gender as a key factor in their studies. Stress studies using clinically developed survey instruments consistently show that females report significantly higher levels of psychological and physical stress than their male counterparts (for a review of the literature, see Derogatis and Savitz, 1999). Moreover, these studies have revealed that male and female employees possess different conceptualizations and adaptations to stress. First, male and female workers often have different views on what is stressful—the source of stress (Stotland, 1991). Second, male and female workers usually adopt different coping strategies when they are under stress (Barnett et al., 1987, p. 350). It is argued that females are more likely to use "emotional-focused" coping strategies compared to males who are more proficient with "problem-focused" coping strategies (Billings and Moos, 1981; Stone and Neale, 1984). It is possible that the gender differences found in the perceptions and coping mechanisms used to deal with stress among male and female workers in non-police-related occupations might also be found among male and female police officers.

Gender and Stress in Police Work

Research shows that gender is a key explanatory factor in predicting the sources and coping strategies of stress among police officers (Pendergrass and Ostrove, 1984; Brown and Campbell, 1990). For example, previous literature reveals that female police officers are likely to encounter higher levels of harassment, overt hostility, and other negative social interactions on the job compared to their male counterparts (Deaux and Ullman, 1983; Balkin, 1988; Martin, 1990). A common explanation for this maltreatment of female officers is that police organizational culture, in general, is adversarial toward them. Moreover, the negative side of police work may bear its mark more on female police officers than their male counterparts. Wexler and Logan (1983, p. 48) revealed that, "The sources of stress mentioned were negative attitudes of male officers, training, exposure to tragedy and trouble, group blame, and rumors." Therefore, both the internal organizational culture and external work environment are much less favorable to female officers.

The studies that were previously discussed suggest that stress may have different effects on male and female police officers. However, there has been little research focused specifically on psychological and physical stress between male and female police officers, using the same measurement. Most of the previous studies on police stress and gender focus on male or female officers separately due to limitations of the collected data (e.g. Wexler and Logan, 1983).

Sources Associated with Occupational Stress Among Police Officers

In this section, we highlight five major convergent and divergent sources of police stress identified in the literature. It is evident that police work is often cited as one of the most stressful occupations (Eisenburg, 1975; Selye, 1978; Alkus and Padesky, 1983; Loo, 1984; Kroes, 1985; Violanti, 1985; Reese, 1986; Dantzer, 1987; Goodman, 1990; Burke, 1993). The sources associated with stress in police work are well documented by scholars and practitioners (Symonds, 1970; Cruse and Rubin, 1973; Kroes et al., 1974; Reiser, 1974; 1976). Major sources of police stress that are frequently highlighted in the literature include:

- stress from the work environment;
- availability of peer support and trust;

- social and family influence;
- bureaucratic characteristics of police organizations; and
- accessibility of coping mechanisms.

The first major source of stress identified in police work is associated with the unique work environment of police officers. The danger associated with police work is usually highlighted in surveys of law enforcement officers where police officers are asked to rank-order a list of possible stressors. Not surprisingly, the death of a partner or having to take a life in the line of duty are typically among the top stressors identified by officers (Coman and Evans, 1991; Violanti and Aron, 1993). Other elements of stress often mentioned in the literature include making violent arrests and gruesome crime scenes (Violanti and Aron, 1993). Overall, violent and unpredictable incidents involved in police work are commonly considered to be the leading sources of both psychological and physical stress among law enforcement officers.

Next, a substantial body of literature addresses the important role of peer support and trust of coworkers and supervisors in buffering the effects of stress related to police work (House and Wells, 1978; LaRocco et al., 1980; House, 1981; Dignam et al., 1986; Ganster et al., 1986; Quick et al., 1992; Morris et al., 1999). Researchers have argued that peer support is especially salient to police officers because the nature of their work requires them to place their lives in the hands of fellow police officers in dangerous situations and because work-related stress may only be completely comprehensible to fellow police officers (Ellison and Genz, 1983; Graf, 1986). Further, research indicates that police officers who perceive themselves as having a strong work-related peer support system also perceived their jobs as being less stressful (LaRocco et al., 1980; Graf, 1986). With respect to gender, peer support from fellow officers is regarded as especially important to female and minority officers who are "breaking and entering" into an occupation that has traditionally been dominated by white male officers (Walker, 1985; Martin, 1990).

Bureaucratic characteristics of police organizations are identified as a third major source of stress among police officers (Violanti and Aron, 1993). Studies have identified the unique characteristics of police agencies as a significant factor predicting stress among police officers (Spielberger et al., 1981; Maslach, 1982; Martelli et al., 1989; Brown and Campbell, 1990). Organizational stressors include the events precipitated by police administration that are troublesome to members of the organization. Given the bureaucratic nature of police organizations (such as impersonal rules, and a distinct chain of command) individual input at the workplace is often reduced to a minimal level (Coman and Evans, 1991). Furthermore, Golembiewski and Kim (1991) make the argument that the quasi-military nature of police organizations tends to breed alienation among police officers. This is especially problematic as police officers are required to exercise considerable discretion while being tightly controlled by a plethora of administrative rules surrounding their work.

The fourth major source of stress in police work involves work/family relationships. Research on work/family interface have long recognized that the personal lives of police officers are affected by the unique nature of police work, which, in turn, makes officers perceive their job as more psychologically and physically stressful (Hughes et al., 1992; Galinsky et al., 1993; 1996). Several studies have identified work-family conflict as an important predictor of psychological burnout among police officers (Jackson and Maslach, 1982; Burke, 1989; 1993). This is particularly true for female officers because the demands of their domestic role as wife and mother are greater than those of male police officers (Martin, 1980, p. 200). For example, research findings suggest that marriage is distinctly beneficial for most husbands but much less for most wives (Bernard, 1972), and married women experience more strain than do married men (Gove and Tudor, 1973). However, very few studies have empirically examined this issue within the context of gender and police work.

The final source of police stress concerns the availability and choice of coping mechanisms adopted by male and female police officers in order to reduce their stress. Although coping literature is replete with varied definitions of the concept of coping, most researchers agree that only the conscious use of a cognitive or behavioral strategy that is intended to reduce perceived stress or improve a person's resources to deal with stress reflects the coping process (Evans et al., 1993; Anshel, 2000).

A review of the literature on stress reveals that individuals in a variety of professions usually take two approaches to reduce psychological and physical stress (Burke, 1993). The first approach focuses on positive coping strategies that usually involve gaining family and social support in an attempt to reduce stress. A few examples of positive coping strategies include support group meetings, sharing stressful experiences with others (including family members), and religious-based support groups. The second approach used to cope with stress includes negative coping strategies. Generally, negative coping strategies involve self-destructive methods to reduce stress, including increased cigarette smoking and avoidance of friends and family members. Violanti et al. (1985) also observed that certain stress-related job "demands" of policing are also associated with alcohol use. They argued that psychological and physical stress is directly or indirectly related to alcohol use. Similarly, Haar and Morash (1999) found that male and female officers use different coping methods, attempting to reduce their stress at the workplace.

Not surprisingly, positive coping mechanisms are considered to be the more appropriate approach to reduce psychological and physical stress. Several studies indicate that improper or maladaptive coping contributes to the intensity of perceived stress instead of reducing stress levels (Lazarus, 1990; Aldwin, 1994). In addition, failure to cope effectively with stress can lead to long-term and chronic stress (Loo, 1984). Police officers who use maladaptive coping skills (e.g. excessive alcohol intake, smoking, overeating, or drug use) are more likely to experience chronic, long-term stress (Hurrel, 1986).

Consequently, ongoing and long-term police stress can result in burnout, reduced motivation and, ultimately, withdrawal from police work (Maslach, 1976; Violanti and Aron, 1993).

After reviewing the body of literature on police stress and gender, it is clear that we do not clearly know how some of the main sources of stress related to police work impact both male and female officers. Using a comparison of both male and female officers, the current study explores the impact of work environment, coping mechanisms, and work-family conflict on psychological and physical stress of male and female police officers.

Methodology

The current study utilizes data that was originally used in Gershon's (1999) study titled "Police stress and domestic violence in police families in Baltimore, Maryland, 1997–1999." We acquired this data set from Inter-university Consortium for Political and Social Research's (ICPSR #2976) Web site.

The sampling strategy that was used in data collection for Gershon's study involved three steps:

1. obtain the total number of sworn employees in each precinct for all shifts;

2. attend one or two roll calls for each shift in all nine of the Baltimore precincts and main headquarters to obtain a convenience sample of volunteers; and

3. distribute self-administered questionnaires to police officers who volunteered to participate in the study.

The reported response rate was 68 percent in the original study (see Gershon, 1999 for more details). The five-page instrument distributed to Baltimore police officers included questions regarding symptoms of psychological and physical stress and likely stressors, perceptions of current stress levels, coping mechanisms to deal with stress, and health outcomes related to stress.

Dependent Variable

The instrument developed to measure police stress in Gershon's (1999) survey was adopted with minor modifications from the brief symptom inventory (BSI), a brief form of the Symptom Check List 90 (Derogatis and Melisaratos, 1983). The original BSI instrument comprised 53 items, which measure nine dimensions of psychological and physical symptoms of stress. Each of the items is rated on a five-point scale of distress ranging from not at all (0) to extremely troublesome (4). The BSI was developed in 1975 and is designed to assess the psychological symptom patterns of community residents and psychiatric and medical patients (Derogatis and Savitz, 1999). Its psychometric validity has been tested and sustained in numerous empirical studies reported in the USA (for a review see Derogatis and Savitz, 1999).

Gershon's (1999) survey includes three of the nine dimensions of stress symptoms and uses a four-point scale of distress ranging from never (1) to always (4). The first dimension is somatization, a scale that reflects the psychological distress arising from perception of bodily dysfunction. Complaints typically focus on cardiovascular, gastrointestinal, respiratory, and other systems with strong autonomic mediation. Aches, pains, and discomfort localized in the gross musculature are also frequent manifestations of stress. The second dimension is anxiety, a scale in which general indicators such as restlessness, nervousness, and panic attacks are represented. The third dimension is depression, a scale that reflects a broad range of the elements constituting the clinical depressive syndrome. Symptoms of dysphoric effect and mood are represented, as are signs of withdrawal of interest in activities, lack of motivation, and loss of vital energy (for a detailed discussion of dimensions see Derogatis et al., 1973). Survey items contained in each scale are presented in Appendix 1.

Independent Variables

The current study also includes six independent variables in three major contexts including:

1. work environment;
2. work-family conflict; and
3. stress coping mechanisms.

Three variables are used to represent the characteristics unique to the police work environment. First, negative exposures related to police work are used to measure the dangerous or negative aspects of work events that police officers often experience (e.g. making violent arrests, shooting someone, attending police funerals, etc.). Second, camaraderie is a measure of peer support and trust within police officers' immediate work groups (e.g. cooperation between units, and trust between police partners). And third, unfairness measures police officers' perceptions of treatment as an officer both within the context of bureaucratic nature of police organization and by the media.

Work-family conflict and its impact on psychological and physical stress of individual police officers are measured by spillover. Unhappiness in someone's personal life and workplace burnout are thought to have significant influence on stress levels. This would include those situations where police officers are too physically and emotionally exhausted to deal with their spouses or significant others, and they begin to treat family the way that they treat suspects at work. This study examines how the "spillover" of conflict associated with family and work impacts stress of both male and female police officers.

This study also uses two measures of coping mechanisms including constructive and destructive coping mechanisms. Constructive coping is a measure of direct, positive, and active responses to work-related stress (e.g. talk to spouse, relative, and friends about the problem; make a plan of action and follow it; pray for guidance and strength; etc.). Destructive coping measures the negative and avoidance techniques used to deal with work-related stress (e.g.

stay away from everyone; yell or shout at spouses/significant others or family members; smash or break things; increased smoking, drinking, and/or gambling; or pretend that nothing is wrong).

Five demographic variables are used as control measures in this analysis:

1. ethnicity;
2. marital status;
3. education status;
4. rank; and
5. years of service.

Previous studies suggest that the rank of officers and years of police service are important occupational characteristics associated with exposure to stressors and experience of their consequences (Robinson, 1981; Gudjonsson and Adlam, 1985; Fielding, 1987; Brown and Campbell, 1990). Other studies found inconsistent and weak relationships of stress and individual demographic characteristics (e.g. Maslach, 1982; Burke and Richardsen, 1993; Burke, 1993). We include these five control variables to ensure that the potentially intervening effects of respondent demographic background or work experience are not accounting for any observed relationships between work environment, work-family conflict, coping mechanisms, and the reporting of stress symptoms among officers. See Appendix 2 for the correlation matrix of all the variables included in this study.

Findings

Table 1 reports the major demographic characteristics of the survey respondents. The survey sample includes 943 male officers (86 percent) and 157 female officers (14 percent). There are 696 officers who identified themselves as white (66 percent), and 355 officers who identified themselves as African American (34 percent). Few respondents are in the other racial categories. For the simplicity of comparison, percentages for the variable ethnicity are calculated based on white and African American officers only. About 60 percent of officers in this survey are married. The majority of the respondents (70 percent) do not have a college degree. A total of 18 percent of the survey respondents stated their ranks as sergeant or higher. The average length of police service is about 12 years.

Our first research question examines the levels of clinically developed measures of stress between male and female officers in the Baltimore City Police Department. Table 2 presents the results of a comparison between male and female police officers on all of the dependent and independent variables using t-tests. The findings indicate that female officers have statistically significant higher levels of stress in two of the three indexes measuring psychological and physical stress. The means of depression and somatization among female officers (1.58, 1.54) are both higher than those of their male counterparts (1.47, 1.36), respectively. However, no statistically significant difference was found between male and female officers on anxiety.

Among the three sets of independent variables, statistically significant differences were found between male and female officers in all three measures of work environment. Male officers were found to have experienced

Table 1   Descriptive statistics of demographic variables

Variables	Mean (SD)	n	%
Gender			
Female = 0		157	14.3
Male = 1		943	85.7
Ethnicity			
White = 0		696	66.2
African American = 1		355	33.8
Marriage			
Not married = 0		441	40.1
Married = 1		658	59.9
Education attainment			
BA and + = 0		326	29.8
Less than BA = 1		768	70.2
Rank			
Supervisor = 0		202	18.4
Officer = 1		898	81.6
Years of service	11.52 (9.28)		

Table 2   Testing the differences between male and female police officers in Baltimore PD

	Baltimore PD Scale mean (SD)	Male officers Scale mean (SD)	Female officers Scale mean (SD)	*t*-test
Dependent variable				
Somatization	1.39 (0.38)	1.36 (0.36)	1.54 (0.45)	4.58*
Anxiety	1.27 (0.36)	1.27 (0.36)	1.26 (0.37)	−0.16
Depression	1.47 (0.39)	1.45 (0.38)	1.58 (0.45)	3.56*
Work environment				
Negative exposures	1.33 (0.65)	1.34 (0.65)	1.22 (0.61)	−2.21*
Camaraderie	3.60 (0.80)	3.62 (0.80)	3.44 (0.84)	−2.70*
Unfairness	3.00 (0.66)	3.04 (0.66)	2.81 (0.62)	−3.98*
Work-family conflict				
Spillover	2.38 (0.78)	2.40 (0.78)	2.30 (0.77)	−1.43
Coping				
Constructive coping	2.39 (0.60)	2.35 (0.60)	2.66 (0.57)	5.98*
Destructive coping	1.55 (0.33)	1.56 (0.33)	1.50 (0.32)	−2.17*

Note: * $p < 0.05$

more work-related negative exposures (1.34) and tended to report higher levels of camaraderie (3.62) than do their female counterparts (1.22, 3.44), respectively. Male officers reported a higher level of unfairness in the department (3.04) than their female counterparts (2.81). There were no statistically significant differences detected between male and female officers in the means of spillover. And finally, we found statistically significant gender differences in coping mechanisms employed by police officers. Female officers seemed to use more constructive coping (2.66) than male officers (2.35). Although statistically significant, the differences in the destructive coping measures were rather marginal when male (1.56) and female officers (1.50) are compared.

Tables 3 and 4 show the results of separate multivariate analyses used to answer our second research question (whether the sources of stress and coping strategies are indeed similar between the two gender groups). Both the unstandardized and standardized (beta) coefficients are reported to document the relative contribution of each individual variable to the equations for the three dimensions of stress.[1] In both the male and female police officer samples, the R^2 statistics for all of the regression models are statistically significant, ranging from 0.24 on the anxiety dimension (female sample) to 0.34 on the depression dimension (male sample).

In the male police officer sample, the results of regression analysis indicate that the majority of the independent variables have statistically significant impact on all three stress indexes. More specifically, we found that four variables are particularly important in predicting the levels of both psychological and physical stress among male officers. These four variables include:

1. negative exposures to police work;
2. camaraderie (work environment);
3. spillover effect (work-family conflict); and
4. destructive coping (coping strategy).

Moreover, all of the signs of the four statistically significant variables are pointed in the hypothesized directions (see Table 3). We also discovered that married male officers have less psychological stress compared to unmarried male officers. And it appears that the years of service in the police force is a statistically significant contributor to depression, as reported by male officers.

In comparison, our regression analysis using the female officer sample revealed some more interesting findings (see Table 4). First, none of the work environment measures yielded statistically significant impact on female police officer stress. It seemed that female officers' stress was not influenced by the three variables measuring work environment.[2] In addition, it is also interesting to note that none of the demographic variables were statistically significant predictors of female officers' psychological and physical stress.

Second, similar to those findings from the male officer sample, spillover (work-family conflict) and destructive coping (coping strategy) were statistically significant contributors to female officer stress. However, unlike those

Table 3   Regression analyses, male officers sample

| | Physical stress | | Psychological stress | | | |
| | Somatization | | Anxiety | | Depression | |
	b	β	b	β	b	β
Work environment						
Negative exposures	0.086	0.157*	0.088	0.163*	0.067	0.115*
Camaraderie	−0.076	−0.174*	−0.043	−0.099*	−0.074	−0.159*
Unfairness	−0.007	−0.013	−0.008	−0.016	0.035	0.062
Work-family conflict						
Spillover	0.102	0.227*	0.090	0.204*	0.102	0.214*
Coping						
Constructive coping	0.010	0.016	0.015	0.025	−0.006	−0.009
Destructive coping	0.259	0.238*	0.330	0.308*	0.339	0.294*
Demographic						
Ethnicity	−0.059	−0.075	−0.041	−0.054	−0.034	−0.041
Marriage	−0.033	−0.045	−0.064	−0.089*	−0.060	−0.078*
Education	0.011	0.014	0.012	0.016	−0.000	−0.000
Rank	0.021	0.024	0.014	0.017	−0.002	−0.002
Years of service	0.001	0.031	−0.000	−0.021	0.003	0.075*
Adjusted R^2 =	0.288*		0.276*		0.340*	

Note: * $p < 0.05$

Table 4   Regression analyses, female officers sample

| | Physical stress | | Psychological stress | | | |
| | Somatization | | Anxiety | | Depression | |
	b	β	b	β	b	β
Work environment						
Negative exposures	0.083	0.102	0.047	0.070	0.093	0.116
Camaraderie	−0.051	−0.093	−0.037	−0.082	−0.057	−0.107
Unfairness	−0.023	−0.031	0.044	0.071	0.030	0.041
Work-family conflict						
Spillover	0.104	0.174*	0.112	0.226*	0.117	0.199*
Coping						
Constructive coping	0.067	0.080	−0.057	−0.082	−0.127	−0.154*
Destructive coping	0.510	0.345*	0.365	0.299*	0.516	0.355*
Demographic						
Ethnicity	0.051	0.054	−0.009	−0.011	0.039	0.042
Marriage	0.059	0.063	0.072	0.090	0.103	0.111
Education	−0.008	−0.008	−0.020	−0.024	−0.082	−0.083
Rank	0.102	0.073	0.031	0.027	0.103	0.075
Years of service	0.012	0.156	0.003	0.047	0.007	0.093
Adjusted R^2	0.297*		0.241*		0.333*	

Note: * $p < 0.05$

found in the male officer sample, constructive coping is now a statistically significant "buffer" to depression for female officers. It is important to point out that although fewer variables are significant in predicting stress levels of female officers, the explanatory power of the two variables (i.e. spillover and destructive coping) are high judging by their respective beta weights. The variance explained measures (R^2) obtained from the three regression analyses using the female sample (R^2 = 0.30, 0.24, and 0.33 respectively) are similar to those obtained using the male officer sample (R^2 = 0.29, 0.28, and 0.34 respectively).

Discussion and Conclusions

In regard to our first research question, the findings of this study indicate that female officers do have statistically significant higher levels of somatization and depression compared to their male counterparts, respectively. These findings are generally consistent with relevant previous research findings in the area of psychology and mental health (e.g. Derogatis and Savitz, 1999). Nevertheless, we find no evidence to suggest that male and female police officers differ statistically in the clinically developed measure of anxiety.[3]

To answer our second research question, a multivariate analysis examines the sources of stress and coping strategies used by male and female officers. We found both convergent and divergent effects of work environment, work-family conflict, and coping strategies on the physical and psychological stress of police officers. In both male and female officer samples, there appears to be convergent impact of spillover and destructive coping on all three measures of stress (somatization, anxiety, and depression). Judging from the signs and values of the standardized regression coefficients (beta), the impact of spillover and destructive coping are consistently the largest, which suggests that both are among the most important job stressors in police work.

There are unmistakable signs of divergent effects of some work environment, coping, and demographic variables on stress that appear to be gender specific. For example, in the analysis using the female officer sample, neither the work environment variables nor the demographic variables are statistically significant predictors of any measures of stress. Yet, unlike the corresponding finding from male officer sample, constructive coping has been found to reduce depression among female officers.

To further our understanding of the intricate nature of police work environment, we compared the percentage of male and female police officers that agreed to specific individual items (see Appendix 3 for analysis of item responses). The results of comparison between the two groups revealed that constructive coping was found to be a statistically significant stress-reducing factor for one type of female police officer stress—depression. About half of all the female officers in the sample indicated that they have frequently or always used the following coping strategies:

- rely on your faith in God to see you through this rough time (female— 61.9 percent; male—35.3 percent);

- pray for guidance and strength (female—59.1 percent; male—28.5 percent);
- talk with your spouse, relative or friend about the problem (female—52.3 percent; male—37.1 percent); and
- make a plan of action and follow it (female—48.0 percent; male—44.2 percent).

Apparently, there are differences between male and female officers in using constructive coping strategies. Male police officers appear to rely far less on spiritual guidance and on consulting spouse, other family members, and friends when dealing with stress. We suggest that this observation has significant policy implications.

Policy Implications

The results of this study provide the basis for several policy implications related to police stress and gender. First, our findings suggest that police administrators should pay attention to the convergent factors that lead to police officer stress. Stressors such as work-family conflict and negative coping are common among both male and female officers. To ameliorate the stress associated with work-family conflict, police management should play a leading role in creating greater flexibility in accommodating police officers' professional, personal, and family needs. In more practical terms, efforts need to be made to actively solicit input from both police officers and their family members. For example, police stress training sessions targeting work-family conflict should consider the possibility of involving both police officers and their spouses/significant others.

Second, with regard to improving police officers' coping skills, police stress management programs should be tailored to fit the specific needs of a police department. A sensible approach would involve the following three major components:

1. assessment of police officers' physical and psychological stress, which includes identifying both internal and external stressors;
2. monitoring police officers' adaptive and maladaptive coping skills; and
3. effective use of appropriate intervention strategies such as peer counseling.

In particular, peer counseling could be a realistic and effective way to deal with police officer stress (Klyver, 1983). Some male police officers are notoriously shy in seeking professional help for fear of being viewed as weak by fellow officers (Graf, 1986).

Finally, police stress management programs could also benefit from learning the divergent impact of work environment and coping mechanisms on police stress that is gender specific. Our study indicates that work environment has had greater impact on stress of male police officers. While negative exposures to work-related incidents remain a significant stressor to male officers, camaraderie among colleagues could counteract its negative impact on the well-being of male police officers. Although we did not find a statistically significant impact of work environment on female officers' stress in this study, the signs of the indicators of work environment were similar in both gender groups. Additionally, it is encouraging that constructive coping has been found to have a significant impact on reducing depression for female police officers. The constructive coping techniques used by female officers that result in decreased depression could be promoted among male police officers in pursuit of similarly positive impact on their stress. In sum, employee stress is an important issue that no police agency can afford to overlook. Stress management in policing is essential because police work is such a highly stressful profession. In addition, police officers unable to deal effectively with stress might fail to provide efficient quality police services to citizens.

We would like to point out three caveats in regard to the findings of our study. First, we acknowledge that the findings derived from our analysis were based on a large police department located on the East Coast. Therefore, the results might be more informative to large police agencies, compared to medium-sized or smaller police agencies. Second, we would caution the possible risk of model specification errors. Third, although we are able to test our hypotheses based on larger sub-samples of male ($n = 943$) and female officers ($n = 157$) than many of the previous police stress and gender studies, we would prefer even greater numbers from broader jurisdictions in future studies on this topic.

We invite other police scholars and practitioners to join in the study of police stress management with an eye on further exploring possible group (e.g. gender, race) differences. Longitudinal and cross-sectional studies are needed to both increase our understanding of the sources of police stress and to develop more effective responses to manage police officer stress. We hope that our study of the convergent and divergent impact of work environment, work-family conflict, and coping mechanisms on female and male officer stress is a step forward in police stress research.

NOTES

[1] Multicollinearity is a potential serious problem associated with the use of ordinary least square (OLS) regression analysis. Accordingly, the variance inflation factor (VIF) often is used to detect whether collinearity exists among independent variables. Some researchers use a VIF score of 4 or greater as an indication of noteworthy multicollinearity (Fisher and Mason, 1980; Judge et al., 1988). The collinearity statistics run on theses data showed that none of the VIF values exceeded 2. It is safe to say that multicollinearity was not a problem in our analysis.

[2] Our reviewers correctly pointed out that since we are using a convenience sample originated from a single site the generalizability of our findings might be limited.

[3] To our best knowledge, there is no prior study in policing using similar clinical measures of stress as used in our current study. This renders a difficult exercise for us to compare our findings to the existing literature in the field of policing.

REFERENCES

Aldwin, C. (1994), *Stress, Coping and Development*, Guilford, New York.

Alkus, S. and Padesky, C. (1983), "Special problems of police officers: stress related issues and interventions," *Counseling Psychologist*, Vol. 11, pp. 55–64.

Anshel, M. H. (2000), "A conceptual model and implications for coping with stressful events in police work," *Criminal Justice and Behavior*, Vol. 27, pp. 375–400.

Balkin, J. (1988), "Why policemen don't like policewomen," *Journal of Police Science and Administration*, Vol. 16, pp. 29–38.

Barnett, R. C., Niener, L. and Baruch, G. K. (1987), *Gender and Stress*, The Free Press, New York.

Bernard, J. (1972), *The Future of Marriage*, Bantam Books, New York.

Billings, A. G. and Moos, R. H. (1981), "The role of coping responses and social resources in attenuating the stress of life events," *Journal of Behavioral Medicine*, Vol. 4, pp. 139–57.

Brown, J. A. and Campbell, E. A. (1990), "Sources of occupational stress in the police," *Work and Stress*, Vol. 4, pp. 305–18.

Burke, R. J. (1989), "Career stages, satisfaction and well-being among police officers," *Psychological Reports*, Vol. 65, pp. 3–12.

Burke, R. J. (1993), "Work-family stress, conflict, coping and burnout in police officers," *Stress Medicine*, Vol. 9, pp. 171–80.

Burke, R. J. and Richardsen, A. M. (1993), "Psychological burnout in organizations," in Golembiewski, R. T. (Ed.), *Handbook of Organizational Behavior*, M. Dekker, New York, pp. 263–98.

Coman, G. and Evans, B. (1991), "Stressors facing Australian police in the 1990s," *Police Studies*, Vol. 14, pp. 153–65.

Crank, J. P. and Caldero, M. (1991), "The production of occupational stress in medium-sized police agencies: a survey of line officers in eight municipal departments," *Journal of Criminal Justice*, Vol. 19, pp. 339–49.

Cruse, D. and Rubin, J. (1973), *Determinants of Police Behavior: A Summary*, Criminal Justice Monograph, U.S. Department of Justice, No. 2700-00215, U.S. Government Printing Office, Washington, DC.

Dantzer, M. L. (1987), "Police-related stress: a critique for future research," *Journal of Police and Criminal Psychology*, Vol. 3, pp. 43–8.

Deaux, K. and Ullman, J. C. (1983), *Women of Steel*, Praeger, New York.

Derogatis, L. and Melisaratos, N. (1983), "The brief symptom inventory: an introductory report," *Psychological Medicine*, Vol. 13, pp. 595–605.

Derogatis, L. and Savitz, K. (1999), "The SCL-90-R: brief symptom inventory and matching clinical rating scales," in Maruish, M. (Ed.), *The Use of Psychological Testing for Treatment, Planning and Outcomes Assessment*, Lawrence Erlbaum Associates Inc., Mahwah, NJ.

Derogatis, L., Lipman, R. and Covi, L. (1973), "SCL-90: an outpatient psychiatric rating scale-preliminary report," *Psychopharmacology Bulletin*, Vol. 9, pp. 13–28.

Dignam, J. T., Barrera, M. and West, S. C. (1986), "Occupational stress, social support, and burnout among correctional officers," *American Journal of Community Psychology*, Vol. 14, pp. 177–93.

Eisenburg, T. (1975), "Job stress and the police officer: identifying stress reduction techniques," in Kroes, W. H. and Hurrell, J. J. Jr. (Eds.), *Job Stress and the Police Officer: Identifying Stress Reduction Techniques*, HEW Publication No. NIOSH 760187, U.S. Government Printing Office, Washington, DC.

Ellison, K. W. and Genz, J. L. (1983), *Stress and Police Officer*, Charles Thomas Publishers, Springfield, IL.

Evans, B. J., Coman, G. J., Stanley, R. O. and Burrows, G. D. (1993), "Police officers' coping strategies: an Australian police survey," *Stress Medicine*, Vol. 9, pp. 237–46.

Fielding, N. G. (1987), *Joining Forces: Police Training Socialization and Occupational Competence*, Routledge, London.

Fisher, J. E. and Mason, R. L. (1980), "The analysis of multicollinear data in criminology," in Fox, J. A. (Ed.), *Methods in Quantitative Criminology*, Academic Press, New York, pp. 99–125.

Galinsky, E., Bond, J. T. and Friedman, D. E. (1993), *The Changing Workforce. Highlights of the National Study, II*, Families and Work Institute, New York.

Galinsky, E., Bond, J. T. and Friedman, D. E. (1996), "The role of employers in addressing the needs of employed parents," *Journal of Social Issues*, Vol. 52, pp. 111–36.

Ganster, D. C., Fusilier, M. R. and Mayes, B. T. (1986), "Role of social support in the experience of stress at work," *Journal of Applied Psychology*, Vol. 7, pp. 102–11.

Gershon, R. (1999), "Police stress and domestic violence in police families in Baltimore, Maryland, 1997–1999," computer file, ICPSR version, Johns Hopkins University (producer), Baltimore, MD, Inter-University Consortium for Political and Social Research (distributor), Ann Arbor, MI.

Golembiewski, R. and Kim, B. (1991), "Burnout in police work: stressors, strain, and the phase model," *Police Studies*, Vol. 14, pp. 74–80.

Goodman, A. M. (1990), "A model for police officer burnout," *Journal of Business and Psychology*, Vol. 5, pp. 85–99.

Gove, W. R. and Tudor, J. F. (1973), "Adult sex roles and mental illness," *American Journal of Sociology*, Vol. 78, pp. 812–35.

Graf, F. A. (1986), "The relationship between social support and occupational stress among police officers," *Journal of Police Science and Administration*, Vol. 14, pp. 178–86.

Gudjonsson, G. H. and Adlam, K. (1985), "Occupational stressors among British police officers," *Police Journal*, Vol. 58, pp. 73–85.

Haar, R. N. and Morash, M. (1999), "Gender, race and strategies of coping with occupational stress in policing," *Justice Quarterly*, Vol. 16, pp. 303–36.

House, J. S. (1981), *Work Stress and Social Support*, Addison-Wesley, Reading, MA.

House, J. S. and Wells, J. A. (1978), "Occupational stress, social support, and health," in McLean, A., Black, G. and Colligan, M. (Eds.), *Reducing Occupational Stress: Proceedings of a Conference*, National Institute of Safety and Health, Washington, DC, publication No. 78–140, pp. 8–29.

Hughes, D., Galinsky, E. and Morris, A. (1992), "The effects of job characteristics on marital quality: specifying linking mechanisms," *Journal of Marriage and Family*, Vol. 54, pp. 31–42.

Hurrel, J. J. (1986), "Some organizational stressors in police work and means for their amelioration," in Reese, J. T. and Goldstein, H. A. (Eds.), *Psychological Services for Law Enforcement*. National Symposium on Police Psychological Services, FBI Academy, Quantico, VA.

Jackson, S. E. and Maslach, C. (1982), "After-effects of job-related stress: families as victims," *Journal of Occupational Behavior*, Vol. 3, pp. 63–77.

Judge, G. G., Hill, R. C., Griffiths, W. E., Lutkepohl, H. and Lee, T. C. (1988), *Introduction to the Theory and Practice of Econometrics*, 2nd ed., Wiley, New York.

Klyver, N. (1983), "Peer counseling for police personnel: a dynamic program in the Los Angeles Police Department," *Police Chief*, Vol. 50, pp. 66–8.

Kroes, W. H. (1985), *Society's Victim: the Police Officer*, Charles Thomas, Springfield, IL.

Kroes, W. H., Margolis, B. L. and Hurrell, J. J. (1974), "Job stress in policemen," *Journal of Police Sciences and Administration*, Vol. 2, pp. 145–55.

LaRocco, J., House, J. and French, J. (1980), "Social support, occupational stress, and health," *Journal of Health and Social Behavior*, Vol. 21, pp. 202–18.

Lazarus, R. S. (1990), "Theory-based stress measurement," *Psychological Inquiry*, Vol. 1, pp. 3–13.

Loo, R. (1984), "Occupational stress in the law enforcement profession," *Canadian Mental Health*, pp. 10–13.

McGreedy, K. (1974), "Selection practices and the police role," *Police Chief*, Vol. 41, pp. 41–3.

Martelli, T. A., Waters, L. K. and Martelli, J. (1989), "The police stress survey: reliability and relation to job satisfaction and organizational commitment," *Psychological Reports*, Vol. 64, pp. 267–73.

Martin, S. E. (1980), *Breaking and Entering: Policewomen on Patrol*, University of California Press, Berkeley, CA.

Martin, S. E. (1990), *On the Move: The Status of Women in Policing*, The Police Foundation, Washington, DC.

Martin, S. E. (1993), "Female officers on the move: a status report on women in policing," in Dunham, R. and Alpert, G. (Eds.), *Critical Issues in Policing: Contemporary Readings*, 2nd ed., Waveland Press Inc., Long Grove, IL, pp. 327–47.

Maslach, C. (1976), "Burnout," *Human Behavior*, Vol. 23, pp. 16–22.

Maslach, C. (1982), *Burnout: The Cost of Caring*, Prentice Hall, Englewood Cliffs, NJ.

Morris, A., Marybeth, S. and DuMont, K. (1999), "Contextual factors affecting the organizational commitment of diverse police officers: a levels of analysis perspective," *American Journal of Community Psychology*, Vol. 27, pp. 75–105.

National Center for Women and Policing (2000), *Equal Denied: The Status of Women in Policing: 1999*, National Center for Women and Policing, Los Angeles, CA.

Pendergrass, V. and Ostrove, N. (1984), "Survey of stress in women in policing," *Journal of Police Science and Administration*, Vol. 12, pp. 303–9.

Quick, J. C., Murphy, L. R., Hurrell, J. J. and Orman, D. (1992), "The value of work, the risk of distress, and the power of prevention," in Quick, J. C., Murphy, L. R. and Hurrell, J. J. Jr. (Eds.), *Stress and Well being at Work: Assessments and Interventions for Occupational Mental Health*, American Psychological Association, Washington, DC, pp. 3–14.

Reese, J. T. (1986), "Policing the violent society: the American experience," *Stress Medicine*, Vol. 2, pp. 233–40.

Reiser, M. (1974), "Some organizational stresses on policemen," *Journal of Police Science and Administration*, Vol. 2, pp. 156–9.

Reiser, M. (1976), "Stress, distress, and adaptation in police work," *The Police Chief*, January, pp. 24–7.

Robinson, P. (1981), "Stress in the police service," *Police Review*, Vol. 20, pp. 2254–9.

Selye, I. (1978), "The stress of police work," *Police Stress*, pp. 1:1–3.

Spielberger, C. D., Westberry, L. G., Grier, K. S. and Greenfield, G. (1981), *The Police Stress Survey: Sources of Stress in Law Enforcement*, Human Resources Institute, Tampa, FL.

Stone, A. A. and Neale, J. M. (1984), "New measure of daily coping: development and preliminary results," *Journal of Personality and Social Psychology*, Vol. 46, pp. 892–906.

Stotland, E. (1991), "The effects of police work and professional relationships on health," *Journal of Criminal Justice*, Vol. 19, pp. 371–9.

Symonds, M. (1970), "Emotional hazards of police work," *American Journal of Psychoanalysis*, Vol. 30, pp. 155–60.

Violanti, J. M. (1985), "The police stress process," *Journal of Police Science and Administration*, Vol. 13, pp. 106–10.

Violanti, J. M. and Aron, F. (1993), "Sources of police stressors, job attitudes and psychological distress," *Psychological Reports*, Vol. 72, pp. 899–904.

Violanti, J. M. and Aron, F. (1994), "Ranking police stressors," *Psychological Reports*, Vol. 75, pp. 824–6.

Violanti, J. M., Marshall, J. R. and Howe, B. (1985), "Stress, coping, and alcohol use: the police connection," *Journal of Police Science and Administration*, Vol. 2, pp. 106–10.

Walker, S. (1985), "Racial minority and female employment in policing: the implications of glacial change," *Crime and Delinquency*, Vol. 31, pp. 555–72.

Wexler, J. G. and Logan, D. D. (1983), "Sources of stress among women police officers," *Journal of Police Science and Administration*, Vol. 13, pp. 98–105.

Appendix 1. Composite Index Construction

Dependent Variables

Response categories are rated from 1 (never) to 4 (always).

Somatization (alpha = 0.76):

Questions. In the past six months, how often did you have:

- Pains or pounding in your heart and chest.
- Faintness or dizziness.
- Headaches or pressure in your head.
- Nausea, upset stomach, stomach pains.
- Trouble getting your breath.
- A lump in your throat.

Anxiety (alpha = 0.85):

Questions. In the past six months, how often did you have:

- Suddenly scared for no reason.
- Feeling that something bad was going to happen to you at work.
- Spells of terror or panic.
- Feeling so restless you could not sit still.

Depression (alpha = 0.67):

Questions. In the past six months, how often did you have:

- Loss of sexual interest or pleasure.
- Feelings of low energy or slowed down.
- Feelings of being trapped or caught.
- Blame yourself for things.

- Feeling blue.
- Feeling no interest in things.
- Feeling hopeless about the future.
- Thoughts of ending your life.
- Crying easily.

Independent Variables

Negative exposures (alpha = 0.79):
   Questions. If you have ever experienced any of the following, please indicate how much it emotionally affected you. Please check N/A if you have not experienced it.

- Making a violent arrest.
- Shooting someone.
- Being the subject of an IID investigation.
- Responding to a call related to a chemical spill.
- Responding to a bloody crime scene.
- Personally knowing the victim.
- Being involved in a hostage situation.
- Attending a police funeral.
- Experiencing a needle stick injury or other exposure to blood and body fluids.

Response categories are: 0 (N/A), 1 (not at all), 2 (a little) and 3 (very much).

Camaraderie (alpha = 0.53):
   Questions: Please check the box that best describes how much you agree with the following statements:

- There is good and effective cooperation between units.
- I can trust my work partner.

Original response categories are from 1 (strongly agree) to 5 (strongly disagree). Categories have been reversed coded in current study.

Unfairness (alpha = 0.60):
   Questions. Please check the box that best describes how much you agree with the following statements:

- Compared to my peers (same rank), I find that I am likely to be more criticized for my mistakes.
- I feel that I am less likely to get chosen for certain assignment because of "who I am" (e.g. race, gender, sexual orientation, physical characteristics).
- Within the department, gender-related jokes are often made in my presence.

- When I am assertive or question the way things are done, I am considered militant.
- Media reports of alleged police wrong-doing are biased against us.
- The department tends to be more lenient in enforcing rules and regulations for female officers.

Original response categories are from 1 (strongly agree) to 5 (strongly disagree). Categories have been reversed coded in current study.

Spillover (alpha = 0.65):
Questions. Please check the box that best describes how much you agree with the following statements:

- I often get home too physically and emotionally exhausted to deal with my spouse/significant other.
- I catch myself treating my family the way I treat suspects.
- At home, I can never shake off the feeling of being a police officer.
- I expect to have the final say on how things are done in my household.

Original response categories are from 1 (strongly agree) to 5 (strongly disagree). Categories have been reversed coded in current study.

Constructive coping (alpha = 0.66):
Questions. When dealing with stressful events at work, how often do you:

- Talk with your spouse, relative or friend about the problem.
- Pray for guidance and strength.
- Make a plan of action and follow it.
- Exercise regularly to reduce tension.
- Rely on your faith in God to see you through this rough time.

Response categories are from 1 (never) to 4 (always).

Destructive coping (alpha = 0.57):
Questions. When dealing with stressful events at work, how often do you:

- Stay away from everyone; you want to be alone.
- Smoke more to help you relax.
- Yell or shout at your spouse/significant other, a family member, or a professional.
- Let your feelings out by smashing things.
- Hang out more with your fellow officers at a bar.
- Gamble.
- Increase your sexual activity.
- Try to act as if nothing is bothering you.

Response categories are from 1 (never) to 4 (always).

Appendix 2. Correlation Matrix

Table A1

	1	2	3	4	5	6	7	8	9	10	11	12	13	14
1. Somatization	1.000													
2. Anxiety	0.612*	1.000												
3. Depression	0.663*	0.674*	1.000											
4. Negative exposure	0.277*	0.267*	0.287*	1.000										
5. Camaraderie	-0.267*	-0.205*	-0.289*	-0.119*	1.000									
6. Unfairness	0.217*	0.250*	0.295*	0.258*	-0.263*	1.000								
7. Spillover	0.383*	0.402*	0.422*	0.206*	-0.153*	0.350*	1.000							
8. Constructive coping	-0.074*	-0.113*	-0.146*	-0.041	0.078*	-0.153*	-0.237*	1.000						
9. Destructive coping	0.435*	0.490*	0.485*	0.253*	-0.159*	0.287*	0.474*	-0.124*	1.000					
10. Ethnicity	-0.057	-0.093*	-0.074*	-0.155*	0.012	-0.058	-0.072*	0.326*	-0.082*	1.000				
11. Marriage	-0.008	-0.030	-0.027	0.198*	-0.025	0.052	0.014	-0.022	-0.021	-0.157*	1.000			
12. Education	0.030	0.045	0.018	-0.077*	0.024	0.070*	0.089*	-0.035	0.070*	0.079*	0.002	1.000		
13. Rank	-0.064*	-0.041	-0.084*	-0.257*	0.102*	-0.026	-0.035	-0.003	-0.009	0.148*	-0.134*	0.223*	1.000	
14. Years of service	0.139*	0.085*	0.160*	0.473*	-0.185*	0.062	0.017	-0.132*	0.071*	-0.219*	0.272*	-0.105*	-0.476*	1.000

Note: $*p < 0.05$

Appendix 3. Analysis of Selected Item Responses

Constructive coping (percentage responded that they have frequently or always done the following things when dealing with stressful events at work):

- Rely on your faith in God to see you through this rough time (male—35.3 percent; female—61.9 percent).
- Pray for guidance and strength (male—28.5 percent; female—59.1 percent).
- Talk with your spouse, relative or friend about the problem (male 37.1 percent; female—52.3 percent).
- Make a plan of action and follow it (male—44.2 percent; female—48.0 percent).
- Exercise regularly to reduce tension (male—37.3 percent; female—27.9 percent).

Spillover (percentage strongly agree or agree with the followings items):

- I often get home too physically and emotionally exhausted to deal with my spouse/significant other (male—42.4 percent; female—41.7 percent).
- I catch myself treating my family the way I treat suspects (male—74.2 percent; female—81.2 percent).
- At home, I can never shake off the feeling of being a police officer (male—63.3 percent; female—71.1 percent).
- I expect to have the final say on how things are done in my household (male—61.3 percent; female—59.3 percent).

Destructive coping (percentage responded that they have frequently or always done the following things when dealing with stressful events at work):

- Stay away from everyone; you want to be alone (male—10.5 percent; female—13.1 percent).
- Smoke more to help you relax (male—11.3 percent; female—13.0 percent).
- Yell or shout at your spouse/significant other, a family member, or a professional (male—5.6 percent; female—6.5 percent).
- Let your feelings out by smashing things (male—1.2 percent; female—1.9 percent).
- Hang out more with your fellow officers at a bar (male—5.5 percent; female—1.3 percent).
- Gamble (male—1.1 percent; female—1.2 percent).
- Increase your sexual activity (male—14.4 percent; female—8.5 percent).
- Try to act as if nothing is bothering you (male—28.2 percent; female—21.4 percent).

Negative exposures (percentage responded that the following items affect them emotionally very much):

- Attending a police funeral (male—53.5 percent; female—64.5 percent).
- Being the subject of an IID investigation (male—34.9 percent; female—27.3 percent).
- Experiencing a needle stick injury or other exposure to blood and body fluids (male—29.7 percent; female—29.7 percent).
- Making a violent arrest (male—19.4 percent; female—18.8 percent).
- Personally knowing the victim (male—15.7 percent; female—20.6 percent).
- Responding to a bloody crime scene (male—15.2 percent; female—18.1 percent).
- Shooting someone (male—8.9 percent).
- Being involved in a hostage situation (male—8.1 percent; female—6.5 percent).
- Responding to a call related to a chemical spill (male—4.6 percent; female—3.9 percent).

Camaraderie (percentage strongly agree or agree with the followings items):

- There is good and effective cooperation between units (male—27.8 percent; female—33.5 percent).
- I can trust my work partner (male—6.2 percent; female—11.9 percent).

21

Toward an Understanding of the Physical Hazards of Police Work

Steven G. Brandl & Meghan S. Stroshine

In the literature, there exist various claims and debates concerning the dangerousness of the police occupation and its dangerousness in relation to other occupations. Most of the extant studies on the topic have come to the conclusion that policing is dangerous (see Fridell & Pate, 1997, p. 603) or, at the very least, that certain tasks of the job are dangerous (Edwards, 1995; Garner & Clemmer, 1986; Hirschel, Dean, & Lumb, 1994; Kaminski & Sorensen, 1995; Konstantin, 1984; Lester, 1981; Stanford & Mowry, 1990). This conclusion is most often arrived at through the analysis of assault and homicide data. Defining dangerousness in this narrow manner, however, is quite unlike other occupations. In most other occupations, the hazards associated with the job are defined in terms of any injuries and illnesses that occur during the course of the job (e.g., Bureau of Labor Statistics, 2000), including those that result from violence (National Institute for Occupational Safety and Health, 1992, 1997; Peek-Asa, Howard, Vargas, & Kraus, 1997) and accidents (Centers for Disease Control, 1998, 2001).

Part of the reason researchers have defined the dangerousness of the police occupation in such a narrow manner is that police officers have a rather unique occupational reality; assaults and homicides are an issue in the police occupation but are not for most other occupations. Whereas it may be true that assaults and homicides pose a greater risk for police officers given the nature of their job, the exclusion of injuries that are the result of accidents presents at least two problems. First, defining dangerousness strictly in terms of assaults and homicides likely distorts an accurate picture of the physical dangers of the job and may severely underestimate the hazards of police work. This is problematic both conceptually and practically. Conceptually, an under-

Police Quarterly 6(2) (June 2003): 172–191, copyright © 2003 by Sage Publications, Inc. Reprinted by permission of Sage Publications, Inc.

standing of the dangers faced by officers is central to understanding the nature of police work and all of its complexities (Skolnick, 1994). Dealing with danger—potential or actual—is a critical factor shaping how police perceive themselves, their role, and the citizens with whom they come into contact (Skolnick, 1994). If one wishes to draw accurate conclusions about the nature of police work and the dangerousness of the police occupation, one must not focus exclusively on injuries and deaths that result from felonious acts; the dangers posed by accidents must also be considered. Practically, the injuries and deaths of police officers have enormous costs. Regardless of how injuries or deaths are sustained (accidentally or feloniously), these incidents translate into lost wages, medical expenses, insurance claims, and decreases in productivity. Of course, these assaults as well as accidents may also have dramatic consequences for officers and their families. It is reasonable to expect that some of the injuries sustained by officers could be prevented, if research is used to develop proper training and policy (Bayley & Garofalo, 1989; Edwards, 1995; Edwards & Tewksbury, 1996; Feldstein, Valanis, Vollmer, Stevens, & Overton, 1993; Fyfe, 1979; Hirschel et al., 1994; Kaminski, Edwards, & Johnson, 1998; Kaminski & Sorensen, 1995; Sherman, 1980). Without examining accidental deaths and injuries, however, it is not possible for police managers to address adequately the totality of the risks faced by police officers.

A second problem that emerges from relying solely on assaults and homicides to define the dangers associated with the policing profession is that it becomes difficult to accurately compare the dangerousness of police work to other occupations. This is problematic because dangerousness is a relative phenomenon. Danger is most meaningful when one can compare the hazards of one occupation with the hazards of another.

In short, operationalizing danger strictly as assaults and homicides precludes an appreciation of both the absolute dangers of policing (by overlooking a potentially significant area of threat) as well as the relative dangers of policing (by preventing the comparison of the danger in police work to danger in other occupations). These issues are addressed in the current study by (a) expanding the conceptualization of dangerousness to include injuries that occur as a result of accidents; (b) comparing accidental injuries to those that result from felonious acts; and (c) comparing injury incidents of varying natures and causes across occupations, fire fighting in particular. By analyzing the nature and frequency of police injuries sustained either by accident or assault for police officers and comparing these to injuries sustained by firefighters, one may develop a more complete appreciation of the relative physical hazards of police work.

Literature Review

The Absolute Dangers of Police Work

As noted, most studies on the dangerousness of police work have examined assaults and homicides (e.g., Edwards, 1995; Fridell & Pate, 1997;

Hirschel et al., 1994; Meyer, Magedanz, Dahlin, & Chapman, 1981; Uchida, Brooks, & Kopers, 1987). These studies have shown that assaults are most common in disturbance and arrest situations, that the injuries are usually relatively minor, and that they are most commonly inflicted via person weapons (e.g., hands and feet).

Alpert and Dunham (1999) analyzed injury incidents that occurred in situations in which the police used physical force in controlling subjects and in which subjects used force against the police. They found that the most common type of force used by subjects was striking or hitting the police officer (44%), followed by pushing or pulling the officer (27%) and grabbing or holding the officer (20%). The most common injuries sustained by officers were bruises or abrasions, followed by sprains or strains and lacerations. Of the injured officers, 2% were bitten by the suspect, 2% suffered broken bones, and 1% were injured by gunshots.

Kaminski and Sorensen (1995) took a different approach and identified factors that differentiated between assaults that involved a physical attack and resulted in officer injury and assaults that involved a physical attack but did not result in officer injury. Using data originally collected and analyzed by Uchida et al. (1987), the researchers found that officers were more likely to be injured as a result of an assault when more than one officer was involved, when the suspect/assailant used bodily force as opposed to a weapon, when the suspect was under arrest or was fighting with officers, and when the suspect was sober. The researchers also found that there was a curvilinear relationship between officer height and odds of being injured; the odds of injury decreased up until the officer was 70 inches tall, then the odds of injury increased. In addition, officers with more years of service were generally less likely to be injured when assaulted. Officer weight, age, gender, and education were not related to the odds of injury.

On an ongoing basis, the FBI regularly reports on the killings, assaults, and other deaths of police officers in their annual publication, *Law Enforcement Officers Killed and Assaulted* (Federal Bureau of Investigation, 1998). The FBI report shows that for the years 1989 through 1998, 682 officers were feloniously killed in the line of duty. Almost the same number of officers were killed accidentally (*n* = 636), most often in motor vehicle, motorcycle, or aircraft accidents. More than a half a million officers (623,887) were assaulted in this 10-year time frame. Relatively little attention is given to accidents in the report, even though accidents are a cause of a large proportion of all deaths. No information is provided about accidents that did not result in deaths. In short, because of the focus on assaults, homicides, and deaths in the previous research, little is known about the nature and frequency of accidental and nonfatal injuries to police officers.

One exception is a study conducted by Brandl (1996), which compared accidental injuries to ones that resulted from felonious acts. Brandl examined more than 2,000 incidents resulting in police officer injuries or deaths. He found that a relatively small proportion of injury incidents resulted from assaults (10%), about one-half of all incidents resulted from accidents (e.g., 54%) (e.g., automobile accidents, slips, and falls), and the remaining incidents resulted from uncooperative or resisting subjects (36%) (e.g., officer was injured during a foot pursuit of subject). In addition, Brandl found that the most serious injuries were most often due to accidents, most medical treatment was due to accidents. and most days off were the result of accidents. For example, Brandl found that 52 incidents resulted in broken bones during the study period. Of these, 6 were as a result of assaults, 21 were due to accidents, and 25 were the result of uncooperative suspects. Medical attention was sought by officers in 50% of accidents, 43% of incidents with uncooperative suspects, and 37% of assaults. Fourteen percent of assaults resulted in at least 1 day off of work due to the injury, 18% in uncooperative suspect incidents, and 20% in accidents. As Brandl's study attests, there is clearly value to examining accidental injuries and deaths in police work. Failure to do so results in an incomplete and inaccurate picture of the dangers of police work.

The Relative Dangers of Police Work

Few studies have empirically compared injuries sustained by police officers to injuries sustained by incumbents of other occupations. *The Census of Fatal Occupational Injuries* (Bureau of Labor Statistics, 2000) showed that policing ranked 8th of the 10 most dangerous industries,[1] but of course, this conclusion does not take into consideration nonfatal incidents. Violanti, Vena, and Marshall (1996) compared the cause of death among police and other municipal workers. This study showed that a larger proportion of police officers died as a result of suicide and homicide than other municipal workers, but a smaller proportion died as a result of accidents. No comparisons were provided with regard to nonfatal injuries. Peek-Asa et al. (1997) examined assaults across occupations and found that, not surprisingly, police departments reported the highest rates among the 9 industries that reported any assaults.[2] The police group was calculated to be 73.1 times more likely to be assaulted at work than the overall industry average. The researchers also found that most injuries that resulted from assaults, regardless of the occupation, were relatively minor, most being contusions, sprains, and strains. No comparisons were provided for deaths or accidents. Finally, Feuer and Rosenman (1986) examined the rate and causes of death among a sample of retired police officers and firefighters and found that the mortality of these two groups did not differ from that of the general population, with the exception of increased rates of skin cancer and heart disease among firefighters and increased heart disease among police officers. Although this study does make comparisons between the police and firefighters, no comparisons are provided with regard to accidents, assaults, or homicides. Indeed, given the current state of the research, we know little about the physical risks of policing—particularly the risks posed by accidents and other nonfatal incidents—compared to other occupations.

Study Objectives

In this study, we explore the absolute dangers associated with police work by broadening the definition of danger typically used by researchers in this area. Specifically, we examine injuries that occurred as a result of assaults, resisting subjects, and accidents. In doing so, we provide a more comprehensive picture of the dangers associated with police work than that currently found in the literature (cf. Brandl, 1996).

This study also explores the relative dangers of police work by comparing the injuries reported by police officers to those reported by firefighters in the same Midwestern municipality. Police officers and firefighters were compared for several reasons. First, both organizations share common characteristics: Both are responsible for providing emergency uniformed services to the public, both have the same source of funding (i.e., municipal tax revenue), both have similar compensation levels (i.e., parity), and both are occupations in which the nature of the work poses hazards above and beyond those typically found in the workplace. In particular, police officers deal with suspects who may or may not peacefully acquiesce to the instructions of police officers. Similarly, firefighters find themselves at risk during the course of fighting fires and assisting people in precarious situations. Clearly, other municipal employees do not have such responsibilities or corresponding risks. Second, police and fire departments have been previously compared to each other in the past (e.g., Feuer & Rosenman, 1986; Fyfe, 1995). Finally, in this study, police officers (police officers and detectives) and firefighters (firefighters and heavy equipment operators) about whom data were collected were employed by the same municipality, resulting in injury report forms and associated reporting procedures that enabled consistent comparisons. In short, it appears reasonable that if police officers are to be compared with other municipal employees, firefighters would be would be most appropriate. By analyzing the nature and frequency of police injuries sustained by either accident or assault with those sustained by firefighters, one is able to develop a more complete appreciation of the relative hazards of police work.

Method

Data

At the time of the study (1997), the police and fire departments served a population of approximately 600,000, of which approximately 40% were members of racial minority groups (30% of the population was African American). The largest segment of the population was employed in the manufacturing sector. The median annual household income was approximately $41,000, with about 84% of families above the poverty level (of 2000). The overall crime rate in the city most often ranks in the lower half of the 25 most similarly sized municipalities in the country. In 1997, the police department employed more than 2,000 sworn officers (of which about 1,700 were patrol officers or detectives), and the fire department employed approximately 1,000 sworn members (of which about 700 were firefighters or heavy equipment operators).

Data Source

As mandated under worker's compensation laws and departmental policies, city employees were required to complete a standard Report of Accident form upon sustaining a work-related injury (via an accident or assault). The report was typically completed by the employee's supervisor at or near the time the incident occurred. The report contained data on the employee's demographic characteristics, employment information, the date and time of the incident, a description of injuries, whether medical attention was sought, and a narrative that explained the circumstances of the incident.

In a single report, several specific injuries may have been documented (e.g., officer fell and received abrasions to hands and knees). Therefore, although each report documented one incident for a particular individual, several injuries may have been sustained and recorded in the report. If more than one employee was injured (or killed) as a result of the same incident (e.g., motor-vehicle accident), a separate report documenting the particular injuries sustained would have been filed for each individual. As such, the unit of analysis in this study was the injury incident.

Data Collection

Injury incidents that occurred in 1997 were analyzed. For the police, a data coding form was completed on all reports that identified a police officer or detective as the injured party. For the fire department reports, a coding form was completed on all reports in which it was determined that a firefighter or heavy equipment operator was the injured party. These four positions represent line-level personnel in each of the respective departments. As a result of the coding process, a total of 1,054 police injury reports and 530 fire department injury reports were included and analyzed in the study.

Variables

The data for the study were obtained from the injury reports and were transcribed as recorded by the supervisor who completed the reports. Specifically, the variables of interest consisted of (a) nature of the injury incident, (b) nature of the most serious injury sustained, (c) total number of injuries sustained, (d) activity that resulted in the injury incident, (e) whether medical attention was sought as a result of the incident, and (f) whether time was lost from work as a result of the incident (for police only).[3]

The nature of the injury incident was defined as either as a result of an accident, a resisting subject, or an assault. The incident was considered a result of an assault on the employee if it appeared that the employee was directly injured by the intentional assaultive acts of the subject. Specifically, if the employee was hit, kicked, bit, shot, stabbed, or spat on, the injury was considered a result of an assault. An injury incident was considered a result of a resisting subject if it was indicated in the report that the subject was fleeing, resisting (arrest or treatment), or was otherwise uncooperative. In all other instances, the injury incident was considered a result of an accident.

The nature of the most serious injury sustained had the following values: laceration/abrasion, sprain/strain, contusion, other muscle pain, contact with bodily fluid,[4] other contact with infectious disease, broken bones/dislocated joints, other pain, human bite, dog bite, contact with hazardous material, smoke/fume inhalation, bee/wasp sting, torn ligaments/tendons, eye injury (other than black eye), gunshot wound, burns, electrical shock, exhaustion/heat stroke, or other injury. The process of determining what constituted the most serious injury when more than one injury was identified was not often clear-cut. Specific medical details on the injuries were usually not provided in the reports. In some cases, it was easier to identify the more serious injury (e.g., fractured ribs vs. sprained finger) than in others (puncture to foot vs. contusion to elbow). When intuitively such a determination was difficult to make, the first injury listed on the report was considered most serious.

As for the total number of injuries sustained, injuries were counted separately if it appeared that each injury would likely require separate treatment. As common examples, pain and contusion to foot was considered one injury, whereas contusion to foot and laceration to hand were considered two injuries.

The activity that led to the incident assumed several values: controlling/arresting subject, conducting investigation, apprehending fleeing subject (on foot), vehicle accident, processing prisoner (e.g., controlling prisoner in lockup), other vehicle-related (e.g., slammed hand in car door), during training, on departmental premises (e.g., slip and fall), other physical activity (e.g., changing tire, foot patrol), assisting citizen/victim (e.g., first aid), when using police/fire equipment (not at fire/crime scene), during fire rescue/discovery, doing forced entry, fighting fire/injured at scene (e.g., using equipment at a fire scene), during shooting incident, post-shooting incident (related to stress), other work-related stress (usually self-diagnosis on report), and other activity (e.g., slip and fall where activity engaged in is not specified).

Medical attention was considered to have been sought and received if a treating practitioner (e.g., a medical doctor) was identified in the report. Finally, the number of work days lost due to the incident/injury was coded as it appeared in the report.

Results

The results of the analyses are presented in Tables 1 through 3. Table 1 reports the results of the analyses on police injury incidents, Table 2 shows the analyses on police incidents disaggregated by the nature of the incident, and Table 3 provides a comparison of police and fire personnel injury incidents.

It is seen in Table 1 that just greater than 10% ($n = 110$) of all police injury incidents were the result of an assault, approximately 39% ($n = 413$) were due to subjects who were resisting or otherwise uncooperative, and the remaining 50% ($n = 531$) were a result of accidents. With regard to the nature of the most serious injury sustained by police officers, five types of injuries were common and distinguishable in frequency from the others: laceration/abrasion (19.4% of all injuries), sprain/strain (18.9%), contact with infectious disease (18.3%),[5] contusion (16.6%), and other muscle pain (15.6%). These five types of injuries account for 88.8% of all injuries to police officers and detectives. In addition, it is seen that there were no deaths, three gun shot wounds, and no knife wounds.

Table 1 also shows the activities that led to the injury incidents. The most common activities resulting in injury incidents for the police were as follows: controlling/arresting suspect (43.8%), conducting investigation (14.1%), apprehending fleeing suspect on foot (11.6%), and vehicle accident (8.7%). These four categories account for 78.2% of all incidents. By far, the most common activity resulting in injury to police personnel was controlling/ arresting suspects.

As depicted in Table 1, approximately one-half of all incidents ($n = 516$) were serious enough to warrant immediate medical attention; however, 87.7% ($n = 909$) did not result in any time lost from work. Finally, on average, police officers sustained 1.43 injuries per incident (1,507 separate injuries were documented in the 1,054 reports/incidents). Considering the total number of patrol officers and detectives in the department, there were 0.610 incidents reported per officer.

Table 2 shows the key variables disaggregated by the nature of the incident. In assaults against the police, the most common injuries were contusions (37.3%), human bites (19.1%), and contacts with infectious disease (17.3%). When incidents resulted from a resisting subject, lacerations/abrasions (27.1%) and sprains/strains (24.9%) were the most common injuries reported. In accidents, contact with infectious disease was the most prevalent injury (24.7%), followed by other muscle pain (18.1%). Perhaps surprisingly, Table 2 also shows that many of the most severe injuries were not the result of assaults. For example, of the 28 incidents that involved broken bones/dislocated joints, only 2 resulted from assaults. Similarly, none of the 5 torn ligaments/tendons resulted from assaults, and none of the 3 gunshot wounds resulted from assaults.

The activities resulting in injuries varied according to the nature of the injury incident. Controlling/arresting subject was the activity that most commonly led to assaults (90.0%). In incidents resulting from a resisting subject, controlling/arresting subjects (68.3%) and apprehending fleeing suspects (29.1%) were most common preceding activities. In accidents, conducting investigations (28%), followed by vehicle accidents (15.7%) and controlling/ arresting subjects (15.0%), was most common.

Table 2 also shows that medical attention was most likely sought as a result of assaults (67.0%) and least likely in accidents (47.8%). However, the opposite pattern held for time lost from work: Accidents were most likely to result in time off work (13.8%), and assaults were least likely (7.5%).

Table 1   Characteristics of injury incidents for police officers

	n	%
Nature of injury incident	1,054	100.0
Accident	531	50.4
Resisting subject	413	39.2
Assaultive subject	110	10.4
Nature of most serious injury	1,054	100.2
Laceration/abrasion	205	19.4
Sprain/strain	199	18.9
Contact with infectious disease	193	18.3
Contact with bodily fluid	98	
Blood-to-blood contact	16	
Other contact with infectious disease	95	
Contusion	175	16.6
Other muscle pain	164	15.6
Broken bones/dislocated joints	28	2.7
Human bite	22	2.1
Other pain	10	0.9
Contact with hazardous material	8	0.8
Smoke/fume inhalation	7	0.7
Torn ligaments/tendons	5	0.5
Eye injury (other than black eye)	4	0.4
Gunshot wound	3	0.3
Burns	2	0.2
Knife wound	0	0.0
Death	0	0.0
Other	29	2.8
Activity resulting in injury	1,050	100.2
Controlling/arresting subject	460	43.8
Conducting investigation	148	14.1
Apprehending fleeing subject (on foot)	122	11.6
Vehicle accident	91	8.7
Processing prisoner	52	5.0
Other vehicle related	36	3.4
During training	31	3.0
On department premises	23	2.2
Other physical activity	22	2.1
Assisting citizen/victim	17	1.6
Using equipment (not at fire scene)	12	1.1
During fire rescue/discovery	6	0.6
Doing forced entry	3	0.3
Fighting fire/at fire scene	1	0.1
During shooting incident	1	0.1
Other	26	2.5
Medical attention sought	1,016	100.0
No	500	49.2
Yes	516	50.8
Time off work due to injury	1,037	100.0
No	909	87.7
Yes	128	13.3

Rate of injury incidents (per officer) = 0.610
Number of injuries per incident = 1.43

Note: Missing data excluded from the table; percentages may not sum to 100 due to rounding.

Table 2   Characteristics of injury incidents for police officers by nature of incident

	Assaultive subject		Resisting subject		Accident	
	n	%	n	%	n	%
Nature of most serious injury	110	100.0	413	99.8	531	100.2
Laceration abrasion	13	11.8	112	27.1	80	15.1
Sprain/strain	3	2.7	103	24.9	93	17.5
Contact with infectious disease	19	17.3	43	10.4	131	24.7
Contact with bodily fluid	19		40		39	
Blood-to-blood contact	16		0		0	
Other contact with infectious disease	0		3		92	
Contusion	41	37.3	66	16.0	68	12.8
Other muscle pain	10	9.1	58	14.0	96	18.1
Broken bones/dislocated joints	2	1.8	15	3.6	11	2.1
Human bite	21	19.1	1	0.2	0	0.0
Other pain	1	0.9	2	0.5	7	1.3
Contact with hazardous material	0	0.0	4	1.0	4	0.8
Smoke/fume inhalation	0	0.0	0	0.0	7	1.3
Tore ligaments/tendons	0	0.0	4	1.0	1	0.2
Eye injury (other than black eye)	0	0.0	1	0.2	3	0.6
Gunshot wound	0	0.0	0	0.0	3	0.6
Burns	0	0.0	1	0.2	1	0.2
Knife wound	0	0.0	0	0.0	0	0.0
Death	0	0.0	0	0.0	0	0.0
Other	0	0.0	3	0.7	26	4.9
Activity resulting in injury	110	99.9	413	100.1	528	100.0
Controlling/arresting subject	99	90.0	282	68.3	79	15.0
Conducting investigation	0	0.0	0	0.0	148	28.0
Apprehending fleeing subject	2	1.8	120	29.1	0	0.0
Vehicle accident	2	1.8	6	1.5	83	15.7
Processing prisoner	5	4.5	2	0.5	45	8.5
Other vehicle related	0	0.0	2	0.5	34	6.4
During training	0	0.0	0	0.0	31	5.9
On department premises	0	0.0	0	0.0	23	4.4
Other physical activity	0	0.0	0	0.0	22	4.2
Assisting citizen/victim	1	0.9	0	0.0	16	3.0
Using equipment (not at fire scene)	0	0.0	0	0.0	12	2.3
During fire rescue/discovery	0	0.0	0	0.0	12	1.1
Doing forced entry	0	0.0	0	0.0	3	.6
Fighting fire/at fire scene	0	0.0	0	0.0	1	.2
During shooting incident	1	0.9	0	0.0	0	0.0
Other	0	0.0	1	0.2	25	4.7
Medical attention sought	106	100.0	402	100.0	508	100.0
No	35	33.0	200	49.8	265	52.2
Yes	71	67.0	202	50.2	243	47.8
Time off work	107	100.0	407	100.0	523	100.0
No	99	92.5	359	88.2	451	86.2
Yes	8	7.5	48	11.8	72	13.8

Note: Missing data excluded from the table; percentages may not sum to 100 due to rounding.

Table 3 Characteristics of injury incidents for police officers and firefighters

	Police		Fire	
	n	%	n	%
Nature of injury incident	1,054	100.0	530	100.0
Accident	531	50.4	526	99.2
Resisting subject	413	39.2	0	0.0
Assaultive subject	110	10.4	4	0.8
Nature of most serious injury	1,054	100.2	530	100.1
Laceration/abrasion	205	19.4	46	8.7
Sprain/strain	199	18.9	151	28.5
Contact with infectious disease	193	18.3	44	8.3
Contact with bodily fluid	98		11	
Other contact with infectious disease	95		33	
Contusion	175	16.6	40	7.5
Other muscle pain	164	15.6	132	24.9
Broken bones/dislocated joints	28	2.7	11	2.1
Human bite	22	2.1	1	0.2
Other pain	10	0.9	5	0.9
Contact with hazardous material	8	0.8	7	1.3
Smoke/fume inhalation	7	0.7	22	4.2
Torn ligaments/tendons	5	0.5	1	0.2
Eye injury (other than black eye)	4	0.4	21	4.0
Gunshot wound	3	0.3	0	0.0
Burns	2	0.2	18	3.4
Knife wound	0	0.0	1	0.2
Death	0	0.0	0	0.0
Other	29	2.8	30	5.7
Activity resulting in injury	1,050	100.2	530	99.9
Controlling/arresting subject	460	43.8	0	0.0
Conducting investigation	148	14.1	0	0.0
Apprehending fleeing subject (on foot)	122	11.6	0	0.0
Vehicle accident	91	8.7	8	1.5
Processing prisoner	52	5.0	0	0.0
Other vehicle related	36	3.4	62	11.7
During training	31	3.0	27	5.1
On department premises	23	2.2	54	10.2
Other physical activity	22	2.1	17	3.2
Assisting citizen/victim	17	1.6	79	14.9
Using equipment (not at fire scene)	12	1.1	50	9.4
During fire rescue/discovery	6	0.6	7	1.3
Doing forced entry	3	0.3	9	1.7
Fighting fire at fire scene	1	0.1	199	37.5
During shooting incident	1	0.1	0	0.0
Other	26	2.5	18	3.4
Medical attention sought	1,016	100.0	524	100.0
No	500	49.2	264	50.4
Yes	.516	50.8	260	49.6
Rate of injury incidents (per officer or firefighter)	0.610		0.717	
Number of injuries per incident	1.43		1.09	

Note: Missing data excluded from the table; percentages may not sum to 100 due to rounding.

Table 3 allows for a comparison of injuries reported by police and fire department personnel. Table 3 shows that more than 99% of fire department personnel injury incidents were the result of accidents; only 4 (of 530, or 0.8%) incidents were due to an intentional assaultive act on the part of a subject. Furthermore, for fire department personnel, two types of injuries were common and distinguishable from the others: sprain/strain (26.4%) and other muscle pain (25.0%). These two types of injuries account for 51.4% of all injuries to firefighters and HEOs. Contacts with bodily fluid (especially (blood-to-blood contacts), human bites, and dog bites were more likely to occur among police officers; whereas smoke/fume inhalation, eye injuries, and burns were more likely to occur among firefighters. Like the police department, the fire department did not experience any work-related deaths in 1997.

It is seen in Table 3 that the most common activities resulting in injury incidents for firefighters or heavy equipment operators were as follows: fighting fire/while at fire scene (37.5%), assisting citizen/victim (14.9%), other vehicle related (11.7%), and while on department premises (10.2%). These four categories accounted for 74.3% of all incidents. Of the injuries that occurred as a result of fighting fire/while at fire scene, the greatest proportion resulted from using equipment at the scene (75 of the 199 injury incidents, or 37.7%; results not tabled).

Table 3 also shows that similar to the police, fire department personnel sought medical attention as a result of the incident in 49.6% (260 of 524) of the incidents. Finally, on average, fire department personnel sustained 1.09 injuries per incident (578 injuries reported in 530 incidents). Considering the total number of personnel in the department, there were 0.717 incidents reported per employee.

Conclusion

On the basis of this descriptive study, several conclusions can be drawn. First, based on the analysis of injuries to police officers, it is seen that assaults on officers—the focus of much previous research—are relatively rare events, as are serious injuries and deaths. The overwhelming majority of incidents, regardless of the task engaged in, are not as a result of assaults and, of course, do not result in deaths. Rather, most injury incidents are a result of accidents. Particularly prevalent in accidents are contacts with infectious diseases (24.7%, $n = 131$). This is a dimension of danger that is rarely captured in the conceptualization of danger used by most police researchers. Yet these incidents—which include exposures to relatively minor diseases such as chicken pox or head lice to far more serious diseases such as hepatitis or HIV—are part and parcel of dealing with the public. The frequency of these incidents, however, highlights the continuing need for proper education and training for officers (see Edwards & Tewksbury, 1996). Contact with persons having HIV, for example, may be a less frightening experience for officers who have received training on the disease and the different means by which the virus may be transmitted. Officers may also take the precaution of wearing gloves at all times to reduce the likelihood of coming into contact with bodily fluids.

Second, felonious incidents differ from other types of incidents. Most of the most serious injuries sustained by police officers are not a result of assaults. As noted, the most serious injuries are most often due to accidents, most medical treatment is due to accidents, and most days off of work are as a result of accidents. These findings are consistent with those reported by Brandl (1996). Little question, if all or even some portion of assaults could be prevented through policies and training, which is the intent of much of the prior research in identifying high-risk or dangerous activities, there would still exist a large percentage of injury incidents to police officers. Simply put, consideration of the physical hazards of police work must include not only assaults and homicides but also accidents.

Third, with regard to a comparison of police and fire department personnel injuries, the frequency (i.e., rate) of incidents reported by police and fire department personnel is similar, but the nature of the injuries and the causes of the injuries are not. The differences in activities that lead to injuries for police and fire personnel reflect important differences in the nature of the occupations and the tasks that are expected to be performed. As such, it is, at a minimum, safe to conclude that the risks, dangers, and physical demands of police work and fire fighting are different. In particular, the police are much more likely to be injured during confrontations with antagonistic people. As such, a relatively large proportion of the actual risks of police work derive from, at least indirectly, the actions of people, with those actions resulting in injuries to police officers. In contrast, most of the risks of fire fighting are associated with using equipment (vehicles, hoses, ladders, axes, etc.), assisting citizens, and performing living activities (preparing meals, cleaning, maintenance, etc.). It is worthwhile to note that when fire department personnel are injured in interactions with citizens, it is most often a result of providing some sort of assistance to them (e.g., first aid). Accordingly, despite the common comparison between firefighters and police officers and the similarities of their occupations, policing and fire fighting are clearly different jobs in terms of their dangers and demands. In this regard, perhaps police work could be more accurately compared to the work of correctional officers or custodial personnel in mental institutions.

Fourth, in considering further the comparison of police and fire department personnel injuries, specifically the nature of the injuries sustained, how these injuries occur, and the significance of these injuries, it is important to realize that there is not only a physiological dimension to injuries but a psychological one as well. With regard to the physiological dimension, one could debate the significance of police officers' typical contusion/abrasion/laceration injuries versus firefighters' typical muscle sprains and strains—different medical opinions may lead to different conclusions. More meaningful, perhaps, is the likely difference in the psychological effects that stem from the typical injuries sustained by police officers and firefighters. Of particular relevance here are those injuries that occur as a result of an assault on the officer or an otherwise resisting, combative subject. One might expect that injuries that occur as a result of one person doing harm to another person are more psychologically significant than injuries that occur as a result of physical exertion. Although this expectation could not be tested given the nature of the data collected here, previous research does support this contention. Briefly, Violanti (1994) found that police officers ranked being physically attacked the third most significant stressor in their work, just behind killing someone in the line of duty and having a fellow officer killed. According to Cullen, Link, Travis, and Lemming (1983), heightened perceptions of danger among police officers contribute to increased work stress and, furthermore, to the manifestation of depression. McMurray (1990) reported that officers who were assaulted expressed increased levels of alienation and decreased levels of job satisfaction and work-related support. In short, even though injuries that result from assaults are relatively rare in police work (and even more so in fire fighting), the likely psychological effects of injuries that result from these interactions may likely have dramatic long-term negative consequences for officers' physical and emotional well-being and, as such, may be much more significant than injuries that occur in other ways.

   This study provides direction for future research. First, as demonstrated in this study, in assessing the physical dangers of police work, one needs to include not only assaults and homicides but also injuries that result from accidents. Second, it is necessary to measure the psychological effects of physical injuries. Future research that seeks to document the hazards of police work would be well advised to broaden the conceptualization of risk/hazards to include psychological effects. Third, it would be worthwhile to examine the long-term physiological impact of injuries. Although injuries are usually minor, long-term cumulative effects may have reaching and lasting consequences. Fourth, it may be useful to compare injuries across police departments of different sizes with different workloads, policies, and structures. In addition, further cross-occupational comparisons may cast additional light on the relative dangers of police work. A final important direction for future research is to examine individual-level variation in injury incidents (Hansen, 1989). Kaminski and Sorensen (1995) took a first step in this direction when they examined individual-level variation in whether officers were injured as a result of an assault, but they did not address the larger questions, namely the following: Are some officers at more risk of accidents, assaults, or other injuries than others? Are some officers more at risk of ill psychological effects of injuries than other officers? Are there accident-, assault-, or injury-prone officers? What characteristics do they share? Studies designed to address these issues may contribute to our understanding of the dangers of police work.

NOTES

[1] The other industries identified were agriculture, mining, construction, manufacturing, transportation, wholesale trade, retail trade, finance, and services. No further details are provided regarding the nature of the jobs within these occupations.

[2] The other industries identified were hotel management, bus driver, school bus driver, retail, hospitals, schools, correctional facilities, and private security.

[3] Given the work schedule of firefighters and heavy equipment operators (two 24-hour shifts a week) and the manner in which the fire department injury reports were completed, it was not possible to determine for fire department personnel whether work time was lost as a result of the injury incident.

[4] A "blood-to-blood" contact occurred when a subject's blood came into contact with the employee's blood, either by aggravating an existing wound or as a result of a new wound.

[5] Note that approximately one-half of contacts with infectious disease involved actual contact with bodily fluid. Sixteen of these incidents involved blood-to-blood contact.

REFERENCES

Alpert, G. P., & Dunham, R. G. (1999). The force factor: Measuring and assessing police use of force and suspect resistance. In *Use of force by police: Overview of national and local data*. Washington, DC: National Institute of Justice.

Bayley, D. H., & Garofalo, J. (1989). The management of violence by police patrol officers. *Criminology, 27*, 1–23.

Brandl, S. G. (1996). In the line of duty: A descriptive analysis of police assaults and accidents. *Journal of Criminal Justice, 24*, 255–264.

Bureau of Labor Statistics. (2000). *Census of fatal occupational injuries*. Washington, DC: U.S. Department of Labor, Bureau of Labor Statistics.

Centers for Disease Control. (1998). Surveillance for nonfatal occupational injuries treated in hospital emergency departments—United States, 1996. *Morbidity and Mortality Weekly Report, 47*, 302–306.

Centers for Disease Control. (2001). Fatal occupational injuries—United States, 1980–1997. *Journal of the American Medical Association, 285*, 2440–2444.

Cullen, F. T., Link, B. G., Travis, L. F., & Lemming, T. (1983). Paradox in policing: A note on perceptions of danger. *Journal of Police Science and Administration, 11*, 457–462.

Edwards, T. D. (1995). Felonious killing of state police and highway patrol officers: A descriptive and comparative evaluation. *American Journal of Police, 14*, 89–105.

Edwards, T. D., & Tewksbury, R. (1996). HIV/AIDS: State police training practices and personnel policies. *American Journal of Police, 15*, 45–62.

Federal Bureau of Investigation. (1998). *Law enforcement officers killed and assaulted*. Washington, DC: Government Printing Office.

Feldstein, A., Valanis, B., Vollmer, W., Stevens, N., & Overton, C. (1993). The back injury prevention project pilot study. *Journal of Occupational Medicine, 35*, 114–120.

Feuer, E., & Rosenman, K. (1986). Mortality in police and firefighters in New Jersey. *American Journal of Industrial Medicine, 9*, 517–527.

Fridell, L. A., & Pate, A. M. (1997). Death on patrol: Killings of American law enforcement officers. In R. G. Dunham & G. P Alpert (Eds.), *Critical issues in policing*. Long Grove, IL: Waveland.

Fyfe, J. (1979). Administrative interventions on police shooting discretion: An empirical examination. *Journal of Criminal Justice, 7*, 309–324.

Fyfe, J. (1995). Good policing. In B. Forst (Ed.), *The socioeconomics of crime and justice.* New York: M. E. Sharpe.

Garner, J., & Clemmer, E. (1986). *Danger to police in domestic disturbances.* Washington, DC: U.S. Department of Justice.

Hansen, C. (1989). A causal model of the relationship among accidents, biodata, personality, and cognitive factors. *Journal of Applied Psychology, 74,* 81–90.

Hirschel, J. D., Dean, C. W., & Lumb, R. C. (1994). The relative contribution of domestic violence to assault and injury of police officers. *Justice Quarterly, 11,* 99–117.

Kaminski, R. J., Edwards, S. M., & Johnson, J. W. (1998). The deterrent effects of oleoresin capsicum on assaults against the police: Testing the velcro-effect hypothesis. *Police Quarterly 1,* 1–20.

Kaminski, R. J., & Sorensen, D. W. (1995). A multivariate analysis of individual, situational and environmental factors associated with police assault injuries. *American Journal of Police, 14,* 3–48.

Konstantin, D. (1984). Homicide of American law enforcement officers. *Justice Quarterly, 1,* 29–45.

Lester, D. (1981). Occupational injuries, illnesses, and fatalities in police officers. *Police Chief, 48*(10), 43, 63.

McMurray, H. L. (1990). Attitudes of assaulted police officers and their policy implications. *Journal of Police Science and Administration, 17,* 44–48.

Meyer, C. K., Magedanz, T., Dahlin, D., & Chapman, S. (1981). A comparative assessment of assault incidents: Robbery related ambush and general police assaults. *Journal of Police Science and Administration, 9,* 1–18.

National Institute for Occupational Safety and Health. (1992). *Homicide in U.S. workplaces: A strategy for prevention and research* (DHHS Publication No. 92-103). Morgantown, WV: U.S. Department of Health and Human Services, Public Health Services, Center for Disease Control, National Institute for Occupational Safety and Health.

National Institute for Occupational Safety and Health. (1997). *Current Intelligence Bulletin 57: Violence in the workplace risk factors and prevention strategies* (DHHS Publication No. 96-100). Morgantown, WV: U.S. Department of Health and Human Services, Public Health. Services, Center for Disease Control, National Institute for Occupational Safety and Health.

Peek-Asa, C., Howard, J., Vargas, L., Kraus, J. F. (1997). Incidence of non-fatal workplace assault injuries determined from employer's reports in California. *Journal of Occupational and Environmental Medicine, 39,* 44–50.

Sherman, L. W. (1980). Perspectives on police and violence. *Annals, 452,* 1–12.

Skolnick, J. H. (1994). *Justice without trial: Law enforcement in a democratic society.* New York: Macmillan.

Stanford, R. M., & Mowry, B. L. (1990). Domestic disturbance danger rate. *Journal of Police Science and Administration, 17,* 244–249.

Uchida, C. D., Brooks, L. W., & Kopers, C. S. (1987). Danger to police during domestic encounters: Assaults on Baltimore County police, 1984–86. *Criminal Justice Policy Review, 2,* 357–371.

Violanti, J. M. (1994). Ranking police stressors. *Psychological Report, 75,* 824–826.

Violanti, J. M., Vena, J. E., & Marshall, J. R. (1996). Suicides, homicides, and accidental death: A comparative risk assessment of police officers and municipal workers. *American Journal of Industrial Medicine, 30,* 99–104.

22

Beyond Boston
Applying Theory to Understand and Address Sustainability Issues in Focused Deterrence Initiatives for Violence Reduction

Marie Skubak Tillyer, Robin S. Engel, & Brian Lovins

In the mid-1990s, Boston implemented Operation Ceasefire as part of a gun project designed to reduce youth homicides. A major component of this initiative was "pulling levers," a focused deterrence strategy that aimed to directly and accurately communicate new consequences of violence to at-risk youth. The project was successful, resulting in a 63% decline in homicides among youths 24 years and younger (Braga, Kennedy, Waring, & Piehl, 2001). This success led to the adoption of focused deterrence initiatives by many cities as a response to violence (e.g., Braga, McDevitt, & Pierce, 2006; Braga, Pierce, McDevitt, Bond, & Cronin, 2008; Kennedy & Braga, 1998). The initial use of focused deterrence strategies by a handful of jurisdictions has led to a national movement in the United States.[1] Although focused deterrence has received considerable mainstream media visibility, academic attention, and federal support, little is known about why these initiatives work. Furthermore, despite early successes, many cities have been unable to sustain the results. The assumption of many researchers and practitioners has been that sustainability issues can be traced back to problems associated with institutionalization of the program; that is, full implementation of the strategies was discontinued and thus the early success was not sustained (Kennedy, 2007).

On its face, this explanation makes sense, and therefore this was the impetus to design a violence reduction initiative in Cincinnati, Ohio, that would address these institutionalization issues through a series of business management strategies. Yet as this initiative moved forward, it became appar-

Crime & Delinquency 58(6) 973–997. 2010 Reprints and permission: sagepub.com/journalsPermissions.nav DOI: 10.1177/0011128710382343.

401

ent that institutionalization of the process was a necessary, but insufficient, solution for long-term success. Rather, we argue that the focused deterrence strategy as currently implemented in multiple cities may actually be a short-term violence reduction tool that must be supplemented and properly managed to leverage long-term success.

This article describes the focused deterrence research to date and the efforts made in Cincinnati, Ohio, to institutionalize the initiative, including the incorporation of several business management strategies. Though important, the Cincinnati experience has demonstrated that institutionalization of focused deterrence does not necessarily deliver long-term success in violence reduction. We turn to criminological theory to better understand why focused deterrence works in the short term and how to enhance the model to ensure sustained success in violence reduction. We then draw on the principles of effective intervention from the correctional rehabilitation literature to demonstrate how to improve the focused deterrence model by targeting for change in both the environment and the individual.

Focused Deterrence

Originating in Boston, focused deterrence is based on the premise that a majority of serious violence is committed by repeat offenders organized to some degree in groups or gangs (Kennedy, 1997). The violence that escalates within the street group context can be largely attributed to respect issues (e.g., Anderson, 1999; Bourgois, 2003), rather than resulting directly from the illicit drug trade. Although a violent incident may result from a single individual's actions, in reality this group dynamic defines the behaviors of individuals, how they will be received by their peers, and how they will respond to their antagonists.

Focused deterrence is grounded in a clear rejection of violence by the community and other stakeholders. This intolerance for violence is displayed in two ways. The first involves mobilizing law enforcement to create predictable consequences for individuals associated with groups or gangs that engage in violence. Law enforcement aims to exploit the lengthy criminal records of these individuals by "pulling every lever" legally available when violence occurs (Braga et al., 2001). Because these individuals break the law frequently, they are vulnerable to a wide range of legal sanctions (Kennedy, 1997). This is operationalized as a coordinated law enforcement effort among multiple agencies that prioritizes groups that engage in violence. The second display of the intolerance for violence is presented as an offer of help for those who want to opt out of a lifestyle that puts them at risk for violent offending and victimization, though this component of the model has been described in less detail in the literature.

A defining feature of focused deterrence initiatives is the direct and accurate communication of the strategy to the target population. Compliance with the new rules is promoted by advertising directly to those individuals and groups at risk for violent offending and victimization (Kennedy, 1997). In other words, individuals and groups are put on notice that law enforcement is mobilized to take out any group that engages in violence and help is available to those who want it. This advertising is done through offender notification meetings, probation and parole officers, and gang outreach workers. Individuals are notified that if any member of their group commits a homicide, the entire group will become the focus of a coordinated law enforcement effort. In essence, focused deterrence exploits the existing group structure to encourage these groups to police themselves in order to avoid becoming the priority of law enforcement.

Numerous crime reduction initiatives have been developed using the focused deterrence model, with the most well-known being Boston's Operation Ceasefire (Braga et al., 2001). Two complementary strategies were used to combat the gun violence. First, law enforcement aggressively pursued illegal firearms traffickers who supplied youth with guns. Second, the officials employed a "pulling levers" strategy that involved directly informing gangs that violence would not be tolerated and that every available legal lever would be pulled when violence occurred. Social services were offered from various sources. Using interrupted time-series analysis, Braga et al. (2001) report a 63% (from 3.5 to 1.3) decrease in the monthly average of homicide victims aged 24 years and younger, a 32% decrease in the monthly count of calls about shots fired, and a 25% decrease in the monthly count of gun assaults. All these declines were statistically significant. When Boston's youth homicide trend was compared with those of 39 other large U.S. cities for the same time period, only three other cities experienced a statistically significant decline at the time of the intervention and none had an estimated effect as large as Boston's (Braga et al., 2001).

Minneapolis employed a similar pulling levers strategy, explicitly and directly informing gangs that violence would not be tolerated and responding to acts of violence by pulling every lever legally available. This message was coupled with an offer for social services and community-based interventions. Using interrupted time-series designs, Kennedy and Braga (1998) report a reduction in the June, July, and August yearly totals of homicide victims, as well as a reduction in pre- and postintervention yearly totals of all homicide victims.

Officials in Lowell, Massachusetts, used a pulling levers strategy to combat general gang violence, as well as Asian gang violence. The police took advantage of the importance of illegal gaming among Asian street gangs and used it as a lever to pull. Gambling businesses run by older gang members were targeted in response to the violence. Braga et al. (2006) report a 24% reduction in gun assaults (from 49 to 37) and a 50% reduction in homicide (from 4 to 2, a change that would not achieve statistical significance) following the intervention. A recent impact evaluation found that the Lowell strategy was associated with a statistically significant reduction in gun-related homicides and aggravated assaults, a reduction not experienced by seven other Massachusetts cities that were used in the comparison (Braga et al., 2008).

In Indianapolis, a focused deterrence strategy was used to target illegal gun carrying and use among known groups of chronic offenders (Chermak & McGarrell, 2004; McGarrell, Chermak, Wilson, & Corsaro, 2006). Resources were focused on chronic offenders with connections to gangs, guns, and drug markets. While social services and job opportunities were offered, there was also an effort to incarcerate impact players known to be particularly dangerous and unlikely to accept social services. Using an interrupted time-series design, McGarrell et al. (2006) report a 34.3% decline in monthly homicides following implementation (comparing 27 months pre-/postintervention). This decline was statistically significant; none of the six control series experienced a significant change in homicide rates during this same period. Corsaro and McGarrell (2009) examined whether this downward trend was similar across gang and nongang homicides, which would suggest that some unmeasured influence, rather than the intervention, was responsible for the decline. Using a difference of coefficients test to compare the coefficients from ARIMA (auto regressive integrated moving average) analyses of the two trends, they found that the decline in gang homicides was significantly greater than that of nongang homicides (Corsaro & McGarrell, 2009).

In Chicago, increased federal prosecutions for convicted felons who carried or used guns, coupled with increased length of sentences in these prosecutions, were used in conjunction with a focused deterrence message delivered through offender notification meetings, letters, school programs, and community and media outreach. Offenders were offered various social services, job training, and educational opportunities. Using a quasi-experimental design with near-equivalent control groups, Papachristos, Meares, and Fagan (2007) report a 37% decline in quarterly homicide rates in the treatment area. In addition, a recent evaluation reports shooting declines ranging from 16% to 34% across treatment sites in Chicago (Skogan, Hartnett, Bump, & Dubois, 2009).

The success in violence reduction across some of these cities, however, appears to be short-lived. This lack of sustainability has been attributed to implementation issues by some involved in these initiatives (Kennedy, 2007). Failure to institutionalize the roles and processes leads actors to abandon the strategy over time, and thus, the results are only temporary. The following section details the numerous ways in which issues of institutionalization have been addressed in Cincinnati to improve the likelihood of long-term success in violence reduction.

Searching for Sustainability through Process Institutionalization: The Cincinnati Experience

In 2007, public officials, criminal justice practitioners, and researchers in Cincinnati designed and implemented the Cincinnati Initiative to Reduce Violence (CIRV, pronounced "serve"). As Kennedy (2007) conveyed to the U.S. Congress in February 2007, "Not all jurisdictions have implemented the strategies properly. Many that have, including Boston, the first and still best-known site, have let effective interventions fall apart . . . This has highlighted the need for attention to institutionalization and sustainability" (p. 3). This testimony came during the planning stages of CIRV, leaving the team acutely aware of the need for a comprehensive plan to address issues of institutionalization to sustain the violence reduction over time.

Implementation and sustainability issues have plagued many criminal justice reform efforts (Feeley, 1983; Horney & Spohn, 1991; Walker, 1993). Contributing to the failure of many initiatives is the lack of planning, competing and/ or ambiguous goals, the scarcity of resources, work overload, and the failure to address the underlying structural conditions of the neighborhoods in which reforms are typically targeted (Brown, 1981; Eisenstein & Jacob, 1977; Feeley & Simon, 1992; Lipsky, 1980; Sherman et al., 1997). The success and failures in court reform in particular have been documented across several decades (Feeley, 1983). The lessons learned from process evaluations of court reform efforts are especially relevant to multidisciplinary teams attempting to implement focused deterrence initiatives because court reform involves multiple organizations with different, and often competing, goals and objectives. For example, Cissner and Farole (2009) reviewed 13 court reform process evaluations and identified four key issues related to effective implementation and sustainability: (a) engaging in comprehensive planning, (b) identifying key stakeholders, (c) responding to emerging challenges, and (d) recognizing the need for leadership. These best practices that are associated with effective implementation and sustainability in court reform are similar across criminal justice reform efforts, including focused deterrence initiatives.

Given that sustainability was a pressing concern for both the champions and the funders of CIRV, the CIRV team needed to develop systems and processes to guard against the issues that had plagued similar initiatives in the past. To this end, the team recruited two types of experts: social science researchers and business management consultants. These experts were included in the early planning stages and have been intimately involved in daily operations ever since. Based on the sustainability issues well documented in both the management and criminal justice literatures, they counseled the CIRV team to use innovative approaches to reduce the likelihood of team collapse, including (a) development of an organizational structure, (b) utilization of corporate strategic planning principles for managing the work, and (c) systematic data collection to assist in decision making and outcome evaluation. Although these approaches may not necessarily be unique to CIRV, they are a working set of promising solutions to address issues of institutionalization and sustainability in violence reduction. Ultimately, the CIRV faced the same challenges documented in the court reform process evaluations reviewed by Cissner and Farole (2009). Based on the approaches described below, however, the CIRV team survived the initial obstacles that resulted in implementation failures in other multiagency reform efforts.

Organizational Structure

Perhaps the greatest threat to focused deterrence initiatives, and prevention strategies more generally, is that implementation simply ceases as those doing the work move on to other jobs or tasks. Focused deterrence initiatives require a high level of commitment across several agencies, and it is crucial that this commitment is transmitted through the ranks. There is high turnover at the top of many organizations, as well as among the political officials who support the initiatives. The CIRV team sought to ensure that the work would be institutionalized in positions, rather than individuals, to improve the likelihood of continued implementation. Furthermore, the team needed to clearly define the decision-making process and the division of labor. In the early planning stages, dozens of law enforcement agencies, social service providers, nonprofit organizations, government offices, community organizations, and religious institutions were identified through a systematic stakeholder analysis (Brugha & Varvasovszky, 2000). With homicide being a central concern to so many in the city, it was initially unclear the level of responsibility and decision making power each of these stakeholders should have.

To address this, the management consultants recommended developing an organizational structure to define the decision-making processes and division of labor. This helped articulate the roles needed to complete the work to ensure efficient and effective use of personnel and resources. The roles were defined in terms of skills and resources rather than by an individual's name. In addition, this allowed the team to distinguish among stakeholders and the level of responsiveness each required. To this end, CIRV initially adopted a four-tiered organizational structure composed of a Governing Board, two co-chairs, a Strategy/ Implementation (S/I) Team, and four Strategy Teams—law enforcement, services, community, and systems.

The Governing Board consisted of high-ranking city officials (Mayor, City Manager, and Council member). These individuals funded the initiative and were ultimately responsible for its success or failure. The positions that these individuals held precluded them from being involved in the daily tasks of CIRV, yet their political capital and public support of the initiative were crucial. Therefore, the Governing Board was responsible for providing resources to the initiative, as well as overcoming the barriers that hinder the success of the initiative.

The second layer consisted of the CIRV co-chairs. Originally, these two highly recognizable and influential members of the community represented the public face of the initiative. Unfortunately, the roles, responsibilities, and decision-making power of the co-chairs were not initially well-defined or clearly understood by all team members. This role confusion led to many problems within the team and ultimately threatened the sustainability of the initiative. Clarification of the roles and responsibilities occurred nearly 2 years after the initiative was launched and only after a full year of incompatibility, mission creep (i.e., departing from the program goals and objectives), and infighting among team members. The organizational structure, designed by the business management consultants, assisted greatly and ultimately salvaged the initiative through a process and renewal effort to change portions of the organizational structure that were perceived as nonfunctioning. The limited roles and responsibilities of the co-chairs, who essentially serve as the primary spokespersons of the initiative, are now better articulated and understood by team members. While CIRV team membership has changed as a result, the initiative has been institutionalized within the key organizational units that contribute the bulk of the effort toward the initiative.

The third layer is the S/I Team, which consists of the owners of each individual strategy and the expert consultants. The S/I Team is responsible for making key decisions, developing strategies, securing necessary resources, and continuously monitoring the results. In short, the S/I Team is tasked with the daily operations of CIRV and reports to the Governing Board on a regular basis to provide progress updates and request needed resources.

Finally, the CIRV Strategy Teams are each responsible for executing a particular strategy. Specifically, the law enforcement team was tasked with forming a law enforcement partnership to identify and focus enforcement on chronic violent groups. The services team was responsible for forming and continually improving a life-change system that engages members of violence-prone groups and moves them to an employment-based lifestyle. The community team was responsible for forming a partnership to work with affected communities to articulate norms and expectations that explicitly reject violence. The systems team was expected to develop and implement a system that ensured permanence and quality assurance.

Applying Corporate Principles

Once the organizational structure was in place, the business management consultants introduced the corporate principles of OGSM—objectives, goals, strategies, and measures (Snow & Hambrick, 1980). These strategic planning principles helped organize, prioritize, and delegate the work. In addition, the CIRV team adopted a series of balanced scorecards (BSC), an approach that has been used by many organizations as a "decision support tool at the strategic management level" (Martinsons, Davison, & Tse, 1999, p. 71). This approach encourages organizations to determine a series of objectives, goals, strategies, and measures that are not necessarily tied directly to lag financial indicators in businesses. The purpose is to create an easy to understand matrix to hold teams accountable for more immediate performance evaluations. Designed to balance long-term and short-term goals with multiple indicators of performance, this approach better links measurements to the overall strategy (Kaplan & Norton, 1993, 1996).

Applying corporate principles that direct business environments to the public policy arena was at first a difficult fit. Many of the CIRV partners represented criminal justice and social service organizations not accustomed to this type of managerial oversight. Furthermore, it was unclear how the collective CIRV team (a coalition of representatives from multiple agencies with differing goals and objectives) would hold one another accountable for their respective tasks and outcomes. The development of the BSC system was an attempt to provide accountability and transparency to the process, as well as build alignment among team members.

Similar to the organizational structure discussed above, the use of these corporate principles proved to be an important component of institutionalizing the CIRV process. The planning process allowed participants to align themselves to specific team goals and understand what was expected of them and how they would be held accountable for particular results. This initial planning process proved critical as team members began to stray from the initiative's objectives and goals. Many successful initiatives suffer from this "mission creep" over time as they fail to maintain a strategic focus that will lead to planned outcomes. The use of the OGSM model and BSC system essentially protects against internal team collapse.

Systematic Data Collection

The social science researchers immediately recognized the need for systematic data collection. For many focused deterrence strategies documented in the literature, an evaluation was conducted after implementation to test the initiative's impact on violence. While this type of evaluation research is important, it does not necessarily provide guidance or recommendations to teams during the implementation stages (Mears, 2007). Therefore, the CIRV team collected data at the onset to measure several process and impact measures to ensure program integrity and inform continual-improvement plans. Process measures included the extent to which the message was delivered to the target population, the level of law enforcement action that was being taken against violent groups linked to a homicide, and details regarding the delivery of services to those who were requesting help. In addition, it was necessary to track and report program impact measures to evaluate the effectiveness of the strategy. For example, the researchers tracked the number of homicides, the number of group (gang)-related homicides, and the number of victims of nonfatal shootings over time. Like the process measures, the impact measures informed continual-improvement plans. Finally, these data were critical for demonstrating the value of the program, gaining political and public support, and securing continued funding.

With the goals of institutionalization and sustainability in mind, researchers also led the development of the CIRV best-practices guides, which systematically report the systems and processes developed to date and reflect the lessons learned in Cincinnati. These best practices are captured in a set of dynamic documents, each with an owner responsible for periodically reviewing and updating the document as the process is refined.[2] The intention of these guides is to institutionalize the systems and processes beyond the tenure of the individuals involved and to avoid repeating the mistakes of the past or failing to benefit from the lessons learned by others.

Using Theory to Interpret Program Findings: Reducing Offender Opportunity and Motivation

Similar to other implementation sites, Cincinnati enjoyed early successes in homicide reduction, reporting a 61% decline (from 33 to 13) in group/gang member–involved (GMI) homicides in the first 6 months following implementation compared with the same months the previous year (Engel, Baker, Tillyer, Eck, & Dunham, 2008). Institutionalization of the roles and processes of CIRV through the business management strategies described above was credited with contributing to this immediate and substantial reduction, and the actors involved believed that these steps would insulate them from the sustainability issues that seemed to plague other sites. Yet as the initiative moved forward, it became increasingly clear that institutionalization of the process was a necessary, but insufficient, solution for long-term success. Over time, the reductions in GMI homicides became less substantive. Comparing the 23 months pre-/postinitiative, the reduction in GMI homicides was 35%. While it is possible that problems in implementation produced an initiative that was less potent over time, the CIRV team implemented a series of best practices known from the management literature and real-world corporate experiences to guard against such team deficiencies. Thus, the possibility looms that focused deterrence approaches inherently work in the short term but possibly not in the long term.

To better understand why focused deterrence strategies work in the short term, as well as why success tends to diminish over time, we turn to two complementary theoretical perspectives—routine activities theory (Cohen & Felson, 1979) and the rational choice perspective (Clarke & Cornish, 1985). Based on our interpretation of the program findings, we present a revised strategy that is consistent with criminological theory, as well as informed by the extant literature on offender rehabilitation, to enhance sustainability in violence reduction.

Routine Activities Theory and the Rational Choice Perspective

According to routine activities theory, crime results from motivated offenders and suitable targets converging in time and space in the absence of capable guardianship (Cohen & Felson, 1979). In short, a crime event can be conceptualized as a motivated offender interacting with criminal opportunities. The major prevention implication is that addressing the opportunity structures for crime can lead to a reduction in crime, without addressing the motivational tendencies of potential offenders (Felson & Clarke, 1998). Virtually all prevention research coming out of this theoretical tradition has focused on understanding the opportunities for crime and how to alter them in a way that reduces the likelihood of subsequent crime events.

The rational choice perspective suggests that offender decision making is composed of two decision points (Clarke & Cornish, 1985). The involvement decision, which is the offender's recognition of the willingness to commit a specific form of crime, is based on bounded rationality. Though the offender makes decisions based on perceived costs and benefits of his or her actions, these perceptions are shaped by prior learning and experiences (Clarke & Cornish, 1985). The event decision, which is the offender's selection of a particular crime opportunity, is also based on a rational choice process influenced by the offender's perceptions of costs and benefits surrounding a specific criminal opportunity. As with the involvement decision, rationality is bounded; prior experiences, individual information-processing abilities, and situational factors shape how the offender perceives specific criminal opportunities. Like routine activities theory, a major prevention implication of the rational choice perspective is to alter the opportunities for crime in a way that will be perceived by offenders and thus alter their rational choice decision to commit crime. Situational crime prevention techniques are based on this logic (Cornish & Clarke, 2003). These techniques aim to systematically alter the environment in a way that reduces the opportunity for crime by increasing the efforts and risks of crime, reducing the rewards and provocations for crime, and removing the excuses for crime (Clarke, 1983; Cornish & Clarke, 2003).

In sum, the primary prevention implication to be drawn from these perspectives is that reducing the opportunities for crime will in turn reduce crime (Felson & Clarke, 1998). In effect, focused deterrence strategies aim to do just that—alter the opportunities for crime to deter motivated offenders. Tillyer and Kennedy (2008) suggest many mechanisms by which focused deterrence programs might reduce street group violence. For example, these strategies make it more difficult to enlist co-offenders, as the group-focused law enforcement strategy makes one's associates less likely to provide weapons, act as lookouts, or dispose of weapons following a homicide because they fear that their acts will make them the priority of law enforcement.

Theoretically speaking, focused deterrence initiatives, and the group-focused law enforcement strategy in particular, aim to reduce violence by altering the opportunity structure in a number of ways. Yet the prevention implications to be drawn from routine activities theory and the rational choice perspective are not limited to opportunity reduction. Routine activities theory suggests that crime is the *interaction* of a motivated offender and a criminal opportunity. The rational choice perspective suggests that offender motivation, realized through the involvement decision, is shaped by prior learning and experiences. Thus, each of these theoretical frameworks suggests that opportunity reduction is not the only way to prevent crime. Rather, addressing offender motivation would also presumably prevent the occurrence of crime.

In short, there appear to be two general mechanisms by which focused deterrence could reduce violence: opportunity reduction and the treatment of offenders. Opportunity reduction is primarily operationalized through the group-focused enforcement strategy. As explicated by Tillyer and Kennedy (2008), the strategy aims to increase the risks and efforts of violence while reducing the rewards, provocations, and excuses. The institutionalization hypothesis, which suggests that sustainability problems can be traced back to lack of institutionalization of the program (i.e., full implementation of the strategy ceases, and thus the early success is not sustained), is largely grounded in an opportunity perspective of crime reduction. By institutionalizing the process to ensure that law enforcement continues to implement the strategy, the risk of consequences for those involved in violence remains high. The business management strategies described above aim to address this by ensuring the institutionalization of the process and, in turn, the continued removal of criminal opportunities for violence.

Addressing Offender Motivation: Using Rehabilitative Principles within a Focused Deterrence Approach

The second mechanism by which focused deterrence could reduce violence is addressing motivation by treating the offender. The availability of social services in many of these initiatives seems to be aimed at addressing motivation, yet there is no evidence in the literature that services have been delivered in a way that is consistent with best practices in correctional rehabilitation for addressing criminogenic needs. In fact, there appears to be an implicit assumption that availability of legitimate opportunities alone (via jobs and social services) will lead to desistance. This may be the case for some in the short term, but it is unlikely for most in the long term.

Traditionally, members affiliated with violent groups/gangs have been somewhat removed from social services, either because of their unfamiliarity and/or frustration with how to navigate the system or because agencies will not provide services to those with violent criminal histories. One major task of the CIRV team was to develop a comprehensive services program that provides individualized, streamlined services to this population in an effective, efficient, and respectful manner. Initially, the CIRV team planned to provide employment opportunities to prior offenders willing to accept the opportunity for an employment-based lifestyle. Referred to as *clients*, these individuals were partnered with a street worker advocate (i.e., ex-offenders with street knowledge and credibility, employed by the City of Cincinnati to provide coaching and mentoring to assist in the extraction of individuals from violent street life) and provided a free 3-week job training workshop, along with assistance in securing employment. Several key figures on the CIRV team believed that employment was the key to violence reduction. Initially, the services component of CIRV was hailed as a great success, as large numbers of individuals contacted street workers and entered the job training program. Over time, however, it was discovered that at least some of those seeking employment opportunities were not truly within the target population of violent group/gang members and, furthermore, that acquisition of employment alone would not change the underlying attitudes and beliefs that led to violence.

For months, the CIRV Services Team floundered, with no clear mission, guiding principles, or course of action. Experts in correctional rehabilitation were consulted to better understand the underlying criminogenic needs of offenders and the forms of treatment most effective for those engaged in violence. At first glance, it appeared that a focused deterrence approach (based on reducing opportunity through group consequences) could not easily partner with a correctional rehabilitative approach (based on reducing motivation through individual treatment). The theoretical underpinnings, explanations of the causes of violent behavior, and perceived effective treatments differ widely across these two perspectives; even the units of analysis—groups versus individuals—differ. Interestingly, the initial concerns surrounded identifying the appropriate target population. While the law enforcement team was most interested in individuals engaged with violent street groups/gangs, the services team was concerned with providing services to any individual with a criminal record, regardless of propensity for violence. The different foci of these teams threatened to dismantle the overall partnership.

Ultimately, the members of the CIRV Governing Board decided that the target population for the initiative was to be individuals engaged in violent groups/gangs. This focus resulted in the need for risk assessments, a standard practice in the correctional rehabilitation field. Based on the obvious need for risk assessment screening tools for entrance into the CIRV Services program, the larger CIRV partnership began to understand and embrace the evidence-based rehabilitative principles that serve as the foundation of correctional rehabilitation. The CIRV Services program needed to restructure the delivery of services to ensure that offenders received services effective in reducing future criminal behavior. To meet this challenge, the Services program adopted the principles of effective intervention (Andrews & Bonta, 2003; Andrews et al., 1990; Gendreau, 1996; Gendreau, Smith, & Goggin, 2000), which covers four core components of effective correctional treatment—risk, need, responsivity, and fidelity.

The first, the risk principle, acknowledges that offenders vary in terms of recidivism risk and that higher risk offenders should receive more intensive services (Gendreau, 1996). To ensure adherence to the risk principle, a program must assess offenders on a validated risk assessment.[3] A valid risk assessment allows the program to identify those who are higher risk and assist in determining what level of service is appropriate for them. The Services Team decided that the program would be most effective by addressing those offenders who were higher risk for both criminal and violent behavior. Therefore, the team implemented a composite risk assessment (LSI-R) and a violence screener called the Violence Triage Tool. The Violence Triage Tool (Davies & Dedel, 2006) was adopted to provide the street worker advocate a means to assess the likelihood of an offender to engage in violent behavior. Once identified as a potential candidate for CIRV Services, the program completed a more detailed assessment of each offender, using the LSI-R, which provides a composite risk score of static and dynamic factors. Those offenders who scored high violence/moderate to high risk were then accepted into the program.

In addition to addressing the risk principle, the program also adopted the second principle, the need principle. The need principle suggests that programs should target criminogenic needs or those needs that are highly correlated with recidivism. Results of numerous meta-analyses have identified these correlates to re-offending (Dowden & Andrews, 2000; Gendreau, Little, & Goggin, 1996; Lipsey, 1995). Generally, these needs are organized by primary targets (antisocial attitudes, antisocial associates, and antisocial personality) and secondary targets (family, employment/education, substance abuse, and prosocial leisure activities; Andrews & Bonta, 2003). Evaluation research of correctional programs supports the need to target a range of criminogenic needs. Gendreau, French, and Taylor (2002) found that programs that targeted four to six criminogenic needs had a mean effect size of .31, compared with an effect size of –.02 for programs that targeted three or fewer criminogenic needs. Furthermore, Landenberger and Lipsey (2005) found that programs targeting aggression and interpersonal problem-solving skills (categorized as personality factors) were significantly related to reductions in recidivism. Similarly, Dowden and Andrews (2000) found that programs that targeted antisocial attitudes were associated with significant reductions in violent recidivism. Once presented with the results of these studies, the Services Team decided that it was important to expand the program from an employment-focused program to one that addressed a broader range of criminogenic needs. Although employment was still targeted, antisocial attitudes, antisocial peers, and personality factors were identified as the primary targets for change. To address these additional needs, the services team established a partnership with a local social service agency that delivers a wide array of services to offenders.

Third, the responsivity principle consists of two primary components: general and specific. General responsivity suggests that most offenders respond well to cognitive-behavioral and social learning models, whereas specific responsivity states that offenders have different learning styles and present barriers to successfully engaging in treatment. To address the responsivity principle, the Services Team adopted a cognitive–behavioral treatment (CBT) model and planned to formally address offender motivation to continue engaging in violence. CBT is based on a combination of cognitive and behavioral therapies and has been used to address problem areas in human behavior since the 1950s. Results from meta-analyses show that CBT has significant impacts on reducing problematic behaviors ranging from anxiety and depression to aggression and posttraumatic stress disorder (Butler, Chapman, Forman, & Beck, 2006). As for offender populations, CBT has demonstrated significant impacts on reducing future criminal behavior (Dowden & Andrews, 1999; French & Gendreau, 2006; Gendreau & Ross, 1987; Izzo & Ross, 1990; Landenberger & Lipsey, 2005; Lipsey & Wilson, 1998; Palmer, 1975; Wilson, Bouffard, & MacKenzie, 2005).

There are several reasons why CBT, when compared with other interventions, is more effective with high-risk, violent offenders. First, CBT is based on addressing how individuals maintain their present condition based on their current thoughts; a change in their thoughts, values, and beliefs can change their behavior. Second, CBT is learning focused. The assumption is that offenders lack prosocial skill sets. Problem solving, weighing the pros and cons of a situation, and delaying gratification are areas in which offenders show significant deficiencies (Maruna, Lebel, Mitchell, & Naples, 2004).

CBT is designed to teach offenders how to manage their lives more effectively through structured skill building and the use of reinforcement and punishment. Third, CBT is active. A typical offender is impulsive, risk seeking, and unmotivated to change. CBT engages offenders in the change process, challenging them to try prosocial alternatives (Spiegler & Guevremont, 1998).

In addition to adopting a new treatment model, the Services Team refocused its efforts on addressing the offender's motivation to change. A significant barrier in working with serious, violent offenders is their unwillingness to change their criminal behavior. Street worker advocates were trained in techniques such as motivational interviewing to help the offender see the importance of adopting a prosocial lifestyle (Miller & Rollnick, 2002).

The last principle, the fidelity principle, was the most difficult to implement. The fidelity principle suggests that programs need not only adopt the aforementioned principles but must also ensure that they are implemented effectively. Programs that do not adhere to the fidelity principle have been found to be less effective and potentially harmful to offenders (Lowenkamp, Latessa, & Holsinger, 2006). The steps adopted to address the fidelity of the model include (a) using a validated risk instrument, (b) training of street worker advocates on core correctional practices, (c) holding monthly staff meetings to monitor the services being delivered, (d) monitoring the progress made by those in the program, and (e) developing a centralized data collection process to track offenders.

Although adherence to the principles of effective intervention is not a magic bullet, it does significantly increase the likelihood of reducing recidivism (Andrews & Dowden, 2006). Some argue that highly antisocial offenders (e.g., psychopaths) are untreatable, but recent evidence suggests that programs that serve very high-risk offenders can still have an impact on recidivism (Dolan & Doyle, 2007). Therefore, programs such as the CIRV services program, which serve some of the most serious, violent offenders, can significantly affect recidivism if they adhere to the risk, need, responsivity, and fidelity principles.

The redesigned CIRV Services Team accepted 30 new clients from September to December 2009. These clients are primarily male (98.3%), Black (100%), single (100%), and unemployed (96.7%) and have less than a high school education (60.0%). These demographics mirror those of the more than 400 clients who were provided CIRV employment services from July 2007 to September 2009 under the previous system. It is of interest that the average age of the new clients (32.6 years) is significantly more than that of the law enforcement–identified population of adult, violent group/gang members in the city (27.1 years). This raises the possibility that those individuals seeking services may eventually "age out" of crime, regardless of CIRV intervention (Farrington, 1986; Hirschi & Gottfredson, 1983; Sampson & Laub, 1992; Warr, 1993, 1998). Furthermore, LSI-R scores indicate that only 30% were classified as "high" risk/needs, again indicating that individuals self-selecting for services are likely not the most active or potentially violent of those targeted for intervention using the focused deterrence approach. Multiple evaluation designs are in the planning stages to track previous and future CIRV clients over time, including a comparison with a matched sample of known offenders who do not self-select for CIRV-provided services. The results from these analyses will be instrumental in understanding the impact of providing social services to reduce violence within a focused deterrence approach.

Discussion

Using routine activities theory and the rational choice perspective, we have argued that there are two general mechanisms to reduce violence: reducing opportunities and addressing offender motivation. Given that this theoretical framework suggests an *interactive* process between opportunity and motivation, simply addressing the opportunity structures for violence using the group-focused law enforcement strategy should in theory reduce violence. The business management strategies described in detail above aim to do just this through institutionalization of the strategy. Yet in practice, blocking opportunities for violence in these settings for the long term becomes more difficult. Despite the best efforts, institutionalization issues arise. The ability of the law enforcement strategy to reduce violence is grounded in the group members' belief that every homicide will trigger the multiagency group-focused law enforcement response. Even with the business management strategies to improve institutionalization, resource limitations alone will often preclude a full response for every homicide in the long term.

This leads to the other mechanism by which focused deterrence might prevent violence—addressing offender motivation. The success of these programs may lie in their ability to use the opportunity reduction that is provided by the law enforcement strategy to leverage the compliance of offenders to engage in correctional rehabilitation treatment to address offender motivation. By targeting both opportunity and motivation, the number of paths for such initiatives to long-term success in violence reduction increase.

To empirically examine our hypothesis that violence reduction initiatives can maximize crime prevention potential by integrating the opportunity-reducing elements of traditional focused deterrence strategies with the motivation-reducing elements of correctional rehabilitation programs, future research should go beyond simply examining the changes in citywide violence. Studies should also examine whether there are differences in subsequent risks of being involved in violence—as a perpetrator or a victim—between those individuals who are engaged in programs that adhere to the principles of effective intervention and those who are not. Such research would shed light on whether integrating the best practices from policing and corrections warrants further attention by policy makers, criminologists, and practitioners.

The model discussed here largely emphasizes the importance of individual choice: The institutionalization efforts are designed to create consistent consequences for engaging in violence, and the principles of effective intervention aim to help individuals develop the skills to make better decisions. Yet, as Felson (1986) notes, "People make choices, but they cannot choose the choices available to them" (p. 119). In other words, people are embedded within broader social contexts that structure their lives and the opportunities available to them. For example, the concept of collective efficacy suggests that community factors such as high residential mobility, concentrated disadvantage, and racial exclusion erode trust among residents and their willingness to intervene in neighborhood problems (Sampson, Raudenbush, & Earls, 1997). Communities lacking collective efficacy struggle to exercise informal social control, as well as secure the necessary resources to address neighborhood concerns, thus leading to higher rates of violence.

In addition, the perceived legitimacy of law enforcement action is central to the deterrent reach of sanctions: Fair and reasonable action can enhance deterrence, whereas inconsistent and discriminatory acts undermine it. Tyler's (1990) research on why people obey the law suggests that perceptions of legitimacy independently increase compliance with the law, beyond the fear of sanctions. This highlights the detrimental effects of the strained relationship between inner-city residents and the police (Anderson, 1999; Brunson & Miller, 2006); if residents perceive police action as arbitrary and unpredictable, it carries far less moral weight.

Despite the research establishing the importance of such factors in understanding crime, translating such research into policy that can be readily implemented by criminal justice actors remains a challenge. The revised focused deterrence model offers some progress in that the improved integration of criminal justice and social services potentially broadens the legitimate opportunities available to at-risk individuals. In addition, the model aims to improve the legitimacy of law enforcement by making police action commensurate with criminal behavior and consistent across cases, bringing together the community and the police as a united front against violence, and communicating sanction risk to offenders in a stern, yet respectful, tone.

The efforts in Cincinnati to improve the social service element of the program, however, underscore a larger issue in criminal justice policy responses to violence. Despite system interventions, individuals are embedded within (or will eventually return to) homes, schools, neighborhoods, and cities with systemic disadvantages that jeopardize their ability to succeed. This suggests an additional explanation for the variation in success both between and within focused deterrence initiatives: available legitimate opportunities and structural constraints within the broader social context. Though the CIRV project is an important step in criminal justice system responses to violence, these initiatives must be part of larger social reforms. Much work remains to be done to translate criminological research findings into feasible criminal justice policies that can be effectively implemented and sustained.

ACKNOWLEDGMENTS

The authors would like to thank the members of the Cincinnati Police Department and the larger Cincinnati Initiative to Reduce Violence (CIRV) team for their thoughtful insights and tremendous efforts to reduce gang violence in Cincinnati.

NOTES

1. In June 2009, officials from John Jay College launched the National Network for Safe Communities (NNSC), a coalition of officials from 30 jurisdictions committed to implementing focused deterrence initiatives. It has also been estimated that 75 jurisdictions are using one or both of the NNCS's core strategies related to gang violence reduction and closing of drug markets through focused deterrence approaches (John Jay College of Criminal Justice, 2009). In 2009, Department of Justice (DOJ) agencies, including the National Institute of Justice (NIJ) and the Bureau of Justice Administration (BJA), offered federal funding opportunities for jurisdictions willing to adopt and/or expand these types of initiatives. In addition to academic outlets, stories regarding the success of focused deterrence initiatives have appeared in the local and national media, including publications such as *Wall Street Journal*, *New Yorker Magazine*, and *Newsweek* (Fields, 2009; Seabrook, 2009; Smalley, 2009). The momentum surrounding focused deterrence approaches for reducing violence indicates that a national movement is under way.
2. To date, the CIRV best practices include the following 14 documents: (1) CIRV overview, (2) homicide reviews, (3) intelligence development, (4) law enforcement's response to group member–involved homicides, (5) services delivery, (6) communicating to the target population, (7) call-in sessions, (8) communicating to the community, (9) best-practice system, (10) strategic planning, (11) quarterly reviews, (12) organizing for success, (13) sustainability, and (14) forming and sustaining the law enforcement team.
3. There are several validated risk assessments available for adults and juveniles. They include the Level of Service Inventory–Revised (LSI-R), the Correctional Management Profiling for Alternative Sanctions (COMPAS), the Wisconsin Risk/ Need Assessment, and the Ohio Risk Assessment System (ORAS).

REFERENCES

Anderson, E. (1999). *Code of the street: Decency, violence, and the moral life of the inner city.* New York, NY: W. W. Norton.

Andrews, D. A., & Bonta, J. (2003). *The psychology of criminal conduct.* Cincinnati, OH: Anderson.

Andrews, D. A., & Dowden, C. (2006). Risk principle of case classification in correctional treatment: A meta-analytic investigation. *International Journal of Offender Therapy and Comparative Criminology, 50,* 88–100.

Andrews, D. A., Zinger, I., Hoge, R. D., Bonta, J., Gendreau, P., & Cullen, F. T. (1990). Does correctional treatment work? A clinically relevant and psychologically informed meta-analysis. *Criminology, 28,* 369–404.

Bourgois, P. (2003). *In search of respect: Selling crack in El Barrio* (2nd ed.). New York, NY: Cambridge University Press.

Braga, A. A., Kennedy, D. M., Waring, E. J., & Piehl, A. M. (2001). Problem-oriented policing, deterrence, and youth violence: An evaluation of Boston's Operation Ceasefire. *Journal of Research in Crime and Delinquency, 38,* 195–225.

Braga, A. A., McDevitt, J., & Pierce, G. L. (2006). Understanding and preventing gang violence: Problem analysis and response development in Lowell, Massachusetts. *Police Quarterly, 9,* 20–46.

Braga, A. A., Pierce, G. L., McDevitt, J., Bond, B. J., & Cronin, S. (2008). The strategic prevention of gun violence among gang-involved offenders. *Justice Quarterly, 25,* 132–162.

Brown, M. K. (1981). *Working the street: Police discretion and the dilemmas of reform*. New York, NY: Russell Sage Foundation.

Brugha, R., & Varvasovszky, Z. (2000). Stakeholder analysis: A review. *Health Policy and Planning*, 15, 239–246.

Brunson, R., & Miller, J. (2006). Young black men and urban policing in the United States. *British Journal of Criminology*, 46, 613–640.

Butler, A., Chapman, J., Forman, E., & Beck, A. (2006). The empirical status of cognitive-behavioral therapy: A review of meta-analyses. *Clinical Psychology Review*, 26, 17–31.

Chermak, S., & McGarrell, E. (2004). Problem-solving approaches to homicide: An evaluation of the Indianapolis Violence Reduction Partnership. *Criminal Justice Policy Review*, 15, 161–192.

Cissner, A., & Farole, D. (2009). *Avoiding failures of implementation: Lessons from process evaluations*. Washington, DC: Bureau of Justice Assistance.

Clarke, R. V. (1983). Situational crime prevention: Its theoretical basis and practical scope. Crime and Justice, 4, 225–256.

Clarke, R. V., & Cornish, D. B. (1985). Modeling offenders' decisions: A framework for research and policy. *Crime and Justice*, 6, 147–185.

Cohen, L. E., & Felson, M. (1979). Social change and crime rate trends: A routine activities approach. American Sociological Review, 44, 88–100.

Cornish, D. B., & Clarke, R. V. (2003). Opportunities, precipitators and criminal decisions: A reply to Wortley's critique of situational crime prevention. In M. J. Smith & D. B. Cornish (Eds.), *Theory for practice in situational crime prevention* (pp. 41–96). Monsey, NY: Criminal Justice Press.

Corsaro, N., & McGarrell, E. F. (2009). Testing a promising homicide reduction strategy: Re-assessing the impact of the Indianapolis "pulling levers" intervention. *Journal of Experimental Criminology*, 5, 63–82.

Davies, G., & Dedel, K. (2006). Violence risk screening in community corrections. *Criminology & Public Policy*, 5, 743–770.

Dolan, M., & Doyle, M. (2007). Psychopathy: Diagnosis and implications for treatment. *Psychiatry*, 6, 404–408.

Dowden, C., & Andrews, D. (1999). What works in young offender treatment: A meta-analysis. *Forum on Correctional Research*, 11, 1–6.

Dowden, C., & Andrews, D. (2000). Effective correctional treatment and violent reoffending: A meta-analysis. *Canadian Journal of Criminology*, 42, 449–468.

Engel, R. S., Baker, S. G., Tillyer, M. S., Eck, J., & Dunham, J. (2008). *Implementation of the Cincinnati Initiative to Reduce Violence (CIRV): Year 1 Report*. Cincinnati, OH: University of Cincinnati Policing Institute.

Eisenstein, J., & Jacob, H. (1977). *Felony justice: An organizational analysis of criminal courts*. Boston: Little, Brown.

Farrington, D. P. (1986). Age and crime. *Crime and Justice*, 7, 189–250.

Feeley, M. M. (1983). *Court reform on trial: Why simple solutions fail*. New York, NY: Basic Books.

Feeley, M. M., & Simon, J. (1992). The new penology: Notes on the emerging strategy of corrections and its implications. *Criminology*, 30, 449–474.

Felson, M. (1986). Linking criminal choices, routine activities, informal control, and criminal outcomes. In D. B. Cornish & R. V. Clarke (Eds.), *The reasoning criminal: Rational choice perspectives on offending* (pp. 119–128). New York, NY: Springer-Verlag.

Felson, M., & Clarke, R. V. (1998). *Opportunity makes the thief* (Police Research Series, Paper 98). London, England: Home Office.

Fields, G. (2009, June 13). Cities join unorthodox anticrime program. *Wall Street Journal*, p. A3.

French, S., & Gendreau, P. (2006). Reducing prison misconducts. *Criminal Justice and Behavior*, 33, 185–218.

Gendreau, P. (1996). The principles of effective intervention with offenders. In A. T. Harland (Ed.), *Choosing correctional options that work: Defining the demand and evaluating the supply* (pp. 18–32). Thousand Oaks, CA: SAGE.

Gendreau, P., French, S., & Taylor, A. (2002). *What works (what doesn't) revised 2002: The principles of effective correctional treatment*. Unpublished manuscript, University of New Brunswick, St. John, New Brunswick, Canada.

Gendreau, P., Little, T., & Goggin, C. (1996). A meta-analysis of the predictors of adult offender recidivism: What works! *Criminology*, 34, 575–608.

Gendreau, P., & Ross, R. R. (1987). Revivification of rehabilitation: Evidence from the 1980s. *Justice Quarterly*, 4, 349–407.

Gendreau, P., Smith, P., & Goggin, C. (2000). Treatment programs in corrections. In J. Winterdyk (Ed.), *Corrections in Canada: Social reaction to crime* (pp. 238–263). Toronto, Ontario, Canada: Prentice Hall.

Hirschi, T., & Gottfredson, M. (1983). Age and the explanation of crime. *American Journal of Sociology*, 89, 552–583.

Horney, J., & Spohn, C. (1991). Rape law reform and instrumental change in six urban jurisdictions. *Law & Society Review*, 25, 117–153.

Izzo, R., & Ross, R. (1990). Meta-analysis of rehabilitation programs for juvenile delinquents: A brief report. *Criminal Justice and Behavior*, 17, 134–142.

John Jay College of Criminal Justice. (2009, June 15). *John Jay College launches "National Network for Safe Communities" to reduce violent crime and overt drug markets and to build a new standard of practice for reducing crime in the US* [Press release]. New York, NY: Author. Retrieved from http://www.jjay.cuny.edu/2666.php.

Kaplan, R. S., & Norton, D. P. (1993). Putting the balanced scorecard to work. *Harvard Business Review*, September/October, 134–147.

Kaplan, R. S., & Norton, D. P. (1996). Using the balanced scorecard: Measures that drive performance. *Harvard Business Review*, January/February, 75–85.

Kennedy, D. M. (1997). Pulling levers: Chronic offenders, high-crime settings, and a theory of prevention. *Valparaiso University Law Review*, 31, 449–484.

Kennedy, D. M. (2007, February 15). *Making communities safer: Youth violence and gang interventions that work* (Prepared testimony before the house judiciary subcommittee on crime, terrorism, and homeland security). New York, NY: John Jay College of Criminal Justice.

Kennedy, D. M., & Braga, A. A. (1998). Homicide in Minneapolis. *Homicide Studies*, 2, 263–290.

Landenberger, N., & Lipsey, M. (2005). The positive effects of cognitive-behavioral programs for offenders: A meta-analysis of factors associated with effective treatment. *Journal of Experimental Criminology*, 1, 451–476.

Lipsey, M. (1995). What do we learn from 400 research studies on the effectiveness of treatment with juvenile delinquents? In J. McGuire (Ed.), *What works: Reducing reoffending: Guidelines from research and practice* (pp. 35–62). Chichester, England: Wiley.

Lipsey, M., & Wilson, D. (1998). Effective intervention for serious juvenile offenders: A synthesis of research. In R. Loeber & D. P. Farrington (Eds.), *Serious and violent juvenile offenders: Risk factors and successful interventions* (pp. 313–345). Thousand Oaks, CA: SAGE.

Lipsky, M. (1980). *Street-level bureaucracy: Dilemmas of the individual in public services.* New York, NY: Russell Sage Foundation.

Lowenkamp, C. T., Latessa, E., & Holsinger, A. (2006). The risk principle in action: What we have learned from 13,676 offenders and 97 correctional programs. *Crime & Delinquency,* 52, 1–17.

Martinsons, M., Davison, R., & Tse, D. (1999). The balanced scorecard: A foundation for the strategic management of information systems. *Decision Support Systems,* 25, 71–88.

Maruna, S., Lebel, T. P., Mitchell, N., & Naples, M. (2004). Pygmalion in the reintegration process: Desistance from crime through the looking glass. *Psychology, Crime, and Law,* 10, 271–281.

McGarrell, E. F., Chermak, S., Wilson, J. M., & Corsaro, N. (2006). Reducing homicide through a "lever-pulling" strategy. *Justice Quarterly,* 23, 214–231.

Mears, D. (2007). Towards rational and evidence-based crime policy. *Journal of Criminal Justice,* 35, 667–682.

Miller, W., & Rollnick, S. (2002). *Motivational interviewing: Preparing people for change.* London, England: Guildford Press.

Palmer, T. (1975). Martinson revisited. *Journal of Research in Crime and Delinquency,* 12, 133–152.

Papachristos, A., Meares, T., & Fagan, J. (2007). Attention felons: Evaluating Project Safe Neighborhood in Chicago. *Journal of Empirical Legal Studies,* 4, 223–272.

Sampson, R. J., & Laub, J. H. (1992). Crime and deviance in the life course. *Annual Review of Sociology,* 18, 63–84.

Sampson, R. J., Raudenbush, S. W., & Earls, F. (1997). Neighborhoods and violent crime: A multilevel study of collective efficacy. *Science,* 277, 916–924.

Seabrook, J. (2009, June 22). Don't shoot. The New Yorker, p. 32.

Sherman, L. W., Gottfredson, D., MacKenzie, D., Eck, J., Reuter, P., & Bushway, S. (1997). *Preventing crime: What works, what doesn't, what's promising in criminal justice.* Washington, DC: Office of Justice Programs, U.S. Department of Justice.

Skogan, W. G., Hartnett, S. M., Bump, N., & Dubois, J. (2009). *Evaluation of ceasefire-Chicago.* Washington, DC: U.S. Department of Justice.

Smalley, S. (2009, February 9). Always on my mind. *Newsweek,* p. 53.

Snow, C. C., & Hambrick, D. C. (1980). Measuring organizational strategies: Some theoretical and methodological problems. *Academy of Management Review,* 5, 527–538.

Spiegler, M. D., & Guevremont, D. C. (1998). *Contemporary behaviour therapy* (5th ed.). Pacific Grove, CA: Brooks/Cole.

Tillyer, M. S., & Kennedy, D. M. (2008). Locating focused deterrence approaches within a situational crime prevention framework. *Crime Prevention and Community Safety,* 10, 75–84.

Tyler, T. R. (1990). *Why people obey the law.* New Haven, CT: Yale University Press.

Walker, S. (1993). Taming the system: The control of discretion in criminal justice 1950–1990. New York, NY: Oxford University Press.

Warr, M. (1993). Age, peers, and delinquency. *Criminology,* 31, 17–40.

Warr, M. (1998). Life-course transitions and desistance from crime. *Criminology,* 36, 183–216.

Wilson, D., Bouffard, L. A., & MacKenzie, D. (2005). A quantitative review of structured, group-oriented, cognitive-behavioral programs for offenders. *Criminal Justice and Behavior,* 32, 172–204.

23

Campus Policing

Andrea Allen

Campus Police

College and university campuses are generally thought of as safe academic retreats. These proverbial ivory towers, however, are not impervious to crime (Sloan & Fisher, 2011). In 2012 there were more than 18,556 burglaries, 3,983 sex offenses, 3,243 motor vehicle thefts, 2,615 aggravated assaults, 1,664 robberies, 699 arsons, and 13 murders perpetrated on campuses nationwide (USDOE, 2013).

Campus police are responsible for responding to and controlling crimes on college and university campuses, although they sometimes respond to incidents involving students off campus. In 2012, campus officers made more than 52,000 arrests. The most frequent violations involved liquor laws, followed by drug abuse, and then weapons violations (USDOE, 2013). Arrest rates are not available for Part I crimes (those listed in the opening paragraph). Campus police also meted out more than 250,000 disciplinary actions to students for the three types of violations mentioned above. Disciplinary actions are processed through an institution's student judicial authority. Sanctions can involve educational activities (e.g., taking classes or writing research papers), restitution, community service, probation, suspension, and expulsion.

Official statistics may underestimate the magnitude of campus officers' work. When more than one offense is committed in a single incident, only the most serious offense is counted in campus crime statistics (USDOE, 2011). This rule of reporting is known as the Hierarchy Rule and is based on the FBI's *Uniform Crime Reporting (UCR) Handbook*. For example, if a student in possession of a small amount of marijuana is caught breaking into another student's dorm room, only the burglary is counted. Furthermore, campus agencies are not required to report many offenses, such as public drunkenness and certain traffic violations. If unreported, the offenses do not appear in campus crime sta-

Prepared especially for *Critical Issues in Policing* by Andrea Allen.

tistics. In addition, the majority of crimes generally do not come to the attention of law enforcement—the dark figure of crime is absent from official statistics.

Despite a wealth of research on crime in the college context, few studies examine campus policing. If the responsibilities and activities of campus and municipal police are essentially similar, then the lack of research on campus policing is not a problem; research on municipal police would also apply to campus policing. To a degree, campus policing does mirror that of municipalities. However, there are also distinct differences. For this reason, it is important for scholars to research campus policing to identify similarities and differences. Research findings could help substantiate or refine current explanations of police work as a profession.

This article presents what is known about campus policing and points to areas for future empirical inquiry. After a review of the history of campus police, the similarities and differences between campus and municipal policing are identified, ending with a discussion of fruitful areas for research.

History of Campus Police

Colleges in the nineteenth century used faculty members to monitor student behavior outside the classroom and to enforce college rules and regulations (Gehrand, 2008). This proctor system presented problems because the role of faculty members was to encourage students to communicate. The adversarial role of monitoring behavior restricted open communication and was eventually discontinued.

In 1894, Yale University hired the first campus police officers—two city policemen from New Haven, Connecticut, who were charged with patrolling the campus (Powell, 1994; Sloan, 1992). Townspeople in New Haven suspected students of stealing bodies from a cemetery for anatomical training at Yale University Medical School. Hostilities between students and people in New Haven escalated. William Wiser and James Donnelly of the New Haven Police Department volunteered to work on Yale's campus. The university was pleased with the success of the two officers in working with the students and in preventing campus issues from aggravating the townspeople. They hired the officers to work at the university, where they became an integral part of campus life (Gehrand, 2008).

For roughly the next 50 years, campus policing followed the "watchman" system. Watchmen had no formal law enforcement training. They were frequently attached to the physical plant or grounds departments, and their duties included maintenance of facilities as well as enforcing campus rules. Local police were called to handle major infractions on campus. Relationships between students, the college, and the local police were often contentious. Some institutions turned to private detectives to investigate theft or serious misconduct on campus (Gehrand, 2008). Night watchmen were present when the faculty and college administrators were not on campus. Often they did not report violations to the administration.

By the 1930s, the orientation of campus policing began to change when universities created "pseudo-police officers" (Sloan, 1992, p. 86). In addition to their custodial duties (e.g., protect property, secure facilities, respond to break-ins and vandalism), a secondary task was introduced: patrol campus for violations of the student code of conduct (Fisher & Sloan, 2007; Sloan, 1992).

Campus policing experienced even greater changes during the 1950s as the number of colleges and universities and also student enrollment rates increased dramatically (Sloan, 1992). Military personnel returning from service in World War II used the educational benefits of the GI Bill to enroll at colleges and universities, changing the student demographics significantly. Half of the students were veterans, and 78% were male. Administrators felt the need to adjust their response to campus security. To institute a "real" police presence on campus, they hired retired municipal officers to act as campus security directors. Many campus police officers still reported to building and grounds departments and were housed in the basements of campus buildings with little access to equipment. There was very little training and no networks to exchange information with other campuses (Gehrand, 2008).

By the late 1960s and early 1970s, widespread student protests over the Vietnam War created the need for changes in campus policing (Sloan, 1992; Fisher & Sloan, 2007). Protest incidents at Kent State and other universities exposed the inadequate training of campus police. This time frame also included a deadly campus shooting. On August 1, 1966, Charles Whitman, an ex-Marine, ascended to the top of the clock tower on the campus of the University of Texas, where he was enrolled as a student. Armed with three rifles, two pistols, and a sawed-off shotgun, he shot and killed 11 people and wounded 32; he also killed 3 people inside the building. University administrators formed campus police forces by selecting experienced officers from municipal departments to develop, staff, and oversee campus enforcement operations (Fisher & Sloan, 2007). These newly established campus police departments emulated the organizational and operational styles of municipalities, which helped to professionalize and legitimize them (Bromley & Reaves, 1998, 1999; Fisher & Sloan, 2007; Paoline & Sloan, 2003; Reaves & Goldberg, 1996; Sloan, 1992).

State legislatures passed laws authorizing colleges and universities to staff their departments with sworn officers (Bordner & Petersen, 1983). New officer recruits were required to become POST (Peace Officer Standards Training) certified, granting them the same police powers as officers in municipal departments (Fisher & Sloan, 2007; Sloan, 1992). Campus officers were issued distinct uniforms with badges and carried weapons and handcuffs like municipal officers (Sloan, 1992). It was during this era that campus officers became more law enforcement oriented, although they continued protecting university property (Bromley, 2007).

From the late 1980s to the early 1990s, campus police experienced another period of change following media reports that lax security practices were the reason for burgeoning campus crime rates. In particular, the murder of freshman Jeanne Ann Clery in 1986 focused public attention on the issue of campus safety (Sloan & Fisher, 2011). Clery was raped, tortured, and strangled to death by a man, with whom she was not acquainted, who entered her dorm room in an attempt to burglarize it (Carter & Bath, 2007). Reports stated that the perpetrator was able to access Clery's room because several of the building's doors had been propped open and left unlocked. In 1990, Congress passed the Crime Awareness and Campus Security Act, renamed the Jeanne Clery Disclosure of Campus Security Policy and Campus Crime Statistics Act in 1998. The Clery Act, as it is known, requires colleges and universities to report crimes and notify the public about campus incidents (Sloan & Fisher, 2011).

Also during this era, many campus police departments adopted a community oriented policing approach in order to better identify crime problems and foster relationships between the police and campus community (Bromley, 2007; Fisher & Sloan, 2007). Community policing relies on problem-solving techniques and promotes partnerships, "which are valued on college campuses . . . where a culture of inquiry and discourse is fostered" (Woolfenden & Stevenson, 2011, p. 3). To help accomplish the goals of community policing, officers implemented bicycle and foot patrols, in addition to vehicle and motorcycle patrols (Peak, Barthe, & Garcia, 2008). In effect, campus law enforcement became much more proactive, perhaps even more so than municipal departments (Sloan & Lanier, 2007; Trojanowicz & Carter, 1988).

Since the early to mid-1990s, campus police have become much more law enforcement oriented, with a greater number of officers being armed (see e.g., Reaves, 2015). Many departments adopted the same weapons as municipal police (including handguns, OC or pepper spray, tasers, and batons). Similar to their municipal counterparts, campus officers have become highly trained in law enforcement tactics/skills, such as active shooter training, self-defense, high-visibility policing, and chemical weapons protection. Extended training in the use of weapons is viewed as necessary to protect campuses from internal and external threats, as well as to enforce state and local laws (Bromley, 1995; Peak et al., 2008; Sloan & Fisher, 2011).

Campus police are also expected to provide security for computer networks housing personal records of students, faculty, and staff. They provide escort services to keep students safe while walking on campus, and they maintain emergency calling systems (Bromley, 1995; Sloan & Fisher, 2011). Since the 9/11 attacks, campus law enforcement agencies have increasingly implemented systems and response strategies to handle large-scale incidents (e.g., terrorist attacks, natural disasters) on and around campus (Peak et al., 2008).

Characteristics of Campus Police Agencies

There is a wide variance in the role, structure, and professionalism of police operations on college and university campuses (COPS, 2005). Two major sources provide information on campus policing: The Bureau of Justice Statistics conducts *The Survey of Campus Law Enforcement Agencies*. This is the largest study and was conducted in 1995 (Reaves & Goldberg, 1996), in 2004–2005 (Reaves, 2008), and in 2011–2012 (Reaves, 2015). The International Association of Campus Law Enforcement Administrators (IACLEA), founded in 1958, surveys its 1,200 institutional and 2,000 individual members (Peak et al., 2008).

The *Survey of Campus Law Enforcement Agencies* inquires about a range of topics including agency functions, hiring practices, employee characteristics, types of equipment used, computers and information systems, expenditures, salaries, policies, and special programs. The 2011–2012 sample included 905 agencies serving 4-year colleges/universities with 2,500 or more students. Survey results show that about 68% of the agencies had sworn personnel—individuals who possess full arrest powers granted by the state or local government (Reaves, 2015). About two-thirds of campuses were served by armed officers. Of agencies using only nonsworn officers, 1 in 10 were armed. Public institutions were more than twice as likely to employ sworn officers as private institutions (92% vs. 38%). Of full-time sworn personnel, about 83% were male and 17% were female. More than 68% of officers were white, followed by blacks (21%), Hispanics (7.5%), and persons identified as other (3%). About 20% of agencies required officers to have at least some college education; 3% required a 4-year college degree. On average, new officers were required to complete 1,027 hours of training. Two-thirds of the hours were spent in the classroom and one-third in the field.

The previous survey compared campus police agencies to municipal agencies (Reaves, 2008). For campus departments with at least 10 but less than 100 full-time sworn officers, information was compared with local police departments similar in size using 2003 data from the BJS *Law Enforcement Management and Administrative Statistics Survey*. In terms of hiring procedures, local police departments more often used personal (e.g., psychological evaluation, written aptitude test, polygraph exam) and physical (e.g., medical exam, drug test, physical agility test) screening tests than campus agencies. Yet campus police were more likely to assess recruits' community-relation skills, such as their ability to solve problems, understand cultural diversity, and manage conflicts. Comparatively, campus police were more likely to have a college degree requirement for new officers than were local police. Local police required more training hours (1,092 vs. 981). Entry-level salaries for campus officers were about 6% lower than those of local police. Campus police chiefs were paid about 2% more than local police chiefs. And campus agencies (92%) were more likely than local police (63%) to use computers for functions such as investigations, dispatch, information sharing, resource allocation, fleet management, and crime mapping.

The most recent IACLEA survey of campus police departments was conducted in 2006 (Peak et al., 2008). However, only a 34% response rate was achieved, so the generalizability of the findings to all campus agencies is limited. Nevertheless, results indicate that more than 82% of the responding agencies had staff with the power to arrest and investigate crimes. Almost 20% had statewide jurisdiction. Findings also revealed an increase in the number of full-time sworn officers since 1986—the first year the survey was administered (Peak, 1987). Responding agencies also reported a change in the kinds of activities they performed; in 1986, the most commonly reported duty was parking enforcement, but in 2006 the number one task was investigations. Agencies also reported performing several new activities including training, Clery Act crime reporting, traffic/accident investigations, and handling hazardous materials.

In 2013, the Department of Justice awarded a grant to establish the National Center for Campus Public Safety. The goal is to provide a centralized resource for campus police chiefs and directors of public safety on the latest thinking in school safety. The center will promote innovative practices for the development of comprehensive response strategies and bring together professional associations, advocacy organizations, and community leaders responsible for ensuring safety on campus.

How Campus Policing Is Unique

Municipal and campus police wear uniforms, carry the same types of weapons, engage in similar operations (e.g., directed patrol, community policing, problem solving), possess the power to arrest, and adopt similar policies (e.g., use of force) and codes of conduct (Bromley, 2003; Bromley & Reaves, 1998; Paoline & Sloan, 2003; Sloan, 1992). However, there are features of the campus context that make campus policing unique.

Campus police patrol largely homogenous, middle-class populations (Miller & Pan, 1987; Trends in Higher Education, 2011). This differs from municipal officers working, for instance, in socially disadvantaged urban areas, although many suburban communities have similar compositions. The demographics of this group generally mean less involvement in violent crime (Truman, Langton, & Planty, 2013). What sets campus police apart from municipal police in practically every community is that the former patrols a population made up almost entirely of 18- to 24-year-old students. This age group represents the height of criminal involvement for the average person and is also the most heavily involved in alcohol and illicit drug consumption (FBI, 2013).

Campus police handle few serious crimes relative to many municipal police, especially those operating in urban or socially disadvantaged communities. The majority of campus crimes are property offenses (Dowdall, 2007). While violent crimes are not particularly common, those that do occur are often cases of sexual and domestic assault (e.g., Abbey, Zawacki, Buck, Clinton, & McAuslan, 2001; Shorey, Stuart, & Cornelius, 2011). Alcohol-involved crime is the most prominent of all offense types. In fact, the majority of crimes on campus involve alcohol (Dowdall, 2007). Part of the reason for this is college students drink at a high frequency and in large amounts (binge drinking). Of course many college students are not old enough to drink legally. The 2011

Core Alcohol and Drug Survey found that 63.4% of underage students (ages 18–20) used alcohol in the past month, and 44.8% of college students reported binge drinking in the past two weeks (CORE Institute, 2013). Research also shows that drinking, especially heavily, increases students' likelihood of being involved in alcohol-related crime as a victim or perpetrator of violent, property, or public order offenses (Allen & Jacques, 2013a).

There have been horrific instances of mass shootings, defined as four or more victims (Fox & Levin, 1998). On April 16, 2007, a student at Virginia Tech, Seung Hui Cho, fatally shot 32 individuals (27 students and five faculty members) and wounded another 17. Several other mass shootings have occurred across colleges and universities. Both municipal and campus police worry about shooters attempting to kill people in a confined and populated area. When school is in session, campus police confront the challenges of patrolling highly populated and concentrated locales, some of which stretch over 500 acres and have hundreds of buildings. Recent data show there were about 2.5 officers per 1,000 students at public 4-year institutions with 15,000 students or more (Reaves, 2015), whereas the ratio for municipal and township police departments is 3.7 officers per 1,000 residents (Reaves, 2011). Though the fewer number of campus officers relative to students makes sense given that campuses have far fewer serious crimes than do many municipal districts, the personnel restraints may hamper officers' ability to respond rapidly to active shooters.

Though campus police possess the same traditional police powers as municipal departments, and emulate their organizational and operational styles, campus patrol officers must perform in accordance with the expectations of both university and campus law enforcement administrators, who generally resist aggressive enforcement and severe sanctioning (Wolf, Mesloh, & Henych, 2007). Administrators restrict police activity so that students will not be dissuaded from attending a university with a reputation for overzealously enforcing student conduct policies and the law (Bordner & Petersen, 1983). This orientation sets campus police apart from some municipal police that adopt a more legalistic style, subscribing to "a single standard of community conduct—that which the law prescribes—rather than different standards for" different groups, such as college students versus outsiders (Wilson, 1968, p. 172). Campus police may be constrained in terms of the quantity and severity of their enforcement actions. Still, campus police must control crime; if they do not, a school's image can be tarnished and student enrollment rates affected (Carr & Ward, 2006).

Another unique feature of campus policing is job role orientation. From 1950 to 1965, campus security adopted the *in loco parentis* doctrine. This involves officers acting "in the place of the parents" while students are at school. In theory, officers are supposed to protect students from "outsiders" (i.e., persons not affiliated with the university), who are perceived as the biggest threat to student and campus safety (Sloan, 1992; Sloan & Fisher, 2011). Outsider offenders are arrested, whereas student offenders are handled through the university's judicial system (Sloan, 1992). Whether and to what extent campus officers today abide by the *in loco parentis* doctrine is unknown.

Campus police perform a variety of duties, several of which are unique to them. They are responsible for protecting property to a greater extent than are municipal officers. While both campus and municipal police scour property looking for suspicious activity (e.g., person peering into a window), the former group is more often charged with safeguarding a vast swath of buildings by ensuring that doors are locked and the infrastructure is secure. As noted above, some campuses sprawl upwards of 500 acres and have tens or hundreds of buildings, so this can be a time-consuming and difficult task (Reaves, 2008; Sloan, Lanier, & Beer, 2000).

Many campus police departments also serve as security for large-scale events on campus, including concerts, football, and basketball games. Personnel are generally supplemented with officers from surrounding local, state, and federal law enforcement agencies. Many college football games draw thousands to campus on game day; for example, the University of Michigan, with the largest college stadium, hosts over 109,000 individuals. The heavy police presence is intended to deter crime and terrorist acts, as well as handle any incidents that occur at the event. Campus police are also responsible for handling crimes committed on campus away from the event.

Before concluding this article with a discussion of potential areas for research on campus policing, there is a vitally important issue that affects all campuses and the officers charged with the safety of students. As discussed above, the Clery Act requires colleges and universities to publish annual reports on security policies and campus crime statistics, including sexual assaults. In 2009, the Center for Public Integrity investigated two- and four-year institutions and found that 77% of them reported zero rapes in 2006. Some avoided the Clery requirement by coding acquaintance rape as "nonforcible" and excluding rapes at off-campus parties (Gray, 2014a). In April 2011, the Department of Education sent a letter to institutions of higher learning warning that they were at risk of losing federal funding for violating Title IX if they did not adequately address sexual assault. In May 2012, the U.S. Assistant Attorney General for Civil Rights announced a federal investigation into the University of Montana, where 80 rapes had been reported in the previous 3 years. The federal investigation scrutinized how city police officers and county officials handled campus assaults. After reaching a settlement a year later, the university overhauled its system for handling sexual assault. The mayor and police chief in Missoula implemented trauma training for police officers, created a less intimidating interview room for victims, and made provisions for including trained counselors to participate in victim interviews.

The problem is not new. In 1987, a psychology professor at Kent State found that 1 in 4 women on 32 college campuses had been the victim of attempted or completed rape (Gray, 2014a). Most women knew their attackers, and the focus turned to "date rape." Unfortunately, that phrase contains within it an implication of accidental behavior that just happened to go too far. The reality is that perpetrators often plan to take advantage of victims who are inexperienced with drinking or drugs. Almost 1.8 million freshman women arrive on college campuses in the fall; the risk of sexual assault is most acute during the first six weeks on campus (Gray, 2014b).

In May 2014, the government released a list of 55 institutions (including Ohio State University, Harvard, and Princeton) under federal scrutiny for their handling of sexual-assault complaints. One of the most consistent findings is that college students rarely report assaults; one study found that only 12% of rapes of college women were reported to law enforcement. Another finding is that the group of perpetrators is relatively small and that more than half were repeat offenders.

Campus police face a daunting problem. Campus life provides students with newfound freedom and a culture in which alcohol consumption, including binge drinking, may be common. Schools may fear that bad publicity will hurt their college rankings and the number of applicants. If schools report sexual assaults as required by the Clery Act, they could look less safe than competitors that take advantage of loopholes. Administrators and defense lawyers point out that the circumstances of alleged assaults are often unclear—too much alcohol affects memories of the specifics of the incident, and there are usually no impartial witnesses (Phelps, 2014). Even if there is a finding of sexual assault, some schools are reluctant to expel the perpetrator. If the punishment is minimal, the message is that sexual violence is not perceived as serious. On the other hand, when circumstances are murky, someone could be expelled without a sufficient standard of proof.

In April 2014, a White House task force published *Not Alone*, which provided detailed guidance for colleges on how to prevent sexual assaults, model policies for handling allegations, rules governing confidentiality of accusers, surveys to determine the number of assaults, and a Web site with data on college sexual assaults. One of the aspects highlighted is bystander awareness and advice on how to partner with local law enforcement. Senator Kirsten Gillibrand summarized the problem:

> There is a pervasive lack of understanding when it comes to the true nature of campus sexual assault. These are not dates gone bad or a good guy who had too much to drink. This is a crime largely perpetrated by repeat offenders, who instead of facing a prosecutor and a jail cell remain on campus after a short-term suspension, if punished at all. (Gray, 2014a, p. 28)

Fruitful Areas for Research on Campus Policing

While there is ample research on campus crime, little attention has been given to campus police. More than 20 years ago, John Sloan observed:

> Considering the fact that modern campus police have existed for some 20 years, it is surprising that so few . . . investigations of them have been

> attempted. Further, . . . most of the investigations of the campus police
> are outdated. . . . Finally, each of these studies is limited in that they
> focus on the operation and characteristics of the agency with little atten-
> tion to the characteristics, attitudes, or behaviors of officers. (1992, p. 92)

Little has changed today. The discussion below suggests several avenues for future scholarship.

One potential line of research would be a systematic study of the nation's campus police departments. The goal of such a project would be to determine how campus crime and policing behaviors—such as initiating stops or sanc-tioning suspects—are affected by differences between campus departments. For instance, do organizational-level variables (e.g., operations, size, bureau-cratization), campus community-level factors (e.g., demographics, geo-graphic location), and officer characteristics (e.g., average rank, age, education) influence procedures and sanctions? Moreover, it would be useful to simultaneously collect comparative information from municipal depart-ments located around the campuses. To what extent do the characteristics, actions, and effects of campus departments parallel those of municipal departments? And what explains any apparent differences or similarities?

Another path for future research on campus policing is to explore offi-cers' situational decision making. One area for exploration would be to con-sider what affects officers' decisions to initiate a stop, be it traffic or pedestrian. Once a person has been stopped and a police–citizen encounter is underway, what influences officers' handling of suspects, including sanction-ing and use of force? Also, it would be useful to look at campus officers' han-dling of victims they encounter. Do encounters between campus police and citizens—whether with suspects, victims, or bystanders—unfold in a similar fashion to, and for the same reasons as, those of municipal police? Research that uncovers similarities and differences could improve knowledge of what factors contribute to policing decisions.

Moon and Corley (2007) conducted research along these lines. They built on the traffic stop literature by analyzing campus officers' sanctioning decisions in more than 10,000 traffic stops. Some prior research with munici-pal police has found officers are more likely to severely sanction older drivers (Alpert et al., 2006), males (Smith, Makarios, & Alpert, 2006), and racial/ethnic minorities (Engel & Calnon, 2004). Similarly, Moon and Corley (2007) found campus officers were more likely to issue a legal sanction over a verbal warning to older drivers and Asians than whites, although no other direct race effects were observed. They also examined the effect of demo-graphic subgroups—based on race and gender—on sanctioning outcomes and found that Asian males had increased odds of receiving a legal sanction relative to white males. These findings suggest that campus policing may not be all that dissimilar from municipal policing, at least not with respect to traf-fic stop sanctioning. Future research could confirm the results or point to other outcomes.

Another useful area for research is the influence of officer attitudes and theories of crime on their decision making. An attitude is "affect for or against a psychological object" (Thurstone, 1931, p. 261), whereas a theory is an idea about how one thing affects another (Homans, 1967). No study has yet examined the effect of campus officers' attitudes on policing. One study, however, has investigated the influence of theories of crime on officer behavior. Based on qualitative data collected from officers of a large southeastern university, Andrea Allen and Scott Jacques (2013b) found that participants explained three particularly common crimes on campus—petty larceny, underage drinking, and drug possession—as due to a variety of factors, including opportunity, students being too trusting of others, lack of parental supervision, and the presence of a party culture, among others. Prior research with municipal police indicates they, too, draw on many factors to explain crime. Wilson (1968) noted municipal police explain various crimes as the result of the weather, economic conditions, the demographic composition of the community, and family and peer group controls. Officers interviewed by William Westley (1970) referenced ethnicity and upbringing. A notable limitation of all these studies, and thus one to explore moving forward, is how officers' theories affect their approach to policing.

Finally, researchers may also analyze students' perceptions of campus police. Some scholarship suggests that campus police are frequently perceived as being "security guards" and not "real cops" (see Heinsler, Kleinman, & Stenross, 1990; Hinkle & Jones, 1991). Such perceptions may affect how students interact with campus police. For example, if a student perceives campus police as illegitimate or relatively powerless, that individual may be less likely to comply with their orders. James Wada, Ryan Patten, and Kimberlee Candela (2010) conducted the most recent study on the perceived legitimacy of campus police. The authors surveyed hundreds of undergraduate students from a large institution in the Pacific Northwest about their perceptions of campus and municipal police and found the latter are perceived as more legitimate than the former. Whether these findings generalize to other institutions remains unanswered, as is the effect of perceptions on encounters between campus police and citizens.

Conclusion

Campus police are an easily recognizable presence—as are municipal police. In both instances, the public has opinions about the profession but is largely uninformed about the reality of both types of policing. Research into the functions of campus police can illuminate the responsibilities of this specialized police force. Knowledge about the particulars of one type of policing also sheds light on the factors that affect the behavior of other police units. Do campus police differ from municipal police? If so, what influences create the differences? The research agenda outlined above should help elucidate this issue.

REFERENCES

Abbey, A., Zawacki, T., Buck, P. O., Clinton, A. M., & McAuslan, P. (2001). *Alcohol and sexual assault.* Washington, DC: National Institute of Health, National Institute on Alcohol Abuse and Alcoholism.

Allen, A., & Jacques, S. (2013a). Alcohol-related crime among college students: A review of research and fruitful areas for future work. *Criminal Justice Studies, 26,* 478–494.

Allen, A., & Jacques, S. (2013b). Police officers' theories of crime. *American Journal of Criminal Justice.* DOI: 10.1007/s12103-013-9219-1.

Alpert, G. P., Becker, E., Gustafson, M. A., Meister, A. P., Smith, M. R., & Strombom, B. A. (2006). Pedestrian and motor vehicle post-stop data analysis report. Los Angeles, CA: Analysis Group.

Bordner, D. C., & Petersen, D. M. (1983). *Campus policing: The nature of university police work.* Maryland: University Press of America.

Bromley, M. L. (1995). Analyzing campus crime and police resources: Implications for policy-makers. *Criminal Justice Policy Review, 7,* 185–201.

Bromley, M. L. (2003). Comparing campus and municipal police community policing practices. *Journal of Security Administration, 26,* 37–75.

Bromley, M. L. (2007). The evolution of campus policing: Different models for different eras. In B. S. Fisher & J. J. Sloan, III (Eds.), *Campus Crime: Legal, social, and policy perspectives* (2nd ed.), pp. 280–303. Springfield, IL: Charles C. Thomas Publisher.

Bromley, M. L., & Reaves, B. A. (1998). Comparing campus and city police operational practices. *Journal of Security Administration, 21,* 41–54.

Bromley, M. L., & Reaves, B. A. (1999). Comparing the practices and policies of sworn and non-sworn campus police departments within the context of the campus security act of 1990. *Criminal Justice Policy Review, 9,* 261–278.

Carr, J. L., & Ward, R. L. (2006). ACHA campus violence white paper. *NASPA, 43,* 380–409.

Carter, S. D., & Bath, C. (2007). The evolution and components of the *Jeanne Clery Act*: Implications for higher education. In B. S. Fisher & J. J. Sloan, III (Eds.), *Campus crime: Legal, social, and policy perspectives* (2nd ed.), pp. 27–44. Springfield, IL: Charles C. Thomas Publisher.

COPS (Community Oriented Policing Services). (2005). Summit on campus public safety. Retrieved from http://www.cops.usdoj.gov/Publications/NationalSummitonCampusPublicSafety.pdf

CORE Institute. (2013). Executive Summary: Core Alcohol and Drug Survey. Retrieved from http://core.siu.edu/_common/documents/report11.pdf

Dowdall, G. W. (2007). The role of alcohol abuse in college student victimization. In B. S. Fisher & J. J. Sloan, III (Eds.), *Campus Crime: Legal, social, and policy perspectives* (2nd ed.), pp. 261–279. Springfield, IL: Charles C. Thomas Publisher.

Engel, R. S., & Calnon, J. M. (2004). Examining the influence of drivers' characteristics during traffic stops with police: Results from a national study. *Justice Quarterly, 21,* 49–90.

FBI. (2013). Crime in the United States: Uniform crime reports, table 38. Retrieved from http://www.fbi.gov/about-us/cjis/ucr/crime-in-the-u.s/2012/crime-in-the-u.s.-2012/tables/38tabledatadecoverviewpdf

Fisher, B. S., & Sloan, J. J. (2007). Campus crime policy: Legal, social, and security contexts. In B. S. Fisher & J. J. Sloan, III (Eds.), *Campus crime: Legal, social, and policy perspectives* (2nd ed.), pp. 3–22. Springfield, IL: Charles C. Thomas Publisher.

Fox, J. A., & Levin, J. (1998). Multiple homicide: Patterns of serial and mass murder. *Crime & Justice, 23,* 407–455.

Gehrand, K. A. (2008). Higher education policing: The new millennium. International Association of Campus Law Enforcement, pp. 67–68. Retrieved from http://www.iaclea.org/visitors/PDFs/IACLEA-ContentPages_67-126.pdf

Gray, E. (2014a, May 26). America's campuses are dangerous places. *Time,* p. 14.

Gray, E. (2014b, September 1). Taking assault seriously. *Time,* pp. 20–29.

Heinsler, J. M, Kleinman, S., & Stenross, B. (1990). Making work matter: Satisfied detectives and dissatisfied campus police. *Qualitative Sociology, 13,* 235–250.

Hinkle, D. P., & Jones, T. S. (1991). Security guards or real cops: How some major universities are facing the nineties. *Law and Order, 39,* 141–146.

Homans, G. C. (1967). *The nature of social science.* New York: Harbringer, Brace & World.

Miller, J. L., & Pan, M. J. (1987). Student perceptions of campus police: The effects of personal characteristics and police contacts. *American Journal of Police, 6,* 27–44.

Moon, B., & Corley, C. J. (2007). Driving across campus: Assessing the impact of drivers' race and gender on police traffic enforcement actions. *Journal of Criminal Justice, 35,* 29–37.

Paoline, E. A., & Sloan, J. J. (2003). Variability in the organizational structure of contemporary campus law enforcement agencies: A national-level analysis. *Policing, 26,* 612–639.

Peak, K. (1987). Campus policing in America: The state of the art. *Police Chief, 54,* 22–24.

Peak, K. J., Barthe, E. P., & Garcia, A. (2008). Campus policing in America: A twenty-year perspective. *Police Quarterly, 11,* 239–260.

Phelps, T. (2014, April 30). Guide on college sex assault draws praise, concerns. *Chicago Tribune,* p. 14.

Powell, J. (1994). The beginning—Yale Campus Police Department—1894. *Campus Law Enforcement Journal, 24,* 2–5.

Reaves, B. A. (2008). *Campus law enforcement, 2004–05.* Special Report, U.S. Department of Justice, Office of Justice Programs, Bureau of Justice Statistics, February, NCJ 219374.

Reaves, B. A. (2011). *Census of state and local law enforcement agencies, 2008.* U.S. Department of Justice, Office of Justice Programs, Bureau of Justice Statistics, December, NCJ 233982.

Reaves, B. A. (2015). *Campus law enforcement, 2011–12.* U.S. Department of Justice, Office of Justice Programs, Bureau of Justice Statistics, January, NCJ 248028.

Reaves, B., & Goldberg, M. (1996). Campus law enforcement agencies, 1995. Washington, DC: Office of Justice Programs, U.S. Department of Justice.

Shorey, R. C., Stuart, G. L., & Cornelius, T. L. (2011). Dating violence and substance use in college students: A review of the literature. *Aggression and Violent Behavior, 16,* 541–550.

Sloan, J. J. (1992). The modern campus police: An analysis of their evolution, structure, and function. *American Journal of Police, 11,* 85–104.

Sloan, J. J., III, & Fisher, B. S. (2011). *The dark side of the ivory tower: Campus crime as a social problem.* New York: Cambridge University Press.

Sloan, J. J., & Lanier, M. M. (2007). Community policing on university campuses: Tradition, practices, and outlook. In B. S. Fisher & J. J. Sloan, III (Eds.), *Campus crime: Legal, social, and policy perspectives* (2nd ed.), pp. 261–279. Springfield, IL: Charles C. Thomas Publisher.

Sloan, J. J., Lanier, M. M., & Beer, D. L. (2000). Policing the contemporary university campus: Challenging traditional organizational models. *Journal of Security Administration, 23,* 1–48.

Smith, M. R., Makarios, M., & Alpert, G. P. (2006). Differential suspicion: Theory specification and gender effects in the traffic stop context. *Justice Quarterly, 23,* 271–295.

Thurstone, L. L. (1931). The measurement of social attitudes. *The Journal of Abnormal and Social Psychology, 31,* 249–269.

Trends in higher education. (2011). Family income by selected characteristics, 2011. Retrieved from http://trends.collegeboard.org/college-pricing/figures-tables/family-income-selected-characteristics-2011

Trojanowicz, R., & Carter, D. (1988). *The philosophy and role of community policing.* Michigan State University: National Neighborhood Foot Patrol Center.

Truman, J. L., Langton, L., & Planty, M. (2013). *Criminal victimization, 2012.* US Department of Justice, Office of Justice Programs, Bureau of Justice Statistics. NCJ 243389.

USDOE (U.S. Department of Education, Office of Postsecondary Education). (2011). *The handbook for campus safety and security reporting.* Washington, DC: Author.

USDOE (U.S. Department of Education, Office of Postsecondary Education). (2013). *Campus safety and security data analysis cutting tool.* Washington, DC: Author.

Wada, J. C., Patten, R., & Candela, K. (2010). Betwixt and between: The perceived legitimacy of campus police. *Policing: An International Journal of Police Strategies & Management, 33,* 114–131.

Westley, W. A. (1970). *Violence and the police: A sociological study of law, custom and morality.* Cambridge: MIT Press.

Wilson, J. (1968). *Varieties of police behavior: The management of law and order in eight communities.* Cambridge, MA: Harvard University Press.

Wolf, R., Mesloh, C., & Henych, M. (2007). Fighting campus crime: Perceptions of polite canines at a metropolitan university. Retrieved from http://www.lesslethalweapons.org/articles/PerceptionsofPoliceDogs.pdf

Woolfenden, S., & Stevenson, B. (2011). Establishing appropriate staffing levels for campus public safety departments. Office of Community Oriented Policing Services, U.S. Department of Justice.

24

Police Response to Persons with Mental Illness

Wesley G. Jennings & Edward J. Hudak

Prior to the 1960s the mentally ill were virtually "warehoused" in large state psychiatric hospitals in abject living conditions and with little emphasis placed on their treatment (Perez, Leifman, & Estrada, 2003). The nineteenth century marked the beginning in British and American construction of a variety of "welfare institutions," such as insane asylums, workhouses, and prisons designed to provide custodial care for the mentally ill. The housing of these individuals was well intended and developed from a genuine concern for the well-being and safety of the mentally ill. However, the underlying motive was to protect the public from real or perceived abnormal/antisocial behavior.

Nevertheless, little time elapsed before these institutions became severely overcrowded. They subsequently became characterized by their inhumane living conditions and for their insensitive treatment of the mentally ill. This reality combined with the growing concern for the mentally ill; the increased availability of revolutionary psychotropic medications (e.g., Thorazine); the economic cost associated with institutionalizing the mentally ill; and state legislative restrictions on involuntary commitment, permissible length of stay, and community mental health centers were all factors that contributed to an era of immense social reform during the second half of the twentieth century (Aderibigbe, 1997; Murphy, 1989). These driving forces became the foundation for what is known as the deinstitutionalization movement and resulted in a paradigmatic shift in treatment of the mentally ill from "long-term psychiatric hospitalization to more independent living environments" (Krieg, 2001, p. 367; see also Manderscheid, Atay, & Crider, 2009).

The principal humanitarian, treatment-focused, and fiscally efficient determinants, which fueled the deinstitutionalization movement, have since

Prepared especially for *Critical Issues in Policing* by Wesley G. Jennings and Edward J. Hudak.

contributed to the displacement of the mentally ill from within the mental health system and into the criminal justice system. Over the past five decades, the number of mentally ill institutionalized in state psychiatric facilities has markedly declined, from approximately 560,000 in 1955, to fewer than 60,000 today (National Association of State Mental Health Program Directors Research Institute, 2000). Comparatively, there are now more people with mental illnesses institutionalized in our nation's jails and prisons than in all the state psychiatric hospitals combined (Sigurdson, 2000). Roughly 1 out of every 15 individuals in United States' jails suffers from a major mental disorder, such as a major depressive disorder, schizophrenia, or bipolar disorder (Walsh & Holt, 1999; Steadman et al., 1999). The dynamic changes in public policy regarding the mentally ill (e.g., deinstutionalization, budget cuts in federal mental health funding, and legislative changes concerning the rights of mentally ill individuals) now means that a fairly significant segment of the mentally ill population needs a specialized response on behalf of the police (Teplin, 2000). This situation is even further evidenced as there are now more than 5.1 million individuals living in the community on probation and parole (Pew Charitable Trusts, 2009), of which a significant amount have a documented mental health issue.

The purpose of this chapter is to begin with a brief overview of the impact of both deinstitutionalization and the criminalization of the mentally ill on law enforcement. We then examine police interactions with citizens, specifically, the level of discretion police exercise and the training for dealing with persons with mental health issues. The chapter then offers a brief discussion of crisis intervention teams and police officers' use of tasers with the mentally ill. We conclude by providing specific policy modifications for law enforcement departments to better prepare their officers for future encounters with the mentally ill.

The Impact of Deinstitutionalization

According to Lamb and Bachrach (2001, p. 1039), deinstitutionalization comprises three procedural processes: 1) the release of mentally ill individuals from psychiatric hospitals to alternative placement in the community; 2) the diversion of new psychiatric hospital admissions to alternative facilities; and 3) the development of special services for the noninstitutionalized mentally ill.

There is little controversy regarding the "success" of the first two processes. The occupancy of state hospital beds has drastically declined since its height of 339 per 100,000 in 1955. As of 1998, there were only 57,151 occupied state hospital beds for the 275 million persons living in the United States (21 per 100,000). However, the adequacy and availability of quality care for the mentally ill varies substantially. The improved care and services range from facilitating the mentally ill individual's ability to realize a relative degree of normalcy in his or her routine activities, achieve greater satisfaction with life circumstances, and promote positive development to what is more often the case, where community-based care for the mentally ill is either grossly inefficient or absent (Lamb & Bachrach, 2001).

In order to fully understand the impact of deinstitutionalization on law enforcement agencies and their personnel it is important to first identify the basic demographics of the mentally ill. Although it is difficult to ascertain the exact number of persons with mental illness because of the lack of a comprehensive mental health data collection system, some estimates indicate that as many as 1 in 10 persons suffer from some type of mental illness, and that there are between 1 and 4 million seriously mentally ill persons in the United States. The mentally ill live in an array of community settings with varying degrees of care and means of support, including private residences, halfway houses or group homes, bed and board homes, nursing homes, single-room hotels, jails and prisons, and homeless shelters (Murphy, 1989). The prevalence of mental illness and the often poor living conditions of the mentally ill lead almost inevitably to their increased involvement with law enforcement agencies.

Officer's Role as a "Gatekeeper"

According to Lamb, Weinberger, and DeCuir (2002, p. 1266), there are two common-law doctrines that emphasize law enforcement's role in taking the responsibility for persons with mental illness: 1) their power and authority to protect the safety and welfare of the community; and 2) their *parens patriae* obligations to protect individuals with disabilities. The public visibility and the 24 hours a day, seven days a week availability of the police contribute to their often one-dimensional decision making in dealing with persons with mental illness (Lamb et al., 2002). In addition, society's negative attitudes, misperceptions, and general apprehension toward the mentally ill further increases the police's obligation to either recognize the individual's need for treatment and connect him or her with the proper mental health service provider (Husted, Charter, & Perrou, 1995) or determine that the individual's illegal activity warrants an arrest (Arboleda-Florez & Holley, 1988). This assessment procedure places the officer in the position of "gatekeeper" between the mental health system and the criminal justice system (Lamb et al., 2002) and forces a determination that many argue the police are neither trained nor qualified to deliver (Ainsworth, 1995; Bittner, 1967; Green, 1997; Ruiz, 1993).

Criminalization of the Mentally Ill

Abramson first proposed the expression criminalization of the mentally ill in 1972. This has been interpreted as meaning that a criminal justice rather than a mental health response has been adopted (Patch & Arrigo, 1999). This refers to the process by which the mentally ill citizens involved in minor criminal offenses such as disturbing the peace, public drunkenness, and trespassing are disproportionately arrested and prosecuted through the county court system (Bittner, 1967; Lamb & Weinberger, 2001; Teplin & Pruett, 1992).

The principal issue that arises from this flawed method of social control is that the criminal justice system was neither intended or designed to be the initial point of entry into the mental health system (Teplin, 2000). However, there is some evidence to suggest that there has been a trend in mental health laws and legislation in moving some of the emphasis away from safeguarding rights to 'refuse treatment' in an effort to help individuals with a need gain access to the necessary and appropriate mental health services (Carney, 2003). Consequently a number of those individuals suffering from a mental illness are being labeled as a "criminal," as opposed to being directed to suitable treatment resources. This label virtually ensures that such individuals are significantly more likely to be arrested in subsequent cases of disorderliness (Teplin, 2000). The initial arrest, therefore, is typically the precursor of a perpetual cycle that shuffles mentally ill citizens between jail and the streets (Perez et al., 2003). In order to more fully understand this revolving door hypothesis between jail and the streets, it is essential to understand the nature of the interactions between the police and the mentally ill and the options officers have when dealing with encounters of this kind.

Police Interactions with Citizens and the Mentally Ill

Wilson (1968) developed a typology that placed the calls for police intervention into four distinct categories 1) police-invoked law enforcement, 2) police-invoked order maintenance, 3) citizen-invoked law enforcement, and 4) citizen-invoked order maintenance.

Police-invoked law enforcement is a proactive, legally sufficient, and officer-initiated response. The officer's decision to act is based solely on his or her knowledge, perceptions, and personal assumptions about the mentally ill. Given that a substantial portion of the mentally ill are homeless and, as a result of deinstitutionalization, are forced to live on the streets, it follows that they are much more likely to be the recipients of police-invoked intervention. This is due to the combination of their visibility, their behaviors, and their disproportionate concentration in urban environments (Murphy, 1989; Patch & Arrigo, 1999; Wilson, 1968).

Police-invoked order maintenance refers to situations where the officer perceives a need to intervene to allay some sort of social disturbance. Public drunkenness and disorderly conduct are the crimes most commonly associated with this type of intervention (Brown, 1981; Wilson, 1968). Citizen-invoked law enforcement is the type of intervention that is initiated when a citizen makes a complaint. The officer, who is frequently forced to act within what amounts to considerable departmental constraints, usually resolves these instances. In such situations, officers make an attempt to "satisfy" all the parties involved, including the citizen who filed the complaint, the officer's departmental supervisors, and the general public.

The fourth type of intervention, citizen-invoked order maintenance, is relatively devoid of departmental influences because the situations necessitating this type of intervention are isolated events and cannot be anticipated by the officer (e.g. loud music, marital squabbles that prompt neighbor complaints, etc.) (Wilson, 1968; Patch & Arrigo, 1999, p. 29).

Encounters between law enforcement and the mentally ill follow patterns relatively similar to all police calls for service. The majority of the encounters occur during the evening shift followed by the day shift, with the fewest incidents happening during the night shift. However, the mentally ill tend to be most vulnerable and responsible for an increased number of calls for service during the night and weekend hours, as well as on public holidays. This is primarily because this is the time when the primary service resources (e.g., mental health agencies) for the mentally ill are unavailable (Murphy, 1989).

Additionally, police encounters with the mentally ill tend to occur in several key locations, with the individuals displaying a similar pattern of behavior. The majority of police contact with the mentally ill occurs either at or near the individual's place of residence. The most common location is in the street, but incidents also occur in halfway houses, mental health agencies, and public buildings. The behaviors that most frequently characterize the mentally ill during their encounters with law enforcement include bizarre or unusual behavior, confused thoughts and actions, aggressiveness, destructive or violent behavior, and/ or attempted suicide. Furthermore, mentally ill citizens are typically unattached, lack social support mechanisms (most notably family support), diagnosed as psychotic (primarily schizophrenia), difficult to manage (in denial about illness), and/or have alcohol or drug abuse dependency problems (Murphy, 1989).

Overall, Wilson's (1968) proposed typology of police–citizen interactions and the specific characteristics that describe the typical encounters between the police and the mentally ill (Lurigio & Lewis, 1987; Murphy, 1989) underscore the extent of the role that the public, the officer, and the mentally ill have in determining the officer's level of discretion and response. The public (i.e., the citizen) has the right to voice his or her concern or file a formal complaint to the police requesting a response to a situation involving a person with mental illness. The nature of this complaint is variable as is the degree of authenticity that can be attached to it (people can and do lie); however, a perceived and reported public threat necessarily demands a police response.

Despite the mixed research on the use of prediction tools in law enforcement (see Jennings, 2006), some research has revealed several factors related to recidivism among mentally ill persons that might be beneficial when assessing risk. For instance, Lewis, Lurigio, and Riger (1994) followed a random sample of persons with mental illness out of a state psychiatric hospital in Chicago, IL, for a period of 12 months. Their findings showed a 20% recidivism rate, measured by re-arrest one year after their release. Perhaps the more provocative finding was that 75% of all the crimes committed by the former patients were either city ordinance violations (e.g., trespassing, public drunkenness) or property crimes (e.g., theft, burglary). However, upon further analysis, their findings revealed that the former patients who were re-arrested upon follow-up were characterized as having extensive and serious criminal and hospitalization histories.

In a similar study using arrest data, Lurigio and Lewis (1987) categorized the criminal histories of persons with mental illness into three groups: 1) crimes were a by-product of their mental illness (e.g., disturbing the peace, trespassing, intoxication, expressing symptoms of mental disorder in public); 2) crimes were committed for survival purposes (e.g., shoplifting, theft, prostitution); or 3) serious crimes were associated with their manifestation of severe mental illness and alcohol and drug dependency problems (e.g., assault, rape, robbery).

Additionally, the behavior and demeanor of the officer and the person with mental illness are also situationally specific. Nevertheless, regardless of the frequency of contact or the nature and type of police–citizen encounter, recent research has noted police officers' frustration in handling mentally ill offenders and found evidence indicating that officers often cite the lack of coordination between the police and mental health professionals as one of the reasons for their frustration (see Cooper, Mclearen, & Sapf, 2004; see also Borum et al., 1997).

Police Discretion with the Mentally Ill

Generally, an officer has three possible choices upon encountering an irrational person creating a social disturbance. The officer's first response option is to transport the person to a mental hospital. This alternative is usually employed whenever the mentally ill individual is either a danger to him- or herself or to others, or lacks the ability to protect him- or herself from victimization. However, this option often results in a frustrating and time-consuming experience for the officer as he or she has to spend a significant amount of time in the emergency room or the hospital waiting room, and, at times, the mental health professional at the hospital may not necessarily agree with the officer's assessment/"diagnosis" for the individual that the officer transported to the facility. This situation can lead to a decision on behalf of the mental health representative/s of the facility to refuse to admit the individual or release him or her fairly quickly (Lamb et al., 2002, p. 1267; Steadman et al., 2001).

The officer's second alternative is to make an arrest. This decision may appear to be the most severe, however, to many officers, it is preferable as it at least ensures that the individual will be provided with treatment; often the individual is either not dangerous enough to satisfy the strict hospital criteria for admission or was defined as too dangerous by the hospital's standards. The officer's third alternative, which is generally the least invasive and most preferred option, is to informally resolve the problem. However, responsibility for the subject's continued conduct can fall squarely on the officer in today's litigious society. At first glance these may appear to be three distinct alternatives, but the officers still exercise a great deal of discretion when determining which response is appropriate in any given situation (Teplin, 2000, p. 9; Patch & Arrigo, 1999).

Bittner's seminal study on police discretion (1967) found that in encounters with the mentally ill, officers were reluctant to make psychiatric referrals unless an individual was perceived to be violent or a potential harm to him- or herself or someone else. Otherwise, in the majority of police encounters with the mentally ill, the officer chose the more informal alternative of "calming" the individual down.

Since Bittner's (1967) study there have been a host of other researchers who have addressed the factors involved in an officer's decision to arrest a mentally ill individual rather than transport him or her to a mental hospital. These determining factors include the level of the social disturbance, the strictness of legal requirements for involuntary commitment, the willingness of mental health facilities or state hospitals to accept intoxicated patients, the relative complexity of admission procedures, the length of waiting periods in the emergency room, and an officer's perception that there are no other viable community alternatives (i.e., a "mercy booking') (Durham, 1989; Gillig, Dumaine, Stammer, & Hillard, 1990; Laberge & Morin, 1995; Ogloff & Otto, 1989; Teplin, 1984). Regardless of the initial justification for the decision to either arrest or refer a person with mental illness to the state hospital, officers exercise a great deal of discretion and authority when determining which system, either criminal justice or mental health, is employed and by which means, either arrest or civil commitment, the mentally ill citizen will be processed (Patch & Arrigo, 1999). And, Morabito (2007, p. 1586) has gone even further to argue that the previous literature in this vein has "oversimplified police discretion" by not having specified parameters for scenic and temporal variables that are indeed important components of this interaction between the police and persons with mental illness.

Police Training

Most police departments in the early 1980s made attempts to incorporate specialized approaches and specific training curricula for how to more effectively deal with the mentally ill. Deane, Steadman, Borum, Veysey, and Morrissey (1999) found that as many as 88% of law enforcement agencies have some sort of training related to mental illness. Although the training has been proven to change officers' attitudes toward the mentally ill, to enhance their knowledge of mental health-related issues, and to improve their relationships with mental health professionals, the content and quality of the training has not yet been quantitatively evaluated (Borum, 1999; Godschlax, 1984; Hails & Borum, 2003; Murphy, 1989).

In one such example, Deane et al. (1999, p. 100) administered a survey in 1996 to the police departments in the 194 cities in the United States with a population of 100,000 or more to determine the prevalence of specialized responses in dealing with the mentally ill. They found that 96 of the 174 departments that responded to the survey did not have any procedure in place for dealing with the mentally ill. The 78 departments that indicated the presence of specialized response strategies were categorized into one of the three following models:

1. *Police-based specialized police response:* This strategic response involves sworn officers who have special mental health training who can provide crisis intervention services and act as liaisons with the mental health system;

2. *Police-based specialized mental health response:* This strategic response utilizes mental health consultants, hired by the police department. The consultants are not sworn officers, but they provide on-site and telephone consultations to the sworn officers in the field; and

3. *Mental-health based specialized mental health response:* This strategic response is a combination of any other type of response and includes departments that rely solely on mobile crisis teams. The teams are part of the local community mental health service system and provide a response to any special needs at the site of an incident.

Hails and Borum (2003) performed a similar study in an attempt to update the findings from the 1996 survey (Deane et al., 1999). Their questionnaire was administered and responded to by a total of 84 of the 135 medium and large-sized police departments that were surveyed. Hail and Borum (2003) arrived at a similar conclusion to Deane et al. (1999). They found that very little attention and training, especially with new recruits and veteran law enforcement officers, was directed toward understanding and dealing with the mentally ill. This result was alarming considering the amount of media coverage, community tension, and legal liability that arises from situations where the police use deadly force against mentally ill individuals (Hails & Borum, 2003).

Despite the relative national inattention to the need for training officers in dealing with the mentally ill, several model programs do exist. Steadman et al. (2000) provided an analysis of three different study sites, each representing one of Deane et al.'s (1999) previously identified models for emergency response to the mentally ill. The Birmingham Police Department (Birmingham, Alabama) employs the police-based specialized police response model. The department utilizes community service officers to assist police officers with incidents involving the mentally ill. These community service officers are civilians, with some degree or professional training in social work or a related field, who provide 24-hour coverage, seven days a week (including holidays).

The Memphis Police Department (Memphis, TN) illustrates the police-based specialized mental health response model. This department utilizes a crisis intervention team, comprised of specially trained officers, to deal with situations involving the mentally ill. The officers on this team receive 40 hours of specialized training from mental health professionals, family advocates, and mental health consumer groups, and are issued crisis intervention team medallions for immediate identification. Once a member of the crisis intervention team arrives on the scene he or she is automatically designated as the officer-in-charge. This Memphis model has since been replicated in various cities throughout the country.

The Knoxville Police Department (Knoxville, TN) utilizes the mental-health-based specialized mental health response model. This department has a mobile crisis unit that responds to calls from the community, as well as telephone calls and referrals from the jail regarding situations with the mentally ill. The Knoxville mobile crisis intervention unit was able to effectively link almost three-fourths of the mentally ill they encountered with the necessary treatment services, and only 5% of the incidents resulted in an arrest.

Acknowledging the positive results, these three programs were not without their flaws. For example, the findings indicated that they were frequently delayed and that their response times were lengthy, especially on nights and weekends. The limited number of trained staff and poor attendance at other similar assignments was also an issue. However, Steadman et al. (2000) still regarded these innovations as an overall success. More specifically, only 7% of the mental disturbance calls resulted in an arrest and more than half of the mentally ill individuals were either transported to or directed to appropriate treatment services. In addition, the officers were able to facilitate a resolution that enabled the individual to remain in the community without the additional impact of sanctions from the criminal justice system (Steadman et al., 2000).

More recently, Teller, Munetz, Gil, and Ritter (2006) examined police dispatch data logs for two years before and four years after the implementation of a crisis intervention team in Akron, Ohio. Members of the crisis intervention team included police officers and representatives from the local mental health systems. Their results indicated that since the implementation of the specialized training program (i.e., the creation of the crisis intervention team), there was an increase in the number and proportion of calls involving mentally ill persons, an increased transport rate (including voluntary transports) of mentally ill persons experiencing a crisis to local emergency treatment facilities, and no significant differences in the arrest rates pre and post intervention.

In addition, Morabito et al. (2012) provided an analysis of police–citizen encounters with crisis intervention-trained officers (CIT) in Chicago and reported that CIT training yielded some benefits in terms of a reduction in use of force. However, recognition of this benefit was complex as a number of relevant variables (e.g., demeanor, district characteristics, and subject resistance) affected this outcome as well. Furthermore, this benefit was not observed in all areas. Nevertheless, these findings along with the others reviewed above have significant implications for departmental and public policy, especially considering the success demonstrated when the police department and the mental health system work together in a collaborative effort and when CIT training is implemented.

Police Use of Tasers with the Mentally Ill

Considering all of the legislative and policy changes targeting the mentally ill, it is no surprise that the police are now typically the first respondents to a mentally ill individual experiencing a crisis. While the probability of a fatal injury resulting from a police–mentally ill person encounter is rather low, law enforcement experts suggest that the police are often on "heightened" alert when responding to a call involving a mentally ill person because of the perception that the individual is likely to be carrying a weapon (usually a knife) for his or her own protection. Thus, in an effort to reduce the occurrence of fatal injuries and still make the officers feel safe, many police departments are now equipping their officers with tasers.

Tasers are an electroshock device that is considered a "less-than-lethal" weapon (similar to the classification of police batons, etc.). Although tasers vary in size and voltage depending on the brand etc., tasers deliver an electric shock via shooting two darts from the device that are attached with a tether. The range of a police-issued taser is approximately 20 feet, and this distance allows the officers to use this less-than-lethal weapon to de-escalate a potentially dangerous confrontation. Furthermore, this is an alternative to having to put themselves at risk of injury through direct personal contact with the mentally ill individual whose behavior demonstrates a threat and when previous attempts at verbally de-escalating the situation have been unsuccessful.

Munetz, Fitzgerald, and Woody (2006) have provided one specific study examining the deployment of tasers by Akron, OH, police officers who were members of a crisis intervention team. Despite the fact that the Akron CIT police officers responded to over 500 incidents involving mentally ill disturbances, the officers only reported deploying their tasers in 35 instances over the course of the 18-month period. More specifically, 21 of these individuals were already known to the public mental health system, and in most of the incidents the individuals were either considered acutely psychotic or had demonstrated suicidal tendencies. In addition, nearly 1 out of every 3 of these individuals possessed a weapon at the time the taser was administered. Overall, the findings in Munetz et al.'s (2006) study, such as the low prevalence of taser use and the absence of serious injury to any of the mentally ill individuals that were tasered, are also promising results.

Thus, although a considerable amount of public attention has been devoted to a few select cases where an officer either overuses or misuses his or her taser, there can be little argument that deploying a taser is certainly a more favorable option than discharging a firearm in less dangerous confrontations between the police and the mentally ill. Still, researchers often caution and recommend that tasers should only be used when dealing with a person with a mental health issue when it is clear that this "individual is imminently likely to sustain or to cause grievous bodily harm" (Edinger & Boulter, 2011, p. 589).

Policy Implications

The fact that the mentally ill are being criminalized is a dual indictment of the failure of the mental health system and the criminal justice system, neither of which is effectively and appropriately dealing with persons with mental illnesses (Teplin, 2000). The reality of the situation is that neither system has proven itself able to manage mental health crises alone (Wolff, 1998). An integrated and collaborative effort between both systems might therefore prove to be the most beneficial for all parties (i.e., the mentally ill, law enforcement, the courts, corrections, and mental health treatment providers).

The police need to be aware of, and accept, that their primary role in dealing with the mentally ill is law enforcement. Their foremost concern should be ensuring the safety of the individual and the community. Having said this, once they have minimized the disturbance their objective should then shift to locating and transporting the mentally ill individual to the most appropriate treatment facility. Likewise, mental health professionals need to realize that their primary role is to assist the officer in conflict resolution and recommend the most beneficial treatment response. The two agencies would thus benefit from developing an ongoing and reciprocal understanding of the occupational expertise the other possesses (Lamb et al., 2002).

The Criminal Justice/ Mental Health Consensus Project was one of the most comprehensive and involved attempts to investigate police responses to persons with mental illness. Its purpose was to develop recommendations, with bipartisan agreement, to enhance the response of the criminal justice and the mental health systems in dealing with persons with mental illness. Stakeholders included state lawmakers, police chiefs, officers, sheriffs, district attorneys, public defenders, judges, court administrators, state corrections directors, community corrections officials, victim advocates, consumers of mental health services, family members, county commissioners, state mental health directors, behavioral health care providers, and substance abuse experts. The final report was released on June 11, 2002 (Council of State Governments et al., 2002), and Thompson, Reuland, and Souweine (2003) summarized the seven policy statements most germane to mental health professionals and law enforcement agencies for improving their response to the mentally ill:

1. Improve availability of and access to comprehensive, individualized services, when and where they are most needed, to enable persons with mental illness to maintain meaningful community membership and avoid inappropriate criminal justice involvement (mental health);

2. Ensure that people with mental illness who are no longer under the supervision of the criminal justice system maintain contact with mental health services and have support for as long as is necessary (mental health);

3. Provide dispatchers with training to determine whether mental illness may be a factor in a call for service, and use that information to dispatch the call to the appropriate responder (law enforcement);

4. Develop procedures that require officers to determine whether mental illness is a factor in the incident, and whether a serious crime has been committed, while ensuring the safety of all parties involved (law enforcement);

5. Establish written protocols that enable officers to implement an appropriate response based on the nature of the incident, the behavior of the person with mental illness, and available resources (law enforcement);

6. Document accurately police contacts with people whose mental illness was a factor in an incident to promote accountability and to enhance service delivery (law enforcement); and

7. Collaborate with mental health partners to reduce the need for subsequent contacts between people with mental illness and law enforcement.

Conclusions

As noted by Hails and Borum (2003; see also Morabito et al., 2012), understanding the problems regarding traditional police responses to persons with mental illness has resulted in the provision of a better service to the community. Unfortunately, when officers and agencies are not prepared and mistakes are made, lawsuits claiming negligence or deliberate indifference to these citizens are often filed. Nevertheless, properly trained officers or specialists can offer assistance and provide a specialized response in situations where time permits. These respondents are often part of a team and can react when called upon for support. In a barricaded suspect scenario, for example, or in a situation where a citizen needs help, these crisis intervention teams or trained individuals can provide much needed assistance to those in potentially dangerous situations.

Unfortunately, and quite often, officers face real and immediate threats from mentally ill individuals, and it is this threat to the officer or to a citizen that becomes critical and more important than dealing with the mental illness itself. When an individual, whether mentally ill or not, pulls a weapon on an officer, it is clear that the weapon is the most serious threat and must be dealt with for the safety of all those in the area including the mentally ill individual as well as the officer.

Additionally, officers would benefit from realizing that dealing or negotiating with a mentally ill person requires a more specialized and directed response than is generally employed in similar threatening situations involving a "normal" individual. For example, people with mental illnesses may be more apt to respond to and cooperate with an officer who recognizes the issues relevant to their life circumstances. The officer needs to be aware of how to best respond to the individual's threatening behavior in a nonconfrontational and/or nonadversarial manner. Any immediate or aggressive action taken by the officer may inadvertently increase the mentally ill individual's confusion and thereby intensify any abnormal/antisocial behavior. In an excellent review of these issues, Murphy (1989, pp. 9–10) has provided suggestions for officers, should they find themselves in such a situation.

What officers *should* do when managing an encounter with a mentally ill person:

1. Check for any weapons that could be perilous to the officer.
2. Gather as much information as possible before arriving on the scene.
3. Be discreet and avoid attracting attention.
4. Be calm, avoid excitement, and portray a take-charge attitude.
5. Remove as many distractions or upsetting influences from the scene as possible—this includes bystanders and disruptive friends or family members.
6. Gather as much information as possible from helpful witnesses, family members, and friends.

What officers should not do when managing encounters with the mentally ill:

1. Do not become or allow excitement, confusion, or upsetting circumstances. These may frighten the person, inhibit communication, and increase the risk of physical injury to the officer, the subject, or bystanders.
2. Do not abuse, belittle or threaten. Such actions may cause the person to become alarmed and distrustful.
3. Do not use inflammatory words such as "psycho" or "nut house."
4. Do not lie to or deceive the person. This can also cause the person to be distrustful. It may also limit any chances for successful mental health treatment and make any future management of the person by officers more difficult. It can also endanger the safety of other officers.
5. Do not cross-examine the person with a flurry of close-ended (e.g., "yes" and "no") questions. Instead, the person should be asked questions that allow him to explain the problems that are bothering him.
6. Do not dispute, debate or invalidate the person's claims. Do not agree or disagree with the person's statements. Rather, legitimize the person's feelings. For example, if the person claims a waitress is poisoning his/her food, the officer should say: "You believe that other people are trying to kill you?"
7. Do not rush the person or crowd his personal space. Do not touch the person unless you are prepared to use force. Any attempt to force an issue may quickly backfire in the form of violence.
8. Avoid being a "tough guy." Tough methods will usually frighten the person and cause a defensive reaction and possibly violent behavior.
9. Do not let the person upset or trick you into an argument. Ignore any attacks on your character, personal appearance or profession, as these will undermine your ability to communicate and will also provide the person with ammunition for future attacks.

Although these suggestions are not exhaustive (see Landsberg et al., 2002) and do not ensure a noncombative resolution in all situations, they remain useful, and serve to offer some guidance in dealing with the mentally ill.

This chapter has illustrated the profound impact that the process of deinstitutionalization has had on the treatment available to the mentally ill, and the duties and responsibilities of law enforcement. The ensuing and seemingly inevitable criminalization of the mentally ill has further exacerbated their plight. Not only do they suffer from often debilitating illnesses but they are also labeled "criminal," often as a direct result of their illness.

In the midst of a mental health crisis, there is no disputing the existence of a genuine threat to the officer and any individuals in the vicinity. It is therefore the officer's duty to take appropriate action to protect him- or herself and those in harm's way, be it the mentally ill person and/or an innocent bystander. Police departments need to implement ongoing training for their officers to help them recognize the signs of mental illness, training that would include education on the different types and symptoms of various mental illnesses. For example, a situation involving a suicidal individual or a paranoid schizophrenic certainly requires a more immediate and cautious response than a situation involving an individual displaying only mild symptoms of depression. However, a misdiagnosis can and occasionally does have dire consequences: knowing when to act and when to stand back are therefore equally important, and are decisions that become far easier to make with comprehensive training.

Recognizing that characterizing police officers as "street-corner psychiatrists" is often viewed negatively, officers must nonetheless be provided with the necessary tools so that they can best deal with situations involving the mentally ill. Without training, and through no fault of their own, police officers run the risk of mishandling situations, and increasing the risk of injury to themselves, to the public, and also to those citizens who stand to benefit the most from such measures, the mentally ill individuals themselves. Some of the preliminary evidence indicates that using crisis intervention teams and equipping police officers with tasers may likely be successful initiatives when dealing with mentally ill individuals. Yet, more research is needed before departments wholeheartedly accept this practice of carrying tasers. Having said this, considering the lethality of an officer-involved shooting this may be a more acceptable alternative, particularly for officers that are in frequent contact with the mentally ill.

REFERENCES

Abramson, M. L. (1972). The criminalization of mentally disordered behavior: Possible side effects of a new mental health law. *Hospital and Community Psychiatry, 23,* 101–105.

Aderibigbe, Y. A. (1997). Deinstitutionalization and criminalization: Tinkering in the interstices. *Forensic Science International, 85,* 127–134.

Ainsworth, P. (1995). *Psychology and policing in a changing world.* New York: John Wiley & Sons.

Arboleda-Florez, J., & Holley, H. L. (1988). Criminalization of the mentally ill: Initial detention. *Canadian Journal of Psychiatry, 33,* 87–95.

Bittner, E. (1967). Police discretion in emergency apprehension of mentally ill persons. *Social Problems, 14,* 278–292.

Borum, R. (1999). Misdemeanor offenders with mental illness in Florida: Examining police response, court jurisdiction, and jail mental health services. Tampa: FL: Department of Mental Health Law & Policy, Louis del la Parte Florida Mental Health Institute, University of South Florida.

Borum, R., Swanson, J., Swartz, M., & Hiday, V. (1997). Substance abuse, violent behavior, and police encounters among persons with severe mental disorder. *Journal of Contemporary Criminal Justice, 13,* 236–250.

Brown, M. K. (1981). *Working the street.* New York: Russell Sage Foundation.

Carney, T. (2003). Mental health law in postmodern society: Time for new paradigms? Psychiatry, *Psychology, and Law, 10,* 12–32.

Cooper, V. G., Mclearen, A. M., & Zapf, P. A. (2004). Dispositional decisions with the mentally ill: Police perceptions and characteristics. *Police Quarterly, 7,* 295–310.

Council of State Governments, Police Executive Research Forum, Pretrial Services Resource Center, Association of State Correctional Administrators, Bazelon Center for Mental Health Law, & the Center fro Behavioral Health, Justice, and Public Policy. (2002). *Criminal Justice/Mental Health Consensus Project.* New York: Council of State Governments.

Deane, M., Steadman, H., Borum, R., Veysey, B., & Morrissey, J. (1999). Emerging partnerships between mental health and law enforcement. *Psychiatric Services 50,* 99–101.

Durham, M. L. (1989). The impact of deinstitutionalization on the current treatment of the mentally ill. *International Journal of Law and Psychiatry, 12,* 117–131.

Edinger, J., & Boulter, S. (2011). Police use of TASERS in the restrain and transport of persons with a mental illness. *Journal of Law & Medicine, 18,* 589–593.

Gillig, P. M., Dumaine, M., Stammer, J. W., & Hillard, J. R. (1990). What do police officers really want from the mental health system? *Hospital and Community Psychiatry, 41,* 663–665.

Green, T. M. (1997). Police as frontline mental health workers: The decision to arrest or refer to mental health agencies. *International Journal of Law and Psychiatry, 20,* 469–486.

Godschlax, S. (1984). Effect of a mental health educational program upon police officers. *Research in Nursing and Health, 7,* 111–117.

Hails, J., & Borum, R. (2003). Police training and specialized approaches to respond to people with mental illnesses. *Crime & Delinquency, 49,* 52–61.

Husted, J. R., Charter, R. A., Perrou, M. A. (1995). California law enforcement agencies and the mentally ill offender. *Bulletin of the American Academy of Psychiatry and Law, 23,* 315–329.

Jennings, W. G. (2006). Revisiting prediction models in policing: Identifying high-risk offenders. *American Journal of Criminal Justice, 31,* 35–50.

Krieg, R. G. (2001). An interdisciplinary look at the deinstitutionalization of the mentally ill. *The Social Science Journal, 38,* 367–380.

Laberge, D, & Morin, D. (1995). The overuse of criminal justice dispositions: Failure of diversionary policies in the management of mental health problems. *International Journal of Law and Psychiatry, 18,* 389–414.

Lamb, H. R., & Bachrach, L. L. (2001). Some perspectives on deinstitutionalization. *Psychiatric Services, 52*, 1039–1045.

Lamb, H. R. & Weinberger, L. E. (2001). *Deinstitutionalization: Promise and problems.* San Francisco: Jossey-Bass.

Lamb, H. R., Weinberger, L. E., & DeCuir, W. J. (2002). The police and mental health. *Psychiatric Services, 53*, 1266–1271.

Landsberg, G., Rock, M., Berg, L., & Smiley, A. (Eds.). (2002). Serving mentally ill offenders: Challenges and opportunities for mental health professionals. New York: Springer.

Lewis, D. A., Lurigio, A. J., & Riger, S. (1994). The state mental patient and urban life: Moving in and out of the institution. Springfield, IL: Charles C. Thomas.

Lurigio, A. J., & Lewis, D. A. (1987). *Toward a taxonomy of the criminal mental patient.* Evanston, IL: Manuscript prepared for Northwestern University, Center for Urban Affairs and Policy Research.

Manderscheid, R. W., Atay, J. E. & Crider, R. A. (2009). Changing trends in state psychiatric hospital use from 2002 to 2005. *Psychiatric Services, 60*, 29–34.

Morabito, M. S. (2007). Horizons of context: Understanding the police decision to arrest people with mental illness. *Psychiatric Services, 58*, 1582–1587.

Morabito, M. S., Kerr, A. N., Watson, A., Draine, J., Ottati, V., Angell, B. (2012). Crisis intervention teams and people with mental illness: Exploring the factors that influence the use of force. *Crime & Delinquency, 58*, 57–77.

Munetz, M. R., Fitzgerald, A., & Woody, M. (2006). Police use of the taser with people with mental illness in crisis. *Psychiatric Services, 57*, 883–883.

Murphy, G. R. (1989). *Managing persons with mental disabilities: A curriculum guide for police trainers.* Washington, DC: Police Executive Research Forum.

National Association of State Mental Health Program Directors Research Institute. (2000). *Closing and reorganizing state psychiatric hospitals: 2000.* Retrieved January 21, 2004, from www.rdmc.org/nri/SH_RPT.pdf.

Ogloff, R. P., & Otto, R. K. (1989). Mental health interventions in jail. In K. P. Heyman (ed.), *Innovations in clinical practice.* Sarasota, FL: Professional Resource Exchange.

Patch, P. C., & Arrigo, B. A. (1999). Police officer attitudes and use of discretion in situations involving the mentally ill. *International Journal of Law and Psychiatry, 22*, 23–35.

Perez, A., Leifman, S., & Estrada, A. (2003). Reversing the criminalization of mental illness. *Crime & Delinquency, 49*, 62–78.

Pew Charitable Trusts. (2009). One in 31: *The long reach of American corrections.* Philadelphia: Pew Charitable Trusts.

Ruiz, J. (1993). An interactive analysis between uniformed law enforcement officers and the mentally ill. *American Journal of Police, 12*, 149–177.

Sigurdson, C. (2000). The mad, the bad, and the abandoned: The mentally ill in prisons and jails. *Corrections Today, 62*, 70–78.

Steadman, H. J., Deane, M. W., Morrissey, J. P., Westcott, M. L., Salasin, S., & Shapiro, S. (1999). A SAMHSA research initiative assessing the effectiveness of jail diversion programs for mentally ill persons. *Psychiatric Services, 50*, 1620–1623.

Steadman, H. J., Deane, M. W., Borum, R., & Morrissey, J. P. (2000). Comparing outcomes of major models of police responses to mental health emergencies. *Psychiatric Services, 51*, 645–649.

Steadman, H. J., Stainbrooke, K. A., Griffin, P., Draine, J., Dupont, R., & Horey, C. (2001). A specialized crisis response site as a core element of police-based diversion programs. *Psychiatric Services, 52,* 219–222.

Teller, J., Munetz, M. R., Gil, K. M., & Ritter, C. (2006). Crisis intervention team training for police officers responding to mental disturbance calls. *Psychiatric Services, 57,* 232–237.

Teplin, L.A. (1984). Managing disorder: Police handling of the mentally ill. In L. A. Teplin (ed.), *Mental health and criminal justice* (pp. 157–175). Beverly Hills, CA: Sage.

Teplin, L. A., & Pruett, H. (1992). Police as street-corner psychiatrist: Managing the mentally ill. *International Journal of Law and Psychiatry, 15,* 139–156.

Teplin, L. A. (2000). Keeping the peace: Police discretion and mentally ill persons. *National Institute of Justice Journal (July 2000),* 8–15.

Thompson, M. D., Reuland, M., & Souweine, D. (2003). Criminal justice/Mental health consensus: Improving responses to people with mental illness. *Crime & Delinquency, 49,* 30–51.

Walsh, J., & Holt, D. (1999). Jail diversion for people with psychiatric disabilities: The sheriff's perspective. *Psychiatric Rehabilitation Journal, 23,* 153–160.

Wilson, J. Q. (1968). *Varieties of police behavior: The management of law and order in eight communities.* Cambridge, MA: Harvard University Press.

Wolff, N. (1998). Interactions between mental health and law enforcement systems: Problems and prospects for cooperation. *Journal of Health Politics, Policy, and Law, 23,* 133–174.

SECTION V

Community-Based Policing

The role of the community in the organization, maintenance, and control of law enforcement has come full circle since the police were first created as "organized watchers." In those early days of the police, it was the community or neighborhood that was the important focus of policing. Over the years, the inventions of two-way radios, automobiles, and computers made police work more impersonal and removed officers from face-to-face interactions with the community. However, since the 1990s, there has been an emphasis on reintegrating policing back into the neighborhood. In this section, we have included four articles that reflect the significance of community-based or community-oriented policing.

The first article in this section is the classic "Broken Windows" by James Q. Wilson and George L. Kelling. The authors reviewed the impact of reinstituting foot patrols in Newark, New Jersey. They concluded that reinstituting foot patrols had not reduced crime rates but that residents in foot-patrolled neighborhoods felt more secure than residents of other neighborhoods. Wilson and Kelling suggested that order-maintenance policing, historically a focus of policing, should replace the preoccupation with crime control.

Samuel Walker, however, criticizes the misuse of history in recent police patrol analysis. In "'Broken Windows' and Fractured History: The Use and Misuse of History in Recent Police Patrol Analysis," Walker argues that Wilson and Kelling's policy proposals may be worth pursuing, but that they are grounded in a romanticized version of the history of policing and therefore need to be more fully developed.

In the next selection, "Community Policing," Gary Cordner discusses the four dimensions of community policing: philosophical, strategic, tactical, and organizational. He notes that all the research on this topic focuses on the tactical dimension. Cordner suggests that since the evaluations thus far have been positive, research should now focus on the other three elements of community policing.

John Reitzel, Nicole Leeper Piquero, and Alex Piquero assess the problem-oriented policing movement in the final selection. They describe its origins and how it differs from other styles of policing. They also include examples of how to evaluate programs that involve a problem-solving orientation. One of the most interesting aspects of this article is the juxtaposition of community-oriented policing and zero-tolerance policing.

25

Broken Windows

James Q. Wilson & George L. Kelling

In the mid-1970s, the state of New Jersey announced a "Safe and Clean Neighborhoods Program," designed to improve the quality of community life in twenty-eight cities. As part of that program, the state provided money to help cities take police officers out of their patrol cars and assign them to walking beats. The governor and other state officials were enthusiastic about using foot patrol as a way of cutting crime, but many police chiefs were skeptical. Foot patrol, in their eyes, had been pretty much discredited. It reduced the mobility of the police, who thus had difficulty responding to citizen calls for service, and it weakened headquarters control over patrol officers.

Many police officers also disliked foot patrol, but for different reasons: it was hard work, it kept them outside on cold, rainy nights, and it reduced their chances for making a "good pinch." In some departments, assigning officers to foot patrol had been used as a form of punishment. And academic experts on policing doubted that foot patrol would have any impact on crime rates; it was, in the opinion of most, little more than a sop to public opinion. But since the state was paying for it, the local authorities were willing to go along.

Five years after the program started, the Police Foundation, in Washington, DC, published an evaluation of the foot-patrol project. Based on its analysis of a carefully controlled experiment carried out chiefly in Newark, the foundation concluded, to the surprise of hardly anyone, that foot patrol had not reduced crime rates. But residents of the foot-patrolled neighborhoods seemed to feel more secure than persons in other areas, tended to believe that crime had been reduced, and seemed to take fewer steps to protect themselves from crime (staying at home with the doors locked, for example). Moreover, citizens in the foot-patrol areas had a more favorable opinion of the police than did those living elsewhere. And officers walking beats had

From *The Atlantic Monthly*, March 1982, pp. 29–38. Reprinted with permission of James Q. Wilson and George L. Kelling.

higher morale, greater job satisfaction, and a more favorable attitude toward citizens in their neighborhoods than did officers assigned to patrol cars.

These findings may be taken as evidence that the skeptics were right—foot patrol has no effect on crime; it merely fools the citizens into thinking that they are safer. But in our view, and in the view of the authors of the Police Foundation study (of whom Kelling was one), the citizens of Newark were not fooled at all. They knew what the foot-patrol officers were doing, they knew it was different from what motorized officers do, and they knew that having officers walk beats did in fact make their neighborhoods safer.

But how can a neighborhood be "safer" when the crime rate has not gone down—in fact, may have gone up? Finding the answer requires first that we understand what most often frightens people in public places. Many citizens, of course, are primarily frightened by crime, especially crime involving a sudden, violent attack by a stranger. This risk is very real, in Newark as in many large cities. But we tend to overlook or forget another source of fear—the fear of being bothered by disorderly people. Not violent people, nor, necessarily, criminals, but disreputable or obstreperous or unpredictable people: panhandlers, drunks, addicts, rowdy teenagers, prostitutes, loiterers, the mentally disturbed.

What foot-patrol officers did was to elevate, to the extent they could, the level of public order in these neighborhoods. Though the neighborhoods were predominantly black and the foot patrolmen were mostly white, this "order-maintenance" function of the police was performed to the general satisfaction of both parties.

One of us (Kelling) spent many hours walking with Newark foot-patrol officers to see how they defined "order" and what they did to maintain it. One beat was typical: a busy but dilapidated area in the heart of Newark, with many abandoned buildings, marginal shops (several of which prominently displayed knives and straight-edged razors in their windows), one large department store, and, most important, a train station and several major bus stops. Though the area was run-down, its streets were filled with people, because it was a major transportation center. The good order of this area was important not only to those who lived and worked there but also to many others, who had to move through it on their way home, to supermarkets, or to factories.

The people on the street were primarily black; the officer who walked the street was white. The people were made up of "regulars" and "strangers." Regulars included both "decent folk" and some drunks and derelicts who were always there but who "knew their place." Strangers were, well, strangers, and viewed suspiciously, sometimes apprehensively. The officer—call him Kelly—knew who the regulars were, and they knew him. As he saw his job, he was to keep an eye on strangers, and make certain that the disreputable regulars observed some informal but widely understood rules. Drunks and addicts could sit on the stoops, but could not lie down. People could drink on side streets, but not at the main intersection. Bottles had to be in paper bags. Talking to, bothering, or begging from people waiting at the bus stop was strictly forbidden. If a dispute erupted between a businessman and a customer, the businessman was assumed to be right, especially if the customer was a stranger. If a stranger loitered, Kelly would ask him if he had any means of support and what his business was; if he gave unsatisfactory answers, he was sent on his way. Persons who broke the informal rules, especially those who bothered people waiting at bus stops, were arrested for vagrancy. Noisy teenagers were told to keep quiet.

These rules were defined and enforced in collaboration with the "regulars" on the street. Another neighborhood might have different rules, but these, everybody understood, were the rules for *this* neighborhood. If someone violated them, the regulars not only turned to Kelly for help but also ridiculed the violator. Sometimes what Kelly did could be described as "enforcing the law," but just as often it involved taking informal or extralegal steps to help protect what the neighborhood had decided was the appropriate level of public order. Some of the things he did probably would not withstand a legal challenge.

A determined skeptic might acknowledge that a skilled foot-patrol officer can maintain order but still insist that this sort of "order" has little to do with the real sources of community fear—that is, with violent crime. To a degree, that is true. But two things must be borne in mind. First, outside observers should not assume that they know how much of the anxiety now endemic in many big-city neighborhoods stems from a fear of "real" crime and how much from a sense that the street is disorderly, a source of distasteful, worrisome encounters. The people of Newark, to judge from their behavior and their remarks to interviewers, apparently assign a high value to public order, and feel relieved and reassured when the police help them maintain that order.

Second, at the community level, disorder and crime are usually inextricably linked, in a kind of developmental sequence. Social psychologists and police officers tend to agree that if a window in a building is broken *and is left unrepaired*, all the rest of the windows will soon be broken. This is as true in nice neighborhoods as in run-down ones. Window-breaking does not necessarily occur on a large scale because some areas are inhabited by determined window-breakers whereas others are populated by window-lovers; rather, one unrepaired broken window is a signal that no one cares, and so breaking more windows costs nothing. (It has always been fun.)

Philip Zimbardo, a Stanford psychologist, reported in 1969 on some experiments testing the broken-window theory. He arranged to have an automobile without license plates parked with its hood up on a street in the Bronx and a comparable automobile on a street in Palo Alto, California. The car in the Bronx was attacked by "vandals" within ten minutes of its "abandonment." The first to arrive were a family—father, mother, and young son— who removed the radiator and battery. Within twenty-four hours, virtually everything of value had been removed. Then random destruction began— windows were smashed, parts torn off, upholstery ripped. Children began to use the car as a playground. Most of the adult "vandals" were well-dressed, apparently clean-cut whites. The car in Palo Alto sat untouched for more than a week. Then Zimbardo smashed part of it with a sledgehammer. Soon, passersby were joining in. Within a few hours, the car had been turned upside down and utterly destroyed. Again, the "vandals" appeared to be primarily respectable whites.

Untended property becomes fair game for people out for fun or plunder, and even for people who ordinarily would not dream of doing such things and who probably consider themselves law-abiding. Because of the nature of community life in the Bronx—its anonymity, the frequency with which cars are abandoned and things are stolen or broken, the past experience of "no one caring"—vandalism begins much more quickly than it does in staid Palo Alto, where people have come to believe that private possessions are cared for, and that mischievous behavior is costly. But vandalism can occur anywhere once communal barriers—the sense of mutual regard and the obligations of civility—are lowered by actions that seem to signal that "no one cares."

We suggest that "untended" behavior also leads to the breakdown of community controls. A stable neighborhood of families who care for their homes, mind each other's children, and confidently frown on unwanted intruders can change, in a few years or even a few months, to an inhospitable and frightening jungle. A piece of property is abandoned, weeds grow up, a window is smashed. Adults stop scolding rowdy children; the children, emboldened, become more rowdy. Families move out, unattached adults move in. Teenagers gather in front of the corner store. The merchant asks them to move; they refuse. Fights occur. Litter accumulates. People start drinking in front of the grocery; in time, an inebriate slumps to the sidewalk and is allowed to sleep it off. Pedestrians are approached by panhandlers.

At this point it is not inevitable that serious crime will flourish or violent attacks on strangers will occur. But many residents will think that crime, especially violent crime, is on the rise, and they will modify their behavior accordingly. They will use the streets less often, and when on the streets will stay apart from their fellows, moving with averted eyes, silent lips, and hurried steps. "Don't get involved." For some residents, this growing atomization will matter little, because the neighborhood is not their "home" but "the place where they live." Their interests are elsewhere; they are cosmopolitans. But it will matter greatly to other people, whose lives derive meaning and satisfaction from local attachments rather than worldly involvement; for them, the neighborhood will cease to exist except for a few reliable friends whom they arrange to meet.

Such an area is vulnerable to criminal invasion. Though it is not inevitable, it is more likely that here, rather than in places where people are confident they can regulate public behavior by informal controls, drugs will change hands, prostitutes will solicit, and cars will be stripped. That the drunks will be robbed by boys who do it as a lark, and the prostitutes' customers will be robbed by men who do it purposefully and perhaps violently. That muggings will occur.

Among those who often find it difficult to move away from this are the elderly. Surveys of citizens suggest that the elderly are much less likely to be the victims of crime than younger persons, and some have inferred from this that the well-known fear of crime voiced by the elderly is an exaggeration: perhaps we ought not to design special programs to protect older persons; perhaps we should even try to talk them out of their mistaken fears. This argument misses the point. The prospect of a confrontation with an obstreperous teenager or a drunken panhandler can be as fear-inducing for defenseless persons as the prospect of meeting an actual robber; indeed, to a defenseless person, the two kinds of confrontation are often indistinguishable. Moreover, the lower rate at which the elderly are victimized is a measure of the steps they have already taken—chiefly, staying behind locked doors—to minimize the risks they face. Young men are more frequently attacked than older women, not because they are easier or more lucrative targets but because they are on the streets more.

Nor is the connection between disorderliness and fear made only by the elderly. Susan Estrich, of the Harvard Law School, has recently gathered together a number of surveys on the sources of public fear. One, done in Portland, Oregon, indicated that three fourths of the adults interviewed cross to the other side of a street when they see a gang of teenagers; another survey, in Baltimore, discovered that nearly half would cross the street to avoid even a single strange youth. When an interviewer asked people in a housing project where the most dangerous spot was, they mentioned a place where young persons gathered to drink and play music, despite the fact that not a single crime had occurred there. In Boston public housing projects, the greatest fear was expressed by persons living in the buildings where disorderliness and incivility, not crime, were the greatest. Knowing this helps one understand the significance of such otherwise harmless displays as subway graffiti. As Nathan Glazer has written, the proliferation of graffiti, even when not obscene, confronts the subway rider with the "inescapable knowledge that the environment he must endure for an hour or more a day is uncontrolled and uncontrollable, and that anyone can invade it to do whatever damage and mischief the mind suggests."

In response to fear, people avoid one another, weakening controls. Sometimes they call the police. Patrol cars arrive, an occasional arrest occurs, but crime continues and disorder is not abated. Citizens complain to the police chief, but he explains that his department is low on personnel and that the courts do not punish petty or first-time offenders. To the residents, the police who arrive in squad cars are either ineffective or uncaring; to the police, the residents are animals who deserve each other. The citizens may soon stop calling the police, because "they can't do anything."

The process we call urban decay has occurred for centuries in every city. But what is happening today is different in at least two important respects. First, in the period before, say, World War II, city dwellers—because of money costs, transportation difficulties, familial and church connections—

could rarely move away from neighborhood problems. When movement did occur, it tended to be along public-transit routes. Now mobility has become exceptionally easy for all but the poorest or those who are blocked by racial prejudice. Earlier crime waves had a kind of built-in self-correcting mechanism: the determination of a neighborhood or community to reassert control over its turf. Areas in Chicago, New York, and Boston would experience crime and gang wars, and then normalcy would return, as the families for whom no alternative residences were possible reclaimed their authority over the streets.

Second, the police in this earlier period assisted in that reassertion of authority by acting, sometimes violently, on behalf of the community. Young toughs were roughed up, people were arrested "on suspicion" or for vagrancy, and prostitutes and petty thieves were routed. "Rights" were something enjoyed by decent folk, and perhaps also by the serious professional criminal, who avoided violence and could afford a lawyer.

This pattern of policing was not an aberration or the result of occasional excess. From the earliest days of the nation, the police function was seen primarily as that of a night watchman: to maintain order against the chief threats to order—fire, wild animals, and disreputable behavior. Solving crimes was viewed not as a police responsibility but as a private one. In the March, 1969, *Atlantic*, one of us (Wilson) wrote a brief account of how the police role had slowly changed from maintaining order to fighting crimes. The change began with the creation of private detectives (often ex-criminals), who worked on a contingency-fee basis for individuals who had suffered losses. In time, the detectives were absorbed into municipal police agencies and paid a regular salary; simultaneously, the responsibility for prosecuting thieves was shifted from the aggrieved private citizen to the professional prosecutor. This process was not complete in most places until the twentieth century.

In the 1960s, when urban riots were a major problem, social scientists began to explore carefully the order-maintenance function of the police, and to suggest ways of improving it—not to make streets safer (its original function) but to reduce the incidence of mass violence. Order maintenance became, to a degree, conterminous with "community relations." But, as the crime wave that began in the early 1960s continued without abatement throughout the decade and into the 1970s, attention shifted to the role of the police as crime-fighters. Studies of police behavior ceased, by and large, to be accounts of the order-maintenance function and became, instead, efforts to propose and test ways whereby the police could solve more crimes, make more arrests, and gather better evidence. If these things could be done, social scientists assumed, citizens would be less fearful.

A great deal was accomplished during this transition, as both police chiefs and outside experts emphasized the crime-fighting function in their plans, in the allocation of resources, and in deployment of personnel. The police may well have become better crime-fighters as a result. And doubtless they remained aware of their responsibility for order. But the link between order-maintenance and crime-prevention, so obvious to earlier generations, was forgotten.

That link is similar to the process whereby one broken window becomes many. The citizen who fears the ill-smelling drunk, the rowdy teenager, or the importuning beggar is not merely expressing his distaste for unseemly behavior; he is also giving voice to a bit of folk wisdom that happens to be a correct generalization—namely, that serious street crime flourishes in areas in which disorderly behavior goes unchecked. The unchecked panhandler is, in effect, the first broken window. Muggers and robbers, whether opportunistic or professional, believe they reduce their chances of being caught or even identified if they operate on streets where potential victims are already intimidated by prevailing conditions. If the neighborhood cannot keep a bothersome panhandler from annoying passersby, the thief may reason, it is even less likely to call the police to identify a potential mugger or to interfere if the mugging actually takes place.

Some police administrators concede that this process occurs, but argue that motorized-patrol officers can deal with it as effectively as foot-patrol officers. We are not so sure. In theory, an officer in a squad car can observe as much as an officer on foot; in theory, the former can talk to as many people as the latter. But the reality of police-citizen encounters is powerfully altered by the automobile. An officer on foot cannot separate himself from the street people; if he is approached, only his uniform and his personality can help him manage whatever is about to happen. And he can never be certain what that will be—a request for directions, a plea for help, an angry denunciation, a teasing remark, a confused babble, a threatening gesture.

In a car, an officer is more likely to deal with street people by rolling down the window and looking at them. The door and window exclude the approaching citizen; they are a barrier. Some officers take advantage of this barrier, perhaps unconsciously, by acting differently if in the car than they would on foot. We have seen this countless times. The police car pulls up to a corner where teenagers are gathered. The window is rolled down. The officer stares at the youths. They stare back. The officer says to one, "C'mere." He saunters over, conveying to his friends by his elaborately casual style the idea that he is not intimidated by authority. "What's your name?" "Chuck." "Chuck who?" "Chuck Jones." "What'ya doing, Chuck?" "Nothin'." "Got a P.O. [parole officer]?" "Nah." "Sure?" "Yeah." "Stay out of trouble, Chuckie." Meanwhile, the other boys laugh and exchange comments among themselves, probably at the officer's expense. The officer stares harder. He cannot be certain what is being said, nor can he join in and, by displaying his own skill at street banter, prove that he cannot be "put down." In the process, the officer has learned almost nothing, and the boys have decided the officer is an alien force who can safely be disregarded, even mocked.

Our experience is that most citizens like to talk to a police officer. Such exchanges give them a sense of importance, provide them with the basis for gossip, and allow them to explain to the authorities what is worrying them (whereby they gain a modest but significant sense of having "done something" about the problem). You approach a person on foot more easily, and talk to him more readily, than you do a person in a car. Moreover, you can more easily retain some anonymity if you draw an officer aside for a private chat. Suppose you want to pass on a tip about who is stealing handbags, or who offered to sell you a stolen TV. In the inner city, the culprit, in all likelihood, lives nearby. To walk up to a marked patrol car and lean in the window is to convey a visible signal that you are a "fink."

The essence of the police role in maintaining order is to reinforce the informal control mechanisms of the community itself. The police cannot, without committing extraordinary resources, provide a substitute for that informal control. On the other hand, to reinforce those natural forces the police must accommodate them. And therein lies the problem.

Should police activity on the street be shaped, in important ways, by the standards of the neighborhood rather than by the rules of the state? Over the past two decades, the shift of police from order-maintenance to law-enforcement has brought them increasingly under the influence of legal restrictions, provoked by media complaints and enforced by court decisions and departmental orders. As a consequence, the order-maintenance functions of the police are now governed by rules developed to control police relations with suspected criminals. This is, we think, an entirely new development. For centuries, the role of the police as watchmen was judged primarily not in terms of its compliance with appropriate procedures but rather in terms of its attaining a desired objective. The objective was order, an inherently ambiguous term but a condition that people in a given community recognized when they saw it. The means were the same as those the community itself would employ, if its members were sufficiently determined, courageous, and authoritative. Detecting and apprehending criminals, by contrast, was a means to an end, not an end in itself; a judicial determination of guilt or innocence was the hoped-for result of the law-enforcement mode. From the first, the police were expected to follow rules defining that process, though states differed in how stringent the rules should be. The criminal-apprehension process was always understood to involve individual rights, the violation of which was unacceptable because it meant that the violating officer would be acting as a judge and jury—and that was not his job. Guilt or innocence was to be determined by universal standards under special procedures.

Ordinarily, no judge or jury ever sees the persons caught up in a dispute over the appropriate level of neighborhood order. That is true not only because most cases are handled informally on the street but also because no universal standards are available to settle arguments over disorder, and thus a judge may not be any wiser or more effective than a police officer. Until quite recently in many states, and even today in some places, the police make arrests on such charges as "suspicious person" or "vagrancy" or "public drunkenness"—charges with scarcely any legal meaning. These charges exist not because society wants judges to punish vagrants or drunks but because it wants an officer to have the legal tools to remove undesirable persons from a neighborhood when informal efforts to preserve order in the streets have failed.

Once we begin to think of all aspects of police work as involving the application of universal rules under special procedures, we inevitably ask what constitutes an "undesirable person" and why we should "criminalize" vagrancy or drunkenness. A strong and commendable desire to see that people are treated fairly makes us worry about allowing the police to rout persons who are undesirable by some vague or parochial standard. A growing and not-so-commendable utilitarianism leads us to doubt that any behavior that does not "hurt" another person should be made illegal. And thus many of us who watch over the police are reluctant to allow them to perform, in the only way they can, a function that every neighborhood desperately wants them to perform.

This wish to "decriminalize" disreputable behavior that "harms no one"—and thus remove the ultimate sanction the police can employ to maintain neighborhood order—is, we think, a mistake. Arresting a single drunk or a single vagrant who has harmed no identifiable person seems unjust, and in a sense it is. But failing to do anything about a score of drunks or a hundred vagrants may destroy an entire community. A particular rule that seems to make sense in the individual case makes no sense when it is made a universal rule and applied to all cases. It makes no sense because it fails to take into account the connection between one broken window left untended and a thousand broken windows. Of course, agencies other than the police could attend to the problems posed by drunks or the mentally ill, but in most communities—especially where the "deinstitutionalization" movement has been strong—they do not.

The concern about equity is more serious. We might agree that certain behavior makes one person more undesirable than another, but how do we ensure that age or skin color or national origin or harmless mannerisms will not also become the basis for distinguishing the undesirable from the desirable? How do we ensure, in short, that the police do not become the agents of neighborhood bigotry?

We can offer no wholly satisfactory answer to this important question. We are not confident that there *is* a satisfactory answer, except to hope that by their selection, training, and supervision, the police will be inculcated with a clear sense of the outer limit of their discretionary authority. That limit, roughly, is this—the police exist to help regulate behavior, not to maintain the racial or ethnic purity of a neighborhood.

Consider the case of the Robert Taylor Homes in Chicago, one of the largest public-housing projects in the country. It is home for nearly 20,000 people, all black, and extends over ninety-two acres along South State Street. It was named after a distinguished black who had been, during the 1940s, chairman of the Chicago Housing Authority. Not long after it opened, in 1962, relations between project residents and the police deteriorated badly. The citizens felt that the police were insensitive or brutal; the police, in turn, complained of unprovoked attacks on them. Some Chicago officers tell of times when they were afraid to enter the Homes. Crime rates soared.

Today, the atmosphere has changed. Police–citizen relations have improved—apparently, both sides learned something from the earlier experience. Recently, a boy stole a purse and ran off. Several young persons who saw the theft voluntarily passed along to the police information on the identity and residence of the thief, and they did this publicly, with friends and neighbors looking on. But problems persist, chief among them the presence of youth gangs that terrorize residents and recruit members in the project. The people expect the police to "do something" about this, and the police are determined to do just that.

But do what? Though the police can obviously make arrests whenever a gang member breaks the law, a gang can form, recruit, and congregate without breaking the law. And only a tiny fraction of gang-related crimes can be solved by an arrest; thus, if an arrest is the only recourse for the police, the residents' fears will go unassuaged. The police will soon feel helpless, and the residents will again believe that the police "do nothing." What the police in fact do is to chase known gang members out of the project. In the words of one officer, "We kick ass." Project residents both know and approve of this. The tacit police-citizen alliance in the project is reinforced by the police view that the cops and the gangs are the two rival sources of power in the area, and that the gangs are not going to win.

None of this is easily reconciled with any conception of due process or fair treatment. Since both residents and gang members are black, race is not a factor. But it could be. Suppose a white project confronted a black gang, or vice versa. We would be apprehensive about the police taking sides. But the substantive problem remains the same: how can the police strengthen the informal social-control mechanisms of natural communities in order to minimize fear in public places? Law enforcement, per se, is no answer. A gang can weaken or destroy a community by standing about in a menacing fashion and speaking rudely to passersby without breaking the law.

We have difficulty thinking about such matters, not simply because the ethical and legal issues are so complex but because we have become accustomed to thinking of the law in essentially individualistic terms. The law defines *my* rights, punishes *his* behavior, and is applied by *that* officer because of *this* harm. We assume, in thinking this way, that what is good for the individual will be good for the community, and what doesn't matter when it happens to one person won't matter if it happens to many. Ordinarily, those are plausible assumptions. But in cases where behavior that is tolerable to one person is intolerable to many others, the reactions of the others—fear, withdrawal, flight—may ultimately make matters worse for everyone, including the individual who first professed his indifference.

It may be their greater sensitivity to communal as opposed to individual needs that helps explain why the residents of small communities are more satisfied with their police than are the residents of similar neighborhoods in big cities. Elinor Ostrom and her co-workers at Indiana University compared the perception of police services in two poor, all-black Illinois towns—Phoenix and East Chicago Heights—with those of three comparable all-black neighborhoods in Chicago. The level of criminal victimization and the quality of police-community relations appeared to be about the same in the towns and the Chicago neighborhoods. But the citizens living in their own villages were much more likely than those living in the Chicago neighborhoods to say that they do not stay at home for fear of crime, to agree that the local police have "the right to take any action necessary" to deal with problems, and to agree that the police "look out for the needs of the average citizen." It is possible that the residents and the police of the small towns saw themselves as engaged in a collaborative effort to maintain a certain standard of communal life, whereas those of the big city felt themselves to be simply requesting and supplying particular services on an individual basis.

If this is true, how should a wise police chief deploy his meager forces? The first answer is that nobody knows for certain, and the most prudent course of action could be to try further variations on the Newark experiment, to see more precisely what works in what kinds of neighborhoods. The second answer is also a hedge—many aspects of order-maintenance in neighborhoods can probably best be handled in ways that involve the police minimally, if at all. A busy, bustling shopping center and a quiet, well-tended suburb may need almost no visible police presence. In both cases, the ratio of respectable to disreputable people is ordinarily so high as to make informal social control effective.

Even in areas that are in jeopardy from disorderly elements, citizen action without substantial police involvement may be sufficient. Meetings between teenagers who like to hang out on a particular corner and adults who want to use that corner might well lead to an amicable agreement on a set of rules about how many people can be allowed to congregate, where, and when.

Where no understanding is possible—or if possible, not observed—citizen patrols may be a sufficient response. There are two traditions of communal involvement in maintaining order. One, that of the "community watchmen," is as old as the first settlement of the New World. Until well into the nineteenth century, volunteer watchmen, not policemen, patrolled their communities to keep order. They did so, by and large, without taking the law into their own hands—without, that is, punishing persons or using force. Their presence deterred disorder or alerted the community to disorder that could not be deterred. There are hundreds of such efforts today in communities all across the nation. Perhaps the best known is that of the Guardian Angels, a group of unarmed young persons in distinctive berets and T-shirts, who first came to public attention when they began patrolling the New York City subways but who claim now to have chapters in more than thirty American cities. Unfortunately, we have little information about the effect of these groups on crime. It is possible, however, that whatever their effect on crime, citizens find their presence reassuring, and that they thus contribute to maintaining a sense of order and civility.

The second tradition is that of the "vigilante." Rarely a feature of the settled communities of the East, it was primarily to be found in those frontier towns that grew up in advance of the reach of government. More than 350 vigilante groups are known to have existed; their distinctive feature was that their members did take the law into their own hands, by acting as judge, jury, and often executioner as well as policeman. Today, the vigilante movement is conspicuous by its rarity, despite the great fear expressed by citizens that the older cities are becoming "urban frontiers." But some community watchmen groups have skirted the line, and others may cross it in the future. An ambiguous case, reported in *The Wall Street Journal*, involved a citizens' patrol in the Silver Lake area of Belleville, New Jersey. A leader told the reporter, "We look for outsiders." If a few teenagers from outside the neighborhood enter it, "we ask them their business," he said. "If they say they're going down the street to see Mrs. Jones, fine, we let them pass. But then we follow them down the block to make sure they're really going to see Mrs. Jones."

Though citizens can do a great deal, the police are plainly the key to order-maintenance. For one thing, many communities, such as the Robert Taylor Homes, cannot do the job by themselves. For another, no citizen in a neighborhood, even an organized one, is likely to feel the sense of responsibility that wearing a badge confers. Psychologists have done many studies on why people fail to go to the aid of persons being attacked or seeking help, and they have learned that the cause is not "apathy" or "selfishness" but the absence of some plausible grounds for feeling that one must personally accept responsibility. Ironically, avoiding responsibility is easier when a lot of people are standing about. On streets and in public places, where order is so important, many people are likely to be "around," a fact that reduces the chance of any one person acting as the agent of the community. The police officer's uniform singles him out as a person who must accept responsibility if asked. In addition, officers, more easily than their fellow citizens, can be expected to distinguish between what is necessary to protect the safety of the street and what merely protects its ethnic purity.

But the police forces of America are losing, not gaining, members. Some cities have suffered substantial cuts in the number of officers available for duty. These cuts are not likely to be reversed in the near future. Therefore, each department must assign its existing officers with great care. Some neighborhoods are so demoralized and crime-ridden as to make foot patrol useless; the best the police can do with limited resources is respond to the enormous number of calls for service. Other neighborhoods are so stable and serene as to make foot patrol unnecessary. The key is to identify neighborhoods at the tipping point—where the public order is deteriorating but not unreclaimable, where the streets are used frequently but by apprehensive people, where a window is likely to be broken at any time, and must quickly be fixed if all are not to be shattered.

Most police departments do not have ways of systematically identifying such areas and assigning officers to them. Officers are assigned on the basis of crime rates (meaning that marginally threatened areas are often stripped so that police can investigate crimes in areas where the situation is hopeless) or on the basis of calls for service (despite the fact that most citizens do not call the police when they are merely frightened or annoyed). To allocate patrol wisely, the department must look at the neighborhoods and decide, from first-hand evidence, where an additional officer will make the greatest difference in promoting a sense of safety.

One way to stretch limited police resources is being tried in some public-housing projects. Tenant organizations hire off-duty police officers for patrol work in their buildings. The costs are not high (at least not per resident), the officer likes the additional income, and the residents feel safer. Such arrangements are probably more successful than hiring private watchmen, and the Newark experiment helps us understand why. A private security guard may deter crime or misconduct by his presence, and he may go to the aid of persons needing help, but he may well not intervene—that is, control or drive away—someone challenging community standards. Being a sworn officer—a "real cop"—seems to give one the confidence, the sense of duty, and the aura of authority necessary to perform this difficult task.

Patrol officers might be encouraged to go to and from duty stations on public transportation and, while on the bus or subway car, enforce rules about smoking, drinking, disorderly conduct, and the like. The enforcement need involve nothing more than ejecting the offender (the offense, after all, is not one with which a booking officer or a judge wishes to be bothered). Perhaps the random but relentless maintenance of standards on buses would lead to conditions on buses that approximate the level of civility we now take for granted on airplanes.

But the more important requirement is to think that to maintain order in precarious situations is a vital job. The police know this is one of their functions, and they also believe, correctly, that it cannot be done to the exclusion of criminal investigation and responding to calls. We may have encouraged them to suppose, however, on the basis of our oft-repeated concerns about serious, violent crime, that they will be judged exclusively on their capacity as crime-fighters. To the extent that this is the case, police administrators will continue to concentrate police personnel in the highest-crime areas (though not necessarily in the areas most vulnerable to criminal invasion), emphasize their training in the law and criminal apprehension (and not their training in managing street life), and join too quickly in campaigns to decriminalize "harmless" behavior (though public drunkenness, street prostitution, and pornographic displays can destroy a community more quickly than any team of professional burglars).

Above all, we must return to our long-abandoned view that the police ought to protect communities as well as individuals. Our crime statistics and victimization surveys measure individual losses, but they do not measure communal losses. Just as physicians now recognize the importance of fostering health rather than simply treating illness, so the police—and the rest of us—ought to recognize the importance of maintaining, intact, communities without broken windows.

26

"Broken Windows" and Fractured History
The Use and Misuse of History in Recent Police Patrol Analysis

Samuel Walker

A fresh burst of creativity marks current thinking about police patrol in the United States. This revival follows a period of doubt and disorientation in the late 1970s when recent research shattered traditional assumptions about patrol strategy. The most notable proposal for a reorientation of police patrol is set forth in "Broken Windows" by James Q. Wilson and George L. Kelling. Drawing partly on recent patrol experiments and partly on a re-thinking of police history, Wilson and Kelling propose a return to what they see as an older "watchman" style of policing (Wilson and Kelling 1982).

This selection examines the use of history by Wilson and Kelling in their proposal for reorienting police patrol. Because the historical analysis is central to their argument, its viability may well depend upon how well they have interpreted police history. Kelling develops his view of police history even more explicitly in a subsequent article co-authored with Mark H. Moore (Moore and Kelling 1983).

We shall argue here that Wilson, Kelling, and Moore have misinterpreted police history in several important respects. Their proposal calls for a restoration—a return to a former tradition of police patrol. Joe McNamara, Chief of the San Jose police, has already responded to the "broken windows" thesis by arguing that the good old days weren't all that good (McNamara 1982). This selection elaborates upon that point and argues that the tradition of policing cited by Wilson, Kelling and Moore never existed. This does not necessarily

Reprinted with permission of Academy of Criminal Justice Sciences, from *Justice Quarterly*, 1 (1984): 57–90.

mean that the broken windows thesis is completely invalid. But if there is merit in the style of police patrol Wilson and Kelling propose, that style will have to be created anew. There is no viable older tradition to restore. Obviously, this is a far more difficult and challenging proposition than they have suggested.

Policing and Broken Windows

Broken windows are a metaphor for the deterioration of neighborhoods. A broken window that goes unrepaired is a statement that no one cares enough about the quality of life in the neighborhood to bother fixing the little things that are wrong. While a broken window might be a small thing in and of itself, left unrepaired it becomes an invitation to further neglect. The result is a progressive deterioration of the entire neighborhood. Wilson and Kelling cite research in social psychology where abandoned cars were rapidly vandalized when some sign of prior vandalism invited further destructive acts (Zimbardo 1969).

Policing in America has failed, Wilson, Kelling and Moore argue, because it has neglected "the little things," the law enforcement equivalents of broken windows. This neglect is the product of the development of an efficiency-oriented crime control-focused style of policing over the past fifty years. Eric Monkkonen argues that the shift toward crime control began even earlier and was substantially complete by 1920 (Monkkonen 1981).

Two developments in the 1930s launched a radical reorientation of police patrol. The first was the greatly increased use of the patrol car, which took the patrol officer off the street and isolated him from the public. The second was the development of the Uniform Crime Reports system that then became the basic measure of police "success."

By themselves, these two developments might not have exerted such a profound effect on policing. The crucial difference was the influence of O. W. Wilson who forged a coherent theory of police management in the late 1930s. Wilsonian theory emphasized the suppression of crime as the primary mission of policing. Fulfillment of this mission depended upon maximizing the efficiency of patrol coverage. The automobile allowed a patrol officer to cover his beat more often during one tour of duty, and to do so in a more unpredictable fashion than foot patrol.

Wilson became the leading proponent of one-officer cars, claiming that two single officer patrol cars were twice as efficient as one two-officer car. He recommended that patrol beats should be organized according to a workload formula that distributed the work evenly among patrol officers. Finally, he concluded that rapid response time would increase apprehensions and generally enhance public satisfaction with police service (Walker 1977; Fogelson 1977).

Wilson tirelessly propounded his gospel of efficiency from the late 1930s onward. His text *Police Administration* became "the bible" of police management and instructed an entire generation of police executives (Wilson and McLaren 1977). Police departments converted almost entirely from foot to

automobile patrol, invested enormous sums of money in sophisticated communications equipment, and encouraged members of the public to avail
themselves of their service.

Lost in this process were the personal aspects of routine policing. The car
isolated officers from the people in the neighborhoods, which became nothing more than a series of "beat assignments" to the officers. The most profes-
sionalized departments, in fact, took extra measures to de-personalize
policing. Frequent rotation of beat assignments was adopted as a strategy to
combat corruption.

The crime control orientation meanwhile caused the police to concentrate on more serious crimes—primarily, the seven felonies that comprised
the Crime Index. Significantly, the police actively adopted the UCR system
as the measure of their performance. It was not something imposed on them
(Manning 1977). The police lost interest in lesser violations of the law and
routine because they just did not count. These nuisances included drunks,
loud and intimidating groups of teenagers, public drug dealing, and the like.[1]

According to Wilson, Kelling, and Moore, these nuisances are the "broken windows," the little things that convey the message that no one cares
about the quality of life in this neighborhood. Wilson, Kelling, and Moore
base much of their argument on the recent Newark Foot Patrol Experiment
(The Police Foundation 1981). The presence of officers on foot patrol did not
reduce crime, but did make people feel safer. Officers were able to establish
and enforce informal rules of behavior for the neighborhood. It was all right
to be intoxicated in public but not to pass out in the gutter, for example. Wilson and Kelling also cite with apparent approval the technique used by some
Chicago police officers to maintain order in public housing projects: if groups
of teenagers were troublesome, the officers would simply chase them away.
"We kick ass," one officer explained (Wilson and Kelling 1982:35).

The "Broken Windows" article argues that policing should be neighborhood-oriented. More officers should be deployed on foot, and those officers
should concentrate less on catching criminals and more on enforcing informal neighborhood norms of behavior. To a certain extent it advocates a form
of team policing, although with some important differences.

Team policing experiments in the 1970s did not emphasize foot patrol,
gave insufficient attention to street-level patrol tactics, and maintained the
traditional crime control focus. Indeed, the incompatibility of some elements
of team policing with the prevailing organizational structure and management philosophy was one of the factors in the failure of early team policing
experiments (Sherman 1973; U.S. Department of Justice 1977; Schwartz and
Clarren 1977).

"Broken Windows" offers an alternative model precisely because it
focuses on what officers would actually do. It characterizes the recommended style of policing as a return to an earlier (pre-1930s) style of "watchman" or "constabulary" policing. At this point we turn our attention to the
historical analysis that underpins this argument.

The Historical Framework

The historical framework presented by Wilson, Kelling and Moore consists of three components: the near-term, which embraces the last fifteen years; the middle-term, which includes the last fifty years; and the long-term, which involves all of police history before the last fifty years.

Their reading of near-term history is excellent. One of the most important developments of the past fifteen years has unquestionably been the enormous expansion of our knowledge about all aspects of policing. We can now discuss in an informed fashion issues that were *terra incognita* to the staff of the President's Crime Commission (Walker 1983). The most important findings constitute a systematic demolition of the assumptions underlying O. W. Wilson's approach to police management. We have learned that adding more police or intensifying patrol coverage will not reduce crime and that neither faster response time nor additional detectives will improve clearance rates. Few authorities on policing today could endorse the basic Wilsonian idea that improved management in the deployment of patrol officers or detectives is likely to reduce the crime rate.

Wilson's, Kelling's, and Moore's reading of the last fifty years of police history is mixed. They recognize the most significant developments in the period but misinterpret them in important respects. There are substantial implications of this misinterpretation for their proposed style of policing.

The development of American policing from the 1930s through the 1960s was a far more complex process than historians have lead us to believe. Wilson, Kelling, and Moore can be excused in large part because they have simply drawn upon the available historical scholarship. We will focus here on two aspects of police history since the 1930s that have not received sufficient attention. The first involves the impact of the patrol car and the second concerns the crime control orientation of policing.

The Technological Revolution

It is indeed true that American police departments largely converted from foot to automobile patrol between the 1930s and the present. We should, of course, be cognizant of the enormous variations that exist even today. Some departments are almost wholly motorized while others, primarily Eastern cities, still make heavy use of foot patrol (Police Executive Research Forum 1981). And it is also true that car patrols remove officers from the sidewalks, isolate them from casual contacts with ordinary citizens, and damage police-community relations. This analysis is part of the conventional wisdom about policing.

The impact of technology was paradoxical, however. The mid-century revolution in American policing involved not just the patrol car, but the car in conjunction with the telephone and the two-way radio. These served to bring police officers into far more intimate contact with people than ever before. While the patrol car isolated police officers in some respects, the telephone simultaneously increased the degree of contact in other respects. Let us examine this paradox in detail.

In the days of foot patrol, officers had extensive casual contacts with people. But they occurred primarily on the streets or in other public places. The police did not often obtain entry to private residences. The reason for this is obvious: there was no mechanism whereby the ordinary citizen could effectively summon the police. The telephone radically altered that situation with profound ramifications for both policing and public expectations about the quality of life. Stinchcombe (1963) has discussed the impact of privacy considerations on routine police work.

The telephone made it possible for the ordinary citizen to summon the police, and the combination of the two-way radio and the patrol car allowed the police to respond quickly. As we know, the more professional departments acquired a fetish for responding as quickly as possible to all calls. The development of the 911 telephone number was simply the logical conclusion of this effort to advertise and encourage people to use police service. People have in fact availed themselves of this service. The number of calls for service has escalated to the point where serious attention has been given to the idea of restricting or otherwise managing those requests in the last few years (Gay 1977).

Technology radically alters the nature of police-citizen contacts. Most of those contacts now occur in private residences. Albert Reiss reports that 70% of all police-citizen contacts occur in private places, 12% in semi-public, and 18% in open public places (Reiss 1971:16). The police not only gain access to private places, but observe the most intimate aspects of peoples' lives, and are asked to handle their most personal problems.

Research has confirmed that the bulk of police work involves domestic disputes and other problems arising from alcohol, drugs, mental illness, and poverty. Officers refer to all this as "bullshit" or "social work" because it is unrelated to what they believe to be their crime control mission.

Police-citizen contacts became increasingly skewed. The police lost contact with "ordinary" people and gained a great deal of contact with "problem" people, who included not just criminal offenders but those with multiple social problems. David Bayley and Harold Mendelsohn once observed that police officers had more direct knowledge about minorities than did the members of any other occupation. This knowledge was a direct product of the heavy demands upon police service placed by low-income and racial minorities (Bayley and Mendelsohn 1969:156).

Our understanding of the full impact of the telephone on policing remains problematic. Not all experts on policing accept the argument advanced here. Some argue that the police were indeed intimately involved in people's lives prior to the advent of the telephone.[2] Unfortunately, there is no empirical evidence that would permit the resolution of this question. Prior to the late 1950s, there were no observational studies of police patrol activities and thus we have no reliable evidence on what American police officers did on patrol in the pre-telephone era.[3]

The Revolution in Public Expectations

One consequence of the technological revolution in policing has been a parallel revolution in public expectations about the quality of life. The availability of police service created and fed a demand for those services. The establishment of the modern police in the early nineteenth century was an initial phase of this process, which created the expectation that a certain level of public order would, or at least should, prevail (Silver 1967).

The technological revolution of the mid-twentieth century generated a quantum leap in those expectations. Because there was now a mechanism for getting someone (the police) to "do something" about minor disorders and nuisances, people came to expect that they should not have to put up with such minor irritations. Thus, the general level of expectations about the quality of life—the amount of noise, the presence of "strange" or "undesirable" people—has undergone an enormous change. Three generations of Americans have learned or at least have come to believe that they should not have to put up with certain problems.

The police are both the source and the victims of this revolution. They have stimulated higher levels of public expectations by their very presence and their policy of more readily available services. At the same time they are the prisoners of their own creation, swamped with an enormous service call workload. The recent effort to restrict or somehow manage this workload faces the problem of a public that expects rapid police response for any and every problem as a matter of right.

Documenting changes in public expectations concerning the police is difficult given the absence of reliable data about public attitudes or police practices prior to the late 1950s and early 1960s. Several indicators do provide evidence of short-term changes in public expectations. The development of three-digit (911) emergency phone numbers for the police increased the number of service calls. In Omaha, Nebraska, for example, the number of patrol car dispatches increased by 36% between 1969 and 1971, presumably as a result of a new 911 phone number (Walker 1983:110). These figures represent the dispatch of a patrol car, not the number of incoming calls. Omaha police officials estimate that about 35% of all calls do not result in a dispatch.

Additional evidence is found in data on the number of civilian complaints about police misconduct. In New York City, for example, the number of complaints filed with the Civilian Complaint Review Board (CCRB) increased from about 200 per year in 1960–62 to just over 2000 per year in 1967–68 and more than 3000 annually in 1971–74. It would be difficult to believe that the conduct of New York City police officers deteriorated by a factor of 10 or 15 during this period. Rather, the increase is probably the result of a lower threshold of tolerance for police misconduct on the part of citizens and the increased availability of an apparent remedy for perceived misconduct.

During the period under discussion, the procedures of the New York CCRB were reorganized several times. Each reorganization facilitated complaint filing and at the same time heightened public awareness of the availability of this particular remedy (Kahn 1975:113). The data on civilian complaints supports the argument made herein concerning police services generally: the availability of a service or remedy stimulates demand for that service, thereby altering basic expectations.

The Mythology of Crime Control

The conventional wisdom states that police organize their efforts around the goal of crime control. Wilson, Kelling and Moore restate this conventional wisdom, but the matter is a bit more complex.

There is an important distinction between the self-image of the police and the day-to-day reality of routine policing (Goldstein 1977). The emphasis on crime control is and has been largely a matter of what the police say they are doing. Peter Manning argues persuasively that the police consciously created and manipulated this self-image as a way of establishing greater professional and political autonomy (Manning 1977).

As we have seen, however, the day-to-day reality of policing contradicted this self-image. The sharp contrast between the crime-fighting imagery of the police and the peacekeeping reality of police activities was one of the first and most important findings of the flood of police research that began in the 1960s. When Wilson, Kelling, and Moore suggest that the police are completely crime control-oriented they seriously misrepresent the nature of contemporary policing.

The discrepancy between crime control imagery and operational reality also becomes evident when we look more closely at how police departments utilize their resources. The most recent Survey of Police Operational and Administrative Practices reveals enormous variations among departments (Police Executive Research Forum 1981). Many still distribute their patrol officers equally among three shifts, ignoring even the most rudimentary workload formulas, which were first developed by O. W. Wilson over forty years ago (Wilson and McLaren 1977: Appendix J). Departments typically do not revise the boundaries of their patrol districts on a regular basis. Districts remain unchanged for ten or twenty years, or longer. Meanwhile, the composition of the urban environment changes radically, as older areas are depopulated, new residential areas created, and so on.

The Question of Legitimacy

The most important long-term development in American policing, according to Wilson, Kelling and Moore, has been the loss of political legitimacy. There can be little doubt that legitimacy, by which we mean acceptance of police authority by the public, is a major problem today.

The interpretation of police history offered by Wilson, Kelling, and Moore, which purports to explain how that legitimacy was lost, is seriously flawed. The evidence completely contradicts the thrust of their argument.

The police in the nineteenth century were not merely the "adjuncts" of the machine, as Robert Fogelson (1977) suggests, but were central cogs in it. Wilson, Kelling, and Moore maintain that this role offered certain benefits for the police, which reformers and historians alike have overlooked.

As cogs in the machine, the police served the immediate needs of the different neighborhoods. Political control was highly decentralized and local city councilmen or ward bosses exercised effective control over the police. Thus, the police carried out a wide range of services. Historians have rediscovered the social welfare role of the police, providing food and lodging for vagrants (Walker 1977; Monkkonen 1981). The police also performed political errands and were the means by which certain groups and individuals were able to corrupt the political process. These errands included open electioneering, rounding up the loyal voters, and harassing the opponents. Police also enforced the narrow prejudices of their constituents, harassing "undesirables" or discouraging any kind of "unwelcome" behavior.

Wilson, Kelling, and Moore concede that there was a lack of concern for due process, but argue there was an important trade-off. By virtue of serving the immediate needs and narrow prejudices of the neighborhoods, the police gained an important degree of political legitimacy. They were perceived as faithful servants and enjoyed the resulting benefits. All of this was destroyed by the reforms of the twentieth century. The patrol car removed officers from the streets, while the new "professional" style dictated an impersonal type of policing. Legal concerns with due process denied officers the ability to use the tactics of rough justice by which they had enforced neighborhood community norms.

This historical analysis is central to the reorientation of policing presented in the "Broken Windows" article. Wilson, Kelling, and Moore propose that the lost political legitimacy could be re-established by what they view as the older "watchman" style of policing. Unfortunately, this historical analysis is pure fantasy.

Historians are unanimous in their conclusion that the police were at the center of urban political conflict in the nineteenth century. In many instances policing was the paramount issue and in some cases the only issue. Historians disagree only on their interpretation of the exact nature of this political conflict. The many experiments with different forms of administrative control over the police (the last of which survives only in Missouri) were but one part of this long and bitter struggle for political control (Walker 1977; Fogelson 1977).

To say that there was political conflict over the police means that the police lacked political legitimacy. Their authority was not accepted by the citizenry. Wilson, Kelling, and Moore are seriously in error when they suggest that the police enjoyed substantial legitimacy in the pre-technology era.

The lack of legitimacy is further illustrated by the nature of the conflicts surrounding the police. Non-enforcement of the various laws designed to control drinking was the issue that most often roused the so-called "reformers" to action. Alcohol consumption was a political issue with many dimensions. In some respects it was an expression of ethnic conflict, pitting sobersided Anglo-Saxons against the heavy-drinking Irish and Germans. Drinking was also a class issue. Temperance and, later, prohibition advocates tended either to come from the middle class or at least define themselves in terms of the values of hard work, sobriety, thrift and upward mobility (Gusfield 1963). When nineteenth-century Americans fought over the police and the enforcement of the drinking laws, that battle expressed the deepest social conflicts in American society.

In one of the finest pieces of historical scholarship on the American police, Wilbur Miller explores the question of legitimacy from an entirely different angle (Miller 1977). The great difference between the London and New York City police was precisely the extent to which officers in New York were denied the grant of legitimacy enjoyed by their counterparts in London. Miller further argues that the problem of legitimacy was individualized in New York City. Each officer faced challenges to his personal authority and had to assert his authority on a situational level.

Miller does not argue that challenges to police legitimacy were patterned according to class, ethnicity or race. Thus, an Irish-American cop was just as likely to be challenged by a fellow countryman as he was by someone of a different ethnic background. To be sure, the poor, political radicals, blacks, and other people deemed "undesirable" were victimized more often by the police than were other groups, but it does not follow that the police enjoyed unquestioned authority in the eyes of those people who were members of the same class and ethnic groups as police officers.

The Myth of the Watchman

With their argument that the nineteenth century police enjoyed political legitimacy, Wilson, Kelling, and Moore have resurrected in slightly different garb the old myth of the friendly cop on the beat. They offer this older "watchman" style of policing as a viable model for contemporary policing. Quite apart from the broader question of political legitimacy, their argument turns on the issue of on-the-street police behavior.

Historians have not yet reconstructed a full picture of police behavior in the nineteenth century. At best, historians can make inferences about this behavior from surviving records. None of the historical accounts published to date presents a picture of policing that could be regarded as a viable model for the present.

What do we know about routine policing in the days before the patrol car? There is general agreement that officers did not necessarily do much work at all. Given the primitive state of communications technology, patrol officers were almost completely on their own and able to avoid effective supervision (Rubinstein 1974). Evidence suggests that evasion of duty was commonplace. We also know that corruption was the norm. Mark Haller (1976) suggests that corruption was possibly the primary objective of all of municipal government, not just the police department.

Wilbur Miller (1977), meanwhile, places the matter of police brutality in a new and convincing light. His argument that brutality was a response to the refusal of citizens to grant the police legitimacy speaks directly to the point raised by Wilson, Kelling, and Moore.

Recently some historians have attempted to draw a more systematic picture of police law enforcement activities. The most convincing picture is drawn by Lawrence Friedman and Robert Percival (1981) in their study of the Oakland police between 1870 and 1910. They characterize police arrest patterns as a giant trawling operation. The typical arrestee was a white, working class adult male who was drunk and was arrested for intoxication, disturbing the peace, or some related offense. But there was nothing systematic about police operations. The people swept up into their net were simply unlucky—there was no reason why they should have been arrested rather than others whose behavior was essentially the same. Nor was it apparent, in Friedman's and Percival's view, that the police singled out any particular categories of people for especially systematic harassment.

The argument offered by Wilson, Kelling, and Moore turns in part on the question of purpose: what the police saw themselves doing. Historians have established that police officers had a few purposes. The first was to get and hold the job. The second was to exploit the possibilities for graft that the job offered. A third was to do as little actual patrol work as possible. A fourth involved surviving on the street, which meant establishing and maintaining authority in the face of hostility and overt challenges to that authority. Finally, officers apparently felt obliged to go through the motions of "real" police work by arresting occasional miscreants.

We do not find in this picture any conscious purpose of fighting crime or serving neighborhood needs. That is precisely the point made by Progressive era reformers when they indicted the police for inefficiency. Wilson, Kelling, and Moore have no grounds for offering this as a viable model for contemporary policing. Chief McNamara is right: the good old days were not that good.

The watchman style of policing described by Wilson, Kelling, and Moore can also be challenged from a completely different perspective. The idea that the police served the needs of local neighborhoods and thereby enjoyed political legitimacy is based on a highly romanticized view of nineteenth-century neighborhood life. Urban neighborhoods were not stable and homogeneous little villages nestled in the city. They were heterogeneous, and the rate of geographic mobility was even higher than contemporary rates. Albert Reiss (1971:209–210) in *Police and the Public* critiques recent "community control" proposals on these very grounds: they are based on the erroneous impression that neighborhoods are stable, homogeneous, and relatively well-defined.

Summary and Conclusions

In "Broken Windows," James Q. Wilson and George Kelling offer a pro-vocative proposal for reorienting police patrol. Their argument is based pri-marily on an historical analysis of American policing. They propose a return to a watchman style of policing, which they claim existed before the advent of crime control oriented policing in the 1930s. This historical analysis is fur-ther developed in a subsequent article by Kelling and Moore (1983).

In this article we have examined the historical analysis used by these three authors. We find it flawed on several fundamental points.

First, the depersonalization of American policing from the 1930s onward has been greatly exaggerated. While the patrol car did isolate the police in some respects, the telephone brought about a more intimate form of contact between police and citizen by allowing the police officer to enter private resi-dences and involving them in private disputes and problems.

Second, the crime control orientation of the police has been greatly exag-gerated. Crime control is largely a matter of police rhetoric and self-image. Day-to-day policing is, on the other hand, primarily a matter of peacekeeping.

Third, there is no historical evidence to support the contention that the police formerly enjoyed substantial political legitimacy. To the contrary, all the evidence suggests that the legitimacy of the police was one of the major politi-cal controversies throughout the nineteenth century and well into the twentieth.

Fourth, the watchman style of policing referred to by Wilson, Kelling, and Moore is just as inefficient and corrupt as the reformers accuse it of being. It does not involve any conscious purpose to serve neighborhood needs and hardly serves as a model for revitalized contemporary policing.

Where does this leave us? We should not throw the proverbial baby out with the bath water. The fact that Wilson and Kelling construct their "Broken Windows" thesis on a false and heavily romanticized view of the past does not by itself invalidate their concept of a revitalized police patrol. They cor-rectly interpret the lessons of recent police research. Suppression of crime is a will-of-the-wisp that the police should no longer pursue. Enhancement of public feelings of safety, however, does appear to be within the grasp of the police. A new form of policing based on the apparent lessons of the Newark Foot Patrol Experiment, the failures of team policing experiments, and the irrelevance of most official police-community relations programs seems to be a goal that is both worth pursuing and feasible.

Our main point here is simply that such a revitalized form of policing would represent something entirely new in the history of the American police. There is no older tradition worthy of restoration. A revitalized, com-munity-oriented policing would have to be developed slowly and painfully.

There should be no mistake about the difficulty of such a task. Among other things, recent research on the police clearly demonstrates the enormous difficulty in changing police officer behavior and/or the structure and process of police organization. Yet at the same time, the history reviewed here does suggest that fundamental long-term changes in policing are indeed possible. Change is a constant; shaping that change in a positive way is the challenge.

NOTES

[1] James Fyfe argues that prosecutorial and judicial indifference to minor "quality of life" offenses is also responsible for neighborhood deterioration and that the police should not be singled out as the major culprits. By implication, he suggests that reorienting the police role would be futile without simultaneously reorienting the priorities of prosecutors and judges. Personal correspondence, James Fyfe to Walker.

[2] Lawrence W. Sherman accepts this view and dissents from the argument advanced in this article. Personal correspondence, Lawrence W. Sherman to Walker.

[3] The debate is conducted largely on the basis of circumstantial evidence. Sherman, for example, believes that literary evidence is a reliable guide to past police practices and cites *A Tree Grows in Brooklyn* as one useful example. Personal correspondence, Sherman to Walker.

REFERENCES

Bayley, D. and Mendelsohn, H. (1969) *Minorities and the Police.* New York: The Free Press.

Fogelson, R. (1977) *Big City Police.* Cambridge, MA: Harvard University Press.

Friedman, L. M. and Percival, R. V. (1981) *The Roots of Justice.* Chapel Hill: University of North Carolina Press.

Gay, W. (1977) *Improving Patrol Productivity*, Vol. I, Routine Patrol. Washington, DC: Government Printing Office.

Goldstein, H. (1977) *Policing a Free Society.* Cambridge, MA: Ballinger.

Gusfield, J. (1963) *Symbolic Crusade: Status Politics and the American Temperance Movement.* Urbana: University of Illinois Press.

Haller, M. (1976) "Historical Roots of Police Behavior: Chicago, 1890–1925." *Law and Society Review* 10 (Winter): 303–24.

Kahn, R. (1975) "Urban Reform and Police Accountability in New York City, 1950–1974." In *Urban Problems and Public Policy*, edited by R. L. Lineberry and L. H. Masotti. Lexington, MA: Lexington Books.

McNamara, J. D. (1982) "Dangerous Nostalgia for the Cop on the Beat." *San Jose Mercury-News*, May 2.

Manning, P. K. (1977) *Police Work.* Cambridge: MIT Press.

Miller, W. (1977) *Cops and Bobbies.* Chicago: University of Chicago Press.

Monkkonen, E. (1981) *Police in Urban America, 1860–1920.* Cambridge: Cambridge University Press.

Moore, M. H. and Kelling, G. L. (1983) "To Serve and Protect: Learning from Police History." *The Public Interest* 70:49–65.

Police Executive Research Forum (1981) *Survey of Police Operational and Administrative Practices—1981.* Washington, DC: Police Executive Research Forum.

Police Foundation (1981) *The Newark Foot Patrol Experiment.* Washington, DC: The Police Foundation.

Reiss, A. (1971) *The Police and the Public.* New Haven, CT: Yale University Press.

Rubinstein, J. (1974) *City Police.* New York: Ballantine Books.

Schwartz, A. I. and Clarren, S. N. (1977) *The Cincinnati Team Policing Experiment.* Washington, DC: The Police Foundation.

Sherman, L. W. (1973) *Team Policing: Seven Case Studies.* Washington, DC: The Police Foundation.

Silver, A. (1967) "The Demand for Order in Civil Society." In *The Police: Six Sociological Essays*, ed. by David J. Bordua. New York: John Wiley.

Stinchcombe, A. (1963) "Institutions of Privacy in the Determination of Police Administrative Practice." *American Journal of Sociology* 69 (September): 150–60.

U.S. Department of Justice (1977) *Neighborhood Team Policing.* Washington, DC: Government Printing Office.

Walker, S. (1983) *The Police in America: An Introduction.* New York: McGraw-Hill.

————. (1977) *A Critical History of Police Reform: The Emergence of Professionalization.* Lexington: Lexington Books.

Wilson, J. Q. and Kelling, G. L. (1982) "Broken Windows: Police and Neighborhood Safety." *Atlantic Monthly* 249 (March): 29–38.

Wilson, O. W. and McLaren, R. C. (1977) *Police Administration* (4th. ed.). New York: McGraw-Hill.

Zimbardo, P. G. (1969) "The Human Choice: Individuation, Reason, and Order versus Deindividuation, Impulse, and Chaos." In *Nebraska Symposium on Motivation*, edited by W. J. Arnold and D. Levine. Lincoln: University of Nebraska Press.

27

Community Policing
Elements and Effects

Gary W. Cordner

In less than two decades, community policing has evolved from a few small foot patrol studies to the preeminent reform agenda of modern policing. With roots in such earlier developments as police-community relations, team policing, crime prevention, and the rediscovery of foot patrol, community policing has become, in the 1990s, the dominant strategy of policing—so much so that the 100,000 new police officers funded by the 1994 Crime Bill must be engaged, by law, in community policing.

Despite all this activity, four complicating factors have made it extremely difficult to determine the effectiveness of community policing:

- *Programmatic complexity*—There exists no single definition of community policing nor any universal set of program elements. Police agencies around the country (and around the world) have implemented a wide array of organizational and operational innovations under the label "community policing." Because community policing is not one consistent "thing," it is difficult to say whether "it" works.

- *Multiple effects*—The number of intended and unintended effects that might accrue to community policing is considerable. Community policing might affect crime, fear of crime, disorder, community relations, and/or police officer attitudes, to mention just a few plausible impacts. The reality of these multiple effects, as opposed to a single bottom-line criterion, severely reduces the likelihood of a simple yes or no answer to the question "Does community policing work?"

- *Variation in program scope*—The scope of community policing projects has varied from single-officer assignments to department-wide efforts.

This article is a substantial revision (revised especially for *Critical Issues in Policing*) of an earlier article in *Police Forum* (July 1995).

Some of the most positive results have come from projects that involved only a few specialist officers, small special units, or narrowly defined target areas. The generalizability of these positive results to full-scale department-wide implementation is problematic.

• *Research design limitations*—Despite heroic efforts by police officials and researchers, most community policing studies have had serious research design limitations. These include lack of control groups, failure to randomize treatments, and a tendency to measure only short-term effects. Consequently, the findings of many community policing studies do not have as much credibility as we might hope.

These complicating factors are offered not as excuses but rather to sensitize us to the very real difficulty of producing reliable knowledge about the effects of community policing. Additionally, they identify priority issues that need to be addressed in order to substantially improve what we know about the effectiveness of community policing.

What Is Community Policing?

Community policing remains many things to many people. A common refrain among proponents is "Community policing is a philosophy, not a program." An equally common refrain among police officers is "Just tell me exactly what you want me to do differently." Some critics, echoing concerns similar to those expressed by police officers, argue that if community policing is nothing more than a philosophy, it is merely an empty shell (Goldstein, 1987).

It would be easy to list dozens of common characteristics of community policing, starting with foot patrol and mountain bikes and ending with the police as organizers of, and advocates for, the poor and dispossessed. Instead, it may be more helpful to identify four major dimensions of community policing and some of the most common elements within each. These four dimensions of community policing are:

• The Philosophical Dimension
• The Strategic Dimension
• The Tactical Dimension
• The Organizational Dimension

The Philosophical Dimension

Many of its most thoughtful and forceful advocates emphasize that community policing is a new philosophy of policing, perhaps constituting even a paradigm shift away from professional-model policing. The philosophical dimension includes the central ideas and beliefs underlying community policing. Three of the most important of these are citizen input, broad function, and personalized service.

Citizen Input. Community policing takes the view that, in a free society, citizens should have open access to police organizations and input to police policies and decisions. Access and input through elected officials is considered necessary but not sufficient. Individual neighborhoods and communities should have the opportunity to influence how they are policed and legitimate interest groups in the community should be able to discuss their views and concerns directly with police officials. Police departments, like other agencies of government, should be responsive and accountable.

Mechanisms for achieving greater citizen input are varied. Some police agencies use systematic and periodic community surveys to elicit citizen input (Bureau of Justice Assistance, 1994a). Others rely on open forums, town meetings, radio and television call-in programs, and similar methods open to all residents. Some police officials meet regularly with citizen advisory boards, ministry alliances, minority group representatives, business leaders, and other formal groups. These techniques have been used by police chief executives, district commanders, and ordinary patrol officers; they can be focused as widely as the entire jurisdiction or as narrowly as a beat or a single neighborhood.

The techniques used to achieve citizen input should be less important than the end result. Community policing emphasizes that police departments should seek and carefully consider citizen input when making policies and decisions that affect the community. Any other alternative would be unthinkable in an agency that is part of a government "of the people, for the people, and by the people."

Broad Police Function. Community policing embraces a broad view of the police function rather than a narrow focus on crime fighting or law enforcement (Kelling and Moore, 1988). Historical evidence is often cited to show that the police function was originally quite broad and varied and that it only narrowed in recent decades, perhaps due to the influence of the professional model and popular media representations of police work. Social science data is also frequently cited to show that police officers actually spend relatively little of their time dealing with serious offenders or investigating violent crimes.

This broader view of the police function recognizes the kinds of non-enforcement tasks that police already perform and seeks to give them greater status and legitimacy. These include order maintenance, social service, and general assistance duties. They may also include greater responsibilities in protecting and enhancing "the lives of those who are most vulnerable—juveniles, the elderly, minorities, the poor, the disabled, the homeless" (Trojanowicz and Bucqueroux, 1990: xiv). In the bigger picture, the police mission is seen to include resolving conflict, helping victims, preventing accidents, solving problems, and reducing fear as well as reducing crime through apprehension and enforcement.

Personal Service. Community policing supports tailored policing based on local norms and values and individual needs. An argument is made that the criminal law is a very blunt instrument and that police officers inevitably exercise wide discretion when making decisions. Presently, individual officers make arrests and other decisions based on a combination of legal, bureaucratic, and idiosyncratic criteria, while the police department maintains the myth of full or at least uniform enforcement (Goldstein, 1977). Under community policing, officers are asked to consider the "will of the community" when deciding which laws to enforce under what circumstances, and police executives are asked to tolerate and even encourage such differential and personalized policing.

Such differential or tailored policing primarily affects police handling of minor criminal offenses, local ordinance violations, public disorder, and service issues. Some kinds of behavior proscribed by state and local law, and some levels of noise and disorder, may be seen as less bothersome in some neighborhoods than in others. Similarly, some police methods, including such aggressive tactics as roadblocks as well as more prevention-oriented programs such as landlord training, may coincide with norms and values in some neighborhoods but not others.

Even the strongest advocates of community policing recognize that a balance must be reached between differential neighborhood-level policing and uniform jurisdiction-wide policing. Striking a healthy and satisfactory balance between competing interests has always been one of the central concerns of policing and police administration. Community policing simply argues that neighborhood-level norms and values should be added to the mix of legal, professional, and organizational considerations that influences decision-making about policies, programs, and resources at the executive level as well as enforcement-level decisions on the street.

This characteristic of community policing is also aimed at overcoming one of the most common complaints that the public has about government employees in general, including police officers—that they do not seem to care and that they are more interested in "going by the book" than in providing quality, personalized service. Many citizens seem to resent being subjected to "stranger policing" and would rather deal with officers who know them, and whom they know. Of course, not every police-citizen encounter can be amicable and friendly. But officers who generally deal with citizens in a friendly, open, and personal manner may be more likely to generate trust and confidence than officers who operate in a narrow, aloof, and/or bureaucratic manner.

The Strategic Dimension

The strategic dimension of community policing includes the key operational concepts that translate philosophy into action. These strategic concepts are the links between the broad ideas and beliefs that underlie community policing and the specific programs and practices by which it is implemented. They assure that agency policies, priorities, and resource allocation are consistent with a community-oriented philosophy. Three strategic elements of community policing are re-oriented operations, geographic focus, and prevention emphasis.

Re-oriented Operations. Community policing recommends less reliance on the patrol car and more emphasis on face-to-face interactions. One objective is to replace ineffective or isolating operational practices (e.g., motorized patrol and rapid response to low priority calls) with more effective and more interactive practices. A related objective is to find ways of performing necessary traditional functions (e.g., handling emergency calls and conducting follow-up investigations) more efficiently, in order to save time and resources that can then be devoted to more community-oriented activities.

Many police departments today have increased their use of foot patrol, directed patrol, door-to-door policing, and other alternatives to traditional motorized patrol (Cordner and Trojanowicz, 1992). Generally, these alternatives seek more targeted tactical effectiveness, more attention to minor offenses and "incivilities," a greater "felt presence" of police, and/or more police-citizen contact. Other police departments have simply reduced their commitment to any form of continuous patrolling, preferring instead to have their patrol officers engage in problem solving, crime prevention, and similar activities when not handling calls and emergencies.

Many police agencies have also adopted differential responses to calls for service (McEwen, Connors, and Cohen, 1986). Rather than attempting to immediately dispatch a sworn officer in response to each and every notification of a crime, disturbance, or other situation, these departments vary their responses depending upon the circumstances. Some crime reports may be taken over the telephone, some service requests may be referred to other government agencies, and some sworn officer responses may be delayed. A particularly interesting alternative is to ask complainants to go in person to a nearby police mini-station or storefront office, where an officer, a civilian employee, or even a volunteer takes a report or provides other in-person assistance. Use of differential responses helps departments cope with the sometimes overwhelming burden of 911 calls and frees up patrol officer time for other activities, such as patrolling, problem solving, and crime prevention.

Traditional criminal investigation has also been reexamined in recent years (Eck, 1992). Some departments have de-specialized the activity, reducing the size of the detective unit and making patrol officers more responsible for follow-up investigations. Many have also eliminated the practice of conducting an extensive follow-up investigation of every reported crime, focusing instead on the more serious offenses and on more "solvable" cases. Investigative attention has also been expanded to include a focus on offenders as well as on offenses, especially in the form of repeat offender units that target high-frequency serious offenders. A few departments have taken the additional step of trying to get detectives to expand their case-by-case orientation to include problem solving and crime prevention. In this approach, a burglary detective would be as concerned with reducing burglaries through problem solving and crime prevention as s/he was with solving particular burglary cases.

Not all contemporary alternatives to motorized patrol, rapid response, and criminal investigation are closely allied with community policing. Those specific operational alternatives, and those uses of the freed-up time of patrol officers and detectives, that are consistent with the philosophical and strategic foundations of community policing can be distinguished from those that conform to other philosophies and strategies of policing (Moore and Trojanowicz, 1988).

Geographic Focus. Community policing strategy emphasizes the geographic basis of assignment and responsibility by shifting the fundamental unit of patrol accountability from time of day to place. That is, rather than holding patrol officers, supervisors, and shift commanders responsible for wide areas but only during their eight or ten hour shifts, community policing seeks to establish 24-hour responsibility for smaller areas.

Of course, no single officer works 24 hours a day, seven days a week, week in and week out. Community policing usually deals with this limitation in one or a combination of three ways: (1) community police officers assigned to neighborhoods may be specialists, with most call-handling relegated to a more traditional patrol unit; (2) each individual patrol officer may be held responsible for long-term problem solving in an assigned neighborhood, even though s/he handles calls in a much larger area and, of necessity, many of the calls in the assigned area are handled by other officers; or (3) small teams of officers share both call-handling and problem solving responsibility in a beat-sized area.

A key ingredient of this geographic focus, however it is implemented, is permanency of assignment. Community policing recommends that patrol officers be assigned to the same areas for extended periods of time, to increase their familiarity with the community and the community's familiarity with them. Ideally, this familiarity will build trust, confidence, and cooperation on both sides of the police-citizen interaction. Also, officers will simply become more knowledgeable about the community and its residents, aiding early intervention and timely problem identification and avoiding conflict based on misperception or misunderstanding.

It is important to recognize that most police departments have long used geography as the basis for daily patrol assignment. Many of these departments, however, assign patrol officers to different beats from one day to the next, creating little continuity or permanency. Moreover, even in police agencies with fairly steady beat assignments, patrol officers are only held accountable for handling their calls and maintaining order (keeping things quiet) *during their shift*. The citizen's question, "Who in the police department is responsible for *my area*, my neighborhood?" can then only truthfully be answered "the chief" or, in large departments, "the precinct commander." Neither patrol officers nor the two or three levels of management above them can be held accountable for dealing with long-term problems in specific locations anywhere in the entire community. Thus, a crucial component of community policing strategy is to create some degree of geographic accountability at all levels in the police organization, but particularly at the level of the patrol officer who delivers basic police services and is in a position to identify and solve neighborhood problems.

Prevention Emphasis.   Community policing strategy also emphasizes a more proactive and preventive orientation, in contrast to the reactive focus that has characterized much of policing under the professional model. This proactive, preventive orientation takes several forms. One is simply to encourage better use of police officers' time. In many police departments, patrol officers' time not committed to handling calls is either spent simply waiting for the next call or randomly driving around. Under community policing, this substantial resource of free patrol time is devoted to directed enforcement activities, specific crime prevention efforts, problem solving, community engagement, citizen interaction, or similar kinds of activities.

Another aspect of the preventive focus overlaps with the substantive orientation of community policing and problem-oriented operations. Officers are encouraged to look beyond the individual incidents that they encounter as calls for service and reported crimes in order to discover underlying problems and conditions (Eck and Spelman, 1987). If they can discover such underlying conditions and do something to improve them, officers can prevent the future recurrence of incidents and calls. While immediate response to in-progress emergencies and after-the-fact investigation of crimes will always remain important functions of policing, community policing seeks to elevate before-the-fact prevention and problem-solving to comparable status.

Closely related to this line of thinking, but deserving of specific mention, is the desire to enhance the status of crime prevention within police organizations. Most police departments devote the vast majority of their personnel to patrol and investigations, primarily for the purposes of rapid response and follow-up investigation *after* something has happened. Granted, some prevention of crime through the visibility, omnipresence, and deterrence created by patrolling, rapid response, and investigating is expected, but the weight of research over the past two decades has greatly diminished these expectations (Kelling, Pate, Dieckman, and Brown, 1974; Greenwood and Petersilia, 1975; Spelman and Brown, 1982). Despite these lowered expectations, however, police departments still typically devote only a few officers specifically to crime prevention programming, and do little to encourage patrol officers to engage in any kinds of crime prevention activity beyond routine riding around.

Moreover, within both informal and formal police cultures, crime solving and criminal apprehension are usually more highly valued than crime prevention. An individual officer is more likely to be commended for arresting a bank robber than for initiating actions that prevent such robberies. Detectives usually enjoy higher status than uniformed officers (especially in the eyes of the public), whereas, within many police agencies, crime prevention officers are seen as public relations functionaries, kiddie cops, or worse. To many police officers, crime prevention work is simply not real police work.

The preeminence of reactive crime fighting within police and popular cultures is understandable, given the dramatic nature of emergencies, crimes, and investigations. Much of police work is about responding to trouble and fixing it, about the contest between good and evil. Responding to emergencies and fighting crime have heroic elements that naturally appeal to both police officers and citizens. Given the choice, though, almost all citizens would prefer not being victimized in the first place to being dramatically rescued, to having the police successfully track down their assailant, or to having the police recover their stolen property. Most citizens would agree that "an ounce of prevention is worth a pound of cure." This is not to suggest that police should turn their backs on reactive handling of crimes and emergencies, but only that before-the-fact prevention should be given greater consideration.

A final element of community policing's preventive focus takes more of a social welfare orientation, particularly toward juveniles. An argument is made that police officers, by serving as mentors and role models, and by providing educational, recreational, and even counseling services, can affect peoples' behavior in positive ways that ultimately lead to reductions in crime and disorder. In essence, police are asked to support and augment the efforts of families, churches, schools, and other social service agencies. This kind of police activity is seen as particularly necessary by some in order to offset the deficiencies and correct the failures of these other social institutions in modern America.

The Tactical Dimension

The tactical dimension of community policing ultimately translates ideas, philosophies, and strategies into concrete programs, practices, and behaviors. Even those who insist that "community policing is a philosophy, not a program" must concede that unless community policing eventually leads to some action, some new or different behavior, it is all rhetoric and no reality (Greene and Mastrofski, 1988). Indeed, many commentators have taken the view that community policing is little more than a new police marketing strategy that has left the core elements of the police role untouched (see, e.g., Klockars, 1988; Manning, 1988; Weatheritt, 1988). Three of the most important tactical elements of community policing are positive interaction, partnerships, and problem solving.

Positive Interaction. Policing inevitably involves some negative contacts between officers and citizens—arrests, tickets, stops for suspicion, orders to desist in disruptive behavior, inability to make things much better for victims, etc. Community policing recognizes this fact and recommends that officers offset it as much as they can by engaging in positive interactions whenever possible. Positive interactions have further benefits as well, of course: they generally build familiarity, trust, and confidence on both sides; they remind officers that most citizens respect and support them; they make the officer more knowledgeable about people and conditions in the beat; they provide specific information for criminal investigations and problem solving; and they break up the monotony of motorized patrol.

Many opportunities for positive interaction arise in the course of call handling. Too many officers rush to clear their calls, however, often in response to workload concerns and pressure from their superiors, their peers, and dispatchers. As a result, they typically do a mediocre job of handling the immediate incident and make little or no attempt to identify underlying conditions, secure additional information, or create satisfied customers. The prime directive seems to be to do as little as possible in order to clear the call quickly and get back in the car and on the radio, ready to go and do little or nothing at the next call. Getting there rapidly and then clearing promptly take precedence over actually delivering much service or accomplishing anything. Community policing suggests, instead, that officers should look at calls as opportunities for positive interaction, quality service, and problem identification.

Even more opportunities for positive interaction can be seized during routine patrol, if officers are willing to exit their vehicles and take some initiative. Officers can go in and out of stores, in and out of schools, talk to people on the street, knock on doors, etc. They can take the initiative to talk not only with shopkeepers and their customers but also with teenagers, apartment dwellers, tavern patrons, and anybody else they run across in public spaces or who are approachable in private places. Police should insert themselves wherever people are and should talk to those people, not just watch them.

Partnerships. Participation of the community in its own protection is one of the central elements of community policing (Bureau of Justice Assistance, 1994c). This participation can run the gamut from watching neighbors' homes to reporting drug dealers to patrolling the streets. It can involve participation in problem identification and problem solving efforts, in crime prevention programs, in neighborhood revitalization, and in youth-oriented educational and recreational programs. Citizens may act individually or in groups, they may collaborate with the police, and they may even join the police department by donating their time as police department volunteers, reserves, or auxiliaries.

Under community policing, police agencies are expected not only to cooperate with citizens and communities but to actively solicit input and participation (Bureau of Justice Assistance, 1994b). The exact nature of this participation can and should vary from community to community and from situation to situation, in keeping with the problem-oriented approach. As a general rule, though, police should avoid claiming that they alone can handle crime, drug, or disorder problems, and they should encourage individual citizens and community groups to shoulder some responsibility for dealing with such problems.

Police have sometimes found it necessary to engage in community organizing as a means of accomplishing any degree of citizen participation in problem solving or crime prevention. In disorganized and transient neighborhoods, residents are often so distressed, fearful, and suspicious of each other (or just so unfamiliar with their neighbors) that police have literally had to set about creating a sense of community where none previously existed. As difficult as this kind of community organizing can be, and as far from the conventional police role as this may seem, these are often the very communities that most need both enhanced police protection and a greater degree of citizen involvement in crime prevention, order maintenance, and general watchfulness over public spaces.

One vexing aspect of community organizing and community engagement results from the pluralistic nature of our society. Differing and often conflicting interests are found in many communities, and they are sometimes represented by competing interest groups. Thus, the elders in a community may want the police to crack down on juveniles, while the youths themselves complain of few opportunities for recreation or entertainment. Tenants may seek police help in organizing a rent strike, while landlords want police assistance in screening or managing the same tenants. Finding common interests around which to rally entire communities, or just identifying common interests on which to base police practices, can be very challenging and, at times, impossible.

It is important to recognize that this inherent feature of pluralistic communities does not arise because of community policing. Police have long been caught in the middle between the interests of adults and juveniles, landlords and tenants, and similar groups. Sometimes the law has provided a convenient reference point for handling such conflicts, but just as often police have had to mediate, arbitrate, or just take the side of the party with the best case. Moreover, when the law has offered a solution, it has frequently been a temporary or unpopular one, and one that still resulted in the police taking sides, protestations of "we're just enforcing the law" notwithstanding.

Fortunately, nearly all citizens want to be safe from violence, want their property protected, and want some level of orderliness in their neighborhoods. Officers can usually find enough consensus in communities upon which to base cooperative efforts aimed at improving safety and public order. Sometimes, apparently deep conflicts between individuals or groups recede when attention is focused on how best to solve specific neighborhood problems. It would be naive to expect overwhelming community consensus in every situation, but it is equally mistaken to think that conflict is so endemic that widespread community support and participation cannot be achieved in many circumstances.

Problem Solving. Supporters of community policing are convinced that the very nature of police work must be altered from its present incident-by-incident, case-by-case orientation to one that is more problem-oriented (Goldstein, 1990). Certainly, incidents must still be handled and cases must still be investigated. Whenever possible, however, attention should be directed toward underlying problems and conditions. Following the medical analogy, policing should address causes as well as symptoms, and should adopt the epidemiological public health approach as much as the individual doctor's clinical approach.

This problem solving approach should be characterized by several important features: (1) it should be the standard operating method of policing, not an occasional special project; (2) it should be practiced by personnel throughout the ranks, not just by specialists or managers; (3) it should be empirical, in the sense that decisions are made on the basis of information that is gathered systematically; (4) it should involve, whenever possible, collaboration between police and other agencies and institutions; and (5) it should incorporate, whenever possible, community input and participation, so that it is the community's problems that are addressed (not just the police department's) and so that the community shares in the responsibility for its own protection.

The problem solving process consists of four steps: (1) careful identification of the problem; (2) careful analysis of the problem; (3) a search for alternative solutions to the problem; and (4) implementation and assessment of a response to the problem. Community input can be incorporated within any or all of the steps in the process. Identification, analysis, and assessment should rely on information from multiple sources. A variety of alternative solutions should be considered, including, but not limited to, traditional enforcement methods. Typically, the most effective solutions are those that combine several different responses, including some that draw on more than just the police department's authority and resources.

A crucial characteristic of the problem-oriented approach is that it seeks tailored solutions to specific community problems. Arrests and law enforcement are *not* abandoned—rather, an effort is made in each situation to determine which alternative responses best fit the problem. Use of the criminal law is always considered, as are civil law enforcement, mediation, community mobilization, referral, collaboration, alteration of the physical environment, public education, and a host of other possibilities. The common sense notion of choosing the tool that best fits the problem, instead of simply grabbing the most convenient or familiar tool in the tool box, lies close to the heart of the problem solving method.

The Organizational Dimension

It is important to recognize an organizational dimension that surrounds community policing and greatly affects its implementation. In order to support and facilitate community policing, police departments often consider a variety of changes in organization, administration, management, and supervision. The elements of the organizational dimension are not really part of community policing *per se*, but they are frequently crucial to its successful implementation. Three important organizational elements of COP are structure, management, and information.

Structure. Advocates of community policing often look at various ways of restructuring police agencies in order to facilitate and support implementation of the philosophical, strategic, and tactical elements described above. Any organization's structure should correspond with its mission and the nature of the work performed by its members. Some aspects of traditional police organization structure seem more suited to routine, bureaucratic work than to the discretion and creativity required for COP.

The types of restructuring often associated with community policing include:

- *Decentralization*—Authority and responsibility can sometimes be delegated more widely so that commanders, supervisors, and officers can act more independently and be more responsive.

- *Flattening*—The number of layers of hierarchy in the police organization can sometimes be reduced in order to improve communications and reduce waste, rigidity and bureaucracy.

- *De-specialization*—The number of specialized units and personnel can sometimes be reduced, with more resources devoted to the direct delivery of police services (including COP) to the general public.

- *Teams*—Efficiency and effectiveness can sometimes be improved by getting employees working together as teams to perform work, solve problems, or look for ways of improving quality.

- *Civilianization*—Positions currently held by sworn personnel can sometimes be reclassified or redesigned for non-sworn personnel, allowing both cost savings and better utilization of sworn personnel.

Management. Community policing is often associated with styles of leadership, management, and supervision that give more emphasis to organizational culture and values and less emphasis to written rules and formal discipline. The general argument is that when employees are guided by a set of officially sanctioned values they will usually make good decisions and take appropriate actions. Although many formal rules will still probably be necessary, managers will need to resort to them much less often in order to maintain control over subordinates.

Management practices consistent with this emphasis on organizational culture and values include:

- *Mission*—Agencies should develop concise statements of their mission and values and use them consistently in making decisions, guiding employees, and training new recruits.

- *Strategic Planning*—Agencies should engage in continuous strategic planning aimed at ensuring that resources and energy are focused on mission accomplishment and adherence to core values; otherwise, organizations tend to get off track, confused about their mission and about what really matters.

- *Coaching*—Supervisors should coach and guide their subordinates more, instead of restricting their roles to review of paperwork and enforcement of rules and regulations.

- *Mentoring*—Young employees need mentoring from managers, supervisors, and/or peers—not just to learn how to do the job right but also to learn what constitutes the right job; in other words, to learn about ethics and values and what it means to be a good police officer.

- *Empowerment*—Under COP, employees are encouraged to be risk-takers who demonstrate imagination and creativity in their work—this kind of empowerment can only succeed, however, when employees are thoroughly familiar with the organization's core values and firmly committed to them.
- *Selective Discipline*—In their disciplinary processes, agencies should make distinctions between intentional and unintentional errors made by employees and between employee actions that violate core values versus those that merely violate technical rules.

Information. Doing community policing and managing it effectively require certain types of information that have not traditionally been available in all police departments. In the never-ending quality vs. quantity debate, for example, community policing tends to emphasize quality. This emphasis on quality shows up in many areas: avoidance of traditional bean-counting (arrests, tickets) to measure success, more concern for how well calls are handled than merely for how quickly they are handled, etc. Also, the geographic focus of community policing increases the need for detailed information based on neighborhoods as the unit of analysis. The emphasis on problem solving highlights the need for information systems that aid in identifying and analyzing community-level problems. And so on.

Several aspects of police administration under community policing that have implications for information are:

- *Performance Appraisal*—Individual officers can be evaluated on the quality of their community policing and problem solving activities, and perhaps on results achieved, instead of on traditional performance indicators (tickets, arrests, calls handled, etc.).
- *Program Evaluation*—Police programs and strategies can be evaluated more on the basis of their effectiveness (outcomes, results, quality) than just on their efficiency (effort, outputs, quantity).
- *Departmental Assessment*—The police agency's overall performance can be measured and assessed on the basis of a wide variety of indicators (including customer satisfaction, fear levels, problem solving, etc.) instead of a narrow band of traditional indicators (reported crime, response time, etc.).
- *Information Systems*—An agency's information systems need to collect and produce information on the whole range of the police function, not just on enforcement and call-handling activities, in order to support more quality-oriented appraisal, evaluation, and assessment efforts.
- *Crime Analysis*—Individual officers need more timely and complete crime analysis information pertaining to their specific geographic areas of responsibility to facilitate problem identification, analysis, fear reduction, etc.

• *Geographic Information Systems* (GIS)—Sophisticated and user-friendly computerized mapping software available today makes it possible for officers and citizens to obtain customized maps that graphically identify "hot spots" and help them picture the geographic locations and distribution of crime and related problems.

What Do We Know?

Despite the programmatic and evaluation complexities discussed earlier, we do have a substantial amount of information from empirical studies of community policing. Table 1 summarizes the "preponderance of the evidence" on the effects of community policing based on a review of over 60 such studies (recent reviews have also been completed by Normandeau, 1993; Bennett, 1994; Leighton, 1994; and Skogan, 1994).

The first thing to note in table 1 is that almost three-fourths of the 28 cells are blank, indicating that the effects are unknown (completely or substantially untested). Nearly all of the evaluations conducted to-date have focused on the tactical dimension of community policing, leaving us with little or no information on the effects of philosophical, strategic, and organizational changes. This gap in community policing research is undoubtedly caused by a combination of two factors: (1) most community policing efforts, at least until recently, have been limited programmatic and street-level initiatives rather than large-scale strategic or organizational-change initiatives; and (2) evalua-

Table 1   Preponderance of the Evidence on Community Policing

Effects/ Dimensions	Crime	Fear	Disorder	Calls for Service	Community Relations	Police Officer Attitudes	Police Officer Behavior
Philosophical: Citizen Input Broad Police Function Personal Service							
Strategic: Re-oriented Operations Geographic Focus Preventive Emphasis							
Tactical: Positive Interaction Partnerships Problem Solving	MIX	MIX	POS	MIX	POS	POS	MIX
Organizational: Structure Management Information					POS		

POS = positive effects (beneficial effects)
NEG = negative effects
MIX = mixed effects
Blank = unknown (completely or substantially untested)

tion of narrowly-focused programmatic initiatives is much easier and more feasible than evaluation of philosophical and organization-wide change.

The most useful way to summarize the evidence on the effects of community policing is to scan the tactical row of table 1.

Crime

The evidence is mixed. Only a few studies have used experimental designs and victimization surveys to test the effects of community policing on crime; many others have relied on simple before-after comparisons of reported crime or single-item victimization questions drawn from community surveys. Overall, a slight majority of the studies have detected crime decreases, giving reason for optimism, but evaluation design limitations prevent us from drawing any authoritative conclusions.

Fear of Crime

Again the evidence is mixed, but it leans more heavily in the positive direction. A number of studies have employed community surveys to make before-after comparisons of fear and related perceptions, some with experimental designs. Fear has typically been measured using a variety of survey items, lending the studies more credibility. The now widely-accepted view that community policing helps reduce levels of fear of crime and increases perceptions of safety seems reasonably well-founded, although some efforts have failed to accomplish fear reductions.

Disorder

The impact of community policing on disorder, minor crime, incivilities, and signs of crime has not been subjected to careful testing as frequently as its impact on crime and fear. The available evidence suggests, though, that community policing, and especially foot patrol and problem solving, helps reduce levels of disorder, lending partial support to the "broken windows" thesis (Wilson and Kelling, 1982).

Calls for Service

Community policing might reduce calls for service in several ways: problem solving might address underlying issues that generate calls; collaboration might increase call referrals to other government agencies; foot patrols and mini-stations might receive citizen requests directly, thus heading off calls to central dispatch; and workload management might find alternative responses for some types of calls. Although the ability of the last approach (workload management) to reduce the volume of calls dispatched to sworn units for immediate response has clearly been demonstrated (McEwen et al., 1986), the rest of the evidence on the effects of community policing on calls for service is mixed. Several studies have found positive effects but several others have not.

Community Relations

The vast majority of the studies that have looked at the impact of community policing on citizens' attitudes toward the police have uncovered positive effects. Clearly, citizens generally appreciate mini-stations in their neighborhoods, foot patrols, problem-solving efforts, and other forms of community policing. These very consistent findings are all the more remarkable because baseline measures of citizen satisfaction with, and support for, their police are frequently quite positive to begin with, thus offering relatively little room for improvement.

Police Officer Attitudes

A clear majority of the studies that have investigated the effects of community policing on officers' job satisfaction, perceptions of the community, and other related attitudes have discovered beneficial effects. Officers involved in community policing, especially if they are volunteers or members of special units, typically thrive on their new duties and responsibilities. Also, there is some evidence that organizing and managing officers differently (the so-called "inside-out" approach) can have positive effects on their morale and related attitudes (Wycoff and Skogan, 1993).

What is somewhat less certain, however, is (1) whether the positive effects of community policing on officers will survive the long term and (2) whether these benefits are as universal when *all* officers are required to engage in community policing. Whenever community policing is practiced only by specialists, as has generally been the case until recently in most departments, one condition that *is* nearly universal is conflict between the specialists and other members of the agency, frequently reflected in derogatory remarks about "the grin and wave squad."

Police Officer Behavior

Significant anecdotal evidence suggests that foot patrol, problem solving, permanent assignment, mini-stations, and other features of community policing lead to changes in some police officers' behavior, but these behavioral effects have only been lightly documented thus far (Mastrofski, Worden, and Snipes, 1995). Evidence also suggests that many officers resist changing their behavior, out of opposition to the philosophical underpinnings of community policing, doubts that community policing really works, or just plain habit.

Conclusion

A great deal of energy has been invested since 1980 in determining the nature of community policing and its effects. These efforts have paid off to the extent that the scope and variation of community policing is much better understood today and some of its effects have been fairly well documented. Since community policing has evolved significantly during this period, however, some of its elements have been more carefully evaluated than others. In addition, programmatic complexity, multiple effects, variations in scope, and research design limitations have hampered many of the community policing evaluations conducted thus far. Nevertheless, the tactical elements of community policing do seem to produce several beneficial outcomes for citizens and officers, and have the potential to impact crime and disorder. Whether the more philosophical, strategic, and organizational elements of community policing will become firmly rooted, and whether they will ultimately have beneficial effects, is yet to be seen.

REFERENCES

Bennett, Trevor. 1994. "Community Policing on the Ground: Developments in Britain." In Dennis P. Rosenbaum, ed., *The Challenge of Community Policing: Testing the Promises*. Thousand Oaks, CA: Sage, pp. 224–46.

Bureau of Justice Assistance. 1994a. *A Police Guide to Surveying Citizens and Their Environment*. Washington, DC: Bureau of Justice Assistance.

————. 1994b. *Neighborhood-Oriented Policing in Rural Communities: A Program Planning Guide*. Washington, DC: Bureau of Justice Assistance.

————. 1994c. *Understanding Community Policing: A Framework for Action*. Washington, DC: Bureau of Justice Assistance.

Cordner, Gary W. and Robert C. Trojanowicz. 1992. "Patrol." In Gary W. Cordner and Donna C. Hale, eds., *What Works in Policing? Operations and Administration Examined*. Cincinnati, OH: Anderson, pp. 3-18.

Eck, John E. 1992. "Criminal Investigation." In Gary W. Cordner and Donna C. Hale, eds., *What Works in Policing? Operations and Administration Examined*. Cincinnati, OH: Anderson, pp. 19-34.

Eck, John E. and William Spelman. 1987. *Problem Solving: Problem-Oriented Policing in Newport News*. Washington, DC: Police Executive Research Forum.

Goldstein, Herman. 1977. *Policing A Free Society*. Cambridge, MA: Ballinger.

Goldstein, Herman. 1987. "Toward Community-Oriented Policing: Potential, Basic Requirements, and Threshold Questions," *Crime & Delinquency* 25: 236-58.

————. 1990. *Problem-Oriented Policing*. New York: McGraw-Hill.

Greene, Jack R. and Stephen D. Mastrofski, eds. 1988. *Community Policing: Rhetoric or Reality?* New York: Praeger.

Greenwood, Peter W. and Joan Petersilia. 1975. *The Criminal Investigation Process, Volume I: Summary and Implications*. Santa Monica: Rand Corporation.

Kelling, George L., Tony Pate, Duane Dieckman, and Charles E. Brown. 1974. *The Kansas City Preventive Patrol Experiment: A Summary Report*. Washington, DC: Police Foundation.

Kelling, George L. and Mark H. Moore. 1988. "The Evolving Strategy of Policing." *Perspectives on Policing* No. 4. Washington, DC: National Institute of Justice.

Klockars, Carl B. 1988. "The Rhetoric of Community Policing." In Jack R. Greene and Stephen D. Mastrofski, eds., *Community Policing: Rhetoric or Reality?* New York: Praeger, pp. 239-58.

Leighton, Barry N. 1994. "Community Policing in Canada: An Overview of Experience and Evaluations." In Dennis P. Rosenbaum, ed., *The Challenge of Community Policing: Testing the Promises*. Thousand Oaks, CA: Sage, pp. 209-23.

Manning, Peter K. 1988. "Community Policing as a Drama of Control." In Jack R. Greene and Stephen D. Mastrofski, eds., *Community Policing: Rhetoric or Reality?* New York: Praeger, pp. 27–46.

Mastrofski, Stephen D., Robert E. Worden, and Jeffrey B. Snipes. 1995. "Law Enforcement in a Time of Community Policing." *Criminology* 33, 4: 539-63.

McEwen, J. Thomas, Edward F. Connors III, and Marcia I. Cohen. 1986. *Evaluation of the Differential Police Responses Field Test.* Washington, DC: National Institute of Justice.

Moore, Mark H. and Robert C. Trojanowicz. 1988. "Corporate Strategies for Policing." *Perspectives on Policing* No. 6. Washington, DC: National Institute of Justice.

Normandeau, Andre. 1993. "Community Policing in Canada: A Review of Some Recent Studies," *American Journal of Police* 12,1: 57-73.

Skogan, Wesley G. 1994. "The Impact of Community Policing on Neighborhood Residents: A Cross-Site Analysis." In Dennis P. Rosenbaum, ed., *The Challenge of Community Policing: Testing the Promises.* Thousand Oaks, CA: Sage, pp. 167-81.

Spelman, William and Dale K. Brown. 1982. *Calling the Police: Citizen Reporting of Serious Crime.* Washington, DC: Police Executive Research Forum.

Trojanowicz, Robert and Bonnie Bucqueroux. 1990. *Community Policing: A Contemporary Perspective.* Cincinnati, OH: Anderson.

Weatheritt, Mollie. 1988. "Community Policing: Rhetoric or Reality?" In Jack R. Greene and Stephen D. Mastrofski, eds., *Community Policing: Rhetoric or Reality?* New York: Praeger, pp. 153-76.

Wilson, James Q. and George L. Kelling. 1982. "Police and Neighborhood Safety: Broken Windows," *The Atlantic Monthly* (March): 29-38.

Wycoff, Mary Ann and Wesley K. Skogan. 1993. *Community Policing in Madison: Quality From the Inside Out.* Washington, DC: National Institute of Justice.

28

Problem-Oriented Policing

John D. Reitzel, Nicole Leeper Piquero, & Alex R. Piquero

Introduction

To understand the current state of policing and its future direction, it is useful to briefly review its path to the present day. Historically, the policing enterprise has gone through numerous shifts in styles of law enforcement (Monkkonen, 1992; Reiss, 1992; Sherman, 1998). For example, some of the earliest forms of policing focused primarily on maintaining the public order while a dramatic shift after the Second World War altered the focus to a traditional or professional model of law enforcement, which lasted throughout much of the twentieth century. Amidst widespread disrepute with the "professional model" of law enforcement, the riots of the 1960s and the failed police-community relation efforts, particularly in minority, inner-city communities, the policing enterprise began to experiment with different forms of policing practices such as team policing, and in recent years, community and problem-oriented policing as well as community-problem solving policing.

In this article, we focus on the problem-oriented policing movement. In the second section, we describe its origins, how it differs from other styles of law enforcement, and what it looks like in practice. In the third section, we provide examples of several initial evaluations of problem-oriented policing programs. Section four presents three current examples of problem-oriented policing in action, one applied in a public housing setting and the other applied to thwart violent crime. The fifth section outlines several implementation issues associated with successful executions of problem-oriented policing, and the sixth section concludes by outlining the probable future practices of problem-oriented policing and its juxtaposition against zero-tolerance policing.

Prepared especially for *Critical Issues in Policing* by John D. Reitzel, Nicole Leeper Piquero, and Alex R. Piquero.

What Is Problem-Oriented Policing?

Problem-oriented policing originated largely as a function of the research undertaken during the traditional era of law enforcement. Specific concerns were raised regarding police effectiveness, police-community relations, police discretion, and police management and organization. The main concern levied against traditional methods of law enforcement was its reactive nature; that is, under the traditional law enforcement approach, police were reactive or incident-driven. Police aimed to respond to calls for service in a quick fashion and to resolve or dispense of individual incidents in a timely manner. Unlike the reactivity that is the hallmark of traditional law enforcement, the problem-oriented policing philosophy contends that reacting to calls for service is only the first step in police work. Herman Goldstein (1979), a pioneer in the problem-oriented policing movement, argued that police should go further and attempt to find a permanent resolution to the problem that was responsible for the initial call. At its core, the theory underlying problem-oriented policing is straightforward: identify the underlying condition(s) that are generating the repeated calls for service and develop problem-solving approaches that solve the underlying problem (Scott, 2000). To make this explanation more concrete, consider the following dental medicine example.

Suppose that at the beginning of last month you had a toothache. You reasoned that it is just one of those things that happens to you as you get older. You stop by the pharmacy to pick up some over-the-counter medicine to put on the tooth. When you get home, you apply the medicine before bed and when you wake up the next morning you notice that the pain has gone away. You feel, at least initially, that you have taken care of the problem. Now suppose that later that day you get the same toothache. You realize that this may be something more than a minor irritation and call your dentist for an appointment. During an examination, your dentist finds that you have a small cavity and she proceeds to fill it. For the next few weeks, you feel no pain in the tooth and once again assume that you have solved the problem. But just this past week, you again notice a pain in the tooth when you chew on it. Thinking that this is not normal, you call your dentist to get the tooth checked out again. This time, your dentist spots something that she did not see before: a root infection. After you settle down from the agony of having to endure a root canal, the dentist informs you that the problem has been taken care of. This is the essence of problem-oriented policing. Rather than responding to repeated calls-for-service (i.e., toothaches), the dentist has figured out what the underlying problem was (i.e., root infection), and has implemented a strategy that was designed to resolve the problem (i.e., a root canal).

At its core then, problem-oriented policing attempts to deal with the underlying problem(s) that may be responsible for the repeated calls-for-service. Such strategies operate under two assumptions. First, problem solving can be applied by officers throughout the police agency as a normal part of their police work. Second, routine problem-solving efforts can be effective in reducing and solving problems, thus curtailing repeated calls-for-service.

The problem-solving process follows a four-step procedure, referred to as SARA, that is interactive and reciprocal (Scott, 2000). In other words, it is constantly in operation and constantly re-produces itself over time. (See Figure A for an example of the SARA process). In the first stage, *Scanning*, the officer scans the area and identifies a problem. In the second stage, *Analysis*, the officer collects information from various sources in the community as well as from his/her own department and other law enforcement agencies. This is the heart of the problem-oriented process because officers are asked to break down the underlying problem into its component events (i.e., actors, incidents, responses). In the third stage, *Response*, the information obtained in the second stage is used to develop and implement potential solutions to the identified problem(s). In the fourth stage, *Assessment*, the officer evaluates the effectiveness of the response (i.e., did the problem get reduced and/or go away?). Depending on the outcome of the *Assessment* stage, the officer may return to the *Analysis* or *Response* stages to revise the response, collect more data, and/or redesign different problem-solving solutions. This is what makes the problem-solving process interactive and reciprocal. Thus, to the extent that officers address the underlying conditions, fewer incidents and repeat calls-for-service will ensue, and those that do occur, may be less serious. At the very least, information about the problem can help police to design more effective ways of responding to each incident (Eck and Spelman, 1987).

As could be reasoned, the problem-solving process takes as given the fact that the same problem-solving solution may not be transferable across different communities, cities, locations, and businesses. That is, problem-solving solutions need to be tailored to the specific makeup of actors and incidents in particular communities. At the same time, knowledge of effective problem-solving tactics in one locale may serve as a useful baseline for problem-solving tactics in other locales. We return to this point later in the article.

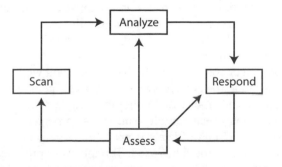

Figure A   The Problem-Solving Process

Early Problem-Solving Evaluations

In the 1980s, the problem-solving movement began to take shape and several police agencies began to adopt such an approach as their policing philosophy. At the same time, the National Institute of Justice, the research arm of the Department of Justice, funded evaluation studies of problem-oriented policing in an effort to gauge the effectiveness of problem-oriented policing. The Institute required that the problem-solving system follow five basic principles (Eck and Spelman, 1987):

1. Officers of all ranks and from all units should be able to use the system as part of their daily routine.

2. The system must encourage the use of a broad range of information, including but not limited to conventional police data.

3. The system should encourage a broad range of solutions, including but not limited to the criminal justice process.

4. The system should require no additional resources and no special units.

5. Any large police agency must be able to apply it.

To examine the effectiveness of problem-oriented policing, the Newport News, Virginia, Police Department was chosen to implement the system. By 1986, a number of problems had been identified. The type of problems varied by location (city vs. neighborhood) and by the type of event (criminal vs. disorder). The department chose two specific problems to concentrate their problem-solving efforts: burglaries from an apartment complex and thefts from vehicles.

Burglaries in Briarfield Apartments

Detective Tony Duke of the Crime Analysis Unit was assigned to study the apartment burglary problem. One of the first things that Detective Duke initiated was a survey of one-third of the households. The results of this survey confirmed that the residents believed burglary to be a serious problem, but others were equally concerned about the physical deterioration of the complex. Inspection of the apartment complex revealed that indeed it was in disrepair. After the survey results were studied, the patrol officer responsible for the area around the apartment complex enlisted the assistance of city agencies and the apartment manager to clean up the complex. Trash and abandoned appliances were removed, abandoned cars were towed, and potholes were filled and streets were swept (Eck and Spelman, 1987). Despite the success of the problem-oriented policing strategy, an evaluation of crime in and around the apartment complex showed a 35 percent reduction in burglaries, the police chief and officials from other city agencies proposed that the apartment complex should be razed. Tenants were provided with temporary housing while a new 220-unit apartment complex, a middle school, and a small shopping center were built in its place.

Vehicle Thefts in Newport News Shipyards

Thefts from vehicles parked near the Newport News shipyards accounted for almost 10 percent of all index crimes reported in Newport News. One officer who was given the task of solving this problem discovered that most of the thefts occurred in a few parking areas. After a number of interviews, the officer was able to identify a small number of suspects for the thefts and provided this information to patrol officers patrolling the area. In addition, the officer interviewed convicted offenders about the factors that made certain automobiles attractive and others unattractive. That information was given to the shipyard workers and a private security force to develop and implement a theft prevention strategy. As a result of these tactics, thefts were reduced by 55 percent since the proactive policing and arrests of repeat offenders began.

The two Newport News case studies provided evidence to many that officers can engage in a practice where they obtain information that underlies designated problems, and then execute concerted responses to help alleviate those problems. The preliminary work in Newport News set forward continued application of problem-solving efforts across many police agencies.

Recent Problem-Solving Efforts

Since the Newport News problem-oriented policing study, the strategy has been extended to varying problems in many different cities and across vastly different police agencies. Here, we discuss four recent efforts aimed at applying problem-oriented policing towards particular locations (public housing in Jersey City, NJ, and Philadelphia, PA) and at particular types of crime (violent crime in Jersey City, NJ, and violent crime, particularly homicide in Richmond, CA).

Problems in Public Housing in Jersey City and Philadelphia

Green-Mazerolle & Terrill (1997) and Green-Mazerolle, Ready, Terrill & Waring (2000) examined problem-oriented policing and public housing problems in Jersey City, New Jersey. In the first study, the researchers created problem-solving teams in six developments, each operating under the assumption that the problems affecting each of the developments varied across sites because of their unique physical, spatial, and cultural characteristics. The teams sought to identify high priority problems within and across each of the six developments that included drugs, graffiti, loitering, among others. Although each of the public housing sites had similar problems, the geographic distribution of the problems varied across the sites. For example, some sites had problems with drugs in lobbies while others had them in stairwells and still others had them in parking lots.

The key finding from the Green-Mazerolle and Terrill study is two-fold. First, officers can identify problems in public housing developments and thereby identify potential solutions to those problems. Second, the problem-solving process has to be applied uniquely across sites due to their varying characteristics. In addition, a number of key findings emerged from the Maze-rolle et al. (2000) study. First, there was a negative correlation between the number of problem-oriented policing activities during each two-week study period and the number of crime calls for service. In other words, when the problem-oriented policing strategies were implemented, crime calls went down. This held even after controlling for the intervention period. Thus, the reduction finding was not significantly related to a general decline in crime rates in Jersey City as those areas under study saw much sharper decreases than the rest of the city. Second, and perhaps most importantly, the two sites where problem-oriented policing activities were implemented had much stronger results (i.e. much better predictive power) than the other sites that relied primarily on public housing or social service activities. Consequently, as they note, it seems that police presence as an authority role in problem solving is an important factor in successful problem-oriented policing strategies.

Problem solving in public housing has also been implemented in Phila-delphia. Greene and his colleagues (1999) implemented and evaluated a problem-solving effort throughout the 11th Street Corridor in five public housing developments in North Philadelphia. Prior to problem solving, the Philadelphia Public Housing Police Department initiated an effort in which the officers assigned to the developments would undergo training in problem-solving and community-policing efforts. Then, the officers would be re-assigned to permanent foot patrol duty throughout the developments. After this was established, five problem-solving teams were created to provide a forum in which the police, residents, other public housing services, and other interested parties were able to discuss public safety concerns, as well as to design and implement local interventions.

The outcome evaluation revealed that the five developments suffered from many similar problems related to drug activity, youth programming, poor lighting, and recreational facilities. Interestingly, the outcome data revealed that the officers engaged in a higher amount of self-initiated radio-activity that is consistent with the proactive philosophy underlying problem-oriented policing. In addition, the residents of the developments noticed this increased level of police activity and reported that the police were instrumen-tal in reducing community problems over the length of the program including drug selling, graffiti, and garbage and litter.

Violence in Jersey City

Shifting toward a problem-oriented study of violent crime places in Jer-sey City, Braga and his colleagues (1999) examined changes in crime within and across twenty-four high-activity, violent crime places that were matched into twelve pairs with one member of each pair allocated to treatment (i.e., problem-solving) conditions in a randomized block field experiment and the other member not allocated to treatment (i.e., the control group). Braga et al.

(1999) describe the extent of violent crime across all of these places as ranging from assault and robbery to drug market violence to street fighting. The dynamics of the places range from transient populations to shoppers to indoor drug markets to middle-class neighborhoods. The physical characteristics of the places vary and include: a shopping mall, a drug house, a tavern, liquor stores, intersections, and college campuses.

After developing an understanding of the problems facing these locations, the officers developed situational interventions as responses to the particular problems. For many, the officers identified both physical and social disorder issues within the places. Although specific tactics and priorities varied across these places, the officers generally attempted to control them by cleaning up the environment through aggressive order maintenance and making physical improvements such as securing vacant lots and removing trash from the street (Braga et al., 1999). (Figure B describes the problem-solving strategies at the treatment places). Outcome data on crime and disorder revealed that the problem-oriented tactics of the officers was successful in reducing crime and disorder at violent places with little evidence of displacement.

Homicides in Richmond, California

In May of 2003, White and colleagues completed a study that examined the effects of problem-oriented policing strategies in reducing homicides (and violence) in the city of Richmond, California. Labeled the Comprehensive Homicide Initiative, and funded by the Bureau of Justice Assistance of the U.S. Department of Justice, the Richmond Police Department (RPD) began instituting a wide variety of problem-oriented policing and some community-oriented policing strategies in the fall of 1995 to combat what had previously been a sharp increase in homicide and violence rates. Though too numerous to list all the individual implementations, the strategies generally fell under headings: (1) Gun, Drug, & Gang-Related Violence (2) Domestic Violence (3) Targeting At-risk Youth and (4) Enhancing Investigative Capabilities. In order to gauge the effectiveness of the problem-oriented policing implementations, the researchers used an interrupted time-series analysis that measured the values of monthly levels of homicides (i.e., the dependent variable) and, for comparative purposes, gauged Richmond's results against all cities in California with over 75,000 residents (N = 75) during the same time period. This allowed them to compare whether the initiatives enacted were, in fact, responsible for the reduction in most "types" of homicides and violence, and it allowed them to tap into some other manifest and latent factors operating in Richmond. Their findings, although somewhat mixed, were noteworthy nonetheless. For instance, homicide rates for almost every type of homicide (e.g. homicides occurring outdoors, drive-by, homicides where the victim had prior convictions, etc.) dropped substantially except for homicides amongst gang members, which increased slightly. Additionally, similar to most homicide rates, the violent crime rate diminished as well. When compared to the other cities, the researchers claimed that while the findings were similar to

Responses
Aggressive Order Maintenance
Drug Enforcement
Required Store Owners to Clean Store Fronts
Public Works Removes Trash on Street
Robbery Investigations
Increased Lighting of Area
Housing Code Enforcement
Erected Fences Around Vacant Lot
Cleaned Vacant Lot
Boarded and Fenced Abandoned Buildings
Hung Signs Explaining Rules (e.g., No Drinking)
Surveillance of Place Using Videotapes
Evicted Troublesome Tenants
Improved Building Security by Adding Locks
Dispensed Crime Prevention Literature
Code Investigation of Tavern
Parking Enforcement
Razed Abandoned Building
Added Trash Receptacles
Changed Style of Trash Cans to Discourage Loitering
Opened and Cleaned Vacant Lot for Youth Recreation
Removed Graffiti from Building
Directed Patrol after School Hours
Removed Trash and Drug Paraphernalia from Alley
Remove Drug Selling Crew's Stashed Guns
Fixed Holes in Fence
Helped Homeless Find Shelter and Substance Abuse Treatment
Removed Piles of Lumber to Discourage Loitering

Source: Braga et al., 1999, Table 2, page 554.

**Figure B   Problem-Oriented Policing Strategies at Treatment Places
(From Most to Least Number of Places)**

only 10 of the 75 cities, those ten had also implemented problem-oriented and/or community-oriented policing. The other cities, excluding 19 cities that had so few homicides as to exclude them from the observation, significantly differed from Richmond. In short, White and colleagues' study is one of only a handful that directly examines the effects of problem-oriented policing strategies on violent crime and/or homicides. However, until we have more conclusive evidence about whether problem-oriented policing works or not, the findings here represent, at best, only tenuous support for problem-oriented policing.

Innovation as a Key to Success

Every year since 1993, the Police Executive Research Forum (PERF) has given individual officers and/or entire police departments the Herbert Goldstein Award for Excellence in Problem-Oriented Policing in recognition of the best problem-oriented policing initiatives (Rojek, 2003). Accordingly, to aid in achieving a more definitive understanding of the types of problem-oriented policing models that are working or that are being recognized as innovative, Rojek (2003) conducted a study of the 53 Goldstein honored proposals awarded since its inception. His study reveals some important findings. Most noteworthy is that the winning proposals share two primary characteristics (in addition to keeping with the principles laid out by Goldstein). They are: (1) they are the most innovative in addressing persistent problems faced by police and (2) they show the most success in "reducing crime, disorder, and public-safety problems" (497).

Relating to the first characteristic, innovation, not only did each of the winning proposals address problems using innovative strategies, but also they did so at three different levels within the Goldstein paradigm (i.e., organizational, programmatic, and technique). For example, while many proposals shared similar techniques, of which Rojek grouped under broader categories for analytical purposes, such as crime prevention through environmental design, community mobilization, targeted enforcement efforts, his findings show that there were over 250 different innovative strategies applied across the 53 initiatives. Moreover, many of the strategies that were implemented may have already existed in some form within individual departments (e.g., targeted enforcement); however, some departments' combined multiple policing strategies in new ways or applied those utilized in other areas to a problem-oriented framework. As such, the innovation displayed by each of the departments seem to hold promise in increasing the technical knowledge base that may aid in improving problem-oriented policing strategies and, related to the second important finding, improve our knowledge about what policing strategies work best in reducing crime and other related problems (Rojek, 2003).

Two other points asserted by Rojek, though not necessarily related to one another, are worthy of mentioning here. First, his analysis of the initiatives runs somewhat counter to Eck's (1993) enforcement conception of problem-oriented policing. He states that problem-oriented policing "does not preclude the use of traditional law enforcement techniques," but rather, the "spirit" of the Goldstein model asserts that traditional enforcement strategies would be included with other types of problem-solving techniques (Rojek, 2003:507). Last, while the findings reveal potential for both reducing crime and disorder and, more generally for problem-oriented policing strategies, more time is needed to see if strategies that are shown to work can be sustained over time, and if not, why some do not work or are not sustained (Rojek, 2003).

Implementation Issues with Problem-Oriented Policing

Problem-oriented policing is a new organizational strategy that seeks to redefine the mission of policing, the principal operating methods, and the key administrative arrangements of police departments (Moore, 1992). Since problem-oriented policing involves a substantial change from traditional methods of law enforcement, some scholars have identified implementation problems that range from limited resources to accountability concerns to difficulty in changing the culture of policing. This last problem, changing the culture of policing, may in fact be the biggest obstacle of all since the traditional law enforcement mentality is deeply entrenched among current administrative arrangements (Moore, 1992). At the same time, there are approaches for changing the culture such that problem-oriented policing can become a viable police strategy. First, the organization must embrace openness as a value, thereby requiring that police become more exposed to the communities they police. Second, the values of the organization must be articulated in a manner so that all members of the police force know what is expected of them as they perform their duties. Third, and perhaps most important, the traditional, reactive method of policing must change from a centralized, reactive organization to one that is decentralized and marked by geographic organization. These changes are likely to alter the face of policing to one less preoccupied with making large numbers of arrests to one more focused on maintaining peace. The guiding principle of problem-oriented policing is to focus on identification and problem-solving techniques, which can lead to a better understanding of the problems that underlie the incidents to which the police are summoned.

With these concerns in hand, a fully problem-oriented police agency will be marked by at least seven characteristics (Eck and Spelman, 1987):

1. Problem solving will be the standard method of policing, not just an occasionally useful tactic.

2. Problem-solving efforts will focus on problems of the public, not police administration.

3. When problems are taken on, police will establish precise, measurable objectives.

4. Police managers will constantly look for ways to get all members of the department involved in solving problems.

5. Officers should consistently undertake thorough analysis using data from many sources, both internal and external to the police agency.

6. Officers will engage in an uninhibited search for solutions to all problems they take on.

7. All members of the department will be involved in problem solving.

Although implementing and sustaining these seven characteristics is likely to take time, police executives and the citizens they service should plan on a long- rather than short-term outlook at how the police define and execute their role. This process should continue, in tandem with the community, until the entire department adopts the problem-solving approach. Importantly, the problem-solving approach should be applied locally and situationally thereby recognizing that conditions, problems, and solutions are context specific such that they may not be translatable to other jurisdictions.

Conclusion

There is a good bit of evidence suggesting that police problem-solving efforts are effective at reducing crime and disorder at problem places (Goldstein, 1990; Sherman and Weisburd, 1995) and that such tactics do not necessarily move problems to surrounding areas (Braga et al., 1999). Thus, focused police efforts that attempt to modify the places, routine activities and situations that promote crime, violence, and disorder may present an effective option for police agencies in altering such negative social ills.

Although extant research on problem-solving tactics appears to support its continued application, the survivability of problem-oriented policing is unknown largely due to other popular, yet politically volatile, police strategies such as zero-tolerance policing. Problem-oriented policing and zero-tolerance policing are two ends of the policing continuum. For example, zero-tolerance policing, with its focus on attacking order maintenance and quality of life issues, is not concerned with (1) problem identification or analysis, (2) identification of underlying conditions and causes, nor (3) consideration of the wide range of possible alternatives to solving the problem. According to Cordner (1998), zero-tolerance policing places an overemphasis on formal control mechanisms, and as such it overrelies on the law enforcement and criminal justice system resources in order to quell social problems. All the while, zero-tolerance policing prefers a relative quick fix to crime and social ill problems with little concern for the long-term effects.

But do the data support the application of zero-tolerance over problem-oriented policing? Although little research has been directed at this issue, police and policy makers have credited zero-tolerance policing with the significant decrease in crime in New York City during the 1990s. Specifically, champions of zero-tolerance policing credit the 37 percent reduction in the Part I Crime Rate between 1990 and 1995 to the get-tough approach of the New York City Police Department and its significant increase in personnel; yet, at the same time, the San Diego Police Department experienced a similar decline with a problem-oriented policing approach and with a much smaller increase in sworn personnel. Thus, given that problem-oriented policing appears to be as successful as zero-tolerance in reducing crime, it may in fact be the preferred strategy for two reasons: (1) it costs less than zero-tolerance tactics, and (2) it requires fewer officers than traditional, enforcement-oriented policing (Cordner, 1998).

So, with this in mind, what does the future of problem-oriented policing look like? A close inspection of police agencies participating in the New England Consortium on Policing provides some evidence. Officers in these agencies are experimenting with computers in patrol cars that assist officers doing problem solving. For example, these problem-oriented policing modules contain information on the problem-solving stages and allow the officer to look up different types of available problem-solving strategies and their effectiveness. The computer program also allows them to input their situation-specific information into the database so other police officers can share in their knowledge. This approach is likely to continue as the use of computers becomes fully integrated into the policing operation and is likely to advance the types of problem-solving exercises and evaluations in the future. Whether this tactic aids in police efforts and leads to effective crime control policies remains an open, empirical question.

In sum, although problem-oriented policing still retains an element of reactiveness (i.e., a continued response to calls-for-service), at the same time it represents a significant shift in police emphasis and practice in that it attempts to identify and remove the problem underlying repeated incidents. In so doing, problem-oriented policing emphasizes a cooperation between the police, the community, and other local agencies. Importantly, problem-oriented policing also recognizes that citizens are concerned with issues much more than crime, like social and physical disorder, that permeate and infiltrate their overall quality of life (Skogan, 1990). By focusing on such concerns, police officers who practice problem-oriented policing can use their local knowledge and experience to improve the communities they serve (Eck and Spelman, 1987).

REFERENCES

Braga, A. A., D. L. Weisburd, E. J. Waring, L. G. Mazerolle, W. Spellman, and G. Gajewski. 1999. Problem-oriented policing in violent crime places: A randomized controlled experiment. *Criminology* 37:541–580.

Cordner, G. 1998. Problem-oriented policing vs. zero tolerance. In T.O. Shelley and A.C. Grant (Eds.), *Problem-Oriented Policing: Crime Specific Problems, Critical Issues, and Making POP Work* (pp. 303–314). Washington, DC: Police Executive Research Forum.

Eck, J., and W. Spelman. 1987. Problem-solving: Problem-oriented policing in Newport News. *Research in Brief*. Washington, DC: National Institute of Justice.

Eck, J. 1993. Alternative futures for policing. In D. Weisburd and C. Uchida (Eds.), *Police Innovation and Control of the Police*. New York: Springer-Verlag.

Goldstein, H. 1979. Improving policing: A problem-oriented approach. *Crime and Delinquency* 25: 236–258.

Goldstein, H. 1990. *Problem-Oriented Policing*. Philadelphia: Temple University Press.

Green-Mazerolle, L., and W. Terrill. 1997. Problem-oriented policing in public housing: Identifying the distribution of problem places. *Policing* 20: 235–255.

Green-Mazerolle, L., J. Ready, W. Terrill, and E. Waring. 2000. Problem-oriented policing in public housing: The Jersey City evaluation. *Justice Quarterly* 17, 1: 129–155.

Greene, J. R., A. R. Piquero, P. Collins, and R. Kane. 1999. Doing research in public housing: Implementation issues from Philadelphia's 11th Street Corridor Community Policing Program. *Justice Research and Policy* 1: 67–95.

Monkkonen, E. H. 1992. History of urban police. In M. Tonry and N. Morris (Eds.), *Modern Policing: Crime and Justice, An Annual Review of Research*. Chicago: University of Chicago Press.

Moore, M. H. 1992. Problem-solving and community policing. In M. Tonry and N. Morris (Eds.), *Modern Policing: Crime and Justice, An Annual Review of Research*. Chicago: University of Chicago Press.

Reiss, Jr., A. J. 1992. Police organization in the twentieth century. In M. Tonry and N. Morris (Eds.), *Modern Policing: Crime and Justice, An Annual Review of Research*. Chicago: University of Chicago Press.

Rojek, J. 2003. A decade of excellence in problem-oriented policing: Characteristics of the Goldstein award winners. *Police Quarterly* 6, 4: 492–515.

Scott, M. 2000. *Problem-Oriented Policing: Reflections on the First 20 Years*. U.S. Department of Justice, COPS Office.

Sherman, L. W. 1998. American policing. In M. Tonry (Ed.), *The Handbook of Crime and Punishment*. New York: Oxford University Press.

Sherman, L., and D. L. Weisburd. 1995. General deterrent effects of police patrol in crime hot spots: A randomized controlled trial. *Justice Quarterly* 12: 625–648.

Skogan, W. 1990. *Disorder and Decline*. New York: The Free Press.

White, M. D., J. J. Fyfe, S. P. Campbell, and J. S. Goldkamp. 2003. The police role in preventing homicide: Considering the impact of problem-oriented policing on the prevalence of murder. *Journal of Research in Crime and Delinquency* 40, 2: 194–255.

SECTION VI

Use of Force

The authority to use force in the line of duty is one of the most controversial aspects of police work. While it is a necessary tool for officers in controlling crime and apprehending criminals, it also is the greatest source of police abuse of authority and citizen complaints. Police officers have the right to use force in certain specific situations, but questions are raised as to when it should be employed and how much force is necessary. The abuse of this authority is one of the most difficult problems facing police administrators today. The beating of Rodney King in Los Angeles in 1991 vividly illustrated the problems and consequences involved with the use of force. The beating and the violent response to the not-guilty verdicts were tragic incidents. The sad truth is that legal and policy-related responses to such abuses have not prevented repeat occurrences.

Article 5 highlighted some of the extreme instances of use of force that occurred in 2014 in which police officers shot and killed civilians. Public protests over perceived police aggression and lack of sanctions rekindled debates over how the police exercise their authority to use force. An instructor for the Washington State Criminal Justice Training Commission (the state police academy) commented that police culture makes it hard for officers to back away from confrontation. He cites the fear of being disrespected as a major contributor to that orientation. He describes a "perfect storm" in which police officers continue to embrace an aggressive, militarized stance of domination and control, while the public is becoming better informed and less likely to defer (Kaste, 2014). People are more likely to ask officers why they should comply with directives, which challenges officers' authority. As people resist, observers may have a camera phone to record officer reactions.

Public demands for transparency on the use of deadly force have increased since the August 2014 shooting death of 18-year-old Michael Brown in Ferguson, Missouri. A *Wall Street Journal* analysis of data from 105 of the country's largest police agencies found more than 550 police killings between 2007 and 2012 that were not included in the records compiled by the Federal Bureau of Investigation for its annual Uniform Crime Reports (UCR). Local agencies are not required to participate (Barry & Jones, 2014). The three sources of information about deaths caused by police (FBI numbers, data from the Centers for Disease Control, Bureau of Justice Statistics

513

information) differ significantly in any given year or state. D. Brian Burghart, editor and publisher of *Reno News & Review*, launched FatalEncounters.org to compile a crowdsourced database of fatal police shootings (Robinson, 2014). The site notes that the FBI statistics do not address where, how often, and under what circumstances police use deadly force—that there is no comprehensive tracking of the taking of life in the line of duty. Burghart identified African American men as the most likely to be killed by police officers in heavily populated areas, while mentally ill men are the most likely to be killed by officers in less populated areas.

Jeffrey Fagan, a law professor at Columbia University, notes, "When cops are killed, there is a very careful account and there's a national database. Why not the other side of the ledger?" (Barry & Jones, 2014). As a spokesman for the Oklahoma City Police Department noted, accurate information could help the police improve tactics, especially when dealing with people who are mentally ill. Mike White, a criminologist at Arizona State University, pointed to another advantage of accurate statistics; the information could help identify poor leadership and a lack of accountability. Better information could contribute to analyses of whether training of officers in the use of force is inadequate and whether the procedures followed are effective. Too many shootings could identify a problem in the culture where an "us versus them" mentality separates police departments from the communities they are sworn to protect (Robinson, 2014).

The full extent to which police abuse of force other than deadly incidents occurs is also difficult to determine—again because all incidents are not reported. A study of emergency room physicians sheds some light on this problem. Researchers surveyed emergency room doctors about suspected use of force by the police on their patients. Almost all doctors (99.8 percent) reported that excessive force against their patients occurred, and 98 percent said that they had cared for patients that they suspected had been abused by the police. Seventy-one percent said that they did not report the incidents because there were no hospital policies or training on what to do (Hutson et al., 2009).

On a more positive side, some researchers have found that the introduction of the Taser® reduced injuries for both officers and suspects in difficult police-citizen encounters (Smith et al., 2008). Occasionally, deaths have occurred to suspects who have been "tasered," but medical evidence is unclear as to the cause of these deaths. Overall, the weapon appears to be an important tool for the police and also reduces injuries to suspects compared to more conventional "hands-on" control tactics. However, there is a risk that the police will misuse this control tactic either by extending the duration of the shock or the number of shocks administered to suspects. Police administrators are in dispute over where Taser® use fits on the force continuum and when and on what suspects the weapon should be used.

Emergency and pursuit driving create multiple challenges for the police and represent another aspect of use of force. Speeding through the streets and on the highways may be a traditional part of police work, but it is an extremely dangerous tactic. In fact, more police officers are killed in vehicular crashes than with firearms. Emergency and pursuit driving deserves critical attention and must be analyzed as a balancing act between the dangers of pursuit driving and the need to immediately apprehend a suspect or get to a location. Many communities are moving to policies that limit dangerous driving to responses to violent crimes (see Schultz, Hudak, & Alpert, 2009). Most recently, the International Association of Chiefs of Police has acknowledged the need for law enforcement and civilian communities to evaluate pursuits and to understand their value and risks (Lum & Fachner, 2008).

James Fyfe wrote "The Split-Second Syndrome and Other Determinants of Police Violence." He delineated the difference between police violence that is clearly extra-legal and violence that is simply the unnecessary result of police incompetence and suggested that much of the problem with the excessive use of force is the result of officers being placed in situations that force the officer to make life and death decisions while under extreme time constraints. He concluded by proposing two principles that can be used to avoid the split-second syndrome: tactical knowledge and concealment.

In "What We Know about Police Use of Force," Kenneth Adams reviews the available research on police use of force. Drawing on a number of studies, he classifies the findings into three categories: what we know with substantial confidence about police use of force, what we know with modest confidence, and what we do not know about police use of force. Although use of force is one of the most serious issues facing law enforcement today, it is applied by the police very infrequently and usually at the lower end of the force continuum without significant injury to the officer or suspect. However, the misuses of force—however rare—cause the serious problems that both citizens and police administrators abhor.

In "Use-of-Force Policy, Policy Enforcement, and Training," Lorie Fridell discusses the challenge for law enforcement executives to optimize the use of force in their agencies: to use force when necessary, not to use force if it can be avoided, and to employ force only in the amounts necessary to achieve legitimate objectives, such as avoiding injury or death. She argues that three elements are essential to optimize the use of force: sound policy, effective mechanisms for enforcing policy and producing accountability, and training that effectively conveys to officers when and how to use force appropriately. Fridell concludes that the policing profession has made tremendous progress in each of these areas over the past several decades.

Jeffrey Noble and Geoffrey Alpert argue in "State-Created Danger: Should Police Officers Be Accountable for Reckless Tactical Decision Making?" that events often occur with little or no warning and no opportunity for the officers to develop a comprehensive plan. This is especially true during the midnight shift. In spite of the lack of opportunity to develop comprehensive plans on how to respond to difficult situations, most often the police respond well and make sound tactical decisions. However, sometimes they make mistakes, and sometimes they create situations where force must be used as self-defense. After analyzing officers' decision making during these types of encounters, Noble and Alpert define acceptable and unacceptable police behavior and tactics. They conclude that officers must be given some leeway to make decisions and some minor mistakes, but that they must be held responsible for errors in judgment that could have been avoided.

REFERENCES

Barry, R., & Jones, C. (2014, December 3). Hundreds of police killings are uncounted in federal statistics. *Wall Street Journal*. Retrieved from http://online.wsj.com/articles/hundreds-of-police-killings-are-uncounted-in-federal-statistics-1417577504

Hutson, H., Anglin, D., Rice, P., Kyriacou, D., Guirguis, M., & Strote, J. (2009). Excessive use of force by police: A survey of academic emergency physicians. *Emergency Medicine Journal, 26,* 20–22.

Kaste, M. (2014, September 25). For police, a debate over force, cop culture and confrontation. National Public Radio. Retrieved from http://www.npr.org/2014/09/25/351373721/police-mental-stamina-metrics-shed-light-on-deadly-force

Lum, C., & Fachner, G. (2008). *Police pursuits in an age of innovation and reform: The IACP Police Pursuit Database.* Alexandria, VA: International Association of Chiefs of Police.

Robinson, E. (2014, December 4). What the police don't want us to know. *Chicago Tribune*, p. 27.

Schultz, D., Hudak, E., & Alpert, G. (2009). Emergency driving and pursuits. *FBI Law Enforcement Bulletin, 78*(4), 1–7.

Smith, M., Kaminski, R., Alpert, G., Fridell, L., MacDonald, J., & Kubu, B. (2008). A multi-method evaluation of police use of force outcomes. A Final Report to the National Institute of Justice. Retrieved from https://www.ncjrs.gov/pdffiles1/nij/grants/231176.pdf

29

The Split-Second Syndrome and Other Determinants of Police Violence

James J. Fyfe

Discussions of police violence are often blurred by the failure to distinguish between violence that is clearly extralegal and abusive and violence that is simply the unnecessary result of police incompetence. This distinction is important because the causes of these two types of violence, and the motivations of the officers involved, vary greatly. Extralegal violence involves the willful and wrongful use of force by officers who knowingly exceed the bounds of their office. Unnecessary violence occurs when well-meaning officers prove incapable of dealing with the situations they encounter without needless or too hasty resort to force.[1]

Extralegal Police Violence

It is tempting but probably simplistic, to conclude that extralegal police violence results exclusively from the aberrations or prejudices of individual officers or their commanders. If this kind of violence were totally—or even primarily—attributable to officers who regard their badges as licenses to vent hostile and anti-social drives, we should be well advised to try to eliminate it by selecting and monitoring officers with greater care.

Certainly, these personnel processes are important, but it is probably useless to rely almost exclusively on them as the strategy for reducing extralegal police violence. First, our skill at predicting human behavior is not highly developed. Except in obviously extreme cases,[2] it is nearly impossible for personnel administrators to determine which police candidates for officers will

Anne Campbell and John Gibbs, eds. *Violent Transactions*. Basil Blackwell, 1986. Reprinted with permission of the publisher.

eventually engage in extralegal violence. Second, as investigators of police corruption have suggested (City of New York, 1972), it is likely that characteristics of police work and police organizations, rather than characteristics of police officers, are the major determinants of police misconduct.[3]

Klockars (1980) makes such an argument in his formulation of a police "Dirty Harry Problem." He argues that some police perceive the procedural limitations under which they work as arbitrary barriers to achievement of one of their most important goals: the protection of good folk through the apprehension and conviction of criminals. Such officers operate on a presumption of suspects' guilt, and become frustrated when legal processes result in acquittals of people who have, in fact, committed the crimes of which they have been accused. Subsequently, to serve what they (and much of the public) see as justice, these officers resort to "dirty means"—fabrication of evidence, intimidation and even torture—to circumvent such perceived barriers to justice as judicial exclusion of illegally obtained evidence, and to make sure that their suspects ultimately receive in court what the officers regard as their just due. Even though the actions of such officers may reflect a widely held view that there should be little distinction between factual guilt and legal guilt (Packer, 1968), they involve, Klockars asserts, wrongful moral choices by the officers themselves. The best way, according to Klockars, of preventing such wrongful choices is to punish the individual officers and the police agencies who make and tolerate them.

As Klockars acknowledges, however, his approach to this kind of violence is not entirely satisfactory. To penalize individual officers who have been trained and socialized by their employers to believe that policing cannot be done by the book and that abuse and misconduct are the most effective means of accomplishing police goals is probably unfair and would almost certainly be ineffective. Extralegal police violence is probably more closely attributable to politically expedient, but morally wrong, definitions of appropriate police conduct at the highest levels of police agencies than to the deviance of street-level officers. Thus, a better way to reduce such violence is to alter the organizational expectations and norms to which the officers who commit abuses conform.

For that reason, Klockars is much more persuasive in his suggestion that police *agencies* bear penalties for extralegal violence than in his qualified advocacy of individual punishment. Certainly, officers who apply wrongful definitions to their work may *deserve* to be punished. But such wrongful definitions are likely to survive them and to dictate the behavior of other officers unless their superiors—and the citizens whose taxes ultimately pay for disciplinary measures against the police—learn that the costs of encouraging or tolerating the use of dirty means to achieve good ends are intolerable.

Thus, as the United States Supreme Court indicated in *Monell vs. New York City Department of Social Services*,[4] one way to correct high-level tolerance or encouragement of public officials' misconduct is to make citizens liable for their employees' misdeeds. Implicit in this approach is the theory that concerned citizens will then demand that officials behave in a manner that is more consistent with both law and their financial interests. But, because the citizenry usually does not comport with this neat theory, this approach is not totally satisfactory either.

Citizens are often apathetic rather than concerned about the operations of their officials, including the police. Many of them simply expect officials to be there when needed, and become concerned only when officials have failed to meet this responsibility, or when they have personally experienced or witnessed what they regard as a grave injustice at the hands of officials. Further, many of the most concerned citizens regard with great distaste and little empathy the people against whom the police employ extralegal violence. The citizens who have the time to devote to civic affairs belong to the middle and upper classes, who rarely are the victims of police abuse; but it is they who sit on the juries that determine whether police have exceeded the bounds of their authority and, if so, whether the citizens—themselves included—should compensate the victims.

There is probably no better way to reform the wrongful behavior of police officers than to hit in the pocket the citizens to whom they are accountable. But this tactic often fails because those same citizens determine whether and how hard their pockets should be hit, and because they often do not regard as peers the victims of police abuse. Consequently, reality demands that more operationally practicable means of reducing extralegal police violence be found.

One such method is simple but rare: the engagement of leaders willing to disabuse the citizenry of their unrealistic expectations of the police. In a democracy, rates of crime, levels of disorder and the safety of "good people" are more closely associated with social conditions than with the number of police or the willingness of the police to employ dirty means to achieve the good ends of order and public safety. Few elected officials or police chiefs, however, are willing to run the risk of appearing to be soft on crime by announcing to apathetic citizens that crime and disorder are *their* problems rather than police problems and that, unless they are willing to give up many of their freedoms, no level of police presence or toughness is likely to improve matters.[5]

Were more mayors and police chiefs willing and courageous enough to do so, the pressures upon them and their personnel to achieve ends that lie beyond their means would dissipate, as would the temptation to bend the rules in attempts to achieve the impossible.[6] Until we grow a new breed of elected executives and police chiefs who are somehow able to change unrealistic public expectations of the police, however, we will not remove the major source of extralegal police violence, but must expect it to continue, however dissipated by other, less direct, approaches.

Incompetence and Unnecessary Police Violence

While extralegal police violence is egregious, it probably occurs far less frequently—and probably less frequently injures sympathetic and factually innocent victims—than does police violence emanating from simple incompetence. Such violence occurs when police lack the eloquence to persuade temporarily disturbed persons to give up their weapons, but shoot them instead. It occurs when, instead of pausing to consider and apply less drastic and dramatic alternatives, officers blindly confront armed criminals in the midst of groups of innocent people. It occurs when officers called to quell noisy but nonviolent disputes act in a way that provokes disputants to violence to which the police must respond in kind. In short, it occurs when well-meaning police officers lack—or fail to apply—the expertise required to resolve as bloodlessly as possible the problems their work requires them to confront.

Much unnecessary violence occurs because many of us, including many police, have not adequately analyzed the role of the police or the problems they confront. Thus, we have not devised adequate solutions to these problems, and have instead settled for a standard of performance from the police that is far below what we should tolerate from other groups.

The Role of the Police

A common conceptualization is that the police, along with the courts and correctional agencies, are a component of the criminal-justice system. This observation is true but, for two major reasons, it may lead to shallow analysis of the police and their problems. First, the courts (excluding civil courts) and correctional agencies devote their efforts exclusively to crime-related matters, but police officers do not. The clients of court personnel are those who have been charged with or victimized by crime; without exception, they are alleged criminals and their presumed victims. The people with whom the officials of correctional agencies interact most directly are those who are awaiting trial on criminal charges, or those who have been convicted of crime; without exception they are alleged or convicted criminals. But, in addition to bringing the alleged perpetrators and victims of crime to the attention of the courts, police regularly interact with people in circumstances in which criminal behavior is doubtful or clearly absent. The clientele of the police includes participants in minor disputes and traffic accidents, those who are lost and in need of travel directions, those who suffer sudden illness or injury, and many others whose problems have nothing whatever to do with crime, criminal law or criminal justice.

In addition, in many cases in which it is clear that some violation of criminal law has occurred, police possess greater discretion to devise informal and unrecorded dispositions of offenders than is true of any other criminal-justice officials. The police officer who sends a disorderly group of teenagers on their way on the grounds that it is more just—or more convenient—than arresting them may do so in the knowledge that no official record of his encounter with them will appear anywhere. What he does and says in such a case disappears into the ozone and, unlike a court or correctional-agency decision to release, cannot be objectively reconstructed by reference to any transcript or detailed official document.

In large measure, the police officer decides which of the people with whom he interacts shall come to the attention of the courts. He exercises a degree of discretion that is usually unrestricted by the prior decisions of any public official.[7] He cannot sentence offenders or impose harsh correctional conditions upon them, but he often has the power to choose between letting them go free and initiating a process likely to result in the imposition of penalties by other officials. He also has great power to impose upon his clientele penalties that do not require court agreement with his actions. Should he decide to arrest rather than to release, nothing a prosecutor, judge, defense attorney or correctional-agency official can do is likely to erase that arrest from the police record. Even when he recognizes that conviction is unlikely, the police officer knows that arrest will result in substantial inconvenience and cost.

But, as has been made clear in several attempts to define the police role, the police cannot be comprehensively discussed or understood in terms of their responsibilities to apprehend criminals or to enforce laws. Their job, Wilson (1968) suggests, includes the duty to see that popular conceptions of order are maintained. The police serve to prevent "behavior that either disturbs or threatens to disturb the public peace or that involves face-to-face conflict among two or more persons" (p. 16).

Goldstein (1977) concurs in part, arguing that law enforcement does not describe the role of the police, but instead defines only one of many methods that they may apply to achieve this goal. Bittner (1970) points out another method employed by police to maintain order: the use or threatened use of legitimate force (that is, as approved by both the government and most of the people served by the police) to coerce individuals to behave in accordance with society's expectations.

Still, the functions of the police are so complex that they are not adequately captured by even the broad "order-maintenance" descriptor. Just as many police tasks have little to do with crime or law, many have little to do with threats to public order, and many involve no coercion or threat or use of force. The police are on duty 24 hours a day, seven days a week, Sundays and holidays included, in order to tackle a variety of problems and crises. These range from tree-bound cats, through lost children and persons locked out of their homes, to people who have been horribly mangled in automobile accidents. In none of these cases is the quality of police response less critical for those concerned—the mother of a lost child, or the man whose femoral artery has been severed in a car crash—than in cases where the police are required to exercise their law-enforcement and order-maintenance responsibilities.

The breadth of police work is what makes Goldstein's definition of the role of the police the most comprehensive and satisfactory. He observes that

> The police function, if viewed in its broadest context, consists of making a diagnostic decision of sorts as to which alternative might be most appropriate in a given case. In this respect the total rule of the police differs little from their role in administering first aid to sick and injured persons. (1977, p. 41)

Goldstein is correct. Police officers, like doctors, lawyers, psychologists and marriage counselors, are human-service workers. Like these others, police are paid to diagnose problems that befuddle the rest of us, to treat those within their competence, and to refer to more specialized agencies and officials those problems that they themselves cannot solve. Just as we call upon the doctor to investigate and treat internal complaints not responsive to our own treatment efforts, so we call upon the police to investigate and treat complaints deriving from certain external conditions that we cannot otherwise ameliorate—noisy neighbors, assault or robbery, the injury of a loved one by a hit-and-run driver.

Police officers, however, treat their clients and professional problems under conditions that do not affect most other human-service workers, and that greatly increase the potential for violence. Police-client interactions are uniquely *urgent, involuntary* and *public*. Unless we and the police fully appreciate the causal relations between these three conditions and violence, we inadequately diagnose police problems. The result is that we witness and experience violence that need not have occurred.

Urgency of Police-Citizen Encounters

Police are generally unable to select the times at which they will perform their services. They are expected to respond to and resolve our problems *now*, while we routinely agree to wait until two weeks from Thursday to obtain help for our medical and legal dilemmas. In Bittner's terms, the police task consists of resolving problems *"that-ought-not-to-be-happening-now-and-about-which-somebody-had-better-do-something-now"* (1974, p. 30). As a consequence, police usually encounter their clients in circumstances analogous to those faced by hospital emergency-room personnel: they deal with people immediately after their problems have come to light, and must treat not only the substance of these problems, but also the shock that accompanies their clients' discoveries that suddenly all is not well.

Involuntariness of Police-Citizen Encounters

The constraint of time usually denies police officers the luxury of picking and choosing their clientele from among those deemed in need of police attention, and places great limits on their ability to refer clients and problems to more highly qualified specialists. When we do get to see our family doctor, he may diagnose but decline to treat a problem that he views as most amenable to resolution by a more specialized colleague. But a police officer summoned to a late-night domestic dispute cannot withdraw with a referral to a better trained and more competent officer who does not come on duty until the morning. Regardless of his ineptness, and because his clientele includes the neighbors who cannot sleep because of the noise, he is duty-bound to establish at least temporary peace before he leaves, even if he has to coerce some of his clients to accept his prescriptions.

Therein lies another unique characteristic of police work: many of those who come to police attention do not seek it, but become unwilling clients through the intervention of third parties or of officers themselves. When this happens, just as officers cannot usually decline clients who come to their attention, so their clients cannot withdraw from treatment no matter how distasteful they find it. Given the choice, very few of the clients arrested or brought to book by the police would consent to this form of treatment.

Public Setting of Police-Citizen Encounters

Unlike even emergency-room personnel, police officers are unable to choose the places in which they perform their services. The work of police patrol officers occurs not in private offices, but in public settings or other locations in which the problems of their clientele have come to light. As a result, police officers suffer the disadvantage of performing in places in which clients' behavior is not constrained by the formality and decorum of a professional setting and the realization that one is on another's territory. The clientele of the police are governed only by the behavioral rules of the street.

Another consequence of the public setting of police work is that officers must be attentive not only to the immediate problems of the clients they have been summoned to treat, but also to third-party reactions to their efforts. If they are to avoid criticism and even interference from bystanders, police officers summoned to restrain emotionally disturbed or drug-crazed persons on the street must do so in a way that is demonstrably proper and humane.

The police officers' concern with the *appearance* of propriety and humaneness is not shared by mental-health professionals who work in residential facilities, or who administer shock therapy to patients in the privacy of their clinics. Nor is it shared by others who must render their services in public places. Ambulance personnel, for example, often perform their work in public, but it rarely involves resolution of disputes or other competing interests, so they need not concern themselves with their audiences' perceptions of their fairness. In addition the work of ambulance personnel usually involves more distastefully gory and less intriguing and public problems than those of the police, so that bystanders watch the proceedings less closely. It is much easier, less nauseating, and more interesting to watch the police subdue a street drunk than it is to watch a team of emergency medical technicians treat a man whose leg has been severed in an automobile accident. Finally, the techniques used by ambulance personnel are far more arcane than are those of the police: few bystanders have any experience or expertise in stanching the flow of blood or treating shock, but nearly everybody has attempted to resolve a dispute, calm an unreasonable or unruly person, and seen the ways in which television police subdue suspects. Consequently, few bystanders feel competent to judge or protest the work of ambulance personnel, but many view themselves as qualified to assess the work of the police. As can be seen from cases where riots have been precipitated by bystanders' dissatisfaction with police actions, some are even willing to demonstrate their disagreement violently and immediately.

Police officers must also be acutely aware that the presence of an audience of bystanders may affect their clients' behavior. In some cases, the embarrassment of having one's problems aired in public may cause—or increase—irrational behavior on the part of the client. In others—the crowd encouraging the young man poised to jump from a high roof comes to mind—bystanders may become direct actors in police encounters. In still others, as Muir observes, police respond to street disputes that are "played out on two levels—in the relationship between the two antagonists, and in the relationship of the crowd to the disputants. Police officers have to perceive both levels" (1977, p. 102). Muir describes a situation in which police arrived at a crowded recreation center and found a bat-wielding young man confronting an aide. This case, which superficially appeared to be an attack by an inner-city youth upon an older authority figure, could be satisfactorily resolved only if the police took time to learn the antagonists' motivations and the importance of the crowd. Here, the young man suspected that the aide had raped his 13-year-old sister, so that

> From the point of view of the brother of the victim of the alleged rape, he was retaliating not only from a desire for retribution but to deter future marauders. . . . The brother was establishing face in the neighborhood, a reputation for dogged revenge; in thrashing his sister's rapist, he was making a harsh example for all the crowd to see. . . . He was publishing his message for those persons that really counted, those who might think they could push his family around. In the brutish neighborhood he and his family inhabited, the brother was making himself "a man of respect." . . .
>
> In the relationship between the crowd and the brother, the crowd's definition of honorable conduct became crucial. Depending on its expectations of him, his attack on the aide would have different meanings. . . . Anyone who had the talent to influence the crowd's philosophy in this matter could make a great deal of difference to what the brother felt he had to do to establish face. (pp. 102–3)

To summarize, then, a proper analysis of the police role requires acknowledgement of many unique characteristics of the work of street-level officers. Policing is a form of human-service work that requires officers to diagnose the problems they confront, and to decide which of several means of solving them—invoking the law, threatening to invoke the law, employing force or, as in Muir's example, attempting to persuade—is most likely to be successful. The broader discretion available to police officers than to other criminal-justice officials, however, is limited by several constraints unique to policing. There is an urgency about police work that does not affect court or correctional-agency officials or most others whose work involves diagnosis and treatment of human ills. The police cannot select the times or places at which they treat their clientele. They often must do so at odd hours and in very public places. Consequently, if they are to avoid criticism or adverse response by third parties, they must be greatly concerned not only with *doing* the right thing, but also with *appearing* to do the right thing. This compounds the difficulties of police work, because the people they treat are often adversaries rather than individuals who have come to the police for help. The people at the core of police problems often do not agree with police diagnoses of those problems or even that any problem exists. They do not see the police as individuals who have come to help them. Once the police have come, however, neither they nor the police may withdraw until the problem at hand is at least temporarily remedied.

The urgent, involuntary, and public relationship between police officer and client creates a high potential for violence. To avert it, police must often apply considerable diagnostic skills, and must learn to manipulate these causal variables in ways that diminish the likelihood that violence will result. If urgency and time constraints sometimes lead to violence, it follows that police should slow the pace of their encounters with citizens so that cooled tempers and the restoration of reason may eventually lead to nonviolent outcomes. If involuntariness sometimes leads to violence, it follows that police should attempt to diminish their clients' feelings that something is being done *to* them, by trying to win their confidence and devising problem solutions that at least appear to be collaborative rather than exclusively coercive. If the public settings of police-citizen encounters sometimes lead to violence, it follows that police should inject as much privacy as possible into these encounters.

There is evidence that attempts by police to manipulate time and involuntariness, and to make more private highly volatile encounters between police and citizens, do reduce violence. Recent police efforts to diagnose and plan for hostage situations and situations involving armed and barricaded persons have led to a high rate of bloodless resolution of these situations. The time-manipulative techniques employed in these situations include avoidance and delay of armed confrontation unless it is clear that lives are in imminent danger. Involuntariness is manipulated by trained negotiators who attempt to determine the motives and win the confidence of their subjects, and to convince them that surrender is in their own best interests. Privacy is introduced into these situations by carefully controlling media access to hostage-takers and *vice versa*, and by clearing the public from the immediate areas. These privacy techniques serve the multiple purposes of protecting uninvolved citizens, eliminating the audiences to whom hostage-takers may wish to play, reducing hostage-takers' loss of face at the time of surrender, and eliminating the possibility that the attention of bystanders or the media will encourage hostage-takers or barricaded persons to further rash actions (see, for instance, Schlossberg and Freeman, 1974).

Despite the apparent success of such defusing techniques, many of us—and many police leaders—often encourage officers to think of themselves as rough and ready men and women of action whose prime function it is to show up quickly at emergencies and to make their diagnoses on the spot. Unless we more strongly encourage officers to develop the requisite diagnostic skills to deal with certain types of situations when they occur, we are likely to witness many more hasty and inaccurate diagnoses and many unnecessarily violent attempts to treat police problems.

Section VI: Use of Force

Police Diagnostic Expertise

As too many experiences have demonstrated, police often do not attempt diagnosis until they are in the midst of treating critical problems. The 1965 Watts riot began when, despite the violent reaction of a large and growing crowd drawn by the protests of the suspect's mother, two police officers persisted in their attempts to arrest a drunken driver whom they had already identified and could presumably retake later under quieter circumstances. The 1971 Attica prison riot resulted in the deaths of 39 inmates and hostages when New York State police officers, who usually work alone or in small groups in rural areas, were armed with shotguns and armor-piercing rifles and directed to storm and retake the tear-gas-filled, heavily-walled yard of a maximum-security prison inhabited largely by inner-city convicts. A block in Philadelphia burned down in 1985 when, in an attempt to evict a radical group, a police helicopter dropped onto the roof of an adjoining wooden house an incendiary device that had apparently never before been used by police in any field situation.

Looking back, it is easy to say that these decisions should not have been made. It would probably have been wiser for the police in Watts to have retreated, and to have returned to make their arrest in quieter and less public circumstances. In Attica and Philadelphia, continued negotiation or less drastic tactics probably would have better served the fundamental police responsibility to protect life than did the hastily devised tactics that were employed.

The Split-Second Syndrome

It is difficult to define the factors that led well-meaning officials to make the bad decisions just reviewed, but it appears that they are reflections of what might be called a "split-second syndrome" that affects police decision-making in crises. This syndrome serves both to inhibit the development of greater police diagnostic expertise and to provide after-the-fact justification for unnecessary police violence. It also serves as a guide to many of the equally unfortunate low-visibility decisions made by individual police officers every day.

The split-second syndrome is based on several assumptions. First, it assumes that, since no two police problems are precisely alike, there are no principles that may be applied to the diagnosis of specific situations. Thus, no more can be asked of officers than that they respond as quickly as possible to problems, devising the best solutions they can on the spur of the moment. This, of course, places an extraordinary burden upon officers, who must make life-or-death decisions under the most stressful and time-constrained conditions.

Second, because of these stresses and time constraints, a high percentage of inappropriate decisions should be expected, but any subsequent criticism of officers' decisions—especially by those outside the police, who can have no real appreciation of the burdens upon officers—is an unwarranted attempt to be wise after the event. Thus, if we are to maintain a police service whose members are decisive in the crises to which we summon them, we had best learn to live with the consequences of the decisions we ask them to make. If we do not, we risk damaging police morale and generating a police service whose members are reluctant to intervene on our behalf.

Finally, the split-second syndrome holds that assessments of the justifiability of police conduct are most appropriately made on the exclusive basis of the perceived exigencies of the moment when a decision had to be taken. So long as a citizen has, intentionally or otherwise, provoked the police at that instant, he, rather than the police, should be viewed as the cause of any resulting injuries or damage, no matter how excessive the police reaction and no matter how directly police decisions molded the situation that caused those injuries or damages.

Thus, should police receive a report of an armed robbery in a crowded supermarket, they should be granted great leeway in their manner of response, because no two armed-robbery calls are precisely alike. If, in the course of responding, they decide that, to prevent the robber from escaping, the best course of action is to confront him immediately in the midst of a crowd of shoppers, they should not be told they should have acted otherwise. When they do challenge the alleged robber and he suddenly reacts to their calls from behind by turning on them with a shiny object in his hand, the only issue to be decided by those who subsequently review police actions is whether, at that instant, the suspect's actions were sufficiently provocative to justify their shooting him. That is so regardless of how the prior actions of the police may have contributed to their peril; regardless of how predictable it was that the suspect would be alarmed and would turn toward the police when they shouted to him; regardless of how many innocent bystanders were hit by bullets; and regardless of whether the reported armed robber was in fact an unhappy customer who, with pen in hand to complete a check for his purchase, had been engaged in a loud argument with a clerk during which he had said that the store's prices were "robbery."

The underpinning of the split-second syndrome, in short, is the assumption that the sole basis on which any use of force by the police needs to be justified is the officers' perceptions of the circumstances prevailing at the instant when they decide to apply force. The officers involved in the incident described above did, of course, possess much information that would lead them to believe that the subject of their call was a robber. When he turned on them, they were entitled, in the heat of the moment, to believe that their lives were in imminent danger. When they made the split-second decision to pull the trigger, they were also entitled to believe that no less drastic action would adequately protect their lives, so they were fully justified in shooting. Under the split-second syndrome, this shooting was a legitimate use of force under provocation.

But such an analysis lends approval to unnecessary violence, and to failure of the police to meet their highest obligation: the protection of life. Split-second analysis of police action focuses attention on diagnoses and decisions made by the police during one frame of an incident that began when the police became aware that they were likely to confront a violent person or situation. It ignores what went before. As the successful application of hostage techniques illustrates, it also ignores the fact that there are general principles that may be applied by officers to a variety of highly predictable, potentially violent situations.

It requires no great diagnostic ability to determine that the officers involved made a significant contribution to the bloody finale of the incident described above. Officers who respond to reports of robberies by charging through the front door and confronting suspects from exposed positions are almost certain to find themselves in great danger, real or perceived, and to face split-second decisions involving their lives, the lives of suspects and the lives of bystanders. Thus, instead of asking whether an officer ultimately had to shoot or fight his way out of perilous circumstances, we are better advised to ask whether it was not possible for him to have approached the situation in a way that reduced the risk of bloodshed and increased the chances of a successful and nonviolent conclusion.

Avoiding Split-Second Decisions

Even though most potentially violent situations encountered by the police are not as clear-cut as the one described in the previous section, opportunities usually do exist for officers to attempt to prevent the potential for violence from being realized. Police are usually assigned to the same geographic areas for long periods, but in my experience they are rarely encouraged to leave their patrol cars when there is little happening and to survey the places in which they might someday be asked to confront potentially violent situations. Were they to do so, they would be able to formulate tentative advance plans for dealing with reported supermarket robberies, warehouse burglaries and the like. Most often, police are directed by radio to scenes of potential violence (Reiss, 1971) and so are usually not on the spot at the time. Thus, even in the few minutes it takes them to get there, they have some opportunity to avoid split-second decisions by analyzing available information and planning their responses in advance of arrival. If they do not, and if they fail to structure their confrontations in a manner that is most likely to avert bloodshed, almost any violence that results is unnecessary, and should be condemned rather than rewarded with headlines, honors and medals.

Two principles, tactical knowledge and concealment, may be useful diagnostic tools in deciding how to deal with potentially violent people and situations.[8] Tactical knowledge includes prior knowledge of the setting and actors involved. Most often, police officers summoned to potentially violent situations have far less tactical knowledge than is desirable. While they usually know only what they have been told over the radio, any potential adversaries know precisely what is happening, where it is happening and who is involved. Since this places officers at a great disadvantage, it is important that they employ techniques for enhancing their tactical knowledge before committing themselves beyond the point of no return. If they fail to do this, they may easily fall prey to the more knowledgeable violent subjects of their calls, or may misinterpret the actions of innocent persons—such as the outraged shopper with a pen—in a way that may create violence where none exists. Like the military, they must be expected to learn as much as possible about the settings in which they may have to intervene.

Concealment includes disguising one's intent or identity, as well as employing actual physical cover or shelter. Officers—especially those in uniform—are usually at a disadvantage where this factor is concerned. When they respond to scenes of potential violence (for instance, armed robberies in progress), they are readily identifiable, while the subjects of their calls (the robbers) usually are not. Consequently, officers should employ all possible means of concealing themselves or their presence until the moment of least hazard. Doing so generally involves confronting from positions of concealment subjects who are temporarily without concealment. In the example of the reported supermarket robbery, this might mean that responding officers should avoid losing concealment by actually entering the supermarket, and should instead surreptitiously take up positions of concealment outside it (for instance, behind parked cars) and wait for their suspect to come to them. The military knows that the safest way to confront potential adversaries is to wait for the appropriate moment to ambush them from positions of concealment, but police are often encouraged to charge up hills.

The use of concealment not only minimizes the risk of officers, bystanders and suspects, but may also prevent tragic mistakes. I can recount several occasions in which officers responding to such calls have neglected to seek concealment, have encountered armed individuals from positions of total exposure, have—with some justification—perceived imminent danger to themselves, and have shot persons later found to be plain-clothes police officers or crime victims who had armed themselves to pursue the actual perpetrators. Many of these tragedies might have been avoided if the officers involved had instead confronted these individuals from positions of physical cover. From such positions, officers make themselves near impossible targets, and are able to give their perceived adversaries opportunities to identify themselves or to drop their weapons without placing themselves in jeopardy.

Application of these principles requires that officers diagnose the most critical problems they face—those that may require the use of extreme force—*before* they occur, and that they attempt to apply to their resolution techniques of tactical knowledge and concealment. We demand that from the military and from the fire service, both of which spend considerable time diagnosing and planning for exigencies that we are someday likely to ask them to resolve. We do not tolerate it when their actions in emergency situations demonstrate that they have been taken by surprise and forced to react on the basis of instinct rather than of careful advance diagnosis and planning. But, when police resort to forcible means to resolve readily foreseeable problems that could have been peacefully resolved with advance diagnosis and planning, we not only tolerate but also often reward their behavior. The police officer who shoots and kills an armed robber is often rewarded for his efforts with a medal. Should he instead kill a shopper with a pen, he is likely to be viewed as the unfortunate victim of a shared tragedy who, under the circumstances, had no choice but to take the action he did.

We should pay less attention to the outcomes of potentially violent situations than to questions of whether officers respond to them in ways likely to reduce the potential for violence. If we do not, we fail to legitimize genuinely unavoidable provoked force, and we reward and encourage an operating-style that eschews advance diagnosis, planning and training, and relies on officers' ability to make the most critical decisions under the worst possible conditions. That operating-style can only lead to frequent bad decisions by officers, who in the heat of the moment cannot reasonably be expected to devise solutions of equal quality to those that could be reached through careful advance planning. These results are grossly unfair to the public and to street-level police officers.

Thus, to reduce unnecessary police violence, we must define the police as diagnosticians, and we must demand that they learn that role thoroughly long before they actually confront someone who they have reason to believe is armed and dangerous. As we have done where hostage situations are concerned, we must define as successful those encounters where the police have done everything reasonably possible to avoid violence, and we must cease rewarding easily avoided split-second violence.

NOTES

[1] As Bittner suggests, it is also necessary to distinguish between all types of violence and "the exercise of provoked force required to meet illegitimate acts" (1970, p. 36). There is little doubt that the police must be granted considerable license to employ such force, and, in our condemnation of what Bittner calls "provocative violence" by officials, we should be careful to avoid retracting the legitimacy of police authority to employ necessary provoked force. The police simply cannot function without this authority. We should take care too to distinguish between legitimate provoked force and incompetence-related violence. The former is that *required* to put down threats against officers or other challenges to official authority. The latter is unnecessary, and occurs only because officers lack the expertise to employ readily available and less drastic means of putting down such threats and challenges.

[2] As a result of bureaucratic procedures or administrative apathy, guns and law-enforcement powers have sometimes been granted to, or not withdrawn from, officer candidates or in-service officers whom personnel investigations have shown to possess gross psychological instability or character flaws. I have reviewed police personnel folders that disclose that officers accused of misconduct had been hired by officials who knew that they had previously been excluded or dismissed from police service in other agencies because of congenital brain defects, extensive criminal records, long histories of drug abuse, assaults on supervisors and coworkers, or giving false sworn statements at previous official investigations of allegations that they had committed extralegal violence.

[3] Friedrich reports that the data he analyzed did "not support the notion that police use of force depends very much on the individual characteristics of the police" (1980, p. 89). Sherman's extensive survey (1980) of studies of police behavior found virtually no empirical support for assertions that individual officer characteristics are measurably related to any type of performance in office.

[4] The major import of the judgment in this case is that public agencies are liable when plaintiffs can demonstrate in court that they have suffered constitutional deprivations at the hands of pub-

lic officials, and that the unconstitutional acts of these officials were directly caused by agency custom and practice. Thus, if an individual were able to demonstrate that he had been unconstitutionally beaten and arrested by a police officer, and that the police department involved had a history of encouraging or tolerating such misconduct, he would presumably be entitled to money damages from both the officer and the government agency that employed him.

5 In addition, elected officials, who serve as intermediaries between citizens and police, may often be tempted to react defensively to judgments against police, regardless of whether such defensiveness is in the citizens' best interests. Consequently, citizens' ire may be redirected at what may be portrayed by elected officials as the arbitrariness of the courts, rather than at the police misconduct that gave rise to judgments against the taxpayers. For an elected mayor to acknowledge that his police department has operated unconstitutionally is not easy. It requires him to admit that the person he appointed as police chief (or who was otherwise determined to have been best qualified for that position) has performed his duties in a manner that violates the fundamental law of the land.

6 See Manning (1977), who argues that the police have assumed—or been given—the "impossible mandate" of responsibility for crime control and order maintenance, and that most police are unwilling to admit that they cannot accomplish it.

7 This is not to suggest that police currently operate with no *a priori* restrictions. As Goldstein (1977) points out, police operations are greatly influenced by legislators, and by the decisions made by prosecutors and judges in prior *similar* matters. My point is that police make decisions about specific individuals and situations before they have come to the attention of other officials.

8 These principles were first articulated in a training-program I developed in 1976 while on the staff of the New York City Police Academy.

REFERENCES

Bittner, E. 1974. Florence Nightingale in Pursuit of Willie Sutton: A Theory of the Police. In H. Jacob (ed.), *The Potential for Reform of Criminal Justice*, Beverly Hills, CA: Sage.

Bittner, E. 1970. *The Functions of the Police in Modern Society.* Rockville, MD: National Institute of Mental Health.

City of New York Commission to Investigate Allegations of Police Corruption and the City's Anti-corruption Procedures. 1973. *Commission Report.* New York: George Braziller.

Friedrich, R. J. 1980. Police Use of Force: Individuals, Situations and Organizations. *Annals of the American Academy of Social and Political Sciences*, 452, 82.

Goldstein, H. 1977. *Policing a Free Society.* Cambridge, MA: Ballinger.

Klockars, C. 1980. The Dirty Harry Problem. *Annals of the American Academy of Political and Social Science*, 452, 33.

Manning, P. 1977. *Police work*, Cambridge: MIT Press.

Monell vs. New York City Department of Social Services. 1978. 436 US 658.

Muir, W. K. 1977. *Police: Streetcorner Politicians.* Chicago: University of Chicago Press.

New York State Commission on Attica. 1972. *Attica.* New York: Bantam Books.

Packer, H. L. 1968. *The Limits of the Criminal Sanction.* Stanford, CA: Stanford University Press.

Reiss, A. J., Jr. 1971. *The Police and the Public.* New Haven, CT: Yale University Press.

Schlossberg, H. and Freeman, L. 1974: *Psychologist with a Gun.* New York: Coward, McCann and Geohagan.

Sherman, L. W. 1980. Causes of Police Behavior: The Current State of Quantitative Research. *Journal of Research in Crime and Delinquency*, 17, 69.

Wilson, J. Q. 1968. *Varieties of Police Behavior: The Management of Law and Order.* Cambridge, MA: Harvard University Press.

30

What We Know about Police Use of Force

Kenneth Adams

Ambrose Bierce, a social critic known for his sarcasm and wit, once described the police as "an armed force for protection and participation."[1] In this pithy statement, Bierce identifies three critical elements of the police role. First, by describing the police as "armed," their ability to coerce recalcitrant persons to comply with the law is emphasized. Because police carry weapons, it follows that the force they use may have lethal consequences. The capacity to use coercive, deadly force is so central to understanding police functions, one could say that it characterizes a key element of the police role.

Second, the primary purpose of police is protection, and so force can be used only to promote the safety of the community. Police have a responsibility for safeguarding the domestic well-being of the public, and this obligation even extends in qualified ways to protecting those who violate the law, who are antagonistic or violent toward the police, or who are intent on hurting themselves. In dealing with such individuals, police may use force in reasonable and prudent ways to protect themselves and others. However, the amount of force used should be proportional to the threat and limited to the least amount required to accomplish legitimate police action.

Third, the concept of participation emphasizes that police and community are closely interrelated. Police are drawn from the community, and as police they continue to operate as members of the community they serve. The community, in turn, enters into a solemn and consequential relationship with the police, ceding to them the power to deprive persons of "life, liberty, and the pursuit of happiness" at a moment's notice and depending on them for public safety. Without police, the safety of the community is jeopardized. Without community support, police are dispossessed of their legitimacy and robbed of their effectiveness.

Use of Force by Police: Overview of National and Local Data. National Institute of Justice Research Report, 1999, NCJ 176330.

This three-element definition of police makes it easy to understand why abuse of force by police is of such great concern. First, there is the humanitarian concern that police are capable of inflicting serious, even lethal, harm on the public. Second, there is the philosophical dilemma that in "protecting" the whole of society, some of its constituent parts, meaning its citizens, may be injured. Third, there is the political irony that police, who stand apart from society in terms of authority, law, and responsibility, also are part of society and act on its behalf. Thus, rogue actions by a few police, if condoned by the public, may become perceived as actions of the citizenry.

Recent developments in policing have elevated concerns about police use of force beyond ordinarily high levels. In particular, community policing, which is becoming widespread as a result of financial incentives by the federal government, and "aggressive" policing, which is becoming widely adopted as a solution to serious crime problems, have come to the fore as perspectives of choice by policing experts. Community policing emphasizes the role of the community as "coproducers" of law and order in conjunction with the police. Communities naturally vary in attributes, and they vary in how they are defined for the purposes of community policing. Consequently, some communities look to add restrictions on police use of force, while others are satisfied with the status quo, and still others seek to ease current restrictions. Regardless of the community's orientation on this issue, community policing means increased levels of accountability and responsiveness in key areas, such as use of force. Increased accountability hinges on new information, and new information stimulates debate.

The other emerging perspective is "aggressive" policing, which often falls under the rubric of broken windows theory, and, as a strategic matter, is concerned with intensifying enforcement against quality-of-life and order maintenance offenses. The influence of aggressive policing can be seen in the proliferation of "zero tolerance" enforcement strategies across the nation. The concern is that the threat posed by petty offenders may be exaggerated to the point that use of force becomes more commonplace and abuses of force more frequent.

The Violent Crime Control and Law Enforcement Act of 1994 mirrored congressional concern about excessive force by authorizing the Civil Rights Division of the U.S. Department of Justice (DOJ) to initiate civil actions against police agencies when, among other conduct, their use of force reaches a level constituting a pattern or practice depriving individuals of their rights. DOJ exercised that authority when, for example, it determined that an urban police department engaged in such conduct and negotiated a consent decree that put in place a broad set of reforms, including an agreement by the department to document its use of force and to implement an early warning system to detect possible abuses.[2]

Use-of-force concerns also are reflected in the attention the media give to possible instances of police abuse. An accumulation of alleged abuse-of-force incidents, widely reported in the media, encourages overgeneralization by giving the impression that police brutality is rampant and that police departments across the nation are out of control. For example, Human Rights Watch states, "Allegations of police abuse are rife in cities throughout the country and take many forms."[3]

Before considering the details of recent research efforts on police use of force, it is useful to summarize the state of our knowledge.[4] We know some details about police use of force with a high degree of certainty. These items represent "facts" that should frame our understanding of the issues. Other details about police use of force we know in sketchy ways, or the research is contradictory. These items should be subject to additional research using more refined methods of inquiry. Finally, there are some aspects of police use of force about which we know very little or next to nothing. These items represent critical directions for new inquiry.

As is often the case with important policy questions, the information that we are most confident of is of limited value. In many cases, it does not tell us what we really need to know, because it does not focus squarely on the important issues or is subject to competing interpretations. Conversely, the information that is most critical for policy decisions often is not available or is very difficult to obtain. Such is the case with police use of force. The issues that most concern the public and policy makers lack the kinds of reliable and solid information that advance debate from the realm of ideological posturing to objective analysis. Nonetheless, it is important to take stock of our knowledge so that it is clear which issues can be set aside and which should be the target of efforts at obtaining new knowledge.

What, then, is the state of knowledge regarding police use of force? We begin with issues about which we have considerable information and a high degree of confidence in our knowledge. Discussed next are issues where knowledge is modest and considerably more research is merited. Finally, we conclude with issues that are critical to debates over police use of force and about which little knowledge exists.

What We Know with Substantial Confidence about Police Use of Force

Police use force infrequently.

Whether measured by use-of-force reports, citizen complaints, victim surveys, or observational methods, the data consistently indicate that only a small percentage of police-public interactions involve the use of force. As Bayley and Garofalo observed, police-citizen encounters that involve use of force and injury are "quite rare."[5]

Because there is no standard methodology for measuring use of force, estimates can vary considerably on strictly computational grounds. Different definitions of force and different definitions, of police-public interactions will yield different rates[6] (see "Working definitions"). In particular, broad definitions of use of force, such as those that include grabbing or handcuffing a suspect, will produce higher rates than more conservative definitions. The Bureau of Justice Statistics' (BJS) 1996 pretest of its Police Public Contact Survey resulted in preliminary estimates that nearly 45 million people had face-to-face contact with police over a 12-month period and that approximately 1 percent, or about 500,000 of these persons, were subjected to use of force or threat of force[7] (see chapter 2 in *Use of Force by Police*). When handcuffing is included in the BJS definition of force, the number of persons increases to 1.2 million.

Expanding and contracting definitions of "police-public" interactions also work to affect use-of-force rates but in an opposite way from definitions of force. Broad definitions of police-public "interactions," such as calls for service, which capture variegated requests for assistance, lead to low rates of use of force. Con-

Working Definitions

Police use of force is characterized in a variety of ways. Sometimes, these characterizations are functionally interchangeable so that one can be substituted for another without doing injustice to the factual interpretation of a statement. At other times, however, differences in terminology can be very consequential to a statement's meaning. For example, "deadly force" refers to situations in which force is likely to have lethal consequences for the victim. This type of force is clearly defined and should not be confused with other types of force that police use.

In contrast, "police brutality" is a phrase used to describe instances of serious physical or psychological harm to civilians, with an emphasis on cruelty or savageness. The term does not have a standardized meaning; some commentators prefer to use a less emotionally charged term.

In this report, the term "excessive force" is used to describe situations in which more force is used than is allowable when judged in terms of administrative or professional guidelines or legal standards. Criteria for judging excessive force are fairly well established. The term may also include within its meaning the concept of illegal force.

Reference also is made to "excessive use of force," a similar, but distinctly different, term. Excessive use of force refers to high rates of force, which suggest that police are using force too freely when viewed in the aggregate. The term deals with relative comparisons among police agencies, and there are no established criteria for judgment.

"Illegal" use of force refers to situations in which use of force by police violated a law or statute, generally as determined by a judge or magistrate. The criteria for judging illegal use of force are fairly well established.

"Improper," "abusive," "illegitimate," and "unnecessary" use of force are terms that describe situations in which an officer's authority to use force has been mishandled in some general way, the suggestion being that administrative procedure, societal expectations, ordinary concepts of lawfulness, and the principle of last resort have been violated, respectively. Criteria for judging these violations are not well established.

To varying degrees, all of the above terms can be described as transgressions of police authority to use force.

versely, narrow definitions of police-public interactions, such as arrests, which concentrate squarely on suspects, lead to higher rates of use of force.

The International Association of Chiefs of Police (IACP) is in the process of compiling statistics on use-of-force data being submitted by cooperating agencies. These data indicate that force is used in less than one-half of 1 percent of dispatched calls for service. From this point of view, one might well consider police use of force a rare event. This figure is roughly consistent with the preliminary estimate reported by BJS, although the IACP figure is subject to the reporting biases that may exist in police agency data. Furthermore, IACP data are not yet representative of the national picture because of selection bias; the estimate is based on a small percentage of police departments that voluntarily report information on use of force.

Garner and Maxwell found that physical force (excluding handcuffing) is used in fewer than one of five adult custody arrests (see chapter 4 in *Use of Force by Police*). While this figure hardly qualifies as a rare event, it can be considered low, especially in light of the broad definition of force that was used.

In characterizing police use of force as infrequent or rare, the intention is neither to minimize the problem nor to suggest that the issue can be dismissed as unworthy of serious attention. Society's ends are best achieved peaceably, and we should strive to minimize the use of force by police as much as possible. However, it is important to put police use of force in context in order to understand the potential magnitude of use-of-force problems. Although estimates may not completely reassure everyone that police are doing everything they can to minimize the use of force, the data do not support the notion that we have a national epidemic of police violence.

Another purpose for emphasizing the infrequent nature of police use of force is to highlight the methodological challenges of trying to count or study infrequent events. In this regard, methodological approaches can vary considerably in terms of cost efficiency, reliability, and precision of information obtained. In BJS's 1996 pilot household survey of 6,421 persons, 14 respondents, or roughly 1 in 450, said that they were subjected to use of force or threat of force by police over a year's time. The household survey approach has the benefit of providing national-level estimates based on data that are free of police agency reporting biases. However, as noted by BJS, the preliminary estimates derived from such a small number of respondents are subject to a wide margin of error. This issue is particularly important if one is interested in tracking changes over time, because a very small change in reporting can have a very large impact on estimates. In the survey's continuing development, the next pilot test will use a sample about 10 times the size of the 1996 pilot test as well as involve a redesigned questionnaire.

Police use of force typically occurs at the lower end of the force spectrum, involving grabbing, pushing, or shoving.

Relatively minor types of force dominate statistics on police use of force. Garner and Maxwell (see chapter 4 in *Use of Force by Police*) observed that police use weaponless tactics in roughly 80 percent of use-of-force incidents and that half the time the tactic involved grabbing the suspect. Alpert and Dunham (see chapter 5) found that in Miami 64 percent of use-of-force incidents involved grabbing or holding the suspect. In the BJS pilot national survey, it was estimated, preliminarily, that about 500,000 people were "hit, held, pushed, choked, threatened with a flashlight, restrained by a police dog, threatened with or actually sprayed with chemical or pepper spray, threatened with a gun, or experienced some other form of force."[8] Three-fifths of these situations, however, involved only holding. Finally, Pate and Fridell's survey of law enforcement agencies regarding use of force and civilian complaints also confirms that minor types of force occur more frequently than serious types.[9]

As a corollary finding, when injuries occur as a result of use of force, they are likely to be relatively minor. Alpert and Dunham (see chapter 5 in *Use of Force by Police*) observed that the most common injury to a suspect was a bruise or abrasion (48 percent), followed by laceration (24 percent). The kinds of police actions that most captivate the public's concerns, such as fatal shootings, severe beatings with fists or batons that lead to hospitalization, and choke holds that cause unconsciousness or even death, are not typical of situations in which police use force. These findings reassure us that most police exercise restraint in the use of force, even if one has concerns over the number of times that police resort to serious violence.

From a police administrator's point of view, these findings are predictable. Officers are trained to use force progressively along a continuum, and policy requires that officers use the least amount of force necessary to accomplish their goals.

Another affiliated finding is that police rarely use weapons. According to Garner and Maxwell (see chapter 4 in *Use of Force by Police*), 2.1 percent of adult custody arrests involved use of weapons by police. Chemical agents were the weapons most frequently used (1.2 percent of arrests), while firearms were the weapons least often used (0.2 percent of arrests). Most police departments collect statistics on all firearm discharges by officers. These data consistently show that the majority of discharges are accidental or are directed at animals. Only on infrequent occasions do police use their firearms against the public. One implication of these findings is that increased training in how to use standard police weapons will be of little value in dealing with day-to-day situations that involve use of force. Training, if it is to be effective in reducing the use of force, needs to focus on how to gain compliance without resorting to physical coercion.

Use of force typically occurs when police are trying to make an arrest and the suspect is resisting.

Research indicates that police are most likely to use force when pursuing a suspect and attempting to exercise their arrest powers. Furthermore, resistance by the public increases the likelihood that police will use force. These findings appear intuitively sound given the mandate that police have regarding use of force. Police may use force when it is necessary to enforce the law or to protect themselves or others from harm. The findings also seem logical in view of police training curriculums and departmental regulations. Alpert and Dunham (see chapter 5 in *Use of Force by Police*) find that police almost always follow the prescribed sequence of control procedures they are taught, except when suspect resistance is high, in which case they tend to skip the intermediate procedure.

The conclusion that police are most likely to use force when dealing with criminal suspects, especially those who are resisting arrest, is based on four types of data: arrest statistics, surveys of police officers, observations of police behavior, and reports by the public about their encounters with police.

Arrest statistics show that resisting-arrest charges often are involved in situations in which officers use force. The interpretation of this finding is ambiguous, however, because officers may bring such charges in an attempt to justify their actions against a suspect. Some commentators even would argue that resisting-arrest charges are a good indication that police officers acted inappropriately or illegally. Because we are relying on official reports by officers who are involved in use-of-force incidents, and because they have self-interest in presenting the situation in the most favorable light possible, we cannot rely on arrest records alone in determining what happened.

Fortunately, other research is available to help clarify the situation. The pilot national household survey by BJS included a series of questions about the respondent's behavior during contact with police.[10] The preliminary analysis revealed that of the 14 respondents in the sample who reported that police used or threatened force against them, 10 suggested that they might have provoked the officer to use force. The provocative behaviors reported by suspects include threatening the officer, assaulting the officer, arguing with the officer, interfering with the arrest of someone else, blocking or interfering with an officer's movement, trying to escape, resisting being handcuffed, and resisting being placed in a police vehicle.

Research by Alpert and Dunham (see chapter 5 in *Use of Force by Police*) confirms that. criminal suspects are not always cooperative when it comes to arrest. In almost all (97 percent) cases in which police officers used force in a Florida jurisdiction, the suspect offered some degree of resistance. In 36 percent of use-of-force incidents, the suspect actively resisted arrest, and in one-quarter of the incidents the suspect assaulted the officer. The researchers observed that the most common type of suspect force was hitting or striking a police officer (44 percent).

Garner and colleagues, after using statistical controls for more than 50 characteristics of the arrest situation, the suspect, and the police officer, found that forceful action by suspects was the strongest and most consistent predictor of use of force by police.[11] Furthermore, they found that while 22 percent of arrests involved use of force by police, 14 percent of arrests involved use of force by suspects. Police officers in Phoenix completed a use-of-force survey after each arrest to generate these data.

Finally, Bayley and Garofalo tallied 36 instances of force used by police or suspects out of 467 police-public encounters observed firsthand by researchers.[12] They found that in 31 incidents police used force against suspects and in 11 incidents suspects used force against police.

One implication of the research is that the decision to use some level of force probably has legal justification in most cases. Force is likely to be used when suspects resist arrest and attempt to flee, Also, in a significant number of instances, suspects use force against the police. These findings leave open the issue of *excessive* force, since issues of proportionality are not clearly addressed. However, the findings do suggest that many debates over excessive force will fall into gray areas where it is difficult to decide whether an officer acted properly, because there is credible evidence that the use of force was necessary.

What We Know with Modest Confidence about Police Use of Force

Use of force appears to be unrelated to an officer's personal characteristics, such as age, gender, and ethnicity.

A small number of studies suggest that use of force by police is not associated with personal characteristics, such as age, gender, and ethnicity. Bayley and Garofalo concluded that use of force is not related to age, although it may be related to experience.[13] Worden, in an analysis of observational data on 24 police departments in 3 metropolitan areas, concluded that the personal characteristics of police officers do not have a substantively significant effect on use of force.[14]

Likewise, Garner and colleagues reported that the race of suspect and officer is not predictive of use of force.[15] However, they found that incidents involving male police officers and male suspects are more likely to involve force. Alpert and Dunham (see chapter 5 in *Use of Force by Police*) found that officer characteristics are of little utility in distinguishing between force and nonforce incidents.

Hence, gender and ethnicity appear unrelated to use of force. Given the limited research in this area, these conclusions should be accepted with caution and additional verification of these findings is needed.

It is widely accepted in criminology that violence, along with a wide variety of other risk-taking and norm-violating behaviors, is a young man's game. Thus, we should expect that young, male police officers should use force more than their female colleagues or older officers. The fact that this is not clearly the case seems surprising.

A lack of relationship between age and gender, on the one hand, and use of force, on the other, may be a function of police hiring and deployment practices. Retirement plans keep the age of police officers lower than that of most other occupations, and seniority, which is derivative of work experience, often brings more choice in work assignments, including duties that limit one's contact with criminal suspects on the street. Both these tendencies serve to constrain variation in the age of police officers who are exposed to potentially violent situations. This may attenuate the relationship between age and use of force. However, it is equally plausible that young male officers are assigned to high-crime areas where frequent use of force is necessary to gain compliance. Finally, it is possible that exposure to the police culture works to encourage the use of force, thus counterbalancing the decline in aggressivity that comes with age as demonstrated in criminological studies. More research is needed to disentangle these relationships.

The finding that an officer's race is unrelated to the propensity to use force runs counter to the argument that racial animosity lies at the heart of police abuse. Indeed, Alpert and Dunham's research (see chapter 5 in *Use of Force by Police*) indicates that officers are more likely to use force against suspects of their own race. The lack of relationship between race and use of force, as well as between gender and use of force, is probably disheartening to those who argue that integration of police agencies along racial and gender lines will do much to reduce the incidence of police violence. Again, more research is needed to understand the situation of minority and female police officers with regard to their use of force.

Use of force is more likely to occur when police are dealing with persons under the influence of alcohol or drugs or with mentally ill individuals. More research is needed.

Police come across a wide variety of situations in their work. They encounter problems that range from relatively minor to serious to potentially deadly. They also interact with people exhibiting various mental states, including persons who are hysterical, highly agitated, angry, disoriented, upset, worried, irritated, or calm.

Two situations that often give police officers cause for concern are when suspects appear to be under the influence of alcohol or drugs and when civilians appear to suffer from serious mental or emotional impairments. The concern stems from the fact that in such situations a person's rational faculties appear impaired. In dealing with problem situations, officers most often talk their way, rather than force their way, into solutions. For this reason, when a civilian is in a highly irrational state of mind, the chances of the police officer having to use force presumably increase and the possibility of injury to both officer and civilian increases as well.

Research carried out for the President's Commission on Law Enforcement and Administration of Justice observed that alcohol use by either a suspect or an officer increased the chances that force will be used.[16] Garner and colleagues found that alcohol impairment by suspects was a consistent predictor of police use of force, while drug impairment predicted increased use of force for some but not all measures of use of force.[17] In contrast, Alpert and Dunham (see chapter 5 in *Use of Force by Police*) observed that alcohol or drug impairment of suspects was unrelated to police use of force or subsequent injury. That finding is interesting because, although impaired civilians did not demonstrate an increased propensity to resist an officer's actions, when they did resist they were more inclined to do so by actively resisting or assaulting the officer.

Part of the disparity in findings between the President's Commission's research and more recent studies may be attributed to the fact that police officers today are better trained in how to deal with impaired civilians. Most police officers now receive training in a variety of violence reduction techniques, and this development is partly attributable to concerns over the President's Commission's findings and over the frequency with which police now are called to respond to large-scale violence, such as riots.

Questions about how police deal with civilians who appear to have impaired mental states are important from administrative and practical points of view. Police officers are expected to exercise restraint in dealing with impaired civilians, while at the same time they need to be cautious about protecting their safety as well as the safety of other civilians. This puts them in a precarious situation, one in which mistakes of judgment or tactics can have grave consequences.

From a practical standpoint, police regularly encounter civilians with impaired mental states, which makes the problem more than academic. Alpert and Dunham (see chapter 5 in *Use of Force by Police*) found that in 42 percent of use-of-force situations, suspects appeared to be under the influence of alcohol or drugs. Overall, the research on whether police use force more frequently in relation to civilians with impaired mental states is inconsistent. Further investigation, with an emphasis on implications for training, could reduce the risk of force and injury for both police officers and civilians.

A small proportion of officers are disproportionately involved in use-of-force incidents. More research is needed.

We often are told that a small number of people are responsible for most of the productive or counterproductive work in an organization. For example, we hear about the 80/20 rule in organizational management. That is, 20 percent of the workers account for 80 percent of the work. Policing has its counterpart explanation for deviant or illegal behavior. It is called the rotten apple or rogue officer theory, and it is often used to explain police corruption. Recently, a variation of this theory has become the principal explanation for use-of-force problems in police departments. In this context, we speak of "violence prone" police officers and we point to these individuals as the reason why a department has problems with the use of force.[18]

People with extraordinary work performance, either good or bad, are noticeable when compared with their colleagues, and their salience leads us to think that their work is highly consequential to the good fortunes or misfortunes of an organization. The utility of this perspective for police managers attempting to deal with illegitimate use of force lies in the presumed concentration of problem behaviors in the workforce. If only a handful of police officers accounts for most of the abuses, then effective solutions targeted at those individuals should deal with the problem. The nature of the solution, be it employee selection, training, oversight, or discipline, is less important than its degree of effectiveness and its ability to be directed at the problem group of employees.

The Christopher Commission, which investigated the Los Angeles Police Department subsequent to the Rodney King incident, highlighted the "violence prone" officer theory.[19] The Commission, using the department's database, identified 44 officers with 6 or more civilian allegations of excessive force or improper tactics in the period 1986 through 1990. For the 44, the per-officer average for force-related complaints was 7.6 compared with 0.6 for all officers identified as having been involved in a use-of-force incident for the period January 1987 through March 1991. The 44 officers were involved in an average of 13 use-of-force incidents compared with 4.2 for all officers reported to be using force.

Put another way, less than one-half of 1 percent of the department's sworn officers accounted for more than 15 percent of allegations of excessive force or improper tactics. The degree of disproportion (30:1) is striking and suggests that focusing efforts on a handful of officers can eliminate roughly 1 out of 7 excessive force incidents. This finding has led many police departments to implement early warning systems designed to identify high-risk officers before they become major problems. Most of these systems use administrative records, such as disciplinary records and citizen complaints, to monitor officer performance for possible problems.

The concept of an early warning system for risk management of problem police officers is not new. In the early 1980s, a report on police practices by the United States Commission on Civil Rights found that "[e]arly warning' information systems may assist the department in identifying violence-prone officers."[20] Consequently, it was recommended that "[a] system should be devised in each department to assist officials in early identification of violence-prone officers."[21]

Until recently, these systems received limited acceptance, owing in part to concerns over possible abuses. The abuses include use of inaccurate information, improper labeling of officers, misuse of confidential records regarding discipline and other personnel matters, and social ostracism by peers and community for officers identified as problematic. There also were concerns about limited resources and about increased legal liability for the organization and individual officers.

As Toch observes, the violence-prone officer paradigm often is based on a variety of loosely articulated theories of violent behavior.[22] The theories include concepts such as racial prejudice, poor self-control, and ego involvement. Furthermore, these theories often overlook the possibility that greater-than-average use of force may be a product of situational or organizational characteristics.

For example, an officer's work assignment may involve a high-crime area that contains a high proportion of rebellious offenders. Also, divisive, dehumanizing views of the world, such as "us-them" and "good guy-bad guy," that facilitate violent behavior may be supported by the organizational culture. Further, administrative views of work roles and products, communicated formally or informally, that emphasize crime control through aggressive police behavior may encourage confrontational tactics that increase the chances of violent behavior by either civilian or police officer. Unless the reasons for violence propensity are accurately identified, the effectiveness of interventions targeted at violent police officers is a hit-or-miss proposition.

Of the 44 officers identified by the Christopher Commission in 1991, 14 subsequently left the department as of October 1997. Of the 30 remaining officers, two had a use-of-force complaint that was sustained after review between 1991 and 1997.[23] This low number may be due to a variety of reasons, such as difficulties in sustaining citizen complaints, reassignment of work duties, negative publicity leading to a change in behavior, or greater circumspection when engaging in misconduct. However, the finding also may reflect regression to the mean. This is a statistical phenomenon postulating that extreme scores gravitate toward the mean or average score, thereby becoming less extreme over time.

For example, groups of police officers who receive many citizen complaints, or who are disproportionately involved in the use of force, or who frequently are given poor performance ratings, will tend to become "better" over time, in the sense of statistically looking more like the "average" officers, even if nothing is done about these problems. Statistical regression represents a serious threat to the validity of early warning systems based on the assumption that extreme patterns of behavior persist over extended periods of time.

What We Do Not Know About Police Use of Force

The incidence of wrongful use of force by police is unknown. Research is critically needed to determine reliably, validly, and precisely how often transgressions of use-of-force powers occur.

We do not know how often police use force in ways that can be adjudged as wrongful. For example, we do not know the incidence of excessive force, even though this is a very serious violation of public trust. We could pull together data on excessive force using police disciplinary records and court documents, for example, but the picture would be sketchy, piecemeal, and potentially deceiving. When it comes to less grave or less precise transgressions, such as "improper," "abusive," "illegitimate," and "unnecessary" use of force, the state of knowledge is even more precarious.

In discussing this issue, we will concentrate on excessive force, because these transgressions are of utmost concern to the public and because well-established professional and legal criteria are available to help us evaluate police behavior. Notwithstanding a generally agreed-upon terminology, we should recognize that developing a count of excessive force that is beyond all dispute is an unworkable task. This is so because difficult judgments are involved in deciding whether use of force fits the criteria for these categories in a given situation, and reasonable people will disagree in such judgments. We clearly need more accurate, reliable, and valid measures of excessive force if we are to advance our understanding of these problems.

Academics and practitioners both tend to presuppose that the incidence of excessive force by police is very low. They argue that, despite their shortcomings, agency statistics provide a useful picture of the use-of-force problem. These statistics show that most officers do not engage in force on a regular basis, that few people are injured by police use of force, that only a small number of people complain about police misconduct involving use of force, and that only a handful of these complaints are sustained.

The argument has appeal. We believe that the vast majority of police officers are professionals who respect the law and the public. If use of force is uncommon, civilian complaints are infrequent, and civilian injuries are few, then excessive force by police must be rare. That conclusion may indeed be correct, but to the extent that it hinges on official police statistics, it is open to serious challenge.

Current indicators of excessive force are all critically flawed. The most widely available indicators are civilian complaints of excessive force and civil lawsuits alleging illegal use of force. Civilian complaints of excessive force are infrequent, and the number of substantiated complaints is very low. These figures are consistent with the argument that excessive force is sporadic. However, complaint mechanisms are subject to selection and reporting biases, and the operation of complaint systems, which typically is managed by police, wields considerable influence on whether people will come forward to complain.

Civil lawsuits against police are exceedingly rare relative to the number of times that police use force. Because the legal process is highly selective in terms of which claims get litigated, lawsuits are a very unreliable measure of illegal use of force. With both civilian complaints and lawsuits, small changes in administrative practices can have a large impact on the magnitude of the problem measured in these ways.

The difficulties in measuring excessive and illegal force with complaint and lawsuit records have led academics and practitioners to redirect their attention to all use-of-force incidents. The focus then becomes one of minimizing all instances of police use of force, without undue concern as to whether force was excessive. From this perspective, other records, such as use-of-force reports, arrest records, injury reports, and medical records, become relevant to measuring the incidence of the problem.

From a theoretical perspective, understanding all use-of-force incidents helps us to put wrongful use of force in perspective. However, because political, legal, and ethical issues are very serious when we are dealing with excessive force, pressures to know the incidence and prevalence of these events with precision will always be present.

As a corollary of our current inability to measure excessive force, we cannot discern with precision changes in the incidence of these events over time and across places. This means that we can neither determine whether excessive force problems are getting better or worse nor determine the circumstances under which those problems are more or less severe.

The impact of differences in police organizations, including administrative policies, hiring, training, discipline, and use of technology, on excessive and illegal force is unknown. Research is critically needed in this area.

A major gap in our knowledge about excessive force by police concerns characteristics of police agencies that facilitate or impede this conduct. Although many of the conditions that arguably lead to excessive or illegal force by police seem obvious, or appear to be a matter of common sense, we still greatly need systematic research in this area. We need to know, for example, which organizational characteristics are most consequential, which characteristics take on added significance in various environments, and which characteristics are redundant or derivative of other characteristics.

Many formal aspects of the organization—such as hiring criteria, recruit training, in-service programs, supervision of field officers, disciplinary mechanisms, operations of internal affairs, specialized units dealing with ethics and integrity, labor unions, and civilian oversight mechanisms—plausibly are related to levels of officer misconduct. It makes sense that poorly educated, badly trained, loosely supervised, and inadequately disciplined officers are likely to be problematic, and that when such officers are in the majority, the organization is on the road toward disaster. Yet, we lack research that systematically addresses these questions.

Less formal aspects of police organizations—officer morale, administrative leadership, peer culture and influence, police-community relations, relations with other government agencies, and neighborhood environments—also plausibly have a part in levels of officer misconduct. Alienated officers who do not have a clear vision of their role and responsibilities and who are working in disorganized agencies and interacting with the public under stressful circumstances probably are more likely to abuse their authority, including their authority to use force. Research that systematically addresses these questions is lacking.

Methodological investigation of relations between organizational elements and use-of-force transgressions will help explain police misconduct at a theoretical level. More importantly, research on these questions will allow us to deal effectively with police misbehavior. Faced with serious misconduct problems in a police agency, we need to focus scarce resources on those aspects of police organizations that are most clearly related to ensuring proper conduct of officers with regard to use of force. Generalized efforts to reform police organizations that are expected to reduce misconduct problems tend to be inefficiently focused and thus appear clumsy, inadequate, and misinformed.

Research must focus on establishing the relative cost-effectiveness of various strategies to reduce or eliminate police misconduct. Furthermore, only strategies that are solidly grounded in theory, practice, and empirical research will provide reliable solutions with predictable costs and benefits.

Influences of situational characteristics on police use of force and the transactional nature of these events are largely unknown. More research is necessary.

Research on police-citizen encounters reveals that use of force by police is situational and transactional. That is, police respond to circumstances as they first encounter them and as they unfold over time. For example, Bayley and Garofalo observed that the situations most likely to involve police use of force are interpersonal disturbance and violent personal crime.[24] Beyond this, however, we do not know much about the types of events that enhance the likelihood that police will use force.

Similarly, we have noted that when suspects attempt to flee or physically resist arrest police are more likely to use force. We also noted that in many cases both police and suspects use force against each other. However, these findings do not address the transactional nature of police-public encounters in that they do not describe the step-by-step unfolding of events and interactions. Knowing that police use force if suspects physically resist arrest, it matters if police use force without provocation and the suspect responds by resisting or vice versa.

A variety of situational elements plausibly are related to police use of force. If police are called to a scene where there is fighting, they may have to or believe they have to use force to subdue the suspects. If they are called to a domestic dispute where emotions are running high, they may have to or believe they have to use force to gain control of the situation. If they are called to intercede with a civilian who is recklessly brandishing a weapon, they may have to or believe they have to use force to protect themselves and others. Use of force in such circumstances maybe justifiable, but to the extent that it is predictable, we can prepare officers for these encounters and devise alternative strategies that minimize or eliminate the use of force.

Some situational factors may increase the chances that force of questionable legitimacy will be used. For example, officers sometimes use force on the slightest provocation following a high-speed car chase, when adrenaline levels are high. They may use force more frequently when they are alone, because they feel more vulnerable or believe that they can get away with it. They may use force more frequently as a way of emphasizing their authority when suspects are disrespectful or when there is a hostile audience to the encounter. At this point, however, knowledge about the types of police-citizen encounters in which police are likely to use force is rudimentary.

Police-public encounters are transactional in the sense that all the actors in a situation contribute in some way to its development and outcome. Understanding the transactional nature of police use of force is important because it emphasizes the role of police actions in increasing the chances that force will be used.

From this perspective, it is possible to minimize the use of force by modifying the behavior and tactics of police officers. By understanding the sequences of events that lead police to use force, we can gain a greater degree of control over those situations and possibly redirect the outcome. But we have only a basic understanding of the transactional nature of use-of-force situations, despite the fact that sequences of actions and interactions are highly germane to determining whether use of force was excessive or illegal.

NOTES

[1] Bierce, Ambrose, *The Devil's Dictionary*, New York: Dover, 1958: 101.

[2] "Justice Department Consent Decree Pushes Police to Overhaul Operations," *Pittsburgh Post-Gazette*, March 1, 1998, C-1.

[3] Based on an investigation in 14 cities, Human Rights Watch described the brutality situation as follows: "[p]olice officers engage in unjustified shootings, severe beatings, fatal chokings, and unnecessarily rough physical treatment in cities throughout the United States, while their police superiors, city officials and the Justice Department fail to act decisively to restrain or penalize such acts or even to record the full magnitude of the problem." Human Rights

Watch, *Shielded from Justice: Police Brutality and Accountability in the United States*, New York: Human Rights Watch, 1998: 1, 27.

4 A previous summary of research on police use of force can be found in McEwen, Tom, *National Data Collection on Police Use of Force*, Washington, DC: U.S. Department of Justice, Bureau of Justice Statistics and National Institute of Justice, April 1996, NCJ 160113.

5 Bayley, David H., and James Garofalo, "The Management of Violence by Police Patrol Officers," *Criminology*, 27(1)(February 1989): 1–27; and Bayley, David H., and James Garofalo, "Patrol Officer Effectiveness in Managing Conflict During Police-Citizen Encounters," in *Report to the Governor, Vol. III*, Albany: New York State Commission on Criminal Justice and the Use of Force, 1987: 131–88.

6 Adams, Kenneth, "Measuring the Prevalence of Police Abuse of Force," in *And Justice For All: A National Agenda for Understanding and Controlling Police Abuse of Force*, ed. William A. Geller and Hans Toch, Washington, DC: Police Executive Research Forum, 1995: 61–97.

7 Greenfeld, Lawrence A., Patrick A. Langan, and Steven K. Smith, *Police Use of Force: Collection of National Data*, Washington, DC: U.S. Department of Justice, Bureau of Justice Statistics and National Institute of Justice, November 1997, NCJ 165040.

8 Ibid.

9 Pate, Antony M., and Lorie A. Fridell, with Edwin F. Hamilton, *Police Use of Force: Official Reports, Citizen Complaints, and Legal Consequences*, Vols. I and II, Washington, DC: The Police Foundation, 1993.

10 Greenfeld, Lawrence A., Patrick A. Langan, and Steven K. Smith, *Police Use of Force: Collection of National Data*.

11 Garner, Joel, John Buchanan, Tom Schade, and John Hepburn, *Understanding Use of Force By and Against the Police*, Research in Brief, Washington, DC: U.S. Department of Justice, National Institute of Justice, November 1996, NCJ 158614.

12 Bayley, David H., and James Garofalo, "The Management of Violence by Police Patrol Officers"; and Bayley, David H., and James Garofalo, "Patrol Officer Effectiveness in Managing Conflict During Police-Citizen Encounters."

13 Ibid.

14 Worden, Robert, "The 'Causes' of Police Brutality," in *And Justice For All: A National Agenda for Understanding and Controlling Police Abuse of Force*, 31–60.

15 Garner, Joel, John Buchanan, Tom Schade, and John Hepburn, *Understanding Use of Force By and Against the Police*.

16 Reiss, Albert J., Jr., *Studies on Crime and Law Enforcement in a Major Metropolitan Area*, President's Commission on Law Enforcement and Administration of Justice, Field Survey No. 3, Washington, DC: U.S. Government Printing Office, 1967.

17 Garner, Joel, John Buchanan, Tom Schade, and John Hepburn, *Understanding Use of Force By and Against the Police*.

18 Toch, Hans, "The 'Violence-Prone' Police Officer," in *And Justice For All: A National Agenda for Understanding and Controlling Police Abuse of Force*, 99–112.

19 Independent Commission on the Los Angeles Police Department, *Report of the Independent Commission on the Los Angeles Police Department*, Los Angeles: Independent Commission on the Los Angeles Police Department, 1991.

20 United States Commission on Civil Rights, *Who's Guarding the Guardians? A Report on Police Practices*, Washington, DC: United States Commission on Civil Rights, 1981: 159.

21 Ibid.

22 Toch, Hans, "The 'Violence-Prone' Police Officer," 112.

23 Office of the Inspector General, Los Angeles Police Commission, "Status Update: Management of LAPD High-Risk Officers," Los Angeles: Los Angeles Police Commission, 1997.

24 Bayley, David, H., and James Garofalo, "Patrol Officer Effectiveness in Managing Conflict During Police-Citizen Encounters."

31

Use-of-Force Policy,
Policy Enforcement, and Training*

Lorie A. Fridell

Introduction

Police officers have the right to use reasonable force—even deadly force—in the course of doing their jobs.[1] At times, they are required to make split-second decisions regarding whether to use force and what type of force to use. The agency executives (that is, chiefs and sheriffs) must provide tools to their officers so that they can make those difficult decisions. The goal of a law enforcement agency executive is not to eliminate use of force by his/her officers, but to "optimize" it (Fridell and Pate, 1997). This means that force is used to the extent necessary so that officers are able to conduct law enforcement functions and do so without injury or death. Force is not used when it could be avoided, and force is used only in the amounts necessary to achieve legitimate objectives.

Critical to achieving force optimization in a department are (1) the adoption of sound and effective policies, (2) implementation of mechanisms to promote policy adherence and accountability, and (3) training to ensure that officers have the knowledge, skills, and judgment to act in accordance with agency policy.

Policy Content

The breadth of activities covered by agency policies and the comprehensiveness of those policies have increased over the years. Policies related to force, particularly deadly force, are no exception. In the late 1960s, the Presi-

*This chapter is a modified version of a chapter entitled "Improving Use-of-Force Policy, Policy Enforcement, and Training" that appeared in Ederheimer, J. A. and Fridell, L. A. (Eds.) (2005). *Chief Concerns: Exploring the Challenges of Police Use of Force*, published by the Police Executive Research Forum.

dent's Commission on Law Enforcement and Administration of Justice (1967) conveyed concern over the lack of policies to guide police in their use of deadly force. The commission noted that many officers were guided only by broad and difficult-to-enforce state statutes (White, 2000). At that time many of the largest agencies had policies on deadly force, but many of these policies, even up to the early 1980s, were very general and ambiguous (Matulia, 1982). Following are a few examples of policies that existed in the 1960s (Chapman, 1967, as cited in White, 2001):

- "Never take me out in anger; never put me back in disgrace."
- "Leave the gun in the holster until you intend to use it."
- "It is left to the discretion of each individual officer when and how to shoot."

A survey conducted in the early 1960s, involving primarily small departments, found that twenty-seven of forty-nine departments had no firearms policies (Chapman and Crockett, 1963). Two decades later, Nielsen (1983) surveyed small departments (serving populations of at least 20,000) as well as large departments in five states. He found that 37% of the responding agencies lacked a written deadly force policy. Over half of the responding agencies in North Dakota and Mississippi reported they had no written policies.

In the 1970s, many agencies began to adopt more restrictive policies and now virtually all agencies, regardless of size, have policies on deadly force and nondeadly force in their "Standard Operating Procedures." These policies are pages in length and, compared to the policies of the past, greatly delimit officer discretion to use force. These policy changes came about as a result of (1) the general movement within policing to control discretion, (2) the call for racial justice in the context of the civil rights movement, (3) the expanded civil liability of municipalities for the actions of their officers, (4) social science research on the impact of force policy on various outcomes, and (5) U.S. Supreme Court decisions (see Fridell, 2008b; Walker and Fridell, 1992).

Policy Enforcement

Not just the content of policies, but the administrative commitment to those policies, is key to optimizing force—both deadly and nondeadly. The words within a Standard Operating Procedure manual may not have any impact unless supported by a clear message from the top echelons of the agency that the policy will be followed. Affirming the importance of clear direction by police leaders, the Independent Commission of the Los Angeles Police Department (also called the "Christopher Commission"), constituted following the Rodney King beating, called "the problem of excessive force in the LAPD . . . fundamentally a problem of supervision, management, and leadership" (1991, 32). Skolnick and Fyfe (1993) describe events in several cities in which the contents of restrictive written policies were overwhelmed by the much more lax unwritten policies of the top administrators (see also Sherman, 1983; Waegel, 1984; White, 2001).

The administrative commitment to optimal use of force by officers comes in the form of accountability mechanisms that convey to sworn personnel that excessive force will not be tolerated and unnecessary force must be avoided. These means of promoting accountability can include monitoring of employees' use of force, a strong system for reviewing complaints, an early intervention system, and departmental rewards for desired behaviors.

Training

Training helps ensure that officers have the skills, judgment, and knowledge to implement policies on the streets of the jurisdiction. The dramatic changes during the past several decades in force policy content and enforcement have been paralleled by equally dramatic changes in training. Advances occurred first in deadly force training and later were applied to training in the use of other types of force.

Rudimentary firearms training for officers can be traced to 1895 when Theodore Roosevelt, serving as the Commissioner of the New York Police Department, established the School of Pistol Practice. Such instruction was not routine, however, until the late 1940s or early 1950s (Morrison, 2002, 2003). For this training, the recruit or in-service officer would, in a standing position, shoot an already unholstered weapon at a static paper bull's eye target (maybe sixty feet away) on command from the training officer during daylight hours. Scharf and Binder (1983, 202) provide one officer's characterization of this type of training: "It's completely unrealistic, a police Disneyland. You have time to set up; no one is trying to kill you and you aren't completely stressed out. . . . Also you're not moving and the target's not moving. Otherwise the training is fantastic here!"

Some of the first improvements to deadly force training attempted to incorporate more realistic features of shooting situations. The Practical Pistol Course advanced this training by having officers shoot from various (and more realistic) distances, from various positions (for example, standing, crouching, kneeling), in the open or from behind barricades, under various lighting conditions, and under time constraints. "Stress courses" incorporated physical exertion in an attempt to enhance the reality of training.

The enhanced reality training still focused on *how* to use force and not *when* to use force. A still relatively recent advancement in force training is the emphasis on when to use force and what level of force to use. This advancement in training first occurred with respect to use of deadly force. An early application of this philosophy was the "shoot/don't shoot" program. An officer was placed in a room where a video portraying an encounter with one or more people was projected on the front wall. The officer was instructed to act as she or he would if the situation happened on the job; all of the scenarios required a decision regarding whether to use deadly force. The better early computer models had officers make use of cover and other tactical skills when responding to the stimuli on the screen. The corresponding application of this advancement for less-lethal force was the introduction of training not just on less-than-lethal tactics and weapons but on their justified utilization in various types of police-citizen encounters.

Modern force training also focuses on avoiding or defusing potentially violent encounters through smart tactics and strong communication skills. Some training programs help officers to make decisions in encounters that might reduce the likelihood that force will be required. In that same vein, agencies are emphasizing the importance of strong communication skills that, in some situations, can be used to de-escalate an otherwise violent encounter (Fyfe, 1987, 1988).

In the next sections, the use-of-force issues facing police and the current best practices in the realms of policy content, policy enforcement, and training are discussed.

Critical Issues in Use-of-Force Policy

Departments and the stakeholders that they serve are discussing and debating several issues that pertain to force policy. These include shooting at drivers of moving vehicles, drawing and pointing firearms, appropriate uses of conducted energy devices (CEDs) (e.g., Tasers), and avoiding unnecessary force.

Shots Fired at Vehicles

An increasing number of agencies have specific provisions in their policies regarding the firing of shots at drivers of moving vehicles. These provisions are prompted by a desire to reduce the potential danger to officers and innocent bystanders of a moving vehicle with a wounded or dead driver. Many policies related to moving vehicles note the officer's role in reducing unnecessary force. The Orange County (FL) policy [General Order 470.0] states that deputies shall not "intentionally place themselves in the path of an oncoming vehicle and (then) attempt to disable the vehicle by discharging their firearms." Similarly, Virginia Beach General Order 12.10 states that "officers shall not intentionally stand and/or step into the path of a vehicle, creating circumstances where the use of deadly force becomes necessary."

The Miami Police Department policy prohibits officers "from discharging their firearms at or from a moving vehicle unless deadly force is being used against the police officer or another person present, by means other than the moving vehicle" [Departmental Order 2, Chapter 6]. This policy recognizes that, if the driver is using the vehicle as deadly force, it is unlikely that shooting the driver will reduce the danger. In other words, it is unlikely that a person (for instance, an officer or other person) who is in imminent danger of being killed by a moving vehicle will be saved if the driver is wounded or killed by a bullet. Instead, it is likely that the vehicle will continue on its deadly path. Some practitioners also advocate this policy because they believe it is the strongest in terms of delimiting the circumstances in which officers can shoot at vehicles and doesn't allow the officer to argue after the fact (truthfully or otherwise) that they could not, despite their best efforts, get out of the way of the moving vehicle.

Drawing and Pointing Firearms

An increasing number of agencies are adding to their use-of-force policy specific provisions regarding when officers can draw and point firearms. According to the Police Assessment Resource Center (2003, 39), "A key purpose in adopting a formal rule is to provide officers with concrete guidelines and, if necessary, to establish a basis for accountability for deviations from the guidelines." Agencies that adopt a formal rule restrict drawing and pointing of firearms to situations where danger is expected; they vary as to their characterization of the degree and certainty of danger required. In its report, the Police Assessment Resource Center (2003) discusses various models including the following from the Los Angeles Police Department and the Metropolitan Police Department in Washington DC, respectively:

> Unnecessarily or prematurely drawing or exhibiting a firearm limits an officer's alternatives in controlling a situation, creates unnecessary anxiety on the part of citizens, and may result in an unwarranted or accidental discharge of the firearm. Officers shall not draw or exhibit a firearm unless the circumstances surrounding the incident create a reasonable belief that it may be necessary to use the firearm in conformance with this policy on the use of firearms. [*Manual of Policy and Procedure*, Vol. 1, § 556.80]

> No members shall draw and point a firearm at or in the direction of a person unless there is a reasonable perception of a substantial risk that the situation may escalate to the point where lethal force would be permitted. [General Order 901.04 at 4]

Policy for Conducted Energy Devices

Over the years, the law enforcement profession has seen an increase in the number of less-lethal weapons available to it (Ederheimer, 2005). These less-lethal weapons increase the force options available to officers, including the options available to police that can "prevent a violent encounter with a citizen from escalating to the use of fatal force" (Fridell and Pate, 1993, 1; see also Ijames and Ederheimer, 2007 and Meyer, 2008). In this vein, departments nationwide are making decisions regarding whether to adopt CEDs such as Tasers[2] and, if adopted, the executives are grappling with the appropriate content of policy guiding their use. According to a recent national survey, approximately half of the law enforcement agencies in the United States deploy at least one CED to personnel; one-third of all municipal and county agencies deploy CEDs to at least half of their line personnel (Fridell, 2008a; Smith et al., 2008). Most agencies using CEDs first deployed them to line personnel after January 2004.

With this surge of interest in CEDs by law enforcement, the debate regarding their use is being played out in court, in the media, and in other public forums.[3] CED critics—including the American Civil Liberties Union and Amnesty International—claim that these weapons are not "less-than-lethal." Amnesty International (2008) reports that since June 2001 more than

330 people in the United States have died after being struck by "police Tasers." It is likely that in many of the CED-proximate deaths the subject's physical condition was such that he or she would have died regardless of the type of force the officer chose to use on him/her. Nonetheless, no one is in a position to state equivocally that CEDs do not contribute to deaths in some circumstances. Of particular concern to critics are multiple or prolonged activations; that is, they are particularly concerned about incidents in which the CED is deployed multiple times or when officers hold down the trigger to produce prolonged activations (American Civil Liberties Union of Northern California, 2005; Amnesty International, 2004).[4]

Advocates claim that CED deployment reduces overall injuries to officers and subjects. A number of law enforcement agencies have reported such reductions following the deployment of CEDs (e.g., police departments in Charlotte-Mecklenburg, Austin, Cape Coral, Cincinnati, and Phoenix and the Orange County Sheriff's Office). Several more scientific reviews have similarly determined that CED deployment reduces officer and subject injuries (Jenkinson, Neeson, and Bleetman, 2006; Smith, Kaminski, Rojek, Alpert, and Mathis, 2007; Smith et al., 2008). Advocates claim that CEDs can displace deadly force or prevent an incident from escalating to the deadly force level. Like the CED-proximate deaths above, however, the CED-proximate saves as well might have occurred with another type of force on the scene.

The challenge for the agency executive is to assess what is known about the costs and benefits of the weapon, consider what we don't yet know, and ultimately develop a policy that guides his/her officers in the use of the CED. A key decision by the executive is where to place CEDs on the agency's use-of-force continuum (see, e.g., Johnson, Warren, Ederheimer, and Fridell, 2007); the placement should reflect an attempt to achieve a balance between potential benefits and potential costs. Linear use-of-force continuums are used by most agencies to guide their officers in the use of force (Fridell, 2008a; Smith et al., 2008); they define various levels of subject resistance (e.g., verbal resistance, passive physical resistance, aggressive physical resistance) and articulate the type of police force that is "reasonable" in response to each (e.g., chemical sprays, CEDs). Many of these continuums present as a staircase with each step up indicating a higher level of subject resistance and therefore a higher level of police force response. There is not a single, standard use-of-force continuum; instead, there are numerous models around the country.

As one example, the Denver Police Department's (DPD) linear force continuum refers to the following levels of resistance by subjects: Psychological Intimidation, Verbal Non-Compliance, Passive Resistance, Defensive Resistance, Active Aggression, and Aggravated Active Aggression (deadly force level). The DPD policy states that CEDs can be used to "incapacitate a combative or physically resistive person whose conduct rises at least to the level of Active Aggression. . . . This use-of-force option becomes necessary when other force options would be inappropriate or ineffective under other circumstances" [Use of Force Policy, 105.00]. The policy also allows for the use of the CED against a "suicidal person who cannot be safely controlled with other force options."

There is variation in the placement of CEDs on use-of-force continuums (Adams and Jennison, 2007; Government Accounting Office, 2005). The survey conducted in 2006 by Smith et al. (2008) used officer-subject scenarios to assess agency policies across the nation. Most agencies do not allow their officers to use the CED against a subject who refuses, without physical resistance, to comply with the officer's commands. There is a 60%–40% split among agencies nationally in terms of whether an officer would be authorized to use a CED against a subject who tenses and pulls against an officer as the officer tries to guide his hands behind his back for handcuffing. Approximately 60% would allow the CED use; 40% would not. Almost all agencies allow their officers to use a CED against a subject who "faces off against the officer with his hands raised in a boxer's stance" (Smith et al., 2008).

Many agencies prohibit or strongly discourage the use of CEDs against specific groups of people—for instance, pregnant women, handcuffed prisoners, children, the elderly, people in high places who might be hurt if they fell, people moving at high speeds such as drivers, and handcuffed prisoners resisting/refusing to enter a police vehicle (Fridell, 2008a; Smith et al., 2008). The Las Vegas policy distinguishes between circumstances in which CEDs should *never be used* and circumstances in which CEDs *should not be used most of the time*. In the latter circumstances, the agency gives officers some discretion to judge whether the potential harm is offset by greater potential gain. Relevant policy provisions are as follows:

At all times the Taser will not be used

- when the subject has come into contact with flammable liquids or is in a flammable atmosphere;
- when the subject is in a position where a fall may cause substantial injury or death;
- to intimidate individuals;
- to escort, provoke, or jab individuals; or
- to awaken unconscious or intoxicated individuals.

Unless there are compelling reasons that can be clearly articulated, Tasers should not be used

- when the subject is operating a motor vehicle;
- when the subject is holding a firearm (Note: SWAT and Detention Services Division are exempt from this provision);
- when a handcuffed prisoner resists/refuses to enter a police vehicle, holding or booking area;
- when the subject is a visibly pregnant woman; or
- when the subject is extremely elderly or impaired.

A national survey of agencies conducted by Smith et al. (2008) found that very few agencies place numerical limits on the length and number of CED activations an officer can use against a subject. The Longmont (CO) Police Department is an exception, stating in Policy 601 that "no person shall be exposed to a single cycle longer than five seconds" and "no person shall be knowingly exposed to more than three five-second cycles."

Avoiding Unnecessary Force

All agencies should train officers to use verbal skills and tactics to reduce the likelihood that force will be required during an incident. Some agencies, in policy and/or training, caution against "officer created jeopardy." For instance, the Philadelphia Police Department's deadly force policy [Directive 10] states that "police officers should ensure their actions do not precipitate the use of deadly force by placing themselves or others in jeopardy by taking unnecessary, overly aggressive, or improper actions." Similarly, the Miami Police Department policy [6.4.7. #10] directs that "police officers shall not unreasonably place themselves in a position where a threat of imminent danger of death or serious physical injury is created when attempting to approach, pursue, stop a motor vehicle or armed subject."

There appears to be an increased emphasis in training and policy on temporary retreat, a viable option that may serve, in part, to reduce unnecessary force. Promoting this option can be challenging in light of many officers' objections to the concept (Geller and Scott, 1992, 310). The Philadelphia Police Department tackles this objection head on in its policy: "Retreating or repositioning is not a sign of weakness or cowardice by an officer." Compared to the immediate use of force, retreating or repositioning "is often a tactically superior police procedure." The Denver Police Department, in the opening narrative of its policy (Use of Force Policy, § 105.00), highlights the importance of avoiding the need for force and the appropriateness of temporary retreat in some circumstances: "When reasonable under the totality of the circumstances, officers should use advisements, warnings, verbal persuasion, and other tactics and recognize that an officer may withdraw to a position that is tactically more secure or allows an officer greater distance in order to consider or deploy a greater variety of force options." In the Summary of Memorandum of Agreement with the Cincinnati Police Department, the U.S. Department of Justice required policy revisions that "will emphasize that de-escalation techniques, such as disengagement, area containment, surveillance, waiting out a subject, summoning reinforcements or calling in specialized units may be an appropriate response to a situation" [para. 3].

Critical Issues in Policy Enforcement

Policy on the use of force may have little impact on police behavior if the agency does not enforce it. To demonstrate a commitment to the judicious use of force, agencies can employ a variety of enforcement mechanisms such as use-of-force reporting, accessible and effective complaint review systems, early intervention systems, and departmental rewards. This section describes these options and identifies successful practices.

Use-of-Force Reporting

Departments document use of force by their officers to a much greater extent than in the past (Pate and Fridell, 1995; Zschoche and Fridell, 2006). In decades past, at best, officers described serious uses of force in their narratives of an incident. Today most agencies require officers to complete separate use-of-force reports for designated force types.[5] Agencies vary with regard to what they designate as "reportable force" (the uses of force that must be reported). The International Association of Chiefs of Police (IACP) model policy on this subject requires force reporting on physical force, chemical force, impact force, use of electronic equipment, and discharge of firearms. The Fresno Police Department (2003, 6) requires force to be reported when

- officers (including canines) use force and a person is injured;
- officers strike a person with a body part (e.g., fist, foot, elbow) or any object (e.g., flashlight, clipboard); or
- officers use (not merely display) a department-issued weapon (e.g., electronic immobilizing device, less-lethal impact projectile, chemical agents, baton, firearm).

The Denver Police Department requires officers to submit a use-of-force report if a firearm is discharged (outside of training); if an impact weapon, carotid compression technique, chemical agent, pepper ball, CED, or shotgun is used; if a canine is used or certain types of physical force, such as a hand strike, leg thrust, or kick; if a person is injured or killed; if a person complains of an injury or may claim injuries in the future; or if the subject is charged with resisting arrest and/or assault on an officer.

According to the IACP (1999) model policy, "All use-of-force reports shall specify the actions of the suspect that necessitated the use of force, the reasons why the officer used force, as well as any suspect complaints of injury, medical treatment received, or refusal of medical treatment" (§ IV.A.2). A key advantage of use-of-force forms over the old system of including narratives in incident reports is the ability to produce aggregate, quantifiable information. Check or code boxes can be tabulated (e.g., check/code boxes on officer/subject injuries, subject characteristics, levels of resistance encountered, and level and type of force used) allowing for the agency production of aggregate reports during specified time periods (e.g., quarterly, semiannually, or annually). Building on these empirical measures, Alpert and Dunham (1997, 2004) developed a system for reporting force that produces a measure of the force used by the officer *relative* to suspect resistance. For instance, if a department denotes five levels of suspect resistance (coded as 1–5) and five levels of officer response (similarly coded as 1–5), the force factor is the level of force used minus the level of resistance. Aggregate data can show how frequently officers respond with levels of force above or below suspect resistance, and/or if they matched the level of suspect resistance. These data can be used to evaluate force used by individual officers, to compare agencies to each other, or to research particular aspects of an agency's force incidents.

An early and meaningful review of the use-of-force forms by immediate supervisors is very important. As Klinger (2004) points out, supervisors should *analyze* these reports, "not just sign off." Supervisors should talk about force incidents with the people involved and with others—thus using the incidents as an opportunity to teach and train. Use-of-force forms are a valuable tool to promote learning. In fact, some agencies include the training unit on the list of entities that receive and review the forms.[6] By examining these forms, the training unit can identify instances or trends related to unnecessary or excessive force. Training can then be tailored to try to avoid past mistakes. Many agencies route the use-of-force forms up the chain of command, and sometimes all the way to the chief. The key to the review system is not the people who receive the forms but the degree to which the readers carefully consider their contents.

Review of Use-of-Force Complaints

To hold officers accountable and promote the prudent use of force, departments must have strong and effective systems of reviewing complaints. A department that is not interested in controlling the use and misuse of force can easily make the complaint review process a frustrating and ineffectual one. Without much proactive effort, it can keep complaints low by making the process unknown to residents, confusing, intimidating, or even risky. Even a department that allows complaints to be filed can institute an investigation process that is weak or intimidating or ensure that sustained complaints result in few consequences to officers.

Human Rights Watch (1998) describes the components of a complaint system that is effective. First of all, "barriers to filing of complaints" are removed. The complaint forms are simple, residents have clear instructions for filing them, and the process is free of intimidation. The Department of Justice consent decree for Detroit requires that the public be able to file complaints using any of a number of different methods—by making a telephone call, sending a facsimile, sending electronic or regular mail, submitting the complaint in person, speaking with a supervisor, and/or by completing a form by themselves. Effective systems make information about how to file complaints available to the public in various ways. This information can be posted in the police department and other public buildings, included on the agency Web site, or described in printed brochures available to individuals and community groups. Human Rights Watch emphasizes that this information should be in the "languages of the community."

A second key aspect of an effective system is meaningful investigation of complaints. Human Rights Watch (1998) calls for investigations that are "prompt, thorough and impartial." Agencies vary widely in the comprehensiveness and quality of their investigations of complaints. Common weaknesses in this process are (1) insufficient investigations (including lack of effort to find and meet with citizen witnesses or complainants), (2) interviews that serve to intimidate complainants and other citizen witnesses, (3) inordinately lengthy investigations, and (4) biased investigations to safeguard peers (Human Rights Watch, 1998; Independent Commission of the Los Angeles Police Department, 1991).

A third important component of an effective system is appropriate disciplinary action. "Light-handed counseling should never replace strong disciplinary actions in serious cases of abuse," according to Human Rights Watch (1998). Such counseling is "a misguided attempt to help officers who should, in fact, be punished or dismissed. Similarly, transfers should not be used as a tool to address an abuse problem."

Agencies that have removed barriers to filing, instituted meaningful investigative processes, and provided for appropriate dispositions for sustained complaints will have gone a long way toward producing a system that is not only effective but credible to the public. Citizen involvement in the complaint review process can also enhance system effectiveness and credibility (see Walker, 2001). Citizen involvement, however, remains a controversial topic. Advocates argue that the involvement of citizens in complaint review systems enhance police accountability and provide for a more independent and effective method for processing complaints. Opponents claim that civilians are not qualified to evaluate complaints of police practices, and that their involvement in such systems undermines the autonomy of the law enforcement agency (Alpert and Dunham, 2004).

Early Intervention Systems

Some departments have adopted early intervention systems (EIS) to identify officers who are at-risk of engaging in inappropriate behaviors, such as unnecessary or excessive use of force. An EIS contains officer-level data on, for instance, vehicle accidents, vehicle stops, searches, sick days, arrests, complaints, and uses of force. This information is regularly monitored in an attempt to identify officers who may be experiencing problems and to provide some type of intervention to help correct an officer's performance—ideally *before* formal disciplinary action is required or a critical incident occurs (Walker, Alpert, and Kenney, 2001). An EIS can be a powerful tool for supervisors and provide a structure of accountability for the entire police department.

In developing a system, agencies must (1) identify appropriate data elements to include, (2) determine "triggering thresholds" (i.e., the level of some measure that will prompt review), and (3) plan responses to thresholds in the form of interventions and monitoring (Walker et al., 2001). The U.S. Department of Justice, in the context of several of its consent decrees and memorandums of agreement (MOAs), recommends including the following force-related elements in an EIS: uses of force, complaints alleging use of force, civil lawsuits alleging use of excessive force, and the outcomes of force investigations and lawsuits regarding force. Assaults on the officer, resisting-arrest arrests, injuries sustained by the officer, and injuries sustained by opponents are other elements that could be included.

The data in the system are of no value unless someone is attending to it. In its consent decrees and MOAs, the Department of Justice requires that supervisors review the EIS data regularly for the officers they supervise. The data also must be reviewed when an officer is being considered for promotion, assigned as a field training officer, transferred to a different command, or applying to serve as an investigator. The Pittsburgh Police Department's early intervention system—Performance Assessment and Review System or PARS—has involved first-line supervisors perhaps more than any other. Under PARS, supervisors are required to log on to the system each day before roll call to identify any officer under their command who has been involved in an incident that is recorded in the PARS system (Walker, 2003). This approach ensures that supervisors are aware of the daily activities of their officers.

Various intervention strategies are available to assist "at-risk officers" who have been identified by EIS: peer counseling, supervisor counseling, training, reassignment, medical screening, and psychological counseling. However, there is no information on the quality, scope, and effectiveness of these interventions as they relate to use of force and other at-risk behaviors.

Departmental Reward Structure

An agency should ensure that it is not rewarding (overtly or subtly) inappropriate or neutral behavior. For example, one West Coast department reported to the author that it had previously given out medals to each and every officer who was involved in a shooting, unless the shooting was found to be in violation of policy. Fortunately, the agency later realized that these awards sent a message that a shooting was always a good thing—something to which each officer should aspire. The agency now gives out medals only for shootings in which the behavior or bravery of the officer was worthy of special commendation.

In addition to scrutinizing awards to ensure that they affirm only positive behaviors, agencies should provide reinforcements for commendable restraint and the use of tactics that lead to a nonforce (or mitigated force) outcome (Geller and Toch, 1995; Klockars, 1995). These reinforcements could come in the form of a report by the officer's supervisor that would go in the officer's file or annual awards that recognize commendable restraint and good tactics. The Toronto Police Use of Force Committee (1998) made such a recommendation: "The chief of police [should] ensure supervisors recognize good judgment by way of formal documentation when officers exercise restraint or minimize the use of force in violent or potentially violent situations" (Recommendation 2.2).

Critical Issues in Use-of-Force Training

In recent decades, the training police officers receive concerning the use of force has advanced considerably in several key respects. For example, the environments in which officers learn and test their firearms skills are more realistic. They receive training, not only on force skills, but also on when to use force and how much force to use. In addition, officers are trained in the use of tactics and verbal skills that can, in some situations, prevent force or reduce the level of force required.

Use-of-force training in the classroom and in other environments should cover the following components:

- Policy/law
- Psychology/physiology of mind/body during stress
- Force skills (marksmanship, defensive tactics)
- Decision making (when to use force and how much to use)
- Tactics and communication skills to prevent or mitigate force events.

Decision-Making Training

Police departments employ various training methods to help officers use good judgment when exercising force. In the classroom, trainers can verbalize appropriate responses or show videos of use-of-force circumstances and engage the class in an analysis of how best to respond. Role playing has become a critical aspect of force decision-making training; computer simulators, "marking cartridges" exercises (e.g., paint balls), and live exercises featuring pseudotargets on the firing range are all popular teaching methods. These methods simulate as closely as possible the interactions officers can have with subjects; in the best methods, some semblance of the physiological and psychological stress produced by real-life incidents is replicated.

As reported above, the first computer simulators portrayed films of subjects to which officers responded with decisions to shoot or not shoot. Advances in these computer simulators have been significant. The modern devices are able to

- use four panels around the officer, simulating 360° action;
- train officers on firearms, CEDs, chemical sprays, batons, and the use of canines;
- use real (untethered) weapons modified with cartridges (e.g., laser cartridges) that produce recoil;
- use weapons that show and record location, lethality, and timing of weapon discharge;
- accommodate training partners and teams (e.g., SWAT teams), not just single individuals;
- modify lighting to produce low-light situations;

- "shoot back" at the officer from the screen with nonlethal "bullets";
- produce interactive options so that the instructor can modify the unfolding of events depending on training needs or the officer's actions; and
- produce audio and videotapes of the sessions for purposes of critique/analysis.

Supplementing or serving as an alternative to computer simulators are the role-playing exercises mentioned earlier in which the trainee(s) interact with live (not filmed) subjects. These exercises might take place in vacant lots or buildings owned by the jurisdiction or in actual venues in the jurisdiction (e.g., in schools after hours). More and more agencies are using "marking cartridges" to simulate the discharging of weapons (usually firearms); the fired paint balls or other markers provide feedback on shooting accuracy. Real weapons can be modified to serve as marking-cartridge weapons, and the exercises can be videotaped and critiqued. Compared to computer simulators, the exercises have several advantages. They allow for greater movement by trainees, they produce higher stress levels (to simulate the stress in real-life use-of-force incidents), they enable officers to be trained in a greater number of force options, and an unlimited number of scenarios can be implemented.

Integrated Training

Agencies with state-of-the-art training programs fully integrate the various aspects and topics associated with force training. In 1996, Arnspiger and Bowers described a major weakness of force training: its disjointedness. Training had improved in terms of the number and types of topics taught and in the effectiveness and sophistication of methods for training officers in knowledge, judgment, and skill. Each topic or skill, however, was still being taught in isolation: officers learned firearm and decision-making skills, then they took a baton course on its usage, and then they took a corresponding course on chemical sprays, defensive tactics course, and so forth. In separate lectures and practice sessions trainees learned about communication skills, the importance of cover, and how to explain use-of-force decisions in court and in reports.

Cutting-edge training in the twenty-first century is integrated. Officers are trained to make decisions about whether to use force and what level of force to use *from the full range of options* (weaponless techniques, baton, chemical spray, CED, and so forth). Full integration also requires that trainees utilize, as appropriate, skills associated with preventing or mitigating the use of force. Whereas early computer simulators trained officers in "shoot/don't shoot," now models allow for officers to select, as appropriate, a wide variety of force options. Officers are able to use flashlights for illumination, take cover, and practice communication skills. The interactive capabilities allow the trainer to produce a prevented or mitigated force outcome based on the good tactics or use of effective communication skills by the trainee. Other role-playing techniques, including those involving marked cartridges, also encompass decision making across all levels of force (e.g., firearms, CED, OC) and require officers to practice tactical and communications skills. With trainers in padded "red suits," trainees can even utilize various forms of impact devices and physical combat techniques.

Intervening with Fellow Officers

Agencies need to provide sufficient levels of supervision and hold supervisors accountable for their officers' use of force. According to the Fresno Police Department (2003), "the key to preventing excessive use of force is to . . . ensure that field supervisors are available and have access to officers in the field." Some executives are holding peers, as well as supervisors, accountable for other officers' use of force on the job. The recently revised force policy of the Miami Police Department contains the following provision:

> At the scene of a police incident, many officers of the department may be present and some officers may not be directly involved in taking police actions. However, this does not relieve any officer present of the obligation to ensure that the requirements of the law and the Department regulations are complied with. Officers are expected to maintain control or intervene if the use of force against a subject clearly becomes excessive. Failure to do so may result in both criminal and civil liability. EXCESSIVE FORCE WILL NOT BE TOLERATED. [Department Order 2, Chapter 6, 6.1.3, emphasis in original]

The Los Angeles Police Department has improved the portion of academy training that teaches recruits how to intercede if a fellow officer is overreacting during an incident or is otherwise out of control. With role playing as a key mechanism, recruits are learning how to prevent and interrupt abuse of force. This training is consistent with the Human Rights Watch (1998) recommendation that officers "be encouraged and trained to intercede when their partners or fellow officers threaten or begin to engage in abuse."

There are difficult issues associated with this training and the real-life implementation of this desired intervention. First, some officers will be very reticent to challenge the actions of their fellow officers—even when it is clear that those actions are outside of policy. Shaping agency culture to set limits on the extent to which officers can and should support and protect their peers presents a very difficult challenge for agency executives. Second, there will be many instances in which it is not clear whether the officer using force is acting within departmental policy or outside of it. Some uses of force will be clearly outside policy, but there will be instances where the second officer at the scene did not observe the factors that led the first officer to use a specified level of force. Moreover, people can reasonably differ with regard to when and at what level force is justified. (Conclusions often cannot be reached regarding whether a use of force was justified until thorough investigations have been completed.) This second issue of whether an officer is acting inside or outside departmental policy will need to be addressed during the training on the need to intervene with peers. Trainers must specify the level of certainty that is appropriate before one officer intervenes with another who is using force.

Conclusion

The challenge for law enforcement executives is to optimize the use of force in their agencies. In this important endeavor, three elements are essential: sound policy, effective mechanisms for enforcing policy and producing accountability, and training that effectively conveys to officers when and how to use force appropriately. The policing profession has made tremendous progress in each of these areas over the past several decades.

Present-day policies are lengthy and detailed—greatly delimiting police power to use force against individuals. While much consensus has been achieved over the years in terms of *general* provisions in use-of-force policy, several issues are being debated regarding force policy content including use of deadly force against moving vehicles, drawing and pointing firearms, appropriate uses of CEDs, and avoiding unnecessary force.

Measures to promote policy adherence and accountability are more prevalent and effective in all realms of policing, including use of force. Most departments require documentation of officers' use of force, although agencies vary in terms of the types of force that must be reported. Similarly, virtually all departments have some form of complaint review; these systems vary in terms of their accessibility and integrity. To promote optimal use of force, some agencies have developed early intervention systems and others are scrutinizing more closely their reward structures.

Training has advanced from the officer shooting in bright light at a bull's eye sixty feet away to participating in technologically advanced, highly realistic judgment and skills training using multiple force options. Agencies strive to provide effective training to help officers make difficult, split-second decisions regarding what types of force to use in the various circumstances they may face, and to encourage and guide officers' intervention when their peers appear to be misusing force.

Despite incredible advances within the law enforcement profession, executives still grapple with critical issues regarding use-of-force policy, policy enforcement, and training. Law enforcement continues to strive—and likely always will strive—toward the optimized use of force.

NOTES

[1] "Deadly force" is force that is likely to cause death or serious bodily injury. Nondeadly force refers to all other types of force.

[2] Taser® is the brand name for the conducted energy device produced by Taser International, Inc.

[3] See Smith, Petrocelli, and Scheer (2007) for a legal analysis of CED-related court decisions.

[4] The electrical charge of the M26 and X26 models produced by Taser International lasts five seconds if the officer pulls the trigger and immediately releases it. An officer, however, can hold down the trigger to produce a longer activation.

[5] Typically, agencies refer to these reports as "use-of-force forms." The Miami Police Department and the Colorado Springs Police Department have labeled them "Response to Resistance Reports" and "Response to Aggression Reports," respectively.

[6] The Police Assessment Resource Center (2003) recommends that the commanding officer of the training division serve on the committee that reviews officer-involved shootings.

REFERENCES

Adams, K. and V. Jennison (2007). What we do not know about police use of Tasers. *Policing: An International Journal of Police Strategies and Management*, 30(3): 447–465.

Alpert, G. P. and R. G. Dunham (1997). *The force factor: Measuring police use of force relative suspect resistance.* Washington, DC: Police Executive Research Forum.

Alpert, G. P. and R. G. Dunham (2004). *Understanding police use of force: Officers, suspects, and reciprocity.* Cambridge, MA: Cambridge University Press.

American Civil Liberties Union of Northern California (2005). *Stun gun fallacy: How the lack of Taser regulation endangers lives.* San Francisco: Author.
http://www.aclunc.org/issues/criminal_justice/police_practices/
stun_gun_fallacy_how_the_lack_of_ taser_regulation_endangers_lives.shtml

Amnesty International (2004). USA: Excessive and lethal force? AI's concerns about deaths and ill-treatment involving police use of Tasers. http://www.amnesty.org/en/library/info/AMR51/139/2004

Amnesty International (2008). *"Less than lethal?": The use of stun weapons in U.S. law enforcement.* London: Author.

Arnspiger, B. R. and G. A. Bowers (November 1996). Integrated use-of-force training program. *FBI Bulletin.* http://www.fbi.gov/publications/leb/1996/nov961.txt

Chapman, S. G. (1967). Police policy on the use of firearms. *The Police Chief*, 16–37.

Chapman, S. G. and T. S. Crockett (1963). Gunsight dilemma: Police firearms policy. *Police*, May–June: 54.

Ederheimer, J. (2005). Use of force tools. In J. Ederheimer and L. A. Fridell (Eds.), *Chief concerns: Exploring the challenges of police use of force*, pp. 57–81. Washington, DC: Police Executive Research Forum.

Fresno Police Department (2003). Reportable use of force project, Final report. Fresno, CA: Author.

Fridell, L. A. (2008a). Less-lethal weapon deployment, policy and training: Results from a national survey. Presentation at the Police Use of Force: Less Lethal Weapons and In-Custody Deaths conference sponsored by the Institute for Law Enforcement Administration, Plano, Texas, September 29–October 1.

Fridell, L. A. (2008b). Deadly force policy and practice: The forces of change. Unpublished manuscript.

Fridell, L. A. and A. M. Pate (1993). Do non-lethal weapons prevent lethal consequences? *The Torch*, 28(2): 1.

Fridell, L. A. and A. M. Pate (1997). Use of force: A matter of control. In M. Dantzker (Ed.), *Police today and tomorrow: Contemporary personnel issues and trends*, pp. 217–256. Oxford, UK: Butterworth-Heinemann.

Fyfe, J. J. (1987). The Metro-Dade Police/Citizen Violence Reduction Project: Summary of findings and recommendations. Paper presented at the Annual Meeting of the American Society of Criminology, Montreal, November.

Fyfe, J. J. (1988). The Metro-Dade Police/Citizen Violence Reduction Project: Final report, executive summary. Submitted by the Police Foundation to the Metro-Dade Police Department, June.

Geller, W. A. and M. S. Scott (1992). *Deadly force: What we know.* Washington, DC: Police Executive Research Forum.

Geller, W. A. and H. Toch, Eds. (1995). *And justice for all: Understanding and controlling police abuse of force.* Washington, DC: Police Executive Research Forum.

Government Accounting Office (2005). *Taser weapons: Use of Tasers by selected agencies.* Report to the Chairman, Subcommittee in National Security, Emerging Threats and International Relations, Committee on Government Reform, House of Representatives. Washington, DC: U.S. Government Printing Office.

Human Rights Watch (1998). *Shielded from justice: Police brutality and accountability in the United States of America.* New York: Author.

Ijames, S. and J. Ederheimer (2007). Less-lethal weaponry and less-lethal force decision making. In J. Ederheimer (Ed.), *Strategies for resolving conflict and minimizing use of force,* pp. 71–96. Washington, DC: Police Executive Research Forum.

Independent Commission of the Los Angeles Police Department (1991). *Report of the Independent Commission of the Los Angeles Police Department.* Los Angeles: Author.

International Association of Chiefs of Police (1999). *Model policy: Use of force.* Arlington, VA: Author.

Jenkinson, E., C. Necson, and A. Bleetman (2006). The relative risk of police use-of-force options: Evaluating the potential for deployment of electronic weaponry. *Journal of Clinical Forensic Medicine,* 13: 229–241.

Johnson, W., M. Warren, J. Ederheimer, and L. A. Fridell (2007). Conducted energy devices: PERF's national studies and guidelines for consideration. In J. Ederheimer (Ed.), *Strategies for resolving conflict and minimizing use of force,* pp. 99–132. Washington, DC: Police Executive Research Forum.

Klinger, D. (2004). Interview with David Klinger, a former police officer, author of numerous articles and books on policing, and a professor at the University of Missouri, St. Louis.

Klockars, C. (1995). A theory of excessive force and its control. In W. A. Geller and H. Toch (Eds.), *And justice for all: Understanding and controlling police abuse of force.* Washington, DC: Police Executive Research Forum.

Matulia, K. (1982). *A balance of forces.* Gaithersburg, MD: International Association of Chiefs of Police.

Meyer, G. (2008). Nonlethal weapons: The promise and the challenge. *Law Enforcement Executive Forum,* 8(4): 41–52.

Morrison, G. B. (2002). Police firearms training survey, 2001: Polices, programs, and practices of state, and large municipal and county departments. Unpublished report.

Morrison, G. B. (2003). Police and correctional department firearm training frameworks in Washington State. *Police Quarterly,* 6(2): 192–221.

Nielsen, E. (1983). Policy on the police use of deadly force: A cross-sectional analysis. *Journal of Police Science and Administration,* 11: 104–108.

Pate, A. M. and L. A. Fridell (1993). *Police use of force: Official reports, citizen complaints, and legal consequences,* Vol. I and II. Washington, DC: The Police Foundation.

Pate, A. M. and L. A. Fridell (1995). Toward the uniform reporting of police use of force: Results of a national survey. *Criminal Justice Review,* 20(2): 123–145.

Police Assessment Resource Center (2003). The Portland Police Bureau: Officer-involved shootings and in-custody deaths. A report submitted to the Portland City Council. http://www.parc.info/pubs/

President's Commission on Law Enforcement and the Administration of Justice (1967). *A national survey of police-community relations: Field surveys V.* Washington, DC: U.S. Government Printing Office.

Scharf, P. and A. Binder (1983). *The badge and the bullet: Police use of deadly force.* New York: Praeger.

Sherman, L. (1983). Reducing police gun use: Critical events, administrative policy, and organizational change. In M. Punch (Ed.), *The management and control of police organizations*, pp. 98–125. Cambridge: MIT Press.

Skolnick, J. and J. J. Fyfe (1993). *Above the law: Police and the excessive use of force.* New York: Free Press.

Smith, M. R., R. J. Kaminski, G. P. Alpert, L. A. Fridell, J. MacDonald, and B. Kubu (2008). A multi-method evaluation of police use of force outcomes: Final report to the National Institute of Justice. Unpublished report.

Smith, M. R., R. J. Kaminski, J. Rojek, G. P. Alpert, and J. Mathis (2007). The impact of conducted energy devices and other types of force and resistance on officer and suspect injuries. *Policing: An International Journal of Police Strategies and Management*, 30(3): 423–446.

Smith, M. R., M. Petrocelli, and C. Scheer (2007). Excessive force, civil liability, and the Taser in the nation's courts: Implications for law enforcement policy and practice. *Policing: An International Journal of Police Strategies and Management*, 30(3): 398–422.

Toronto Use of Force Committee (1998). *Final report.* Toronto: Toronto Police Association.

Waegel, W. B. (1984). The use of lethal force by police: The effect of statutory change. *Crime and Delinquency*, 31: 121–140.

Walker, S. (2001). *Police accountability: The role of civilian oversight.* New York: Wadsworth.

Walker, S. (2003). Early intervention systems for police state of the art conference. Unpublished report to the Office of Community Oriented Policing Services.

Walker, S., G. P. Alpert, and D. J. Kenney (2001). Early warning systems: Responding to the problem police officer. *Research in Brief.* Washington, DC: National Institute of Justice.

Walker, S. and L. A. Fridell (1992). Forces of change in police policy: The impact of *Tennessee v. Garner. American Journal of Police*, XI(3): 97–112.

White, M. D. (2000). Assessing the impact of administrative policy on use of deadly force by on- and off-duty police. *Evaluation Review*, 24(3): 295–318.

White, M. D. (2001). Controlling police decisions to use deadly force: Reexamining the importance of administrative policy. *Crime and Delinquency*, 37(1): 131–151.

Zschoche, R. and L. A. Fridell (2006). Accountability and the use of force. Paper presented at the meeting of the American Society of Criminology, Los Angeles, November.

32

State-Created Danger
Should Police Officers Be Accountable for
Reckless Tactical Decision Making?

Jeffrey J. Noble & Geoffrey P. Alpert

Police officers are called upon to resolve our society's shortcomings by arresting those who commit crimes, manage those with mental illness, and resolve violent and dangerous situations. Often these situations happen in the middle of the night, with little or no warning and no opportunity to develop a comprehensive plan, seek advice, or refer to a manual. The police are expected to intervene quickly and to make what are often critical decisions. For the most part America's police are up to the task, but not all tactical decisions are sound. And while poor judgments based on limited information or insufficient time or even mistakes may be understandable, reckless acts that provoke violence must not be tolerated.

Situations where police officers respond with force to extricate themselves from a dangerous position that they created are particularly troubling. For example, officers who use their bodies as a barricade to prevent a driver from fleeing are not only foolish but are also reckless—a significant problem that is compounded when officers who deliberately place themselves in danger fire their weapons at the vehicle in "self-defense." This is magnified when the police have the opportunity to plan, to summon resources, and to respond in a tactically sound manner but fail to do so through incompetence, laziness, or expediency. This article will review the use of force by police officers and consider the implications of tactically unsound or reckless decision making when the danger necessitating the force was created by the officer.

Prepared especially for *Critical Issues in Policing* by Jeffrey J. Noble and Geoffrey P. Alpert.

Police Tactics

Police officers are the nation's front line in dealing with noncompliant, resistive, combative, mentally ill, and violent subjects. Because these situations are almost always fluid, dynamic, and unique there are no predetermined steps that may be applied in every case to achieve a desired result; it is impossible to prepare a police officer for every imaginable field situation. There are, however, predictable types of behavior and reasonable tactical strategies that allow officers to avoid placing themselves and others at a substantial risk of injury and to decrease the need to impose a significant level of force to resolve the situation. Police management can structure meaningful guidelines and training to achieve these worthwhile goals. The methods and techniques employed by officers to exercise legitimate control are referred to as tactics. Tactics are best described as a sequence of moves that limit the suspect's ability to inflict harm and advance the ability of the officer to conclude the situation in the safest and least intrusive way.

Police officers are trained how to evaluate and manage potentially violent field situations and how to apply tactics to minimize the danger of risk to themselves and others. Officers are trained to formulate a plan whenever possible by gathering information, considering risk factors, assembling sufficient resources, communicating with other officers, and using available time to their advantage. Officers understand the value of cover and concealment, contact and cover strategies, and calm and effective negotiation skills. They are well versed in containing scenes, setting perimeters, isolating suspects and evacuating those in harm's way. Modern police officers are also provided a wide range of tools to minimize the necessity to use serious or deadly force, including less lethal options like pepper spray, Tasers®, and impact projectiles. Tactics are first taught in the police academy and are reinforced and refreshed through continuing professional training. Supervisors debrief officers about tactical situations so that the lessons learned can be applied in other situations. Police tactics are routinely discussed, emphasized, and reviewed at all levels of a police organization. The focus on safety stems from the recognition that when officers perform poorly, they place themselves, community members, and/or suspects at risk of severe or fatal injuries.

Law enforcement continually considers high-risk situations and sometimes makes wholesale changes in recommended tactics based on an incident or a series of incidents. For perspective, consider the 1966 Texas tower incident where Charles Whitman began randomly shooting at people, killing 14 and wounding dozens more.[1] The police response depended on the independent actions of responding officers, which mostly consisted of uncoordinated handgun and rifle fire that had little effect other than to chip away at the tower. Some officers commandeered armored cars to rescue the wounded; others commandeered an airplane that allowed the officers to shoot down on Whitman, but the plane was quickly driven back by Whitman's gunfire. Finally, several officers were able to access the tower through a system of tunnels. After climbing 30 flights of stairs, the officers confronted Whitman, who was killed in an ensuing gun battle.[2]

The Austin police were fortunate to stop Whitman, but the efforts took over 90 minutes. Although the independent, improvised actions of the officers resolved the incident, police departments across the nation recognized the need for a better response to incidents of this magnitude. The Texas tower incident, along with the Watts riots a year earlier, were the impetus for the formation of special teams of police officers equipped and trained to deal with dangerous and unusual criminal incidents. Known by various names and acronyms—Special Weapons and Tactics (SWAT), Hostage Rescue Teams (HRT), Special Response Teams (SRT), Special Emergency Response Teams (SERT), and Special Operations Units (SOU)—tactical teams have proliferated since the Texas tower incident.[3]

Just as the Texas tower incident and the Watts riots of the 1960s were the impetus for the formation of police paramilitary units (PPUs), events in the 1990s dramatically changed the police response to dynamic reactive incidents. North Hollywood (CA), Littleton (CO), Jonesboro (AR) and Atlanta (GA) all shared the common tragedy of ongoing random shootings of unarmed citizens. Individuals exhibiting aberrant human behavior kept firing until there were no more victims in the area or because of an independent act of courage by a uniformed police officer. Law enforcement officials recognized that the traditional tactics of containment, negotiation, and activation of PPUs were ineffective in these situations. Learning from their collective experience, law enforcement trainers developed an "active shooter" rapid response technique.[4]

While the development of PPUs and active shooter response protocols have increased the ability of police officers to resolve certain types of violent behavior, law enforcement has continually worked to improve the tactics employed by officers to resolve a myriad of unpredictable high-risk situations. Although officers are generally well trained, well prepared, and quite capable of resolving violent confrontations in a safe and reasonable manner, mistakes are made. Confronting threats of serious or deadly injury that require immediate action differs significantly from considering theoretical sets of circumstances or situations that allow time to gather resources for a comprehensive response. While it is reasonable to expect mistakes in situations that require split-second decisions, it is unreasonable to allow officers to act recklessly to provoke a violent response.[5]

Unsound Tactical Decision Making

Unsound decisions in the face of predictable violent behavior sometimes set a series of events into motion that can result in tragedy. Officer-created jeopardy often results when dealing with suspects inside vehicles, failing to use available cover, and acting too hastily without waiting for backup. Incidents involving vehicles are perhaps the most common root cause of officer error involving lack of discipline and poor decision making. The officer may engage in provocative acts that cause the suspect to respond in a way that leaves the officer no reasonable alternative other than to use force in self-defense.

Tactical shortcomings involving vehicles include officers using their bodies as barricades, attempting to grab keys from the ignition, forcibly trying to extricate someone from a vehicle, or holding onto a moving vehicle. Unfortunately, there are many court cases over the use of deadly force that illustrate these errors in judgment.

Kimberly Raso, an off-duty officer, attempted to arrest a shoplifter who managed to flee from the store and enter his vehicle.[6] The officer placed her body in front of the vehicle to prevent the suspect's escape after the suspect had already collided with other vehicles. The shoplifter inched his vehicle toward the officer, but when the officer refused to move, the shoplifter suddenly accelerated toward the officer, and the officer fired in self-defense.

Terry Allen left his house after an altercation with his wife and children. He took ammunition and several guns with him and parked in front of his sister's house. The Muskogee Police Department was alerted that Allen was armed and had threatened family members; a radio dispatcher advised that he was suicidal.[7] Instead of containing the scene, seeking a position of cover, and trying to talk the man into surrendering, arriving officers left their cover and tried to wrestle the gun from the man's hand. During the struggle, the man pointed the gun at one of the officers; in response the officers shot and killed the man.

Ernestine Ruffin, a police officer working a prostitution sting, observed a woman believed to be a prostitute entering a vehicle with a man. Ruffin followed the car until it parked, keeping in radio contact with other officers from the vice squad.[8] Ruffin approached the car with a handgun in one hand and opened the car door with her other hand. She ordered the two passengers to place their hands in view. The officer did not wait a few seconds for additional backup, and she did not illuminate the interior of the car with a flashlight. The driver moved suddenly, and Ruffin shot the unarmed suspect, thinking he was reaching for a shotgun (it was a wooden nightstick). The bullet lodged near his spinal cord causing permanent damage.

Officers who fail to seek or who abandon a position of cover are rejecting a basic tenet of officer safety. A position of cover allows officers to attempt to negotiate a peaceful solution while waiting for additional resources that may provide the means to conclude a tense and potentially dangerous situation safely. When officers do not use available cover, tactical situations may quickly escalate into unnecessary use of force. In a 2001 court case, officers were attempting to arrest a man for violating bail.[9] The man claimed he had a gun and exited his home holding something wrapped in towel. Officers initially reacted appropriately by shooting a blunt force round (beanbag) and released a police dog, but neither less-lethal force was effective. Rather than attempting any additional tactics, an officer decided to leave his position of cover to knock the man down. Believing that the man was armed, the officer had no alternative once he left his position of cover than to fire when the man turned in his direction.

Finally, officers are trained to understand that time is a valuable tactical asset. Time allows officers to plan, wait for resources to arrive and be deployed, and to consider alternative tactics. Unnecessary hurried actions are almost always a significant tactical error, particularly when there is clear evi-- dence of the dangers of moving too quickly. Joel Dickerson was intoxicated and fired a handgun nine times inside his home. A neighbor called the police, and the dispatcher issued the highest priority code for officers to respond. McClellan saw the neighbor but failed to ask whether anyone else was inside the house. He parked and waited for backup. The two officers immediately entered the home without waiting for additional backup, without setting a perimeter, and without making any attempts to negotiate the suspect's surrender. Once inside, the man threatened the officers with a handgun, and the officers shot and killed the man. Police radio tapes showed that only one minute had passed from the time that the officers arrived to the time when they shot the man. Entering a home under those circumstances exhibited a wanton disregard for the officers' own safety as well as the safety of others.

Use-of-Force Law

Police officers are entrusted to use some physical coercion to control and apprehend those who are suspected of engaging in criminal activity or those who place the officer or others at risk of being harmed. While the government permits the police the authority to use force on behalf of the community, that force is closely monitored. Any force that is not objectively reasonable is deemed to be excessive.[10] The seminal case on police use of force is *Graham v. Connor.* In that case, the Court held that force claims are analyzed under the Fourth Amendment's reasonableness standard, which balances the "nature and quality of the intrusion on the individual's Fourth Amendment interests against the countervailing government interest at stake."[11] The Court held that the "proper application requires careful attention to the facts and circumstances of each case including the severity of the crime at issue, whether the suspect poses an immediate threat to the safety of officers or others, and whether he is actively resisting arrest or attempting to evade arrest by flight." Reasonableness "of a particular use of force must be judged from the perspective of a reasonable officer on scene, rather than with the 20/20 vision of hindsight."[12]

One aspect of this holding that has not been studied sufficiently is the effect of stress and adrenalin on an officer's perception of an event. While research has shown that stress affects officers' performance and perception, it has not pinpointed the ways in which officers interpret threats under extreme stress.[13] In its holding, *Graham* refers to the Court's prior holding in *Garner* that the question is "whether the totality of the circumstances justified a particular sort of search or seizure.'"[14] Although the standard outlined in *Graham* instructs one to look at the totality of the circumstances to determine if the officer's actions were objectively reasonable, one portion of *Graham* has caused confusion among the circuit courts that have created rules neglecting the totality of the circumstances and focusing analysis only on the final frame. "With respect to a claim of excessive force, the same standard of reasonableness at the *moment* [italics added] applies: 'Not every push or shove, even if it may later seem unnecessary in the peace of a judges' chambers,' (citation omitted) violates the Fourth Amendment. The calculus of reasonableness must embody allowance for the fact that police officers are often forced to make split-second judgments—in circumstances that are tense, uncertain, and rapidly evolving—about the amount of force that is necessary in a particular situation." Some circuit courts have interpreted the word "moment" and "split-second judgment" to limit the analysis of a use-of-force incident to only the facts at the moment of the use of force. These courts hold that the events leading up to the use of force are irrelevant. This is referred to as the "final frame" analysis because only the instant prior to the use of force is considered.[15]

Final Frame

There is little consistency among the circuit courts in determining the scope of actions to be reviewed in a police use-of-force case. Some circuits review the totality of the circumstances to determine reasonableness, others review only the moment force was used, and still others have created their own rules. The circuits that employ a totality of the circumstances analysis include the First, Third, Sixth, Seventh, and Eleventh Circuits. The First Circuit has held that the proper rule is to examine the events leading up to the use of force, not just the moment, because such a rule is more consistent with the Supreme Court's mandate for courts to consider these cases in the totality of the circumstances.[16] The Third Circuit is willing to review evidence of events preceding the seizure and has found that "totality" is an encompassing word that implies that reasonableness should be sensitive to all of the factors bearing on an officer's use of force. "A more fundamental point is that it is far from clear what circumstances, if any, are left to be considered when events leading up to the shooting are excluded. How is the reasonableness of a bullet striking someone to be assessed if not by examining preceding events?"[17]

The Sixth Circuit found that the court should first identify the seizure at issue and then examine whether the force used to effect that seizure was reasonable in the totality of the circumstances—not whether it was reasonable for the police to create the circumstances. The court reasoned that "the time frame is a crucial aspect of excessive force. Other than random attacks, all such cases begin with the decision of a police officer to do something, to help, to arrest, to inquire. If the officer had decided to do nothing, then no force would have been used. In this sense, the police officer always causes the trouble. But it is trouble which the police officer is sworn to cause, which society pays him to cause and which, if kept within constitutional limits, society praises the officer for causing."[18]

The Seventh Circuit reviews the totality of the circumstances[19] and has held that police officers who unreasonably create a physically threatening situation in the midst of a Fourth Amendment seizure cannot be immunized for their use of deadly force.[20] The Eleventh Circuit also looks at the officer's conduct to determine if the officer created the circumstances where it became necessary to use deadly force in self-defense[21] and reviews the totality of the circumstances that include officer's statements.[22]

Other circuits look at the moment of the seizure but add qualifying language that creates a unique analysis in each circuit. The Second Circuit looks at conduct "immediately prior to and at the moment" that the officer used force.[23] The Fourth Circuit found that evidence that an officer may have recklessly created a dangerous situation during the arrest was not relevant to deciding the reasonableness of the behavior,[24] yet they will consider actions "immediately prior" to the use of force.[25] The Eighth Circuit excludes evidence about whether the officers' created the need to use force by mishandling the encounter because that evidence is not related to the reasonableness of the seizure itself. However, it adds to confusion about when prior actions are relevant to the reasonableness standard by stating, "But this does not mean we should refuse to let juries draw reasonable inferences from evidence about events surrounding and leading up to the seizure."[26] The Tenth Circuit looks at the precise moment that force was used but will also consider the officer's conduct prior to the suspect's threat of force if the conduct is "immediately connected" to the suspect's threat of force.[27]

Still other circuits have created their own unique rules to determine how, if, or what circumstances should be considered. The Fifth Circuit found "The constitutional right to be free from unreasonable seizure has never been equated by the Court with the right to be free from a negligently executed stop or arrest. There is no question about the fundamental interest in a person's own life, but it does not follow that a negligent taking of a life is a constitutional deprivation."[28] The Ninth Circuit has created an entirely different test. It will look beyond the moment of the force application and will hold an officer liable for his otherwise reasonable use of force if the officer intentionally and recklessly provokes a violent confrontation. However, it requires that the provocation be an independent Fourth Amendment violation.[29] The requirement is based on a prior Ninth Circuit decision where public health officials obtained an administrative forcible entry warrant to investigate a sewage leak. Upon their arrival, the resident threatened to get a gun, so a SWAT team was summoned. The SWAT officers forced entry into the home and confronted the mentally ill resident who twice tried to shoot the officers. The officers returned fire and killed the man. The court held that the massively disproportionality of the response to the problem of a leaky sewer pipe rendered the entry unreasonable; based on the Fourth Amendment violation of an unlawful, entry the court held the use of force to be unreasonable.[30]

The circuits that advocate an analysis other than the totality of the circumstances are overlooking the holding in *Graham* that requires careful attention to the facts and circumstances of each case including the severity of the crime and whether the suspect is actively resisting or is attempting to evade arrest by flight. These circuits focus only on whether the suspect poses an immediate threat to the officers or others. Such a limited view prevents a thorough analysis of the most intrusive action of the authority of the state—the death of one of its citizens. Most importantly, this wide disparity among the circuits demands some intervention by the Supreme Court to create a rule that may be uniformly applied.

Split-Second Decision Making

There are clearly sound policy reasons for deferring to the tactical decisions of police officers confronted with resistance and little time to consider alternatives. Indeed, the law should not be so strict that it makes officers hesitant to act—increasing the likelihood of injury to the officers, or worse, the unwillingness of officers to act at all, placing the community at risk. Police officers who make split-second decisions in dangerous situations should be provided with a fairly wide zone of protection even if there is a plausible claim that the situation could have been handled better or differently.[31] However, when a situation does not require a split-second decision and it evolves at a pace where reasonable alternatives may be considered and implemented, the law should encourage officers to avoid acting in reckless ways. In fact, officers should be trained and encouraged to reduce the need for making split-second decisions and to slow down the pace of an encounter rather than to intensify it.[32]

Experienced, well-trained, and well-meaning police officers will make informed decisions about whether the use of force is necessary under ideal circumstances. If informed about the situation they will confront and provided sufficient time to develop a rational response, they will implement the appropriate course of action. However, this ideal situation does not often exist. There are always situations where police officers are required to make critical decisions under adverse conditions, with insufficient information, under severe time restraints, and with the potential for significant risk of injury to themselves or others. Even these very difficult factors do not necessarily place the officer in a position whether there is truly only a *split-second* to make a decision.

The idea that police officers will only make key decisions in most potentially violent confrontation at the last instant under acute time stress (known as the *split-second syndrome*) overlooks the thought process of officers in advance of any decision to use force.[33] The reality of policing is that there are very few instances where police officers have only a split second to make a significant use-of-force determination. If an officer is suddenly and without warning confronted by an armed man or if an officer responds to a traffic collision and is instantaneously assaulted by a person suffering from a mental illness, the officer must make split-second decisions to defend him- or herself and others. In these situations of random violent acts, officers may have no control over the preliminary frames and are forced to make split-second decisions to prevent serious bodily injury to themselves or others. In a true instance of split-second decision making, the analysis is much easier to complete as there are no preliminary frames to review.[34]

More frequently officers will have at least some knowledge about the situation that they are about to confront. When officers have both knowledge and time yet still recklessly provoke a violent response, unnecessary force has occurred.[35] In most situations, police officers have three available frames of analysis for the decision-making process: (1) activities prior to any contact with the suspect, (2) contact with the suspect, and (3) the decision whether to use force to control the situation.[36]

Regarding the first frame, police officers rarely stumble onto the scene of a crime without any warning. Most often, they respond to some external stimulus. Typically, information is provided to officers verbally by a witness, through a dispatcher after a community members calls the police, or from their own observations. This communication provides the officer with at least a minimum amount of information and allows the officers to conduct some level of tactical planning. These initial bits of information allow the officer to begin their planning process and to make assessments for subsequent steps. Tactical planning and preparation allows police officers to make sound decisions that will minimize the danger to the officer, to the community, and to the actor who is creating the risky situation. The opportunity to plan for a tactical response can be divided into three categories: those where there are hours, days, or weeks for preparation; those where there are minutes; and those where the officer is confronted instantly.

Police officers are trained to develop plans before taking action whenever possible. The more time available during the planning process, the more comprehensive the plan. The first step in the planning process is to collect as much relevant and reliable information as possible. This information gathering stage may be complex, like conducting undercover reconnaissance to determine the layout of a building prior to the execution of a search warrant. It may be limited to asking the dispatcher for additional information as an officer responds to a call or to a request for another officer for backup. The execution of a search warrant or the monitoring of a scheduled protest allows hours, days, or weeks for extensive planning. For these types of events, one would expect a comprehensive written plan that indicates staffing, supervision, a clear mission statement, and considerable contingency planning. Conversely, when time is limited to a few minutes, the planning process may consist of coordinating the response with other responding officers, efforts to seek additional information, or requests for additional resources.[37]

Concurrently during the information gathering phase, the officer is engaged in analysis. The officer should consider specific risk factors, available resources, the area where the incident is occurring, the speed of the response, and the potential need to contain the scene, isolate the suspect, or evacuate those at risk of harm in the area. The analytical process breaks down the overall incident into its component parts and allows the officer to develop the initial tactical plan. The progression is from observation to orientation to decision making to action.[38]

Officers have an opportunity to continue their decision-making efforts at the point when they initially contact the suspect. The officer is able to make visual observations of the suspect that provide the officer with a wealth of information. It is during these first few critical seconds that the officer will be able to assess whether the suspect is armed or is potentially armed, whether others are at immediate risk, whether the suspect is coherent or irrational, the size of the suspect, the environment, and—importantly—the suspect's response as the officer begins to negotiate by communicating in a calm and deliberate way. Even if this initial contact lasts only a few seconds, the officer has had an opportunity to gain a vast amount of information that may be used in deciding whether the use of force is necessary.

Typically, it is only after these steps that the officer will make a decision to use force. Clearly, all force decisions are made at the last moment and should be based on the totality of the circumstances that the officer confronts and ultimately the actions of the suspect that places the officer or others at risk of immediate harm. Making a force decision early would be imprudent; circumstances may change that eliminate the need for or the level of force necessary. Holding the officer accountable for only the final frame would be equally imprudent because the final frame may not justify the officer's actions. Consider an officer who fires at an individual who reaches for his waistband. This frame alone could never justify the use of force, particularly the use of deadly force. However, if the imaginary motion picture were backed up to the series of frames that led to the final frame where the force was implemented, those frames may reveal facts that would make the officer's action objectively reasonable, justifying the use of force.

Standards

The *Graham* Court clearly articulated the standard of objectively reasonable conduct to differentiate the amount of force that may be exercised and the amount of force deemed to be excessive. However, reasonableness is sometimes an elusive concept. The concept of reasonableness is particularly difficult when applied to a police use of force where the officer lacks a bad motive and the suspect is morally blameworthy. From a police procedural standpoint, there are several significant questions. What is a reasonable error? How should officers be held accountable for their mistakes or negligent acts? Should some higher standard such as gross negligence or recklessness be applied, or should departments employ the standards developed by the circuits who only review the moment that the force was applied, ignoring all of the officer's actions prior to that point?

A mistake is an error that results from a defect in judgment or a deficiency of knowledge. Mistakes in policing most frequently occur when an officer misinterprets information or when factors crucial for the decision-making process are not recognized or identified.[39] Mistakes are a subset of simple negligence. Simple negligence is defined as the failure to exercise ordinary care or a deviation from the conduct of a reasonable person of ordinary prudence under the circumstances.[40] Under such a standard, the intention of the officer is not a factor, and acts of inadvertent behavior could create officer liability. Application of a simple negligence standard would not consider the reality of policing where decisions are made in a rapidly changing and possibly dangerous environment. Such a standard could create a chilling effect on officers who may fear that their well intentioned or inadvertent actions may subject them to civil liability.

Using the benefit of 20/20 hindsight, use-of-force experts are very adept at identifying mistakes or negligent actions that officers could have performed differently. They will point out that the officer could have retreated, used a less-lethal tool like pepper spray, or waited for backup. They will suggest that the officer should have called for more officers, a supervisor, a SWAT team, a negotiator, a K-9, an armored vehicle, or even a helicopter. They will advocate that if officers had all their equipment (or better equipment), if their weapons were holstered safely, if their attention had not been diverted, if they were neither too close nor too far—or any other mitigating factor—the situation could have been resolved peacefully. It is exactly this type of review that the Supreme Court sought to avoid. Subjecting crisis decision making that involved mistakes or simple negligence to hypercritical assessment in the calm and safety of a courtroom could be an obstruction to effective policing.

A standard of recklessness is a more serious transgression against common police practice than simple negligence. Recklessness is a disregard for or indifference to the dangers of a situation or for the consequences of one's actions.[41] Intentional acts involving a known or obvious risk create a high probability that harm will occur.[42] Recklessness should not be confused with bravery, where a person demonstrates a reasonable level of fear, rather than none at all. A reckless officer may be seen by some as heroic—consider an officer who, without regard for his or her own safety, fearlessly charges into a building to confront an armed assailant. This type of reckless display is more often a blunder that places the officer or others at great risk with little true benefit. The reckless act of charging into a situation causes the suspect to react. The suspect is faced with a split-second decision; unlike the officer, the suspect has had no training, has demonstrated poor decision-making skills by failing to immediately surrender or comply with the officer's commands, may be under the influence of a drug or alcohol, and may suffer from a mental deficiency.

Unfortunately, neither simple negligence nor recklessness is an appropriate standard. The application of a simple negligence standard would be too unforgiving to officers who are responding to the actions of a suspect in situations that may be dangerous and volatile. Such a standard may cause officers to refuse to act to avoid the risk of liability while allowing the community to absorb the risk that the police were intended to manage. Recklessness, on the other hand, may be difficult to prove. Gross errors alone do not necessarily indicate the intentional disregard of known and obvious risks.

A gross negligence standard is perhaps the appropriate standard to apply in the determination of objective reasonableness. Gross negligence is not easy to define, but it falls somewhere between simple negligence and reckless-ness.[43] Gross negligence is a conscious and voluntary disregard of the need to use reasonable care to prevent foreseeable grave injury or harm to persons. It is conduct that is extreme when compared with simple negligence, which is a mere failure to exercise reasonable care. Gross negligence is much more than any mere mistake resulting from inexperience, excitement, or confusion—and more than mere thoughtlessness, simple inattention, or inadvertent errors.[44] A standard of gross negligence to determine reasonableness would balance the need to allow officers to make mistakes or acts that may amount to simple negligence with the necessity for a remedy when officers needlessly provoke a violent confrontation.

Effective Realistic Training
to Improve Tactical Decision Making

While it is true that no amount of perfect planning can prevent random violence, it is also true that planning and training can help first responders exercise good judgment and employ effective tactics to save lives, prevent injuries, and resolve dynamic tactical situations. Much of police use-of-force training has been criticized. For example, shooting drills for officers who are comfortably positioned a few yards away from a fixed target have limited utility when dealing with the random violence of a disturbed individual. Two-dimensional interactive videos that test only the "final frame" of an encounter do not teach officers how to plan and coordinate their approach and initial actions. Role playing, although more realistic, does not always create the level of stress that would be generated by the danger and uncertainty of a field situation.[45] Recognizing that police tactics require practical application and have little value if the officer cannot apply his or her learning to field situations, many police organizations have begun to focus their use-of-force training on decision-making models that are applied in the most realistic environment possible.

Technology has improved over the last several years; with video simulators, developers can create much more realistic interactive simulations. Although not as ideal as interacting in the field, this new generation of simulators allows officers to plan their approach, communicate with other officers, and be tested on their tactical decision-making skills. These new simulators use firearms identical to those that officers deploy in the field. The weapons are no longer tethered to a machine; they are carried in the officer's holster to be deployed only when necessary. The trainer has the option to change the video scenarios based on the officer's actions, creating situations that may, or may not, require a force application. This type of "shoot—don't shoot" training reinforces the officer's decision-making skills and forces the officer to consider alternatives other than force to resolve the encounter. But perhaps the greatest innovative aspect of these simulators is the ability to literally shoot back at the officer. Equipped with a compressed air cannon, the trainer can fire plastics projectiles at the student. These plastic balls do not injure the student, but they are painful and serve as an immediate reminder that the officer failed to take appropriate cover when cover was available. The ability to fire back at the officers also places the officers under duress simulating conditions in the field.

The first generation of 360-degree simulators that function as part of a live firing range have also become available for trainers. Over the last decade, these simulators allow the officers to drive their vehicle into a firing range and confront situations that may be occurring in front of them, to their sides, or even behind the officer. This type of simulation allows a greater amount of time to judge the officer's initial actions, to hear his or her plans, and to require the officer to communicate to other officers, witnesses, and suspects alike.

Traditionally, firearms training for police officers involved shooting at a "bull's eye" target. Those targets were changed to silhouettes, which were slightly more realistic, although the officers were standing only a few yards away firing from a position of comfort or perhaps from behind a small barricade. Range masters are now requiring the officers to shoot while moving, while kneeling, from behind objects that may provide cover, or from the open door of a police car. Trainers emphasize the need to use cover, to reload while remaining in a position of cover, and to communicate with other officers who may be engaging the same target.

Finally, technology has helped make role playing more realistic; it has evolved into force-on-force training. Simunition® was designed to train officers to improve their tactical skills and to condition their responses to fear in life-threatening situations through the use of nonlethal training ammunition. Service weapons are converted to fire reduced-energy, nonlethal cartridges that leave a detergent-based, water-soluble marking compound. The markings left after officers fire their weapons allow trainers to assess the lethality of the actions taken. Trainers put officers into scenarios and evaluate responses from the beginning of the interaction. Officers can be trained how to diffuse situations, contain scenes, set perimeters, communicate information, and formulate tactical plans approaches. Trainers offer advice on the effective use of low-light situations, back lighting, the use of a flashlight, cornering, and a myriad of other tactical advantages. The simulations provide immediate feedback to the officers should they fail to take appropriate cover, if they miss their target, or if they engage a target with a poor backdrop. Officers learn to function in stressful situations and to understand the advantages of proper tactics.

Police officers deserve effective policies, training, supervision, and a system of accountability. Policies must be written to guide officers in responding safely to situations that can lead to injury or death. Departments must train officers not to create dangerous situations or to put themselves in situations that require force as self-defense. There are many tactics that may seem reasonable and would provide officers with a quick and simple response to an uncooperative suspect, but if the strategies would result in a use of force that could have been avoided, they should be revised. Reaching into a car that is running to turn it off and to take the keys might seem like a reasonable response, but we learned earlier that such tactics can result in an officer being dragged down the street and then shooting the driver to save his own life. Supervisors must analyze the actions taken by their officers to be sure that policies are followed and to determine if additional training is necessary. Finally, if officers fail to learn policies and procedures and take actions that jeopardize their own safety or that of the public, there must be a system to hold them accountable.

NOTES

[1] Snow, Robert. 1996. *SWAT Teams: Explosive Face-Offs with America's Deadliest Criminals.* New York: DaCapo Press.

[2] Ibid.

[3] Rojek, Jeff and David Klinger. 2005. SWAT Teams. In *The Encyclopedia of Law Enforcement,* Marie Simonetti Rosen, Dorothy Moses Schultz, and M. R. Haberfeld, Eds., pp. 447–448. Thousand Oaks, CA: Sage.

[4] Ibid.

[5] Fyfe, James J., Training to Reduce Police-Civilian Violence. 1996. In *Police Violence: Understanding and Controlling Police Abuse of Force,* William A. Geller and Hans Toch, Eds., pp. 165–179. New Haven: Yale University Press.

[6] *Abraham v. Raso,* 183 F.3d 248 (8th Cir. 1996).

[7] *Allen v. Muskogee, Oklahoma,* 119 F.3d 837 (10th Cir. 1997).

[8] *Greenidge v. Ruffin,* 927 F.2d 789 (4th Cir. 1991).

[9] *Medina v. Cram,* 252 F.3d 1124 (10th Cir. 2001).

[10] Alpert, G. P., and R. G. Dunham. 2004. *Understanding Police Use of Force: Officers, Suspects and Reciprocity.* New York: Cambridge University Press.

[11] *Graham v. Connor,* 490 U.S. 386, 396 (1989).

[12] Ibid.

[13] Meyerhoff, James, William Norris, George Saviolakis, Terry Wollert, Bob Burge, Valerie Atkins, and Charles Spielberger. 2006. "Evaluating Performance of Law Enforcement Personnel during a Stressful Training Scenario." *Annals* 1032: 250–253.

[14] *Tennessee v. Garner,* 471 U.S. 1, 8-9 (1985).

[15] Reiss, Albert. 1968. "Police Brutality—Answers to Key Questions." *Transaction* 5: 10–19; Alpert, G., and L. Fridell. 1992. *Police Vehicles and Firearms: Instruments of Deadly Force.* Long Grove, IL: Waveland Press; Scharf, Peter and Arnold Binder. 1983. *The Badge and the Bullet: Police Use of Deadly Force.* New York: Praeger.

[16] *Young v. City of Providence,* 404 F.3d 4, 22 (1st Cir. 2005).

[17] *Abraham v. Raso,* 183 F.3d 279, 291-92 (3rd Cir. 1999).

[18] *Dickerson v. McClellan,* 101 F.3d 1151, 1161 (6th Cir. 1996).

[19] *Deering v. Reich,* 183 F.3d 645, 652 (7th Cir. 1999).

[20] *Estate of Starks v. Enyart,* 5 F.3d 230 (7th Cir. 1993)

[21] *Gilmere v. Atlanta,* 774 F.2d 1495, 1501 (11th Cir. 1985).

[22] *Brown v. City of Hialeah,* 30 F.3d 1433, 1436 (11th Cir. 1994)

[23] *Nimely v. City of New York,* 414 F.3d 381, 390 (2nd Cir. 2005)

[24] *Greenidge v. Ruffin,* 927 F.2d 789, 792 (4th Cir. 1991).

[25] *Drewitt v. Pratt*, 999 F.2d 774 (4th Cir. 1993).

[26] *Gardner v. Bueger*, 82 F.3d 248, 254 (8th Cir. 1996).

[27] *Allen v. Muskogee, Oklahoma*, 119 F.3d 837 (10th Cir. 1997).

[28] *Fraire v. City of Arlington*, 957 F.2d 1268, 1276 (5th Cir. 1992).

[29] *Billington v. City of Boise*, 292 F.3d 1177 (9th Cir. 2001).

[30] *Alexander v. City and County of San Francisco*, 29 F.3d. 1355 (9th Cir. 1994).

[31] *Roy v. Inhabitants of City of Lewiston*, 42 F.3d 691, 695 (1st Cir. 1994).

[32] Fyfe, Training to Reduce Police-Civilian Violence.

[33] Ibid.

[34] Alpert, Geoffrey P., and William C. Smith. 1994. "How Reasonable Is the Reasonable Man?: Police and Excessive Force." *J. Crim. L. & Criminology* 481(85).

[35] Fyfe, James J. 2015. The Split-Second Syndrome and Other Determinants of Police Violence. Chapter 29 in *Critical Issues in Policing: Contemporary Readings*, 7th ed., Roger G. Dunham and Geoffrey P. Alpert, Eds. Long Grove, IL: Waveland Press, pp. 517–531.

[36] *Greenidge v. Ruffin*, 927 F.2d 789, 792 (4th Cir. 1991).

[37] Rojek, Jeff. 2005. *Organizing to Manage Risk: The Operations of a Police Tactical Unit*. Unpublished Dissertation, University of Missouri-St. Louis; Heal, Charles. 2000. *Sound Doctrine: A Tactical Primer*. New York: Lantern; Clark, J., M. S. Jackson, and P. M. Schaefer, and E. Gail Sharpe. 2000. "Training SWAT Teams: Implications for Improving Tactical Units." *Journal of Criminal Justice* 28: 407–413. Mijares, T. C., R. M. McCarthy, and D. P. Perkins. 2000. *The Management of Police Specialized Tactical Units*. Springfield, MO: Charles C. Thomas; Bayley, David and James Garofalo. 1989. "The Management of Violence by Police Patrol Officers." *Criminology* 27: 1–26.

[38] Boyd, John. 1987. *Organic Design for Command and Control*, http://www.d-n-i.net/boyd/pdf/c&c.pdf.

[39] Noble, Jeffrey J., and Geoffrey P. Alpert. 2008. *Managing Accountability Systems for Police Conduct: Internal Affairs and External Oversight*. Long Grove, IL: Waveland Press.

[40] *Black's Law Dictionary*. 2004. Eighth Edition. St. Paul, MN: Thompson West Publishing, pp. 1061–1062.

[41] Ibid. at 1298.

[42] Zarb, Frank G., Jr. 1998. "Police Liability for Creating the Need to Use Deadly Force in Self-Defense," *86 Mich. L. Rev.* 1982.

[43] Ibid. Note 40 at 1062–1063.

[44] Ibid.

[45] Fyfe, Training to Reduce Police-Civilian Violence.

SECTION VII

The Future of Policing

We began this collection of readings on policing with a discussion of the social contract, as depicted by Jeffrey Reiman. Admittedly, the social contract idea is an idealistic account of what policing should be like in a democratic society. Some would say it is an ideal for the role of the police in a democratic society that has never been achieved. We argued in the first article that it has some historic validity, even if faint. And more importantly, it stands as a noble set of goals to be realized, even if implemented in small increments. If the ideal is accepted and honored, as is the Constitution, it will provide an impetus for achieving the goal written on the sides of many police vehicles: "To Serve and Protect."

In the last section of this book, we include two articles that speak eloquently to this ideal. The first selection, "What a Good Police Department Looks Like: Professional, Accountable, Transparent, Self-Monitoring," is written by a well-regarded police historian, Samuel Walker, who outlines the ideal characteristics of "good" police departments. Walker has a long history of promoting high ideals for police departments. In this article, he lists and discusses the most important characteristics that should guide police departments. Further he argues that effective, professional, and accountable police departments are a possibility for every community. Making each police department the best it can be is simply a matter of identifying the best practices of other departments and implementing them.

The second selection, "The Challenge of Policing in a Democratic Society: A Personal Journey toward Understanding," is written by an unusual police leader, Commissioner Charles Ramsey of the Philadelphia Police Department. Commissioner Ramsey espouses a human rights model of policing, viewing the responsibility of the police as protecting the constitutional rights of the citizens they serve. He teaches that philosophy to the police officers under his command. While Commissioner Ramsey knows that the ideal of a society that is free of crime is probably unachievable, he believes that we should strive to secure everyone's safety and to protect human rights.

We air these important visions for policing in the hopes of contributing, in some small way, to the progressive evolution of an important institution in our society.

33

What a Good
Police Department Looks Like
Professional, Accountable,
Transparent, Self-Monitoring

Samuel Walker

The Purpose of This Guide

This Guide identifies principles, policies and programs that characterize good policing. In each case, it offers an example, with a web site, of a good program or practice that already exists in a police department, and/or an important report on it. This Guide is designed as a community education tool, to help people evaluate the quality of their own police department in terms of the best practices that characterize a good police department. This report does not claim to be the last word on the subject. It aspires to be the first word in a continuing public discussion of what a good police department looks like. Readers and community groups are invited to make suggestions or adapt it to their own purposes.

How to Use This Report

This report is designed as a community organizing tool. It seeks to inform people about what they should look for and expect of their own police department. The report can serve as a check list of the important principles, policies, and programs. Particularly important, the report will help community people have a solid basis of information when they initiate discussions with their police chief, sheriff, mayor, city council members, civic leaders, and the media. Not everyone will agree with this report's definition of what a good police department should look like. People will certainly disagree with

Used by permission of the author.

the some examples offered on particular points. Good! One of the main goals of this report is to initiate an informed discussion of what constitutes a good police department. Let that discussion begin.

Advisory

As you certainly already know, web sites are very unstable: here today, gone tomorrow. As a result, some of the web sites in this report may not be live by the time you seek to access them. In some cases, they simply have a new address and you can try to find them through an original search. We will try to continually monitor the web sites and update sites when necessary. New versions of this report will be duly noted. Please notify us when you encounter dead sites. We will either substitute a new site or send you the latest version of the report. samwalker@unomaha.edu

---

Basic Principles

The Goal: A Professional and Accountable Police Department

No community should settle for anything less than the best, most professional and accountable police department. There is no excuse for not having the best. Many departments have in place some valuable policies and programs, but no department has all of the necessary ones. This guide identifies the best that currently in place across the country.

PATS, for professional, accountable, transparent, and self-monitoring, is a useful acronym for the various elements that constitute a good police department.

- **Professional.** A good police department is professional in the sense that it is effective in serving the public and makes a continuing effort to seek out and adopt the best practices.

- **Accountable.** A good police department holds its officers accountable for their conduct. It achieves this by having state of the art policies on use of force, domestic violence, and other critical incidents. Early intervention systems (EIS) have emerged as the best practice in accountability, and every department should have an EIS system. An independent oversight agency is also an important form of accountability.

- **Transparent.** A good police department is open and transparent. It achieves this by providing information to the public about its operations: by placing its policy manual on its web site, by explaining its various units and what they do, and by facilitating communication with officers who serve in various units.

- **Self-Monitoring.** A good police department has in place procedures for self-monitoring. This involves reviewing and learning from critical incidents, such as shootings or use of force incidents, to determine if there are ways to prevent such incidents from happening in the future. It also involves learning from other police departments and adopting the recognized best practices.

A Professional Police Department

A professional police department adopts the current best practices for responding effectively to crime and disorder, protecting the public, and helping to maintain safe communities. The question is how to achieve these goals. We have learned that the old ways—putting more police on the streets—do not work. Recent innovations have resulted in effective strategies that have been evaluated and found to be effective when properly implemented.

It is now recognized in policing that the police cannot do all themselves. Effective responses involve partnerships with community groups, other private organizations, and other criminal justice agencies.

Problem-Oriented Policing

Problem-oriented policing (POP) is widely recognized as the best way to approach for addressing specific crime and disorder problems. The POP Center in Madison, Wisconsin has a wealth of information about strategies for addressing particular problems. *POP Guides* are available on Sexual Assault of Women by Strangers, Gun Violence Among Young Offenders, Robbery of Convenience Stores, and many other topics.

Go to the PopCenter web site: www.popcenter.org. On the left hand side, click on "What is POP? and learn about its basic principles. Across the top, click on "POP Projects," and then on the right-hand side, explore the collection of Goldstein Award projects. This will give you many examples of exactly what police departments have done.

The *Collaborative Agreement in Cincinnati,* settling several racial profiling suits against the police department, required the department to adopt problem-oriented policing. Read the Collaborative Agreement and see the changes it mandated: http://samuelwalker.net/wpcontent/uploads/2010/06/Collaborative.pdf

Addressing Gun and Gang Violence

Gun violence and gang-related violence is a serious national problem. Recent research has identified a strategy that has proven to be effective when properly implemented. Check out the relevant Pop Guides discussed above. *Focused deterrence* is a strategy for focusing on a small and carefully selected group of individuals known to be active in gangs and violent crime.

One widely cited successful focused deterrence program is the *Cincinnati Initiative to Reduce Violence* (CIRV). Go to the Cincinnati Police Department web site and learn more about CIRV: http://www.cincinnati-oh.gov/police/community-involvement/cincinnati-initiative-toreduce-violence.

Partnerships: A Community-Wide Approach

It is the consensus among police experts that addressing violent crime requires a coordinated community-wide approach. One promising example is

> **What to Look For in the CIRV Program.**
>
> Notice the use of partnerships in the program.
> Notice how it focuses on a small group of known high-level offenders, and does not engage in indiscriminate stops, frisks, or arrests.
> Notice the cooperation among law enforcement and social service agencies.

the *Seattle Youth Violence Prevention Initiative*. Learn more about it here: http://www.seattle.gov/neighborhoods/education/youthInitiative/AboutUs.htm

One of the core principles of both problem-oriented policing and its first cousin community policing is *partnerships*. This includes partnerships with neighborhood groups, social service agencies, and other criminal justice agencies. Experts on policing today recognize that the police cannot do it all by themselves.

A Department Must Reflect the Community It Serves

A professional police department is one that reflects the community it serves, particularly with regard to race, ethnicity, and gender. A professional and transparent department provides information about the demographics of its sworn officers on its web site where people can readily find it and assess how well their department is doing. See the demographics of the Washington, DC, Metropolitan Police Department (go to p. 32 of its Annual Report): http://mpdc.dc.gov/sites/default/files/dc/sites/mpdc/publication/attachments/MPD%20Annual%20Report%202013lowres.pdf

An Accountable Police Department

An accountable police department holds is officers accountable for their actions. It has state of the art policies on critical actions, provides close supervision, reviews officer conduct, and imposes discipline or takes other remedial actions where necessary. There are a variety of accountability policies and procedures that a good department should have, and a department should inform the public about which ones it has in place.

A State of the Art Policy on Use of Physical Force

A department's use of force policy should embody state of the art principles. The policy should provide clear and detailed guidance for officers on the proper use of force in various situations, in a well-organized policy statement. The policy should be readily available to the public (see our discussion of this point, below).

A recent report on the new Collaborative Reform Process involving the COPS Office of the Justice Department and the Las Vegas Metropolitan

Police Department sets forth the standards for use of force policies and procedures for continuous monitoring of policies and practices. Read the COPS/Las Vegas Collaborative Report on Las Vegas at: http://www.cops.usdoj.gov/pdf/e10129513-Collaborative-Reform-ProcessFINAL.pdf

What to Look for in a Use of Physical Force Policy

The use of force policy should address specific police actions. It should, for example, (1) specifically prohibit strikes to the head, (2) emphasize de-escalation techniques, and (3) include a clear statement that only the minimal amount of force should be used to accomplish a lawful police purpose.

These are just a few of the key points. If you study other departments' policies, you will get a better picture of what a good policy looks like.

What to Look for in the Collaborative Reform Report

Notice the weaknesses in the department's force policy.

Notice the criticisms of how the department reviewed use of force incidents.

Notice how use of deadly force incidents is often the result of communication and command failures.

Most important, notice the value of an independent assessment of use of force incidents and the lessons to be learned.

De-Escalating Police–Resident Encounters

One of the most important recent developments in policing has been a commitment to de-escalating encounters between police officers and community residents. Historically, officers responded to perceived or actual challenges to their authority by escalating their actions, often using force where it was not necessary. De-escalation involves responding through verbal or nonverbal tactics or simply ignoring minor challenges.

A good police department should have a de-escalation policy, along with the appropriate training for all officers. Read the important Police Executive Research Forum report on de-escalation: http://www.calea.org/sites/default/files/PERF%20UOF%20De-Escalationv5.pdf

As a result of a consent decree with the Justice Department, the Seattle Police Department revised its use of force policy, incorporating de-escalation as a starting point. See the new policy: http://www.seattle.gov/police/compliance/finishedpolicy/UseofForcePolicy11272013.pdf

A Commitment to Bias-Free Policing

Issues of biased policing affect police departments across the country. This includes bias related to race, ethnicity, gender, and sexual orientation. It includes all police actions: stops and frisks, traffic stops ("driving while black"), arrests, the investigation of sexual assaults and domestic violence incidents. A department should have a formal policy on bias-free policing, make that policy available to the public, and conduct the appropriate training designed to ensure bias-free policing. One recognized training program is *Fair and Impartial Policing* project. Learn about it at: http://www.fairandimpartialpolicing.com/

An Early Intervention System (EIS)

Early intervention systems (EIS) are recognized as a powerful accountability tool. An EIS consists of a computerized database of individual officer performance that permits *identification of officers* who have performance problems (e.g., community member complaints) at rates higher than their peers. For officers so identified, an EIS provides *non-disciplinary interventions* (e.g., counseling, training) designed to correct an officer's performance problems. Read the COPS Report on EIS at: http://www.cops.usdoj.gov/Publications/e07032003.pdf

---

What Is Important about an EIS

1. A small number of officers are responsible for repeated problems such as use of force and resident complaints.
2. An EIS has the capacity to identify those officers.
3. An EIS provides corrective action to improve their performance.

Early intervention systems have been required in all of the Justice Department settlements with police departments. See the details of the EIS, called the Personnel Performance Monitoring System, in the Washington, DC, police department (scroll down to roman numeral VI): http://www.justice.gov/crt/about/spl/documents/dcmoa.php

An Open and Accessible Community Member Complaint Process

Community members should find it easy to file a complaint about their experience with the police. This means the department should provide *widely available information* about the complaint process; provide it in all *languages* appropriate for the community; provide *multiple ways of filing complaints,* including electronically, by mail, by telephone, or in-person at a *non-intimidating location.*

The complaint process should be prominently indicated on a police department's home page. People should not have to hunt for it.

The department needs to have a formal protocol for the complaint process to ensure that possible witnesses are located, medical evidence is obtained and reviewed, officers are not asked leading questions and complainants not asked intimidating questions, and that the determination is closely related to the available facts. Finally, complainants need to be kept informed of the progress of the complaint investigation.

No police department has a perfect community member complaint process. But some are certainly more open and accessible than others. Take a look at the San Jose, CA, Police Department's process: http://www.sjpd.org/COP/IA.html

Mediating Community Member Complaints against the Police

Mediation, which is widely used in many other areas of American life, is a small but growing aspect of policing. With a trained mediator conducting the session, mediation is an opportunity for both the complainant and the police officer to both say what they want to say and to listen to what the other side says. The point of mediation is not discipline, but instead for each side to listen to the other side and to achieve a greater level of understanding.

What to Look for in the Mediated Cases

Scroll down to the list of examples of mediated cases. Look for the kind of complaints that were mediated and the reported outcomes of the mediation process.

Learn more about police complaint mediation from the Washington, DC, Office of Police Complaints: http://policecomplaints.dc.gov/service/mediation-service

Learn more from the U.S. Justice Department report on mediating complaints: http://www.cops.usdoj.gov/pdf/e04021486web.pdf

External Oversight

External oversight is a crucial part of police accountability.

External oversight of the police takes many forms. The traditional approach involves a civilian review board, an independent agency that reviews community member complaints against police officers and makes a recommendation to the department. An alternative, newer approach involves what is often referred to as a police auditor (although the terms monitor or inspector general are also uses). Some external oversight are *hybrids,* investigating individual complaints and auditing the police department.

Whatever form of oversight is adopted, it needs to have sufficient powers to achieve its stated objectives.

This report recommends the *police auditor* approach, because it has the authority to examine the policies, procedures, and practices of a police department. Auditors have the authority to examine any and all data they believe to be important. Police auditors issue public reports, which represent an important element of openness and transparency to police issues. Particularly important police auditors make recommendations for changes in policies, procedures, and practices. The primary goal is to change the department and to prevent future misconduct. And finally, police auditors conduct updates on progress toward implementing prior recommendations.

The LASD Special Counsel.   Since it was created in 1993, the Special Counsel to the Los Angeles Sheriff's Department has established a reputation as one of the best external police oversight agencies in the country. Its work has covered a wide range of issues, including use of force, law suits against the department, the early intervention system, the dangers of foot pursuits, and many more issues. The Special Counsel reports are all readily available from the Police Assessment Resource Center: http://parc.info/losangelescountysheriffsdepartment.chtml. See, for example, the Special Counsel's report on the dangers of foot pursuits: http://parc.info/clientfiles/LASD/16th%20Semiannual%20Report.pdf

The Washington, DC, Office of Police Complaints.   The Office of Police Complaints in Washington, DC, also has a regular program of using community member complaints to identify problems and to make recommendations for reform. See their police recommendations: http://policecomplaints.dc.gov/page/policyrecommendations

The Denver Office or Independent Monitor (OIM) Policy Review.   The Denver Office of Independent Monitor conducts an annual review of policies and practices in the Denver police department that need attention. Read the 2011 OIM Annual Report (and take a look at earlier annual reports): http://www.denvergov.org/Portals/374/documents/OIM2011AnnualReportFORWEB.pdf

A Transparent Police Department

A transparent police department makes available information about its policies and operations that are matters of concern to the public. The department web site is the obvious place for posting such information, and the web site should be easy to navigate for the average person.

Department Policy Manual on the Web

An increasing number of police departments place their policy and procedure manual on their web sites. This allows community members to study polices on use of force, vehicle pursuits, and other critical incidents that are community concerns. Placing the manual on the web is an important step in the direction of openness and transparency, helping to eliminate the feeling that the department is a closed, secretive bureaucracy.

Police departments that have their policy manuals on their web sites include:

- Minneapolis: http://www.minneapolismn.gov/police/policy/index.htm
- Charlotte-Mecklenberg (North Carolina): http://charmcck.org/city/ charlotte/CMPD/resources/DepartmentDirectives/Documents/ CMPDDirectives.pdf

Search other police departments to see if they put their police manual on the web. Study the critical policies on use of force, de-escalation, domestic violence, bias–free policing, and others.

Access to the Department

The Minneapolis Police Department represents a model for providing detailed information about how community members can contact officers who serve their neighborhoods. Go on the web site below and see that the department provides the names and phone numbers of the crime prevention specialists in each neighborhood: http://www.ci.minneapolis.mn.us/police/ crimeprevention/policeoutreachsafe-teams

Self-Monitoring

Continually Reviewing and Updating Policies

We have already discussed the COPS Office / Las Vegas Collaborative Reform Report. Take another look at the recommendation for an annual review and update of use of force policies. The recommendation states:

> Recommendation 5.1: LVMPD should review and update its Use of Force Policy at least annually and as needed to incorporate recent court decisions, analysis of use of force data, and lessons learned from incidents in Las Vegas and other jurisdictions.

Learning from Critical Incidents

Departments should have a formal process in place for learning from critical incidents that have occurred. The review should be independent of the investigation for possible discipline and instead should focus on possible ways to improve policies, training and supervision in ways that would help prevent unnecessary uses of force and/or other adverse outcomes

See for example, the response of the Dallas, Texas police chief to an increase in officer-involved shootings represents an excellent example of a police department responding to and learning from a controversial incident. Two weeks after the shooting of an unarmed suspect, the chief issued an 8-Point Plan for New Policies and Strategic Directions. In addition to developing a foot pursuit policy and strengthening the policy on consent searches, the plan called for researching the "best practices" that have emerged "from around the nation." Read the Dallas 8-Point Plan here: http://samuelwalker.net/wp content/ uploads/2012/08/Dallas8pointplan.pdf

Kansas City Police Department Internal Audits

The Kansas City Police Department has a process for conducting Internal Audits of its operations. Equally important, it shares the audit reports with the public by placing them on its web site. Read the reports here: http://kcmo.gov/police/audit/

What to Look for in Internal Audits

1. Most important is the fact that the department puts its internal reviews on its web site, open to the public.

2. Notice that the 2013 audit of detention practices examined the record-keeping practices and medical attention for detainees.

3. Notice the 2012 audit of the central patrol district. Notice the review of the handling of property, security procedures, resident complaints received, and the 10% rule on staffing. The point is not that the audit found any "smoking guns," but rather that the department has a regular process of auditing itself—*and makes those audits available to the public.*

Strategic Plans

One aspect of self-monitoring is to have a program of periodic strategic plans that identify current or future issues and make recommendations for addressing them.

The Lincoln, Nebraska, Police Department has an excellent series of strategic plans. The 2012–2016 Strategic Plan, for example, recommends updating the police radio system that has not been updated since 1997, utilizing retired officers as a way of preserving the "institutional knowledge" about the department, developing public/private partnerships for training efforts that are constrained by the current budget crisis, and many more. Read the 2012–2016 plan here: http://www.lincoln.ne.gov/city/police/pdf/stratplan.pdf

Community Surveys

A good police department actively engages the community it serves. It can do this in a number of ways, but the basic principle is that it actively seeks out opportunities to engage community groups and leaders, listens to what they have to say, and then acts on what it hears.

A small number of police departments conduct regular surveys of community experiences with and attitudes toward the department. Read the results of the Seattle and New Orleans police departments. The New Orleans surveys are particularly interesting because they indicate a significant improvement in public attitudes in recent years.

- Seattle Service Quality Surveys: http://www.seattle.gov/police/policy/911Survey.htm
- New Orleans Community Surveys: http://www.nola.gov/nopd/about-us/citizen-satisfaction-surveys/

A Word about the Financial Cost of Accountability

A professional, effective and accountable police department is expensive, no doubt about it. Many people will object to the policies and procedures recommended in this report. They will argue that the money is better spent on crime-fighting, or that we just can't afford it in these times of budgetary limits. There are several answers to these arguments.

Merrick Bobb, the highly respected Special Counsel to the Los Angeles Sheriff's Department, put it well: "Money can be spent wisely or imprudently. Money can be spent on short term fixes or, better, on long-term, long-lasting reform that instills a new culture of accountability."

Sam Walker argues that accountable, constitutional policing is a necessary part of effective crime fighting. Police misconduct undermines community trust and the cooperation the police need to combat crime. Read the op-ed piece at: http://samuelwalker.net/wp-content/uploads/2012/09/constitutionalpolicing.pdf

Conclusion

An effective, professional and accountable police department is within the grasp of very community. Each of the various pieces of the puzzle is in place in other departments round the country. Achieving the best possible department is simply a matter of learning from these best practices and adopting them at home. There is no excuse for not doing so.

Your Comments, Criticisms, and Suggestions

If you have any comments, criticisms, or suggestions for changes in this report, please feel free to contact Professor Sam Walker at samwalker@unomaha.edu

34

The Challenge of Policing in a Democratic Society
A Personal Journey toward Understanding

Charles H. Ramsey

The Code

"As a law enforcement officer my fundamental duty is to serve mankind; to safeguard lives and property; to protect the innocent against deception, the weak against oppression or intimidation, the peaceful against violence and disorder; and to protect the Constitutional rights of all people to liberty, equality and justice."

This paragraph is part of the Law Enforcement Code of Ethics (author unknown). I believe it captures the essence of what it means to be a police officer in a democratic society. Unfortunately, the policing profession sometimes loses sight of what I believe is the most challenging element: "to protect the Constitutional rights of all people to liberty, equality and justice."

Police leaders must ensure that their officers fully understand the nature and significance of the commitment this brief phrase suggests. It commits us to a pact with the communities we serve. We make this commitment standing

Ramsey, Charles, *The Challenge of Policing in a Democratic Society: A Personal Journey Toward Understanding*. New Perspectives in Policing Bulletin. Washington, D.C.: U.S. Department of Justice, National Institute of Justice, 2014. NCJ 245992.

Author Note: Charles H. Ramsey is Commissioner of the Philadelphia Police Department, President of the Major Cities Chiefs Association, President of the Police Executive Research Forum and a member of the Harvard/NIJ Executive Session on Policing and Public Safety. This paper draws in part from a speech entitled "The Lessons of the Holocaust: Helping Create Better Police Officers for Today and Tomorrow" delivered by Commissioner Ramsey at the U.S. Holocaust Memorial Museum/Anti-Defamation League Symposium on April 12, 2000, from other more recent speeches delivered by Commissioner Ramsey regarding the character of police service, and from remarks made by him during the Executive Sessions.

before God, swearing allegiance to the principles, values and ethics of the law enforcement profession.

It took me almost 30 years and a visit to the United States Holocaust Memorial Museum to fully comprehend the role police play in protecting the freedoms that we, as Americans, hold dear. Today, I strive to share important lessons about these obligations with my officers—in part through the use of symbolism and ceremonies and in part by telling certain stories. This paper describes some of the most valuable lessons I believe I learned through reflecting on the exhibits at the Holocaust Museum. It also describes some of the ways in which I have sought to convey those lessons to other officers.

The Badge

At the Metropolitan Police Department in Washington, D.C., I established a new ceremony that we conducted for every graduating class of new recruits. Each graduate has a family member attend the ceremony, and that family member pins the badge on the graduating officer's uniform for the first time. The recruits therefore share that moment with the people whom they most care about and who care most about them. They learn to regard the badge as a symbol—a bright and highly visible symbol—of the authority and the trust that the public places in them. The community does not place that level of authority and trust in many people, but it has placed it in them, in us, the police. Every day we wear the badge, we must do everything we can to use our authority wisely and to earn the trust that the community places in us.

The badge identifies each officer not only as a member of a particular police department but also as a member of the policing profession. The badge represents our oath of office, serving as a constant reminder of the values and principles we hold dear. Having family members share in the ceremony, we believe, makes it less likely that officers will tarnish that badge, more likely that they will remember and stay true to their oath.

Inevitably, some do go astray. In Philadelphia, if an officer is found to be corrupt, that badge is taken away and destroyed. That tarnished badge will never be worn again by a member of our department. A new badge is minted, with the same number, to take its place. When recruits receive their badge, they are given the names of every officer who has worn that badge number before them and worn it with honor. The names of officers who tarnished their badge are not included in that list.

We want all officers to know that by wearing the badge they inherit an honorable tradition. They will wear the badge only for a time. But, during the time when they do have that badge, it is incumbent on each of them to keep it untarnished—as a symbol not just of authority but also of pride and integrity. Each officer becomes a part of a legacy of service connecting all of those who wore that badge before them and all those who will wear it after them.

Instilling Values

The law enforcement profession is good at training new recruits. I use the word "training" deliberately. We offer defined curricula in the police academy; we teach skills in self-defense, certify firearms proficiency, and give out multiple directives that explain what to do and what not to do in the line of duty. We can teach officers to be technically proficient, expert marksmen, and well-versed in criminal law and procedure. But it is much more challenging to teach them how to be compassionate, civil and just human beings; how to think, how to feel, how to judge, and how to connect with members of the public whom they will encounter when those people are at their most vulnerable.

As a profession, we institute all kinds of policies and procedures to try to shape the behavior of police officers. And yet many of the same undesirable behavior problems persist, year after year. In my view, we will not change behavior if we do not change attitude, and we will not change attitude if we do not change a person's heart. We need to affect the way in which officers see themselves and their role in society. We need to change what is inside them and help them see things differently.

Teaching our officers to respect the intent of the Constitution and the Bill of Rights—not just the technical aspects of criminal procedure—is an emotional, spiritual and moral experience. They need to understand the importance of and commitment to both the oath they swore and the code of ethics they obligated themselves to live by.

A Visit to the Holocaust Museum

Early in my tenure as Commissioner of the Washington, D.C., Metropolitan Police Department, in 1998, I received an invitation from David Friedman, Executive Director of the Anti-Defamation League in Washington, to visit the United States Holocaust Museum and meet the museum's director, Sara Bloomfield. I took up the invitation and visited the museum one afternoon on my way to the airport. For me it was a powerful and totally unexpected experience. I spent a good part of that first tour walking and talking with Irene Weiss, a Holocaust survivor. To hear her tell her own experiences and memories was remarkable. All of us study the Holocaust in school and from textbooks, but few of us have the opportunity to hear about it firsthand from those who lived through it.

I left the museum overwhelmed with emotion. Something there—particularly in some of the images—haunted me. I left with a strong sense that there were important lessons to be learned, for myself and for every other police officer. But I was not clear at that point what those lessons were. So I went back a few weeks later, unannounced, and toured the museum again on my own. I spent a considerable amount of time there on that second visit, and that is when I started noticing the pictures of police officers and began to understand their involvement in this tragedy.

Having had many years since to contemplate the various exhibits, I now point to three photographs that continue to hold special significance for me. Let me tell you about them and about my reflections on what they have taught me.

Photograph 1: Complicity

The first is a photo on the top floor of the exhibition that shows a police officer and a Nazi militia soldier flanking a muzzled dog.

I would guess that most first-time visitors to the museum mistakenly believe that the Nazi atrocities were carried out almost exclusively by the military, by the infamous SA and SS troops. Most people simply do not realize the integral role that local police played—not just passively permitting atrocities to take place but actively participating in many of them. Over time, the distinctions between local police and the Nazi military became so blurred that the two became synonymous. Even in the early days of the Nazi regime, soldiers and police, though organizationally separate, often worked hand in hand.

At the time of the Holocaust, at least a few Americans began asking the question, "Where were the police?" One of the newspaper blowups on display in the museum is from the *Dallas Morning News* of November 11, 1938. Its banner headline, reporting on the Kristallnacht rampage of two days earlier, reads as follows: "Hysterical Nazis Wreck Hundreds of Jewish Shops, Burn Synagogues in Wild Orgy of Looting and Terror." What is particularly

Photo credit:
Bundesarchiv,
Bild 102-14381 / photo:
Georg Pahl

disturbing is the "kicker" (subheadline) to the story: "Policemen Refuse to Halt Organized Riots in Germany."

What is revealing about that newspaper story is that it expresses the long-held tradition in our own country that if people are rioting and looting and destroying property, it is the job of the police to intervene. It is just so fundamental to our view of the police mission: the protection of life and property.

How then, in Germany in the 1930s, did things get so out of whack that people could loot and destroy in an organized and widespread manner without the police even trying to intervene? In our modern policing paradigm, such complacency on the part of the police seems almost impossible. But it was a reality then, as well as an obvious paradox.

The historical explanations point out a trend at the time toward a nationalization and politicization of policing. The stated reasons for that trend, and for the increasingly repressive tactics the police employed, have an all-too-familiar ring to them. Crime was out of control. Mobsters were in control. Enforcement across different jurisdictions was difficult. The Depression was breeding crime, and this lawlessness demanded a swift and certain response.

The Nazis did not call it "zero tolerance" at the time, but the brand of crime control they practiced was "zero tolerance" taken to its most horrific extreme. The concept quickly moved from "zero tolerance" for criminal behavior to "zero tolerance" for those people believed responsible for crime, disorder and other forms of hardship—in this case, Jews, gays and lesbians, people with mental illness, those with physical and cognitive disabilities, the "Roma" and many, many others.

Of course, the term "zero tolerance" is quite in vogue today. Some people even suggest (quite mistakenly, I would argue) that zero tolerance and community policing are one and the same, or at least closely related. What worries me most about this is that the ideals of democracy are all about tolerance—tolerance for different people, different cultures, different viewpoints. In the name of zero tolerance, many police departments today crack down on nuisance crimes such as drinking in public and other minor misdemeanors and almost always choose underprivileged neighborhoods for this strategy. I certainly do not advocate drinking in public or any other disorderly or criminal behavior. But how many of us ask the questions: Why is this person an alcoholic to begin with? And why doesn't he or she have a home to live in?

If we are to stand for any type of zero tolerance, it should be zero tolerance for the causes of crime and zero tolerance for the types of racist attitudes that led to the Holocaust 70 years ago and continue to feed hate crimes in our communities today. That is the type of "zero tolerance" we, as police officers, should be focusing on.

What followed from the zero tolerance policies in Nazi Germany was the denial of basic human rights and individual freedoms. Almost from the beginning, local police were intimately involved, and they soon became part and parcel of the Nazi reign of repression and terror.

Could the Holocaust have happened without the active cooperation and participation of the local police in Germany? We may never know the answer to that question. But one thing we do know for certain: local police forces began to operate in accordance with a set of values totally contrary to their oath of office and totally contrary to the mission of the police in a free, democratic and pluralistic society.

The Holocaust is probably the most extreme example of just how horrific and far-reaching the consequences can be when police officers violate their oath and fail to protect the basic rights and liberties of citizens. But even small ethical violations on the part of police officers can result in people's rights being denied, their confidence in the police being eroded and their communities becoming less safe.

I have mentioned my reservations about the concept of "zero tolerance." I also have serious reservations about the notion of a "**thin blue line**." The idea is decades old and suggests a fragile but necessary demarcation between good and evil in our communities. The history of the Holocaust shows us that in Nazi Germany the police did become a line, helping to separate the people that Hitler and his political allies defined as good from those they defined as evil.

The problem with reinforcing any kind of line is that you have to put each and every individual you encounter on one side or the other of that line—either the good side or the evil side. That requires police officers to make snap judgments about people based not always on their behavior but sometimes on their appearance, their background, where they live, whom they associate with or other factors.

I believe that much of the tension that surrounds perceived profiling by police based on race or ethnicity stems from this viewpoint. Today, in communities across America, we still face painful issues relating to the perceived profiling by police based on race and ethnicity. The "thin blue line" metaphor does damage. True community policing does not define police officers as a line—thin, blue or otherwise. We are not now, nor should we ever be, something that divides or separates communities.

How then should we help the police officers of today understand their role as defenders of the constitutional rights of all people? How do we help them recognize their own biases and prevent prejudice from influencing their decisions? Unfortunately, the issue of race in our society still divides us. It is difficult to have a discussion on the topic or to get people to see the world through the eyes of someone of another race without a variety of defensive reactions getting in the way. It was my attempt to answer those questions that led me to reflect more carefully on the Holocaust. The events leading up to and including the Holocaust powerfully demonstrate the dangers that can materialize when police offer their allegiance to a person or to a political party rather than holding true to the ethics of their profession.

In cooperation with the Holocaust museum and the Anti-Defamation League, the Metropolitan Police Department established a one-day educational program (which has been running now for more than a decade) called the "Law Enforcement & Society Program." The day begins with a guided tour of the museum's permanent collection, which traces the history of the Holocaust from the Nazi rise to power through the end of World War II and its aftermath. The tour is followed by a group discussion among the police officers, museum historians and educators on the abuse of power under the Nazis and the role of police within the Nazi state. Finally, the session concludes with an interactive conversation between Anti-Defamation League educators and police participants, who are encouraged to discuss their personal reactions and feelings in response to what they have seen. They are prompted to explore in greater depth the role that local police played in the genocide. They discuss how the lessons of the Holocaust can be applied to their own work as police officers today. It gives officers a chance to spend a day at the Holocaust museum and reflect on the role of police in a democratic society. I am told that more than 90,000 law enforcement officers from a range of federal, state and local agencies have been through this program. I hope their visit to the museum was as profound an experience for them as it was for me.

This training reminds officers that local police must never become so politicized—as they were in Nazi Germany—that they regard their primary role as carrying out the will of political leaders or simply looking the other way when political agendas that deny fundamental rights are pushed forward. Our power—our authority as police officers—comes not from the politicians. Our power and authority come from the people. Above all else, our role as police officers is to protect and preserve the rights of the people: the right to assemble, the right to speak, the right to petition and criticize one's government, and the right to be secure in one's home and with one's own possessions and beliefs. Defending these rights for all people, all of the time, ultimately defines us as police officers.

One of the lessons police recruits pick up from the day they spend at the museum is much more intimate and personal. It is a lesson in how to deal with their own personal prejudices—which are normally very private—while they carry out their very public role as police officers.

Nobody enters this profession without some prejudices. That is just human nature, and police officers are human beings too. We all come to this job with certain preconceptions about people, certain stereotypes and even certain prejudices. Exposure to the history of the Holocaust forces our recruits to confront those highly personal feelings in a compelling but supportive way. Nobody is asked to publicly confess any prejudices he or she may hold. We do not call it "sensitivity training" or anything like that, as such labels seem to accuse. But I do believe any person who walks through the Holocaust museum or goes through our training would be hard-pressed not to go home and take a deep look inside themselves, at their own attitudes and values. That is exactly the effect it had on me. Because our recruits take this introspective journey early in their careers, I am convinced they start off being more aware of other people's circumstances, more sympathetic to their predicaments and more tolerant of differences than they might have been otherwise.

Photograph 2: Resignation

Another photo that made a profound impression on me is one of the first you see when you get off the elevator to begin the tour. It is a 1945 photograph of a lone prisoner who has just been liberated from Buchenwald. He is sitting, eating rice from a bowl, and you look at him and he is looking up at whoever took the photograph, and you can look into his eyes and tell that he will never really be liberated because of the immensity and intensity of the suffering he has been through.

Usually, the idea of "liberation" conjures up images of parties and ticker tape parades and wild celebrations in the streets. There were certainly many such images among the museum exhibits, captured by photographers as World War II came to a close. But this liberation photo is obviously quite different. The subject's eyes tell the story of much more than just physical discomfort and exhaustion. They show intense emotional pain, anguish and resignation. Given what this man has been through, there seems to be no room for relief, excitement or joy.

Looking into this man's eyes, I began to wonder what message they held for today's police officers. When we come into a distressed or crime-ridden community to execute a search warrant, make an arrest or board up an abandoned building, are the eyes of the residents all that different from the eyes of this prisoner? Do our residents really view police as "liberators"? Or are we seen as something else, perhaps as a part of the problem, maybe because we did not do enough to prevent their neighborhood from deteriorating in the first place?

Part of the anguish I see in the Buchenwald prisoner's eyes is the conviction that all of this human tragedy and suffering was so unnecessary. It did

Photo credit: United States Holocaust Memorial Museum, courtesy of National Archives and Records Administration, College Park, Maryland. Photo used by permission.

not have to happen, if only the people who were supposed to protect the rights and liberties of the Jewish people had stood up and done something early on, when they could have, when they should have.

That is part of the anguish that many of our own residents feel today. It is great that the police are here now, trying to clean up the problems of crime and disorder that have developed over the years in their communities. But where were the police when these problems were taking hold?

Of course, there are important differences between the two scenarios. In the 1930s and 1940s, local police officers in the Nazi empire not only failed to prevent atrocities from taking place, they actively participated in many of those atrocities, including the murder of innocent people. That type of blatant criminal behavior is not to be found among the vast majority of our police officers today. But the question—then and now—is still the same: Where were the police?

Where were the police when libraries were being looted and books burned? When Jewish businesses were being illegally targeted? When people were being classified and publicly harassed, and ultimately imprisoned and slaughtered? Where were the police?

And where was the rest of the community—the local politicians, other government officials, civic leaders and everyday citizens—most of whom stood by silently and watched it all happen?

In America we might similarly ask: Where were the police when people were being lynched because of the color of their skin, and segregation was the law in states across the South?

Fast-forwarding several decades, where were the police when crack cocaine and other drugs invaded our communities? When gangs armed with powerful automatic and semiautomatic weapons took control of many of our streets? When shootings and homicides became everyday occurrences in far too many of our communities? Where were the police? And, once again, where was the rest of the community when crime was gaining its stranglehold on many of our communities? Do residents' expressions and behaviors toward police in our country's most beleaguered communities now reflect a similar resignation? Is the disconnection between residents and police exacerbated by feelings of abandonment and mistrust?

Whether they pertain to the 1930s or to our times, these are compelling questions. They are questions I think all police officers should be thinking about and talking about.

In our daily routines as police officers, we spend the vast majority of our time with the most vulnerable in our society—people who are poor and undereducated; people who may be newly arrived in our country and may speak a different language; people who are afraid and sometimes hopeless; people who may not appreciate, understand or trust the police. Who but these people have the greatest need of our help? In serving these and other people, we must show compassion and always be mindful of an obvious but sometimes forgotten fact—we are dealing with fellow human beings, not icons on a computer-generated map or numbers in a statistical report. When we start to look at crime victims, witnesses and others as statistics and stop seeing them as human beings, as people in trouble or in need, then we have lost our way.

To serve with compassion means understanding that when someone is the victim of a robbery, burglary, sexual assault or any other crime, his or her life may very well have been changed forever. It means treating each and every one of these individuals with empathy, dignity and respect. It means working tirelessly to help bring some sense of closure to the victims of crime. It means doing everything in our power to ensure that others do not suffer the same fate. And it means understanding that we should never judge others. It means recognizing that fate and circumstance are the only things that separate us from one another as human beings.

I learned a powerful lesson about the importance of respect from a member of my squad when I was a sergeant in the Chicago Police Department. I was having difficulty understanding why some people in our most challenged neighborhoods viewed police negatively rather than seeing us as protectors. This officer told me it all boiled down to the lack of respect some officers showed toward the community. He expressed this truth in a somewhat unusual and compelling way. His explanation went like this: "At the moment of birth everyone is a perfect 10, but once you enter this world, deduct 3 because life is only temporary. If you are born into a dysfunctional family, deduct another 3 because you will have very few positive role models in your life that will help keep you on the straight and narrow. If you are poor or a member of a minority group, deduct another 3 because many doors that lead to success may not be open to you. That takes the person that was once a perfect 10 down to 1. The 1 represents that person's dignity and self-respect." He said to me, "As a police officer, do what you have to do to make an arrest or defuse a situation but *never* do anything that takes away that person's 1 because that is all they have left and they will fight you to hold on to it."

As police officers we must respect the communities that we serve. It is by showing respect and compassion toward others that we develop legitimacy in the hearts and minds of these communities.

Photograph 3: Bystanders

The third photograph that haunts me shows about 15 soldiers standing around a man who is on his knees, about to get shot in the back of the head. He has dug his own grave and is about to fall into it.

Out of the 15 soldiers, maybe 14 of them appear to be looking on to see what is happening. Some of them are actually smiling. But one soldier is looking away. Now, the photographer might just have snapped that picture at that time when that particular soldier happened to look away. But I have wondered, and I would like to think that this soldier knew right from wrong and was saying to himself something like, "Man, this is messed up. I don't even want to be here." It makes me wonder what would have happened if five of those soldiers out of the 15 had said, "Whoa, wait a minute, we are not

Photo credit: United States Holocaust Memorial Museum, courtesy of Sharon Paquette.

doing this." Would that have changed things a little bit? It would surely have taken considerable courage to speak up in those circumstances.

Let us bring this up to date. What about the other officers, the bystanders, when a suspect takes a beating? What is running through those officers' heads? I would guess that there are some with a perverted sense of justice who think everything is fine and that this person deserves this treatment, and I suspect a considerable number know it is not fine and they are deeply uncomfortable. But what will they do? Will they have the courage to intervene, to step forward, to challenge their colleagues, to do the right thing? Feeling uncomfortable will never be enough. This is a call to action.

We look at courage in our business as going up against an armed gunman, into a dangerous situation or facing physical danger. We think less about courage as standing up for what is right. What is more, our systems and organizational cultures often fail to support or reward that kind of courage. When an officer reports misconduct to internal affairs, what kind of reward does he or she get for such courage? Too often, it seems as if the incentives and reward structures are stacked against those who are on the side of right. Too often, those who speak up or say "no" end up ostracized and decide never to do that again because of the way the department treats them, because of the cost that the system imposes on them. At some point that has got to change if we expect reality to be different in 10 or 20 years.

I believe that fundamental change in attitudes and in police culture is possible. Of course, it is hard, and I am not suggesting for a minute it is not. But it takes a different kind of courage, a courage that many people simply do not have as individuals. Collectively, we have to find the strength.

First Responders

Since 9/11, and again in the wake of the Boston Marathon bombing, we hear police (among others) described as first responders. Everyone was struck by the images in Boston of police officers at the scene of the bombing rushing in without hesitation to help the wounded with little or no regard for their own safety.

If we really understand our oath—and the role police must play in protecting human rights, civil liberties and democratic values—then we also have to be the first responders when basic human and civil rights are threatened or denied. Not bystanders. Will we rush in then to intervene, without regard for the personal consequences, just as we do at a bomb scene? Of course, others should follow us and have their role to play, too, but police need to be first, the very first. Our oath as police officers demands that we take this leadership role.

When I went through the academy, I learned about the First Amendment and the Fourth Amendment, not from the standpoint of how important it was for me to protect them but so that I would know how to get around them to do my job.

I remember when we had the "Occupy" demonstrations in Philadelphia as in so many other major cities in the U.S. and abroad. During our department's planning sessions, I was astonished at how quickly and naturally the conversation turned to mass arrest procedures, the importance of having arrest procedures ready for various eventualities and checking that we were ready to deploy them at short notice. So I raised the question, "What is Plan B? Why do we always go to mass arrest procedures? We should have as our goal not to arrest anyone. Whether we agree with the demonstrators or not, these folks have a legitimate right to protest and to air and voice their concerns. Our job is to make sure they can do that, peacefully."

We reminded ourselves that Philadelphia was the birthplace of democracy in the free world. For as long as the demonstration lasted, every day at roll call the sergeant read the First Amendment out loud. Every day! This went on for months, and maybe some people got a bit tired of it; nevertheless, we stuck with it and read the First Amendment each and every day at roll call to remind the officers at the beginning of their shift what their job was.

In my office at police headquarters, I have one picture that makes me particularly proud. It shows a group of our bicycle officers at the National Constitution Center, where a huge stone tablet has the First Amendment engraved on it. These officers chose to take their own picture, as a group, surrounding that tablet. That means a great deal to me.

The public has come to know that we will rush headlong toward danger and will put ourselves in harm's way to protect total strangers. Even if some of our own should fall in the process, the public knows that there will be others to fill in. The heroes who responded to the terror attacks of 9/11 will forever serve as shining examples of this type of service: service with purpose and service with courage.

But our oath to "serve and protect" means much more than protecting life and property. Our oath also carries with it the unique and awesome responsibility of protecting the constitutional rights of all Americans—of safeguarding the very freedoms that we cherish and that set us apart from so many other nations on earth.

In recent years, whenever we see the escalation of crime, drug abuse, youth violence, child abuse, security threats or other serious problems, we hear various calls for the relaxation of the exclusionary rule, the reversal of other Fourth Amendment rights and, most recently, the overhaul of police *Miranda* warnings. All of these suggestions have been made in the name of more effective law enforcement and safer communities.

Yes, the police need to work harder and smarter in controlling crime. But in doing so, we must never compromise our staunch defense of the Constitution and the bedrock freedoms it guarantees. We must never buy into the notion—as the police in Nazi Germany did—that taking away individual rights is somehow the way to solve our crime problems and create safer communities. If our officers leave their day at the Holocaust museum with only one lesson learned, I hope it is that one.

Our Legacy

The ultimate goal of the police is to create a society that is free of crime and where everyone's rights are safe and secure. That is the ideal, something to reach for, but something that we will probably never fully achieve. There will always be challenges and obstacles that get in the way.

Today, the threat of terrorism creates challenges to our physical safety and security as well as to our traditions of fairness, equality and liberty. Faced with such threats, we will increasingly be forced to weigh the issues of individual privacy against the issues of public security. We will be tempted to use new and powerful surveillance technologies just because we can. But should we? Moving forward, we will have to be more thoughtful about which technologies to deploy. Technology is sometimes a benefit, sometimes a curse. Of course, we should pursue effective and appropriate technological solutions to our problems. But we must also consciously decide where the limits lie and do so before we cross those lines. As police weigh conflicting obligations, we need to remind ourselves constantly that our first priority is the protection of constitutional rights.

In closing, let me return to the issue of how we, as police officers, view ourselves and how, as a consequence, others might view us. Earlier in this paper, I expressed my reservations concerning the metaphor of the "thin blue line." As a result of my personal journey, I no longer buy into that metaphor at all. I would prefer that police see themselves as a thread woven through the communities they serve. That metaphor makes police an integral part of the very fabric that holds communities together in a democratic society. Our partnerships and collaborations will mean much more when we view ourselves as a part of the fabric rather than as a separate institution trying to engage the public. As a thin blue line, we might suppress crime in some neighborhoods, but as part of the fabric of society, we are already joined with others in the task of creating safe and healthy places to live and work.

Policing is a noble profession. We always meet the challenges of our time, overcome the obstacles and continue moving forward, all the while staying true to our values and principles. Our legacy is precious and deserves our constant care and attention. One hundred years from now, most people are unlikely to remember any of us as individuals. Our individual names will be on the list of those who wore the badge. But collectively, will we have made an imprint? What will that imprint look like? What legacy will we leave behind, as individuals and as a profession?

I have every confidence that we will be remembered positively—and our imprint will be honorable, memorable and lasting; that is, so long as we remain true to our calling of service to others, to our oath of office, and to the principles and ethics of our profession.

Photo credit: Philadelphia Police Department.

Index

Abbate, Anthony, 95, 110
Accountability
  citizen complaint process and,
    172–173
  Crank's paradox of, 164–165
  evidence-based policing and, 261–262
  external oversight and, 591–592
  financial cost of, 595
  Early Intervention (EI) systems to
    enhance, 244–257, 590
  organizational justice and, 208
  for police use of force, 562–563
  for reckless tactical decision making,
    567–580
  technical advances in, 239
Administration
  combating the code of silence
    through administrative investiga-
    tions, 116–117
  dishonesty among administrators, 201
  nineteenth-century police adminis-
    trative boards, 20
  technical advances in, 239–241
  See also Management
African Americans
  frequency of complaints against
    police by, 167
  percentage satisfied with police
    behavior/response regarding
    requests for assistance, 36–37
  racial profiling and, 190–191
  research on excessive use of force
    against, 167
  underrepresentation on police forces,
    84
  verbal abuse by police, 166

Afrocentric policing
  hidden history of, 333–336
  lack of mainstream outlets for schol-
    arly work on, 332
  police brutality and, 345, 337–339
  race and use of deadly force, 339–348
  scholars of color excluded from dis-
    course on, 348–350
  scholars' perspective on, 332–339,
    349–350
  "shoot first and ask questions later"
    policy, 341–345
  stereotypical perceptions affecting,
    341
  underrepresentation of contributions
    by black police officers, 336–337
Age, and police discretionary behavior,
  133
Alcohol use, ethical dilemmas regarding, 189–190
Allen, A., 421, 431
Alpert, G. P., 3, 51, 79, 106, 125–126,
  129, 131, 135–136, 206, 387,
  537–541, 567
American police
  emergence of community policing,
    26–28
  emergence of police professionalism,
    21–23
  heritage of English law enforcement,
    12–14
  historical overview of, 11–30
  legacy of the 1960s, 25–26
  nineteenth-century police activity,
    17–20
  nineteenth-century reform, 20–21

preventive model of policing, 14–17
twentieth-century evolution of,
23–25
Andrews, D., 413
Archbold, C. A., 362
Arizona v. United States, 191
Arnspiger, B. R., 561
Arrests
1860–1920, 18
sex of suspect and, 62
socioeconomic status and, 61–62
Assaults against police officers, research
on, 86, 387–388
Assholes
behavioral rules upon which "assholes" are recognized, 146–149
interactional origins and consequences of the label, 143–144
justification for identification of and
action taken regarding, 156–157
rubric police use to define, 149–155
stigmatization by the police and vul-
nerability to street justice, 145–146
three stages of stigmatization process, 150–155
Authoritarian personality, 80
Authority
abuse of, 108–109, 164, 166–167
centralization of, 20
citizens' resentment over, 93
as element of police control, 3
as important characteristic in development of police working personality, 89
Klinger's formal authority scale
(FAS), 56–57
normative dimensions of ("good"
policing), 58
police misconduct and abuse of,
53–59, 164
Auto-dialing system/reverse 911, 231
Automated Emergency Dispatch systems (AEDs), 240
Autonomy, ethos of, 91

Bachrach, L. L., 436
"Bad apple" analogy, 111, 168
Badge, as symbol of authority and trust
placed in police by the public, 597

Bahn, C., 93
Baldwin, J., 92
Barker, T., 189, 198, 201
Batts, A., 75
Bayley, D. H., 51, 56, 58, 81, 85, 98,
170–171, 472, 538–539, 545
Beehr, T., 202
Behan, B., 158
Behavior, police. *See* Discretionary
behavior
Bennett, K., 129, 131, 135
Bennett, R. R., 82
Bennett, T., 266
Bentham, J., 15
Beral, H., 175
Bias-free policing, departmental com-
mitment to, 590
Bibbins, George, 347
Bierce, A., 532
Binder, A., 550
Bittner, E., 98, 163, 441, 521–522
Black, D. J., 55–56, 167
Blacks. *See* African Americans
Blue curtain of secrecy/blue wall of
silence, 112–113, 197–198. *See also*
Code of silence
Boba, R., 235
Bonner, H. S., 46, 63
Borum, R., 441–442, 446
Bowers, G. A., 561
Bowers, K. J., 281–282
Bowling, C., 241
Braga, A. A., 1, 504
Brame, R., 132
Brandl, S. G., 136–137, 385, 387–388, 397
Brantingham, P. J., 279
Bratton, W., 191, 207, 278, 304
Bravery, ethos of, 90–91, 98–100
Breda, D. R., 175
Broad Street Riot of 1837, 16
Broderick, J. J., 80–81
Broken windows theory, 455–467,
469–470
"aggressive" policing and, 533
flaws in historical analysis of Wilson
and Kelling, 468–479
as proactive policing, 276
racially offensive connotations of, 335
See also Foot patrol

Brown, M. K., 88, 93, 126, 339
Brown, Michael, 513
Brutality. *See* Police brutality
Bucuvalas, M., 262
Budz, D., 281
Bumphus, V. W., 175, 177
Bureau of Justice Statistics, Police-Public
    Contact Survey (PPCS), 2011, 31
Bureaucracy
    as contributing factor to stress among
        police officers, 365
    effect on police discretionary behav-
        ior, 65
Burghart, D. B., 514

CAD (Computer Aided Dispatch) sys-
    tems, 234, 290
Cain, M., 148
Caldero, M., 192
Calls for service. *See* Requests for assis-
    tance
Campbell Collaboration, 266
Campus policing
    characteristics of campus police
        agencies, 424–426
    fruitful areas for research on, 429–431
    history of, 422–424
    in loco parentis doctrine and job role
        orientation, 428
    responsibilities of campus police, 421
    sexual-assault concerns, 428–429
    uniqueness of, 426–429
    "watchman" system of, 422
Candela, K., 431
Carpenter, B. N., 81
Carter, D., 189, 193, 198, 204
Centralization of authority, 20
Chambliss, W. J., 91
Character. *See* Police character
Chenery, S., 281
Chevigny, P., 168
Cincinnati Initiative to Reduce Violence
    (CIRV), 404–412, 414
Cissner, A., 209
Citizen–police interaction. *See* Police–
    citizen encounters
Citizens
    achieving greater input, in commu-
        nity policing, 483

citizen patrols and order mainte-
    nance, 466
complaints by. *See* Complaints
external oversight function of, 592
fear of violent crime, 457–459
input on police policies and deci-
    sions, 483
overall satisfaction with police
    response/assistance, 8
percentage who believe police are
    ethical, 199–200
perceptions of police behavior fol-
    lowing requests for assistance, 43
police typology of suspicious per-
    sons, assholes, and know noth-
    ings, 145–146
role in assisting the police, 7–8
role in police review process, 175–178
taking responsibility for officials'
    misconduct, 518–519
Civil rights movement, additional
    demands on police during, 23–24
Civil service, 21
Civilian Complaint Review Boards
    (CCRBs), 206, 473
Clark, J., 48
Code of ethics for Law Enforcement
    (IACP), 184–185, 596
Code of silence
    in case of state trooper Donna Watts,
        111–112
    consequences for those who break
        the law by upholding, 117–119
    eliminating through minimization of
        entitlement and impunity, 119
    as essential for police trust and good
        policing
    in *Karolina Obrycka v. City of Chicago*
        case, 110–111
    in the medical profession, 108
    multiple layers of, 107
    Police Foundation survey on atti-
        tudes of police and, 108–109
    preventing misconduct and corrup-
        tion, 114–117
    promoting organizational intoler-
        ance of, 118–119
    social solidarity and, 106–121. *See
        also* Social solidarity

Coercion
  ends-oriented thinking as cause of,
    192
  increase in areas with inequality and
    racial diversity, 130–131
  officer characteristics and likelihood
    of, 137
  race as predictor of, 190
Collective efficacy, 416
Colquhoun, P., 15
Communications, technical advances in,
    230–232
Community
  involvement in order maintenance,
    465–466
  nature of, unethical police conduct
    defined by, 203
  partnerships with police, 489–490,
    587–588
  surveying about their police depart-
    ments, 594
  "untended" behavior leading to
    breakdown of control in, 458
Community-oriented policing
  broad view of the police function in,
    483
  broken windows theory and, 276,
    455–479
  cultivating positive police–citizen
    encounters through, 7
  defining, 26–27, 482
  difficulty in determining effectiveness
    of, 481–482
  discretionary behavior and, 125
  early warning systems and, 253–254
  effects of federal funding on, 27–28
  emphasis on quality, 493
  evidence-based policing and, 267
  in field training and supervision,
    224–225
  geographic focus of, 486
  increased emphasis on face-to-face
    interactions, 485–486
  increased levels of accountability and
    responsibility regarding use of
    force, 532–546
  information management in, 493
  leadership/management styles of,
    492–493

order maintenance better accommo-
    dated through, 53
  organizational dimension of, 491–493
  personalized service aspect of,
    483–484
  philosophical dimension of, 482
  police–community partnerships in,
    489–490, 587–588
  positive impact on neighborhoods,
    124
  proactive/preventive orientation of,
    487
  problem-solving aspect of, 490–491
  strategic dimension of, 484
  street-level drug enforcement inter-
    ventions through, 266
  supervision's impact on patrol offi-
    cers, 224
  tactical dimension of, 488–491
  technical advances in, 240
  territorial imperative and, 128
  See also Broken windows theory;
    Problem-oriented policing
COMPASS crime mapping program,
    293–294
Complaints
  attitude/demeanor of complainants,
    impact on discretionary behavior,
    133
  citizen review boards to monitor,
    206, 591
  considerations involved in decisions
    against filing, 170–171
  contradictory roles of police leading
    to, 163
  establishing a proper process for,
    173–174
  failure to accept as form of code of
    silence, 116–117
  filing, considerations involved in,
    169–171
  increase in, as reflection of height-
    ened public expectations of
    police, 473
  involvement in the complaint pro-
    cess, 558
  mediation of, 591
  nature of complaints against police,
    165–166

open/accessible process for citizens, 590–591

positive and negative aspects of, 172–173

regarding use of force, 557–558

role in addressing police misconduct, 162–180

structure of police review process regarding, 174–178

COMPSTAT/Compstat (computer comparison statistics) model of policing

analysis and management of crime data through, 240, 297, 307

EI systems and, 246, 255

"fudging" of crime statistics, 207

history/uses of, 231–232

proactive nature of, 277

use in generating hot spots maps, 304

Computer-Aided Dispatch (CAD) systems, 234, 290

Computers

crime analysis software, 293–294, 303, 308–309, 313–314

crime mapping with, 235–236

departmental Internet access, 232

in the field, 236–237

GIS mapping programs, 293–294

information technology as key component of evidence-based policing, 262

predictive-policing software/programs, 279–280, 285

record-keeping functions of, 232–233

Concealment, tactical strategy of, 568

Conducted energy devices (CEDs), 238, 552–555. See also Tasers

Conformity, deviant, 79–101. See also Deviance

Constabulary policing, 13–14, 131, 190

Control

authority, power, persuasion and force as elements of, 3

self-perceived police mandate of, 148

Cooper, C., 331

Cope, N., 306

Coping mechanisms, 366–369

COPLINK/Coplink, 233—234, 313

COPS Office, 27–28

Cordner, G. W., 481

Corley, C. J., 430

Correctional treatment, core components of, 412–414

Corrections profession, EI systems and the accreditation process in, 253

Correia, M. E., 241

Corruption

explanations for, 201–203

facilitated by ethos of solidarity and secrecy, 95

individual, organizational, and societal explanations for, 200–203

mandatory reporting policy to combat, 115

mediocrity as cause of, 117

in nineteenth-century policing, 19–20

noble cause, 197–198

organizational intolerance of, 118–119

prevalence, origin, and reason for existence of, 198–200

proactive/reactive investigations to combat, 116–117

rules and regulations to prevent, 114

strong supervision and leadership to combat, 118

See also deviance

Crank, J. P., 91, 164–165, 169, 192

Crash Mapping, 299

Crime analysis

analyst level of training and qualification affecting, 318–320

computerized reporting of crime, 233

factors influencing quality of data for, 314–315

future concerns, 321–322

history of, 302–305

issues for analysts, 314–320

organizational factors affecting, 316–318

software for, 293–294, 303, 308–309, 313–314

tasks and tools of an analyst, 305–314

technical advances in, 234–235

through UCINET, 313

See also Crime mapping

Crime Awareness and Campus Security Act of 1990, 424

Crime control, mythology of, 474

Crime mapping
analyzing spatial trends of crime
with, 309–311
with geographic information systems, 290–300
predictive, 282
technical advances in, 235–236
Crime rate
citizen–police relations impacting, 464
Compstat's impact on, 304
criticism of police for inability to curtail, 25
foot patrol, ineffective in reducing,
453, 455–456
hot spot maps created using, 282
increase between 1960 and 1970, 23
neighborhood, impact on police discretionary behavior, 129–130
overall, reduction of repeat crimes
impacting, 281
police–citizen cooperation to reduce,
229
problem-oriented policing's impact
on, 504, 506
routes and methods of travel impacting, 298
as ultimate measure of police success, ix
CrimeStat III, 236
Criminal Geographic Targeting (CGT),
299
Criminogenic needs, 412–413
Critchley, T. A., 14
Cullen, F. T., 85, 398
Culture vs. subculture, anthropological
paradigm of, 82–83
Culture, police. See Subculture, police

Danger in police work
absolute dangers, 386–388
conclusions regarding, 396–398
exaggerated sense of, disjuncture
between potential for injury and, 85
narrow definition of dangerousness,
385
as part of police worldview, 86–87
relative dangers, 388
research methodology on, 389–391
research results on, 391–396

Davis, E. M., 128
Davis, R., 266
Deadly force
Afrocentric policing perspective on,
343–345
enhanced reality training on use of,
550–551
inadequate policy content on, 549
public outcry over, 99–100
race-based phenomena involving,
339–348
use of CEDs to prevent, 552–553
Deane, M., 441–442
Decentralization, 17, 492
Decision making
split-second, 574–576. See also Split-
second syndrome and police violence
tactical, 578–580. See also Tactical
strategies
training in use of force, 550–551,
560–561
Decker, S. H., 162, 167
Decriminalizing disreputable behavior,
463, 467
DeCuir, W. J., 437
Democracy, challenges of policing in,
596–609
Democratic model of police in society, 6
Desmond, Rudolph, 347
Deviance
ethos of secrecy regarding, 96–97
explanations for, 201–203
individual, organizational, and societal explanations for, 200–203
prevalence, origin, and reason for
existence of, 198–200
social construction of deviant categories, 152
See also Corruption
Diallo, Amadou, 339–340, 344–345
"Dirty Harry" problem, 192, 518
Discretion
citizen complaints about abuse of.
See Complaints
day-to-day ethics involving, 185–187
definition of, 124–125
devising informal/unrecorded dispositions of offenders, 520–521

multifaceted nature of, 163–164
racial discrimination in practice of, 190–192
in treatment of the mentally ill, 439–441
Discretionary behavior
ambiguity/uncertainty of officers' task environments affecting, 59
corrupt. *See* Corruption; Deviance
education's impact on, 135–136
justifications for, 124–125
legal variables affecting, 123
neighborhood variables affecting, 128–130
officer characteristics and outlooks affecting, 63–64, 123, 134–135, 137
organizational variables affecting, 64–66, 127–128
policing styles impacting, 126
research approaches on, 60
situational variables affecting, 60–63, 130–134
suspect demeanor's effect on, 61
threat of reactivity impacting, 52, 66
Discrimination, ethical dilemmas involving, 190–192. *See also* Afrocentric policing; Racial profiling; Racism
Disorderliness and fear, connection between, 458–459
Displaced aggression theory, 137
Domestic violence, complainant requests for leniency regarding, 62
Dorismond, Patrick, 344
Dowden, C., 413
Drug use, ethical dilemmas regarding, 189–190
Dugan, J. R., 175
Dunham, R. G., 3, 51, 54, 106, 126, 129, 131, 135–136, 387, 537–541
Durkheim, D. E., 106
Durose, M., 7, 31

Early Intervention systems/early warning systems
as accountability tool, 248–249, 590
Commission on Accreditation for Law Enforcement Agencies (CALEA) standard on, 248
in community policing, 253–254
concept of early intervention, 244–247
development of, 558–559
goals and impacts of, 249–253
management and accountability improved through, 239, 248–249
police–community relations and, 255
as proactive approach to police misconduct, 179
in problem-oriented policing, 254
for risk management of problem officers, 206, 255, 542
substantial effect on police behavior, 245–246
terminology used in, 247–248
Eck, J. E., 266, 276, 303, 507
Education, impact on police discretionary behavior, 135–136
Elderly, victimization of, 459
Engel, R. S., 124, 219, 401
Ericson, R. V., 126, 229
Estrich, S., 459
Eterno, J., 207
Ethics
categorizing unethical police behavior, 198–200
day-to-day, 185–191
Law Enforcement Code of Ethics, 596
noble cause, 192–198
of public servants, dilemmas of, 184–185
training, combating the code of silence through, 116
of use of geographic information systems, 295
Evidence-based policing, 260–272
agency characteristics, 269–272
defining, 260–264
information technology as key component of, 262
matrix for, 267–269
model of, 268
research supporting, 264–269
External oversight, 591–592

Fagan, J., 514
Fairness/justice, principle of, 185
Farmer, S. J., 202

Farole, D., 209
Felson, M., 415
Female police officers. *See* Gender;
  Women in policing
Ferdinand, T. N., 93
Ferguson, A. G., 284
Feuer, E., 388
Field operations, technical advances in,
  236–238
Field supervision, influence on patrol
  officer behavior, 219–228
Fielding, H., 15
Fielding, J., 15
"Fire brigade" policing, 276
Firearms
  inadequate/nonexistent policy on
    police use of, 549
  policy on drawing and pointing, 552
  policy regarding shots fired at mov-
    ing vehicles, 551
Firefighters, characteristics of injury
  incidents for, 389, 395
First Amendment rights, importance for
  police to uphold, 607–608
First responders, police as, 607–608
Fitzgerald, A., 444
Fixed-site surveillance cameras, 237
Fleet management, computerized, 240
Focused deterrence
  addressing offender motivation, 415
  cognitive–behavioral treatment
    (CBT) model, 413–414
  definition/premise of, 402–404
  implementation and sustainability
    issues, 405–408
  reducing offender opportunity and
    motivation, 409–411
  rehabilitative treatment of offenders,
    411–415
  routine activities theory vs. rational
    choice perspective, 409–411
Fogelson, R., 11, 21, 23
Foot patrol
  increased use in community policing,
    485
  ineffectiveness in reducing crime
    rates, 455–456
  motorized patrol vs., 461–462,
    471–472, 485

order-maintenance function of,
    456–457, 460
  popularity with citizens, 462
Force, use of
  age, gender, and ethnicity as factors
    not associated with, 539–540
  against "assholes," 153–154
  avoiding unnecessary force, 555
  citizen complaints about, 165–166
  critical need for research on, 543–546
  CRSO guidelines for, 165
  deadly. *See* Deadly force
  documenting/reporting, 556–557
  as element of police control, 3
  excessive, 165–167, 195–197, 533
  final-frame analysis of, 572–574
  illegal, police perception of accept-
    ability of, 195
  inadequate policy content on,
    548–549
  International Association of Chiefs
    of Police (IACP) model, 556
  intervening with fellow officers,
    562–563
  with intoxicated individuals, 540–541
  judging reasonableness in, 571–572
  legal standards of objectively reason-
    able conduct, 576–578
  less-than-lethal weapons, 238, 444,
    551–554. *See also* Tasers
  level of police experience impacting,
    135
  low percentage of police–citizen
    encounters involving, 534–536
  with mentally ill individuals,
    540–541
  noble cause ethics and, 195–197
  by patrol officers, impact of supervi-
    sory style on, 223
  physical, state of the art policy on use
    of, 588–589
  policy, critical issues in, 551–555
  policy enforcement on, 549–550
  race of officer affecting, 136
  race of suspect and, 191
  reckless tactical strategies employed
    by police, 567–580
  right of police to use, 4–5
  sex of suspect and, 62

small percentage of officers involved in, 541–543
socioeconomic status and, 130
split-second syndrome and police violence, 517–531
SSO studies regarding, 54
suspect resistance as most common factor precipitating, 537–539
training in, 550–551
working definitions of, 535
Frank, J., 124
Frankpledge system, 12–13
French, S., 413
Fridell, L. A., 75, 125, 537, 548
Friedman, L., 477
Fuhrman, Mark, 336
Furtive gesture rule, 344
Fyfe, J. J., 51, 189, 338, 344, 517, 549

Gang violence, deterrence programs for, 590
Garner, Eric, 99
Garner, J. H., 536–538
Garofalo, J., 51, 58, 538–539, 545
Gates, Darryl, 336
Gender
    differential police treatment of police subjects by, 132
    influence on police behavior, 136
    officer attitudes and, 137
    perceptions of police behavior by, 37
    stress in police work and, 362–384
Gendreau, P., 413
General responsivity, 413
Geographic information systems (GIS)
    in community policing, 494
    crime analysis with, 303
    crime mapping and analysis with, 309
    technology, 235, 289–300
Geographic profiling, 299–300
Germann, A. C., 164
Gershon, R., 367
Gibson, C., 189
Gil, K. M., 443
Glazer, N., 459
Global positioning system (GPS) technology, 238, 241, 291
Goldstein, H., 26, 163, 303, 500, 507, 521–522

Golembiewski, R., 365
Gorta, A., 189
Gould, J. B., 54–55
Graham v. Connor, 571–573, 576
Gratuities, ethical dilemmas involving, 187–189
Greene, J. R., 504
Green-Mazerolle, L., 503
Greenspan, R., 201
Grimmitt, Deon, 347
Gross negligence, 578
Guardian Angels, 465
Gun violence, deterrence programs for, 587
Gurley, Akai, 99

Haarr, R. N., 224
Haberman, C. P., 281
Haggerty, K. D., 229
Haggerty, Latanya, 344
Hails, J., 442, 446
Harris, C., 208
Hawkins, D. F., 130–131
Haynie, D. L., 283
Hazards of police work, 385–398. *See also* Danger in police work
He, N., 362
Hispanics, 36–37, 84
Hobbes, T., 4, 184
Hoffmaster, D., 128
Holocaust, shameful role of police in/lessons for police today, 598–607
Holt, J., 281
Homicide
    felonious killings of officers in the line of duty, 387–388
    impact of problem-solving orientation on homicide rate, 506
Hoover, J. E., 163
Hot spot policing
    calls for service data used in crime analysis, 303–304
    COMPSTAT and intelligence-led policing as forms of, 278
    crime analysis mapping used in, 309–310
    GIS mapping of, 297–299
    hot spot mapping for crime analysis, 304

noteworthy crime reductions resulting from, 1
place-based target control in, 266
problem-oriented policing's impact on homicide rate, 506
prospective hot-spotting, 282
Hudak, E. J., 435
Hudson, J. R., 167
Hughes, E. C., 146
Hunt, J., 87
Hunter, R., 204
Hureau, D. M., 1

IBM SPSS Modeler, 314
Illinois v. Wardlow, 346
Immigration and racial profiling, 191
Impunity, culture of, 95
Individual privacy, weighing against the issues of public security, 608
Industrial Revolution, 14
Injury, characteristics of incidents for police and firefighters, 392–395
Integrity testing, 206
Intelligence analysis, 311–314
Intelligence-led crime reduction model, 317
Intelligence-led policing (ILP), 277, 297, 304–305
International Association of Chiefs of Police (IACP), policy manual for management of effective police discipline, 173–174
International Association of Law Enforcement Intelligence Analysts (IALEIA), 319
Internet access, departmental, 232
Interrogation, deception and coercion used in, 194–195
Isolation, cultural theme of, 92–93, 97–98
i2 Analyst Notebook, 313
Ivkovich, S., 109

Jacques, S., 431
Jeanne Clery Disclosure of Campus Security Policy and Campus Crime Statistics Act of 1998, 424
Jennings, W. G., 435
Johnson, L. B., 24

Johnson, R., 137
Johnson, S. D., 281–282
Jonathan-Zamir, T., 57
Justice/fairness, principle of, 185
Justices of the peace, early American, 13
Juvenile status, effect on imposition of police authority, 62

Kaminski, R. J., 387, 398
Kane, R., 189
Kappeler, V. E., 79
Karolina Obrycka v. City of Chicago, 110–111
Katz, C. M., 238
Kelling, G. L., 26, 176, 335, 338, 455, 468–470, 474, 477
Kelner, J., 108
Kennedy, D. M., 334
Kerner Commission (National Advisory Commission on Civil Disorders), 24
Kerstetter, W. A., 175, 178
Kim, B., 365
"Kin police" model of law enforcement, 12
King, Rodney, 345
Klein, J. R., 128
Klinger, D. A., 56–57, 61, 129, 557
Klockars, C. B., 3, 58, 192, 198, 207, 518
Kochel, T., 131
Koper, C. S., 260, 263, 266
Kreisel, B. W., 178

Lamb, H. R., 436–437
Landenberger, N., 413
Lane, R., 11, 14
Langton, L., 7, 31, 355
Latinos
racial profiling and, 191
Law enforcement
crime control model vs. due process model of, 192
ethical dilemmas of, 183–209
improving ethical decision making in, 203–208
number of agencies/employees, 1, 9
perceived legitimacy of as central to focused deterrence, 416
social contract theory and, 5–7

Law Enforcement Code of Ethics, 596
Lee, H., 207
Lemming, T., 85, 398
Leo, R., 194
Lersch, K. M., 167–168, 179
Less-than-lethal weapons, 238, 444,
    551–554. *See also* Tasers
Leviathan (Hobbes), 4
Lewis, D. A., 439–440
LexisNexis Accurint for Law Enforce-
    ment, 312–313
License plate readers (LPRs), 238
"Lightning Strikes Twice" initiative,
    281
Link analysis of crime through target
    profiles, 313
Link, B. G., 85, 398
Lipsey, M., 413
Locke, J., 184
Logan, D. D., 364
London Metropolitan Police, 15–16
Louima, Abner, 197, 338–339
Love, K., 202
Lovins, B., 401
Lum, C., 260, 264, 267, 303, 309
Lurigio, A. J., 439–440

MacDonald, J. M., 131, 135–136
Making Officer Redeployment Effective
    (MORE) program, 235
Male police officers, research on factors
    contributing to stress in, 370–372
Malpractice, police, 166
Management
    alienation felt by officers promoted
        to positions of, 89
    in community policing, emphasis on
        organizational culture and val-
        ues, 492–493
    hostility between officers and, 100
    indirect encouragement of corrup-
        tion through poor/ill-conceived
        management practices, 207
    minimizing corruption in police
        departments through, 205–206
    organizational, 80/20 rule in, 541
    preventive/preemptory actions
        against problem behavior of offi-
        cers, 239–240

role in creating flexibility in accom-
    modating officers' professional
    and personal needs, 374
as source of police deviance and cor-
    ruption, 200–201
structuring of police tactical strate-
    gies, 568
supervisors as a buffer between offi-
    cers and, 222
supervisory failures contributing to
    tolerance of corruption, 118
See also Administration
Management Awareness Program
    (MAP) for police accountability,
    245, 249
Manning, P. K., 474
Marquart, J., 90
Marshall, J. R., 388
Mastrofski, S. D., 49, 54–55, 57, 63,
    123–125, 128, 130–131, 135, 264
Maxwell, C. D., 124, 536–537
Mayo-Wilson, E., 266
Mazerolle, L., 266, 504
McCluskey, J. D., 57, 130–131, 137
McHugh, P., 152
McLean, S. J., 46, 66
McMurray, H. L., 398
McNamara, J. D., 336
Media
    biased presentation of Afrocentric
        concerns and positions, 349–350
    coverage of police abuse of force, 534
    police perception as a hostile entity,
        91–92
    skewed impression created by cover-
        age of police abuse of force,
        533–534
Mediocrity, as cause of lack of integrity
    in police officers, 117
Mendelsohn, H., 81, 170–171, 472
Mental illness
    Criminal Justice/Mental Health
        Consensus Project, 445
    criminalization of the mentally ill,
        437–438
    deinstitutionalization movement,
        436–437
    increased likelihood of police use of
        force with the mentally ill, 540–541

officers' role as gatekeepers, 437
police-based specialized mental
    health response model, 443
police discretion with the mentally
    ill, 440–441
police interactions with citizens and
    the mentally ill, 438–440
police use of Tasers with the men-
    tally ill, 444
policy implications regarding,
    445–446
recommendations regarding police
    responses to, 446–448
specialized police response model,
    442–443
specialized police training for dealing
    with, 441–443
Metro-Dade Violence Reduction Proj-
    ect, 51
Midwest City study, 48, 50
Mieczkowski, T., 167–168, 179
Military/paramilitary model of polic-
    ing, 85, 87–89, 127
Miller, W. R., 11, 14–16, 476–477
Minorities
    disproportionate representation
        among complainants against
        police, 167
    as frequent victimizations of police
        misconduct, 167
    heavy demands placed upon police
        service by, 472
    increased use of coercion with,
        130–131, 190
    percentage satisfied with police
        behavior/response regarding
        requests for assistance, 36–37
    police discretionary behavior toward,
        130–131, 190–192
    recruitment of officers unable to
        identify with minority groups,
        84–85
    See also African Americans; Hispanics
Misconduct
    abuse of authority, 108–109, 164,
        166–167
    causes of, 168–169
    complaint acceptance to combat, 116
    definitions of, 165–166

departmental accountability vs. offi-
    cer autonomy, 164–165
managing, proactive efforts in,
    178–179
mandatory reporting policy to com-
    bat, 115
mediocrity as cause of, 117
official policy statements regarding,
    173–174
organizational factors affecting levels
    of, 545
organizational intolerance of,
    118–119
police deception concerning, 114–115
Police Executive Research Forum
    (PERF) statement on police mis-
    conduct policy, 174
previous studies of, 166–168
proactive/reactive investigations to
    combat, 116–117
rules and regulations to prevent, 114
types of, 198–199
typology of citizens failing to report,
    170–171
Mistrust/suspicion, 92–93, 97–98, 135
Mobile data/digital terminals (MDTs),
    236–237
Mohler, G. O., 279
Monell vs. New York City Department of
    Social Services, 518
Monkkonen, E. H., 11, 14, 17–19, 333,
    469
Montejo, K., 327
Moon, B., 430
Moore, M. H., 58, 265, 334–335,
    468–470, 474, 477
Morabito, M. S., 441, 443
Morrissey, J., 441
Motorized patrol, 461–462, 471–472,
    485
Moyal, S., 57
Muir, W. K., 58, 126
Munetz, M. R., 443–444
Murphy, G. R., 446
Murphy, P. V., 128

National Advisory Commission on
    Civil Disorders (The Kerner Com-
    mission), 24

National Crime Information Center (NCIC), 308
National Data Exchange (N-DEx), 234, 241
National Intelligence Model (NIM) of policing/crime analysis, 304–305, 313
Near repeat phenomenon, 280–281
Nick Lynch v. Adam Barrett, et al., 109–110
Niederhoffer, A., 81, 168, 335
Nielsen, E., 549
Night watch, early American, 14
911 systems, 230–231
Nix, J., 275
Noble cause ethics, 192 198
　cover-ups and whistle-blowing, 197–198
　interrogation, 194–195
　undercover investigations and testilying, 193–194
　use of force and, 195–197
Noble, J. J., 106, 567
Novak, K. J., 124
Nowicki, D., 124

Oath to serve and protect, significance of, 608
Obrycka, Karolina, 95–96, 110–111
Office of Community Oriented Policing Services (COPS Office), 27–28
Olsen, M., 4
Operations, technical advances in, 236–238
Order-maintenance and crime-prevention, link between, 458, 460–461
Organizational justice, 201–202
Ostrom, E., 48, 465

Packer, H., 192
Paoline, E. A., III, 64, 134–136
Papachristos, A. V., 1, 283
Paramilitary/military model of police training, 85, 87–89, 127, 569
Parks, R. B., 48–49, 124
Partnerships between police and community, partnerships with police, 489–490, 587–588
Pate, A. M., 537
Pate, T., 128

Patrol
　foot patrol vs. motorized patrol, 469–472, 485. *See also* Foot patrol
　influence of supervision on patrol officer behavior, 219–228
　nineteenth-century, 18
　police beliefs regarding nature of, 146–149
　supervision's impact on patrol officers, 224
Patten, R., 431
Payne, B. K., 129, 131, 133, 135, 137
Pease, K., 281
Peek-Asa, C., 388
Peel, R., 15, 17
Peer support, as buffer for effects of stress in police work, 365
Pegnall, N., 281
Pelfrey, W. V., Jr., 289
Percival, R., 477
Perez, D. W., 164, 166
Perry, W. L., 284
Personnel
　allocation, computerized, 240
　BJS statistics on, 9
　management systems, EI systems as, 246
Personnel Assessment System (PAS), 247
Personnel Performance Index, 247
Physical force, state of the art policy on use of, 588–589
Physical hazards of police work. *See* Danger in police work
Piquero, A. R., 109, 202, 499
Piquero, N. L., 189, 499
Police, American. *See* American police
Police behavior
　behavior, factors shaping, 59–66, 80–81. *See also* Discretionary behavior
　character. *See* Police character
　citizen complaints about. *See* Complaints
　citizens' role in assisting, 7–8
　complexity of role and responsibilities of, 8–9
　control, elements of, 3
　crime-control orientation of, 470

danger in politicization of, 602
discretionary. *See* Discretion; Discretionary behavior
as first responders, 607–608
incompetence, as cause of unnecessary violence, 519–520
law-enforcement vs. order-maintenance role of, 125
misconduct. *See* Misconduct
moral mandate of, 148–149
night watchman function of, 460
order-maintenance function of, 460, 462, 466–467
response to persons with mental illness, 435–448
review process, structure of, 174–178
role in society, 3–10, 53, 125–126, 163–164, 520–524, 532
scales of authority, 55–57
socialization and the police subculture, 75–215
subculture of. *See* Subculture, police
tactics of. *See* Tactical strategies
understanding through systematic social observation, 46–73. *See also* Systemic social observation
worldview of, 83–100
Police behavior
in civil rights era, 335
Eurocentric view of, 339
as physical, psychological or legal, 199
protests against and police countermovement regarding, 100
race-based, 337–341, 345, 447–339
research on, 166–167
See also Discretionary behavior
Police character
anthropological paradigm of, 82–83
perspectives on development of, 79–83
psychological paradigm of, 80–81
sociological paradigm of, 81–82
Police deception, continuum of, 114–115
Police departments
basic principles of what a good department should look like, 586
impact of EI systems on, 252–253
internal audits of, 594

percentage using computer for records management, 233
policy and procedure manuals on the web, 592–593
professionalism of, 587–588
reflection of the communities they serve, 588
self-monitoring function of, 593–594
transparency of, 592–593
Police Executive Research Forum (PERF) statement on police misconduct policy, 174
Police investigations, racial bias in process of, 345–348
Police officers
abuse of authority, 108–109, 164, 166–167
actions motivated by race, 340
black, as victims of friendly fire/friendly beatings, 342–343
conformity with a use-of-force continuum, 54
employment selection process for, 83–84
feloniously killed, decrease in, 86
impact of EI systems on, 250
learning to deal with personal prejudices, 602–603
mediocrity as cause of lack of integrity in, 117
minority, high rate of citizen complaints against, 168
officers with performance problems, 248
predominantly middle-class white male background of, 84
race and use of force, 136
stress's impact on. *See* Stress
truthfulness vs. deception of, 114–115
unstable, secrecy dictum protecting, 96
as watchmen, 422, 462, 476–477
Police Services Study (PSS), 48–50
Police work
danger in. *See* Danger in police work
discretionary nature of. *See also* Discretion, 520–525
job-related stress for female officers, 362–384

maintaining the "edge" in, 148
nineteenth-century, 18–19
physical hazards of, 385–398
"real," officer perception of the nature of, 147
situational/discretionary nature of, 163–164
technical challenges for the future, 241–242
video cameras used in, 236–238
Police–citizen encounters
contact, exit, and processing stages of, 56
cooperative aspect of, 7
de-escalation of, 589
drawbacks of observing from video/audio recordings, 67
impact of motorized patrol on, 461–462, 471–472, 485
increased contact with "problem" people vs. "ordinary" people, 472
increasingly explosive nature of, 157–158
judgment matters in, 59
low percentage of instances involving use of force, 534–536
with the mentally ill, 433, 438–440
as moral contests, 151
police discretionary behavior and, 134
race as a factor in. See Afrocentric policing; Racism
research treatment as hypothesized decision premises, 59
as a social transaction, 48
symbolic interaction in, 48
technology's impact on, 471–472
transactional nature of, 545–546
urgent, involuntary, and public nature of, 522–525
use of force in, 195–196
Police–community relations
Afrocentric policing's impact on, 349
community policing's impact on, 124, 488–489
impact of EI systems on, 255
impact of foot patrol vs. motor patrol, 461–462, 471–472, 485
order maintenance and, 463–464

in small vs. large communities, 464–465
strained, within minority communities, 335
Police-Public Contact Survey (PPCS)
data-collection methods for, 40–42
perceptions of police behavior following requests for assistance, 43
standard error computations, 44–45
twenty-first-century changes to, 42–43
Policing
Afrocentric, 331–352
aggressive, 533
bias-free, 590
broken windows theory and, 455–467, 469–470
on campus, 421–431
challenges of, in a democratic society, 596–609
in Colonial America, 13–14
community-oriented, 481–497. See also Community Policing
crime-control orientation of, 474
cultural themes in, 92–94
discrepancy between crime control imagery and operational reality, 474
Eurocentric, 334, 336, 341
evidence-based, 260–272
future of, 583–609
historical framework of, 471
historical overview of, 1–45
hot spot, 1
importance of serving with compassion, 603–605
intelligence-led, 277
loss of political legitimacy in, 474–476
military tactics involved in, 87–89
nineteenth-century, 17–20
predictive, 275–285
preventive model of, 14–17
proactive, 276–278
problem-oriented, 499–510
"professional" or "standard" model of, 276
requests for assistance, 2011. See also Requests for assistance, 31–45
revolution in public expectations regarding, 473–474

SARA model of, 276–277
social contract theory of, 5–7
social solidarity and the code of
    silence, 106–121
styles of, 126
technological innovations in, 229–242
watchman style of, 65, 422, 462, 468,
    470, 476–478
Policing in Cincinnati Project (PCP), 49
Politics
    police as an instrument of, 19, 21
    police as tool of, 25
Pollock, J. M., 183
POPN. *See* Project on Policing Neigh-
    borhoods
Postulates of police culture, 94–100
    ethos of bravery, 98–100
    ethos of isolationism, 97–98
    ethos of secrecy/theme of solidarity,
        94–97
Power
    abuse under the Nazi regime, 602
    delegation by citizens to police, 6–7
    as element of police control, 3
    physical/psychological/legal abuse
        of, 199
Predictive policing
    concerns for the future, 283–284
    defining, 275–276
    geographic profiling, 299–300
    GIS projective analysis, 299
    widespread adoption of, 278–279
Predispositional model of police behav-
    ior, 80
Prenzler, T., 206
Proactive policing, 276–278, 303, 487
Problem-oriented policing, 490–491
    contribution to the community polic-
        ing movement, 26
    definition/origin of, 500–501
    early problem-solving evaluations,
        502–503
    EI systems and, 254
    evidence-based policing and, 267
    hot spot mapping in, 266, 309–310
    impact of supervision on patrol offi-
        cers, 224
    implementation issues with, 508–509
    innovation as key to success in, 507

proactive nature of, 276–278, 303,
    487
problem-solving strategies at treat-
    ment places, 506
professionalism associated with, 587
recent problem-solving efforts,
    503–506
street-level drug enforcement inter-
    ventions through, 266
technical advances in, 240
zero-tolerance policing vs., 509. *See
    also* Zero-tolerance policing
See also Community-oriented policing
Procedural justice, 57–58
Professionalism/professionalization
    Code of Ethics for Law Enforcement
        and, 184–185
    emergence of in policing, 21–23
    legacy/consequences of, 25–26
    police department classified on basis
        of, 127, 587–588
    widening the police mandate in soci-
        ety/amplification of police as
        moral entrepreneurs, 158
Progressive reform, 20–21
Project on Policing Neighborhoods
    (POPN), 49–50, 57, 61, 63, 66–67,
    227
Public. *See* Citizens
Public housing
    fear of crime in, 459
    order-maintenance tactics in, 470
    problem-oriented policing in, 499,
        503–504
Public Safety Partnership and Commu-
    nity Policing Act of 1994, 27
Public security, weighing against the
    issues of individual privacy, 608
Public servants, ethical dilemmas of,
    184–185
Putti, J., 82

Quinney, R., 4

Race, impact on police discretionary
    behavior, 130–131, 136
Racial profiling, 75, 190–191, 256, 340,
    348–350
Racial threat theory, 191

Racism
    complaints regarding racially biased
        policing, 166
    differences in public perceptions of
        police helpfulness regarding calls
        for assistance, 36–37
    discrimination in policing practices,
        190–192
    discriminatory traffic-stop protocol
        people of color, 348
    marginalization of people of color, 340
    Rampart scandal, 336–337
    recruitment of officers unable to iden-
        tify with minority groups, 84–85
    "shoot first, ask questions later" pol-
        icy, 341–345
    See also Afrocentric policing
Radil, S. M., 283
Radzinowicz, L., 14
Rampart scandal, 336–337
Ramsey, C. H., 596
Rasinski, K. A., 176
Ratcliffe, J. H., 277, 281, 317
Rational choice perspective, and focused
        deterrence, 409–411
Raza, S. M., 81
Ready, J., 503
Recklessness
    definition/standard of, 577–578
    reckless tactical strategies employed
        by police, 567–580
Record keeping, technical advances in,
        232–234, 307
Recruitment of officers unable to iden-
        tify with minority groups, 84–85
Reform, Progressive, 20–21
Reiman, J., 5–7
Reisig, M. D., 130–131
Reiss, A. J., Jr., 46–47, 49, 52–53, 153,
        165–167, 171, 472
Reith, C., 12, 14
Reitzel, J. D., 499
Rengert, G. F., 299
Repression, the state as institution of, 4
Requests for assistance
    CAD systems analysis/monitoring
        of, 234, 290
    citizens' perceptions of police behav-
        ior and response, 39–39, 43

differential responses to, 485
    face-to-face contact with officers
        involved in, 33–35
    likelihood of contacting police again
        for similar problems, 39–40
    percentage of police behavior
        deemed "proper" in, 35–38
    percentage of population requesting,
        31–33
    technology's impact on, 472 473
Resource allocation, computerized,
        240–241
Retaliation, mandatory reporting policy
        to combat, 115
Reuland, M. M., 234, 445
Reuss-Ianni, E., 94–98, 100
Reverse 911/auto-dialing system, 231
Reynolds, P. D., 183
Richardson, J. F., 11, 14
Ridgeway, G., 284
Riger, S., 439
Riley, K., 66
Riots
    in civil rights era, 335
    paramilitary control of, 88
    police provocation of, 24, 335
    in 1700s–1800s, 6, 15–16
Risk management, EI systems as a tool
        for, 179, 252, 255, 542
Ritter, C., 443
Ritti, R., 128
Rojek, A., 302
Rojek, J., 106, 162, 507
Role modeling, limiting unethical con-
        duct through, 207
Ronken, C., 206
Rosenbaum, D. P., 124, 129–131
Rosenman, K., 388
Rossmo, D. K., 193, 299–300
"Rotten apple" explanation of police
        deviance and corruption, 200, 338
Rousseau, J-J., 184
Routine activities theory, and focused
        deterrence, 409–411
Rubenstein, J., 148
Russell, K., 169–171

Sacks, H., 145
Sauerman, A., 109

Scanning, Analysis, Response, and Assessment (SARA) model, 276–277, 303, 309, 501
Schafer, J., 63
Scharf, P., 550
Schuck, A. M., 124, 129–131
Schultz, P. D., 240
Scott, M., 75
Scrivner, E., 75
Secrecy, ethos of, 91, 94–97
Seidman, R. B., 91
Sex, differential arrest and use of force, 62
Shane, J., 208
Sheriffs, early American, 13–14
Sherman, L. W., 260–261, 265–266, 303
"Shoot first, ask questions later" policy, 341–345
Silverman, E., 207
Simmel, G., 157
Simple negligence standard, defining, 577
Sisk, M., 175
Skolnick, J. H., 85, 92, 113, 127, 147, 194, 549
Sluder, R. D., 79
Smart policing paradigm, 305
Smith, B. W., 124
Smith, D. A., 127–128
Smith, M. R., 131, 555
Smoot, S., 75
Snipes, J. B., 123–124
Social contract theory, and law enforcement, 5–7, 184
Social isolation, cultural theme of, 92–93, 97–98
Social media
    defining target profiles for crime analysis through, 312
    platforms, police uses for, 232
Social network analysis, 282–283
Social solidarity
    blue wall of silence and, 112–113
    reciprocal silence valued among police officers, 106–107
    social unity vs. "closed shop" mentality, 107–112
Social-control mechanisms, minimizing fear of public places through, 464–465

Society, role of police in, 3–10, 53, 125–126, 163–164, 520–524, 532
Socioeconomic status, and differences in police discretionary behavior and, 129, 132, 166
Solidarity, cultural theme/ethos of, 93–94, 96–97, 113. *See also* Code of silence
Sorensen, D. W., 387, 398
Souweine, D., 445
Sparrow, M., 334
Spelman, W., 276, 303
Split-second syndrome
    assumptions regarding, 526–528
    avoiding split-second decisions, 528–530
    incompetence and unnecessary police violence, 519–520
    lack of police diagnostic experience and, 526
    rationalization of, 91
Squad cars, video cameras in, 237
Stark, R., 165
Steadman, H. J., 441, 443
Stereotypes, and biased police response to minority citizens, 131
Stinchcombe, A., 472
Street justice, 149–155
Stress
    bureaucracy as contributing factor, 365
    coping mechanisms, negative and positive, 366–369
    effect on officers' perception of an event, 571–572
Stroshine, M. S., 62, 126, 129, 131, 135–137, 229, 385
Subculture, police
    Afrocentric perspective in, 341–348
    code of silence and, 106–119
    contribution to deviance and corruption, 200–202
    cultural themes in policing, 92–94
    "Dirty Harry" orientation promoted by, 192, 518
    explanation of excessive force, 208
    looking the other way, 605–607
    misconduct explained by, 168–169
    postulates of police culture, 94–100
    spirit of, 90
Sun, I. Y., 129, 131, 133, 135, 137

Supervision
  accountability for police use of force, 562–563
  in community policing, 492
  EI systems' impact on, 250
  frontline supervisory styles, 220–223
  impact on police discretionary behavior, 65
  performance assessment and review systems for, 559
  technical advances in, 239
Survey of Campus Law Enforcement Agencies, The, 425
Suspect demeanor, impact on police discretionary behavior, 61
Suspicion/mistrust, 92–93, 97–98, 135
Swanton, B., 92–93
Swatt, M., 189
Sykes, R. E., 48
Symbolic interaction, 48
Systematic social observation (SSO)
  conclusions drawn from, 53–66
  definition of, 46–47
  five major studies of, 47–51
  future of, 66–67
  methodological strengths and weaknesses, 51–53
  theoretical underpinnings of, 47–49

Tactical strategies
  effective realistic training to improve, 578–580
  evolution of, for dangerous situations, 567–569
  split-second decision making and, 574–576. *See also* Split-second syndrome
  training and guidelines regarding, 568–569
  unsound tactical decision making, 569, 571
  use-of-force law and, 571–572
Target profiles, link analysis of crime through, 313
Tasers
  ethical issues involving use of, 196–197
  as less-than-lethal weapons, 238
  policy for use of, 552–554
  use with the mentally ill, 444

Taylor, A., 413
TEAMS (Training Evaluation and Management System), 249
Technology
  impact on policing, 471–472
  technological innovations in policing, 229–242
  video simulators to improve training in tactical decision making, 578–580
  See also Computers
Teller, J., 443
Terrill, W., 54, 64, 130, 134–137, 175, 503
Territoriality
  patrolmen's perspective of, 147–148
  rule of, 96–97
  territorial imperative, 128
Testilying, 192
Thin blue line, 89, 197, 601, 609
Thompson, M. D., 445
311 systems, 230–231
Tilley, N., 276
Tillyer, M. S., 401
Toch, H., 542
Townsley, M., 281
Training
  of crime analysts, 318–320
  on ethics and integrity, 116
  integrated, 561–562
  for interactions with the mentally ill, 441–443
  paramilitary model of, 89
  Peace Officer Standards Training (POST) for campus police, 423
  reinforcement of police subculture during, 85
  for response to dangerous and unusual criminal incidents, 568–569
  tactical decision making improved through, 578–580
  typical law enforcement basic program, 86
  in use of force, 550–551, 560–563
Travis, L. F., 85, 398
Tuch, S. A., 7

Uchida, C. D., 11, 387
UCINET, crime analysis through, 313

Uniform Crime Reports system, impact on reorientation of police patrol, 469–470
Urban decay, 459
Use of force. *See* Force, use of

Values, instilling in new recruits, 598
Van Maanen, J., 97, 143
Vandalism of unattended property, 457–458
Vena, J. E.; 388
Veysey, B., 441
Video-camera use in police work, 236–238
Vigilantism, 466
Violanti, J. M., 388, 398
Violence
   reduction, sustainability issues in focused deterrence initiatives, 401–416
   split-second syndrome and, 517–531
   See also Force, use of
Violence Triage Tool, 412
Violent Crime Control and Law Enforcement Act of 1994, 27
Violent crime, deterrence programs for, 587
Violent Criminal Apprehension Program (ViCAP), 308
VIPER (Visibility, Intelligence, Partnerships, Education, and Resources), 232
Vollmer, August, 8, 22
Volpe, J., 197

Wada, J., 431
Wagner, A. E., 162, 167
Walker, S., 6, 11, 14, 18, 23, 25, 163, 175, 177–178, 206, 238–239, 244, 468
War on Drugs, military metaphor/connotations of, 87
Waring, E., 503
Watchman
   myth of, 476–477
   style of policing, 65, 422, 462, 468, 470, 478

Watts, Donna, 111–112
Weinberger, L. E., 437
Weisburd, D., 109, 201, 263, 265, 303, 309
Weiss, C., 262
Weitzer, R., 7
West, P., 175, 178
Westley, W. A., 91, 431
Wexler, J. G., 364
"What works" movement, evidence-based policing as, 265
Whistle-blowing, 106, 109, 113, 197–198, 201
Whitaker, G. P., 48
White, M. D., 506, 514
Whitfield, Michael, 345
Willis, J., 264–265
Wilson, D., 131
Wilson, J. Q., 26, 53–54, 65, 126, 276, 335, 431, 438–439, 455, 468–470, 474, 477, 521
Wilson, O. W., 469, 471
Wolfe, S., 109, 202
Women in policing
   impact of stress on, 362–384
   research on current state of/trends in employment of female officers, 355–361
   use of force when authority was explicitly denied, 87
   See also Gender
Woodworth, J. R., 147
Woody, M., 444
Worden, R. E., 46, 49, 56, 66, 123, 126, 208, 539
Work–family conflict, as cause of stress and burnout among police officers, 366–368
Worldview of police, 83–100
Wu, Y., 129, 131, 133, 137

Young, Cornel, 342

Zero-tolerance policing, 124, 509, 533, 600
Zhao, J., 362
Zimbardo, P., 457–458